MOBILE SUIT

GUNDAM

THE ORIGIN

II

—GARMA—

YOSHIKAZU YASUHIKO

ORIGINAL STORY BY:
YOSHIYUKI TOMINO • HAJIME YATATE

MECHANICAL DESIGN BY:
KUNIO OKAWARA

Mobile Suit Gundam
THE ORIGIN

II
—GARMA—
CONTENTS

SECTION I ———————— 007

SECTION II ——————— 061

SECTION III ——————— 105

SECTION IV ——————— 143

SECTION V ———————— 229

SECTION VI ——————— 273

SECTION VII ——————— 329

SECTION VIII ——————— 373

ILLUSTRATION GALLERY ———— 422

Special contributions from CLAMP ——— 428

Humanity had been emigrating excess populations to space for over half a century.

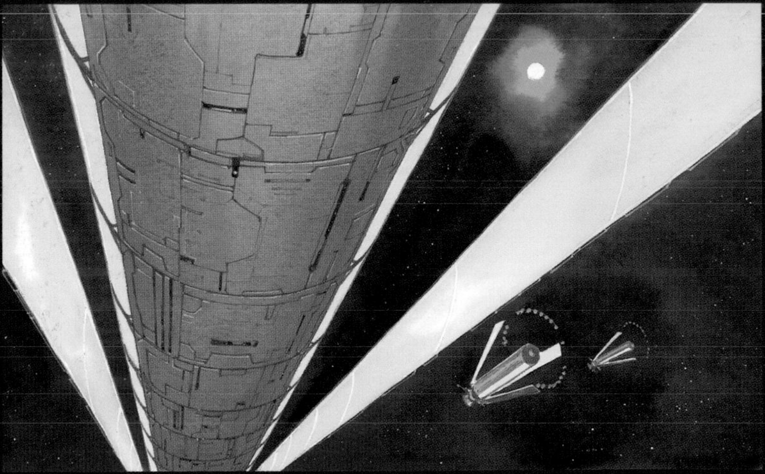

Hundreds of enormous space colonies floated in orbit around the Earth.

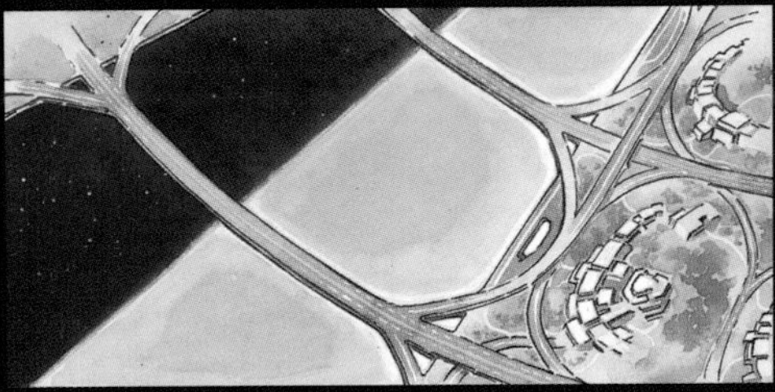

On the terraformed inner walls of the great cylinders,

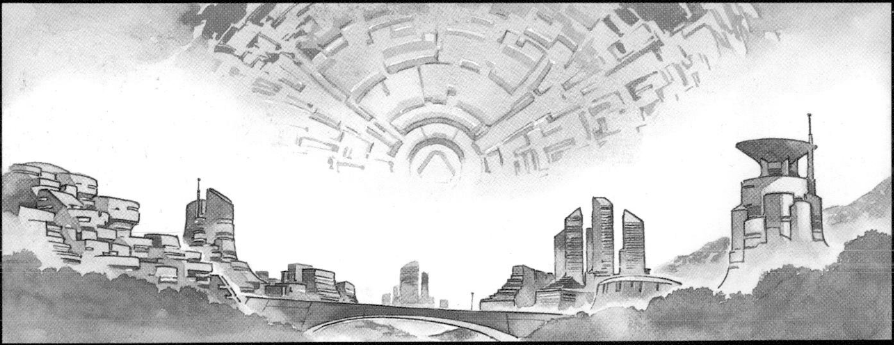

people found new homes.

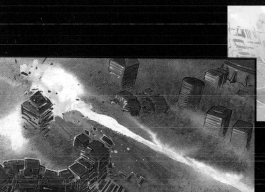

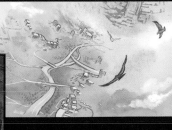

Millions of space colonists lived there, had children, and

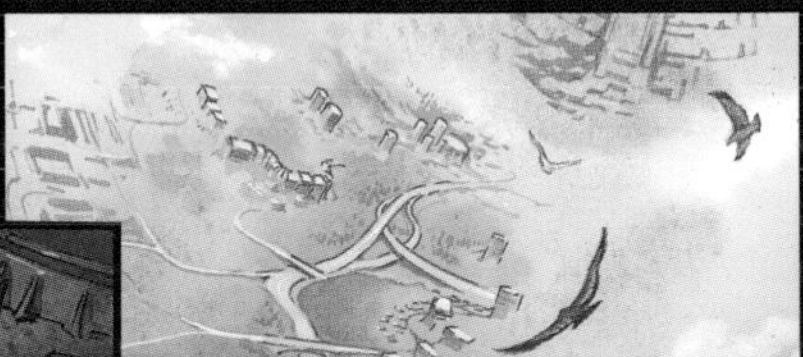

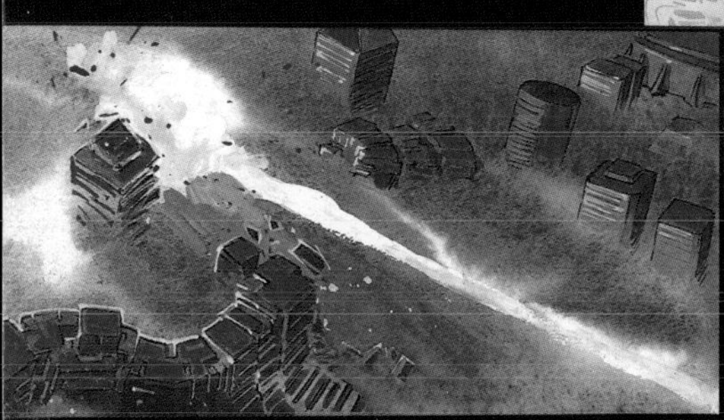

passed on.

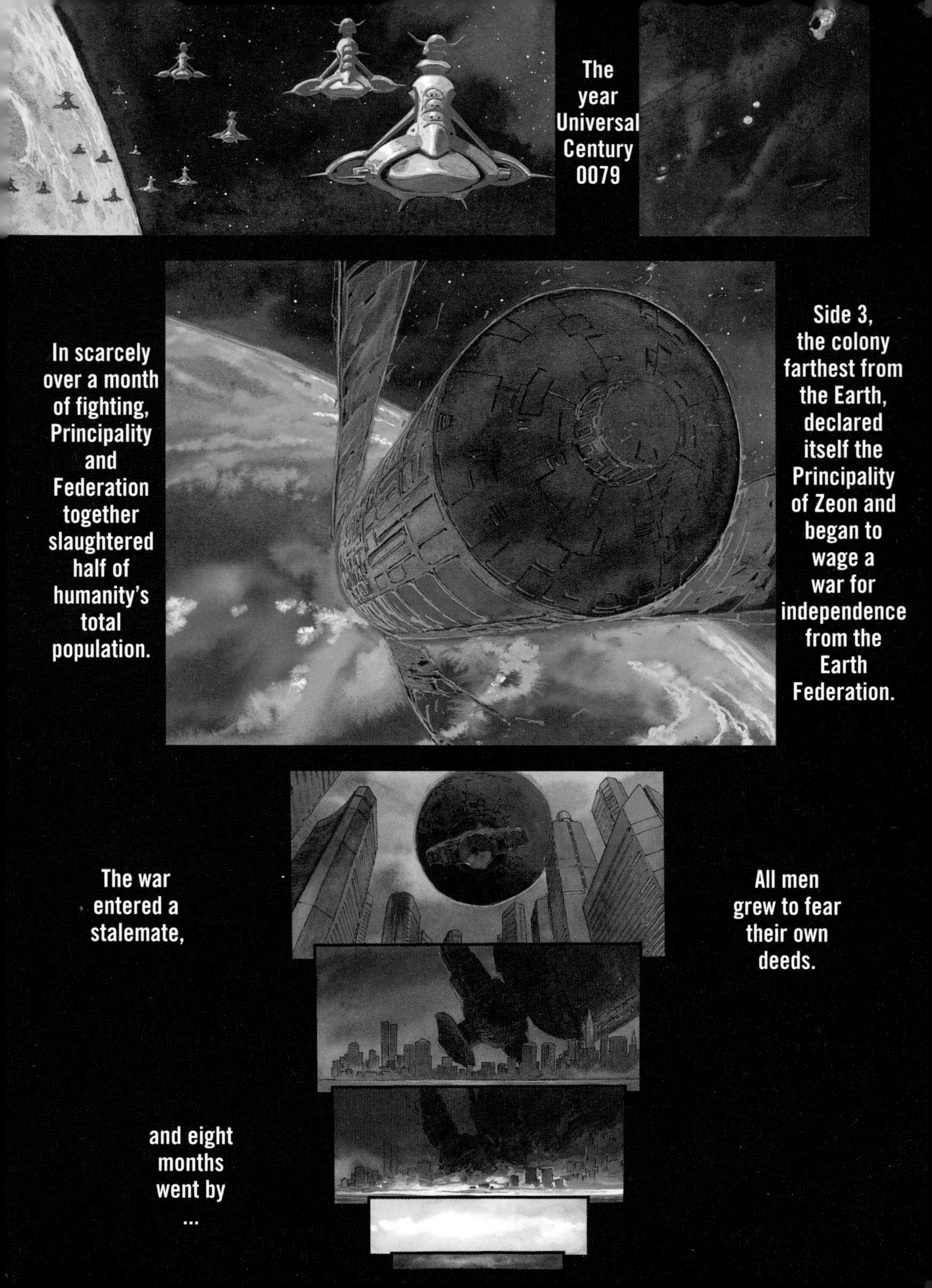
The year Universal Century 0079
Side 3, the colony farthest from the Earth, declared itself the Principality of Zeon and began to wage a war for independence from the Earth Federation.
In scarcely over a month of fighting, Principality and Federation together slaughtered half of humanity's total population.
All men grew to fear their own deeds.
The war entered a stalemate,
and eight months went by ...

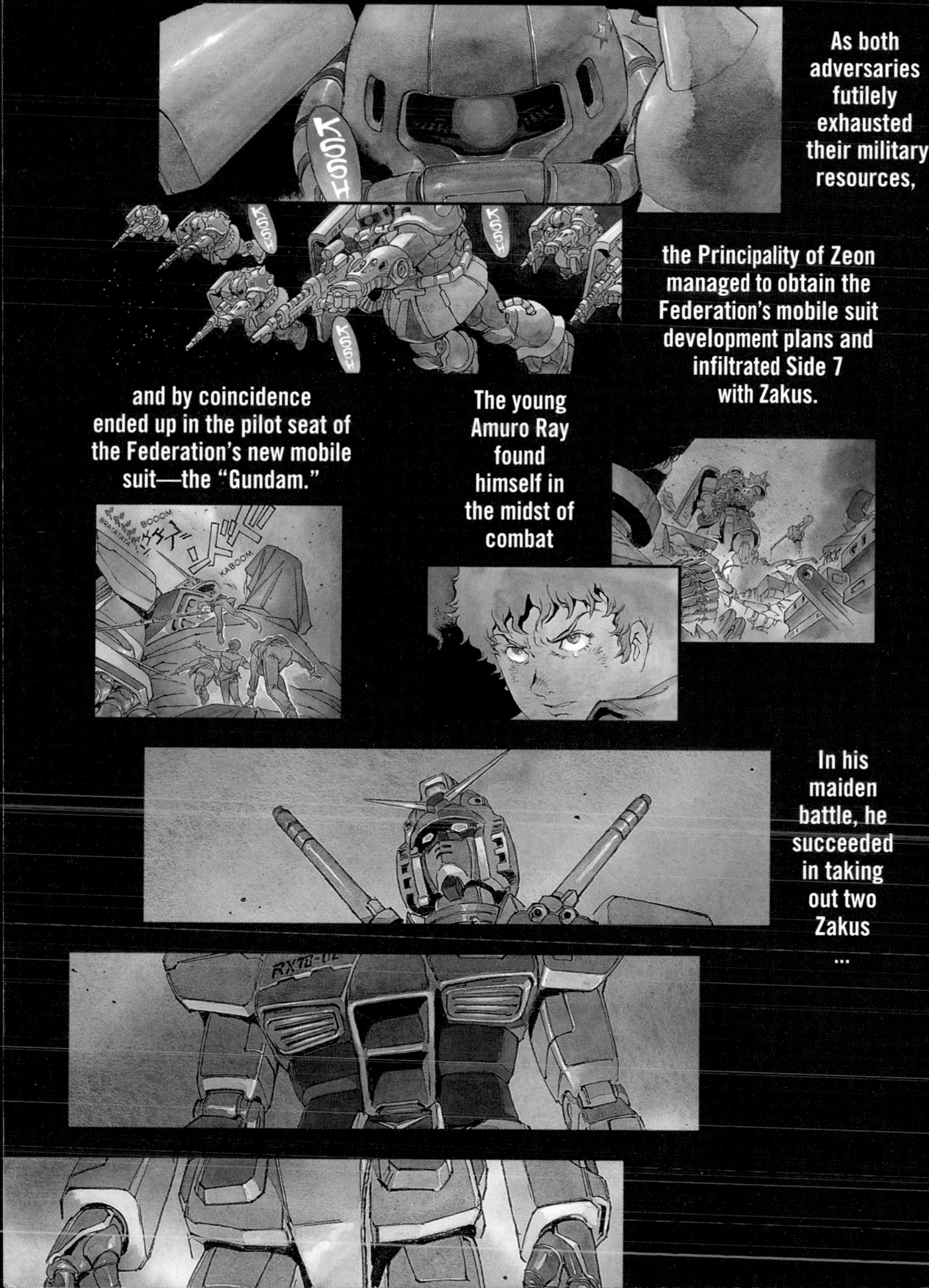
As both adversaries futilely exhausted their military resources,
KSSH
KSSH
KSSH
KSSH
the Principality of Zeon managed to obtain the Federation's mobile suit development plans and infiltrated Side 7 with Zakus.
The young Amuro Ray found himself in the midst of combat
and by coincidence ended up in the pilot seat of the Federation's new mobile suit—the "Gundam."
BOOOM
BRATATATA
KABOOM
In his maiden battle, he succeeded in taking out two Zakus
...
RX78-02

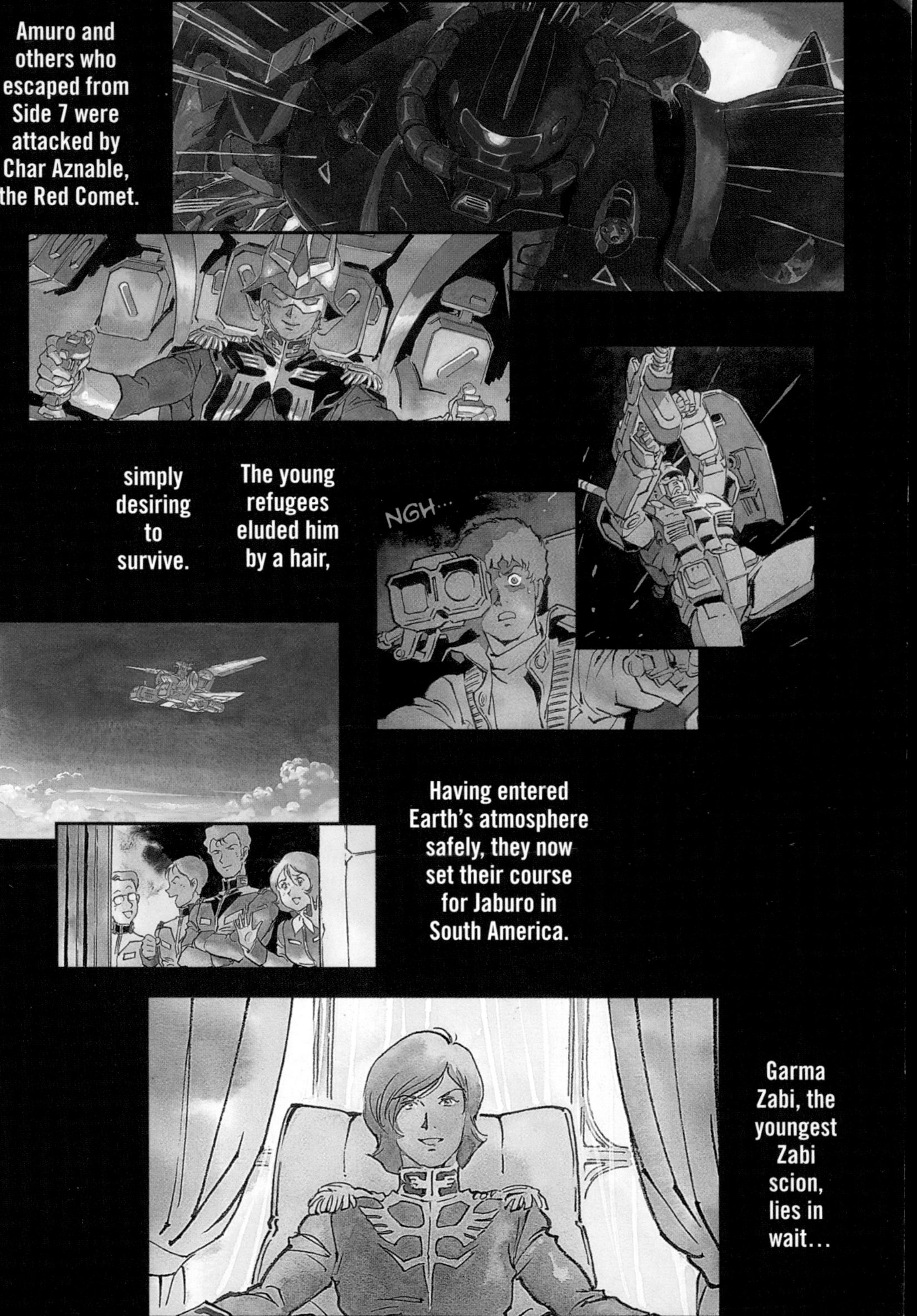
Amuro and others who escaped from Side 7 were attacked by Char Aznable, the Red Comet.
NGH...
The young refugees eluded him by a hair,
simply desiring to survive.
Having entered Earth's atmosphere safely, they now set their course for Jaburo in South America.
Garma Zabi, the youngest Zabi scion, lies in wait...

SECTION I

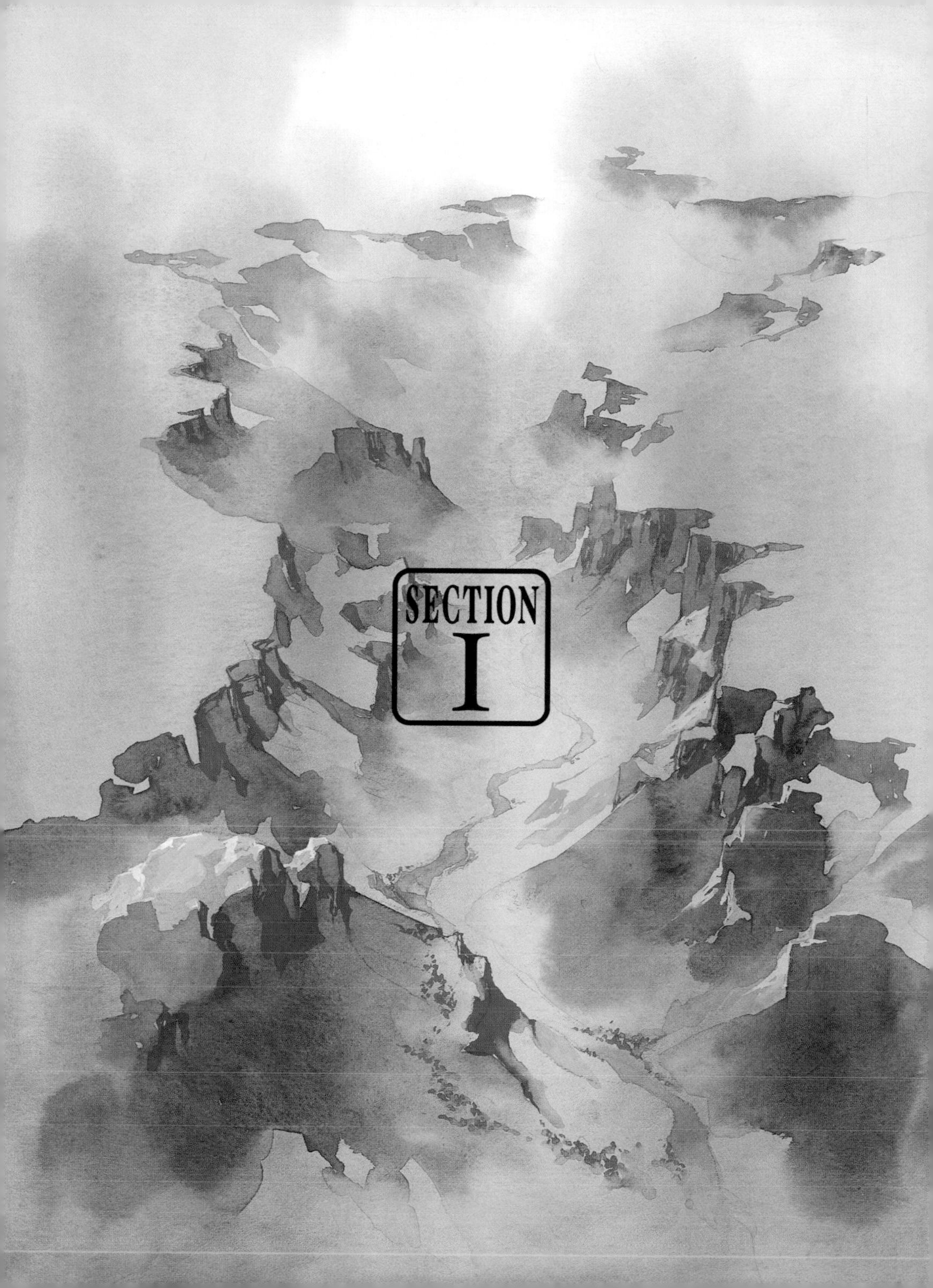

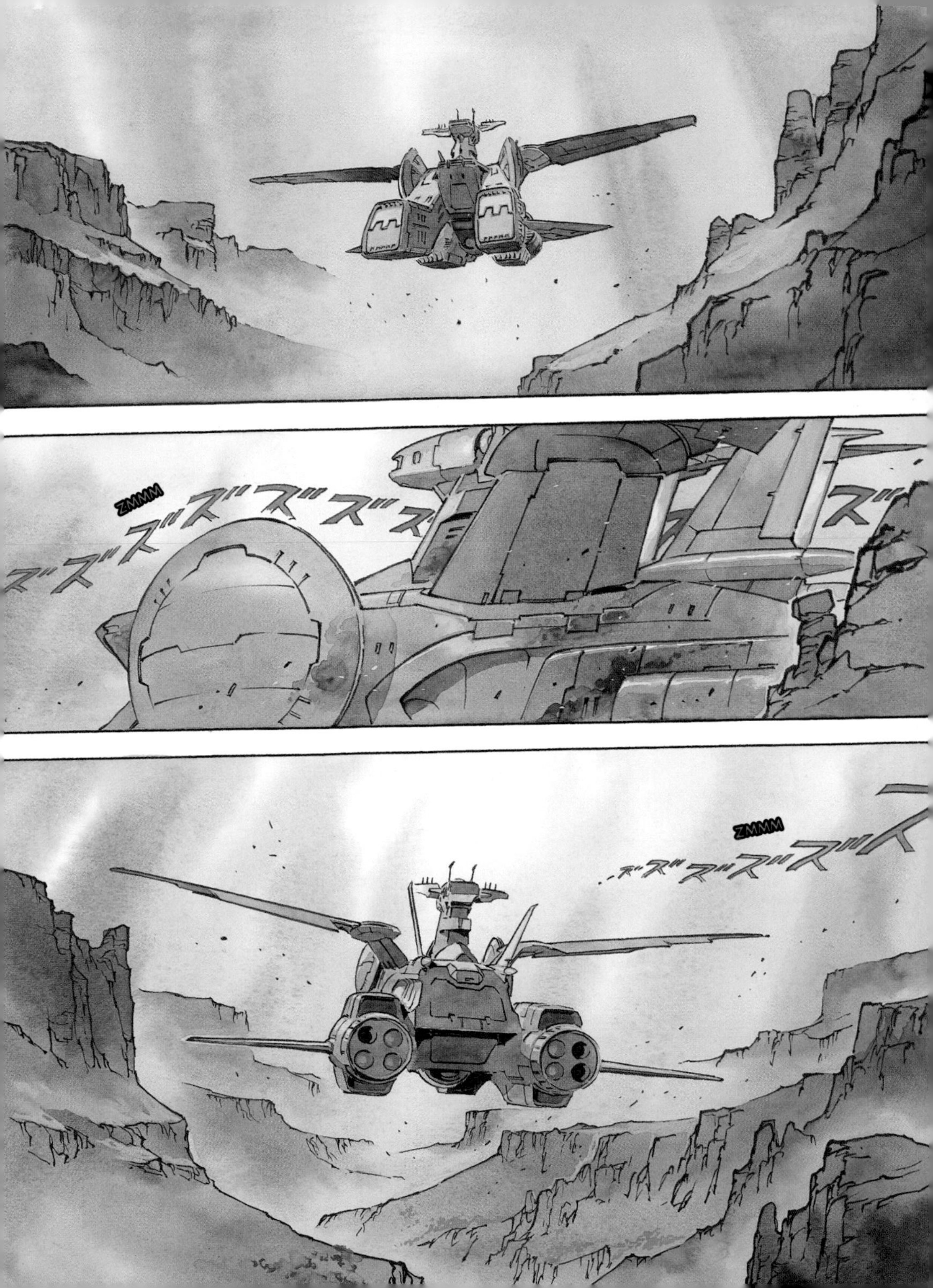
ZMMM
ズズズズズズ
ZMMM
ズズズズズ

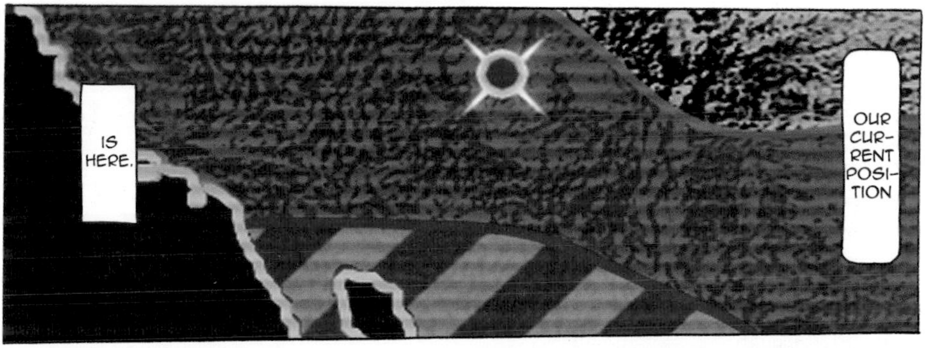
OUR CUR-RENT POSI-TION
IS HERE.

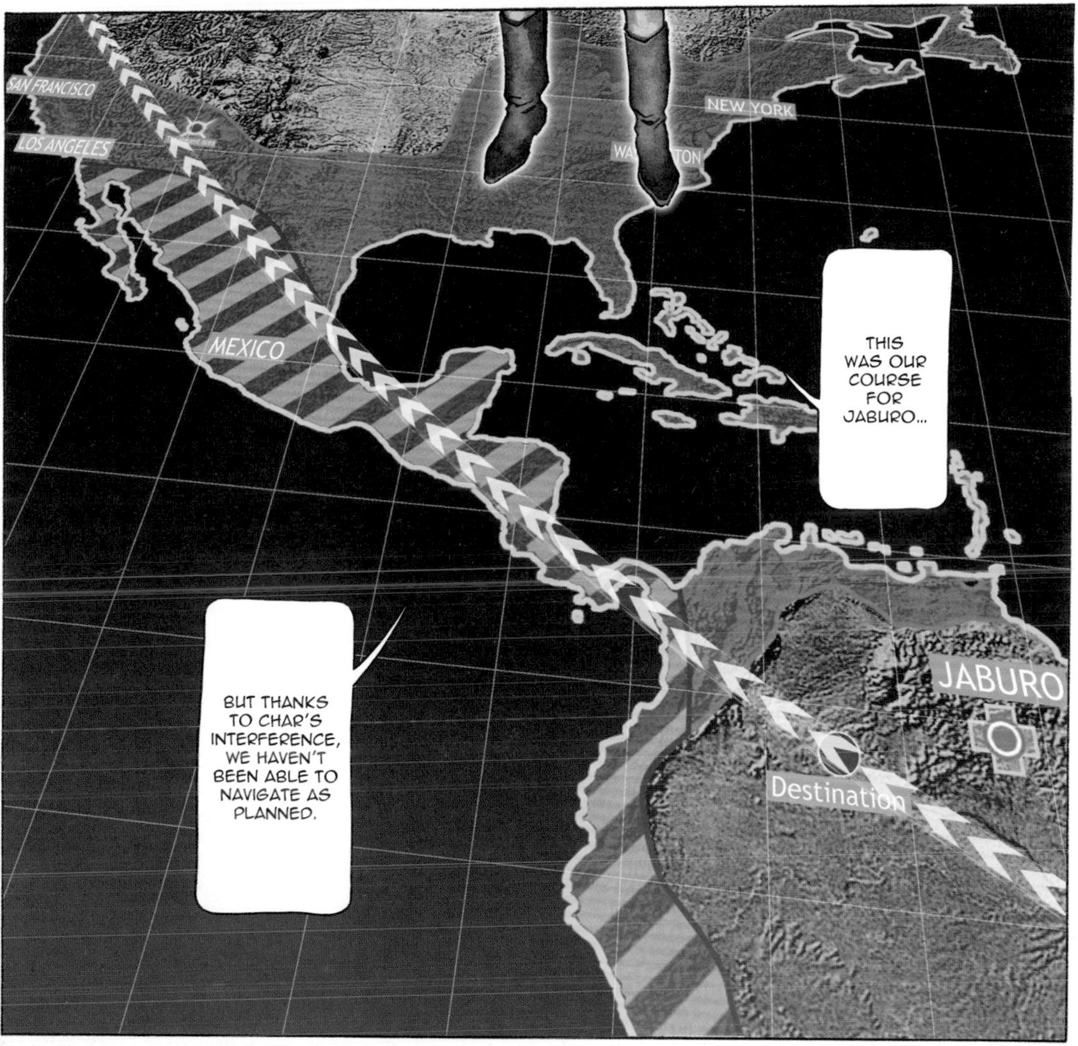
THIS WAS OUR COURSE FOR JABURO...
BUT THANKS TO CHAR'S INTERFERENCE, WE HAVEN'T BEEN ABLE TO NAVIGATE AS PLANNED.
SAN FRANCISCO
LOS ANGELES
NEW YORK
MEXICO
JABURO
Destination

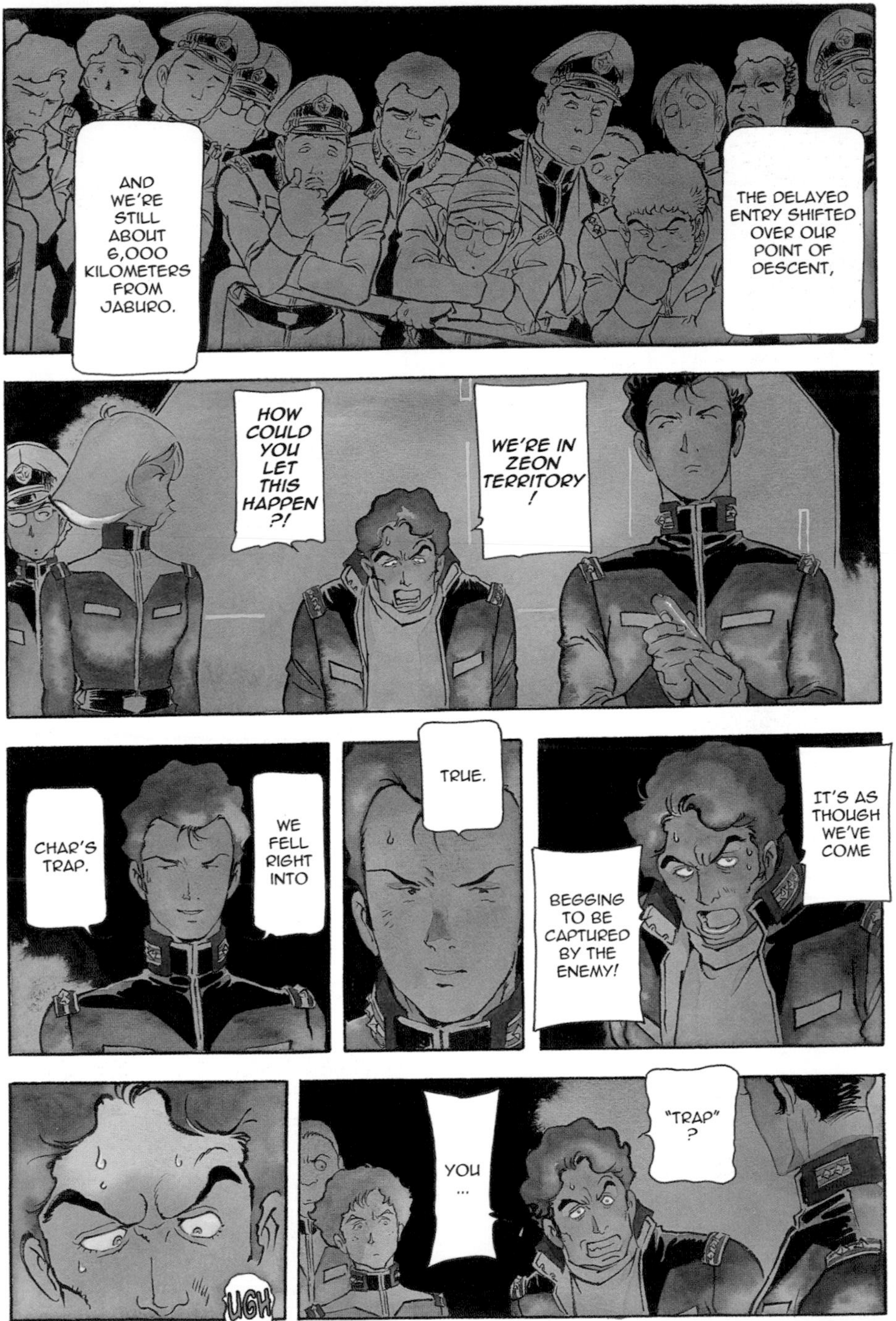
THE DELAYED ENTRY SHIFTED OVER OUR POINT OF DESCENT,
AND WE'RE STILL ABOUT 6,000 KILOMETERS FROM JABURO.
WE'RE IN ZEON TERRITORY!
HOW COULD YOU LET THIS HAPPEN?!
IT'S AS THOUGH WE'VE COME
BEGGING TO BE CAPTURED BY THE ENEMY!
TRUE.
WE FELL RIGHT INTO
CHAR'S TRAP.
"TRAP"?
YOU...
UGH

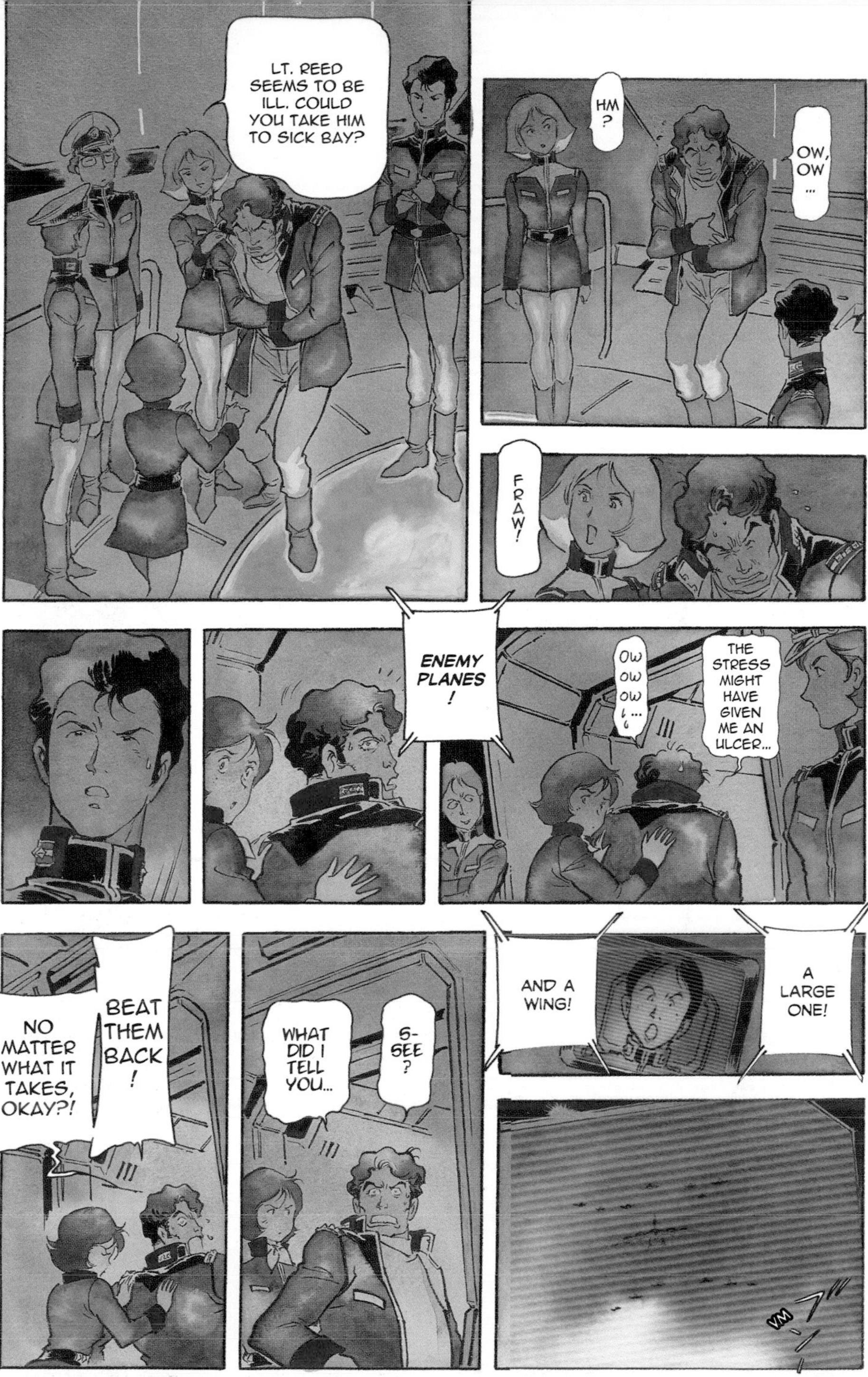
OW, OW ...
HM?
FRAW!
LT. REED SEEMS TO BE ILL. COULD YOU TAKE HIM TO SICK BAY?
THE STRESS MIGHT HAVE GIVEN ME AN ULCER...
Ow ow ow...
ENEMY PLANES!
A LARGE ONE!
AND A WING!
VM
S-SEE?
WHAT DID I TELL YOU...
BEAT THEM BACK!
NO MATTER WHAT IT TAKES, OKAY?!

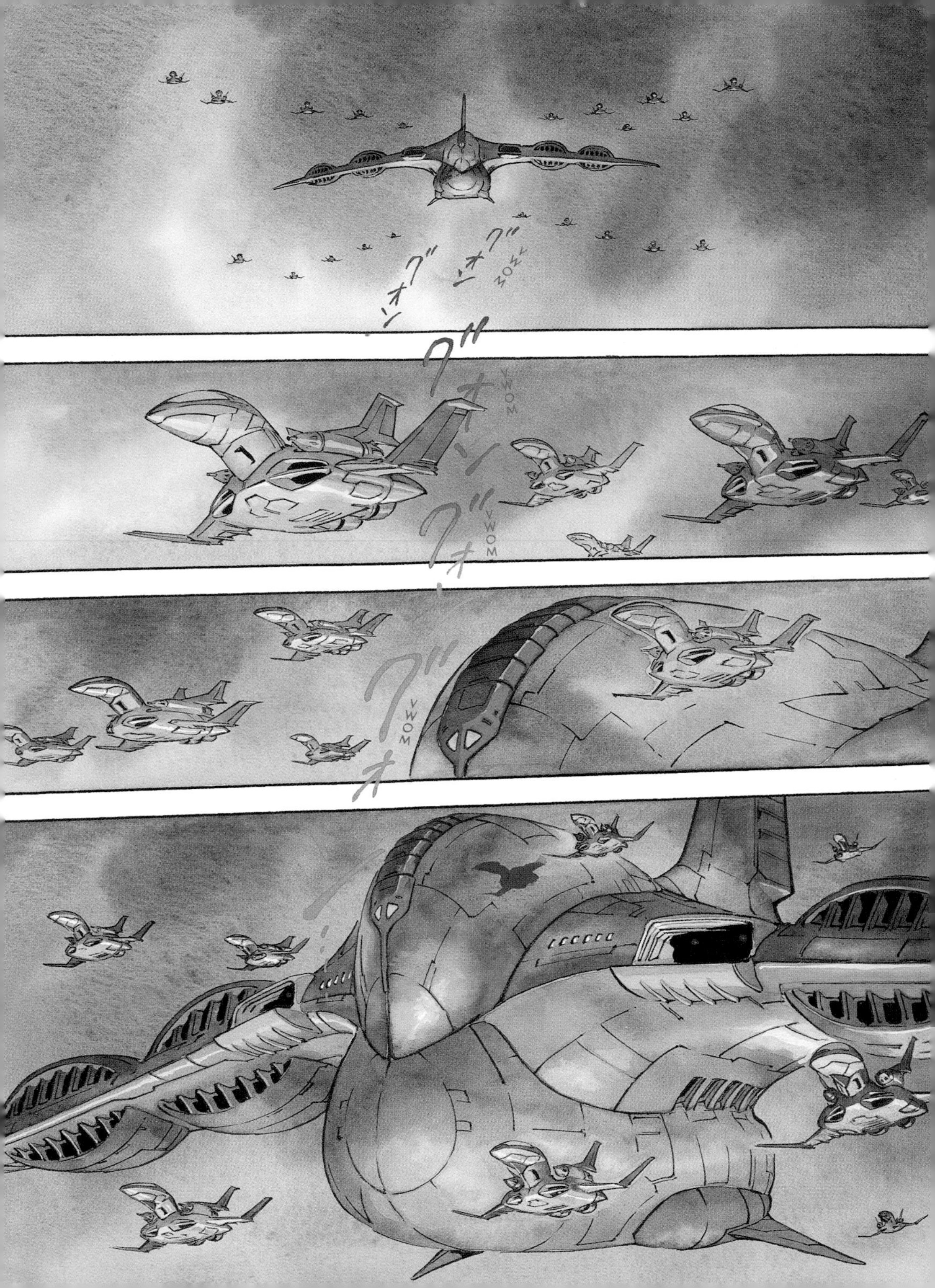
ヴォン
VWOM
ヴォン
ヴォン
VWOM
ヴォ
VWOM
ヴォ
VWOM

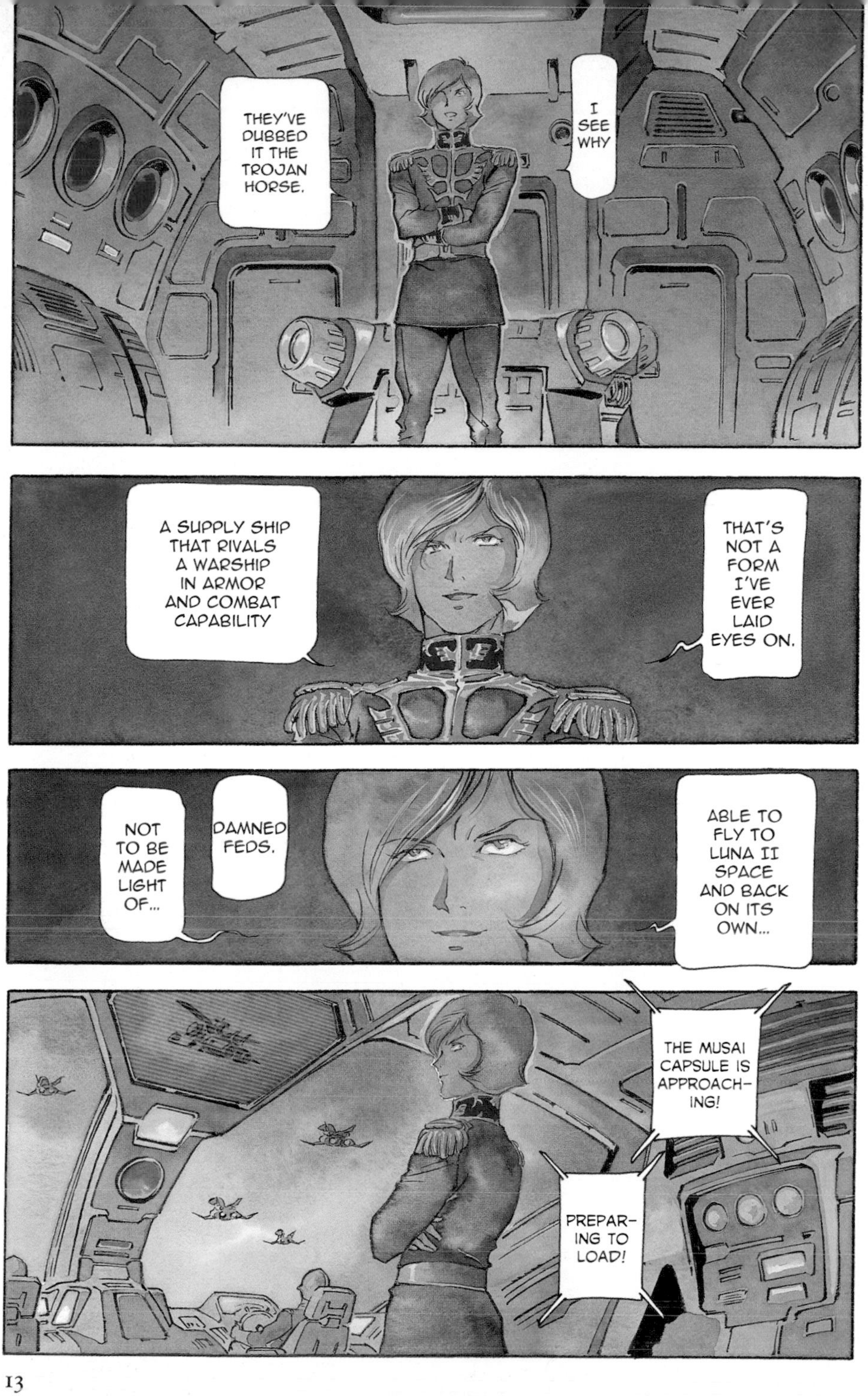
I SEE WHY
THEY'VE DUBBED IT THE TROJAN HORSE.
THAT'S NOT A FORM I'VE EVER LAID EYES ON.
A SUPPLY SHIP THAT RIVALS A WARSHIP IN ARMOR AND COMBAT CAPABILITY
ABLE TO FLY TO LUNA II SPACE AND BACK ON ITS OWN...
DAMNED FEDS.
NOT TO BE MADE LIGHT OF...
THE MUSAI CAPSULE IS APPROACH-ING!
PREPAR-ING TO LOAD!

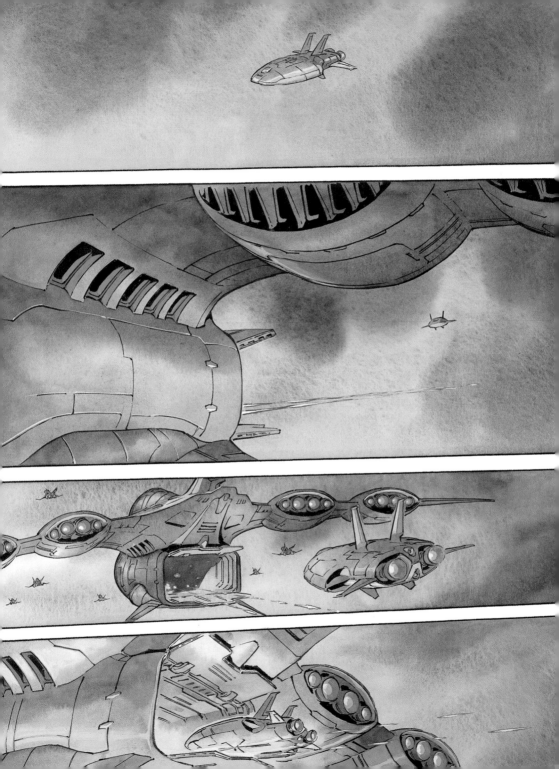

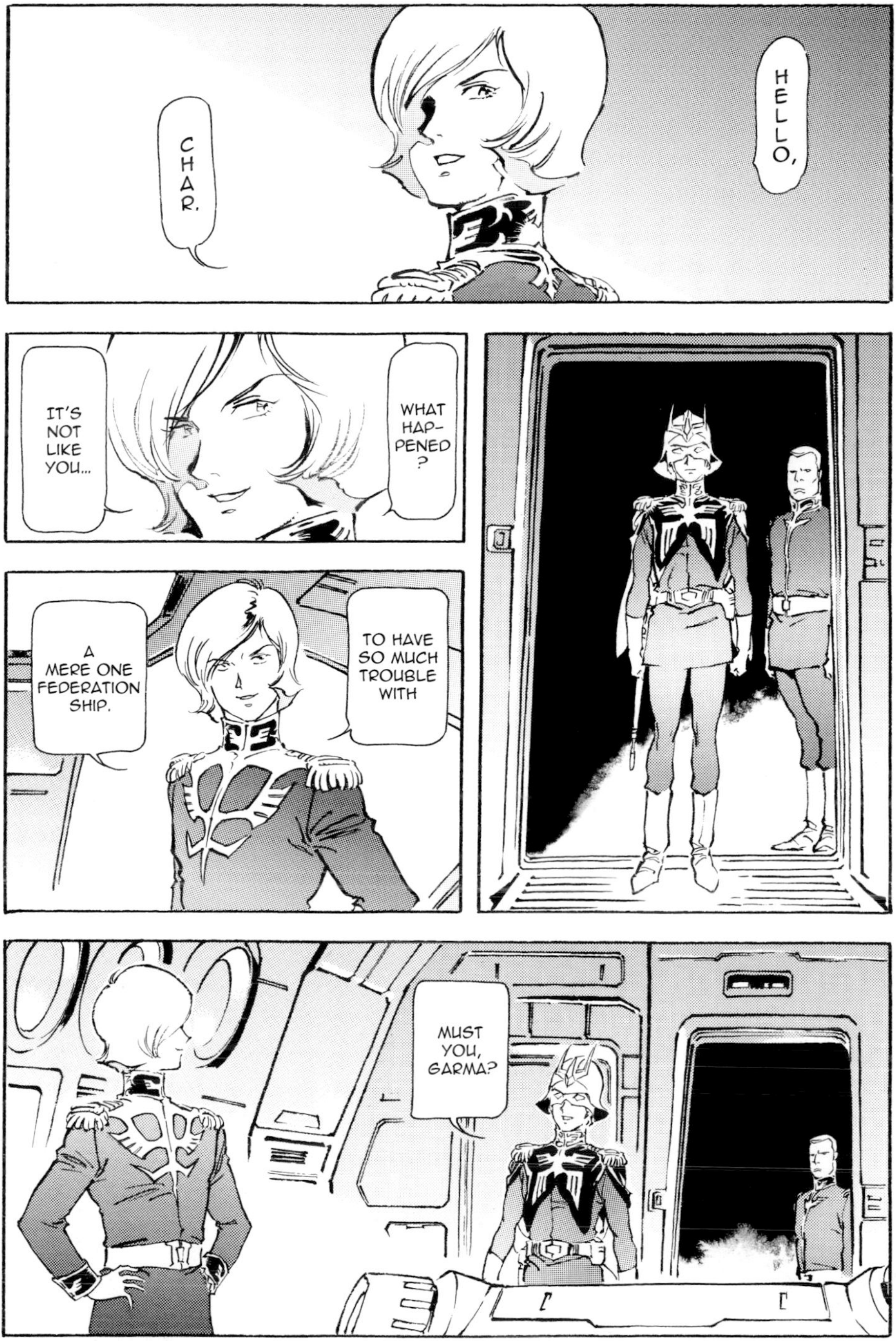
HELLO,
CHAR.
WHAT HAPPENED?
IT'S NOT LIKE YOU...
TO HAVE SO MUCH TROUBLE WITH
A MERE ONE FEDERATION SHIP.
MUST YOU, GARMA?

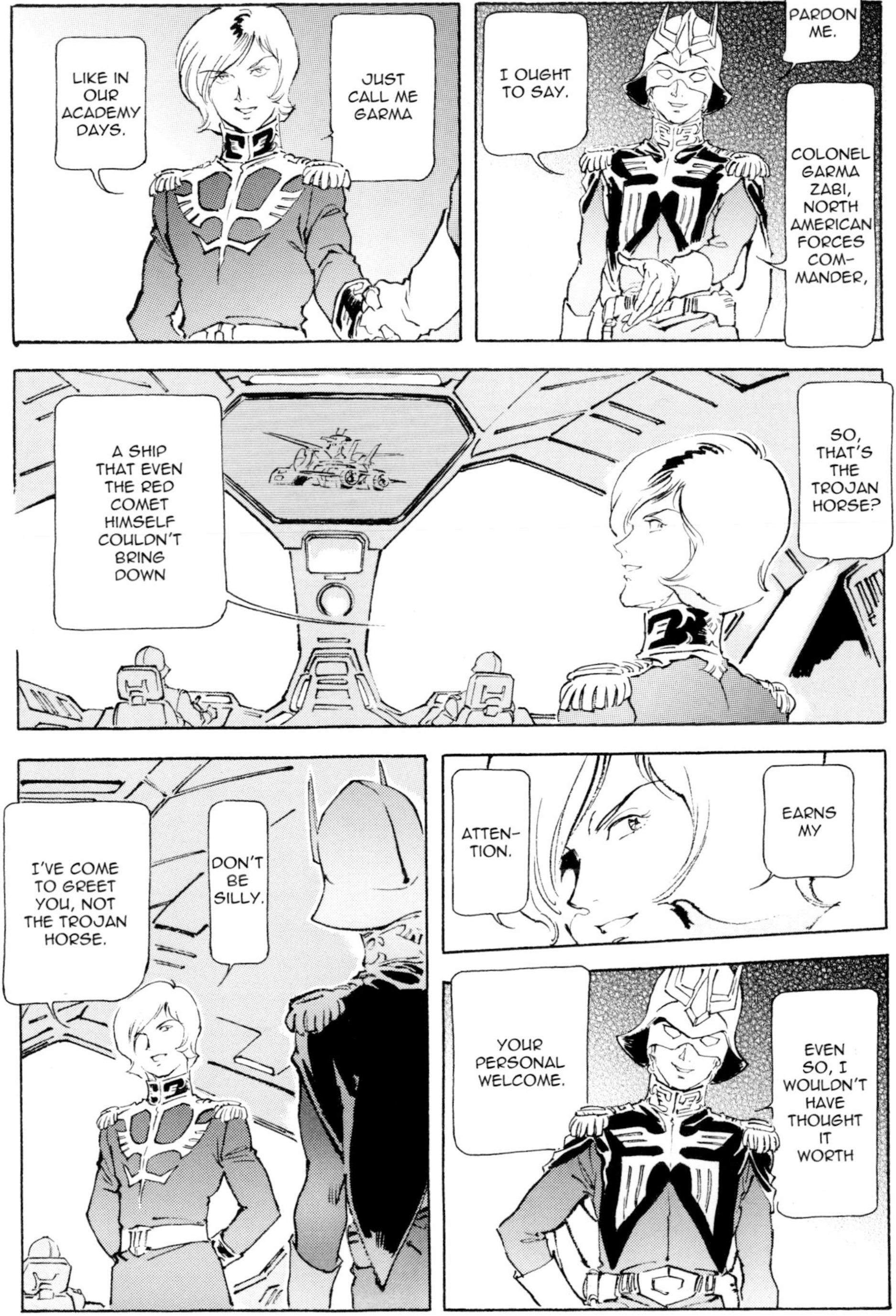
PARDON ME.
COLONEL GARMA ZABI, NORTH AMERICAN FORCES COM-MANDER,
I OUGHT TO SAY.
JUST CALL ME GARMA
LIKE IN OUR ACADEMY DAYS.
SO, THAT'S THE TROJAN HORSE?
A SHIP THAT EVEN THE RED COMET HIMSELF COULDN'T BRING DOWN
EARNS MY
ATTEN-TION.
EVEN SO, I WOULDN'T HAVE THOUGHT IT WORTH
YOUR PERSONAL WELCOME.
DON'T BE SILLY.
I'VE COME TO GREET YOU, NOT THE TROJAN HORSE.

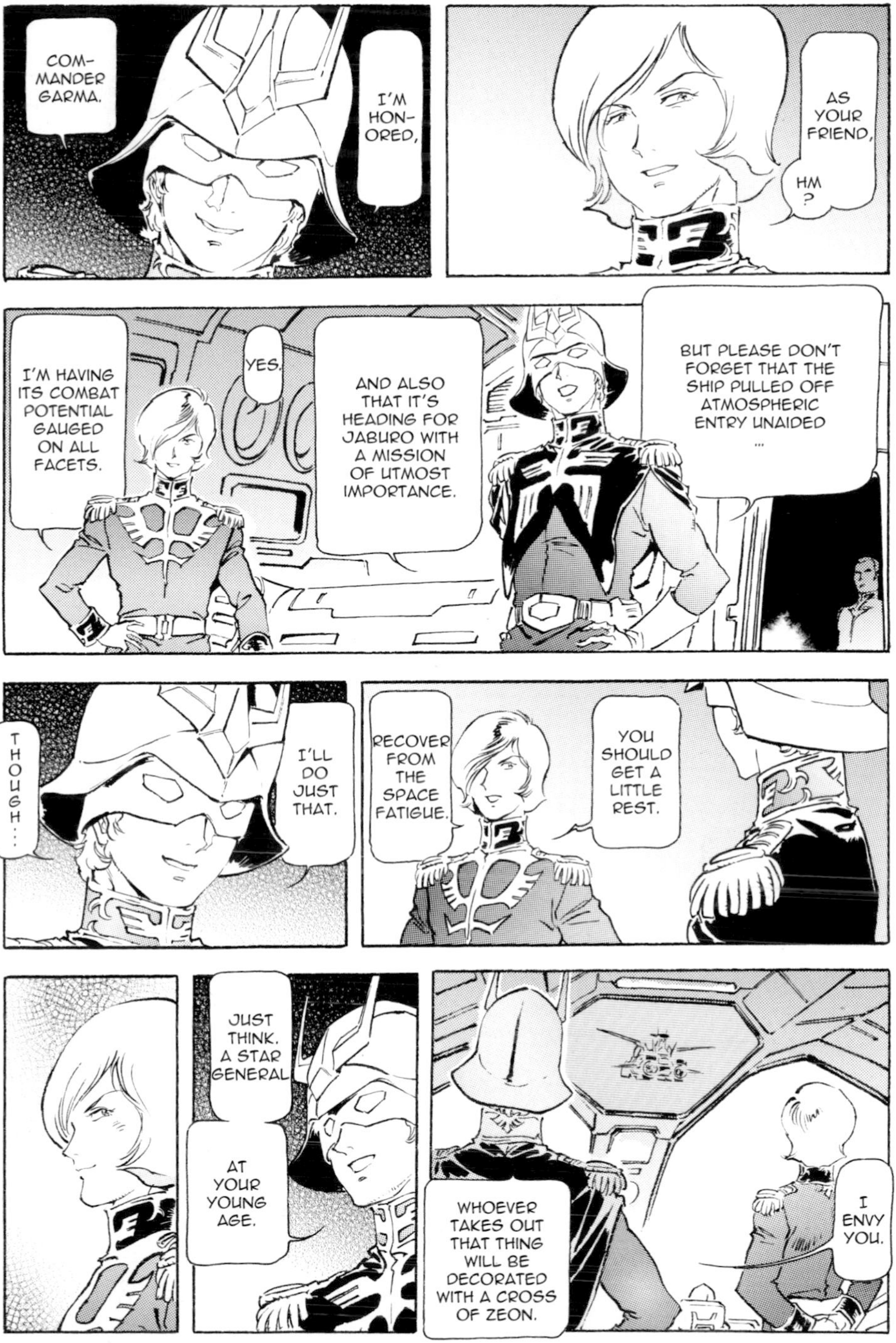
AS YOUR FRIEND,
HM?
COMMANDER GARMA.
I'M HONORED,
BUT PLEASE DON'T FORGET THAT THE SHIP PULLED OFF ATMOSPHERIC ENTRY UNAIDED ...
AND ALSO THAT IT'S HEADING FOR JABURO WITH A MISSION OF UTMOST IMPORTANCE.
YES.
I'M HAVING ITS COMBAT POTENTIAL GAUGED ON ALL FACETS.
YOU SHOULD GET A LITTLE REST.
RECOVER FROM THE SPACE FATIGUE.
I'LL DO JUST THAT.
THOUGH...
I ENVY YOU.
WHOEVER TAKES OUT THAT THING WILL BE DECORATED WITH A CROSS OF ZEON.
JUST THINK. A STAR GENERAL
AT YOUR YOUNG AGE.

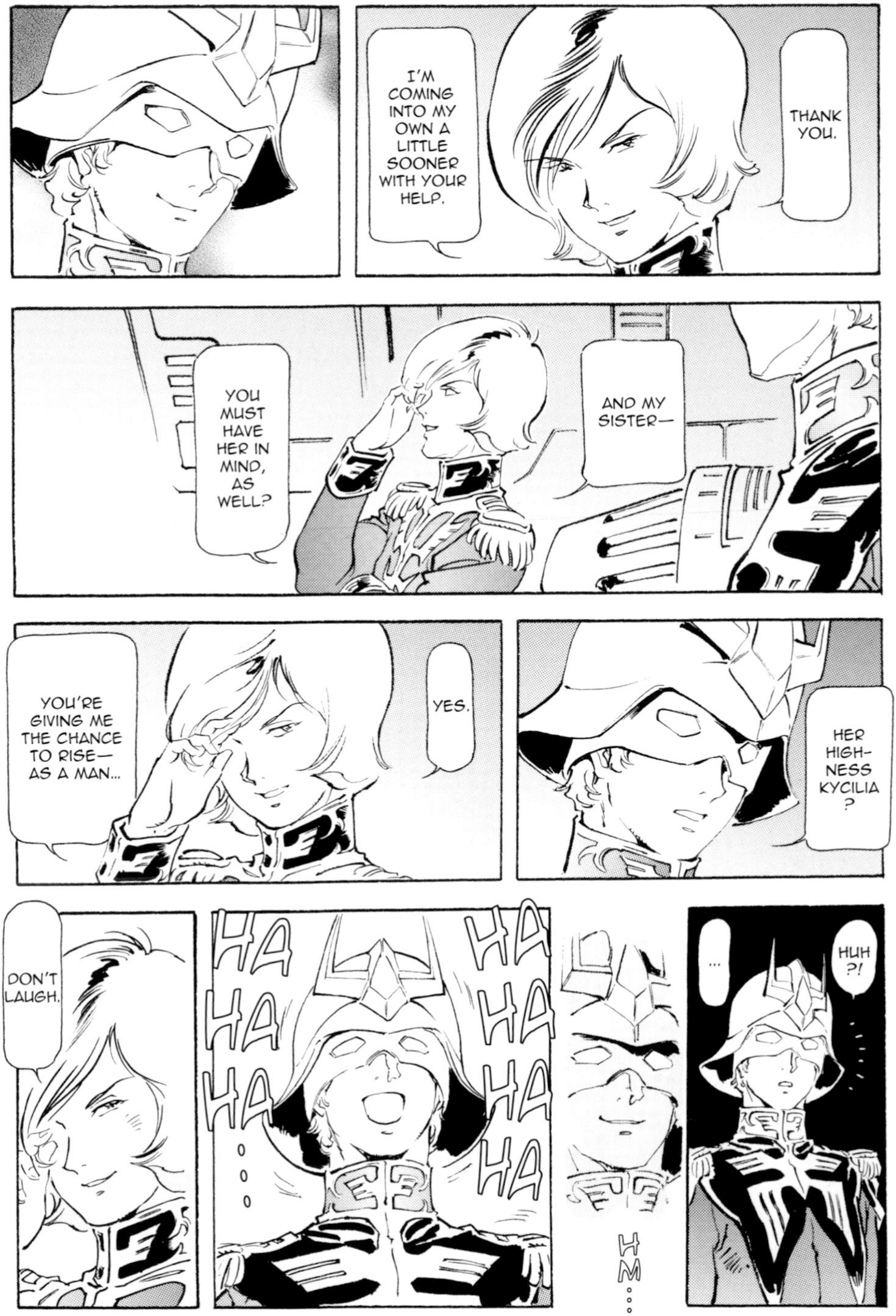
THANK YOU.
I'M COMING INTO MY OWN A LITTLE SOONER WITH YOUR HELP.
AND MY SISTER—
YOU MUST HAVE HER IN MIND, AS WELL?
HER HIGHNESS KYCILIA?
YES.
YOU'RE GIVING ME THE CHANCE TO RISE—AS A MAN...
HUH?!
...
HM...
HA HA HA HA HA
HA HA HA
DON'T LAUGH.

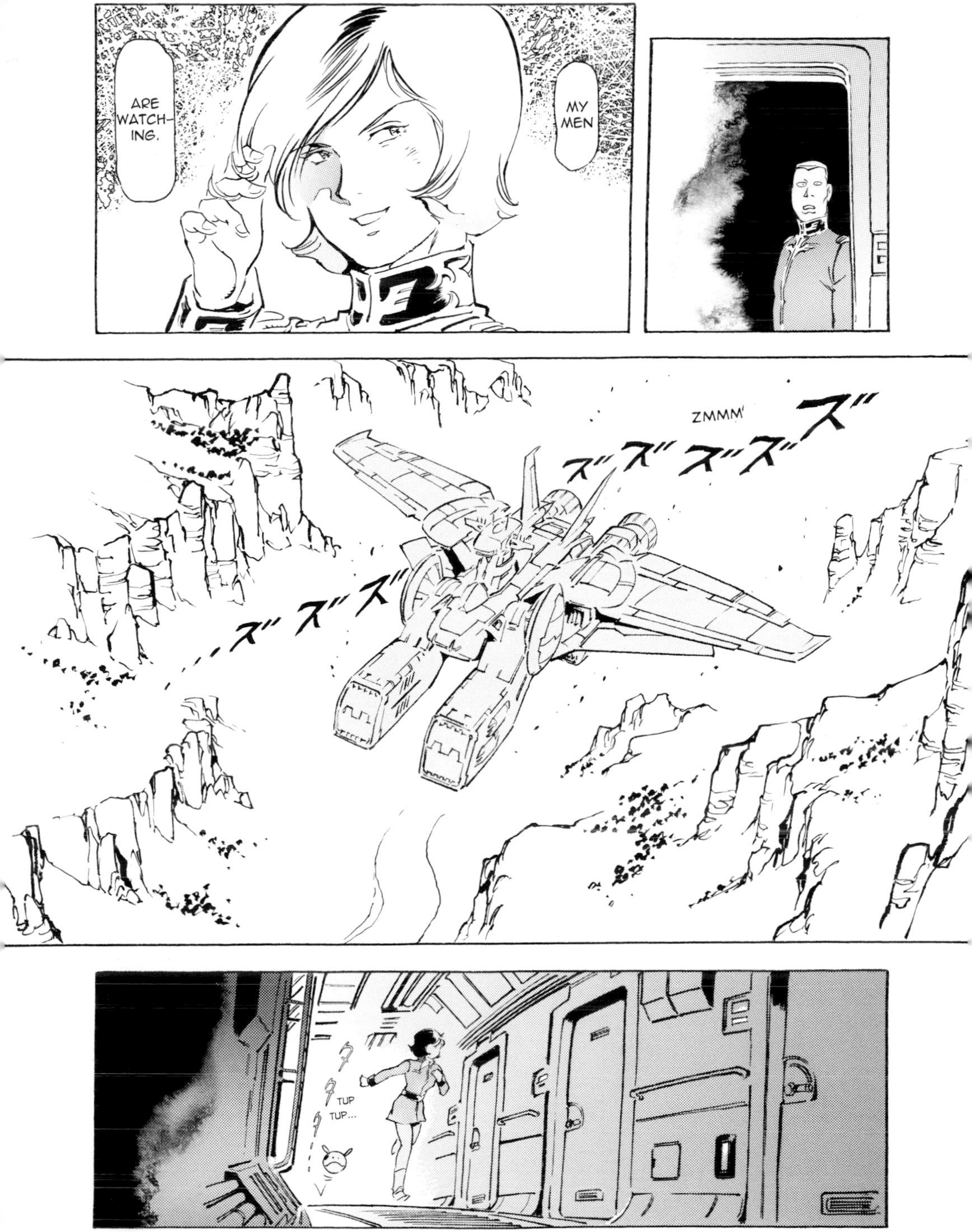
MY MEN
ARE WATCHING.
ZMMM'
ズズズズ
...ズズズ
タタタ
TUP TUP...

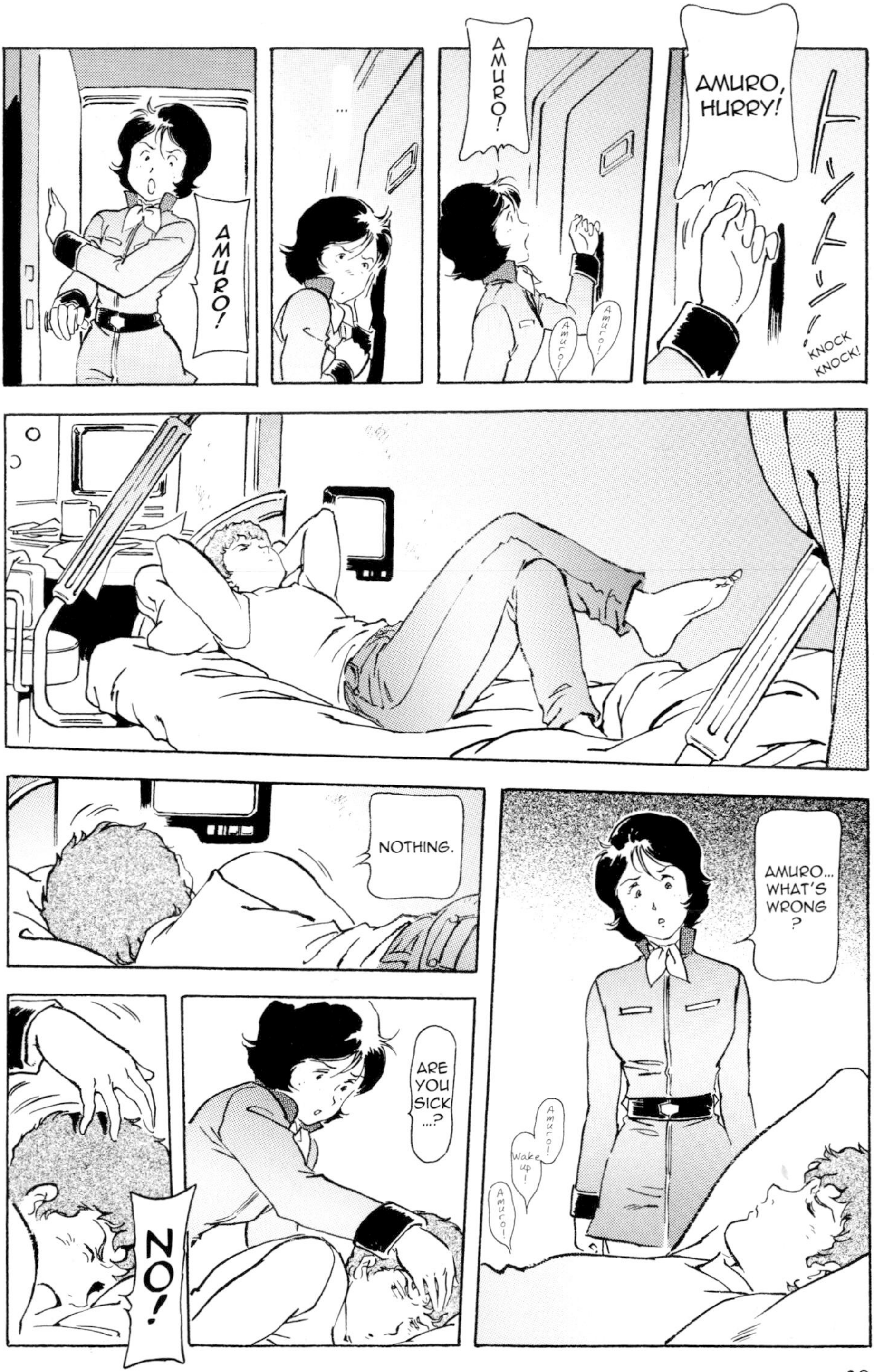

AMURO, HURRY!
KNOCK KNOCK!
AMURO!
Amuro!
Amuro!
...
AMURO!
AMURO... WHAT'S WRONG?
Amuro!
Wake up!
Amuro!
NOTHING.
ARE YOU SICK...?
NO!

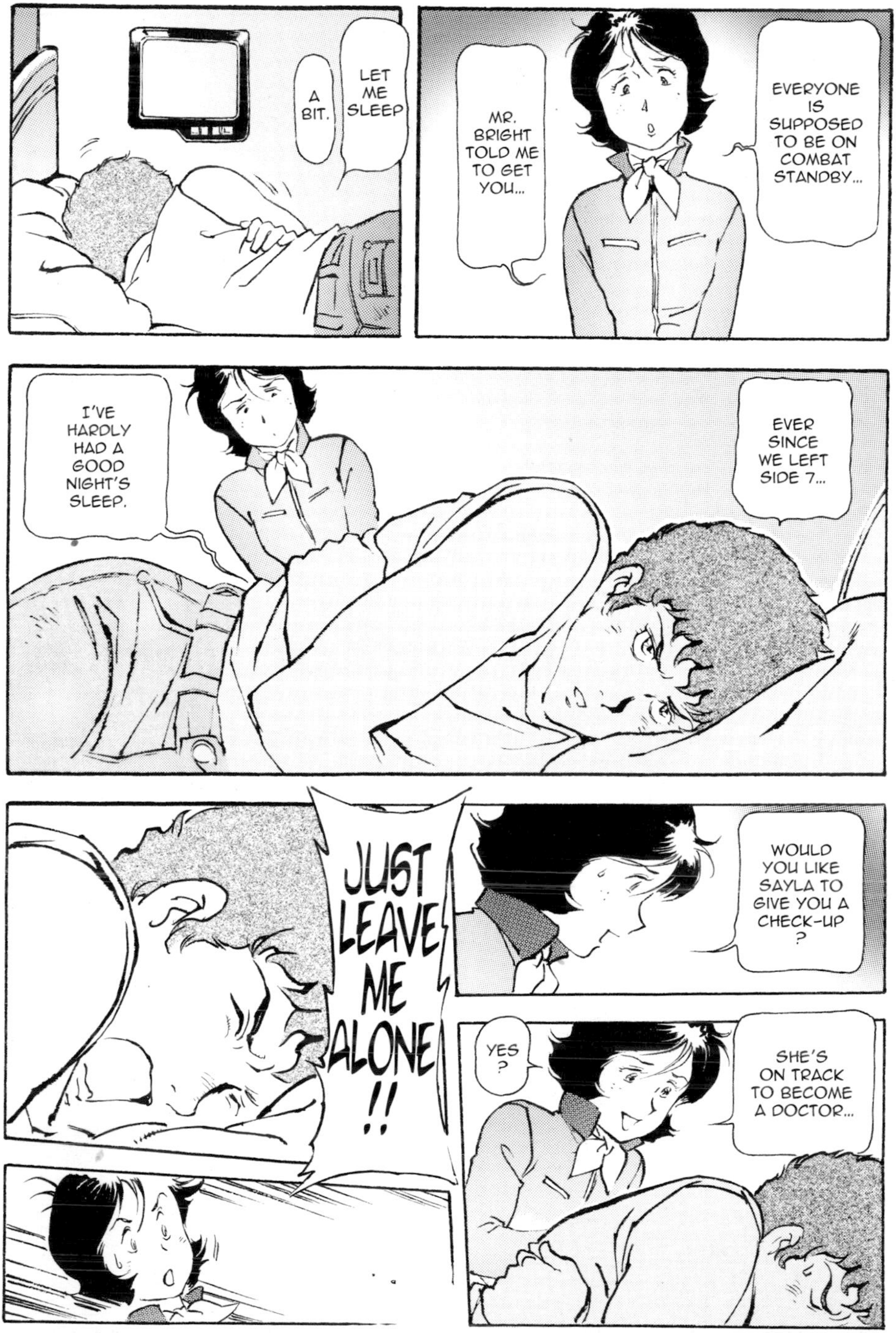
EVERYONE IS SUPPOSED TO BE ON COMBAT STANDBY...
MR. BRIGHT TOLD ME TO GET YOU...
LET ME SLEEP
A BIT.
EVER SINCE WE LEFT SIDE 7...
I'VE HARDLY HAD A GOOD NIGHT'S SLEEP.
WOULD YOU LIKE SAYLA TO GIVE YOU A CHECK-UP?
SHE'S ON TRACK TO BECOME A DOCTOR...
YES?
JUST LEAVE ME ALONE!!

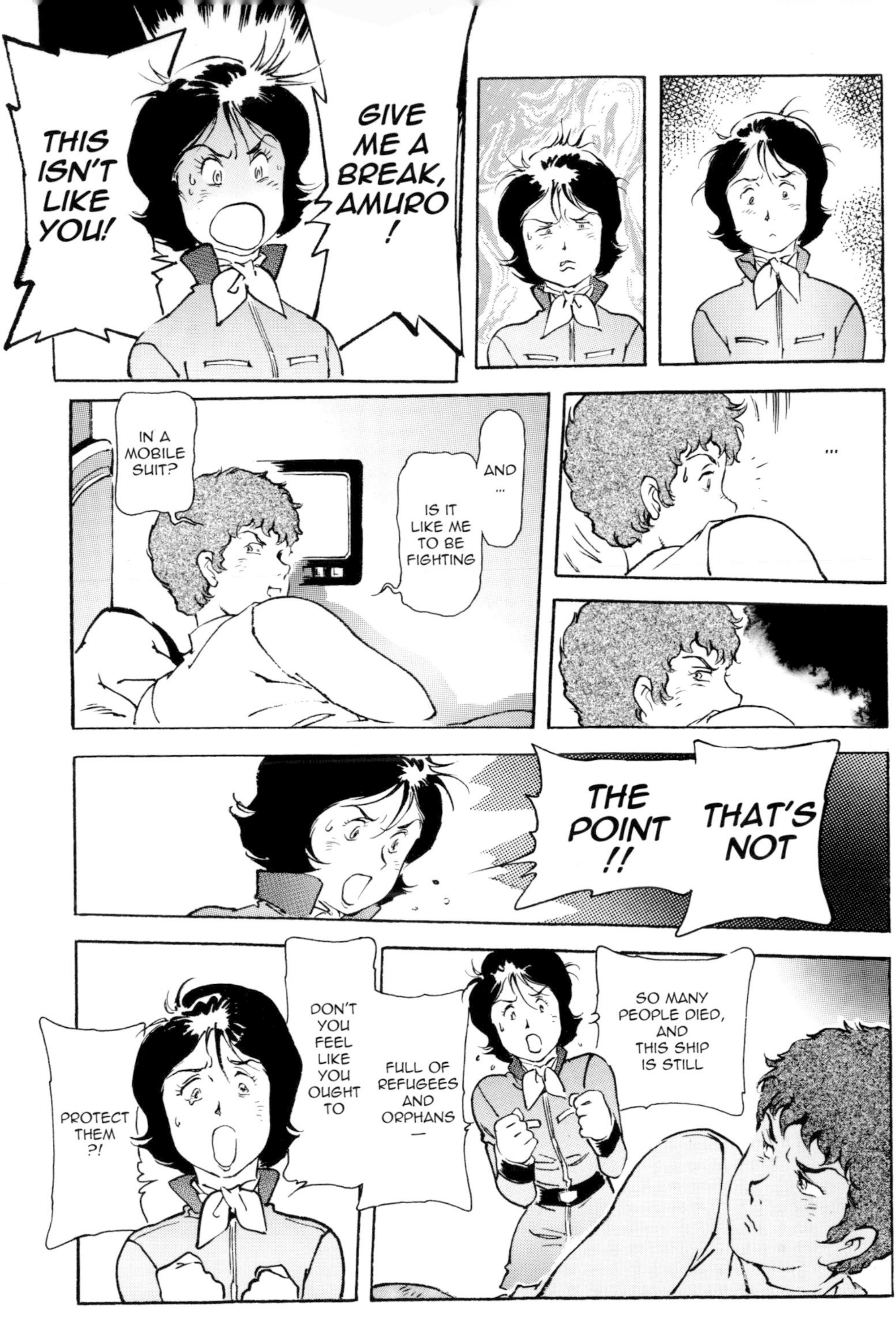
GIVE ME A BREAK, AMURO!
THIS ISN'T LIKE YOU!
...
AND ...
IS IT LIKE ME TO BE FIGHTING
IN A MOBILE SUIT?
THAT'S NOT
THE POINT!!
SO MANY PEOPLE DIED, AND THIS SHIP IS STILL
FULL OF REFUGEES AND ORPHANS —
DON'T YOU FEEL LIKE YOU OUGHT TO
PROTECT THEM?!

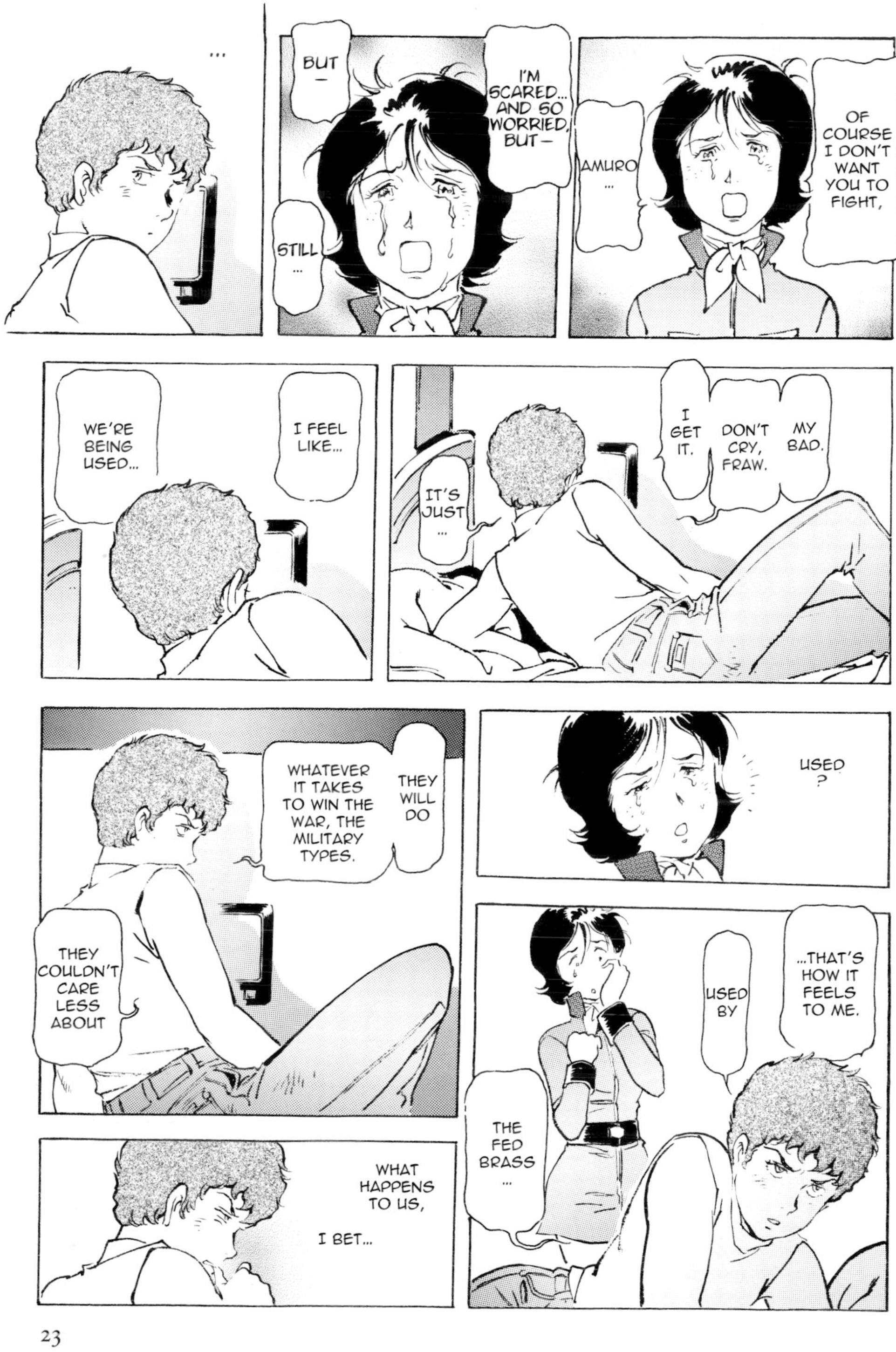
OF COURSE I DON'T WANT YOU TO FIGHT,
AMURO ...
I'M SCARED... AND SO WORRIED, BUT—
BUT —
STILL ...
...
MY BAD.
DON'T CRY, FRAW.
I GET IT.
IT'S JUST ...
I FEEL LIKE...
WE'RE BEING USED...
USED ?
...THAT'S HOW IT FEELS TO ME.
USED BY
THE FED BRASS ...
THEY WILL DO
WHATEVER IT TAKES TO WIN THE WAR, THE MILITARY TYPES.
THEY COULDN'T CARE LESS ABOUT
WHAT HAPPENS TO US,
I BET...

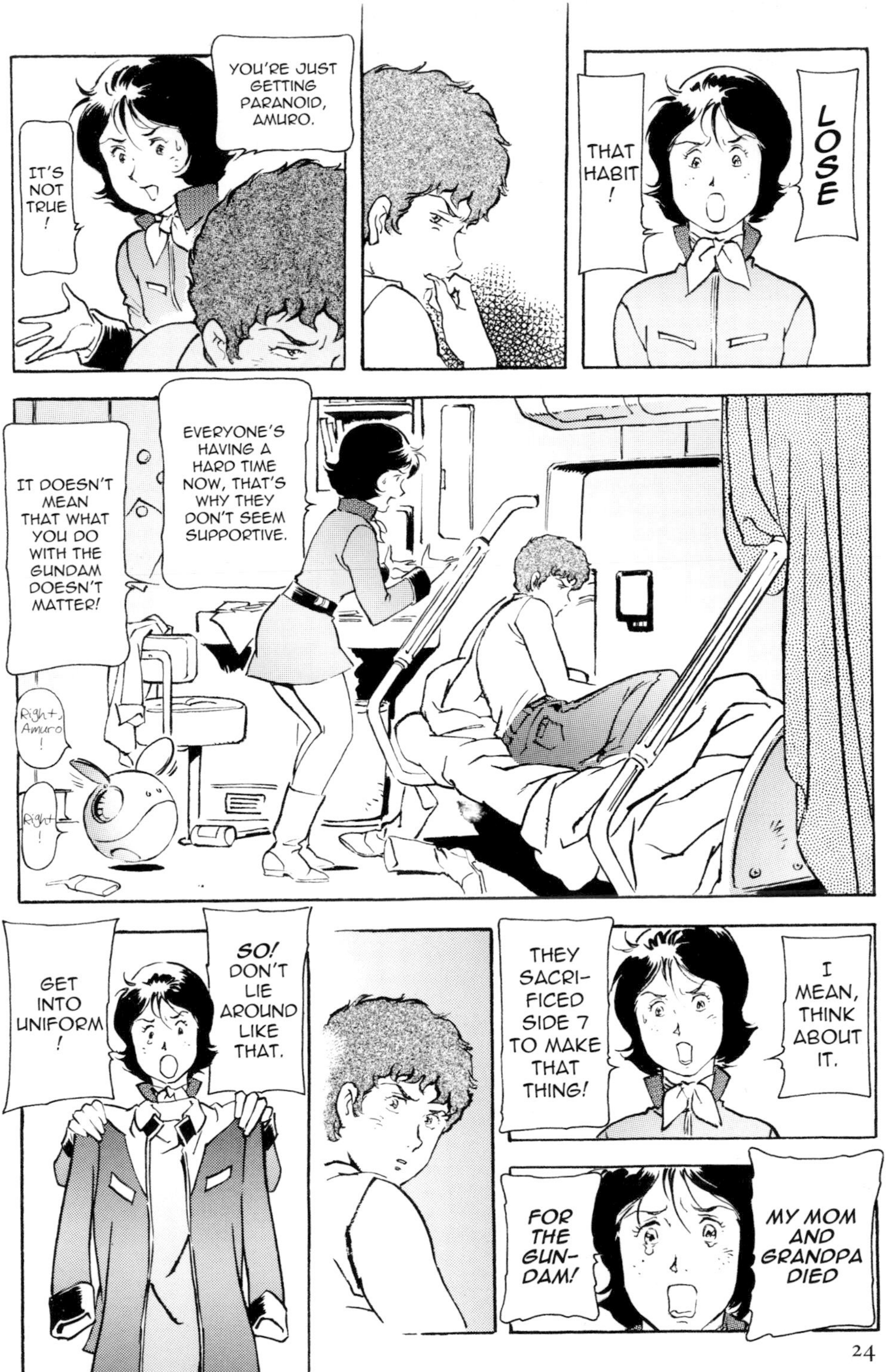
LOSE
THAT HABIT!
YOU'RE JUST GETTING PARANOID, AMURO.
IT'S NOT TRUE!
EVERYONE'S HAVING A HARD TIME NOW, THAT'S WHY THEY DON'T SEEM SUPPORTIVE.
IT DOESN'T MEAN THAT WHAT YOU DO WITH THE GUNDAM DOESN'T MATTER!
Right, Amuro!
Right!
I MEAN, THINK ABOUT IT.
THEY SACRIFICED SIDE 7 TO MAKE THAT THING!
MY MOM AND GRANDPA DIED
FOR THE GUNDAM!
SO! DON'T LIE AROUND LIKE THAT.
GET INTO UNIFORM!

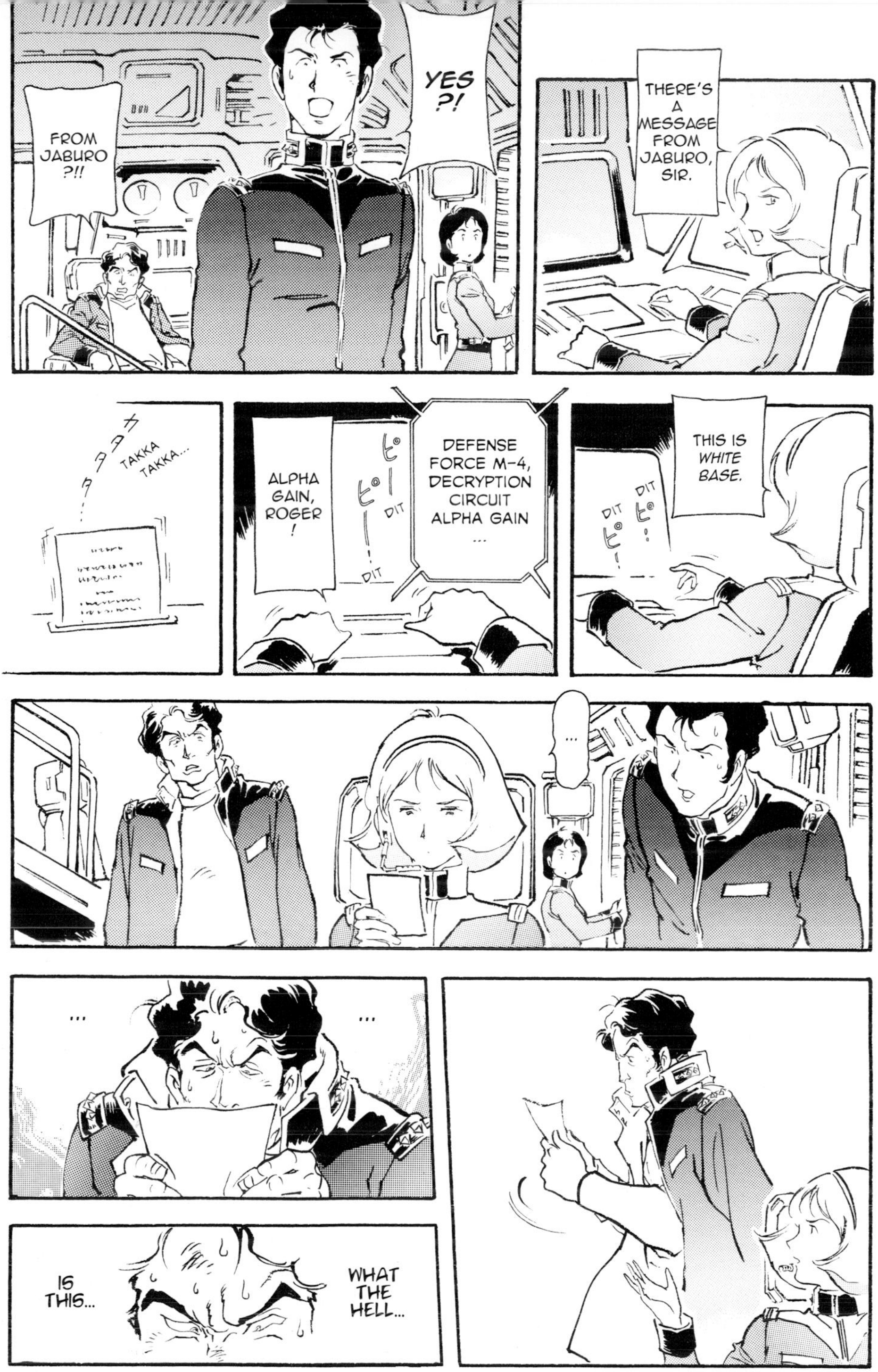
THERE'S A MESSAGE FROM JABURO, SIR.
YES ?!
FROM JABURO ?!!
THIS IS WHITE BASE.
DIT DIT
DEFENSE FORCE M-4, DECRYPTION CIRCUIT ALPHA GAIN ...
ALPHA GAIN, ROGER!
DIT DIT
TAKKA TAKKA...
...
...
...
WHAT THE HELL...
IS THIS...

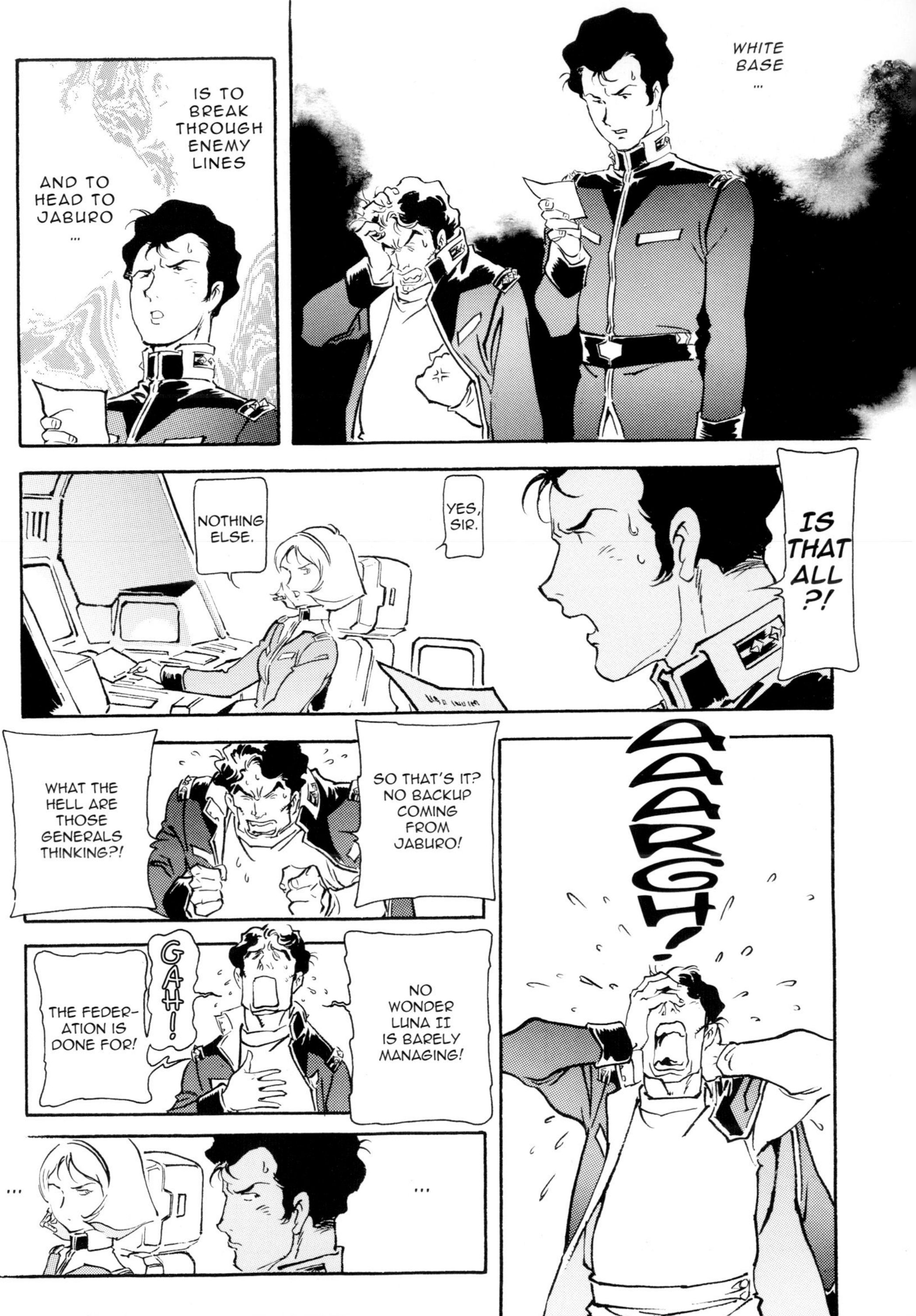
WHITE BASE ...
IS TO BREAK THROUGH ENEMY LINES
AND TO HEAD TO JABURO ...
IS THAT ALL?!
YES, SIR.
NOTHING ELSE.
AAARGH!
SO THAT'S IT? NO BACKUP COMING FROM JABURO!
WHAT THE HELL ARE THOSE GENERALS THINKING?!
NO WONDER LUNA II IS BARELY MANAGING!
GAH!
THE FEDER-ATION IS DONE FOR!
...
...

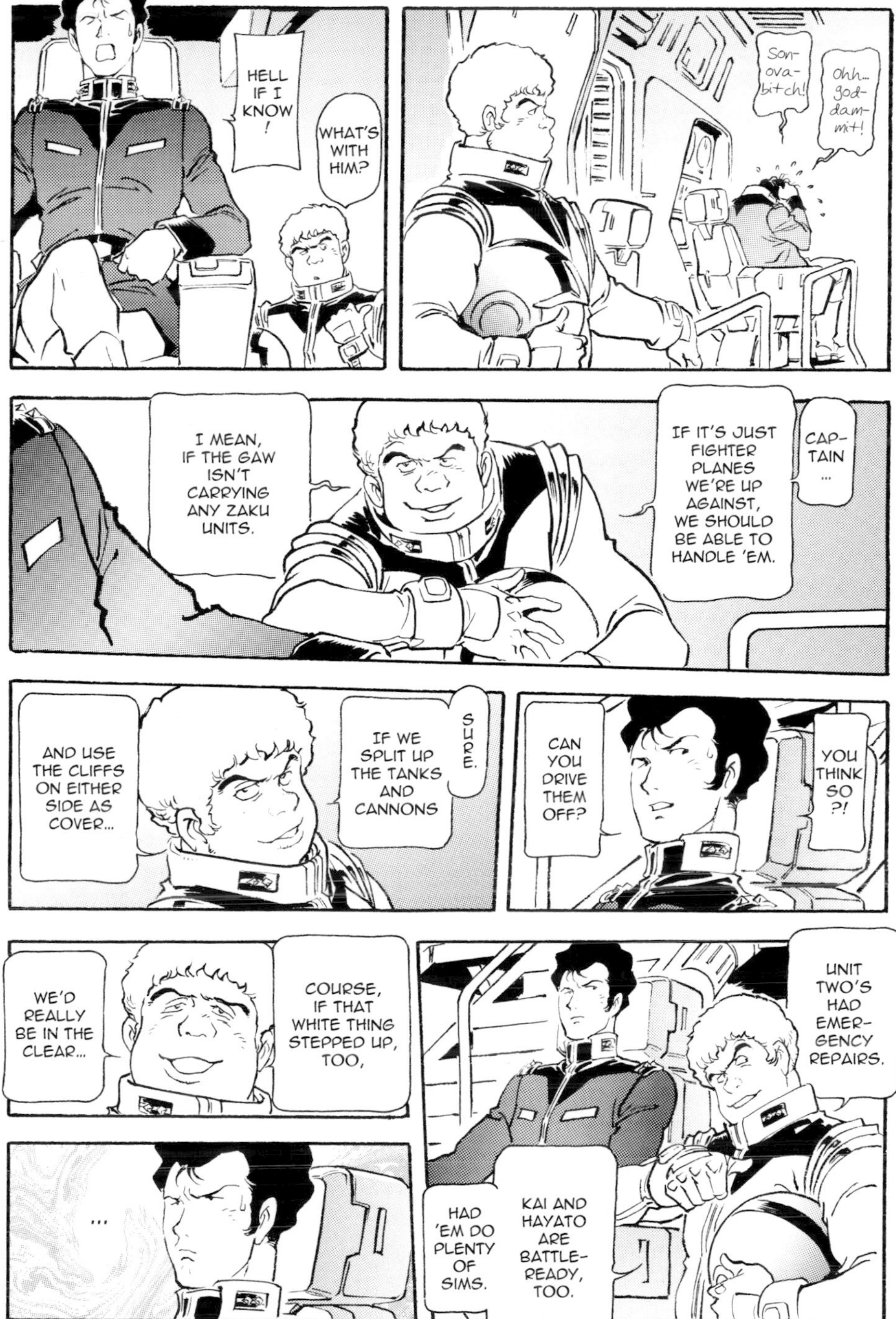
Ohh... god-dam-mit!
Son-ova-bitch!
WHAT'S WITH HIM?
HELL IF I KNOW!
CAP-TAIN...
IF IT'S JUST FIGHTER PLANES WE'RE UP AGAINST, WE SHOULD BE ABLE TO HANDLE 'EM.
I MEAN, IF THE GAW ISN'T CARRYING ANY ZAKU UNITS.
YOU THINK SO?!
CAN YOU DRIVE THEM OFF?
SURE.
IF WE SPLIT UP THE TANKS AND CANNONS
AND USE THE CLIFFS ON EITHER SIDE AS COVER...
UNIT TWO'S HAD EMERGENCY REPAIRS.
KAI AND HAYATO ARE BATTLE-READY, TOO.
HAD 'EM DO PLENTY OF SIMS.
COURSE, IF THAT WHITE THING STEPPED UP, TOO,
WE'D REALLY BE IN THE CLEAR...
...

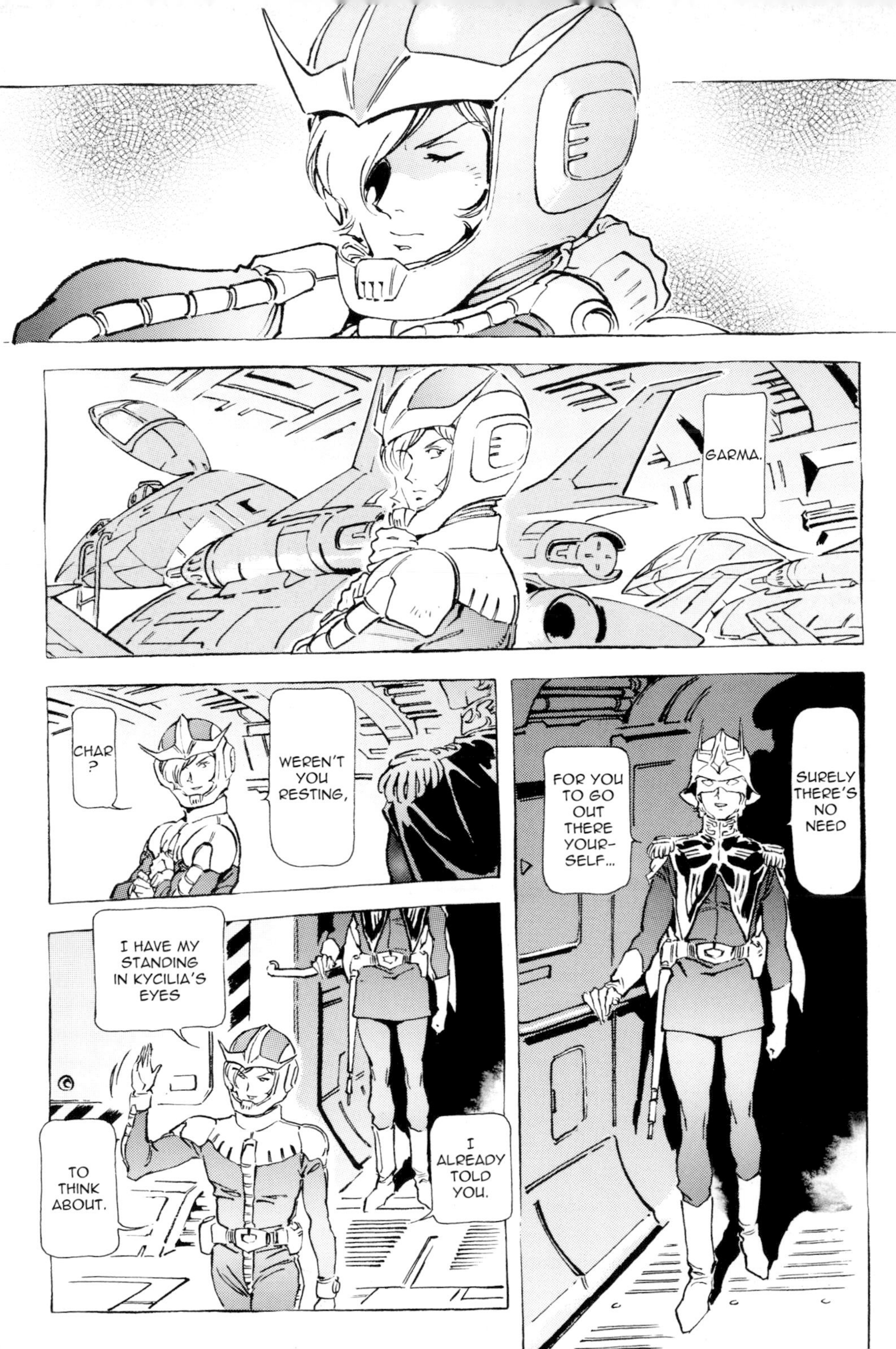
GARMA.
SURELY THERE'S NO NEED
FOR YOU TO GO OUT THERE YOURSELF...
WEREN'T YOU RESTING,
CHAR?
I ALREADY TOLD YOU.
I HAVE MY STANDING IN KYCILIA'S EYES
TO THINK ABOUT.

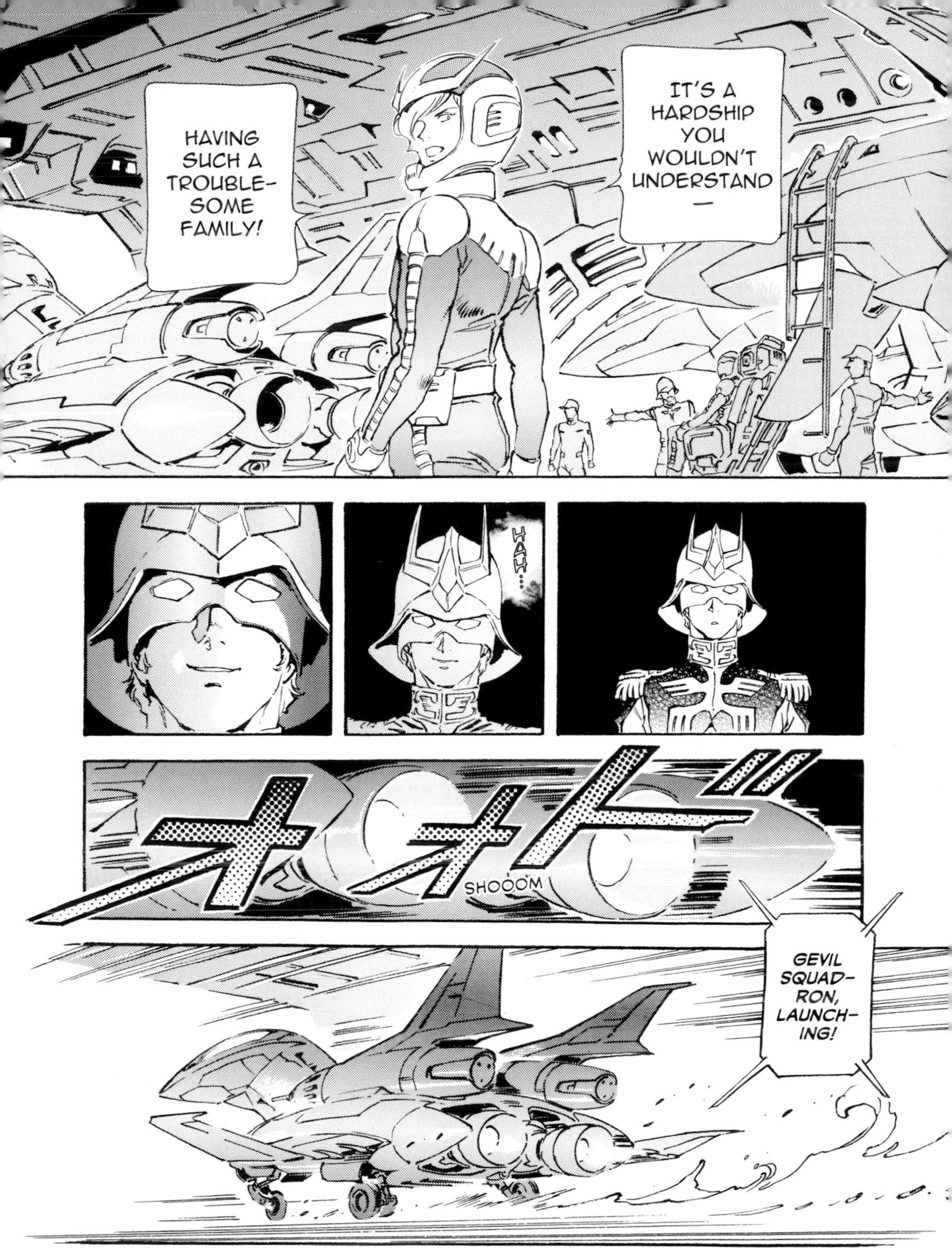
IT'S A HARDSHIP YOU WOULDN'T UNDERSTAND —
HAVING SUCH A TROUBLE-SOME FAMILY!
HAH...
SHOOOM
GEVIL SQUAD-RON, LAUNCH-ING!

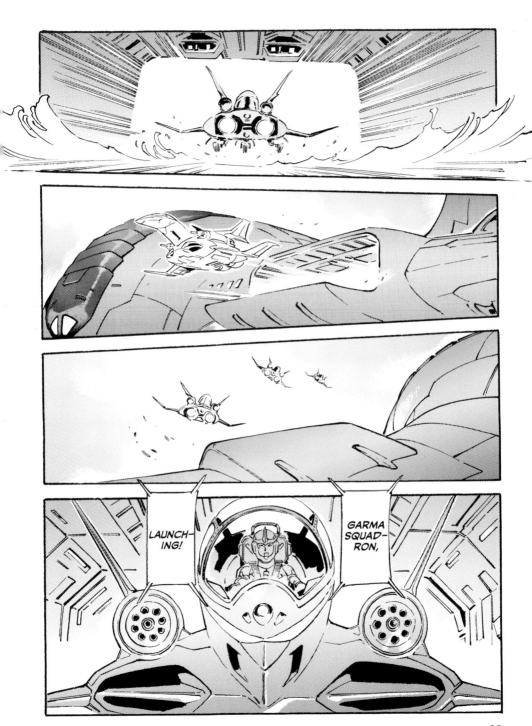

LAUNCH-
ING!

GARMA
SQUAD-
RON,

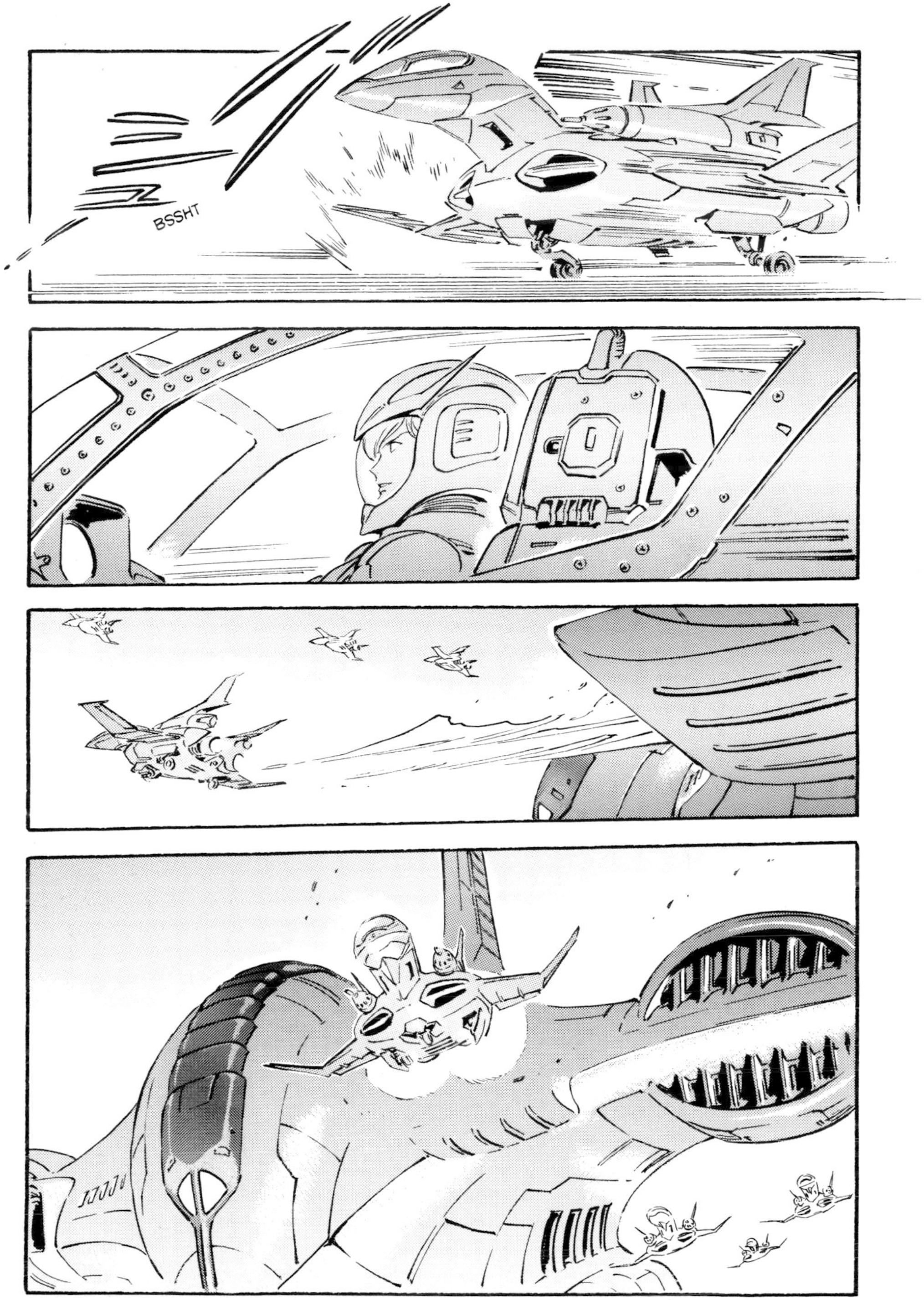
BSSHT

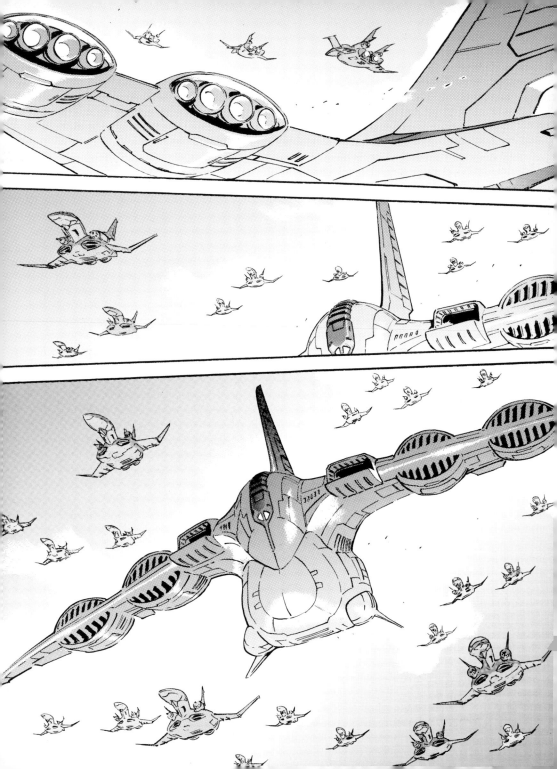

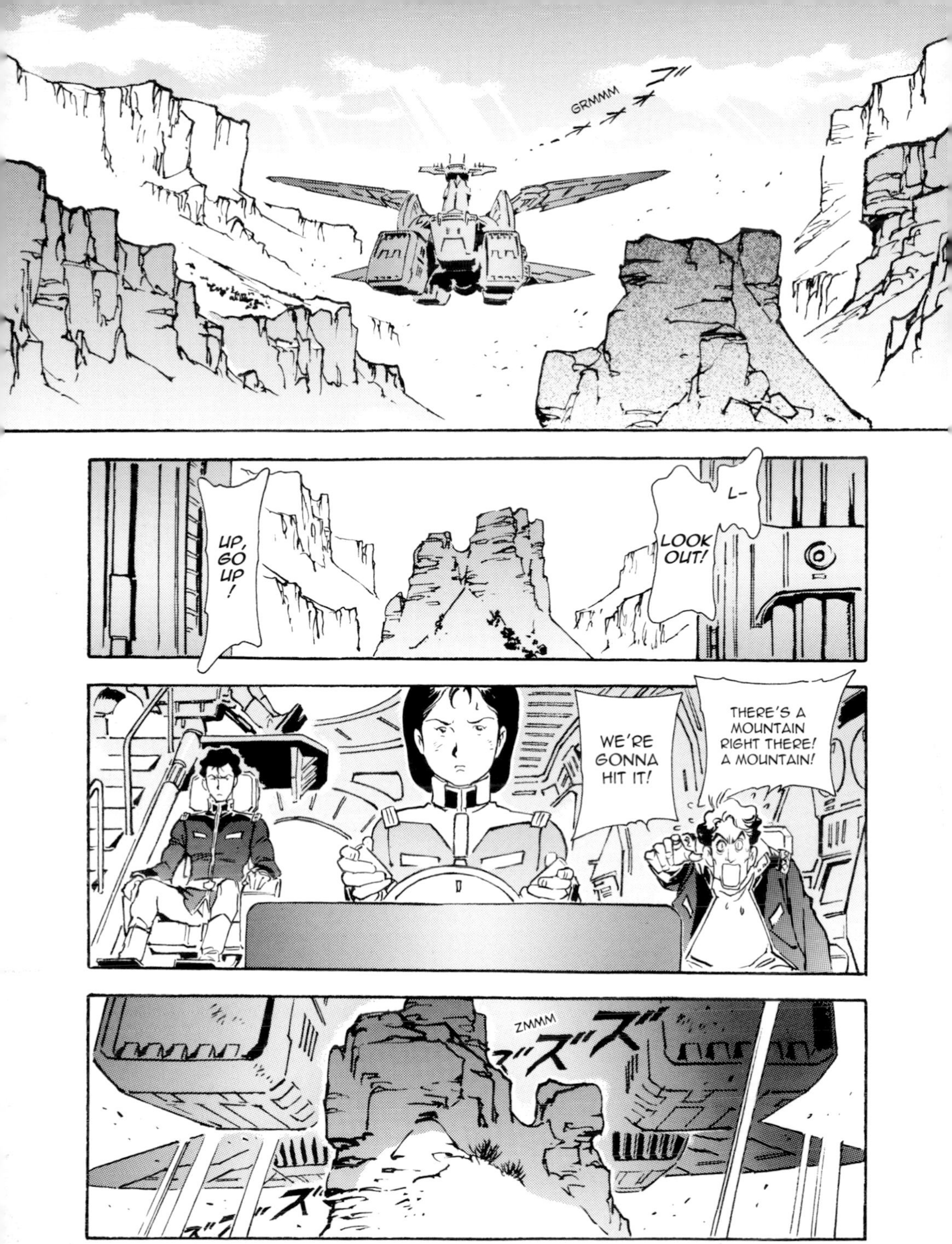
GRMMM
L-
LOOK OUT!
UP, GO UP!
THERE'S A MOUNTAIN RIGHT THERE! A MOUNTAIN!
WE'RE GONNA HIT IT!
ZMMM

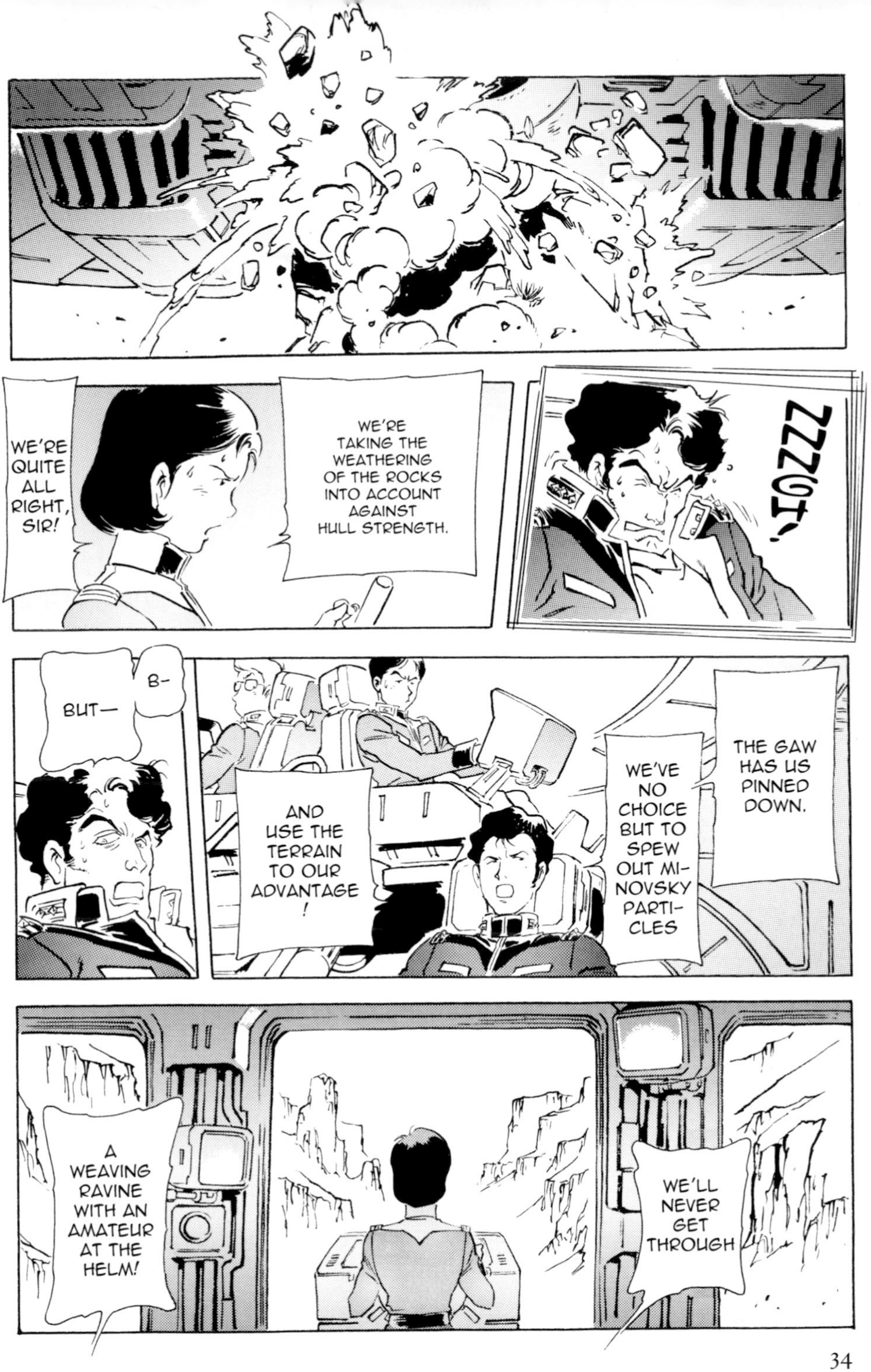
ZZNGH!
WE'RE TAKING THE WEATHERING OF THE ROCKS INTO ACCOUNT AGAINST HULL STRENGTH.
WE'RE QUITE ALL RIGHT, SIR!
THE GAW HAS US PINNED DOWN.
WE'VE NO CHOICE BUT TO SPEW OUT MI-NOVSKY PARTI-CLES
AND USE THE TERRAIN TO OUR ADVANTAGE!
B-
BUT—
WE'LL NEVER GET THROUGH
A WEAVING RAVINE WITH AN AMATEUR AT THE HELM!

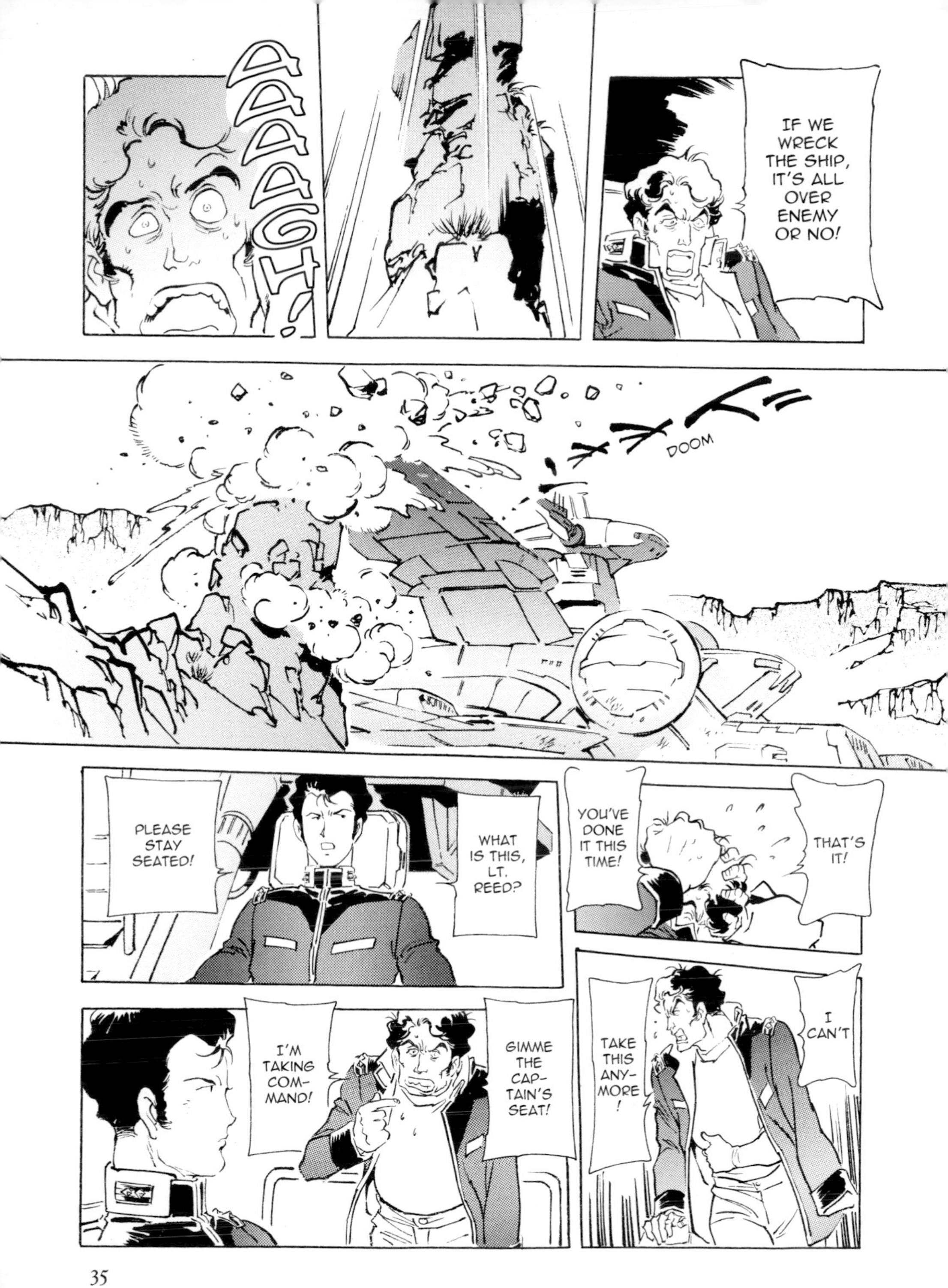
IF WE WRECK THE SHIP, IT'S ALL OVER ENEMY OR NO!
AAAAGH!
DOOM
THAT'S IT!
YOU'VE DONE IT THIS TIME!
WHAT IS THIS, LT. REED?
PLEASE STAY SEATED!
I CAN'T
TAKE THIS ANYMORE!
GIMME THE CAPTAIN'S SEAT!
I'M TAKING COMMAND!

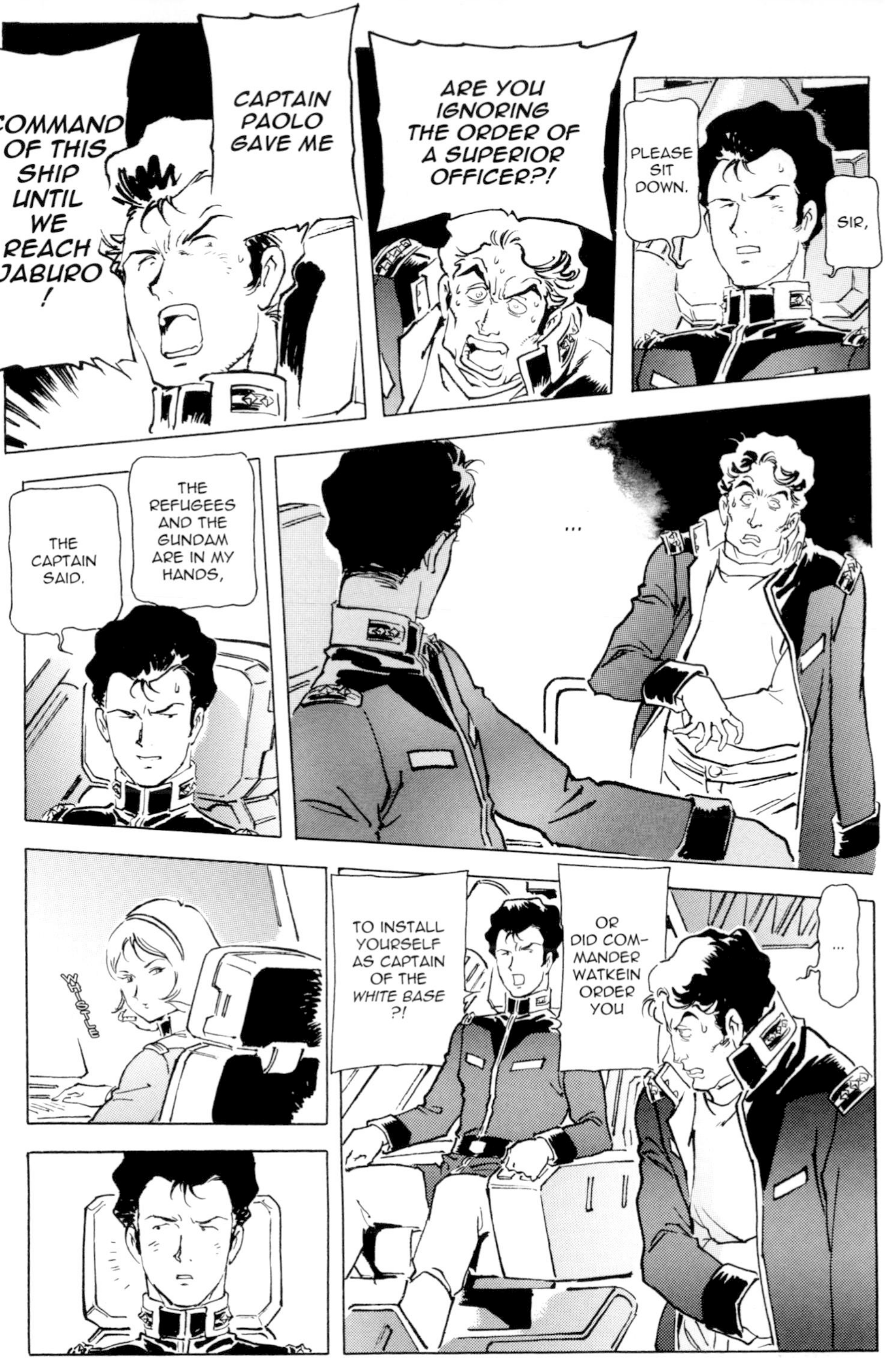
SIR,
PLEASE SIT DOWN.
ARE YOU IGNORING THE ORDER OF A SUPERIOR OFFICER?!
CAPTAIN PAOLO GAVE ME
COMMAND OF THIS SHIP UNTIL WE REACH JABURO!
...
THE REFUGEES AND THE GUNDAM ARE IN MY HANDS,
THE CAPTAIN SAID.
...
OR DID COM-MANDER WATKEIN ORDER YOU
TO INSTALL YOURSELF AS CAPTAIN OF THE *WHITE BASE*?!

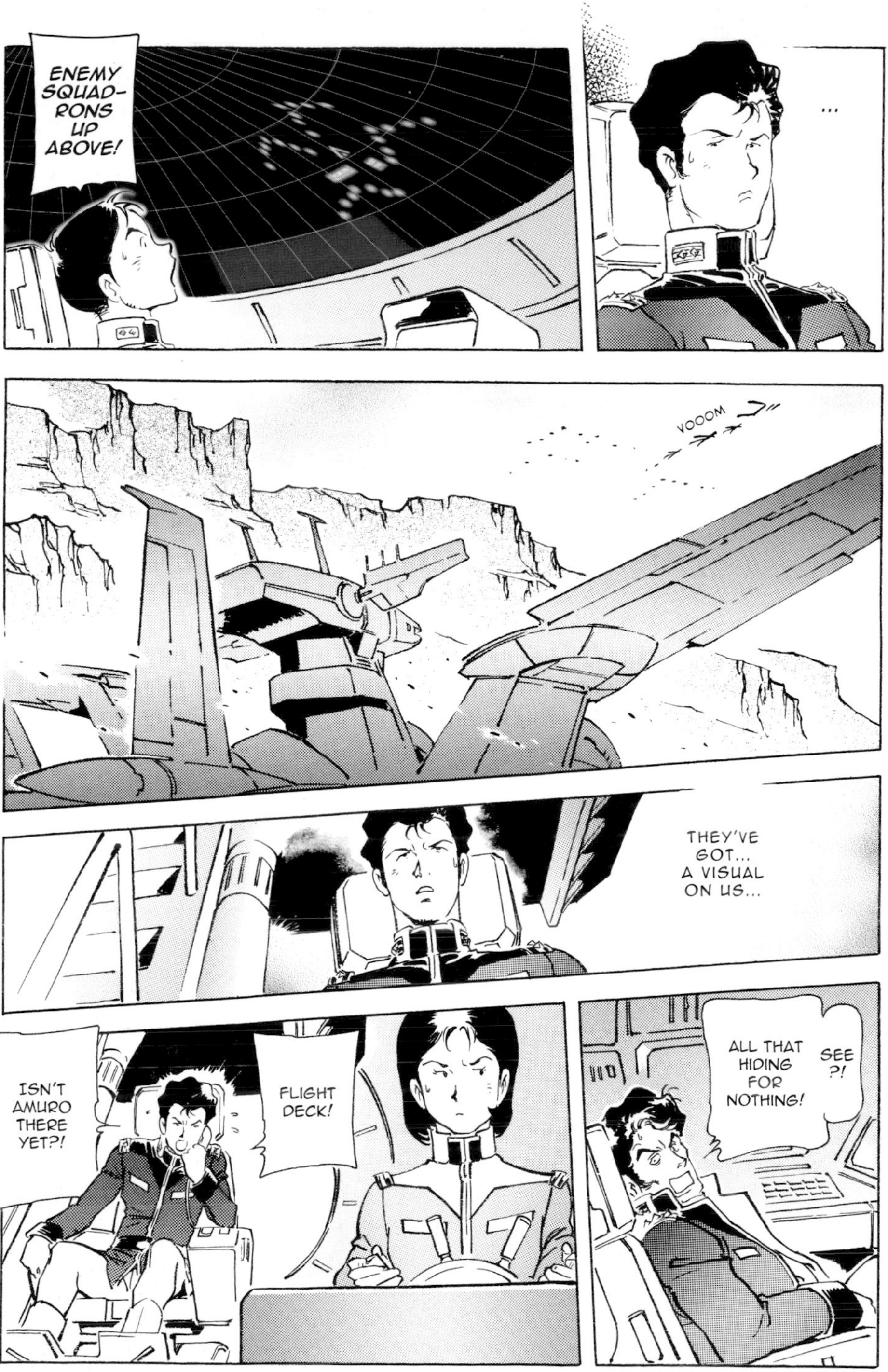
...
ENEMY SQUADRONS UP ABOVE!
VOOOM
THEY'VE GOT... A VISUAL ON US...
SEE?!
ALL THAT HIDING FOR NOTHING!
FLIGHT DECK!
ISN'T AMURO THERE YET?!

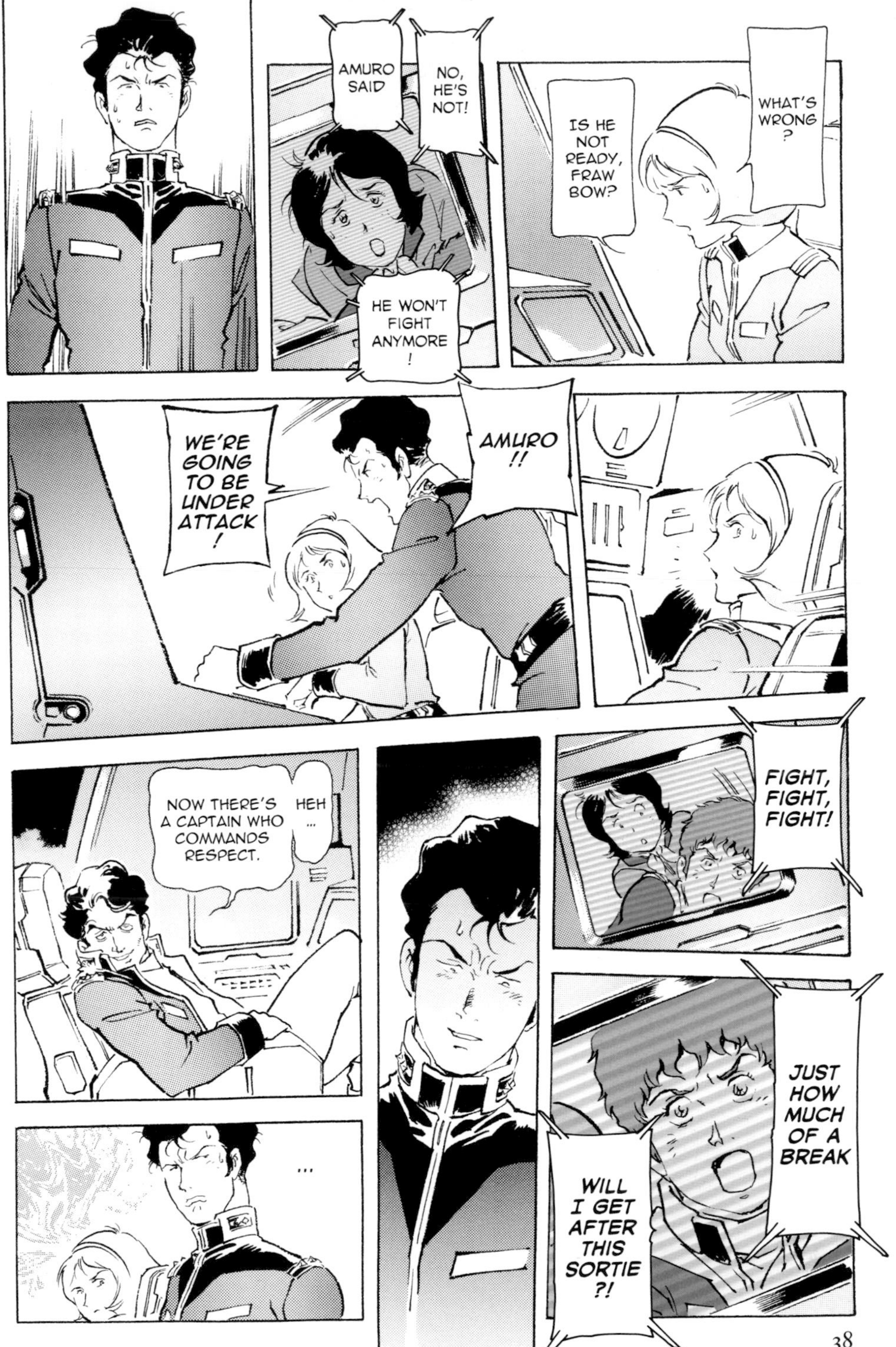
WHAT'S WRONG?
IS HE NOT READY, FRAW BOW?
NO, HE'S NOT!
AMURO SAID
HE WON'T FIGHT ANYMORE!
AMURO!!
WE'RE GOING TO BE UNDER ATTACK!
FIGHT, FIGHT, FIGHT!
JUST HOW MUCH OF A BREAK
WILL I GET AFTER THIS SORTIE?!
HEH...
NOW THERE'S A CAPTAIN WHO COMMANDS RESPECT.
...

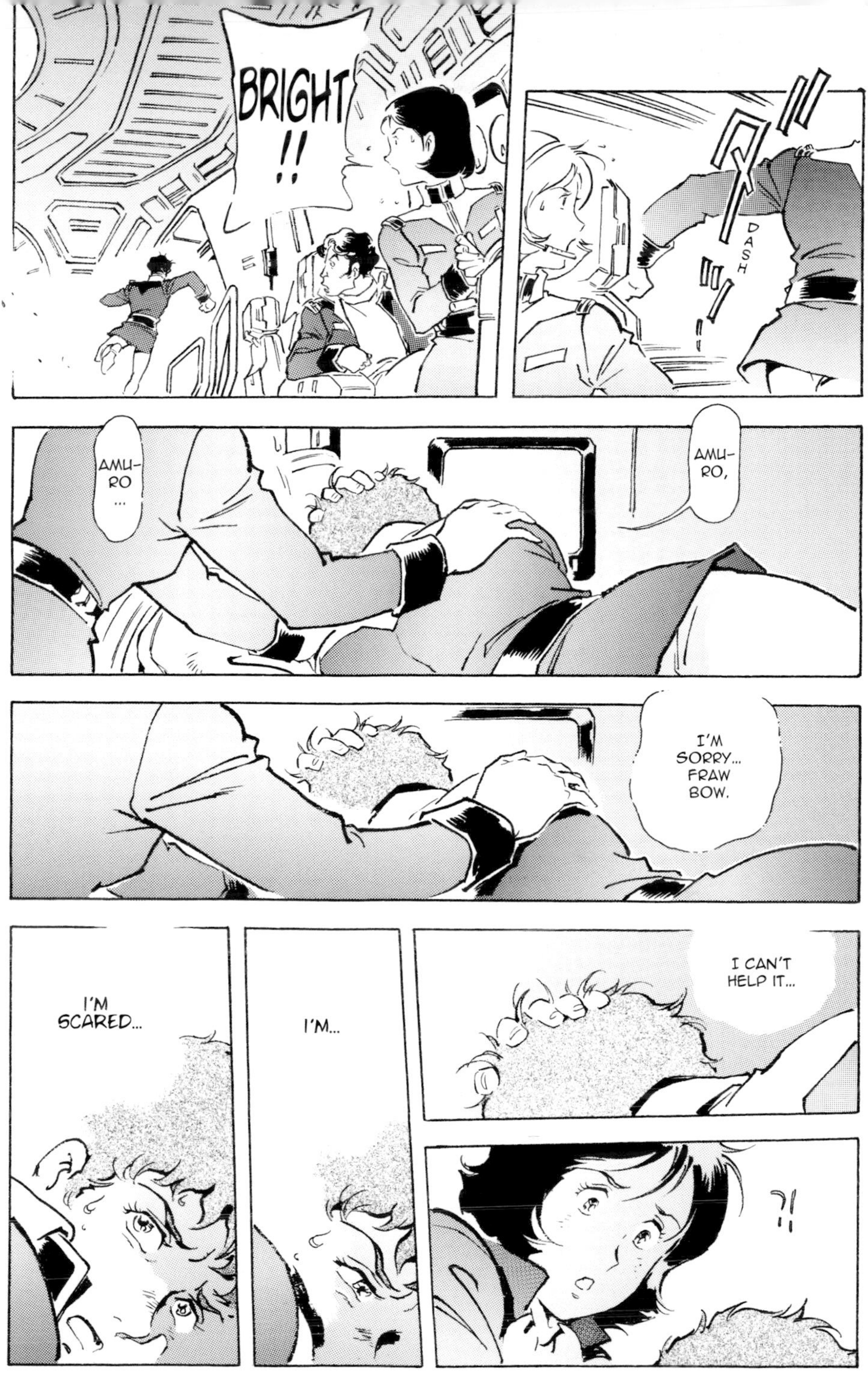
DASH
BRIGHT!!
AMU-RO,
AMU-RO...
I'M SORRY... FRAW BOW.
I CAN'T HELP IT...
?!
I'M...
I'M SCARED...

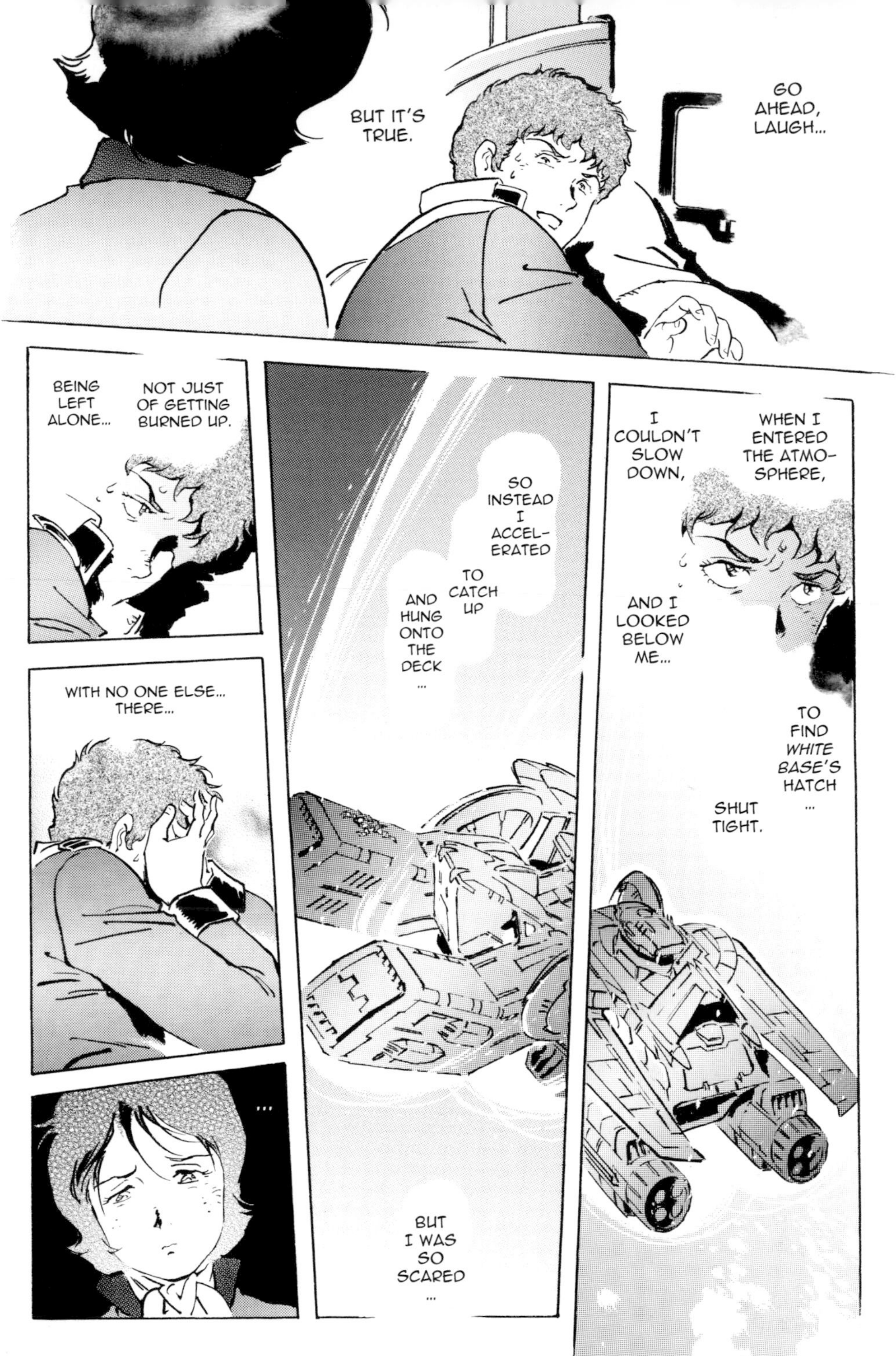
GO AHEAD, LAUGH...
BUT IT'S TRUE.
WHEN I ENTERED THE ATMOSPHERE,
I COULDN'T SLOW DOWN,
AND I LOOKED BELOW ME...
TO FIND *WHITE BASE'S* HATCH...
SHUT TIGHT.
SO INSTEAD I ACCELERATED
TO CATCH UP
AND HUNG ONTO THE DECK...
BUT I WAS SO SCARED...
NOT JUST OF GETTING BURNED UP.
BEING LEFT ALONE...
WITH NO ONE ELSE... THERE...
...

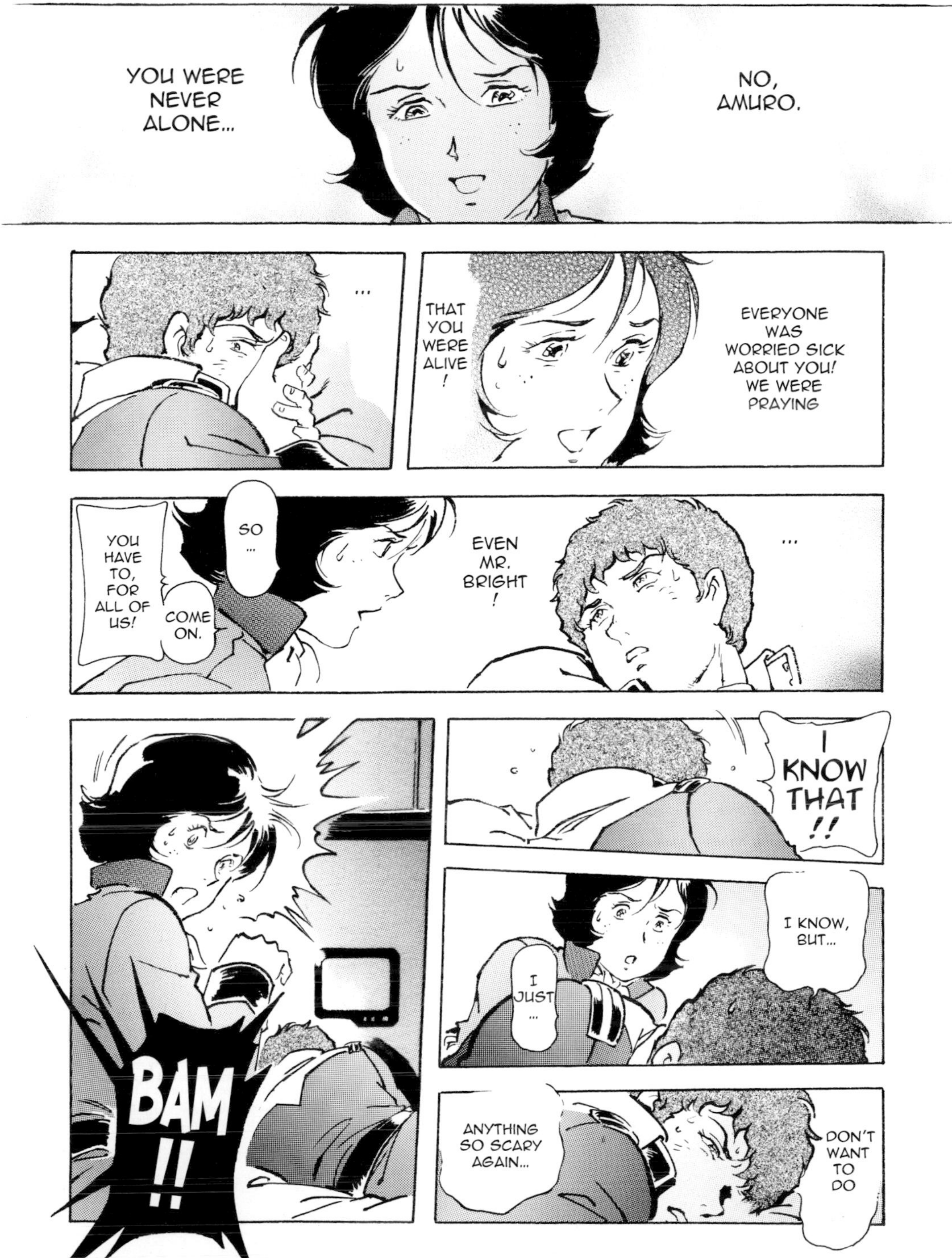
NO, AMURO.
YOU WERE NEVER ALONE...
EVERYONE WAS WORRIED SICK ABOUT YOU! WE WERE PRAYING
THAT YOU WERE ALIVE!
...
...
EVEN MR. BRIGHT!
SO ...
COME ON.
YOU HAVE TO, FOR ALL OF US!
I KNOW THAT!!
I KNOW, BUT...
I JUST ...
DON'T WANT TO DO
ANYTHING SO SCARY AGAIN...
BAM!!

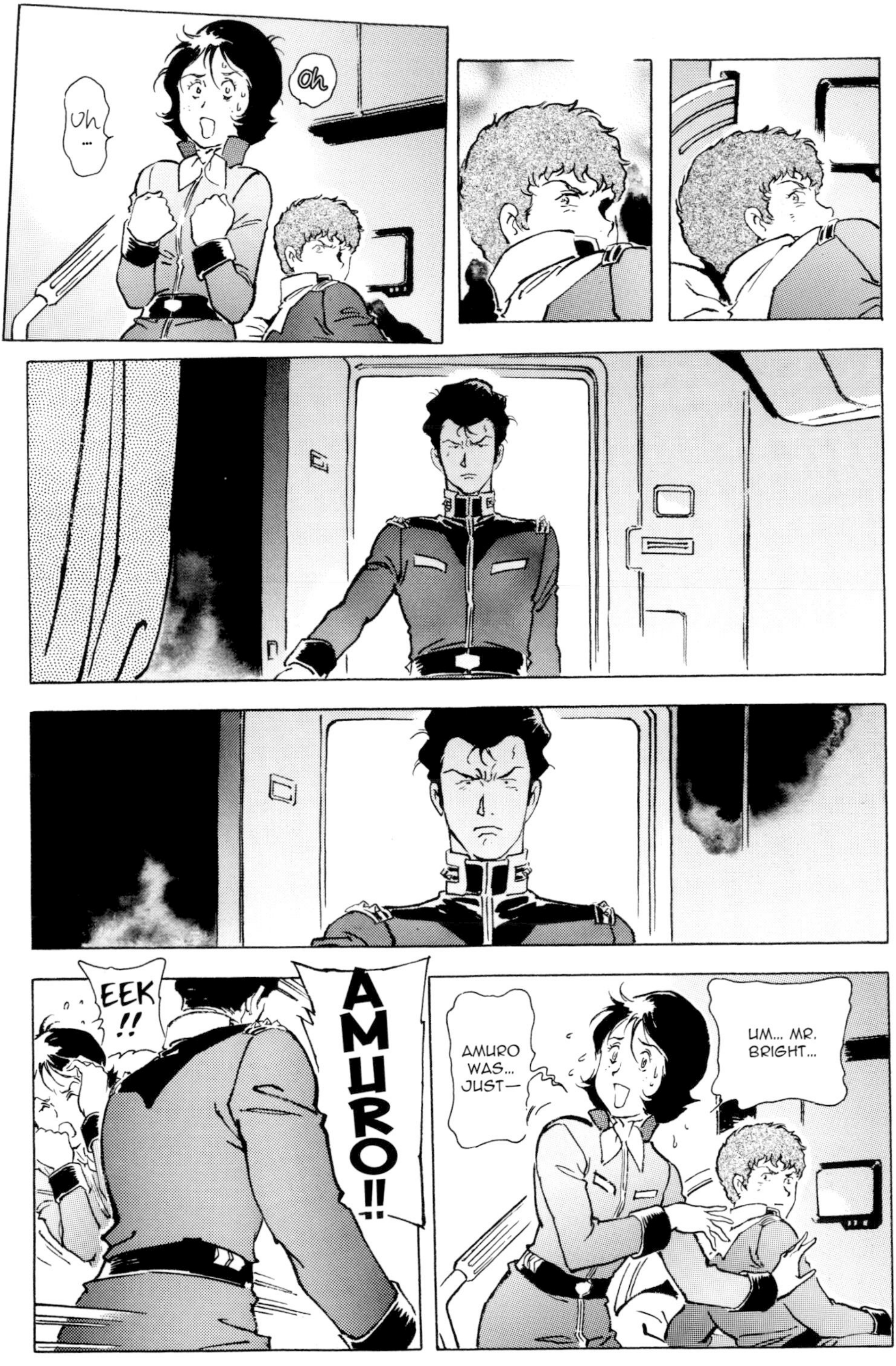
Oh
Uh...
UM... MR. BRIGHT...
AMURO WAS... JUST—
AMURO!!
EEK!!

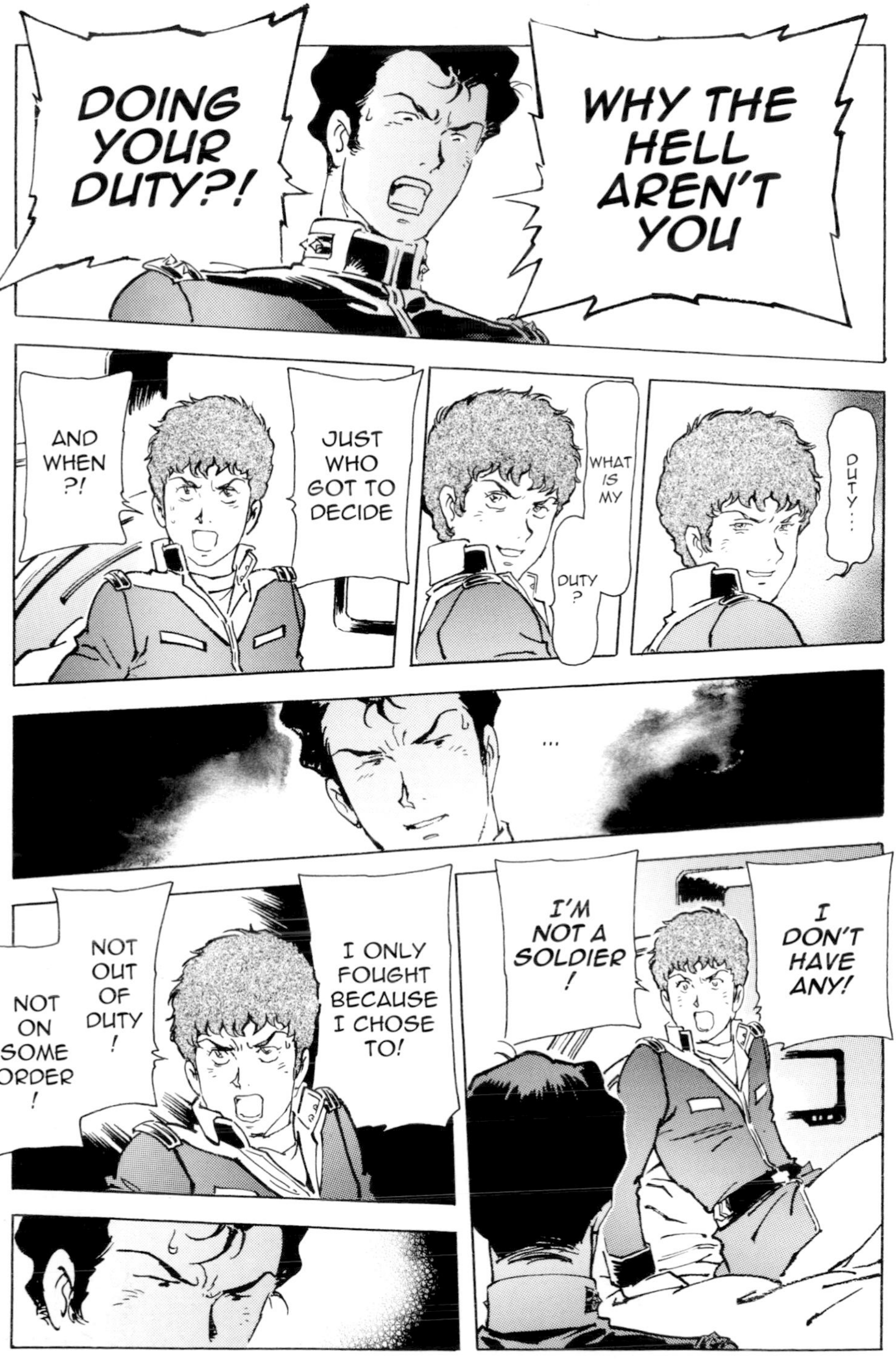
WHY THE HELL AREN'T YOU
DOING YOUR DUTY?!
DUTY...
WHAT IS MY DUTY?
JUST WHO GOT TO DECIDE
AND WHEN?!
...
I DON'T HAVE ANY!
I'M NOT A SOLDIER!
I ONLY FOUGHT BECAUSE I CHOSE TO!
NOT OUT OF DUTY!
NOT ON SOME ORDER!

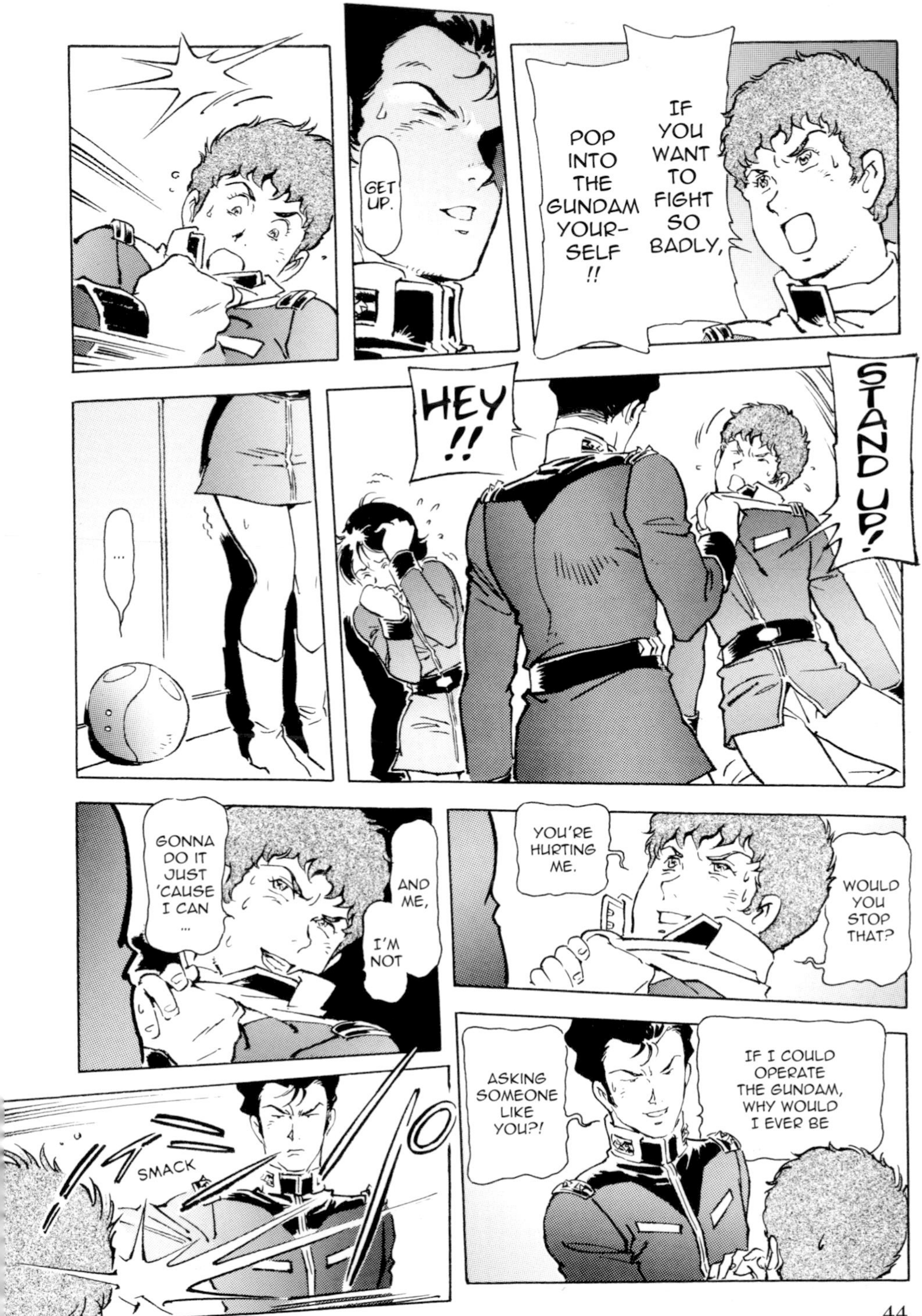
IF YOU WANT TO FIGHT SO BADLY,
POP INTO THE GUNDAM YOURSELF!!
GET UP.
STAND UP!
HEY!!
...
YOU'RE HURTING ME.
WOULD YOU STOP THAT?
IF I COULD OPERATE THE GUNDAM, WHY WOULD I EVER BE
ASKING SOMEONE LIKE YOU?!
AND ME, I'M NOT
GONNA DO IT JUST 'CAUSE I CAN ...
SMACK

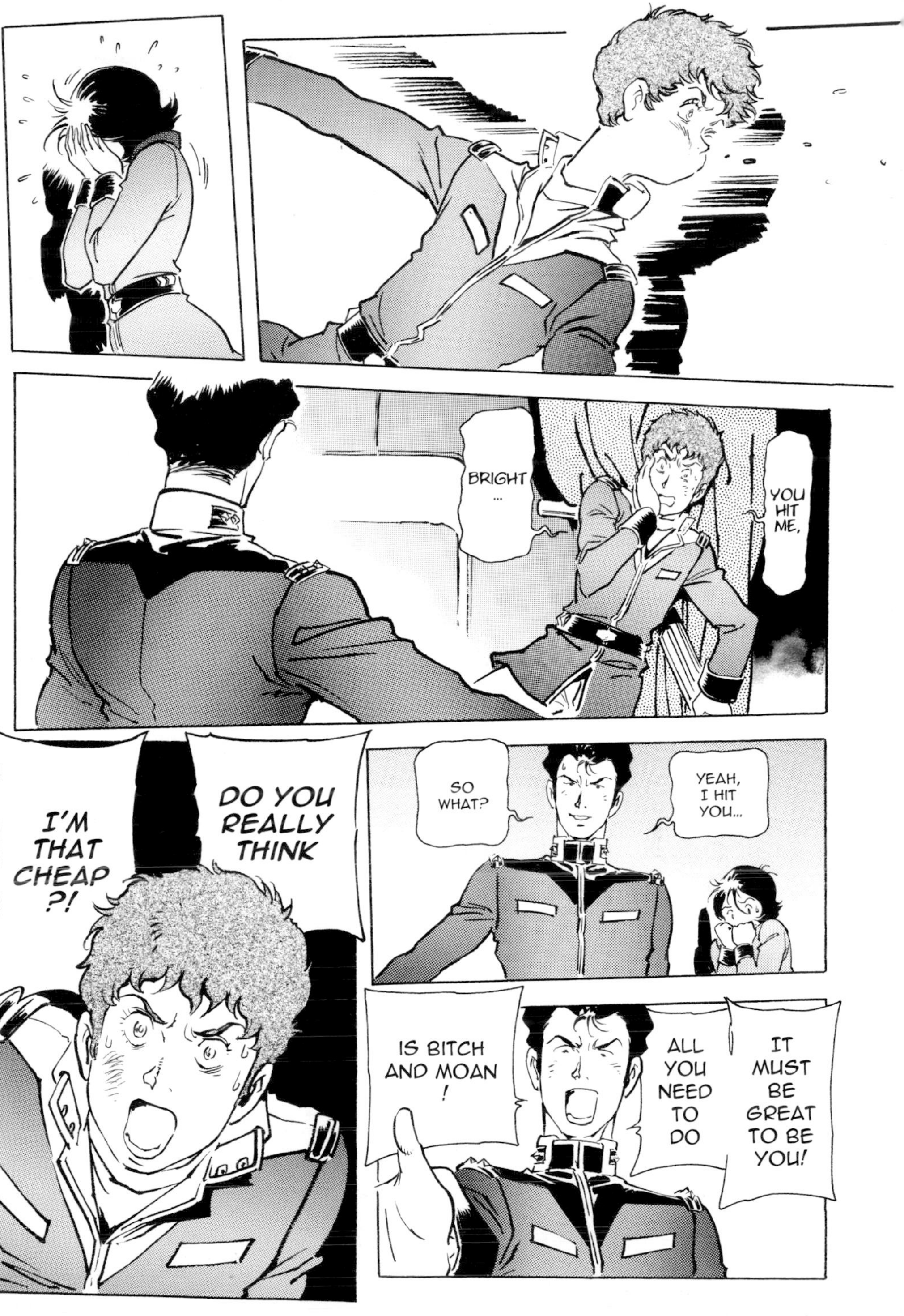
YOU HIT ME,
BRIGHT ...
YEAH, I HIT YOU...
SO WHAT?
IT MUST BE GREAT TO BE YOU!
ALL YOU NEED TO DO
IS BITCH AND MOAN!
DO YOU REALLY THINK
I'M THAT CHEAP ?!

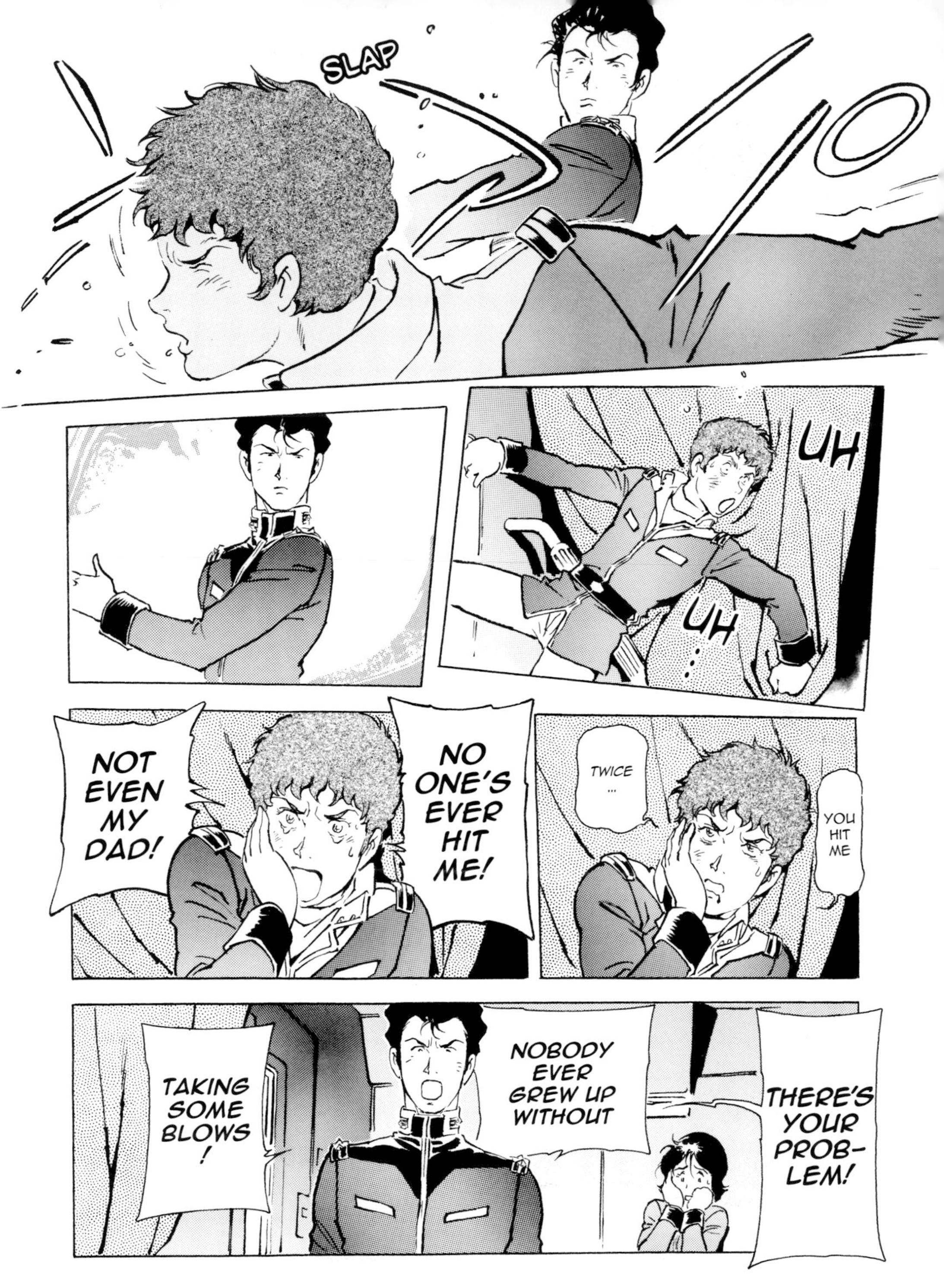
SLAP
UH
UH
...
YOU HIT ME
TWICE ...
NO ONE'S EVER HIT ME!
NOT EVEN MY DAD!
THERE'S YOUR PROB-LEM!
NOBODY EVER GREW UP WITHOUT
TAKING SOME BLOWS!

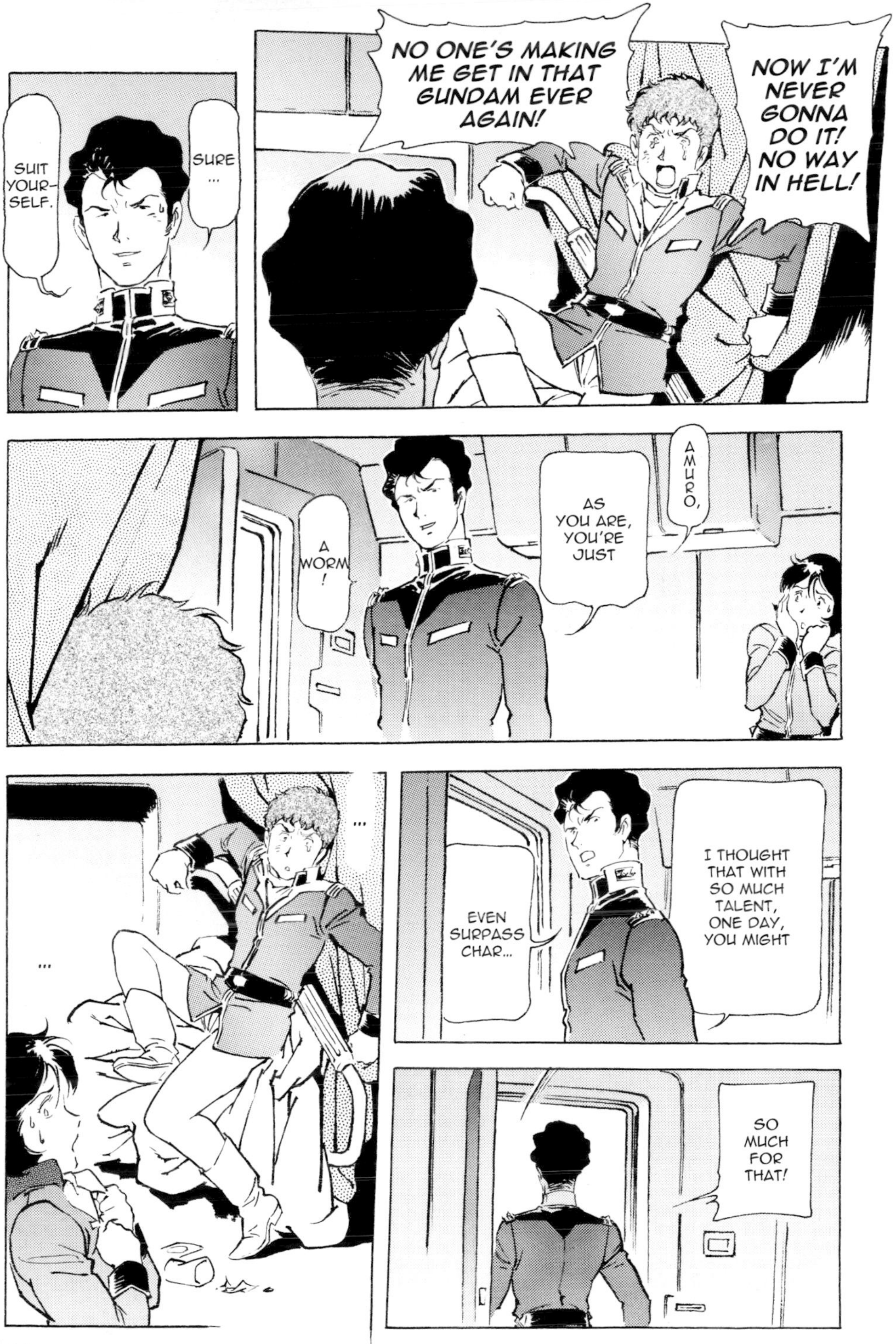
NO ONE'S MAKING ME GET IN THAT GUNDAM EVER AGAIN!
NOW I'M NEVER GONNA DO IT! NO WAY IN HELL!
SURE ...
SUIT YOUR-SELF.
AMURO,
AS YOU ARE, YOU'RE JUST
A WORM!
I THOUGHT THAT WITH SO MUCH TALENT, ONE DAY, YOU MIGHT
EVEN SURPASS CHAR...
SO MUCH FOR THAT!
...
...

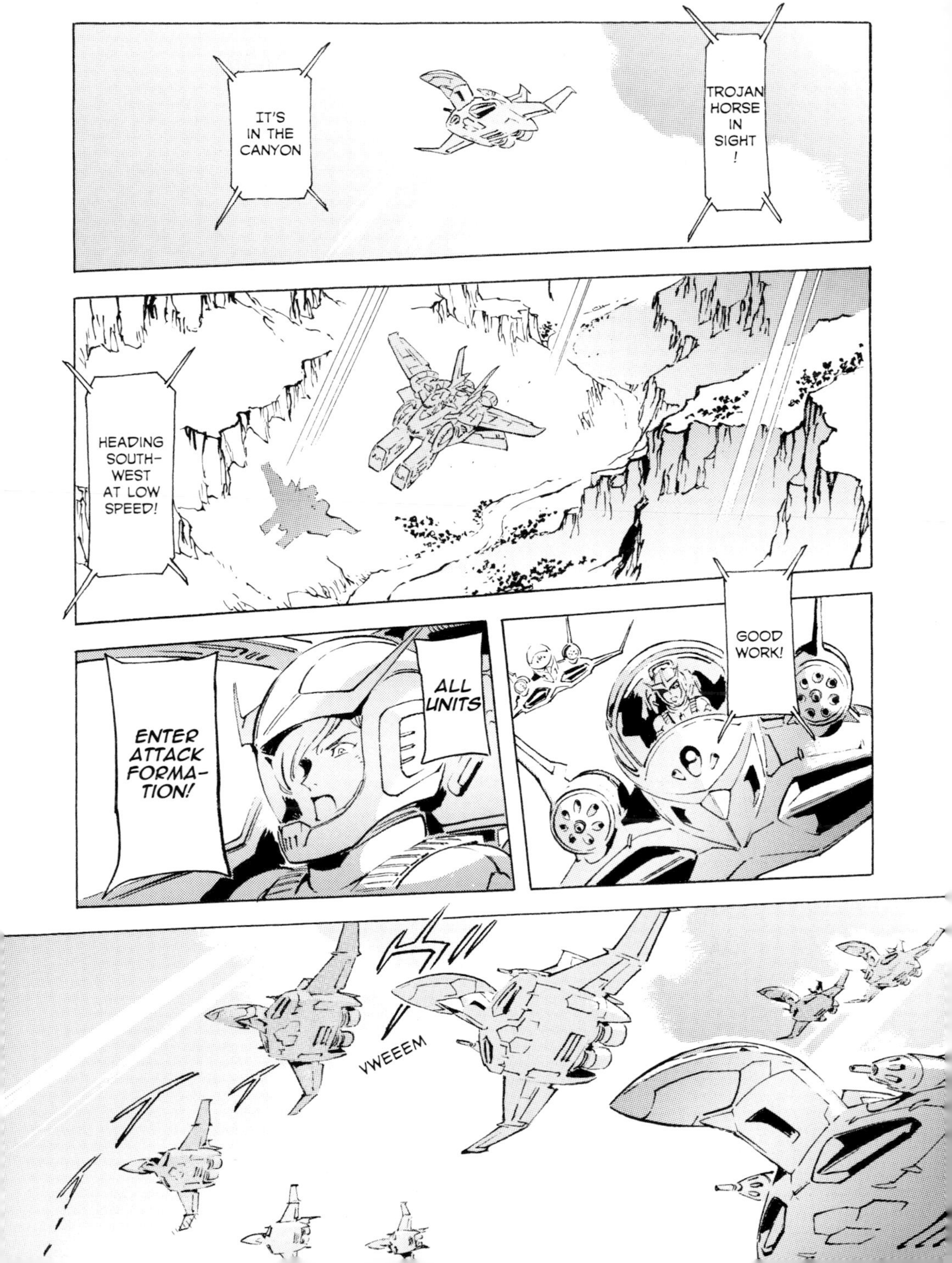
TROJAN HORSE IN SIGHT!
IT'S IN THE CANYON
HEADING SOUTH-WEST AT LOW SPEED!
GOOD WORK!
ALL UNITS
ENTER ATTACK FORMATION!
VWEEEM

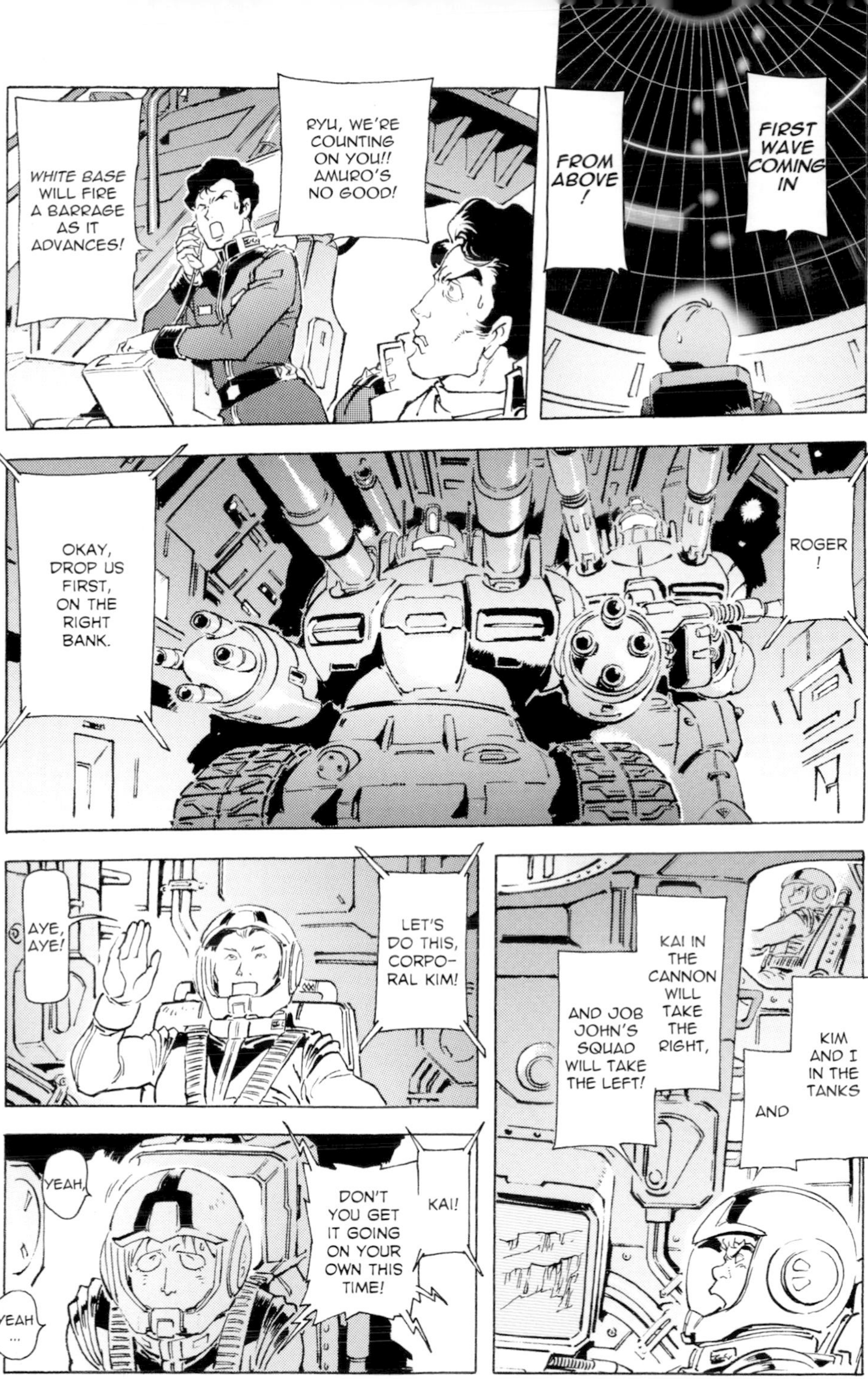
FIRST WAVE COMING IN
FROM ABOVE!
RYU, WE'RE COUNTING ON YOU!! AMURO'S NO GOOD!
WHITE BASE WILL FIRE A BARRAGE AS IT ADVANCES!
ROGER!
OKAY, DROP US FIRST, ON THE RIGHT BANK.
KIM AND I IN THE TANKS
AND
KAI IN THE CANNON WILL TAKE THE RIGHT,
AND JOB JOHN'S SQUAD WILL TAKE THE LEFT!
LET'S DO THIS, CORPORAL KIM!
AYE, AYE!
KAI!
DON'T YOU GET IT GOING ON YOUR OWN THIS TIME!
YEAH,
YEAH...

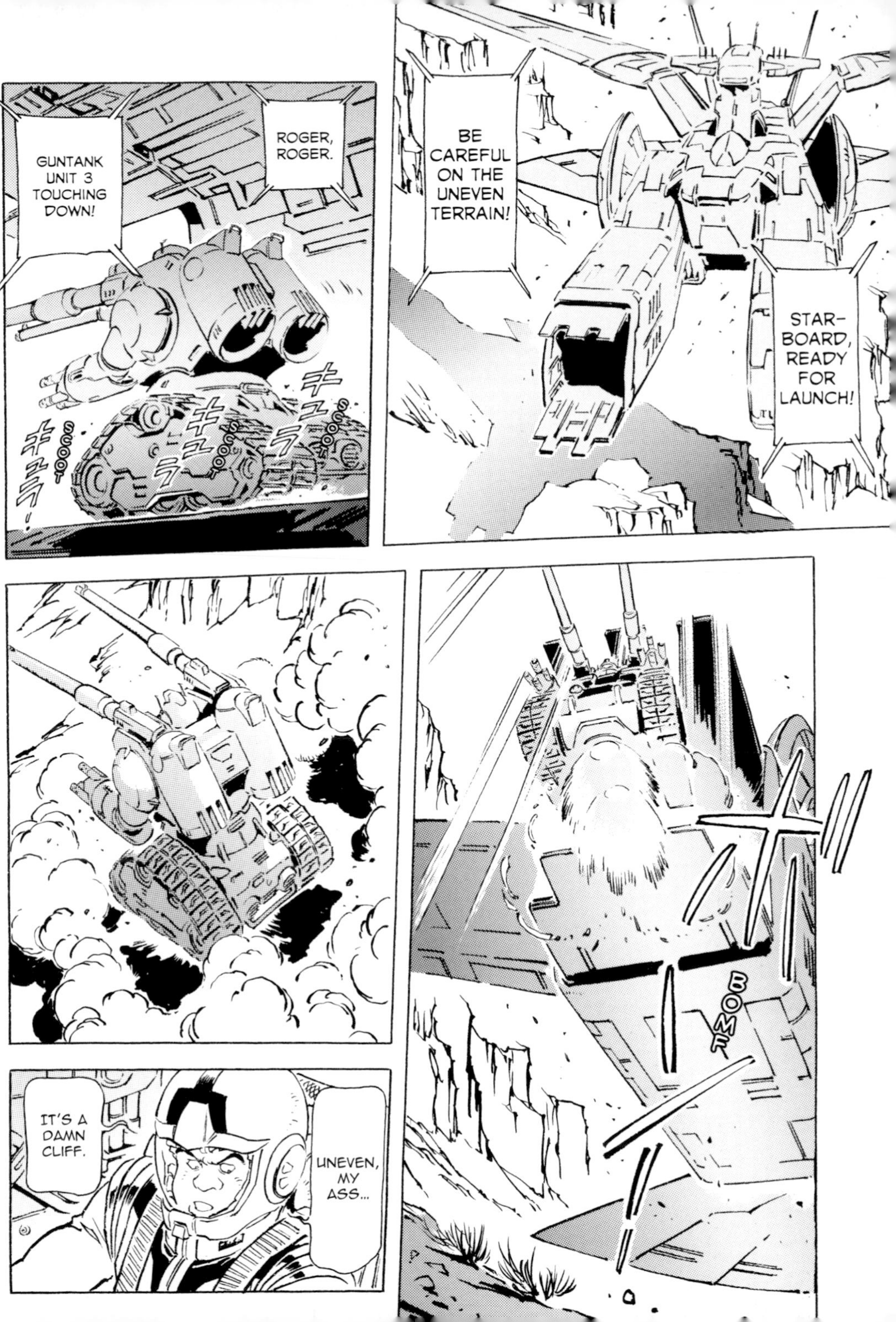
BE CAREFUL ON THE UNEVEN TERRAIN!
STAR-BOARD, READY FOR LAUNCH!
ROGER, ROGER.
GUNTANK UNIT 3 TOUCHING DOWN!
キュラ
SCOOT
キュラ
SCOOT
キュラ!
SCOOT
BOMF
UNEVEN, MY ASS...
IT'S A DAMN CLIFF.

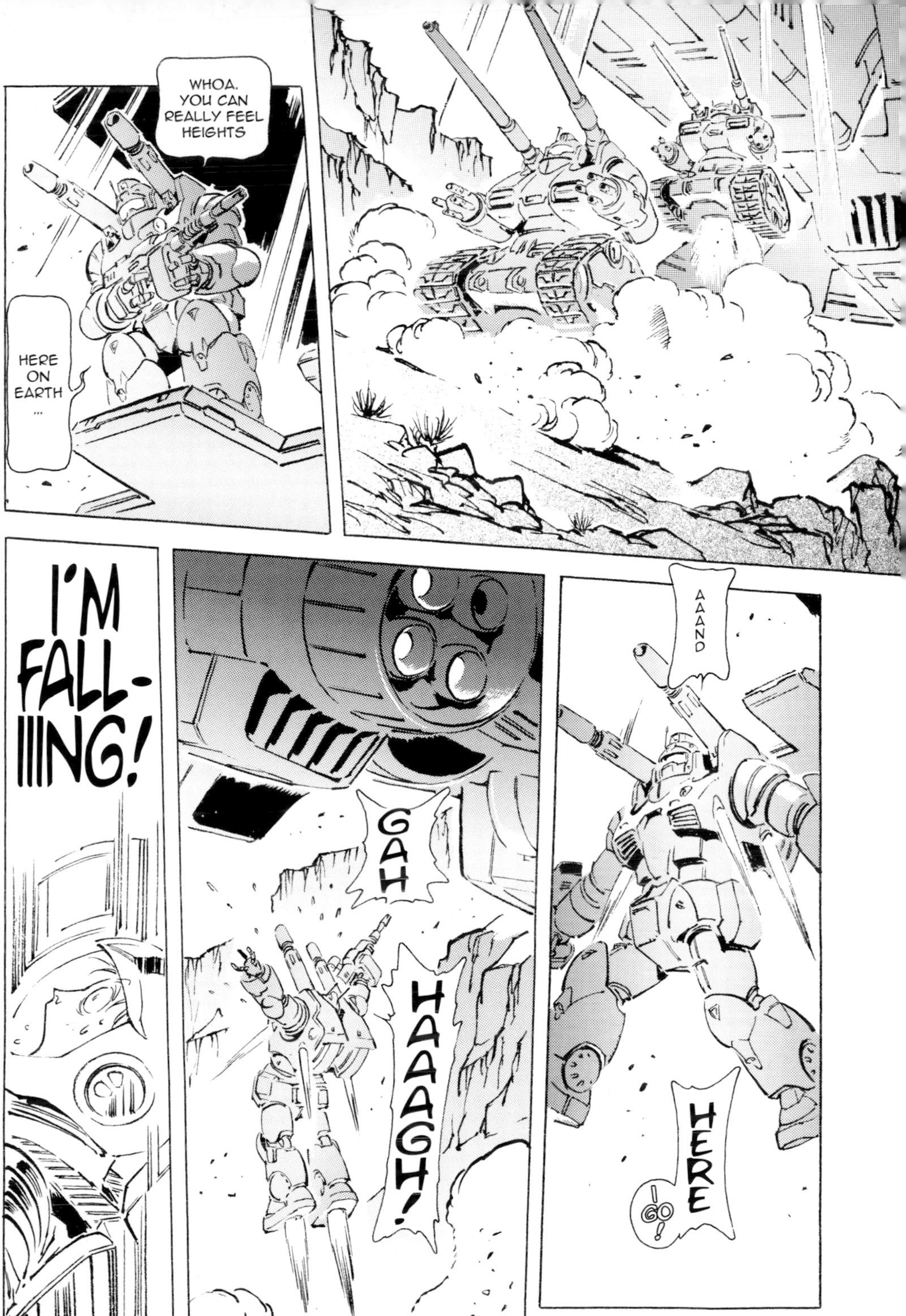
WHOA. YOU CAN REALLY FEEL HEIGHTS
HERE ON EARTH ...
AAAND
HERE I GO!
GAH
HAAAAGH!
I'M FALL-IIING!

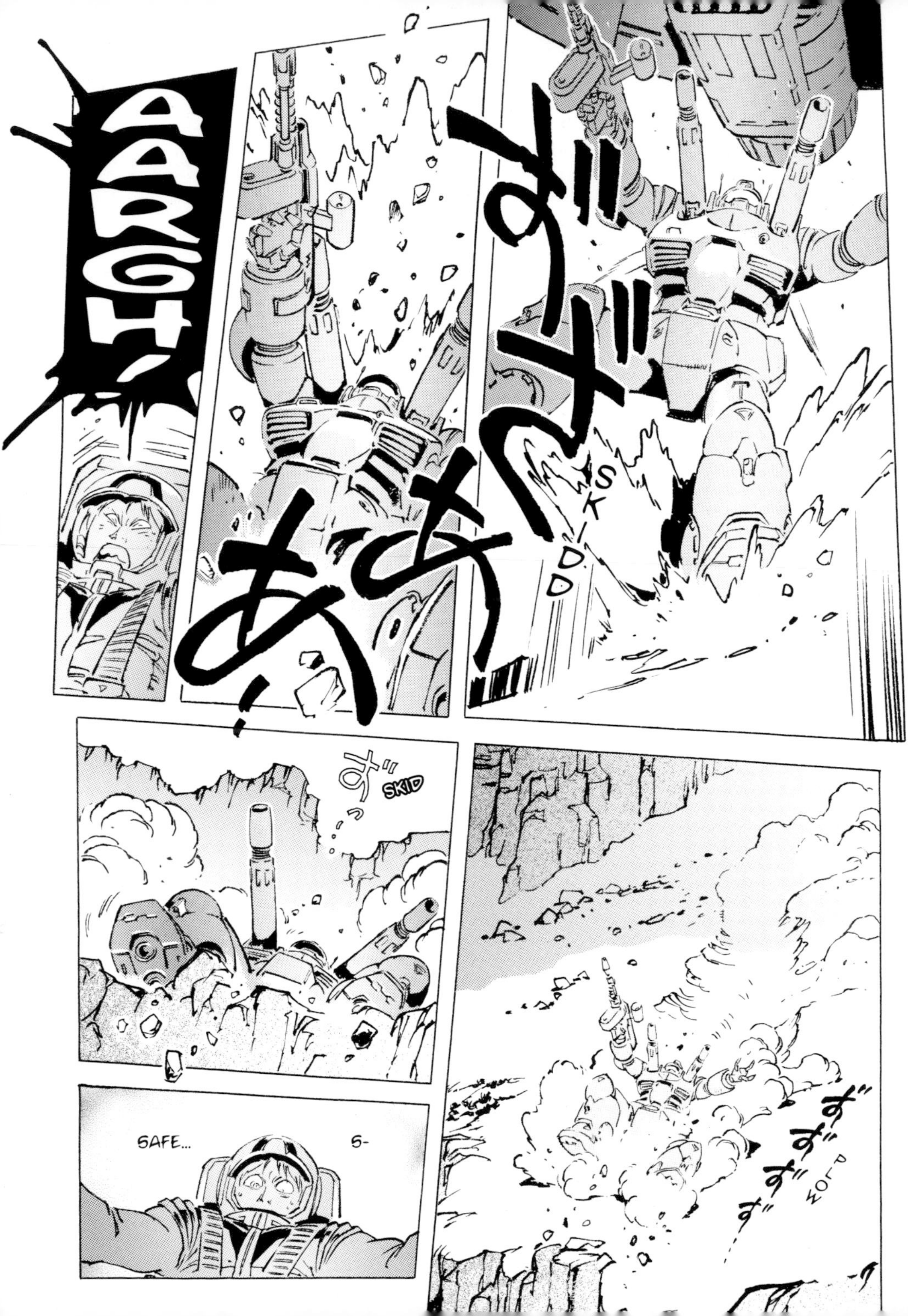
SKIDDD
AARGH!
PLOW
SKID
SAFE... S-

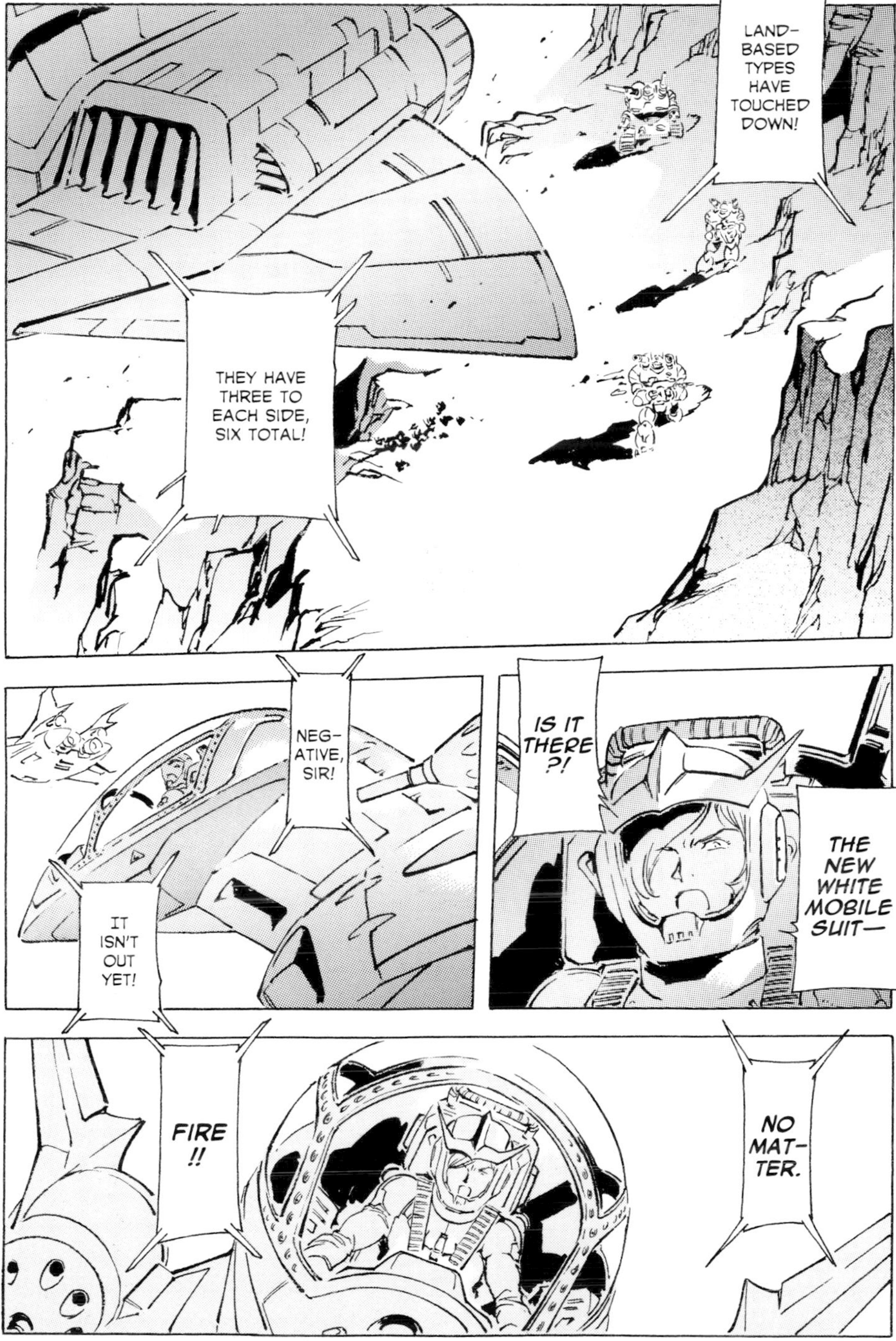
LAND-BASED TYPES HAVE TOUCHED DOWN!
THEY HAVE THREE TO EACH SIDE, SIX TOTAL!
IS IT THERE?!
THE NEW WHITE MOBILE SUIT—
NEG-ATIVE, SIR!
IT ISN'T OUT YET!
NO MAT-TER.
FIRE!!

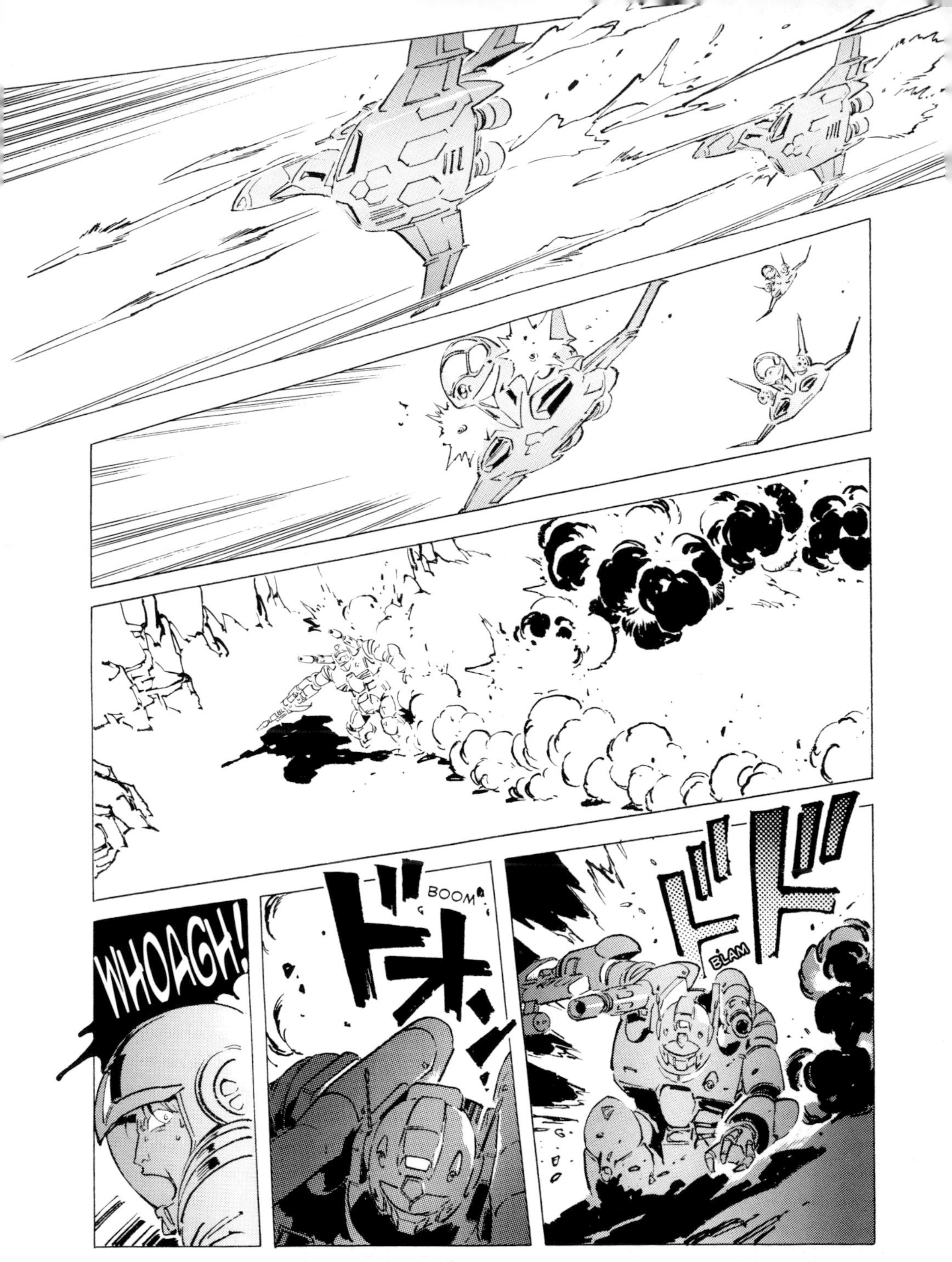
ドド
BLAM
ドオン
BOOM
WHOAGH!

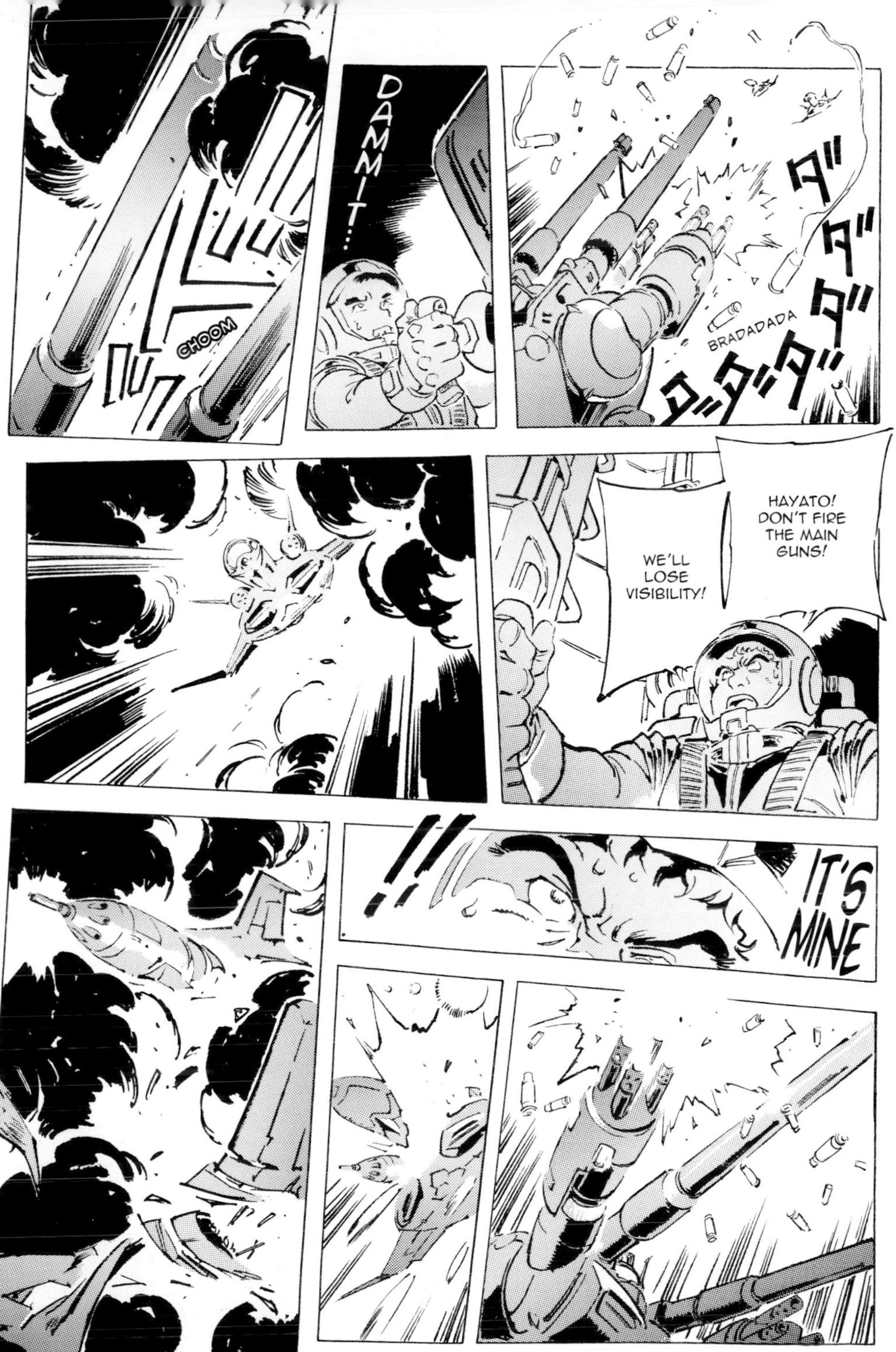
BRADADADA
DAMMIT…
CHOOM
HAYATO! DON'T FIRE THE MAIN GUNS!
WE'LL LOSE VISIBILITY!
!!
IT'S MINE

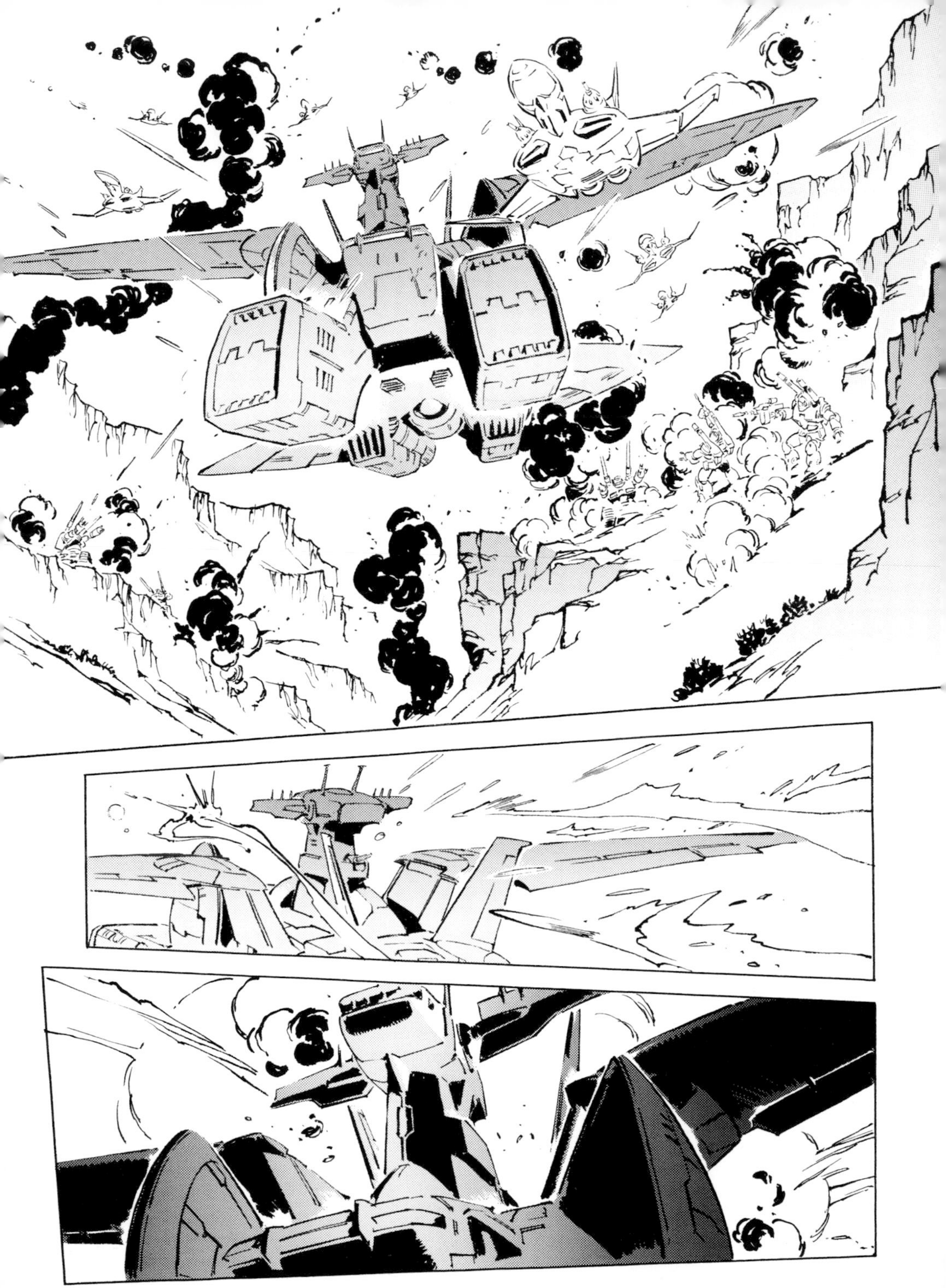

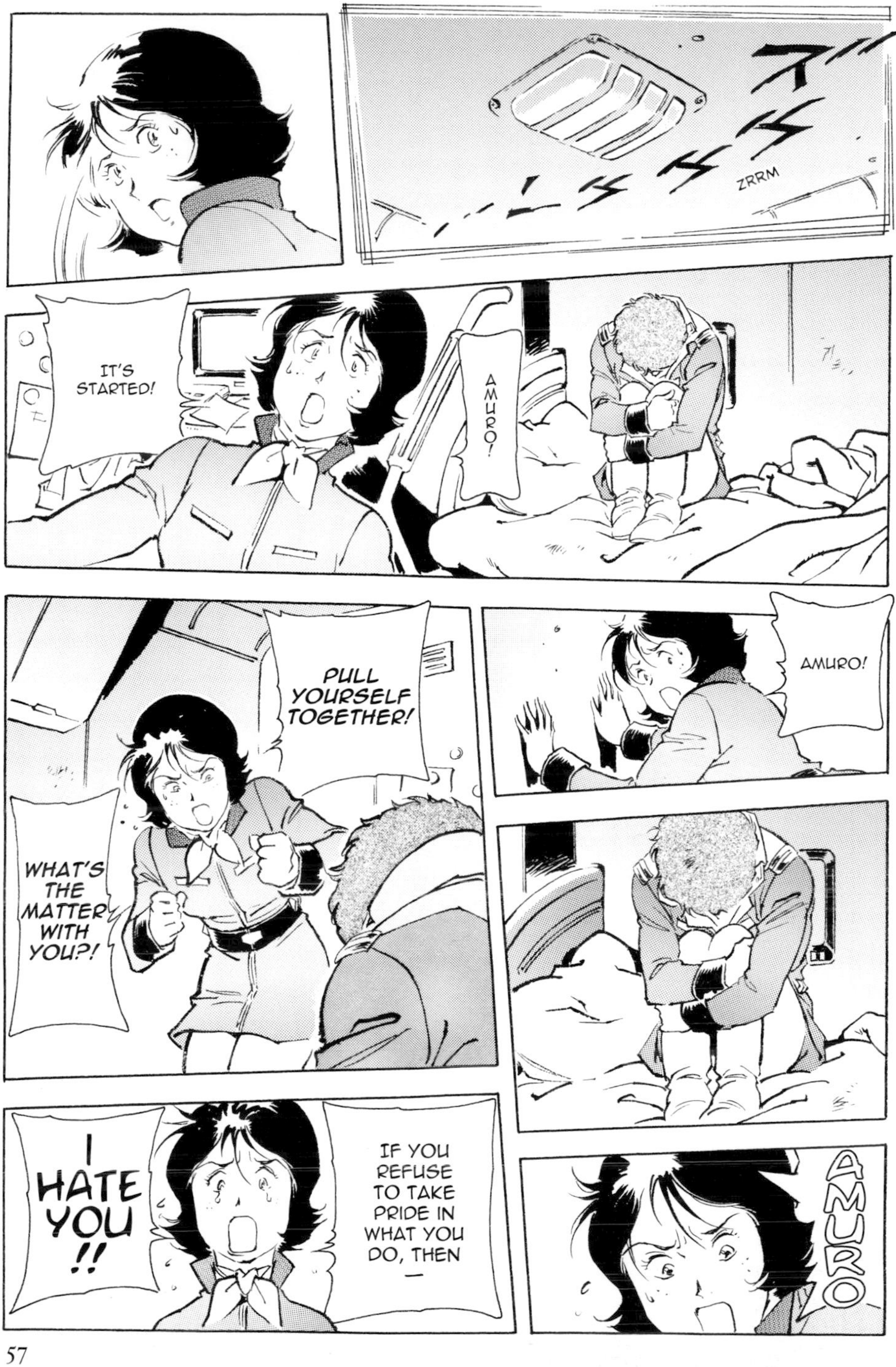
ZRRM
AMURO!
IT'S STARTED!
AMURO!
PULL YOURSELF TOGETHER!
WHAT'S THE MATTER WITH YOU?!
AMURO
IF YOU REFUSE TO TAKE PRIDE IN WHAT YOU DO, THEN —
I HATE YOU!!

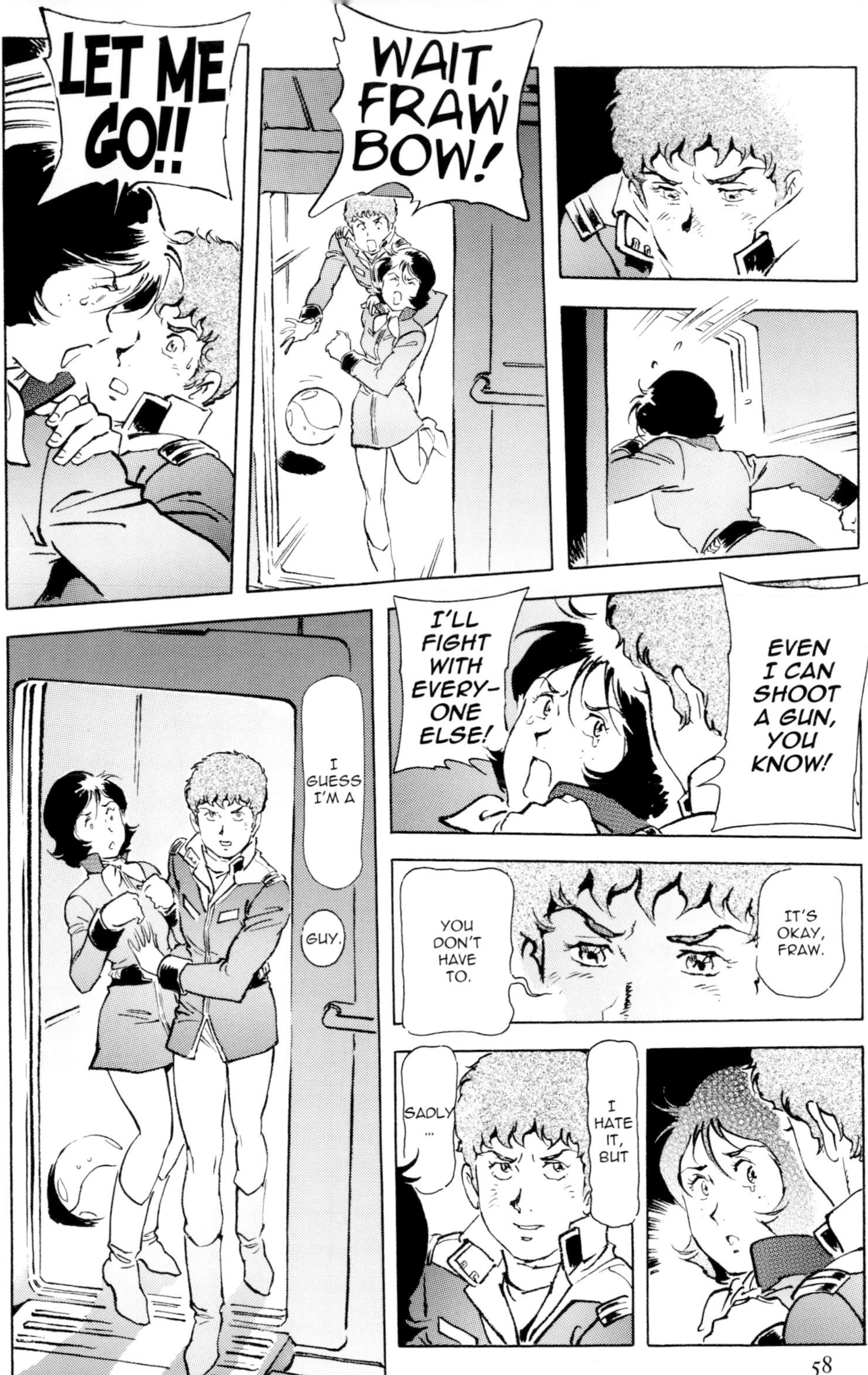

WAIT, FRAW BOW!
LET ME GO!!
EVEN I CAN SHOOT A GUN, YOU KNOW!
I'LL FIGHT WITH EVERY-ONE ELSE!
IT'S OKAY, FRAW.
YOU DON'T HAVE TO.
I HATE IT, BUT
SADLY...
I GUESS I'M A
GUY.

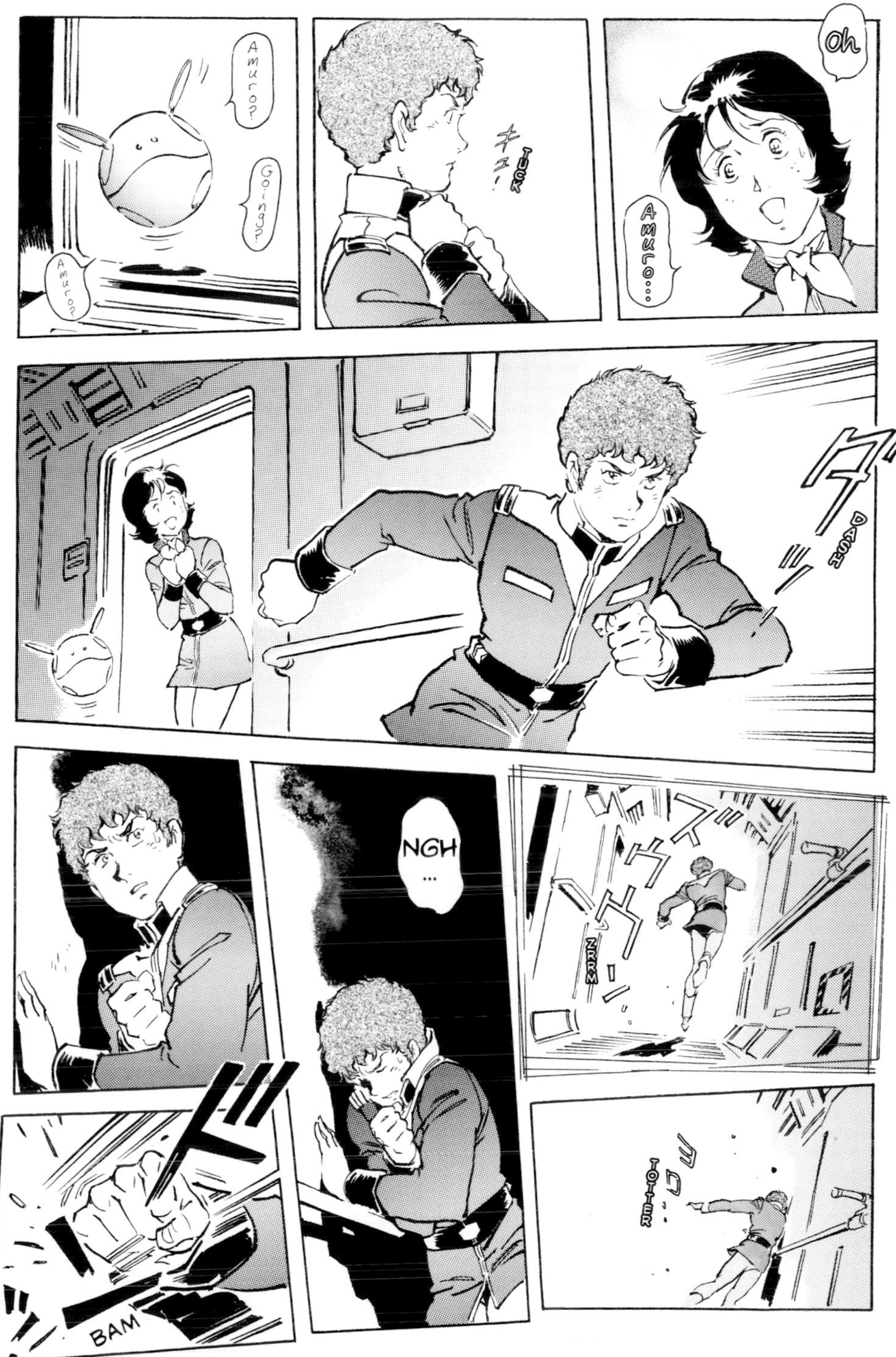
Oh
Amuro...
TUCK
Amuro?
Going?
Amuro?
DASH
ZRRM
TOTTER
NGH...
BAM

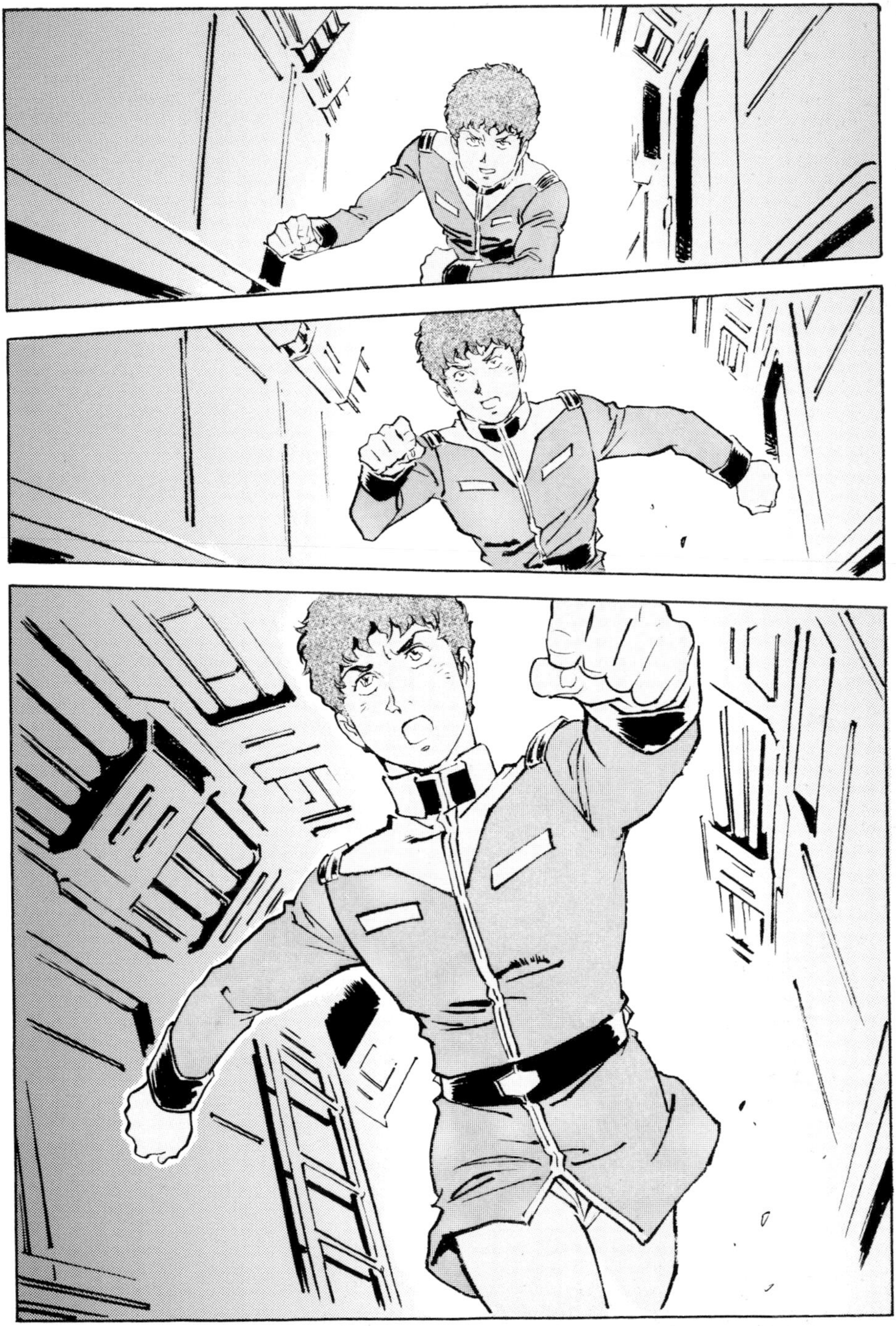

SECTION
II

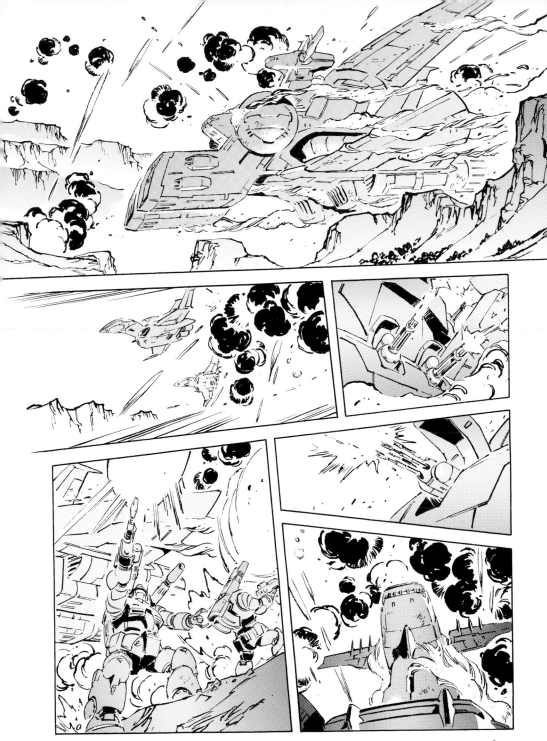

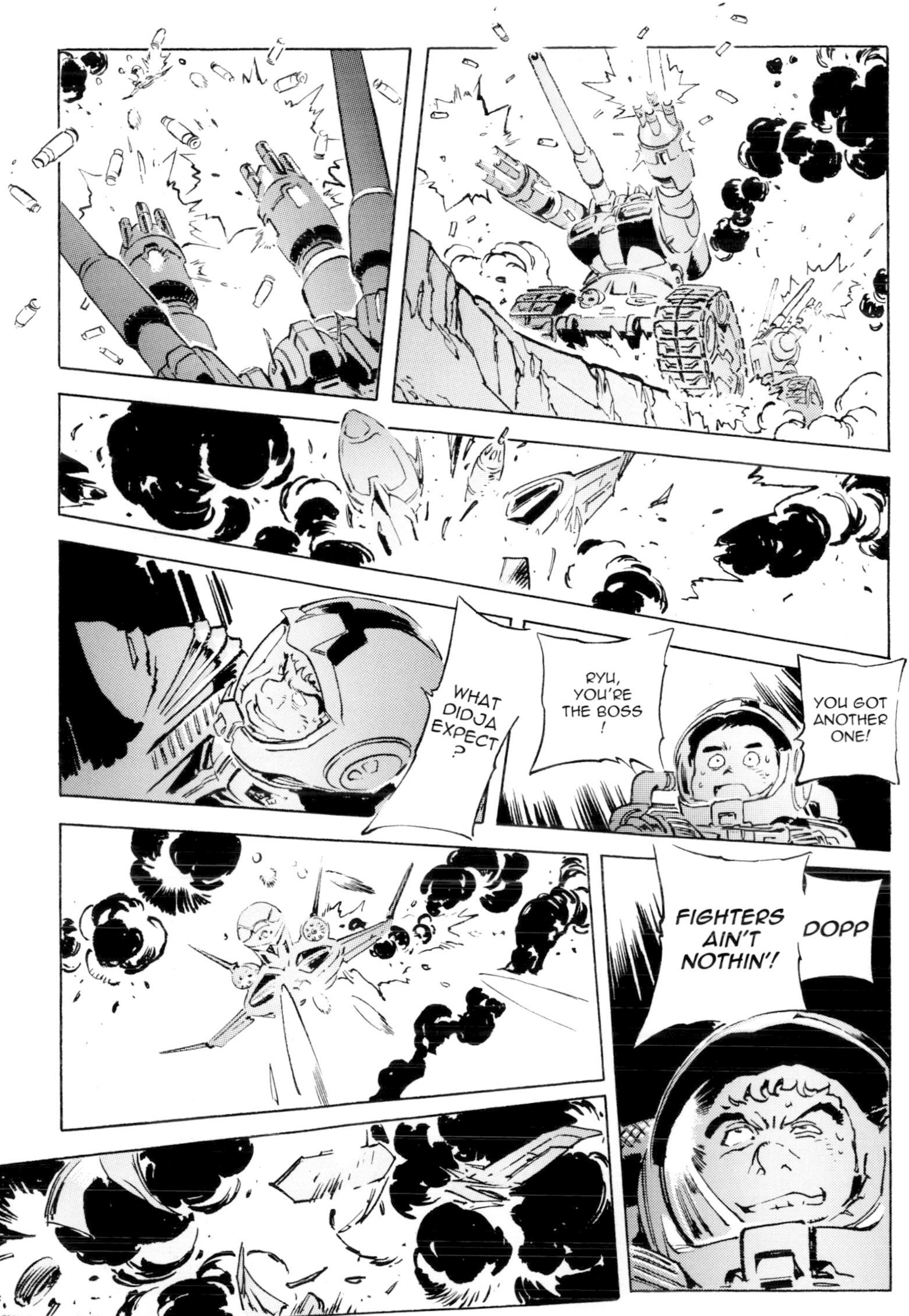
YOU GOT ANOTHER ONE!
RYU, YOU'RE THE BOSS!
WHAT DIDJA EXPECT?
DOPP
FIGHTERS AIN'T NOTHIN'!

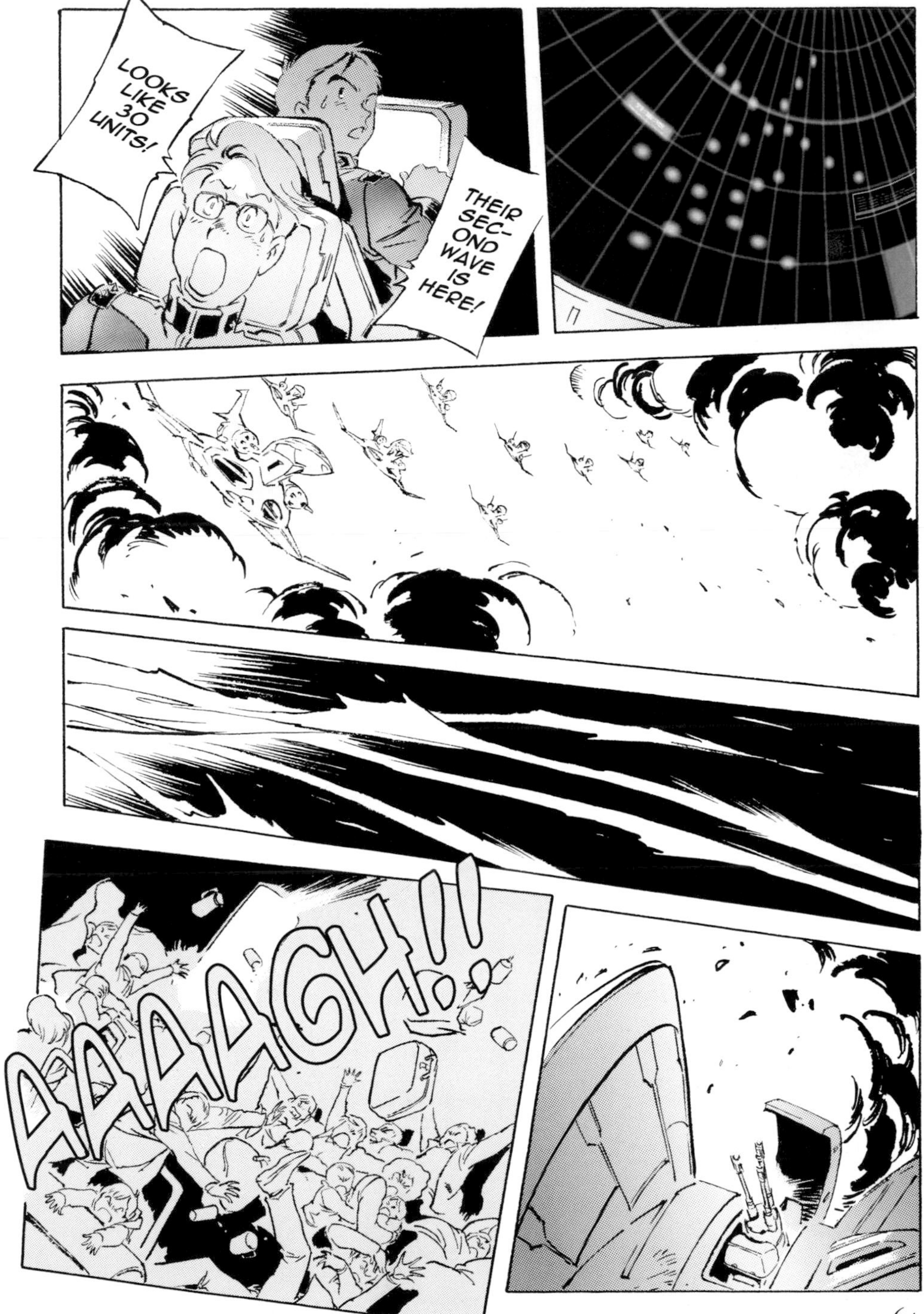
THEIR SEC-OND WAVE IS HERE!
LOOKS LIKE 30 UNITS!
AAAAGH!!

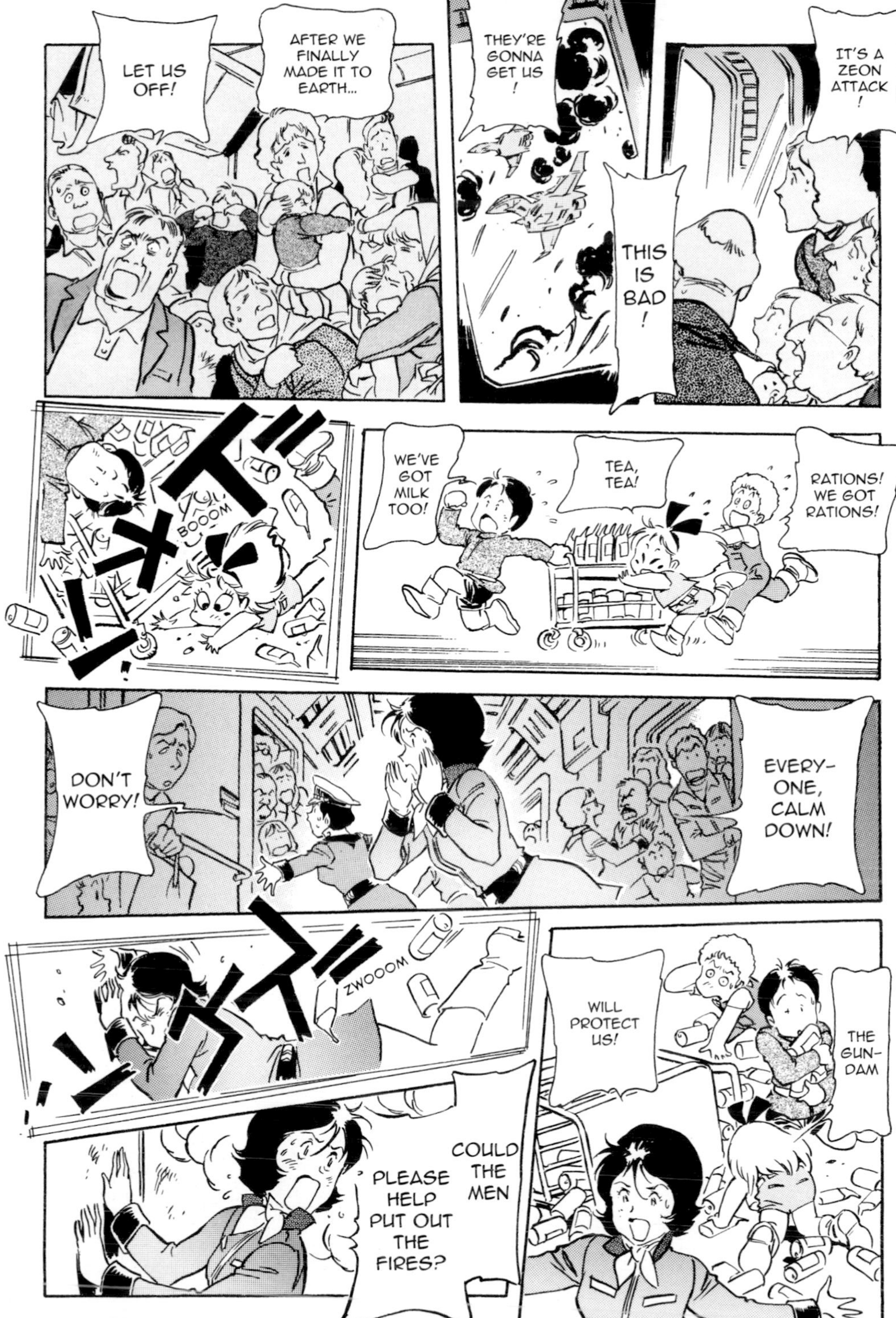
IT'S A ZEON ATTACK!
THEY'RE GONNA GET US!
THIS IS BAD!
AFTER WE FINALLY MADE IT TO EARTH...
LET US OFF!
RATIONS! WE GOT RATIONS!
TEA, TEA!
WE'VE GOT MILK TOO!
BOOOM
EVERY-ONE, CALM DOWN!
DON'T WORRY!
THE GUN-DAM
WILL PROTECT US!
ZWOOOM
COULD THE MEN
PLEASE HELP PUT OUT THE FIRES?

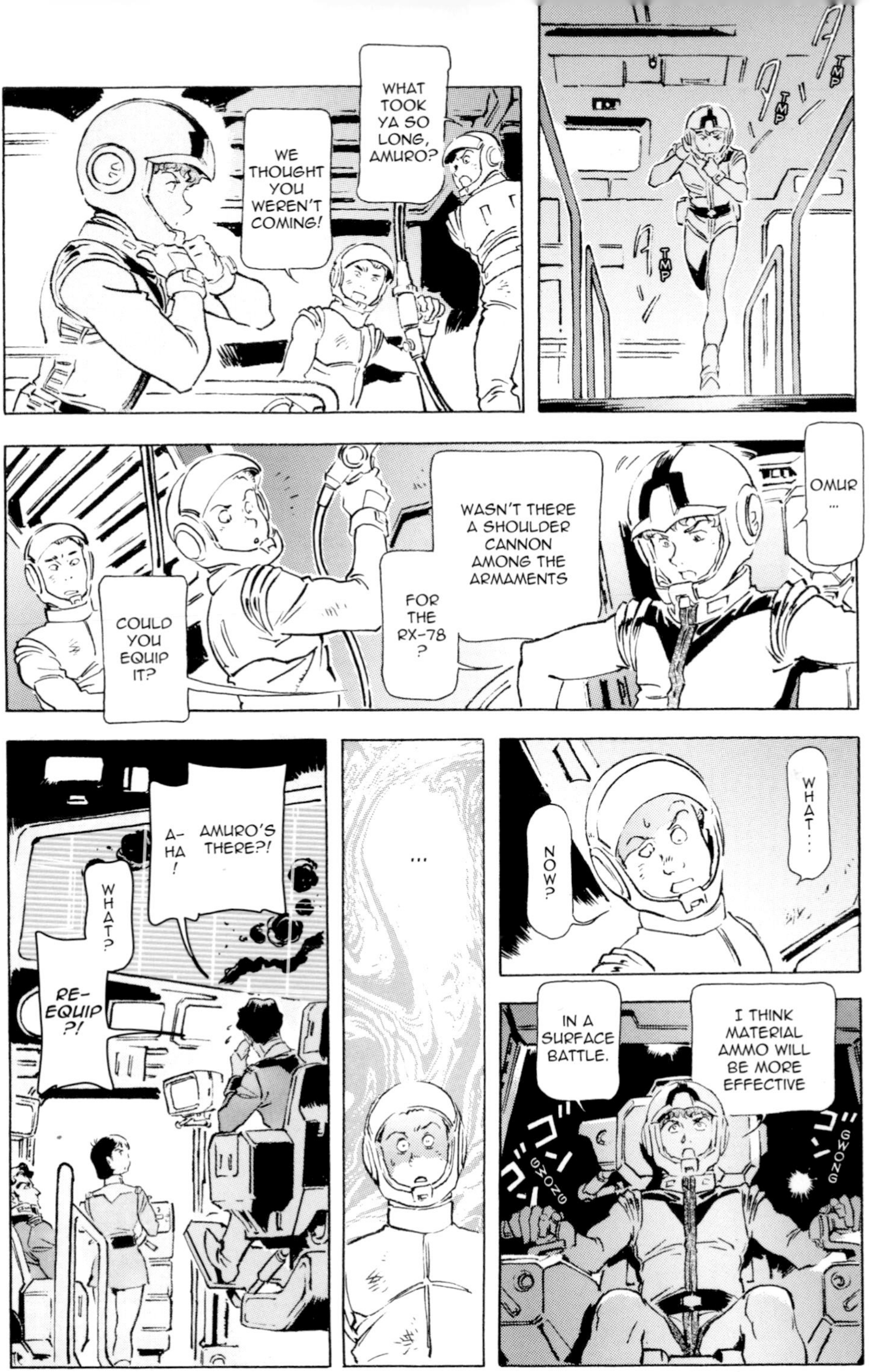
TMP
TMP
TMP
WHAT TOOK YA SO LONG, AMURO?
WE THOUGHT YOU WEREN'T COMING!
OMUR ...
WASN'T THERE A SHOULDER CANNON AMONG THE ARMAMENTS
FOR THE RX-78 ?
COULD YOU EQUIP IT?
WHAT...
NOW?
I THINK MATERIAL AMMO WILL BE MORE EFFECTIVE
IN A SURFACE BATTLE.
GWONG
GWONG
...
AMURO'S THERE?!
A-HA!
WHAT?
RE-EQUIP?!

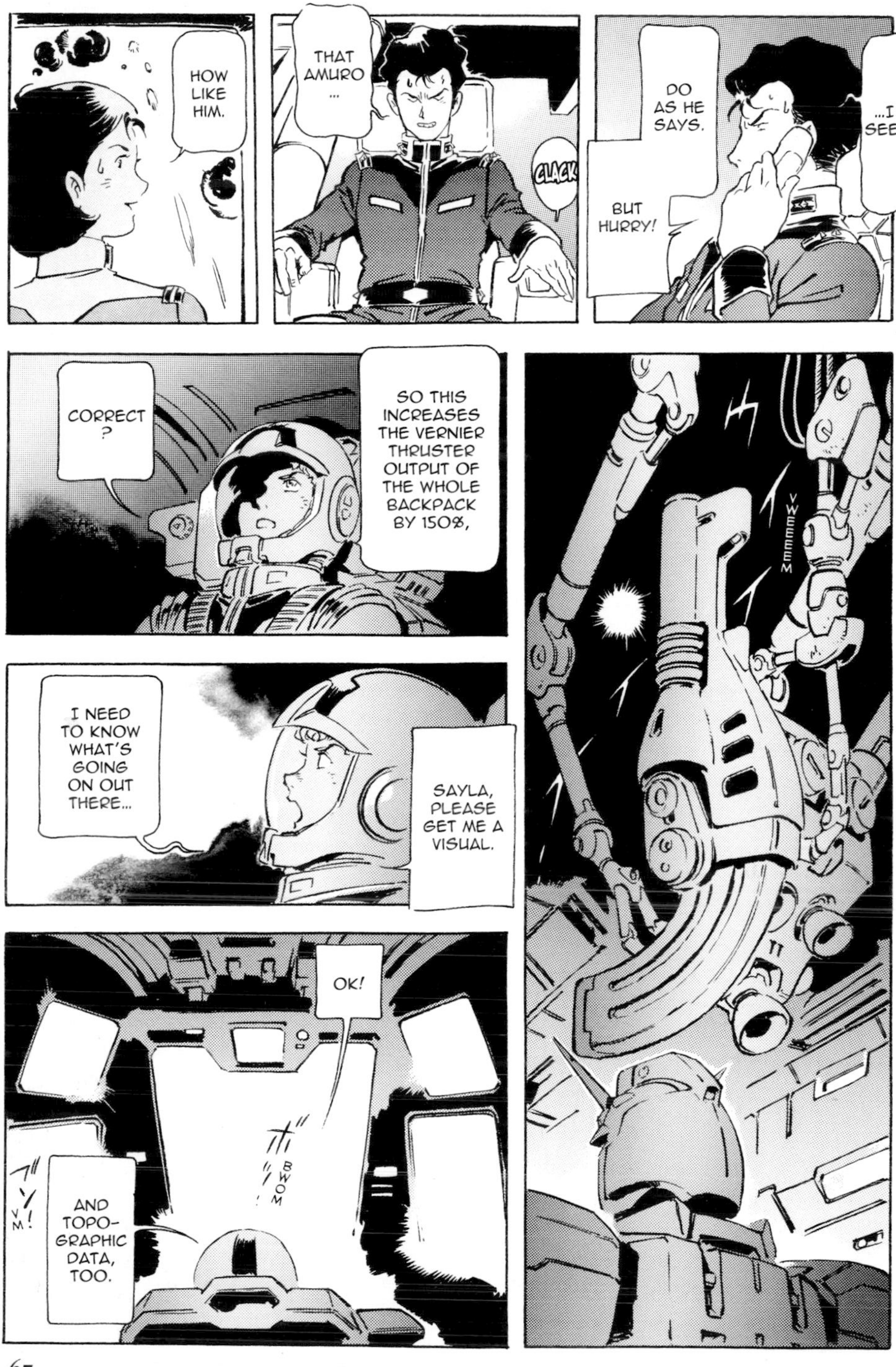
...I SEE.
DO AS HE SAYS.
BUT HURRY!
THAT AMURO ...
CLACK
HOW LIKE HIM.
VWEEEEM
SO THIS INCREASES THE VERNIER THRUSTER OUTPUT OF THE WHOLE BACKPACK BY 150%,
CORRECT?
SAYLA, PLEASE GET ME A VISUAL.
I NEED TO KNOW WHAT'S GOING ON OUT THERE...
OK!
BWOM
AND TOPO-GRAPHIC DATA, TOO.
VM!

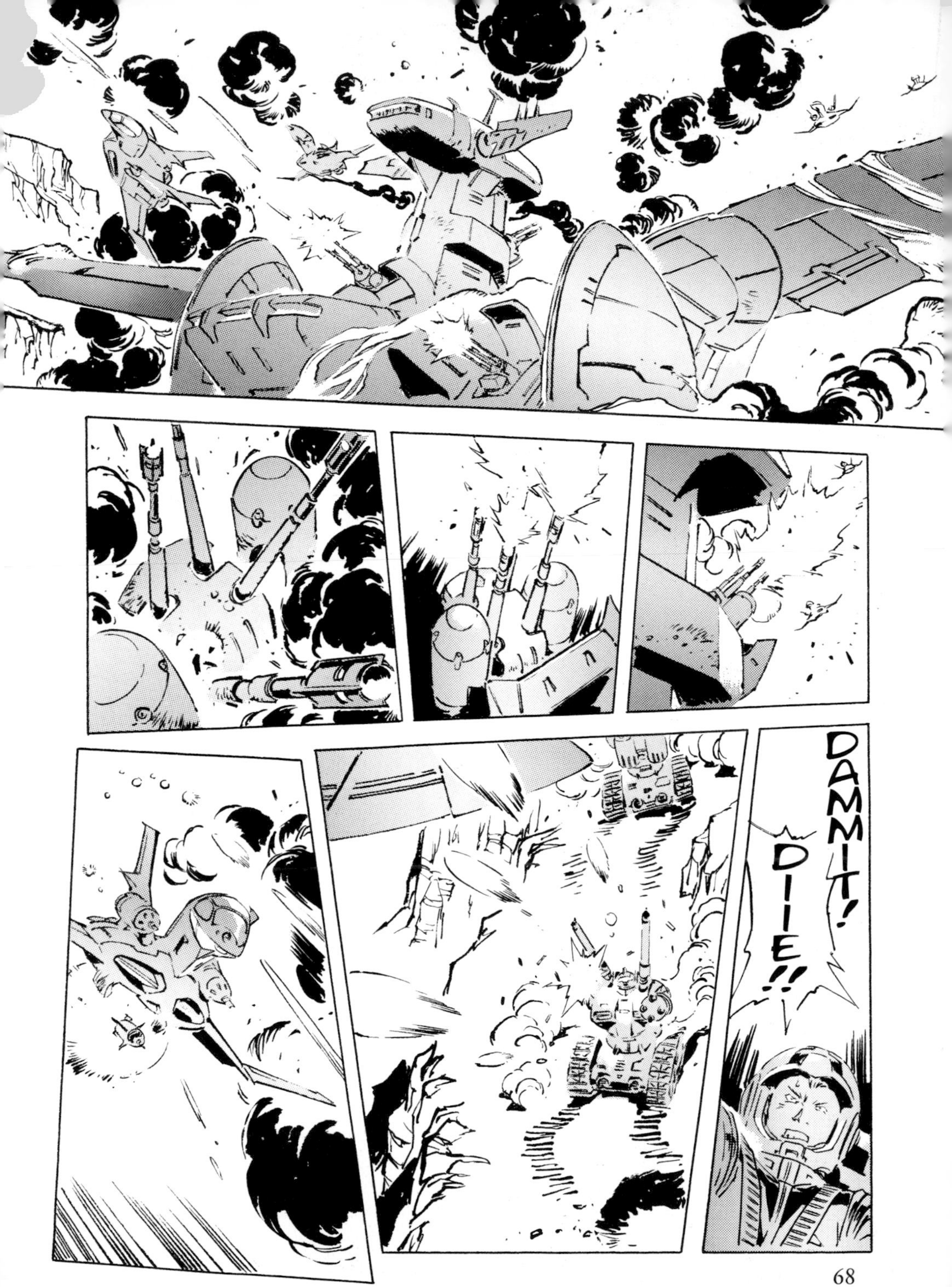
DAMMIT!
DIIE!!

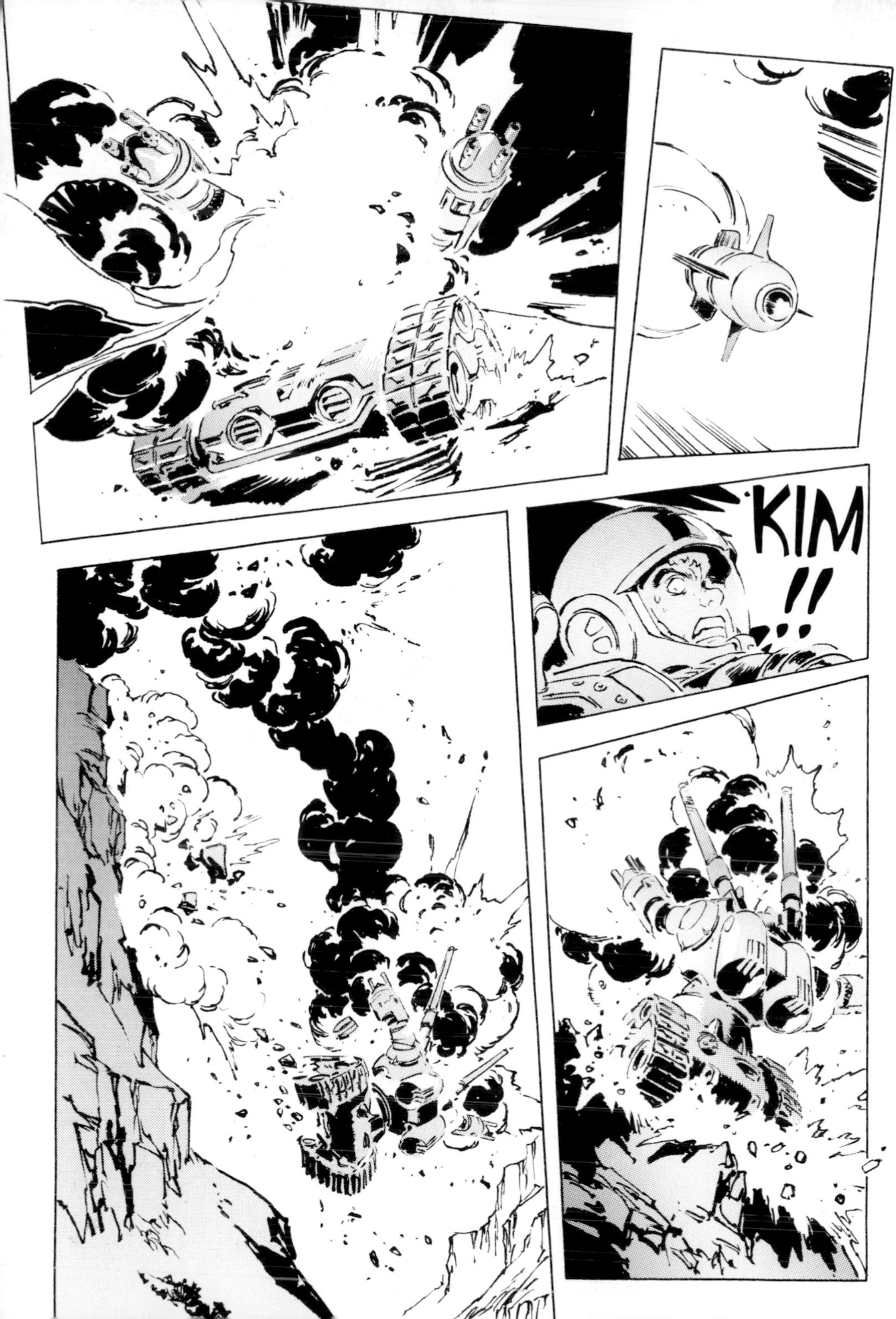
KIM!!

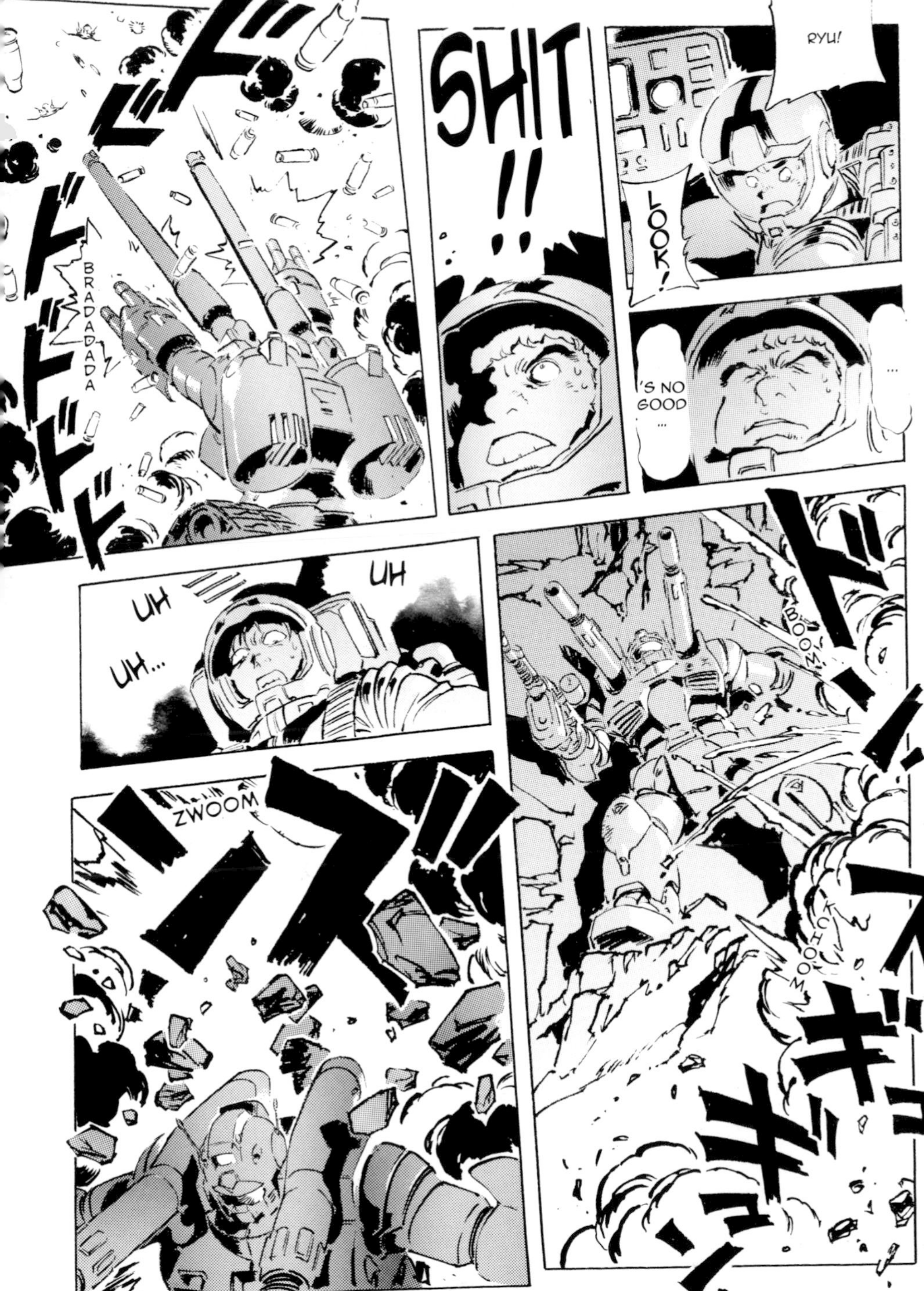
RYU!
LOOK!
...
'S NO GOOD ...
SHIT!!
BRADADADA
BOOM
KCHOOOM
UH
UH
UH...
ZWOOM

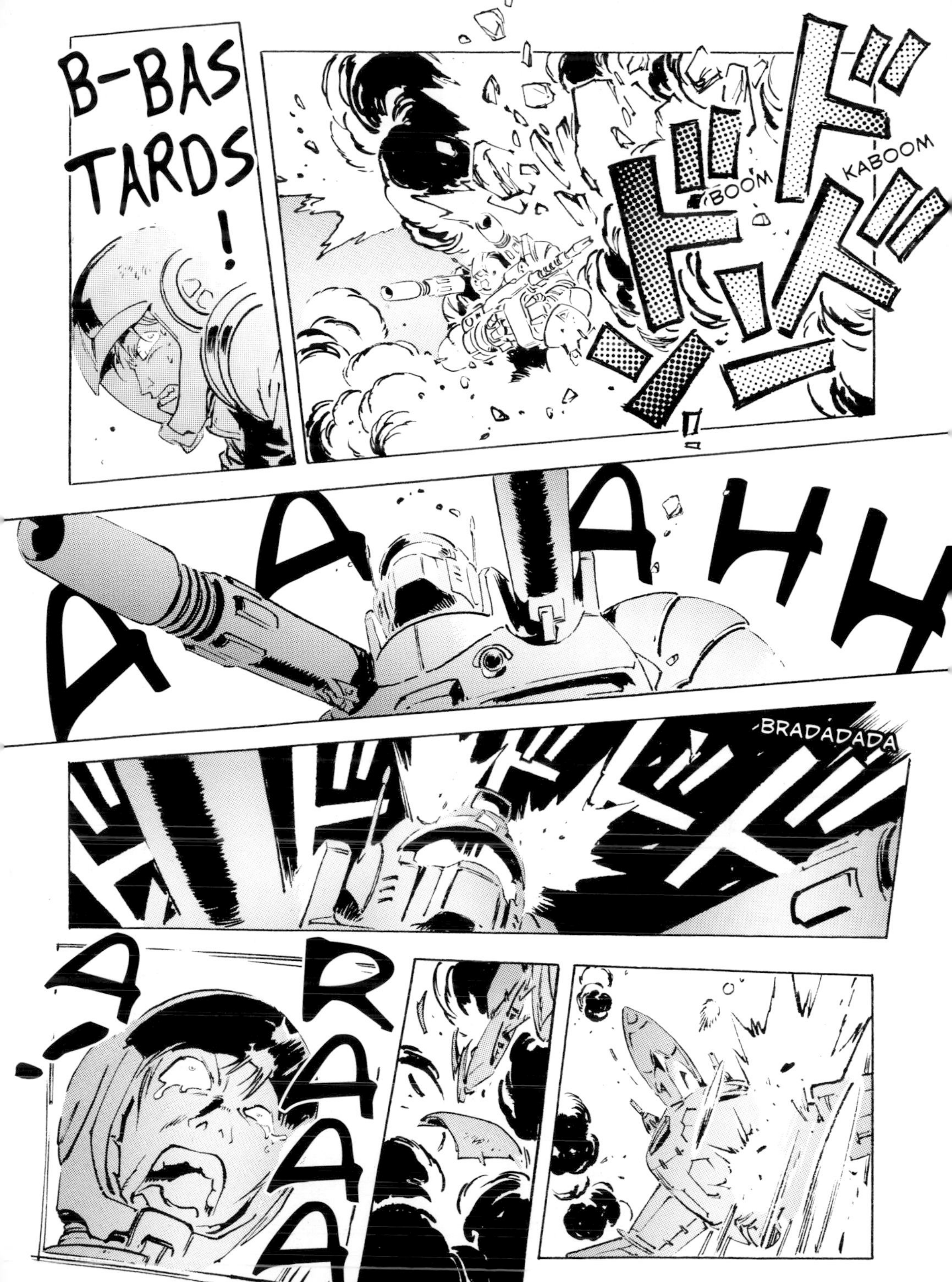
BOOM
KABOOM
B-BASTARDS!
AAAHHH
BRADADADA
ARAAAA

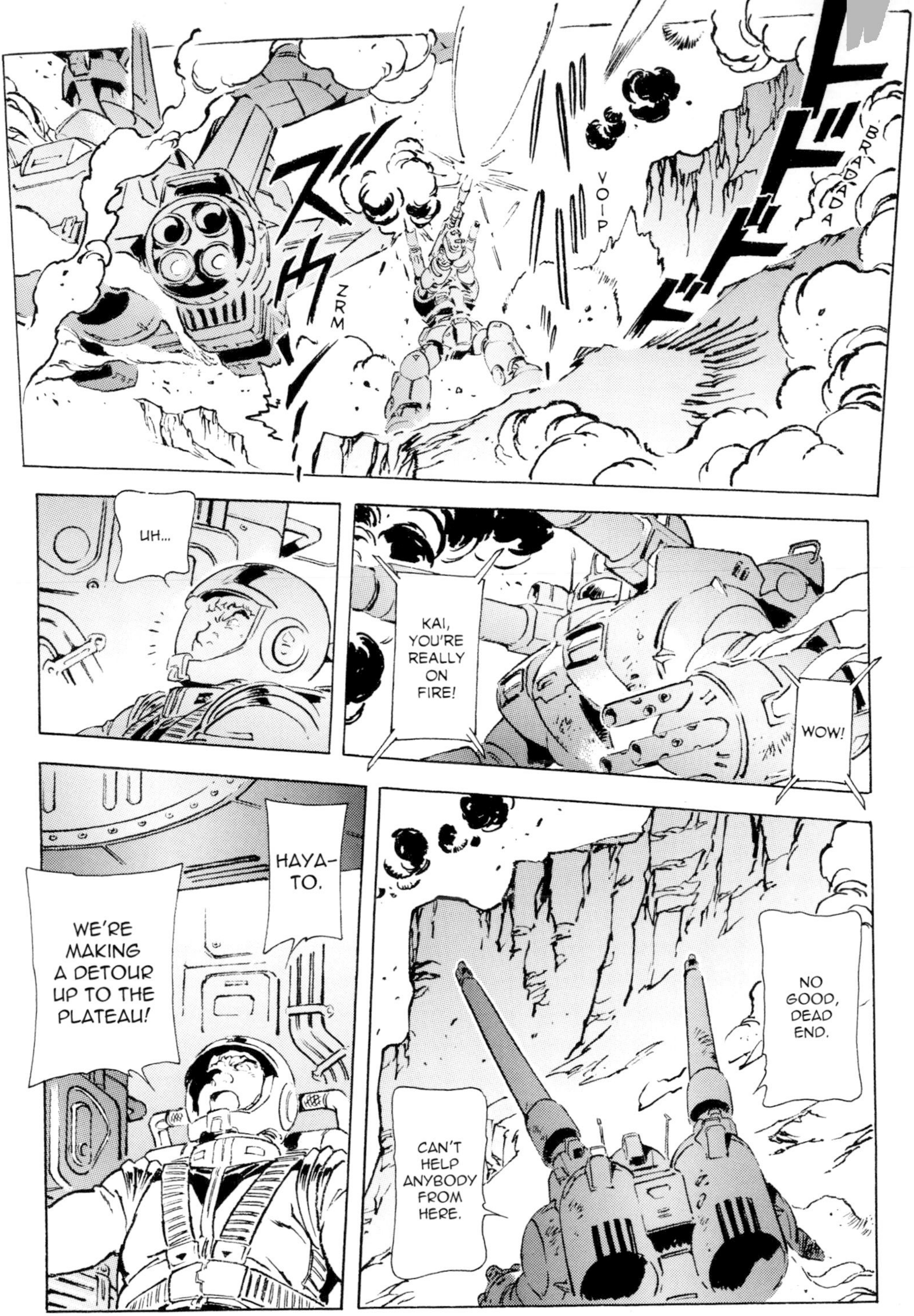

BRADADA
VOIP
ZRM
WOW!
KAI, YOU'RE REALLY ON FIRE!
UH...
NO GOOD, DEAD END.
CAN'T HELP ANYBODY FROM HERE.
HAYA-TO.
WE'RE MAKING A DETOUR UP TO THE PLATEAU!

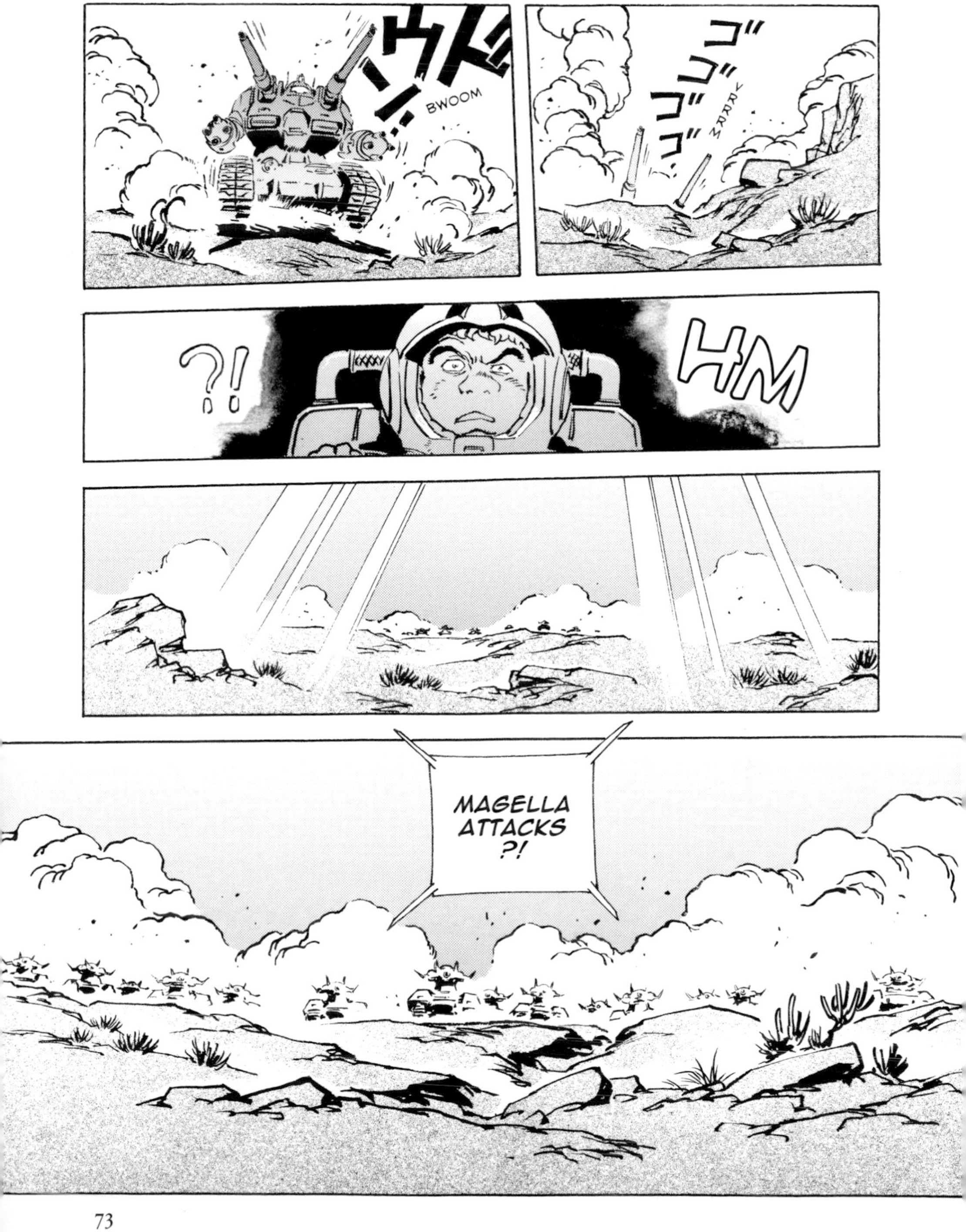
ゴゴゴゴ
VRRRM
ドウン!!
BWOOM
HM
?!
MAGELLA ATTACKS ?!

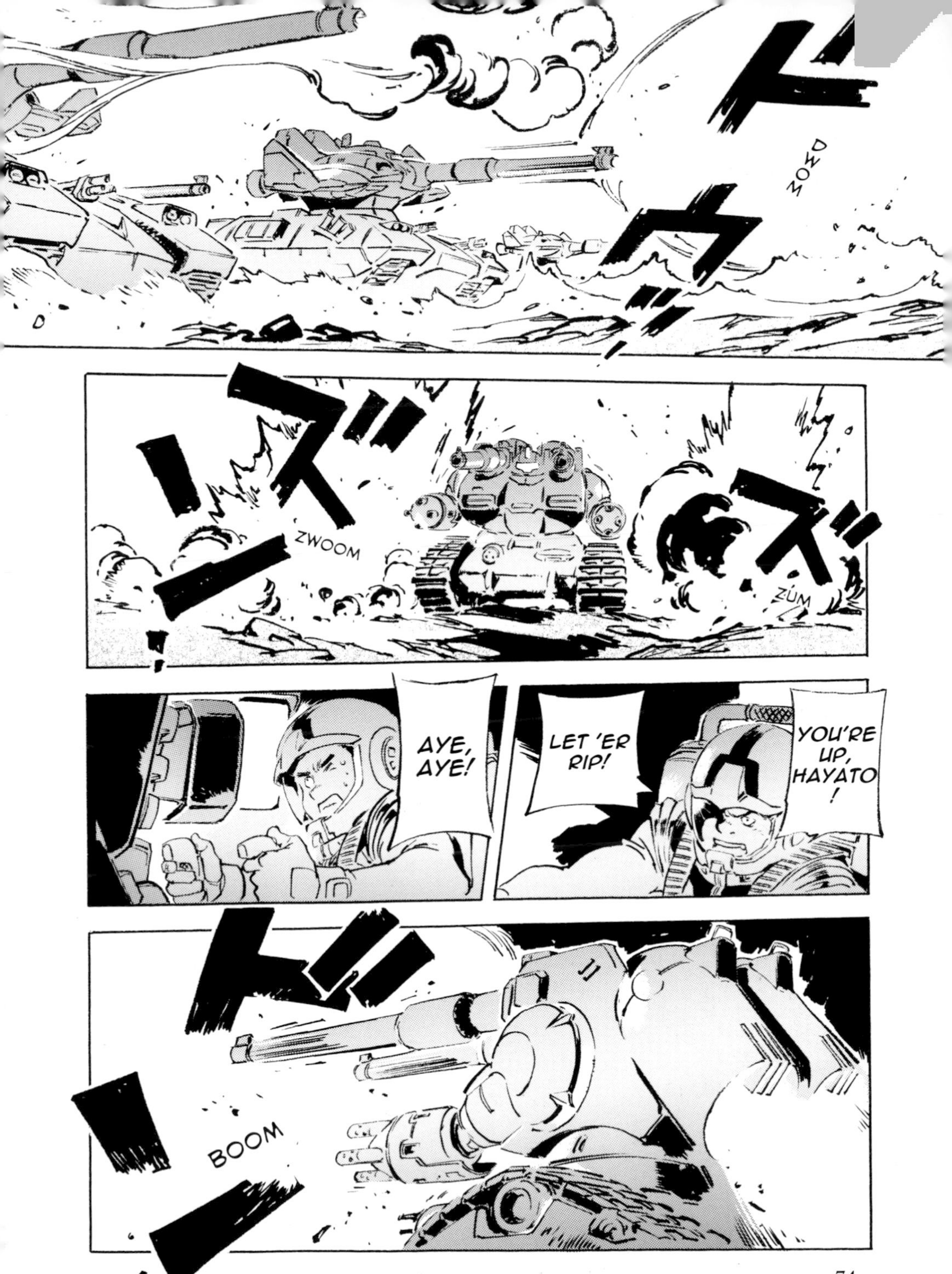
DWOM
ZUM
ZWOOM
YOU'RE UP, HAYATO!
LET 'ER RIP!
AYE, AYE!
BOOM

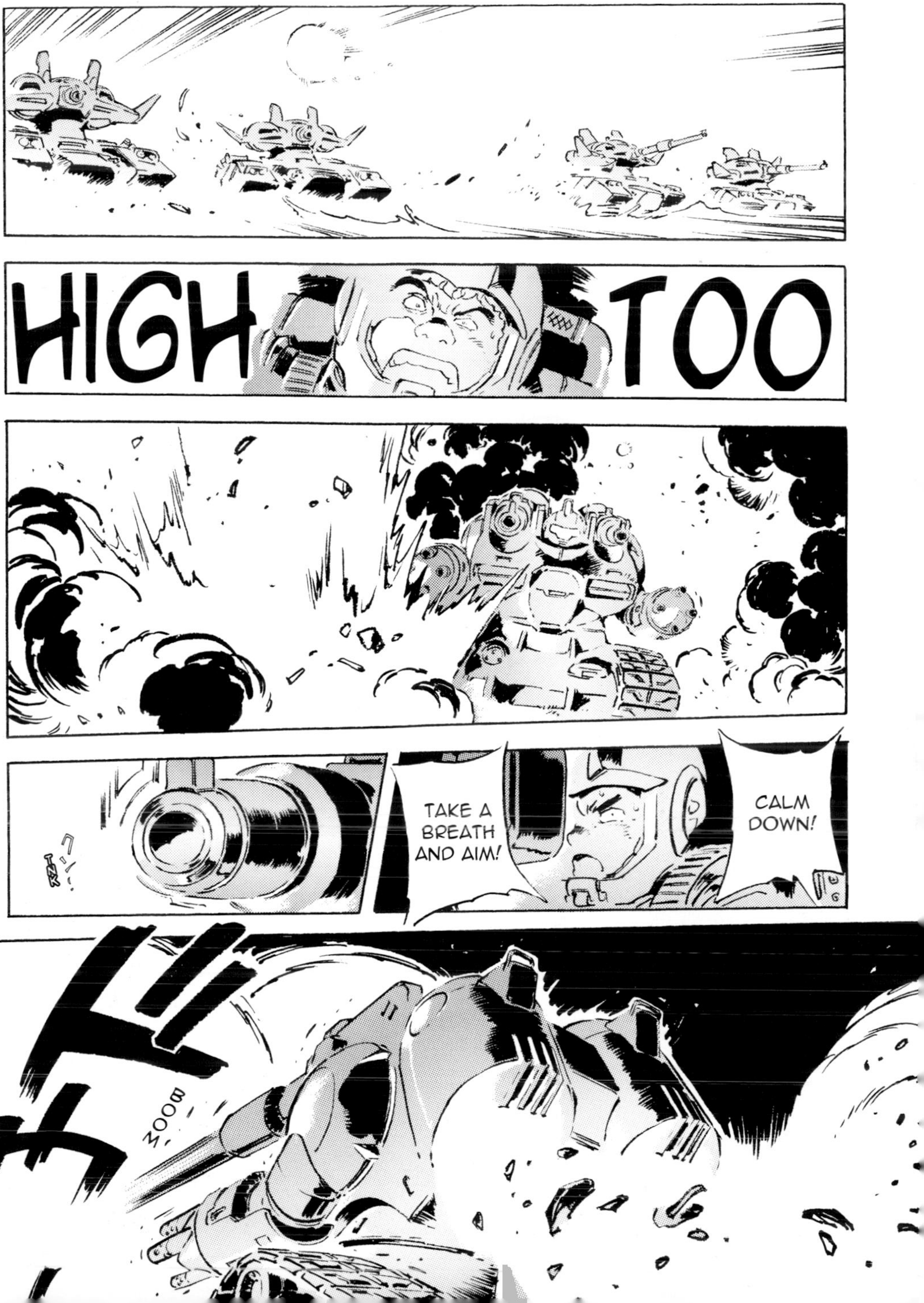
TOO
HIGH
CALM DOWN!
TAKE A BREATH AND AIM!
TNK
BOOM

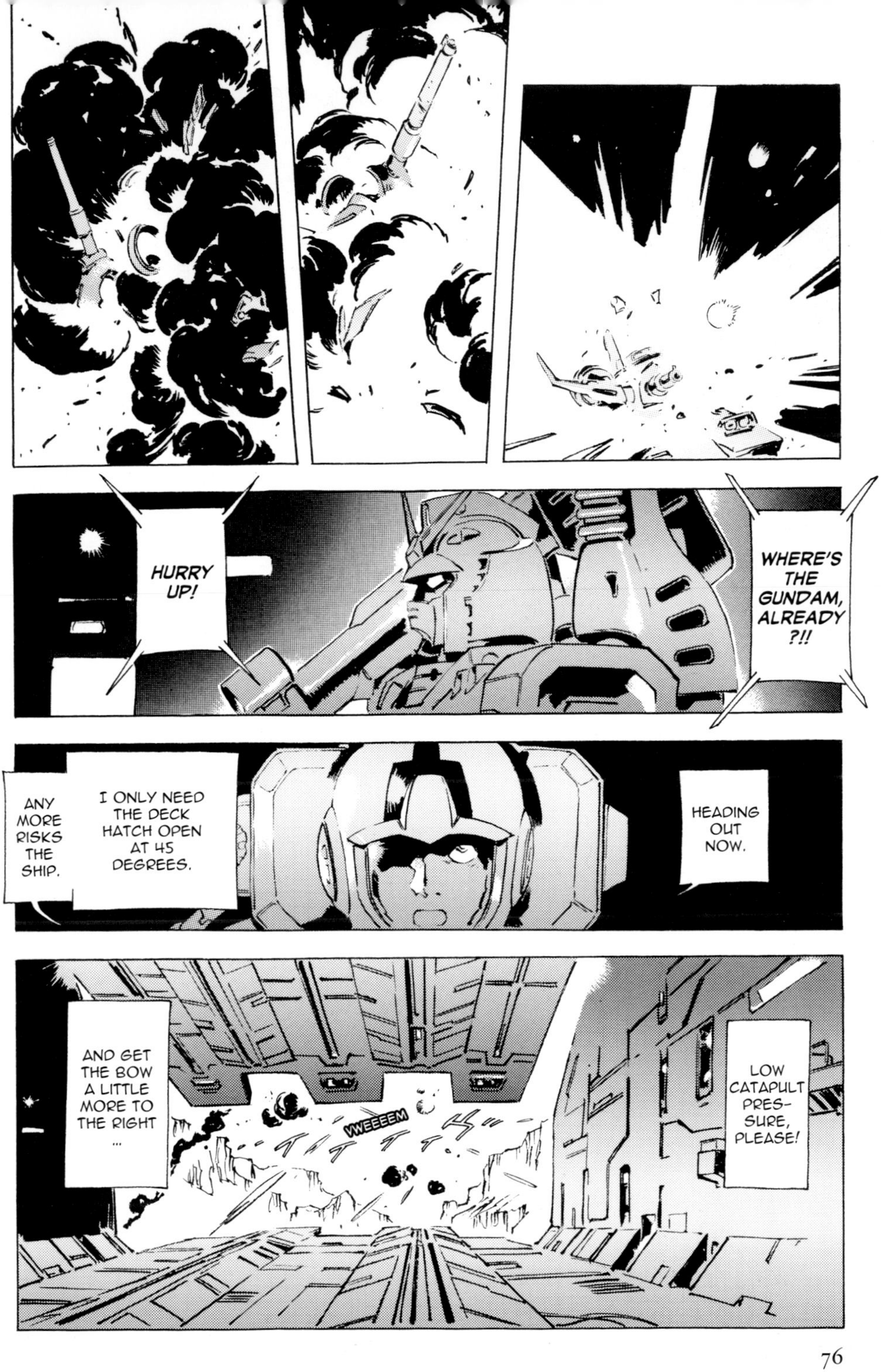
WHERE'S THE GUNDAM, ALREADY?!!
HURRY UP!
HEADING OUT NOW.
I ONLY NEED THE DECK HATCH OPEN AT 45 DEGREES.
ANY MORE RISKS THE SHIP.
LOW CATAPULT PRES-SURE, PLEASE!
VWEEEEM
AND GET THE BOW A LITTLE MORE TO THE RIGHT ...

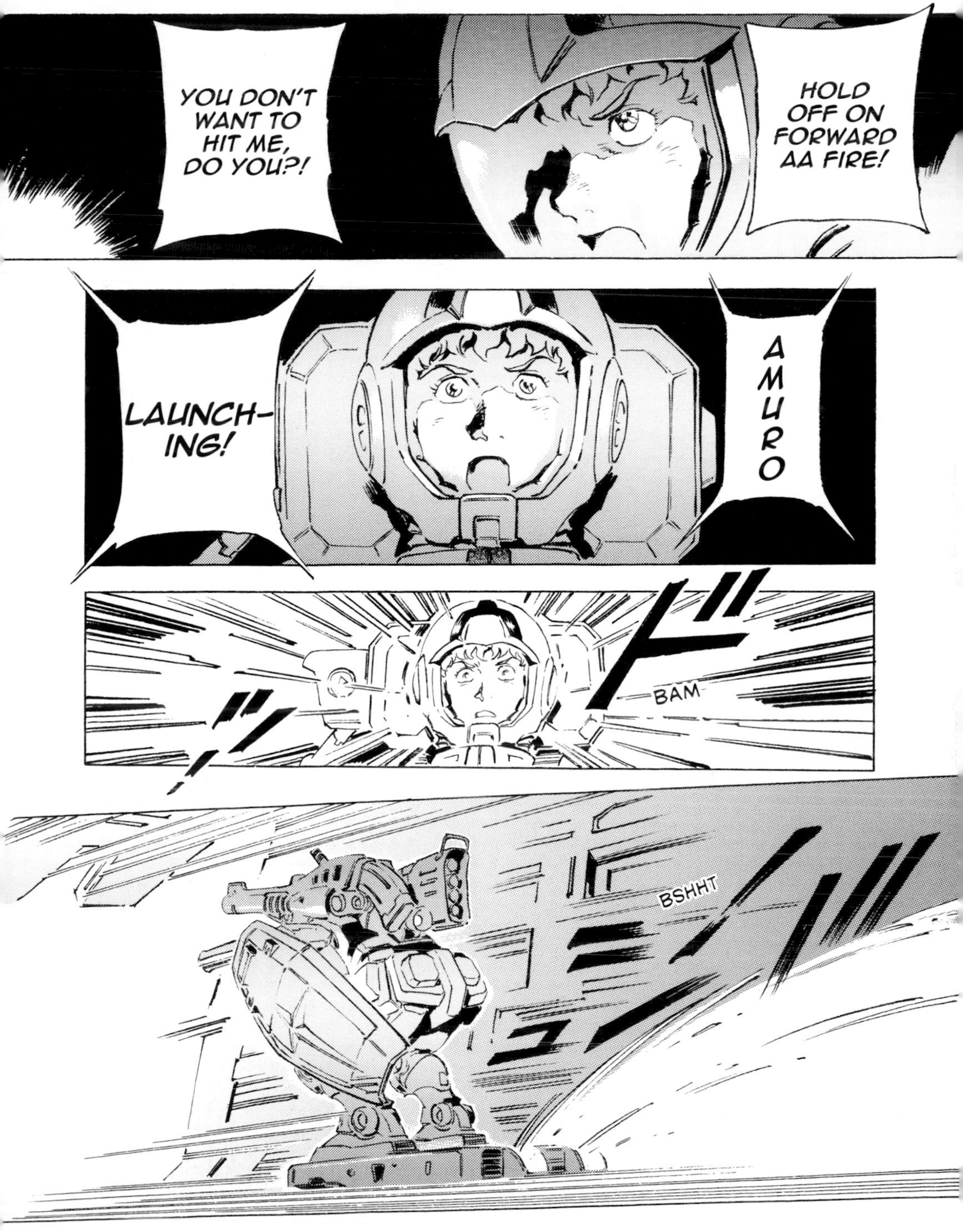
HOLD OFF ON FORWARD AA FIRE!
YOU DON'T WANT TO HIT ME, DO YOU?!
AMURO
LAUNCH-ING!
BAM
BSHHT

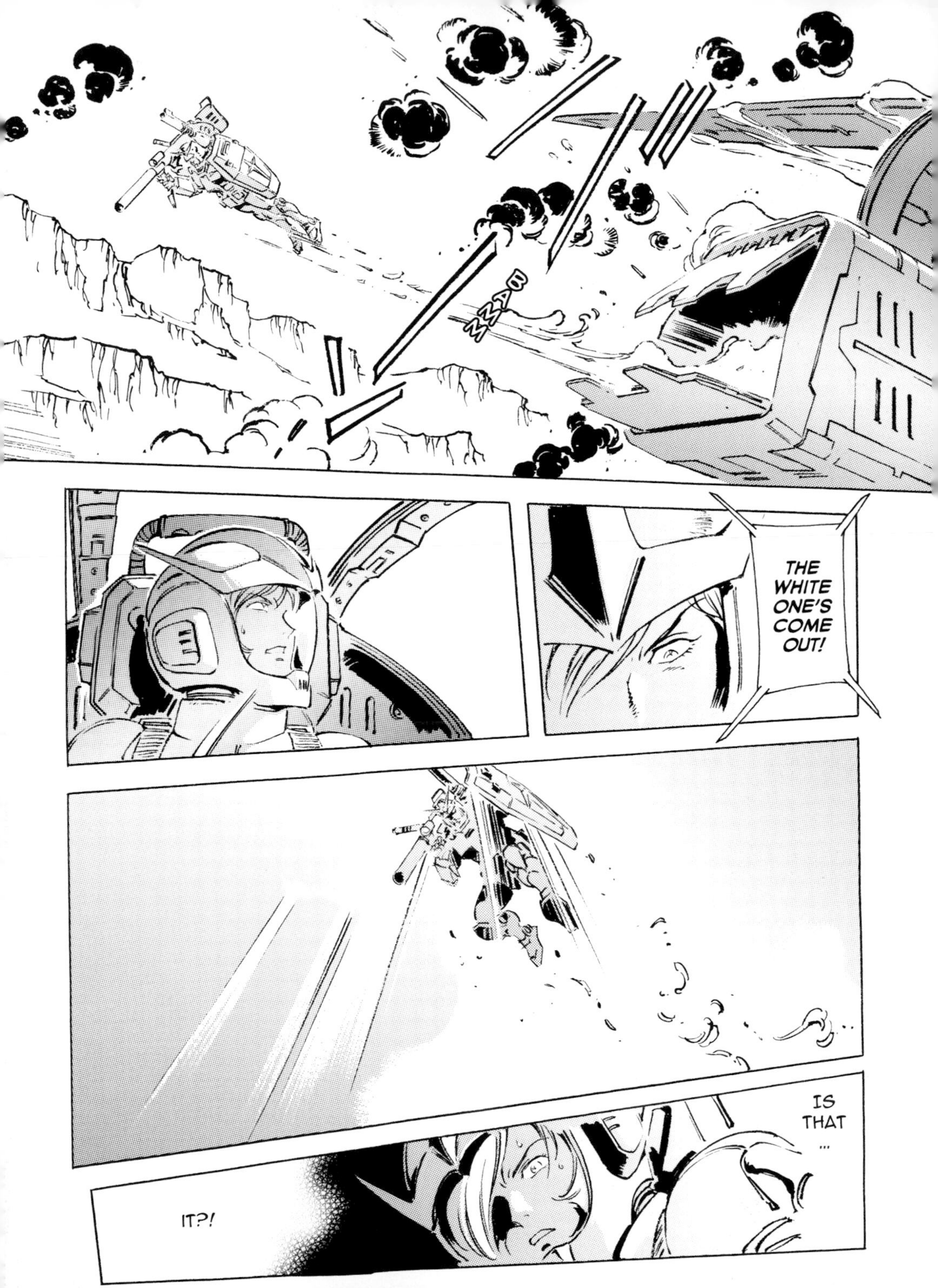
BAMM
THE WHITE ONE'S COME OUT!
IS THAT ...
IT?!

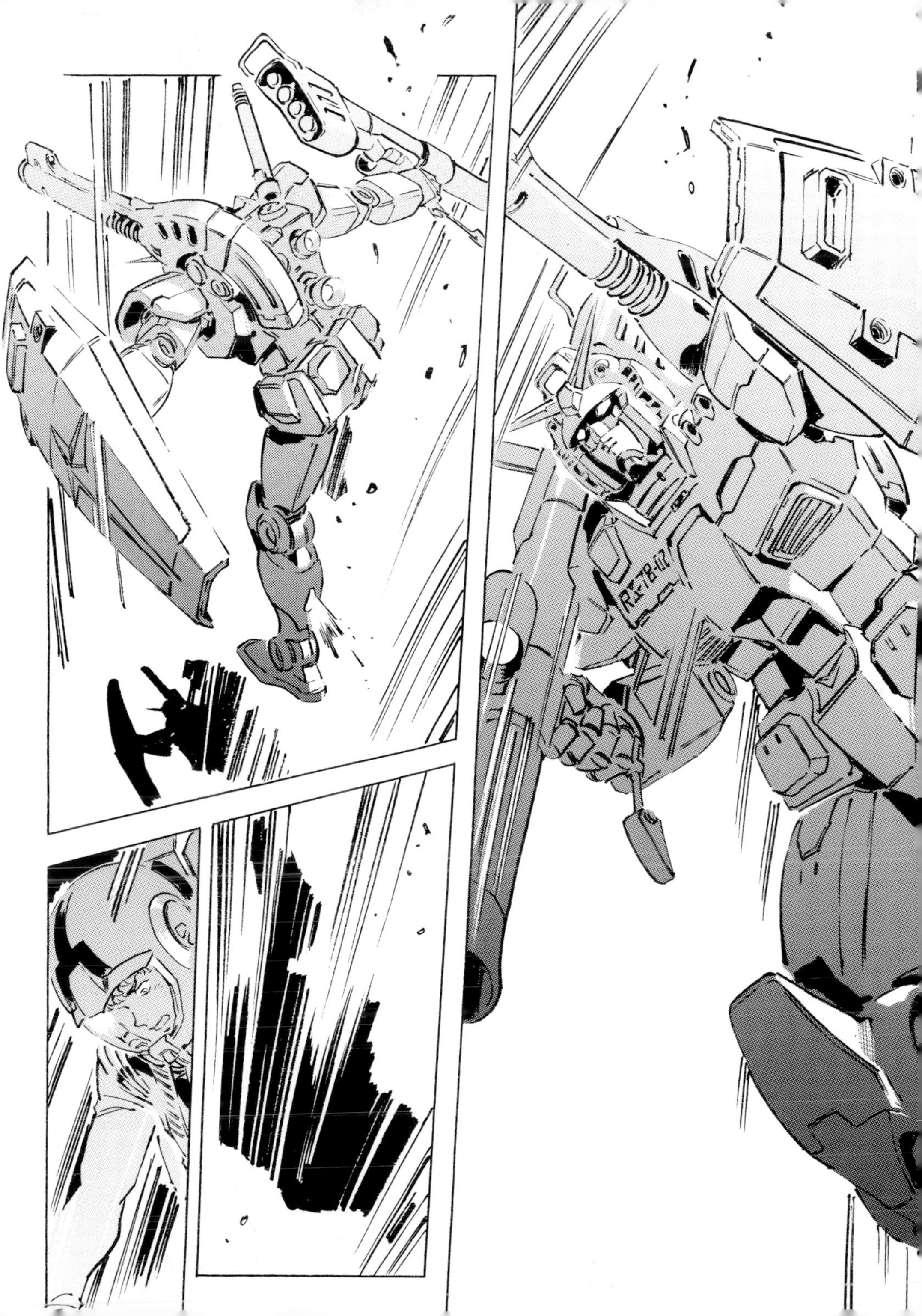
RX-78-02

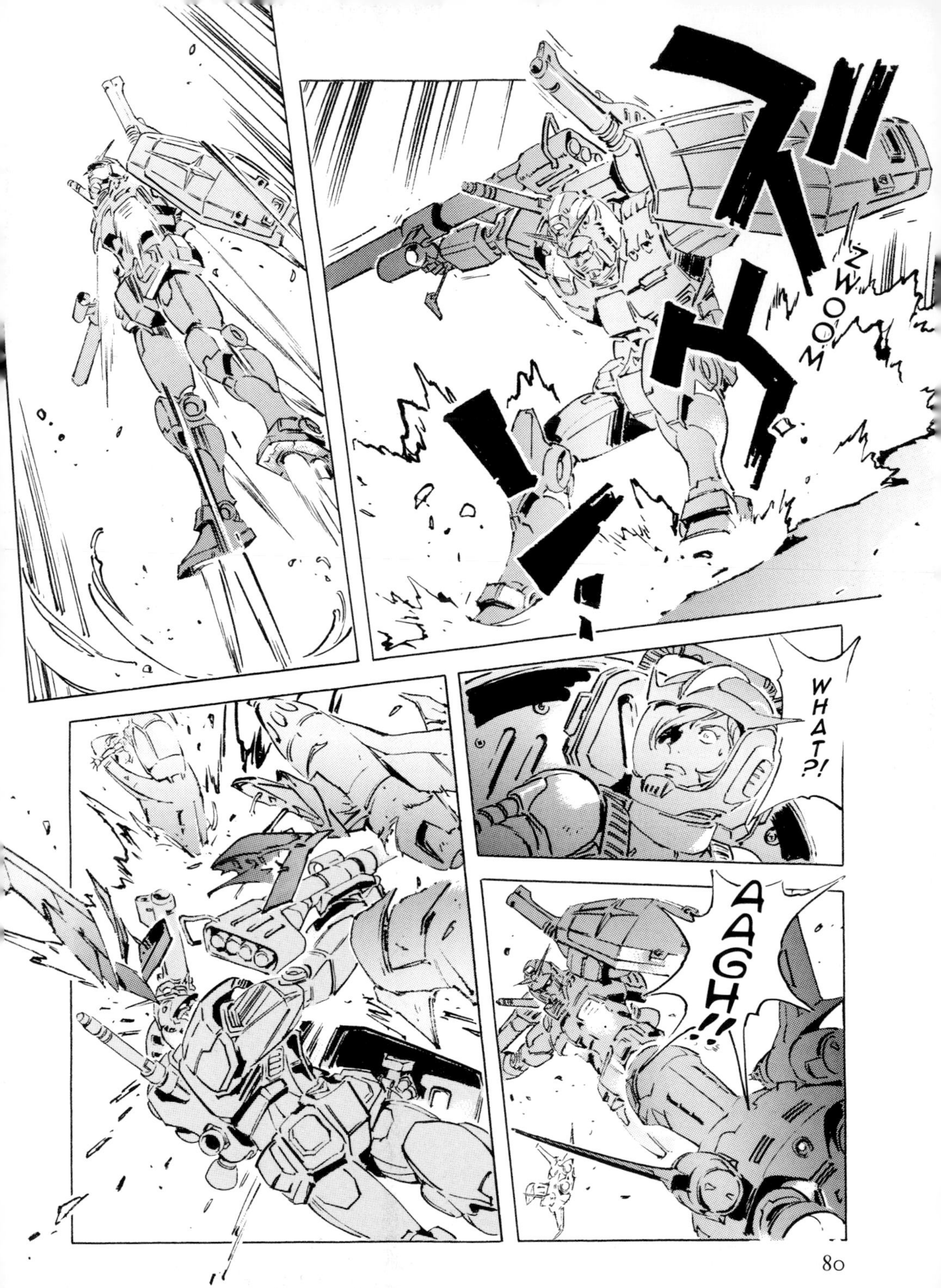

ズドッ
ZWOOM
WHAT?!
AAAGH!!

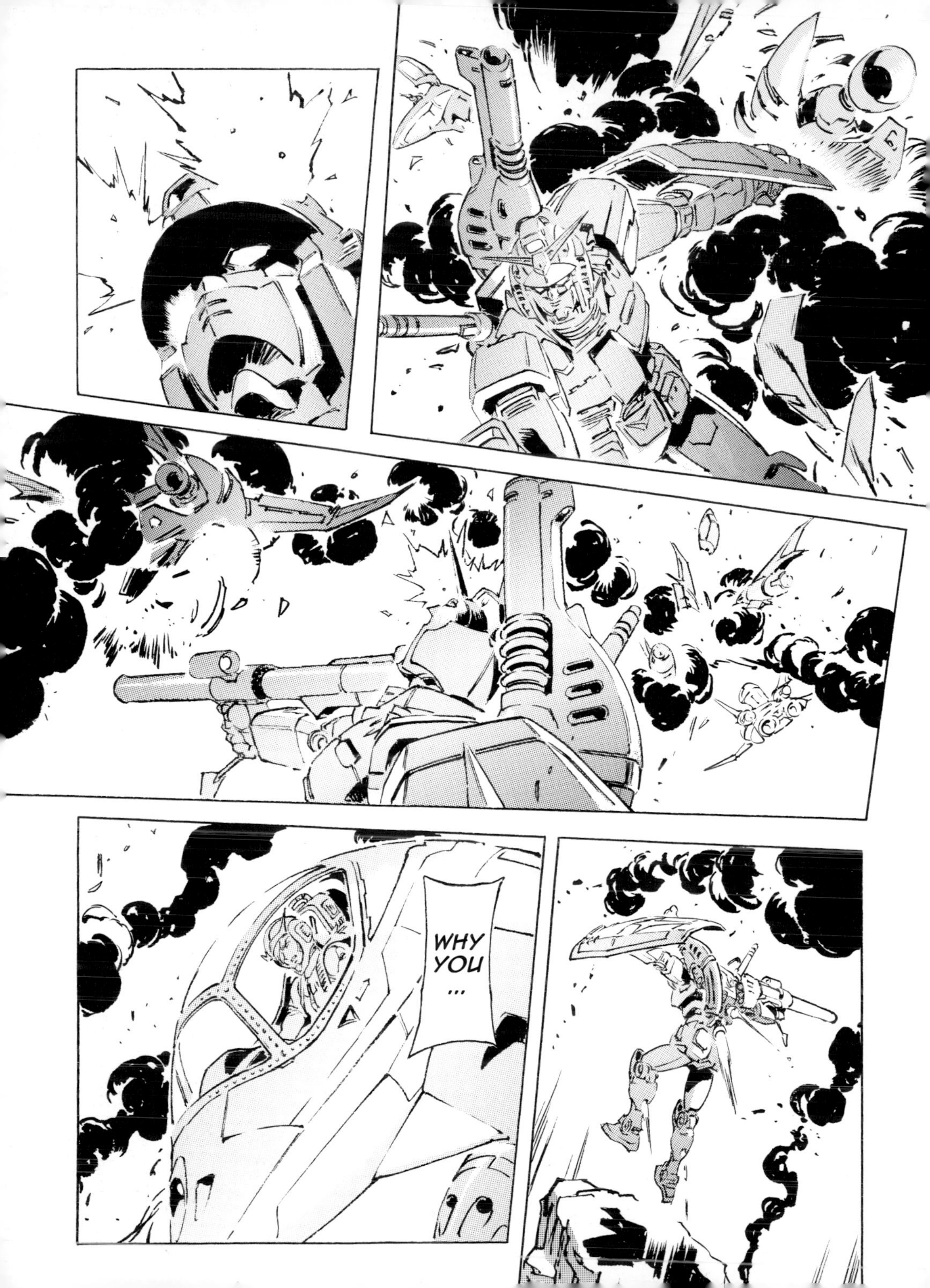
WHY YOU ...

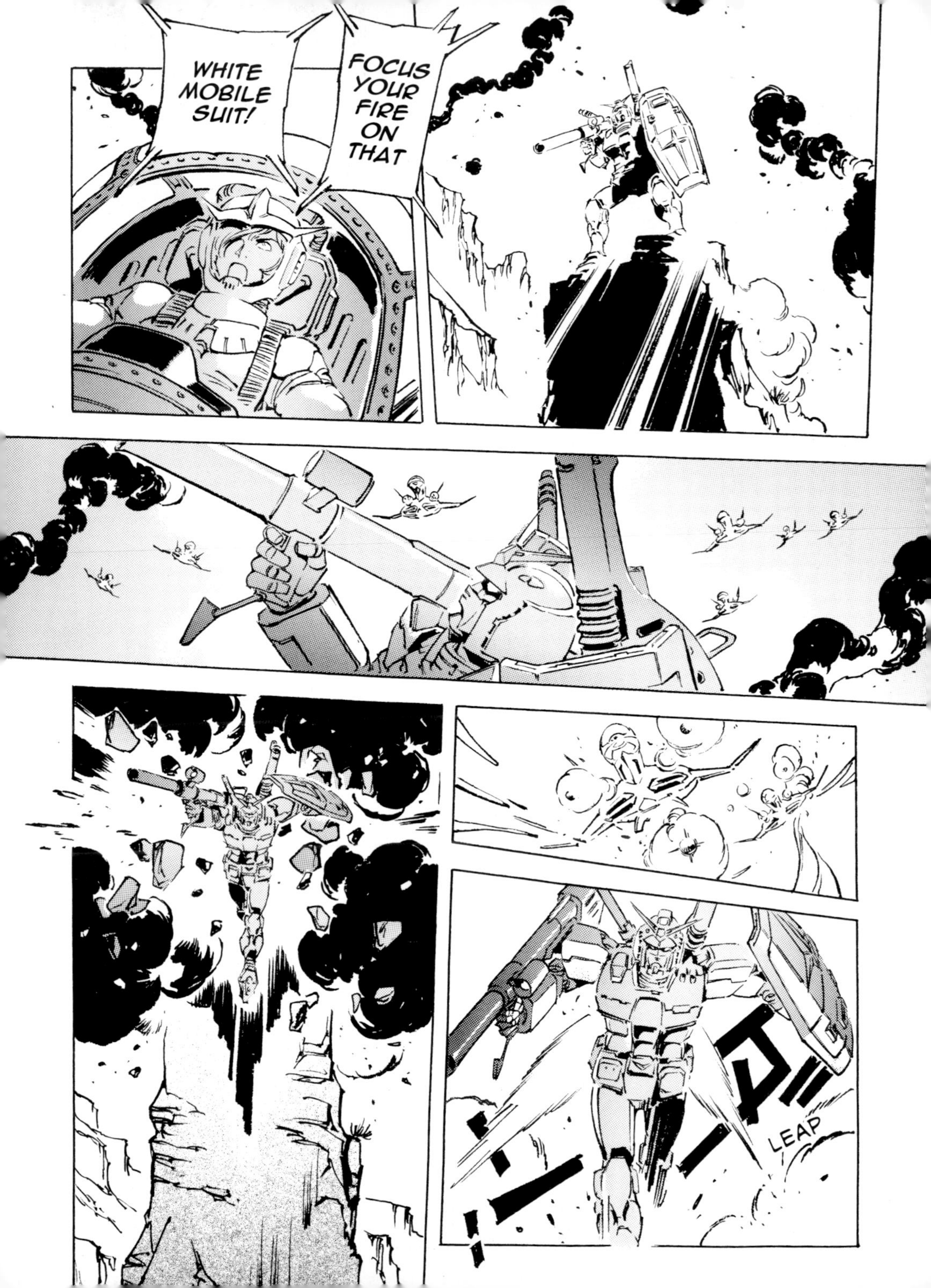
FOCUS YOUR FIRE ON THAT
WHITE MOBILE SUIT!
LEAP

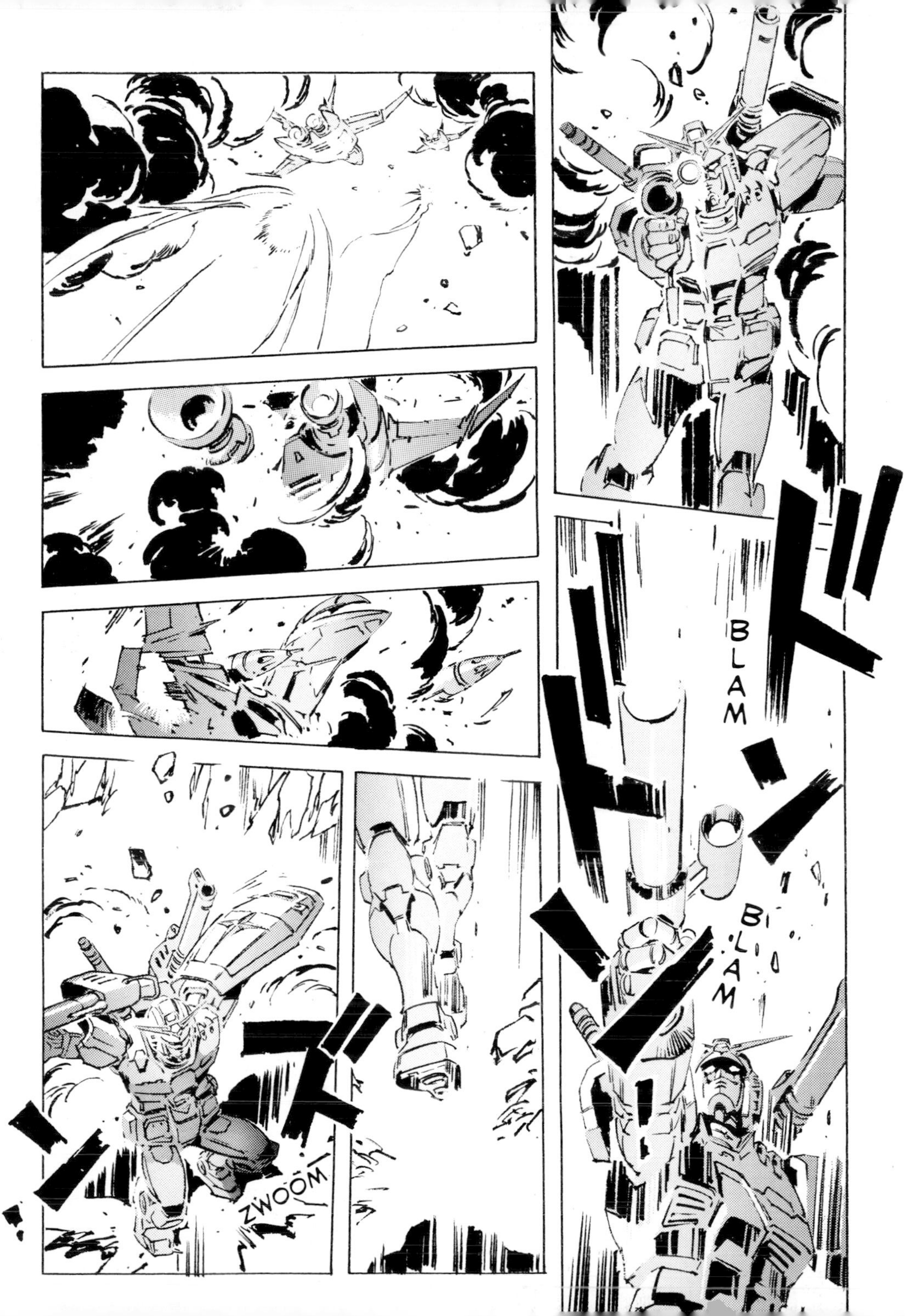
BLAM
BLAM
ZWOOM

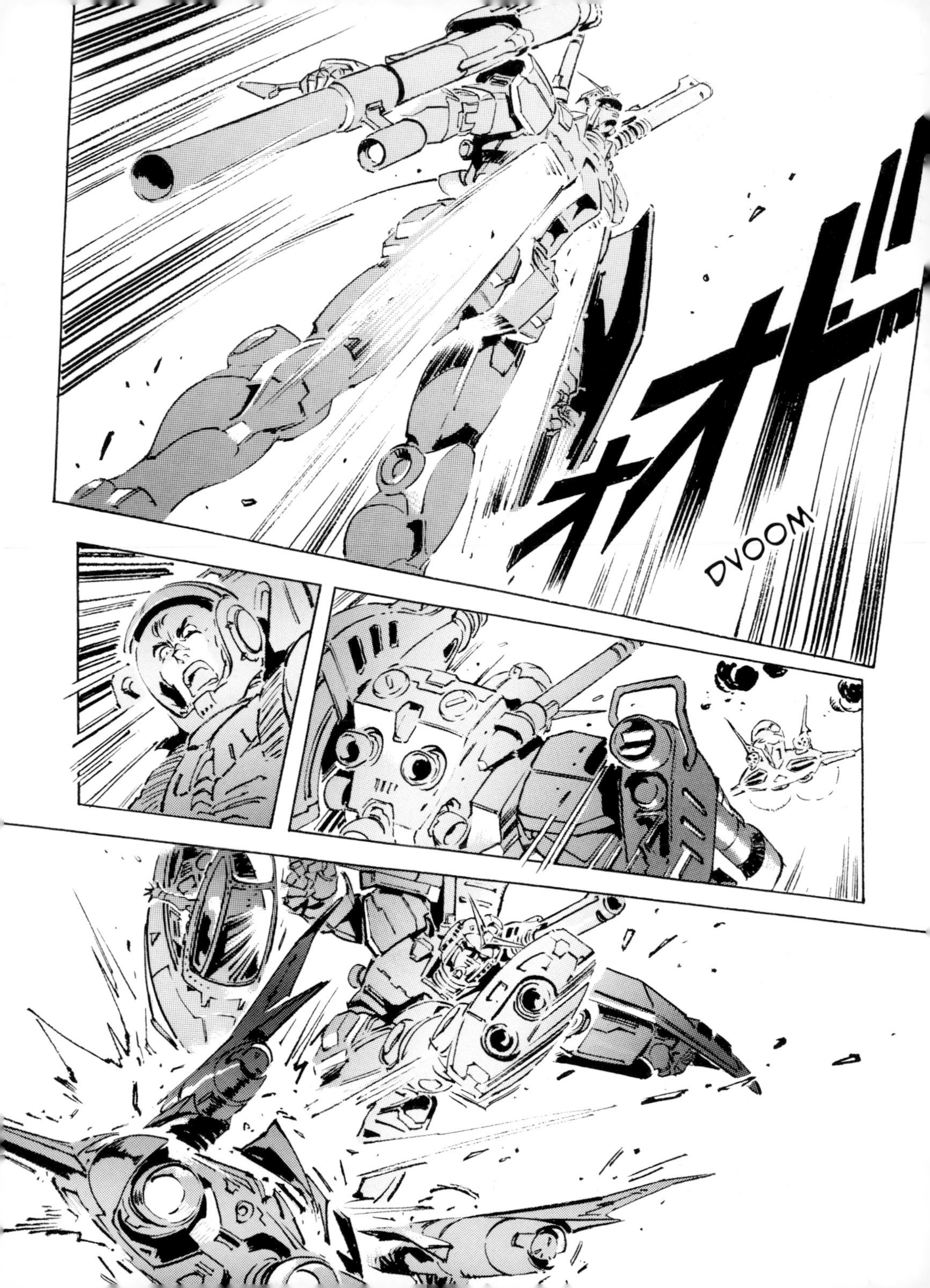
ドオ
DVOOM

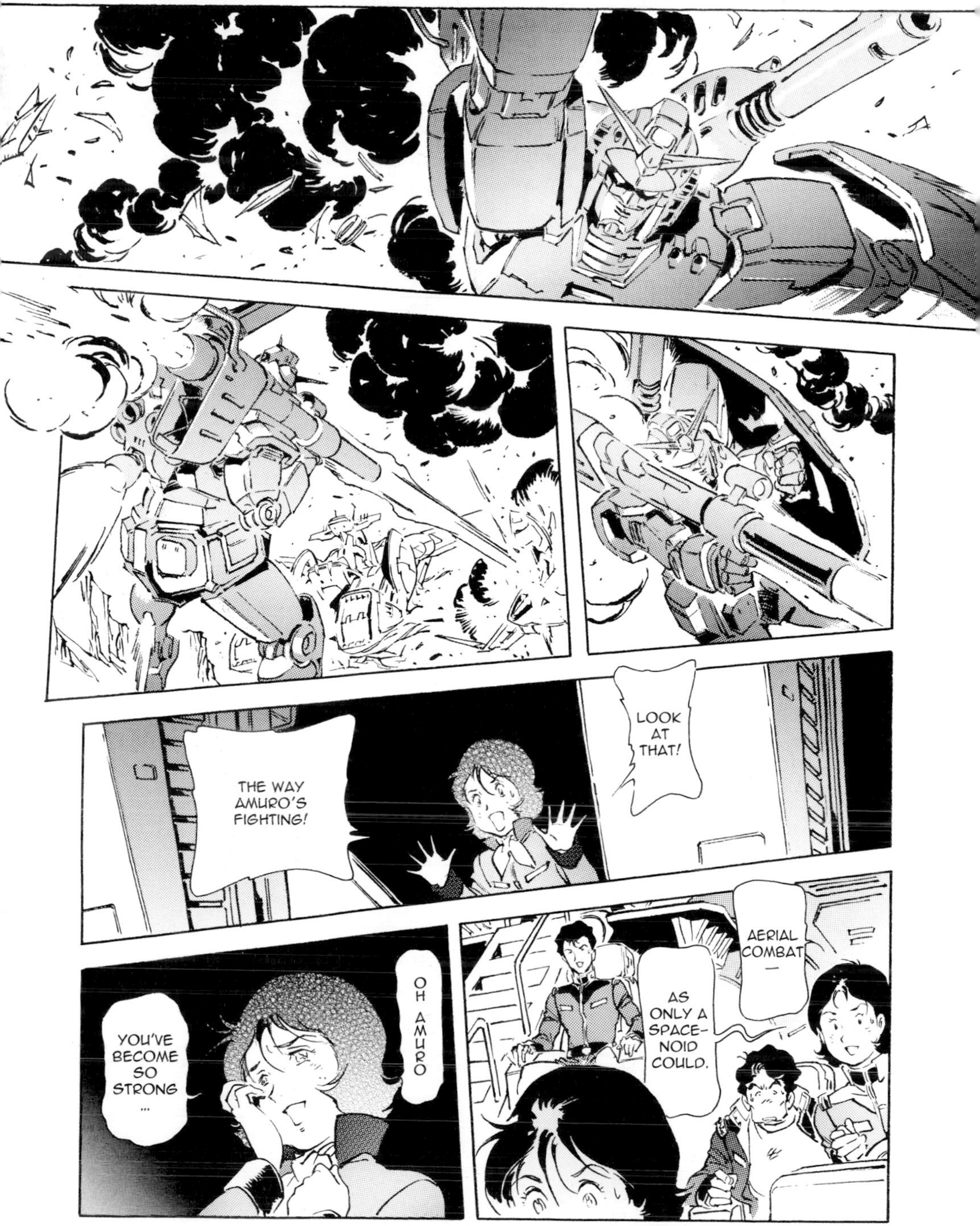
LOOK AT THAT!
THE WAY AMURO'S FIGHTING!
AERIAL COMBAT—
AS ONLY A SPACE-NOID COULD.
OH AMURO
YOU'VE BECOME SO STRONG ...

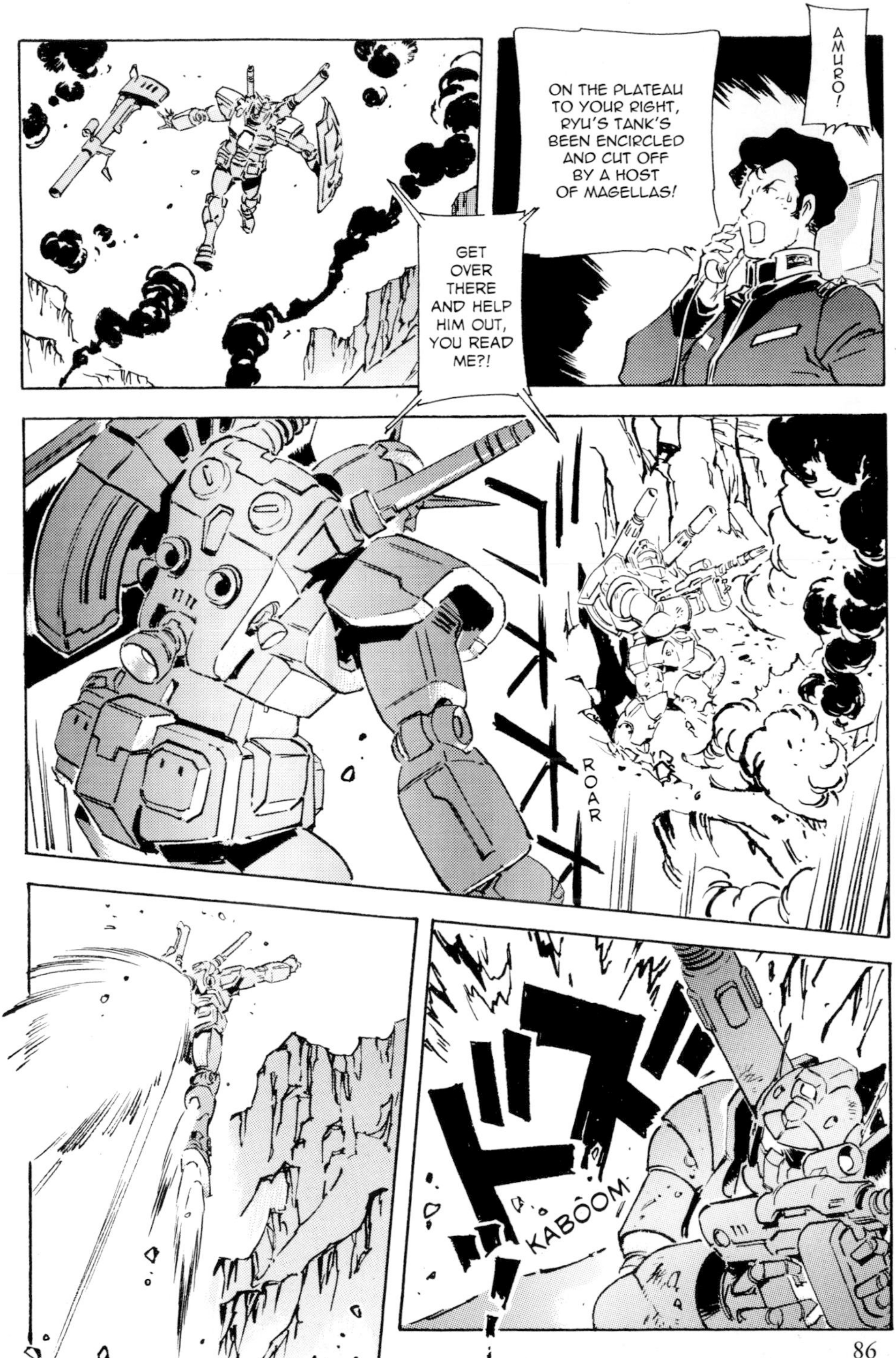
AMURO!
ON THE PLATEAU TO YOUR RIGHT, RYU'S TANK'S BEEN ENCIRCLED AND CUT OFF BY A HOST OF MAGELLAS!
GET OVER THERE AND HELP HIM OUT, YOU READ ME?!
ROAR
KABOOM

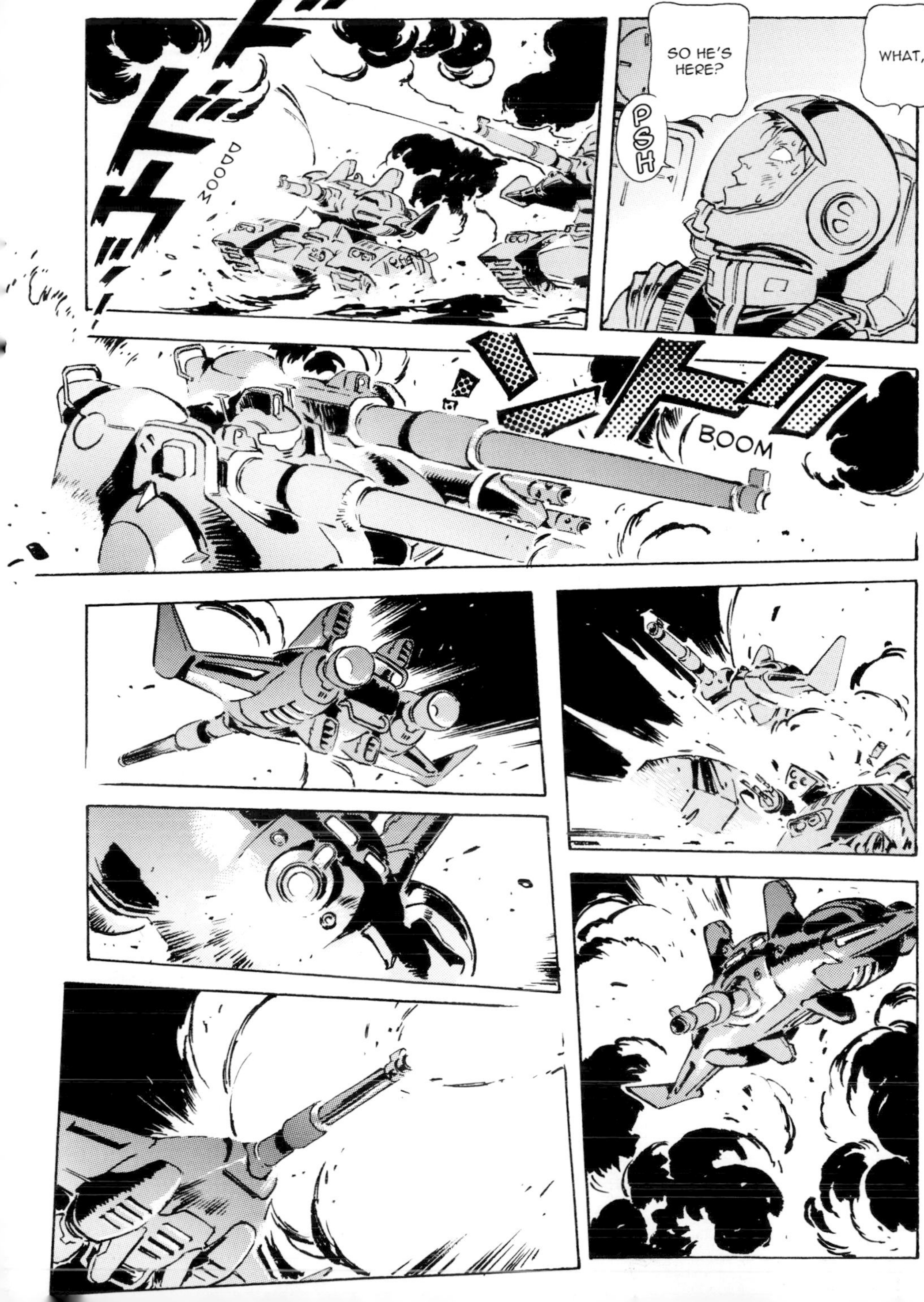
WHAT,
SO HE'S HERE?
PSH
DDOOM
BOOM

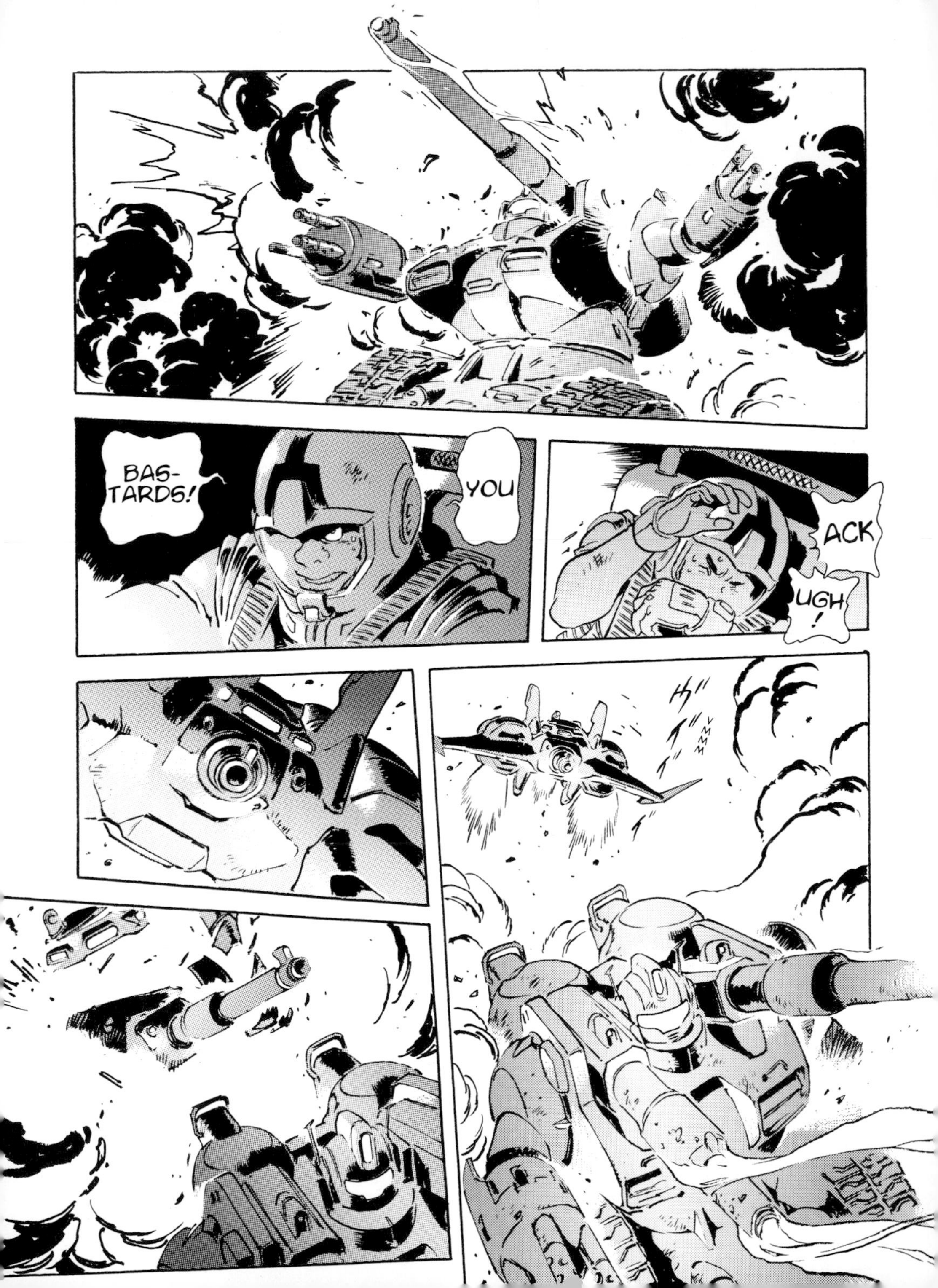
ACK
UGH!
YOU
BAS-TARDS!

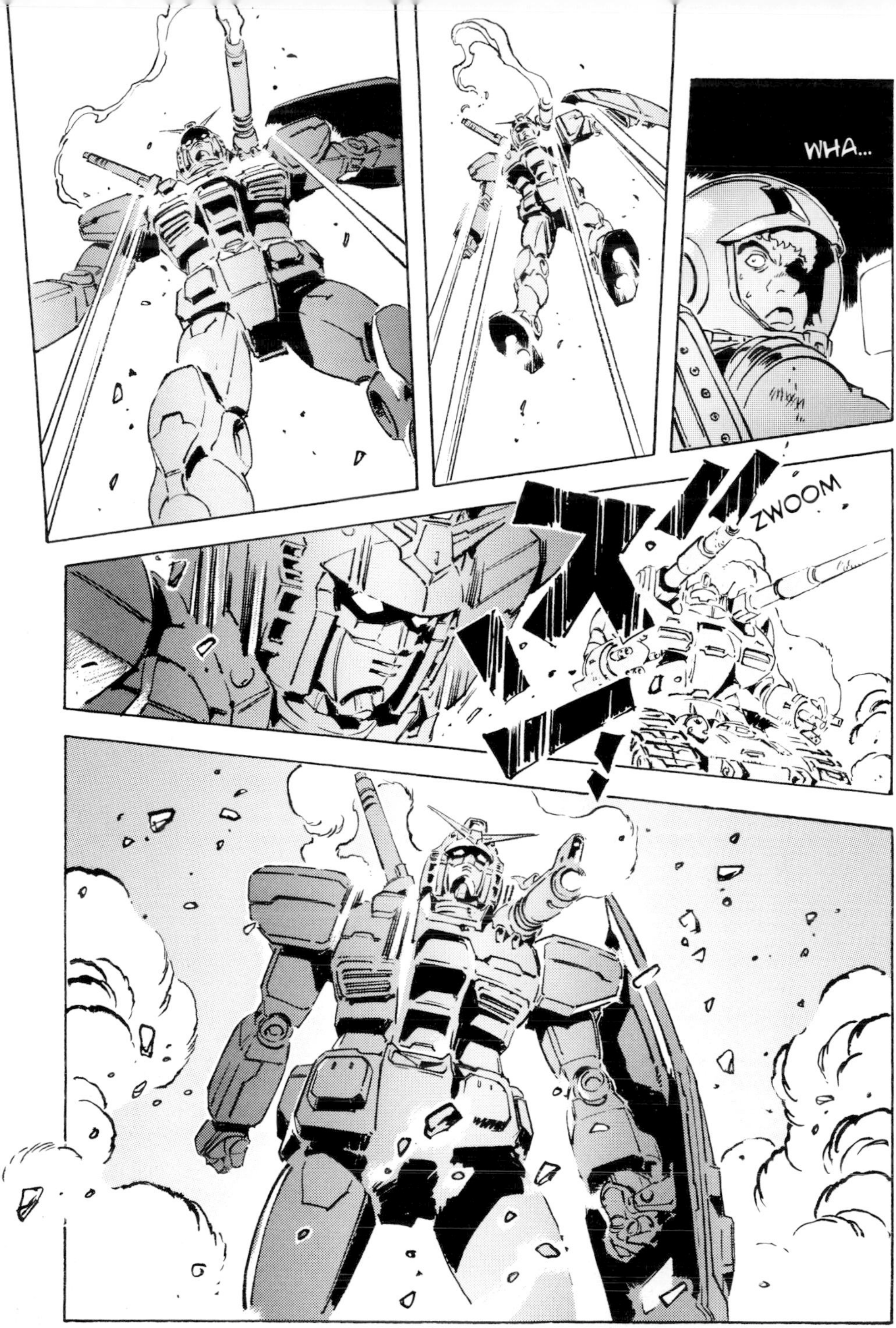
WHA...
ZWOOM

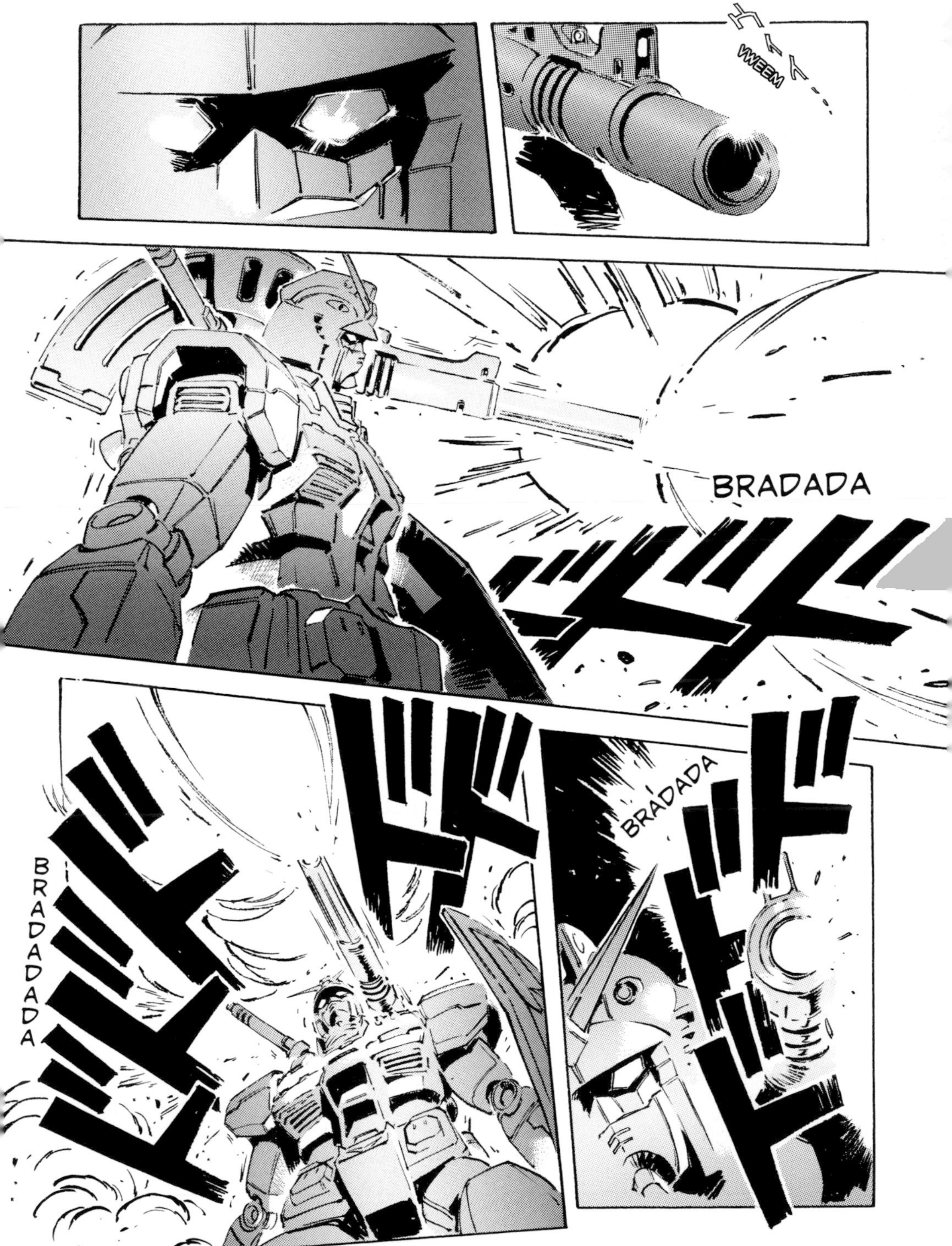
VWEEM
BRADADA
BRADADA
BRADADADADA

BRADADA
ドドド
DA

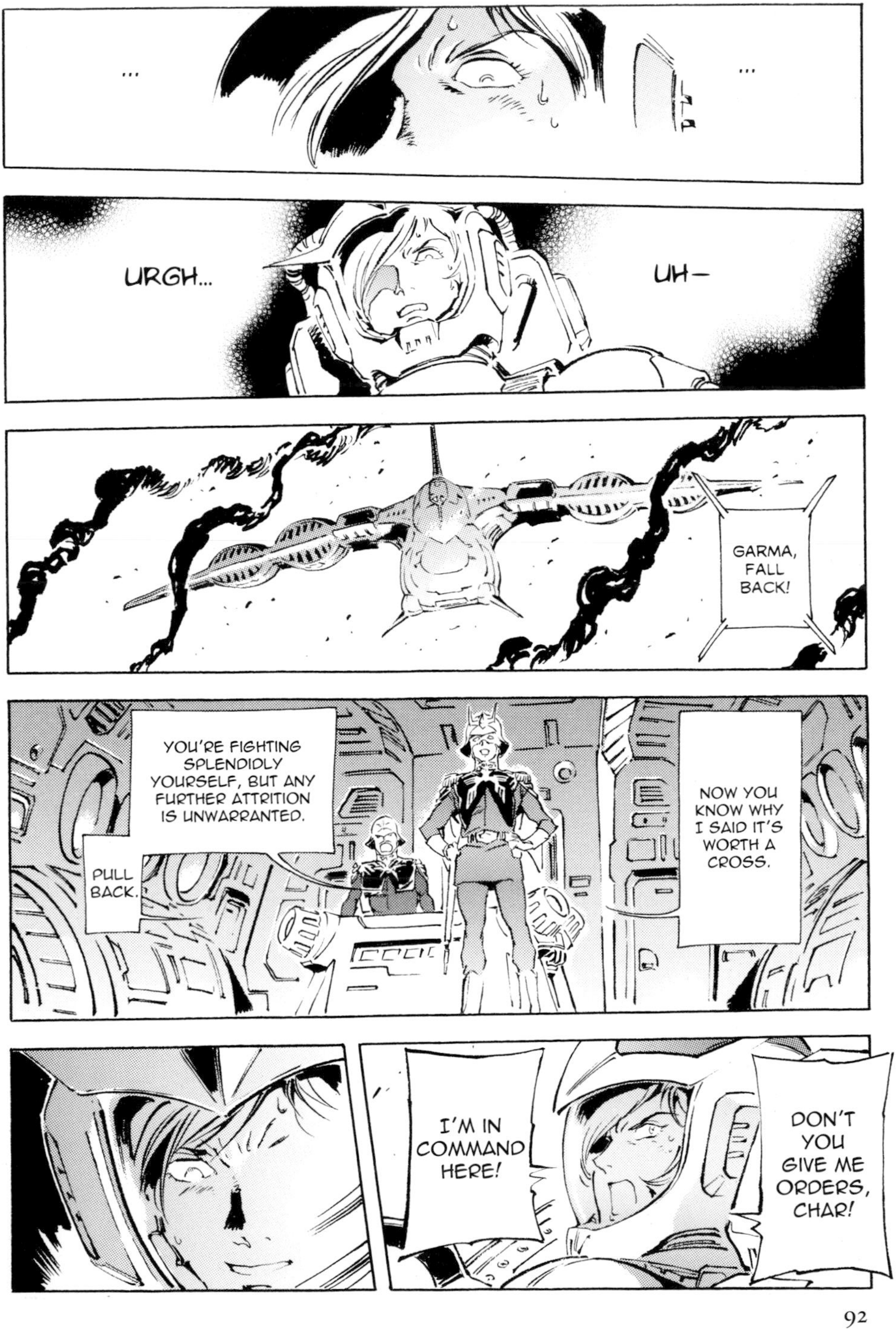
...
...
UH—
URGH...
GARMA, FALL BACK!
NOW YOU KNOW WHY I SAID IT'S WORTH A CROSS.
YOU'RE FIGHTING SPLENDIDLY YOURSELF, BUT ANY FURTHER ATTRITION IS UNWARRANTED.
PULL BACK.
DON'T YOU GIVE ME ORDERS, CHAR!
I'M IN COMMAND HERE!

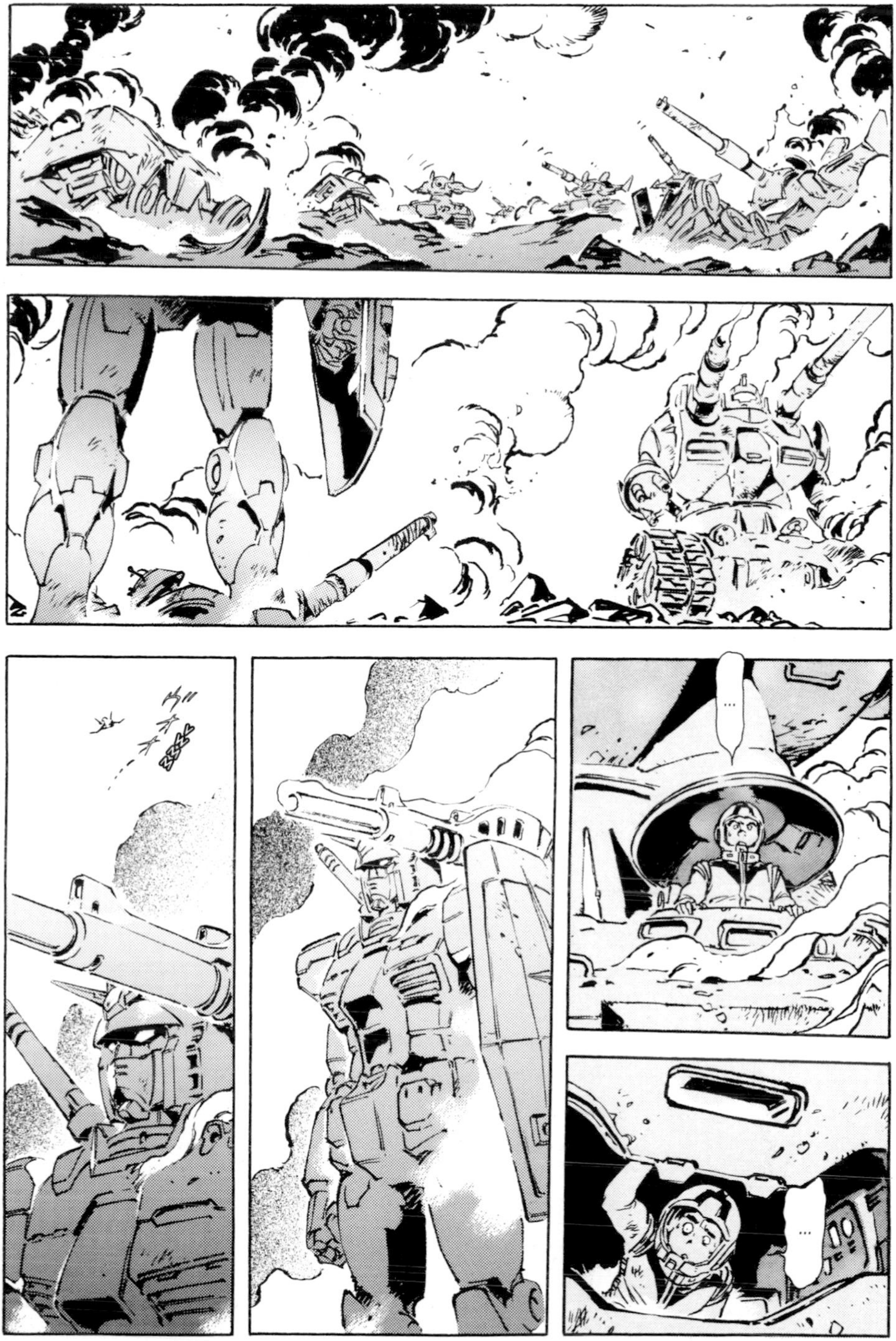
…
…

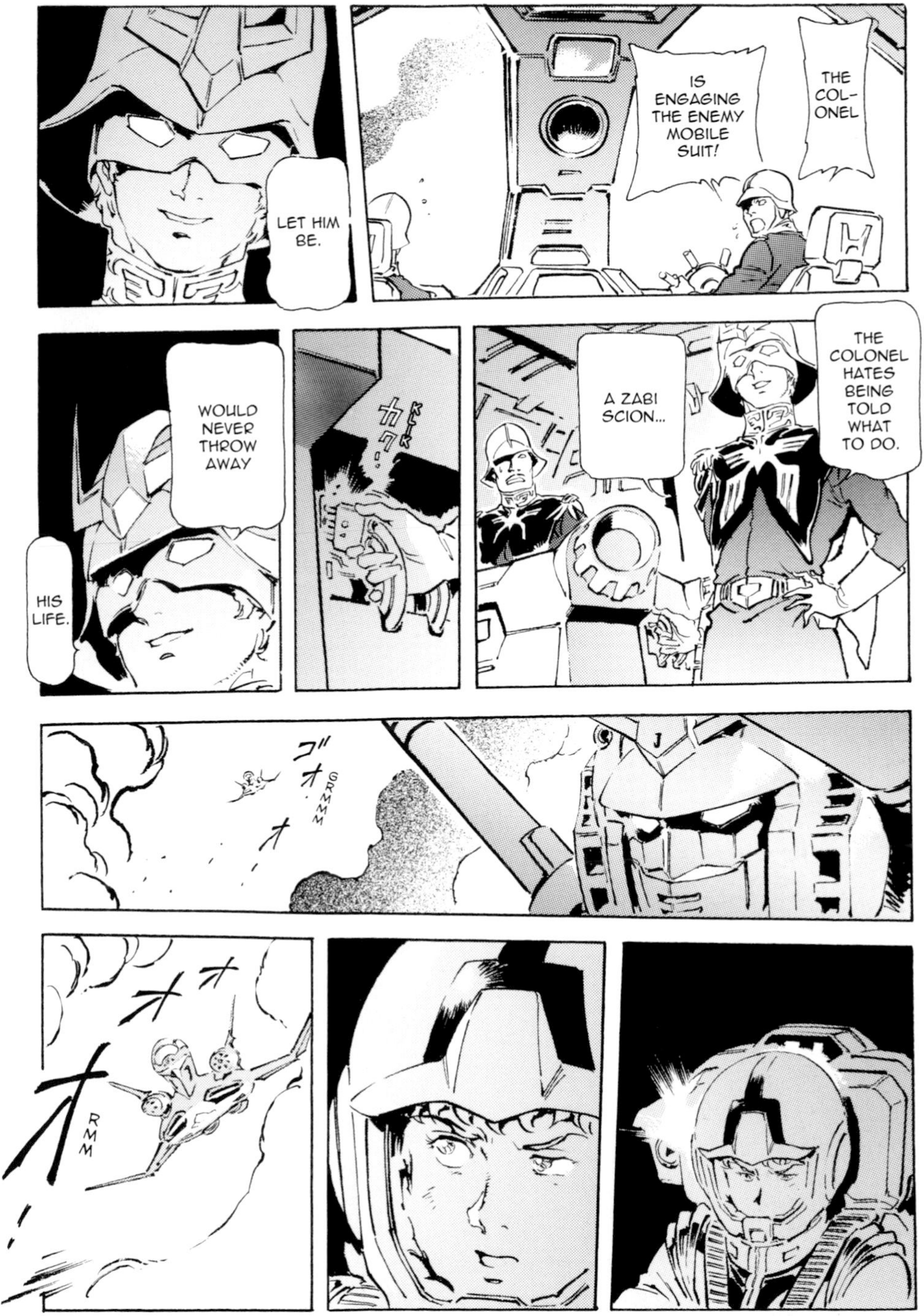
THE COL-ONEL
IS ENGAGING THE ENEMY MOBILE SUIT!
LET HIM BE.
THE COLONEL HATES BEING TOLD WHAT TO DO.
A ZABI SCION...
カク
KLIK
WOULD NEVER THROW AWAY
HIS LIFE.
ゴオ
GRMMM
RMM

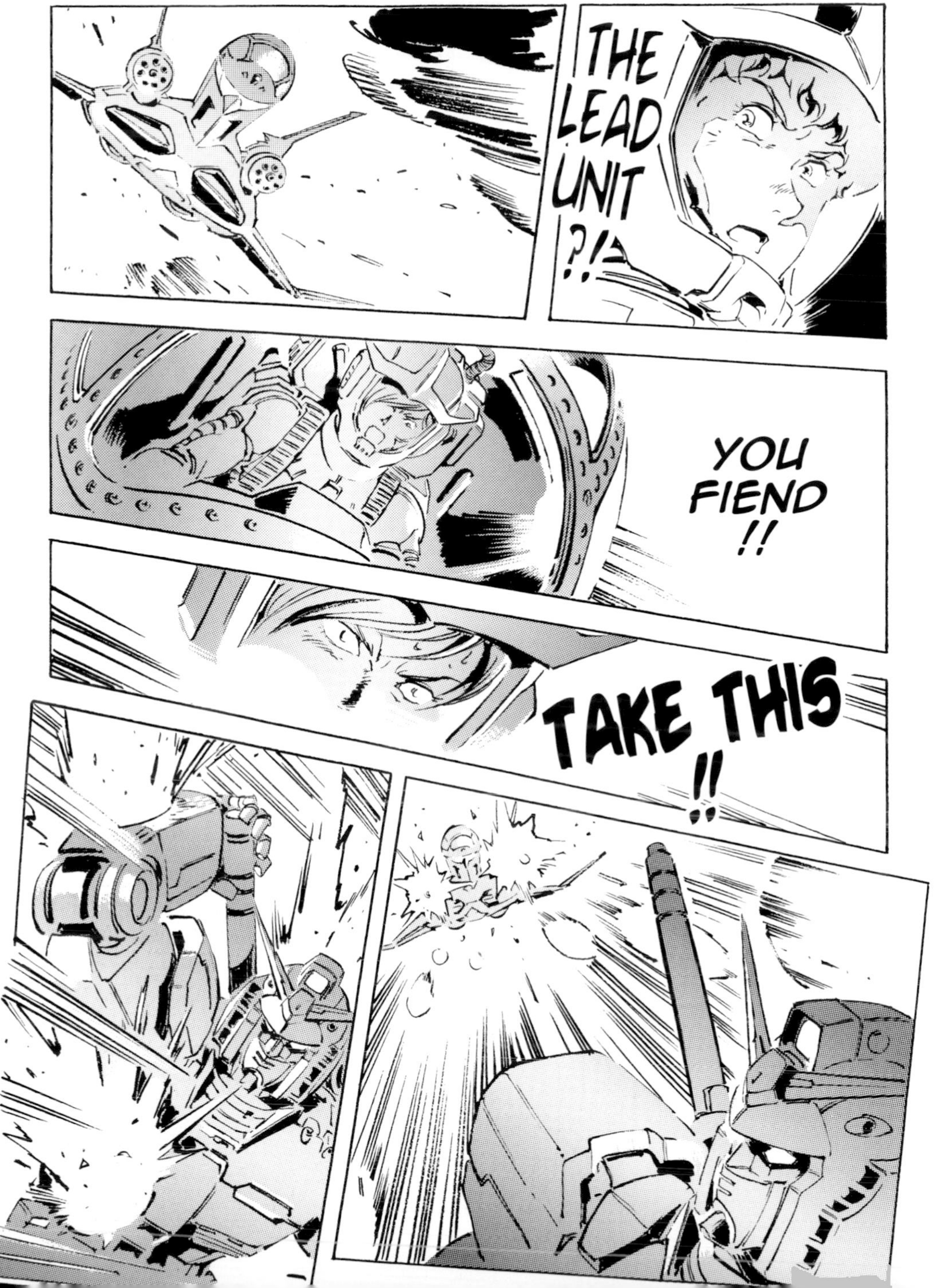
THE LEAD UNIT ?!
YOU FIEND !!
TAKE THIS !!

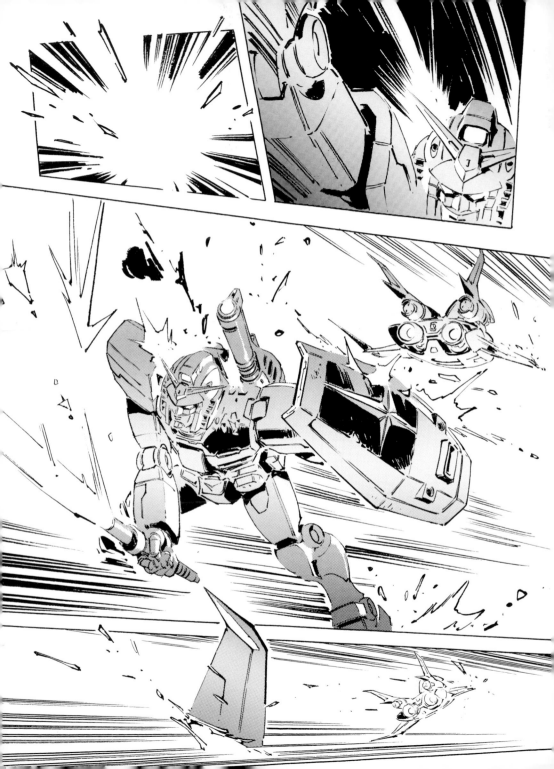

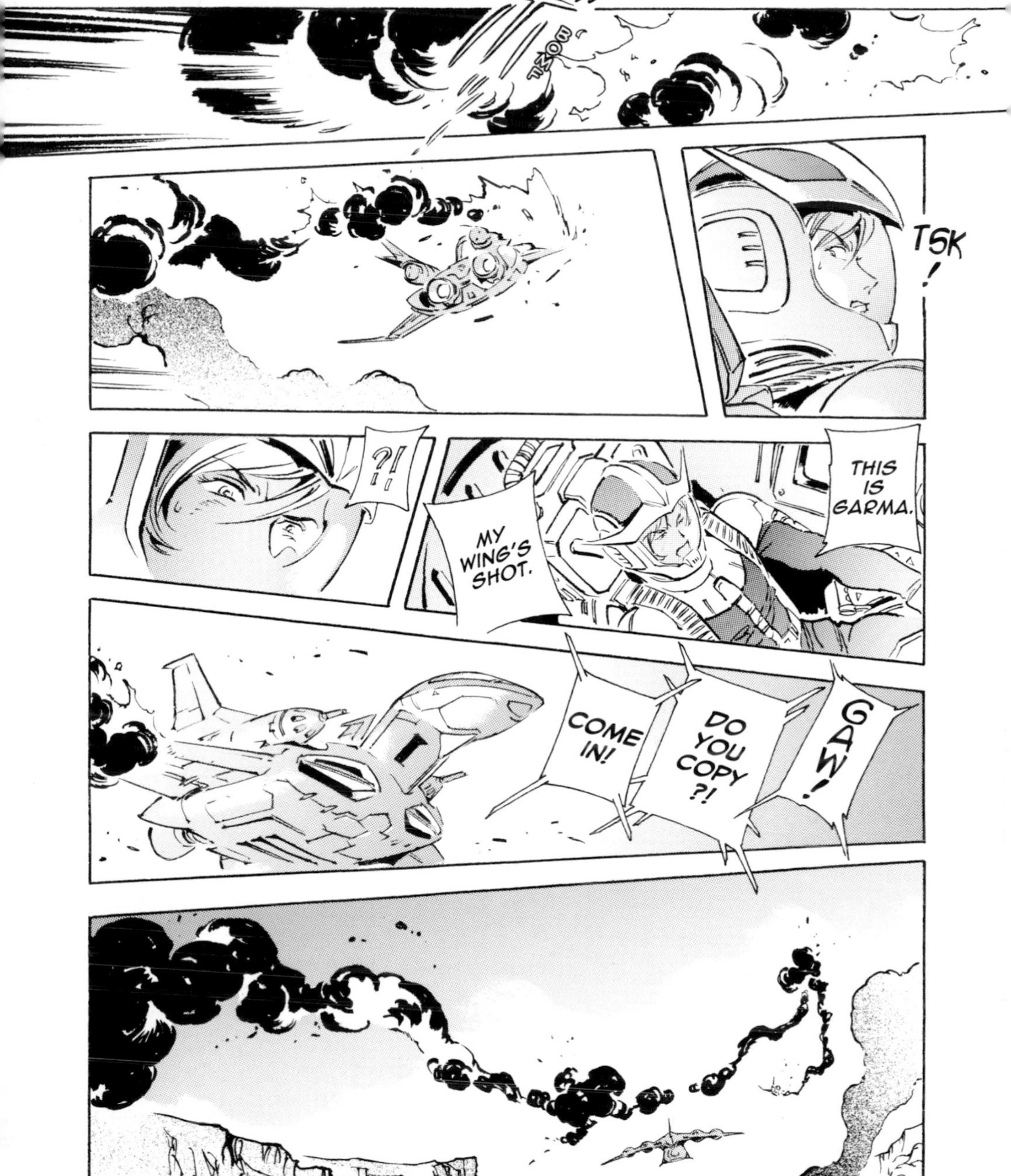
TSK!
THIS IS GARMA.
MY WING'S SHOT.
?!
GAW!
DO YOU COPY?!
COME IN!

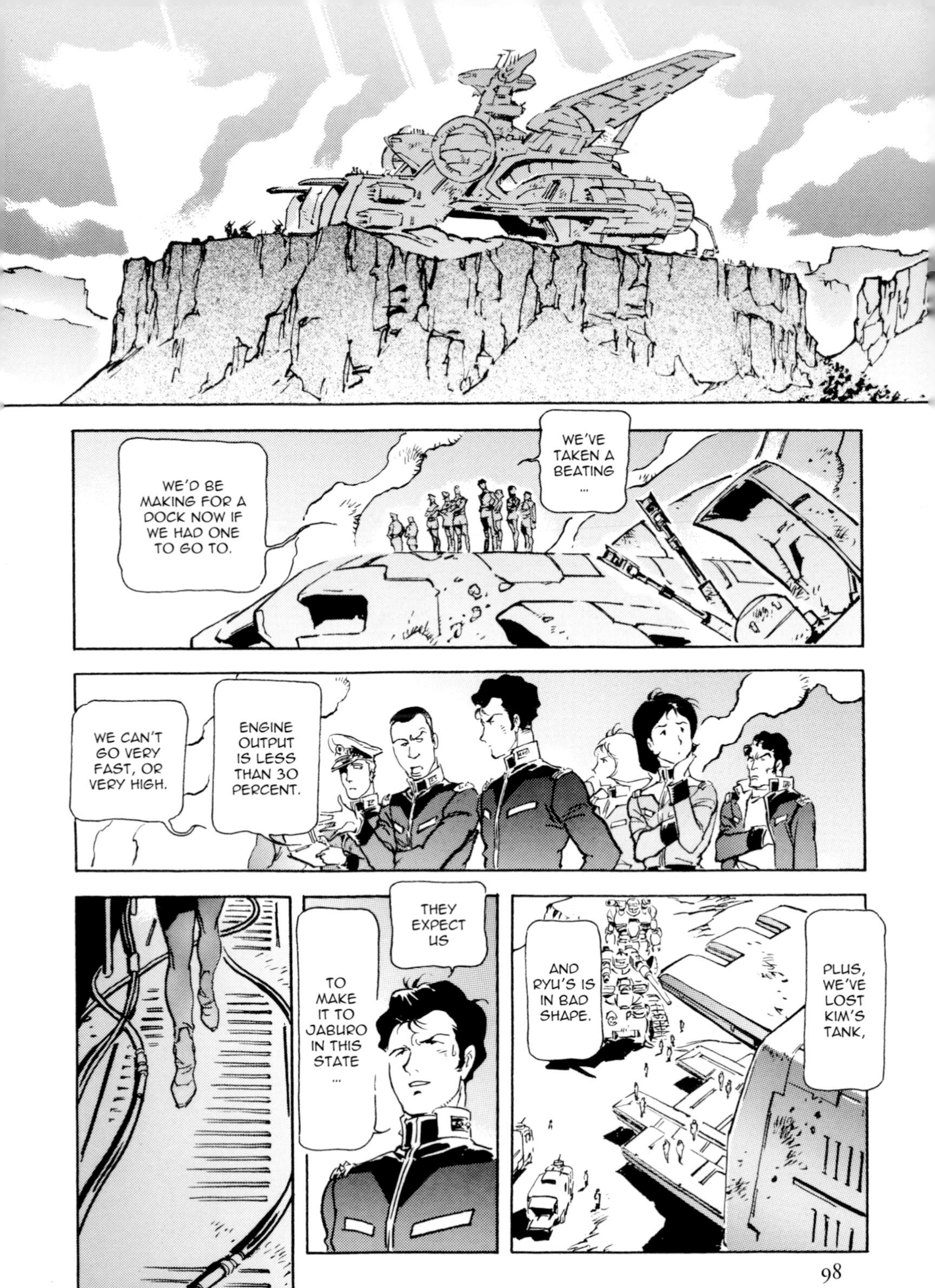
WE'VE TAKEN A BEATING ...
WE'D BE MAKING FOR A DOCK NOW IF WE HAD ONE TO GO TO.
ENGINE OUTPUT IS LESS THAN 30 PERCENT.
WE CAN'T GO VERY FAST, OR VERY HIGH.
PLUS, WE'VE LOST KIM'S TANK,
AND RYU'S IS IN BAD SHAPE.
THEY EXPECT US
TO MAKE IT TO JABURO IN THIS STATE ...

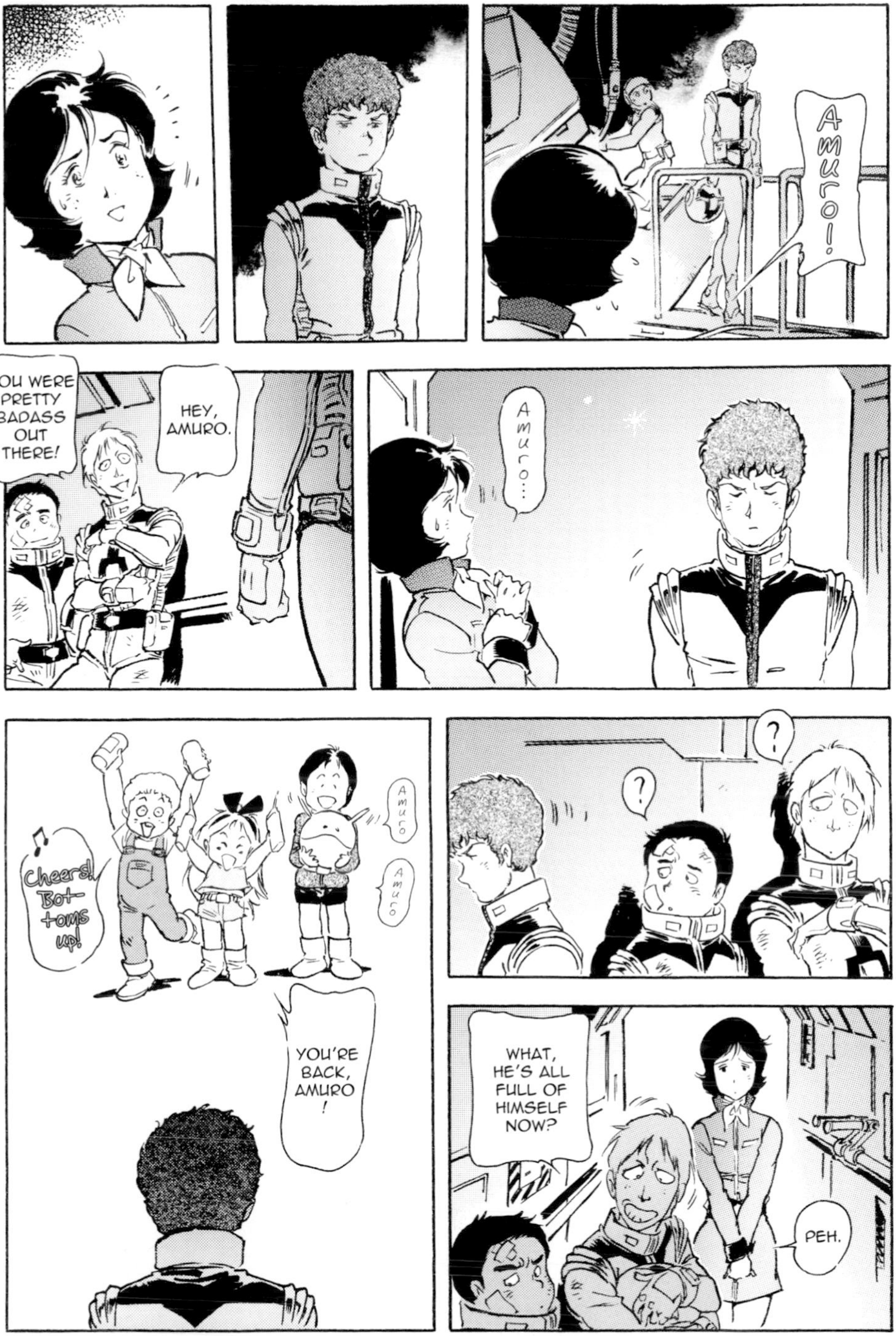
Amuro!
Amuro...
HEY, AMURO.
YOU WERE PRETTY BADASS OUT THERE!
?
?
WHAT, HE'S ALL FULL OF HIMSELF NOW?
PEH.
Amuro
Amuro
Cheers! Bot-toms up!
YOU'RE BACK, AMURO!

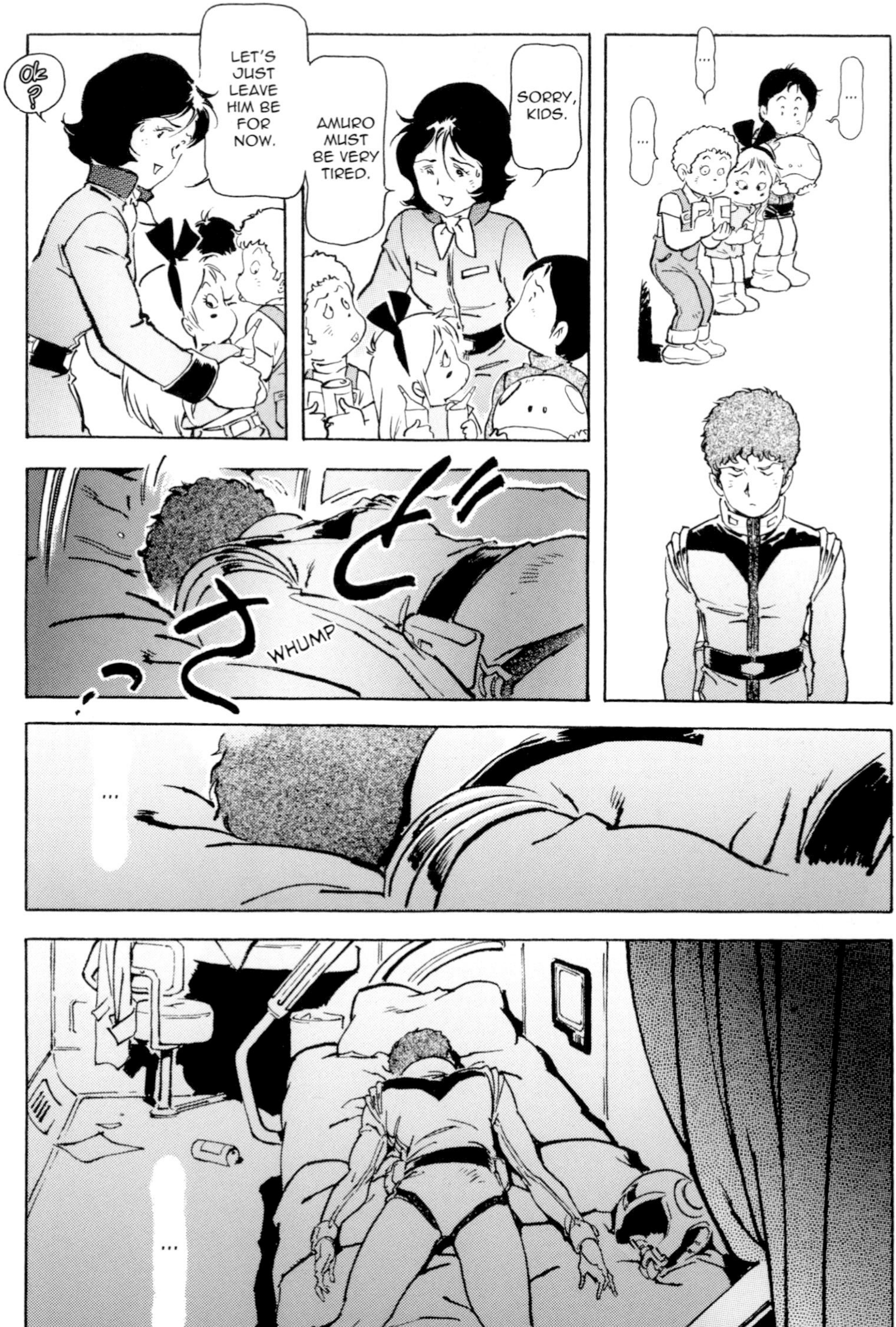
...
...
...
SORRY, KIDS.
AMURO MUST BE VERY TIRED.
LET'S JUST LEAVE HIM BE FOR NOW.
Ok?
WHUMP
...
...

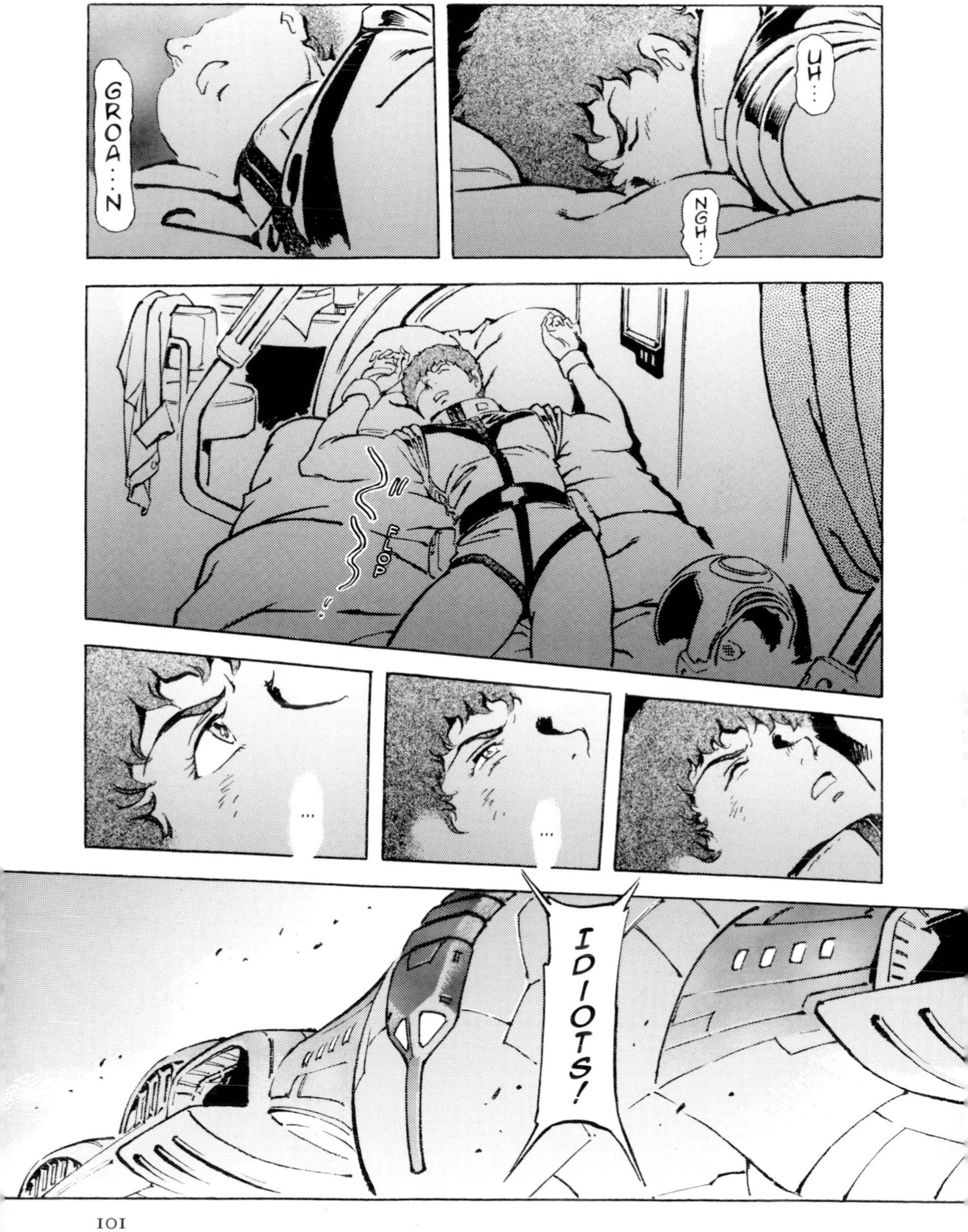
UH…
NGH…
GROA…N
FLOP
…
…
IDIOTS!

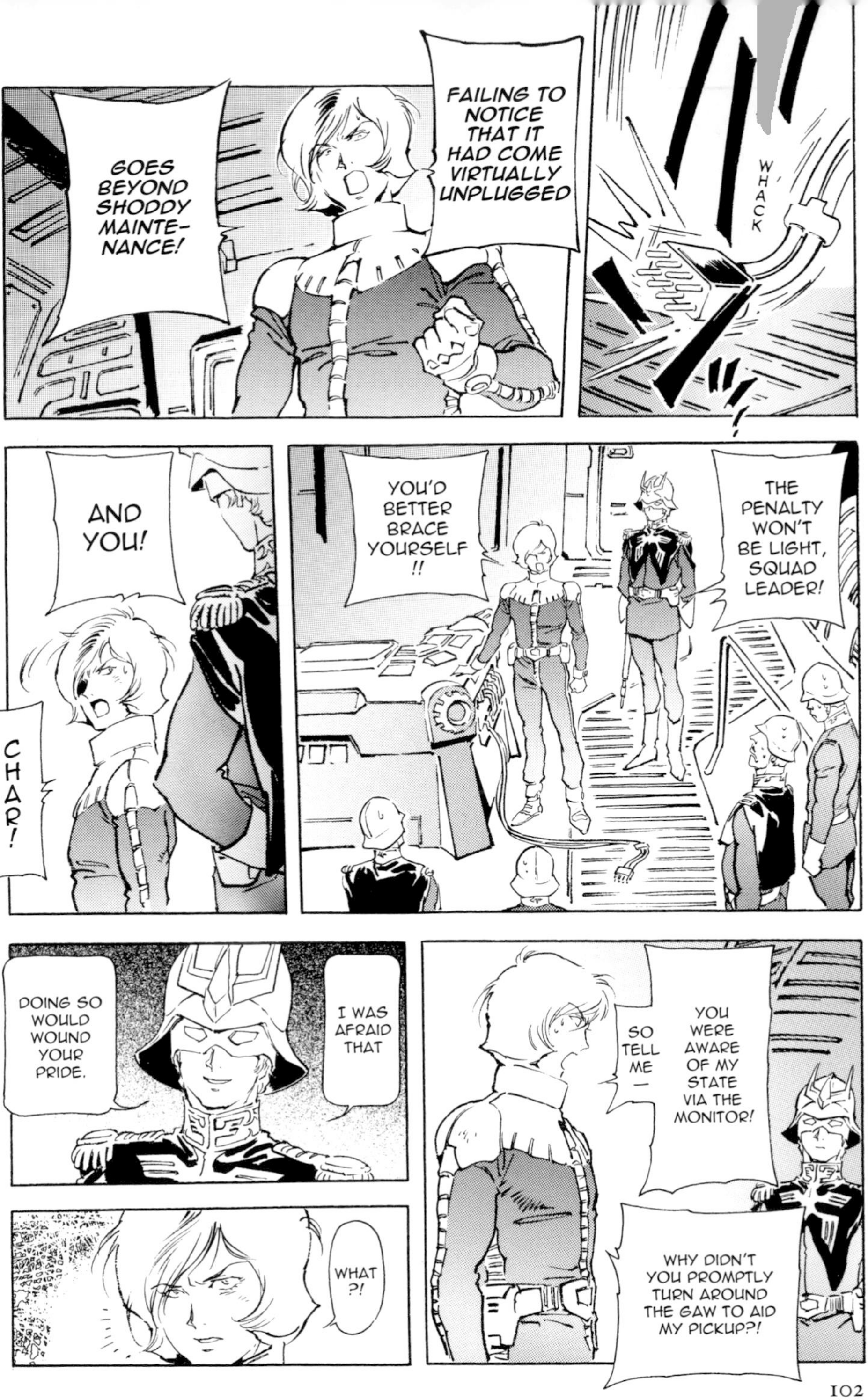
WHACK
FAILING TO NOTICE THAT IT HAD COME VIRTUALLY UNPLUGGED
GOES BEYOND SHODDY MAINTE-NANCE!
THE PENALTY WON'T BE LIGHT, SQUAD LEADER!
YOU'D BETTER BRACE YOURSELF !!
AND YOU!
CHAR!
YOU WERE AWARE OF MY STATE VIA THE MONITOR!
SO TELL ME —
WHY DIDN'T YOU PROMPTLY TURN AROUND THE GAW TO AID MY PICKUP?!
I WAS AFRAID THAT
DOING SO WOULD WOUND YOUR PRIDE.
WHAT ?!

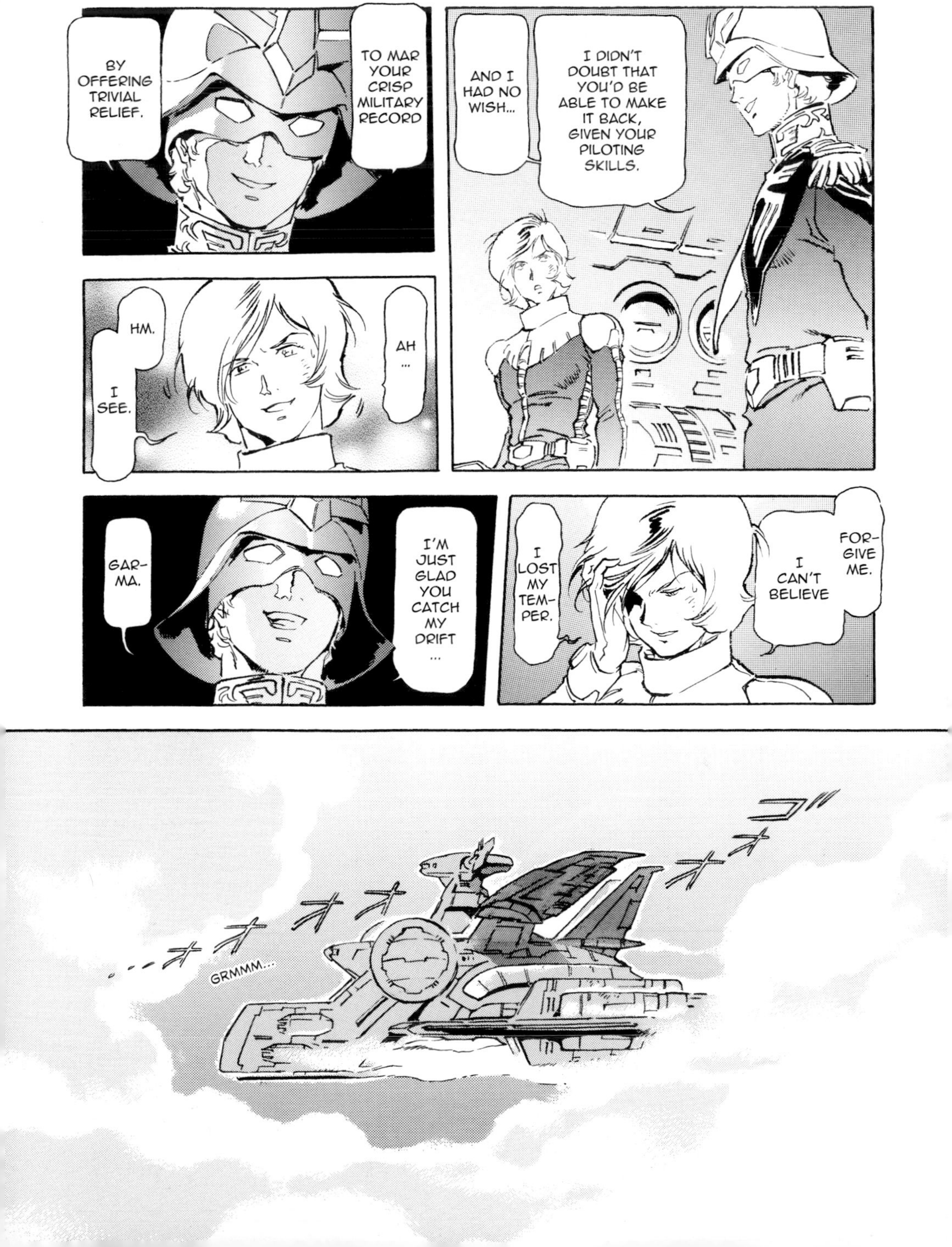
I DIDN'T DOUBT THAT YOU'D BE ABLE TO MAKE IT BACK, GIVEN YOUR PILOTING SKILLS.
AND I HAD NO WISH...
TO MAR YOUR CRISP MILITARY RECORD
BY OFFERING TRIVIAL RELIEF.
AH ...
HM.
I SEE.
FOR-GIVE ME.
I CAN'T BELIEVE
I LOST MY TEM-PER.
I'M JUST GLAD YOU CATCH MY DRIFT ...
GAR-MA.
GRMMM...

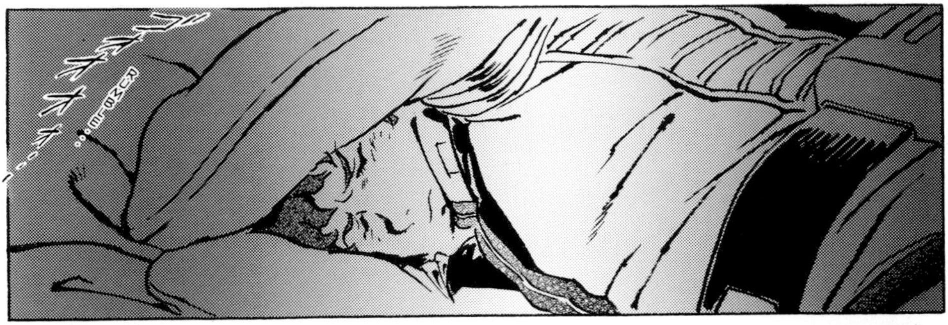

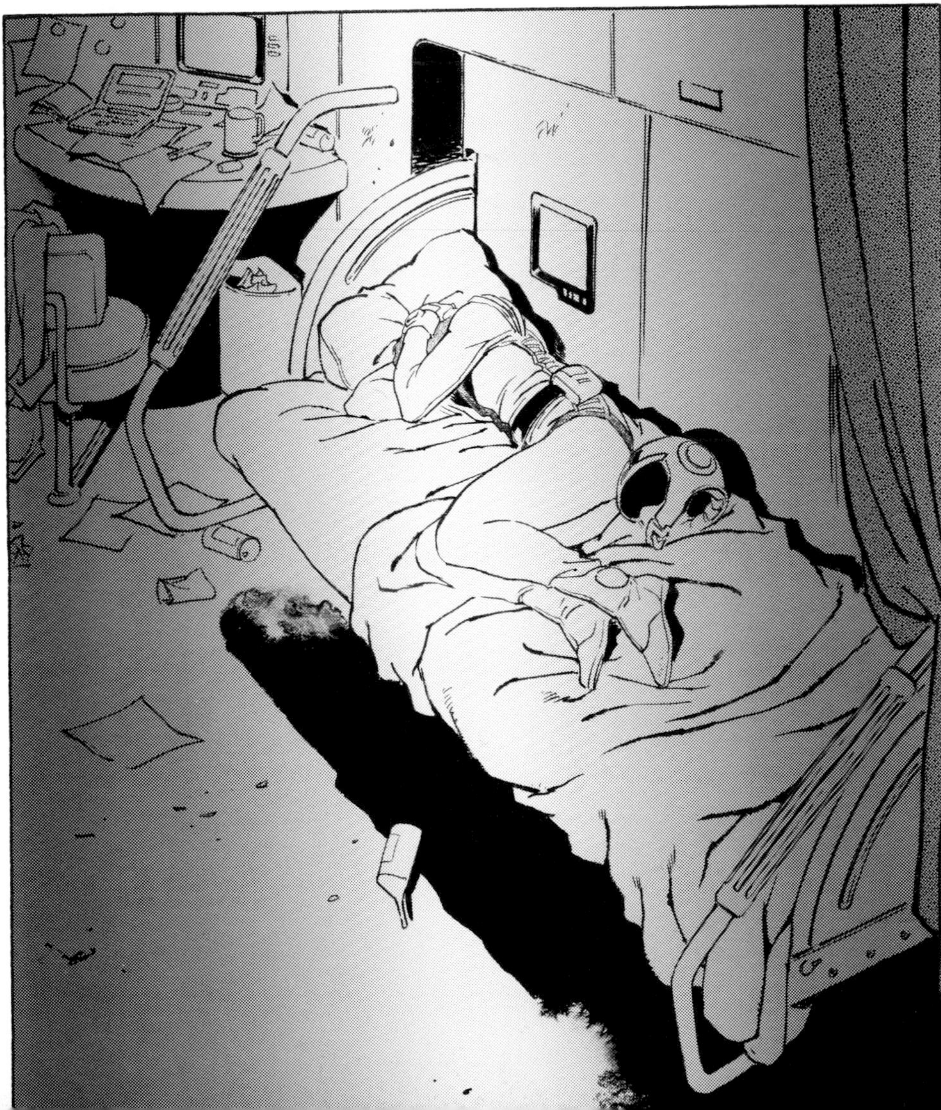

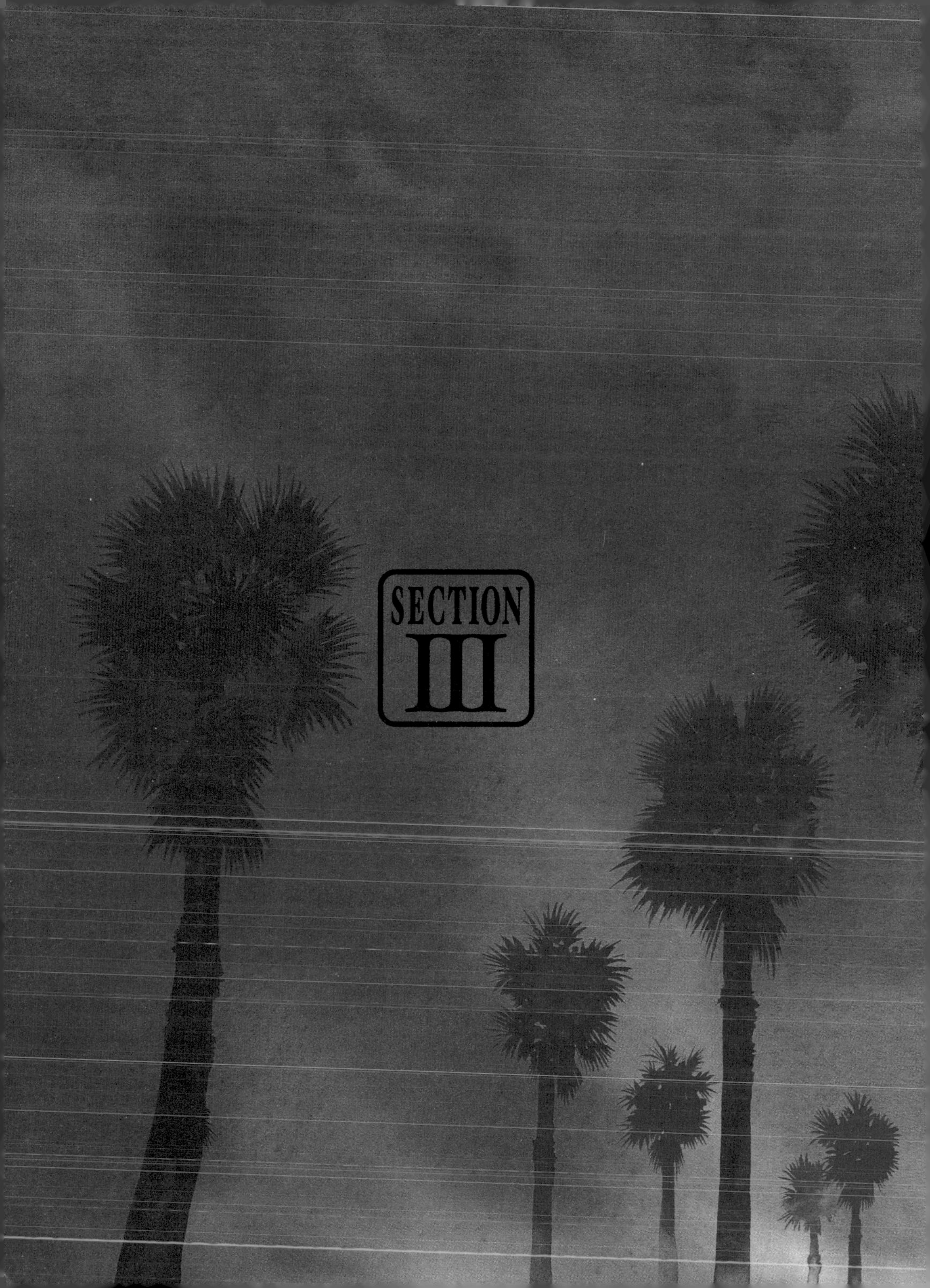

SECTION III

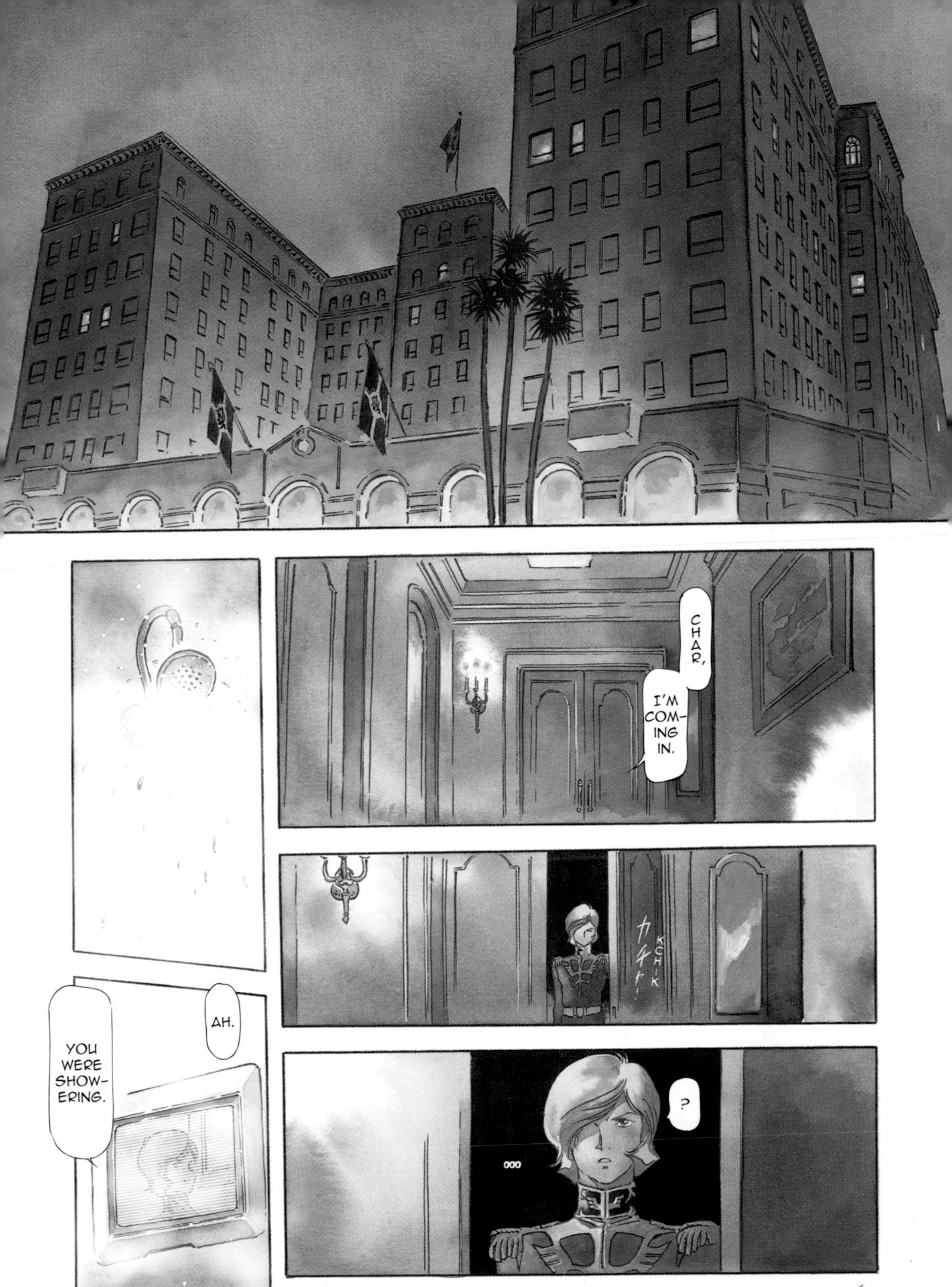
CHAR, I'M COMING IN.
カチャ!
KCHIK
?
...
AH.
YOU WERE SHOWER-ERING.

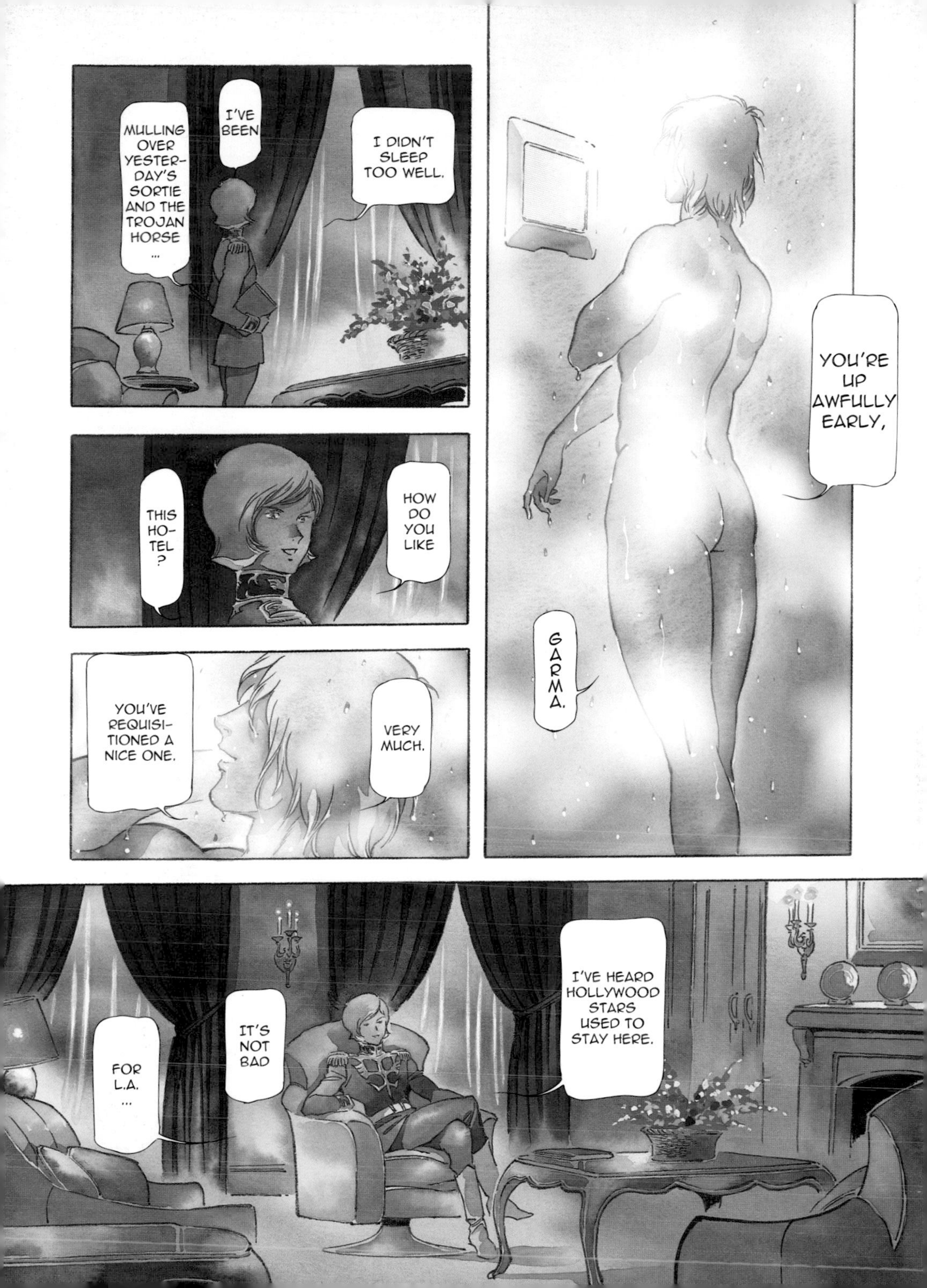
YOU'RE UP AWFULLY EARLY,
GARMA.
I DIDN'T SLEEP TOO WELL.
I'VE BEEN
MULLING OVER YESTER-DAY'S SORTIE AND THE TROJAN HORSE ...
HOW DO YOU LIKE
THIS HO-TEL?
VERY MUCH.
YOU'VE REQUISI-TIONED A NICE ONE.
I'VE HEARD HOLLYWOOD STARS USED TO STAY HERE.
IT'S NOT BAD
FOR L.A. ...

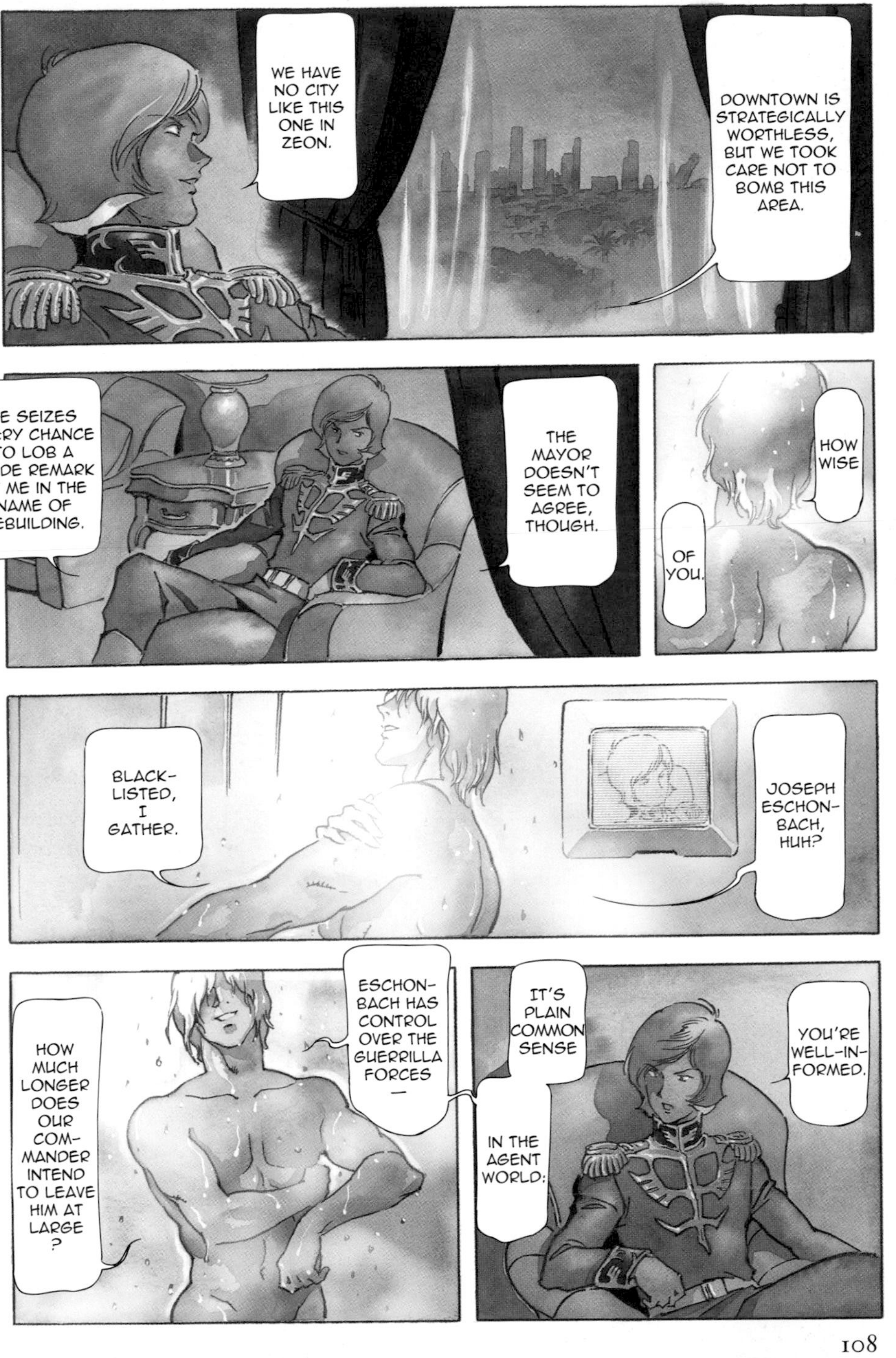
DOWNTOWN IS STRATEGICALLY WORTHLESS, BUT WE TOOK CARE NOT TO BOMB THIS AREA.
WE HAVE NO CITY LIKE THIS ONE IN ZEON.
HOW WISE
OF YOU.
THE MAYOR DOESN'T SEEM TO AGREE, THOUGH.
HE SEIZES EVERY CHANCE TO LOB A SNIDE REMARK AT ME IN THE NAME OF REBUILDING.
JOSEPH ESCHONBACH, HUH?
BLACKLISTED, I GATHER.
YOU'RE WELL-INFORMED.
IT'S PLAIN COMMON SENSE
IN THE AGENT WORLD.
ESCHONBACH HAS CONTROL OVER THE GUERRILLA FORCES —
HOW MUCH LONGER DOES OUR COMMANDER INTEND TO LEAVE HIM AT LARGE ?

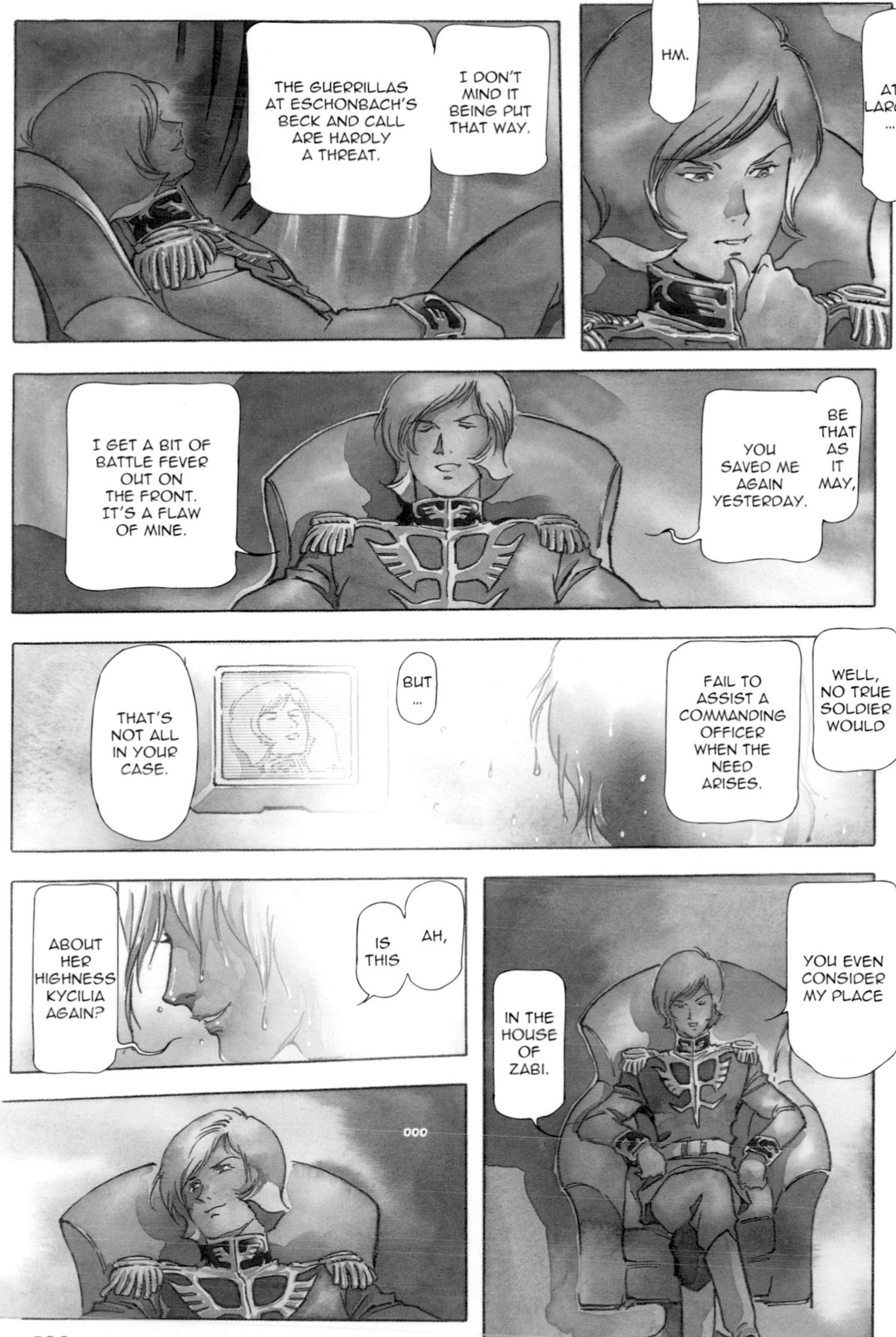
AT LARGE ...
HM.
I DON'T MIND IT BEING PUT THAT WAY.
THE GUERRILLAS AT ESCHONBACH'S BECK AND CALL ARE HARDLY A THREAT.
BE THAT AS IT MAY,
YOU SAVED ME AGAIN YESTERDAY.
I GET A BIT OF BATTLE FEVER OUT ON THE FRONT. IT'S A FLAW OF MINE.
WELL, NO TRUE SOLDIER WOULD
FAIL TO ASSIST A COMMANDING OFFICER WHEN THE NEED ARISES.
BUT ...
THAT'S NOT ALL IN YOUR CASE.
YOU EVEN CONSIDER MY PLACE
IN THE HOUSE OF ZABI.
AH,
IS THIS
ABOUT HER HIGHNESS KYCILIA AGAIN?
ooo

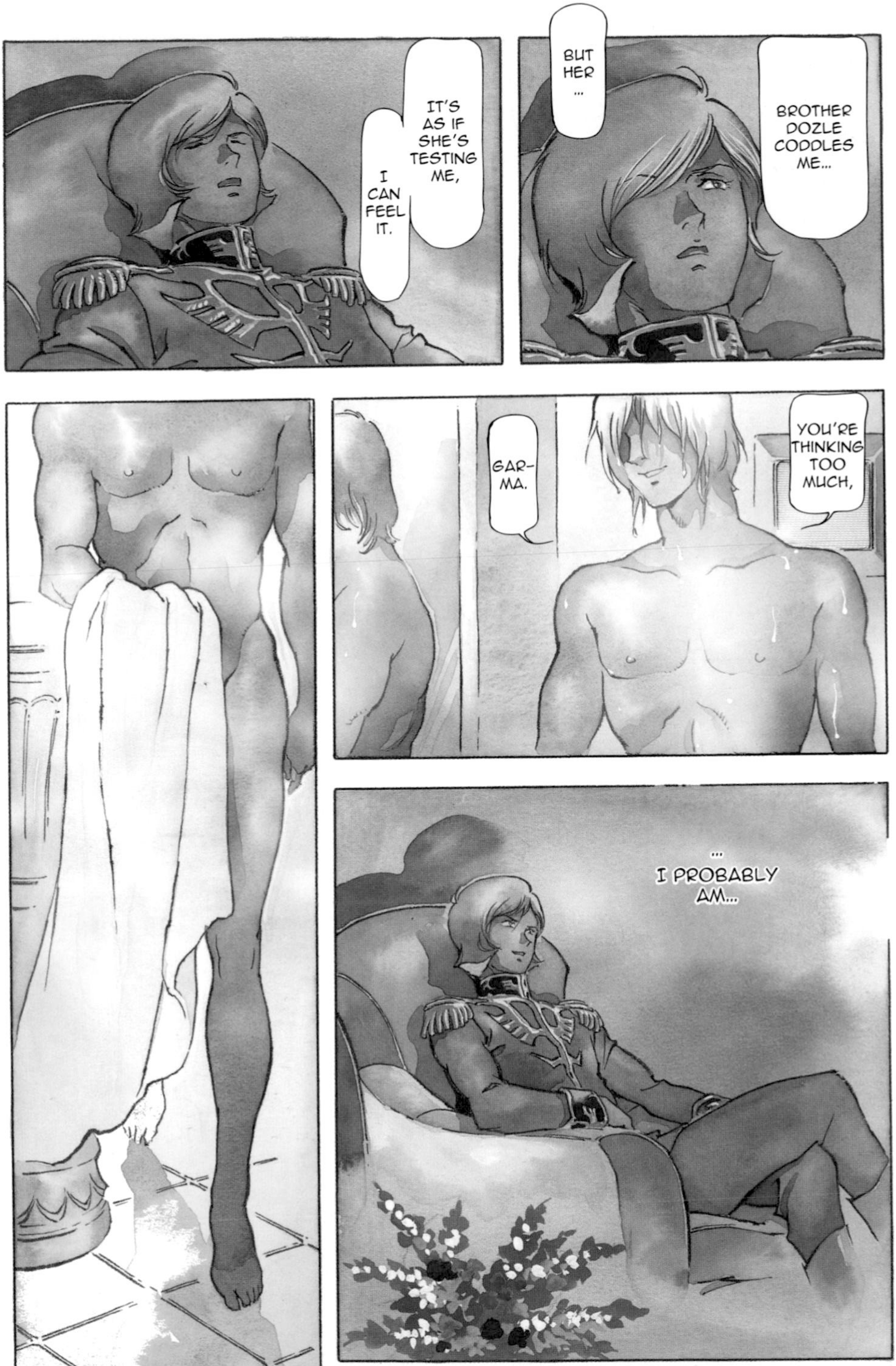
BROTHER DOZLE CODDLES ME...
BUT HER ...
IT'S AS IF SHE'S TESTING ME,
I CAN FEEL IT.
YOU'RE THINKING TOO MUCH,
GAR-MA.
... I PROBABLY AM...

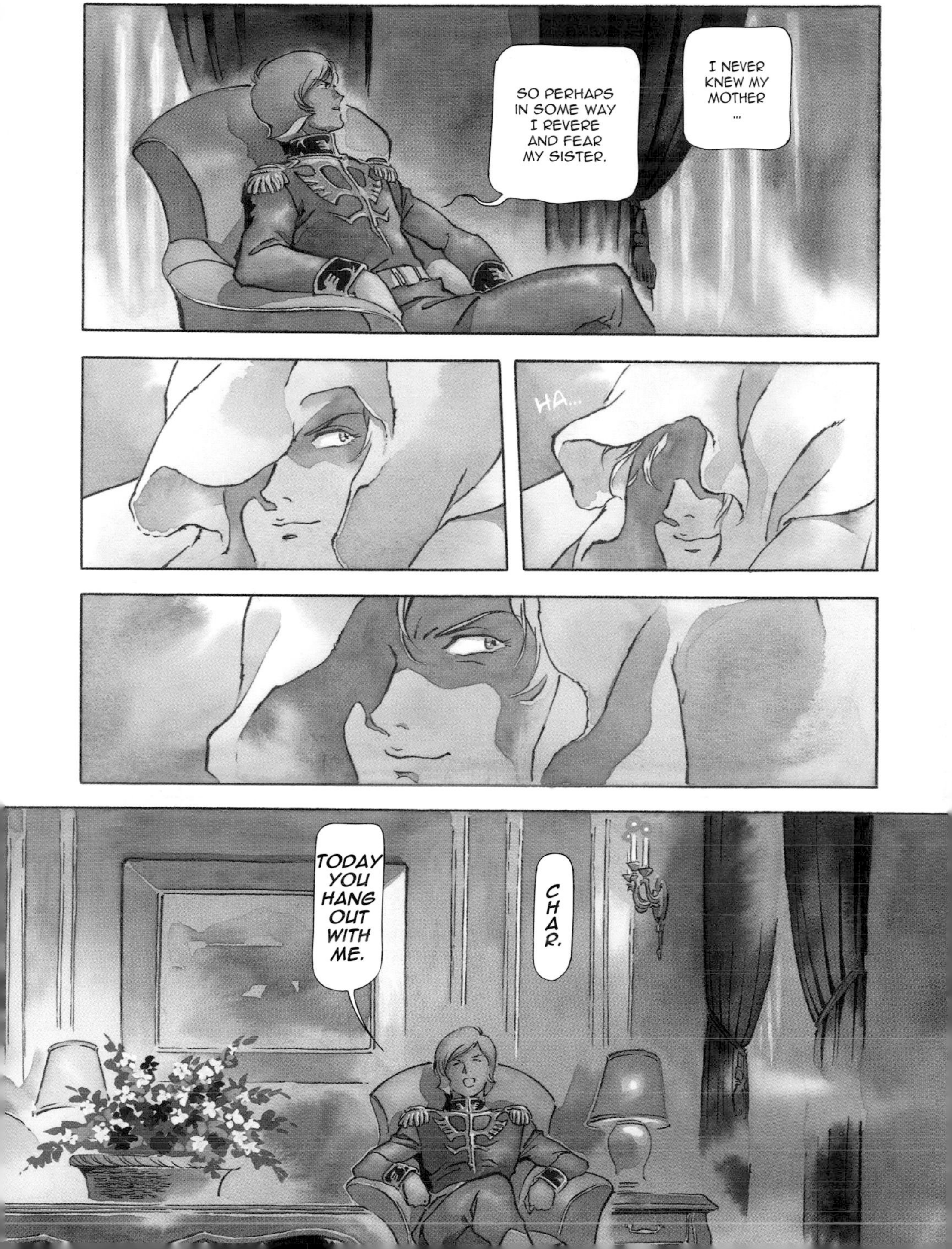

I NEVER KNEW MY MOTHER ...
SO PERHAPS IN SOME WAY I REVERE AND FEAR MY SISTER.
HA...
CHAR.
TODAY YOU HANG OUT WITH ME.

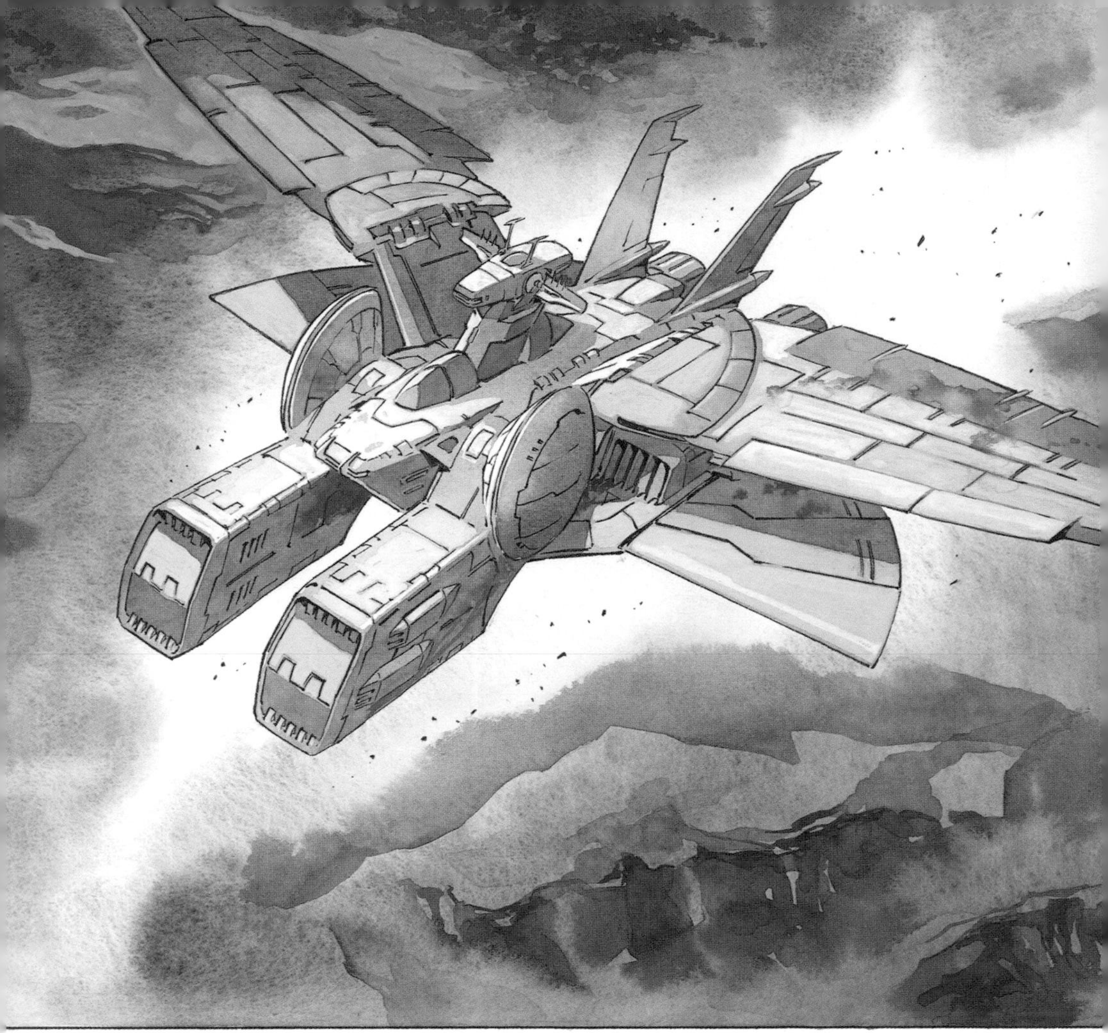

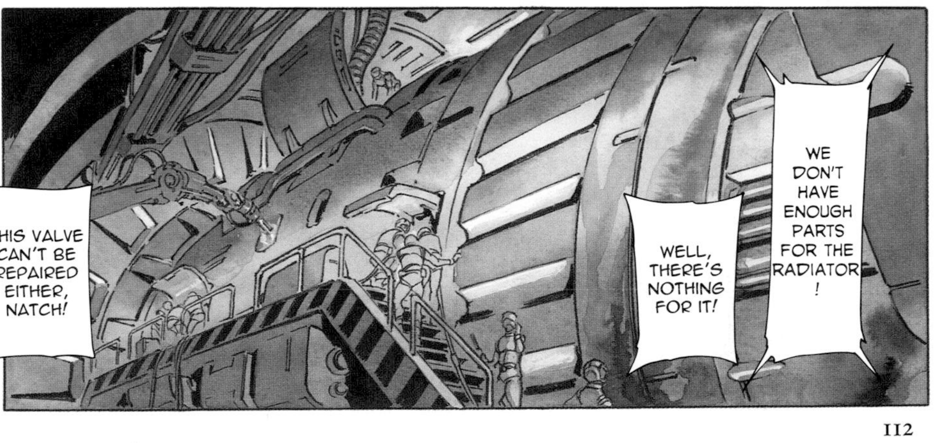
WE DON'T HAVE ENOUGH PARTS FOR THE RADIATOR!
WELL, THERE'S NOTHING FOR IT!
THIS VALVE CAN'T BE REPAIRED EITHER, NATCH!

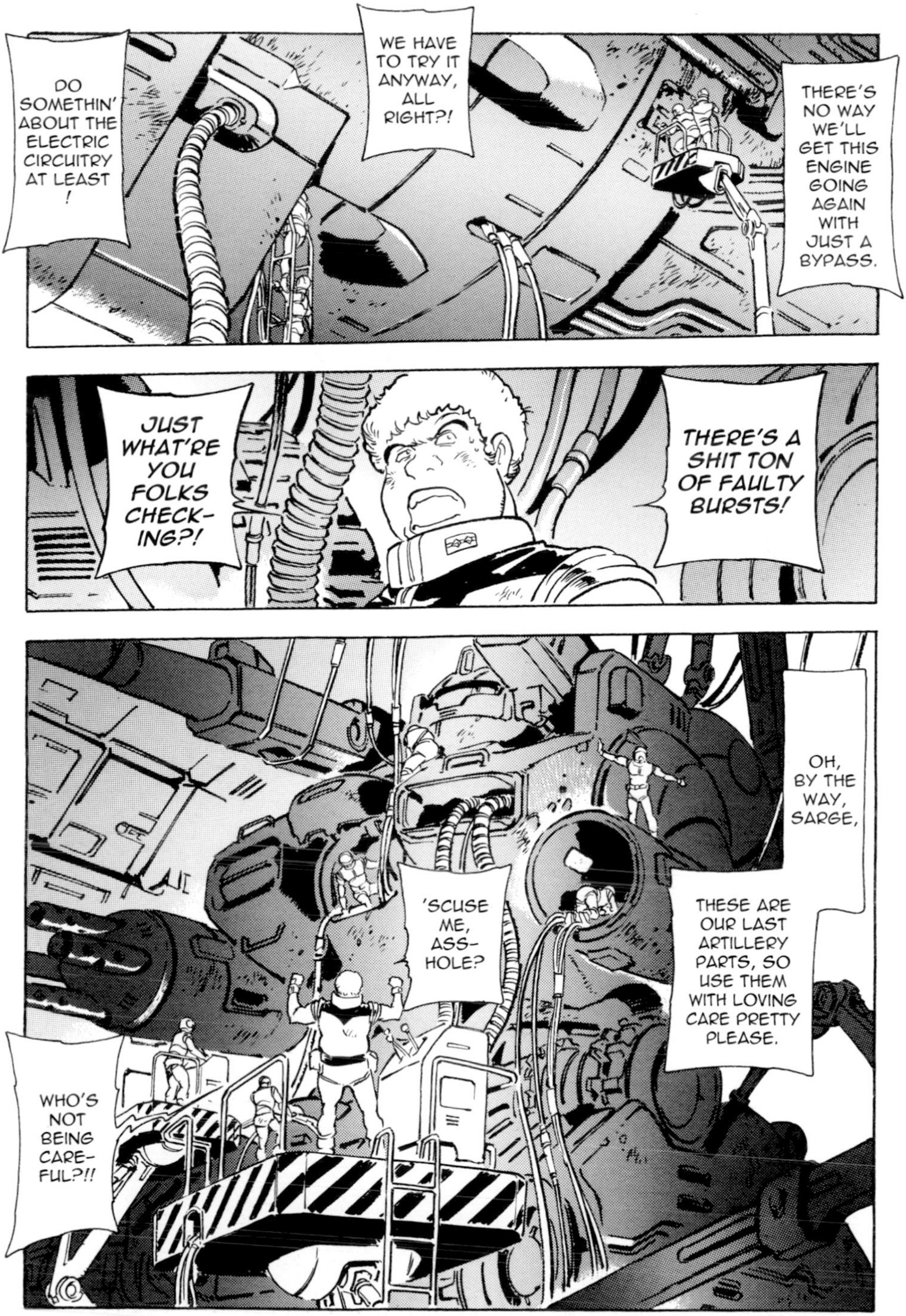
THERE'S NO WAY WE'LL GET THIS ENGINE GOING AGAIN WITH JUST A BYPASS.
WE HAVE TO TRY IT ANYWAY, ALL RIGHT?!
DO SOMETHIN' ABOUT THE ELECTRIC CIRCUITRY AT LEAST!
THERE'S A SHIT TON OF FAULTY BURSTS!
JUST WHAT'RE YOU FOLKS CHECKING?!
OH, BY THE WAY, SARGE,
THESE ARE OUR LAST ARTILLERY PARTS, SO USE THEM WITH LOVING CARE PRETTY PLEASE.
'SCUSE ME, ASSHOLE?
WHO'S NOT BEING CAREFUL?!!

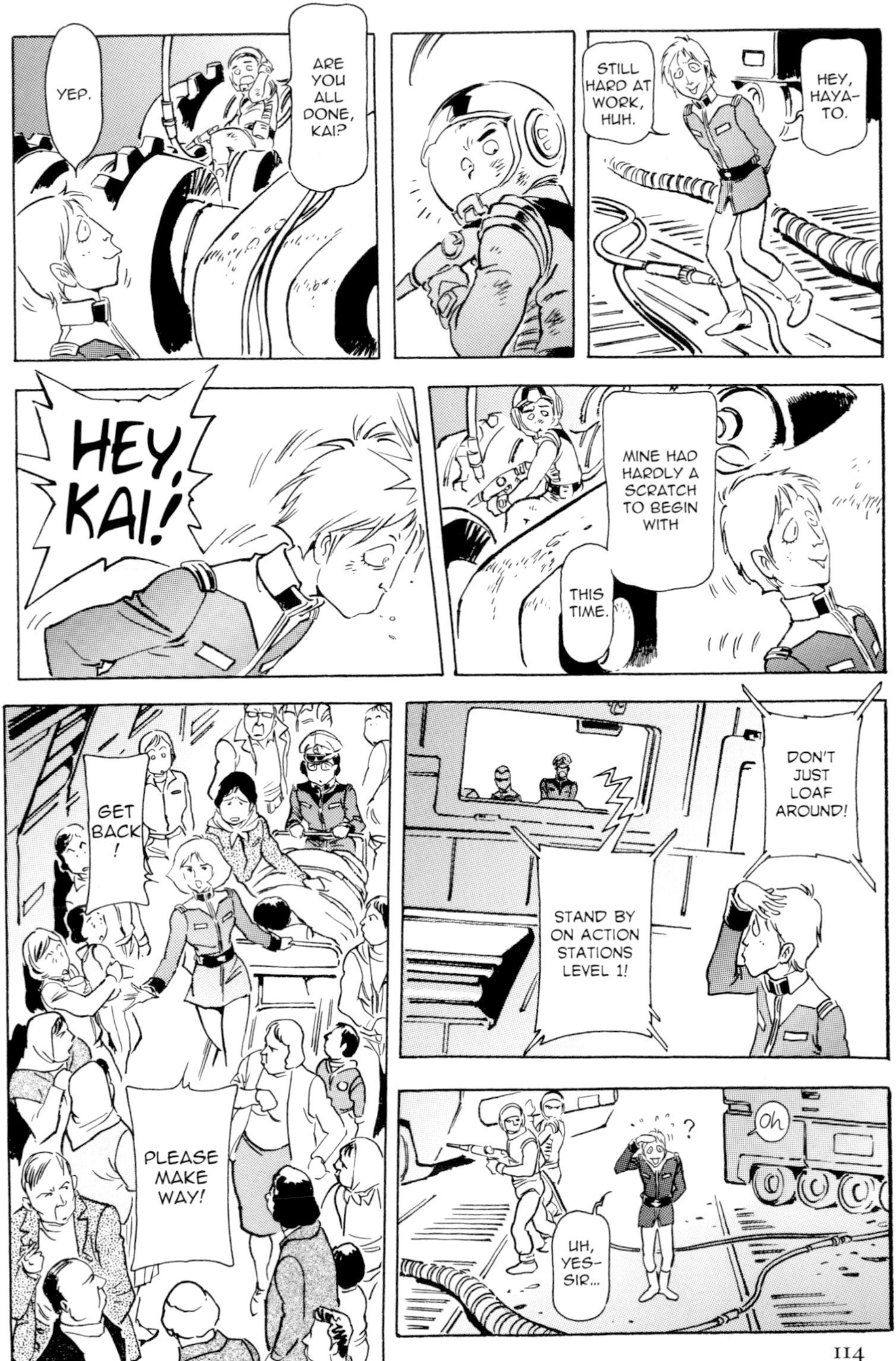
HEY, HAYA-TO.
STILL HARD AT WORK, HUH.
ARE YOU ALL DONE, KAI?
YEP.
MINE HAD HARDLY A SCRATCH TO BEGIN WITH
THIS TIME.
HEY, KAI!
DON'T JUST LOAF AROUND!
STAND BY ON ACTION STATIONS LEVEL 1!
oh
UH, YES-SIR...
GET BACK!
PLEASE MAKE WAY!

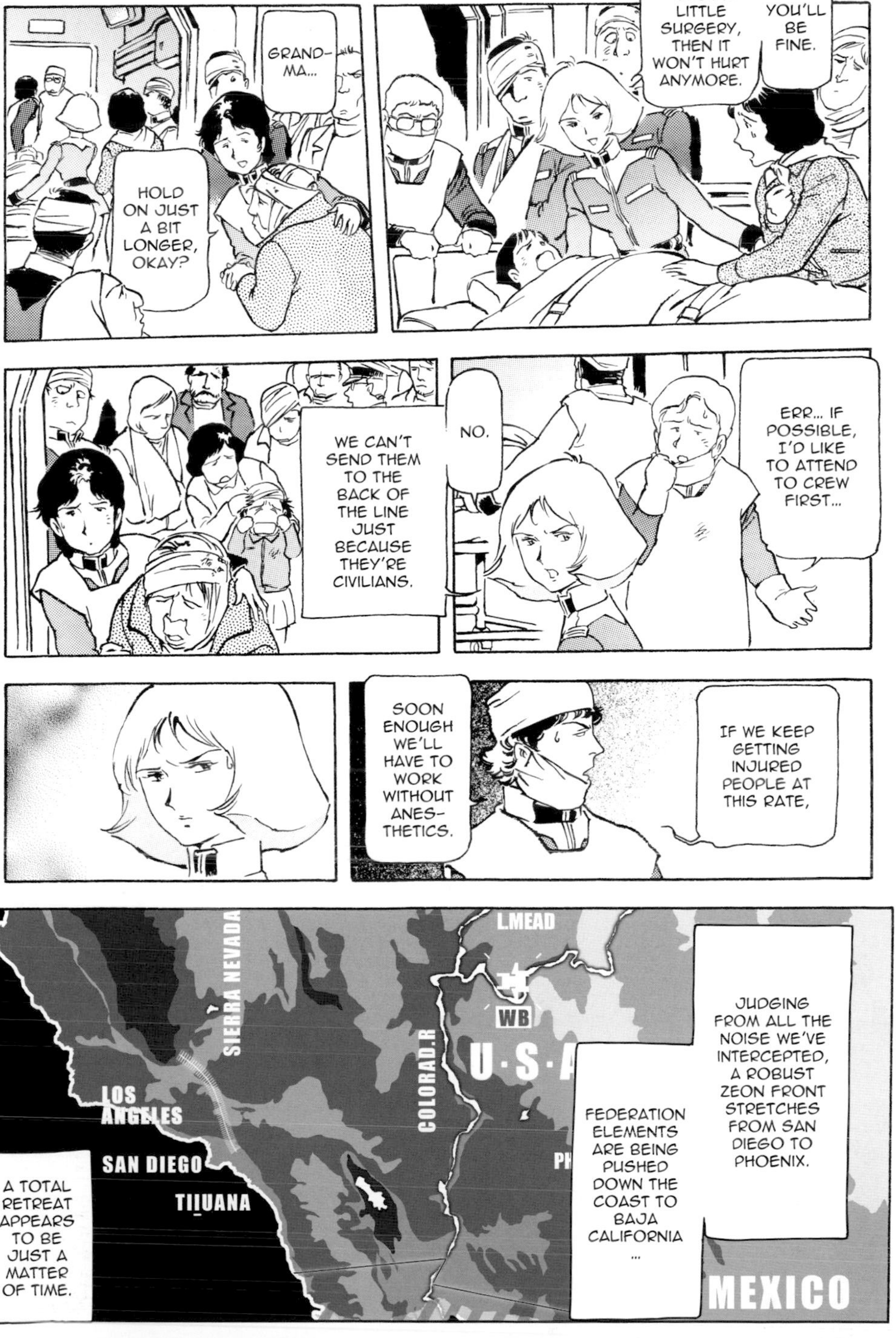
YOU'LL BE FINE.
JUST A LITTLE SURGERY, THEN IT WON'T HURT ANYMORE.
GRAND-MA...
HOLD ON JUST A BIT LONGER, OKAY?
ERR... IF POSSIBLE, I'D LIKE TO ATTEND TO CREW FIRST...
NO.
WE CAN'T SEND THEM TO THE BACK OF THE LINE JUST BECAUSE THEY'RE CIVILIANS.
IF WE KEEP GETTING INJURED PEOPLE AT THIS RATE,
SOON ENOUGH WE'LL HAVE TO WORK WITHOUT ANES-THETICS.
L.MEAD
WB
U·S·A
SIERRA NEVADA
COLORAD.R
LOS ANGELES
SAN DIEGO
TIJUANA
MEXICO
JUDGING FROM ALL THE NOISE WE'VE INTERCEPTED, A ROBUST ZEON FRONT STRETCHES FROM SAN DIEGO TO PHOENIX.
FEDERATION ELEMENTS ARE BEING PUSHED DOWN THE COAST TO BAJA CALIFORNIA ...
A TOTAL RETREAT APPEARS TO BE JUST A MATTER OF TIME.

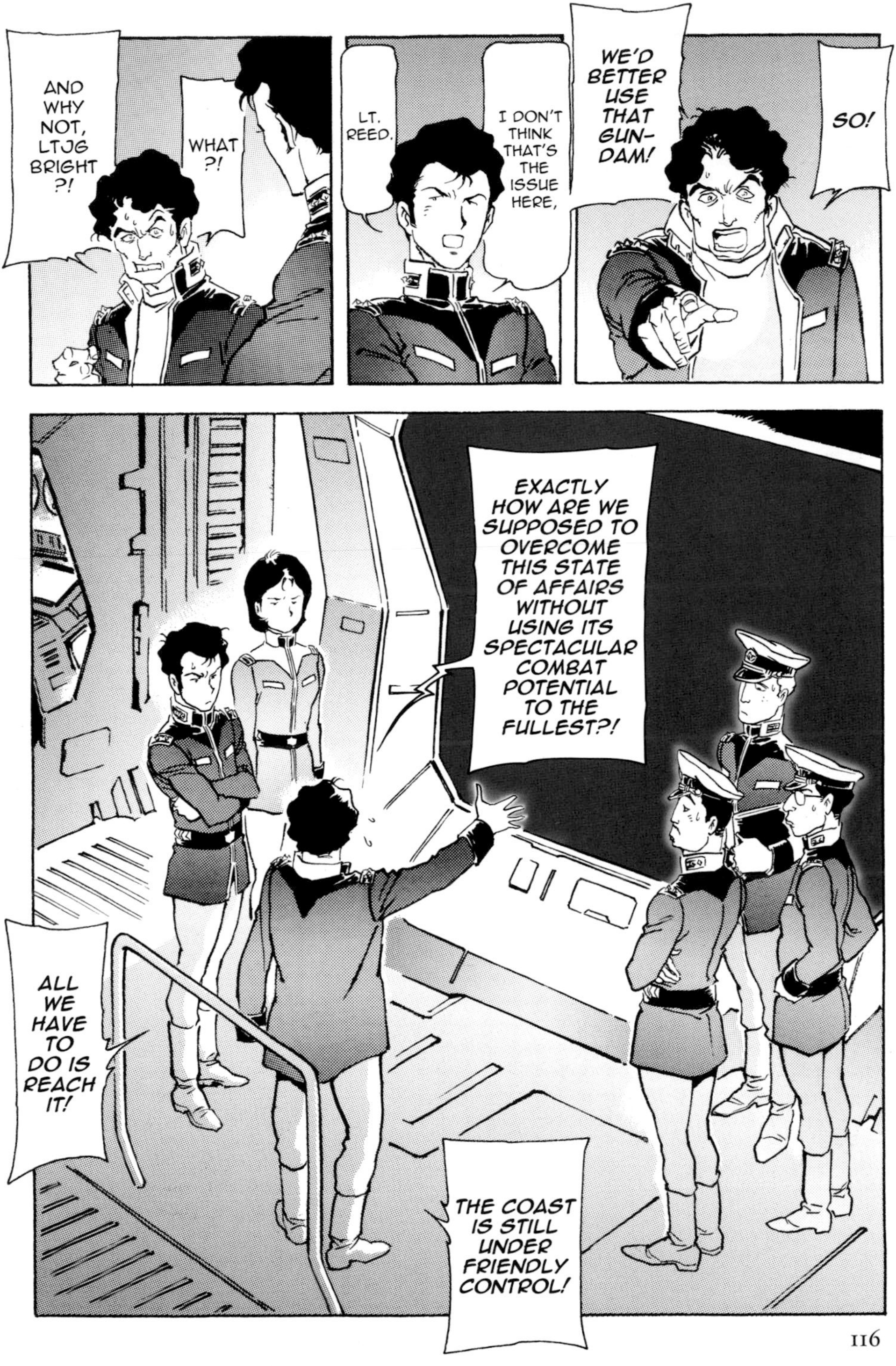
SO!
WE'D BETTER USE THAT GUN-DAM!
I DON'T THINK THAT'S THE ISSUE HERE,
LT. REED.
WHAT?!
AND WHY NOT, LTJG BRIGHT?!
EXACTLY HOW ARE WE SUPPOSED TO OVERCOME THIS STATE OF AFFAIRS WITHOUT USING ITS SPECTACULAR COMBAT POTENTIAL TO THE FULLEST?!
THE COAST IS STILL UNDER FRIENDLY CONTROL!
ALL WE HAVE TO DO IS REACH IT!

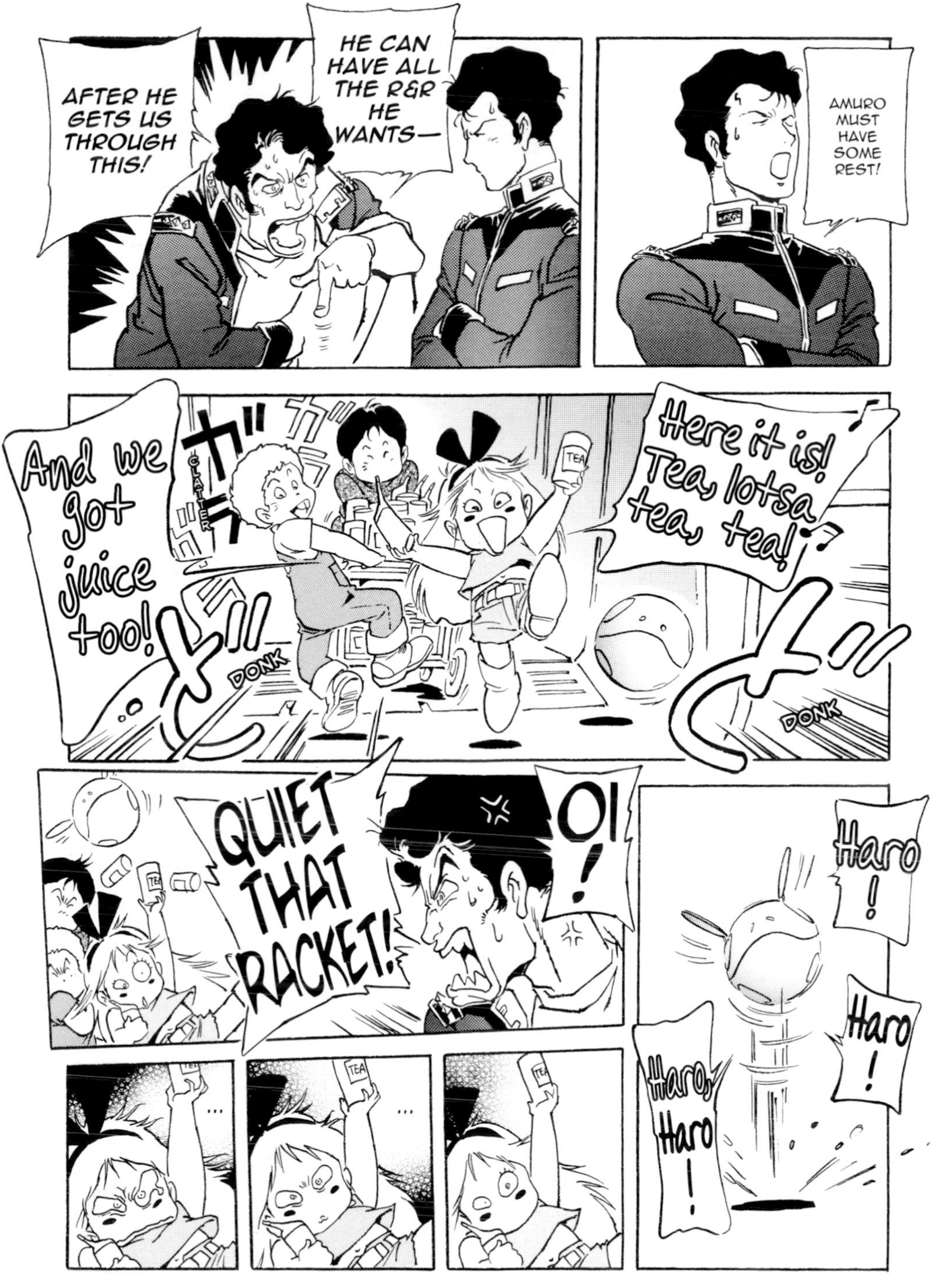
AMURO MUST HAVE SOME REST!
HE CAN HAVE ALL THE R&R HE WANTS—
AFTER HE GETS US THROUGH THIS!
Here it is! Tea, lotsa tea, tea!
CLATTER
And we got juice too!
DONK
DONK
Haro!
Haro!
Haro, Haro!
O!
!
QUIET THAT RACKET!
...
...

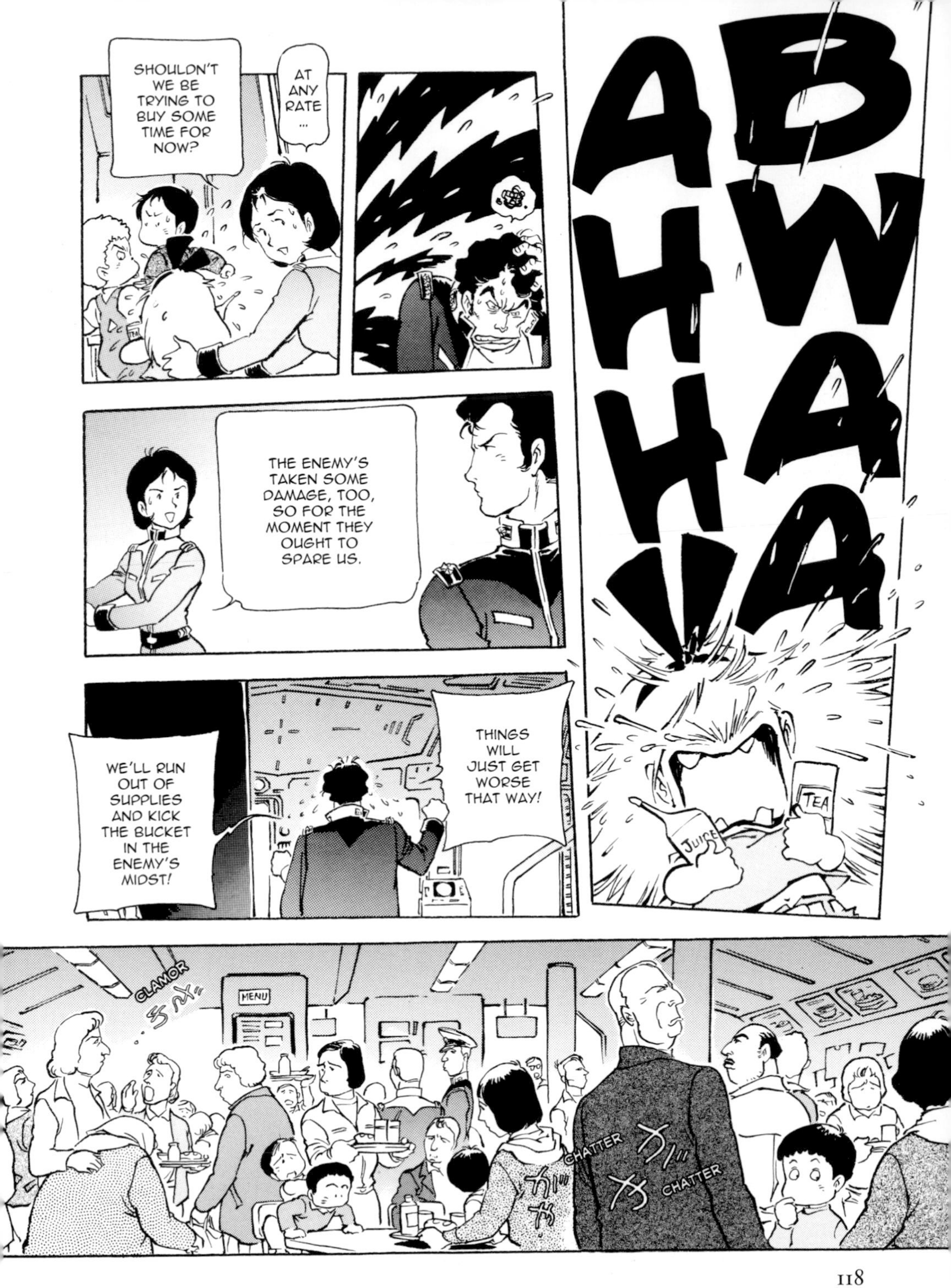

BWAHAHAHAA
JUICE
TEA
AT ANY RATE ...
SHOULDN'T WE BE TRYING TO BUY SOME TIME FOR NOW?
THE ENEMY'S TAKEN SOME DAMAGE, TOO, SO FOR THE MOMENT THEY OUGHT TO SPARE US.
THINGS WILL JUST GET WORSE THAT WAY!
WE'LL RUN OUT OF SUPPLIES AND KICK THE BUCKET IN THE ENEMY'S MIDST!
MENU
CLAMOR
CHATTER
CHATTER

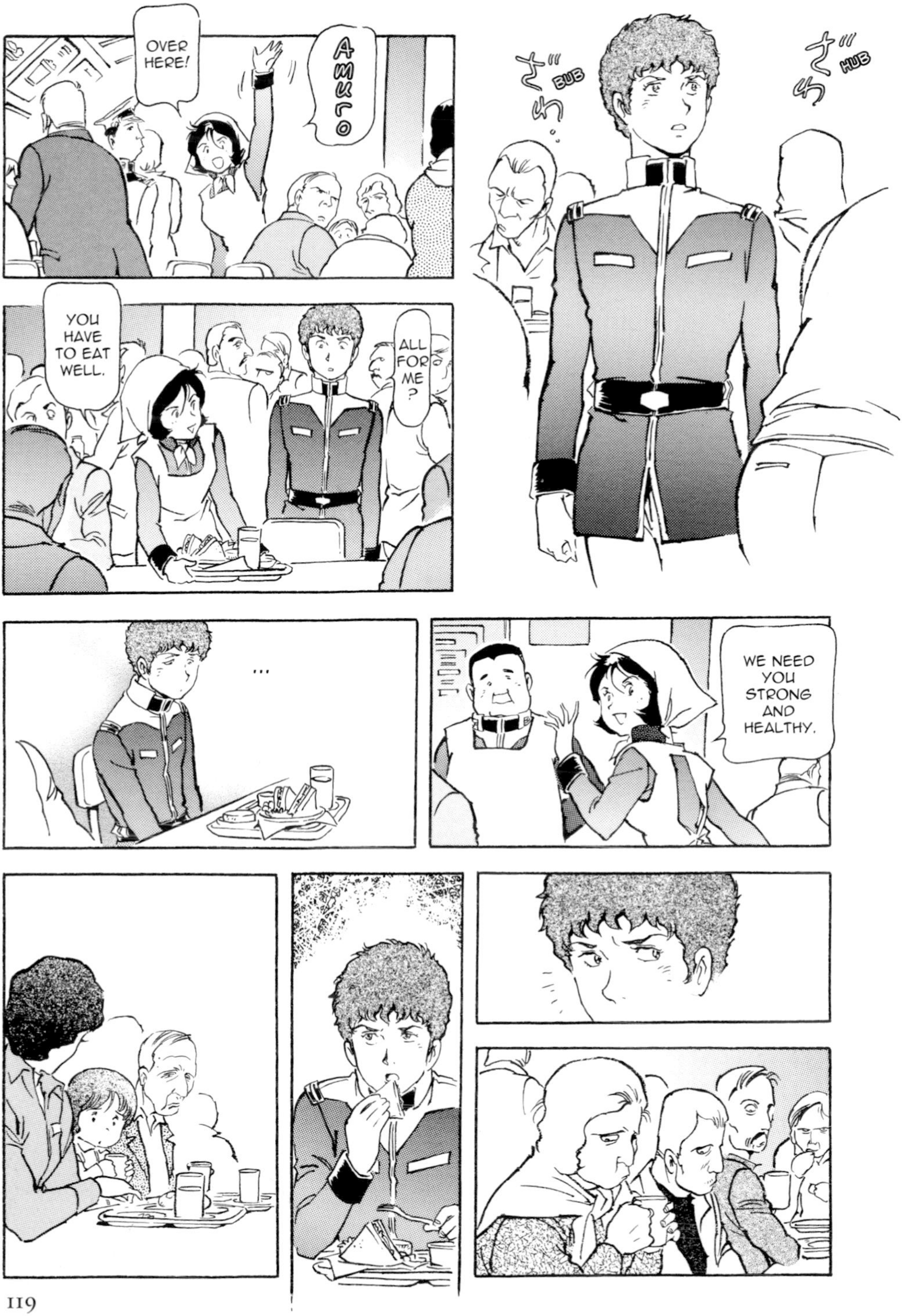
ざわ HUB
ざわ BUB
Amuro
OVER HERE!
ALL FOR ME?
YOU HAVE TO EAT WELL.
WE NEED YOU STRONG AND HEALTHY.
...

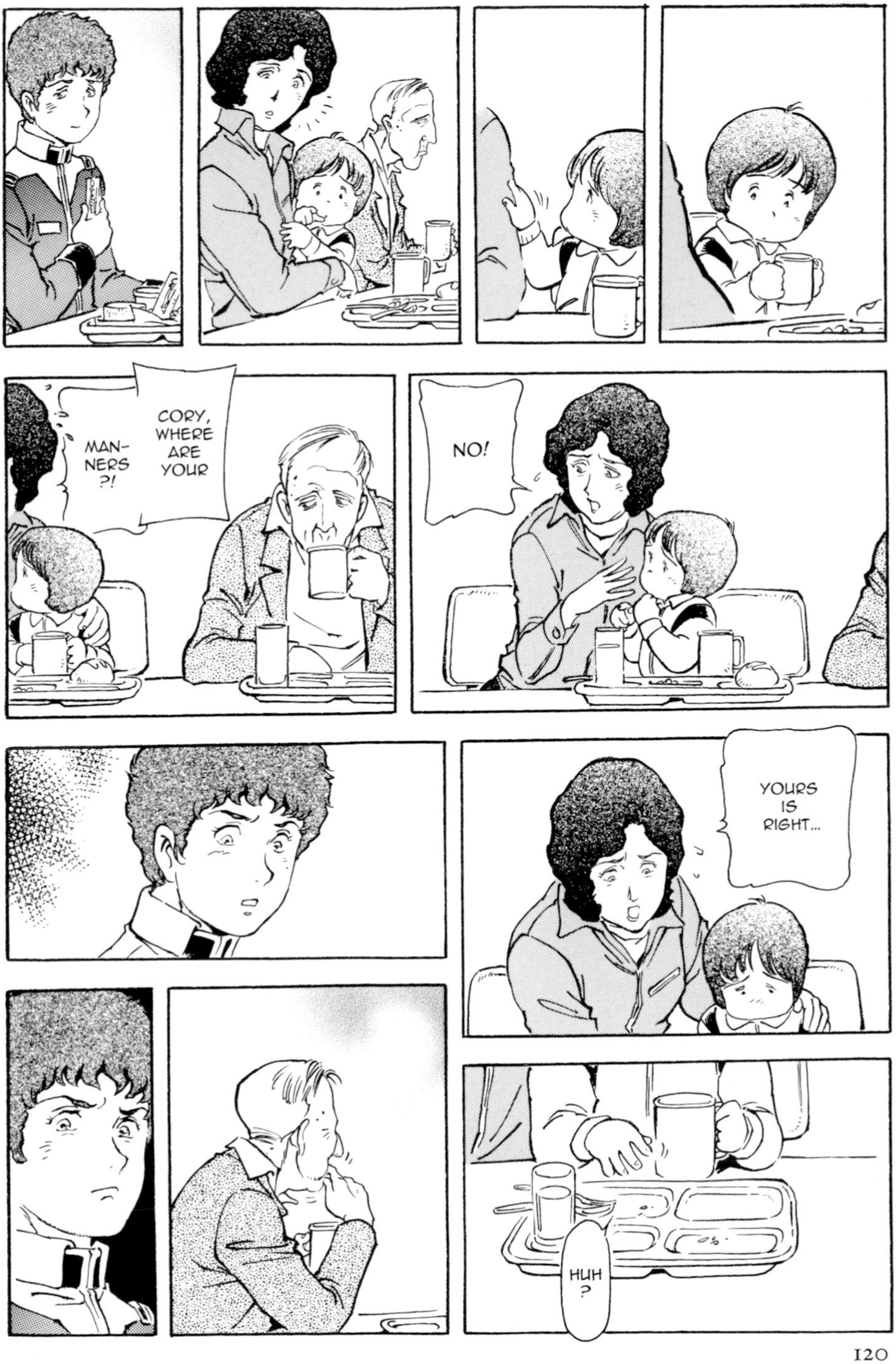
NO!
CORY, WHERE ARE YOUR MANNERS?!
YOURS IS RIGHT...
HUH?

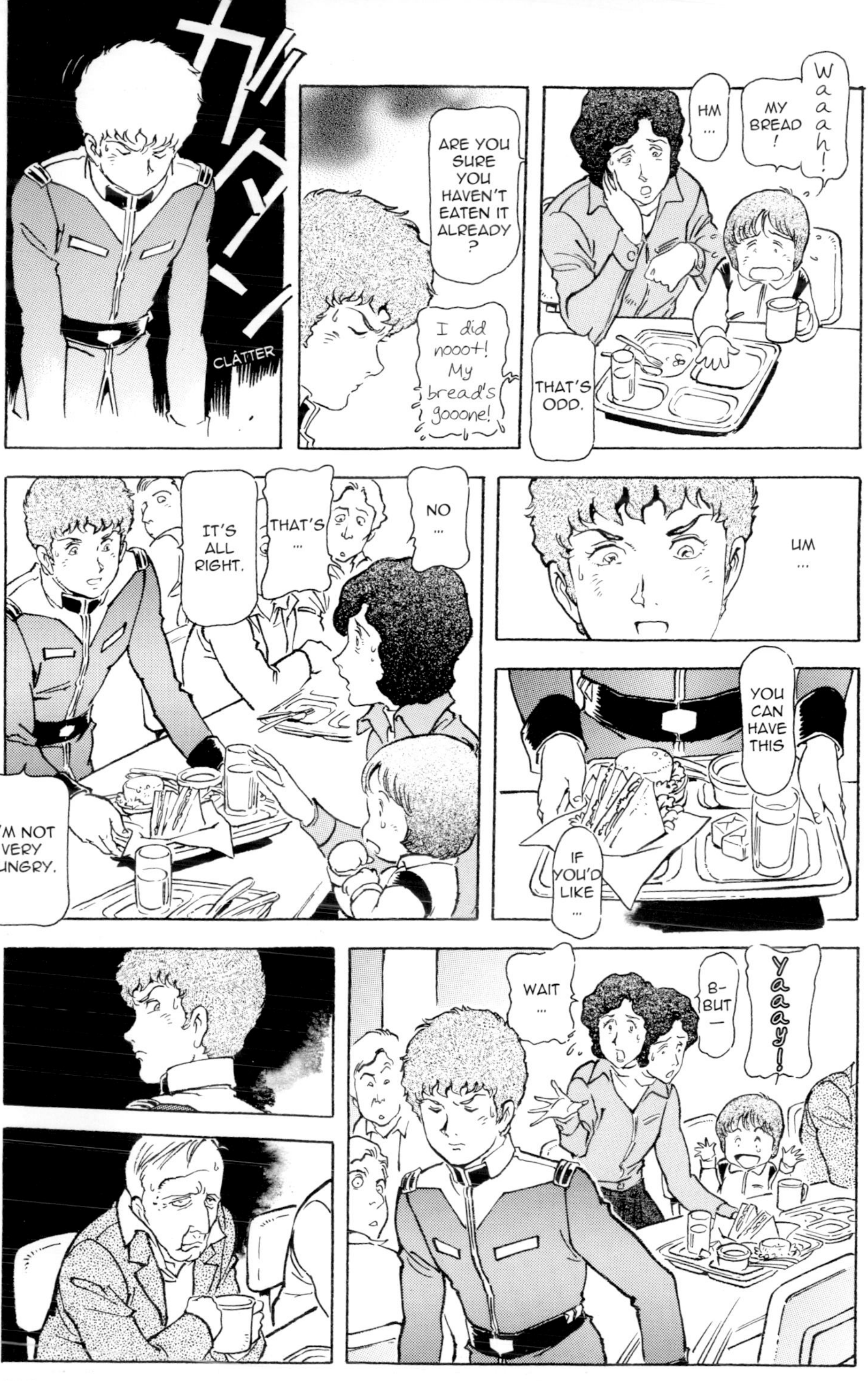

Waaah!
MY BREAD!
HM...
THAT'S ODD.
ARE YOU SURE YOU HAVEN'T EATEN IT ALREADY?
I did nooot! My bread's gooone!
CLATTER
UM...
YOU CAN HAVE THIS
IF YOU'D LIKE...
NO...
THAT'S...
IT'S ALL RIGHT.
I'M NOT VERY HUNGRY.
Yaaaay!
B-BUT—
WAIT...

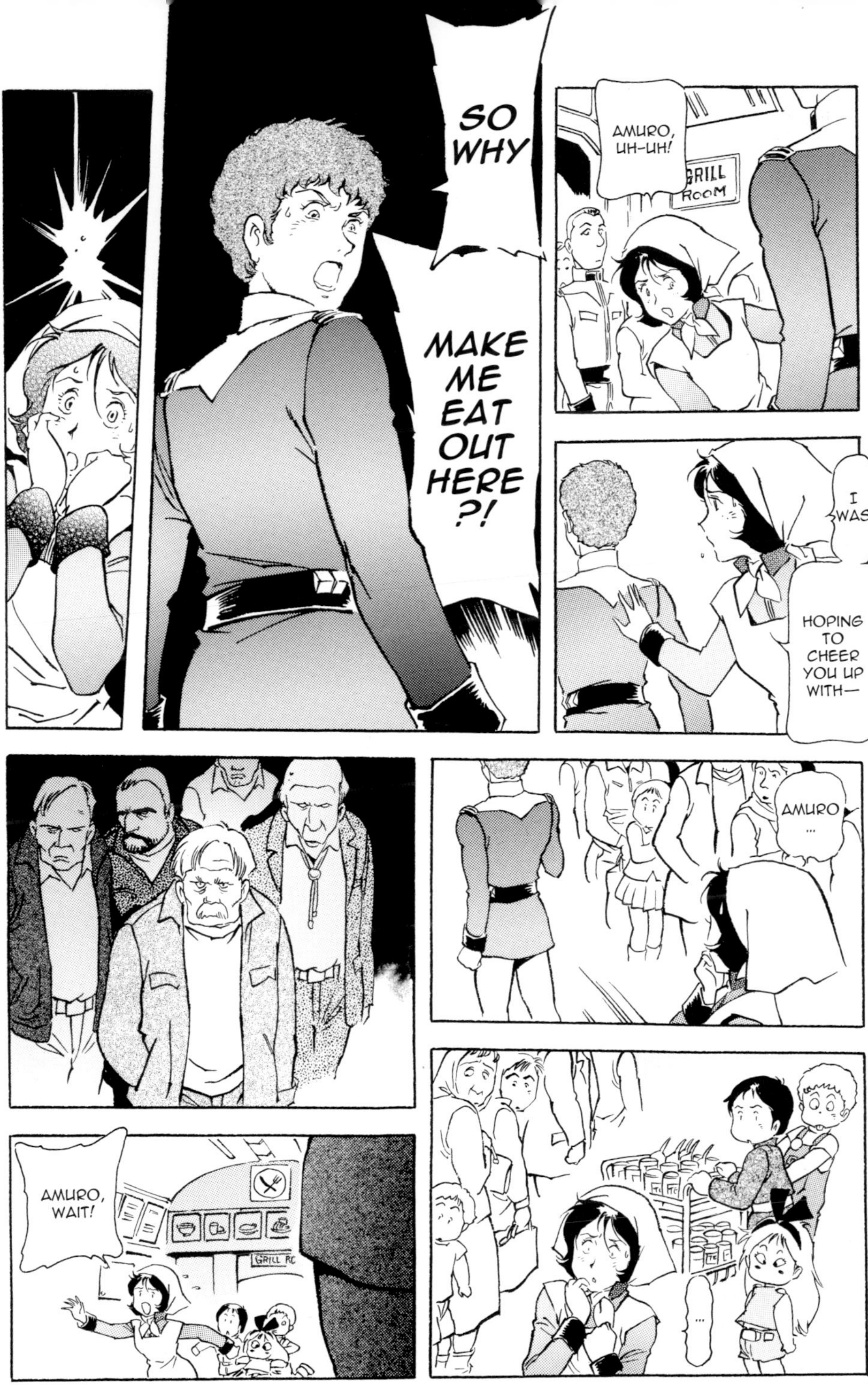
AMURO, UH-UH!
GRILL ROOM
I WAS
HOPING TO CHEER YOU UP WITH—
SO WHY
MAKE ME EAT OUT HERE?!
AMURO ...
...
AMURO, WAIT!
GRILL RO

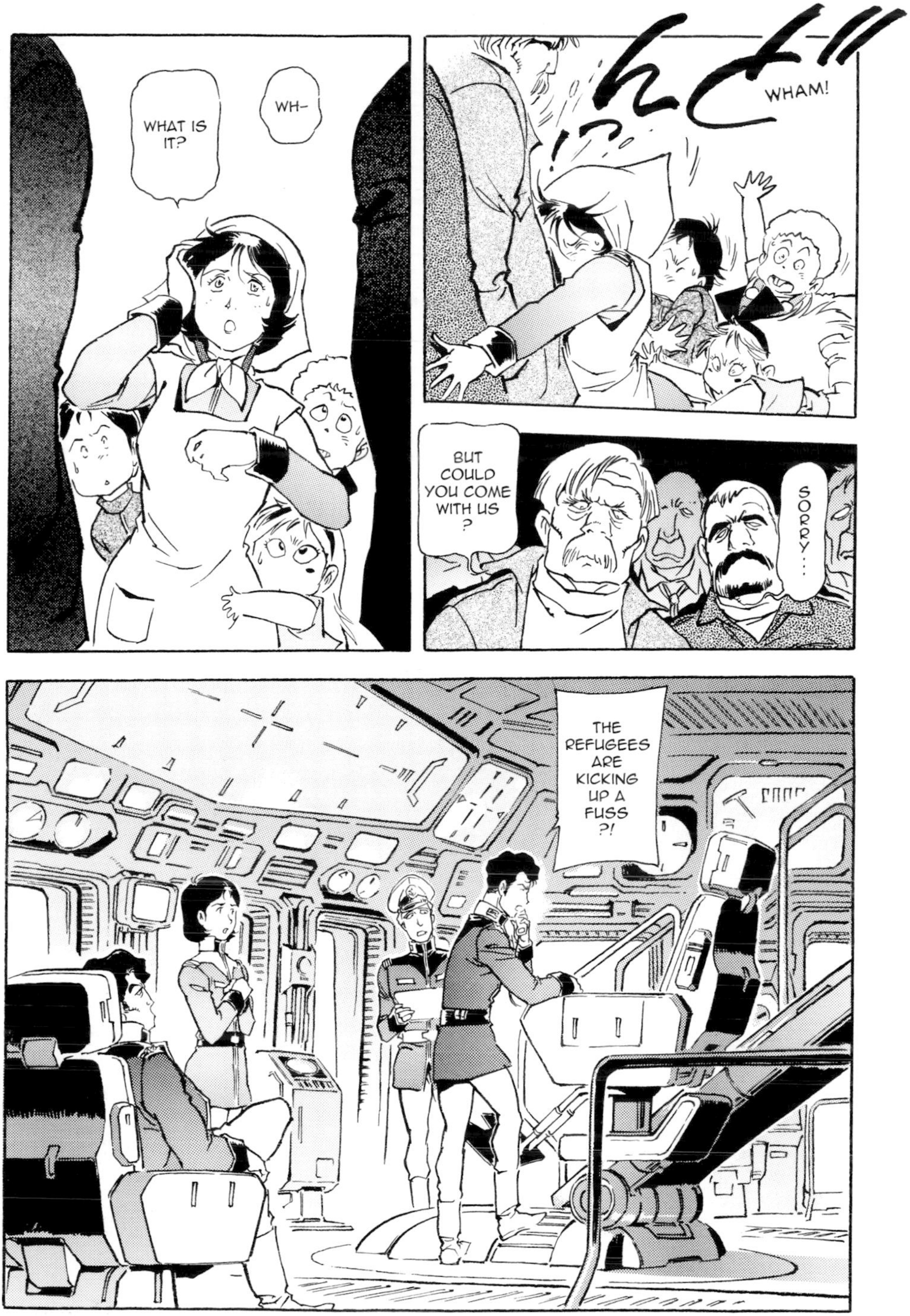
WHAM!
SORRY...
BUT COULD YOU COME WITH US?
WH-
WHAT IS IT?
THE REFUGEES ARE KICKING UP A FUSS?!

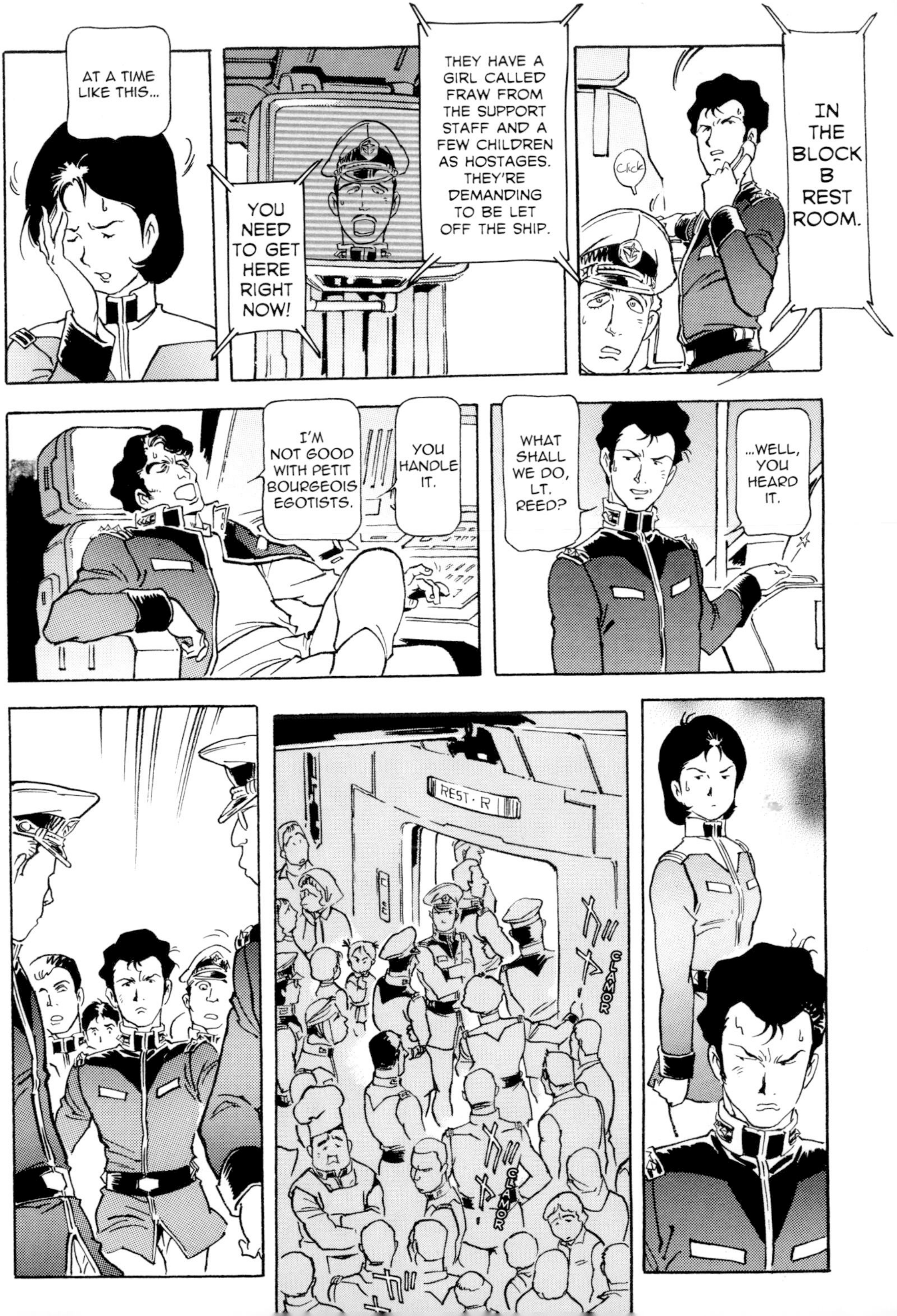
IN THE BLOCK B REST ROOM.
Click
THEY HAVE A GIRL CALLED FRAW FROM THE SUPPORT STAFF AND A FEW CHILDREN AS HOSTAGES. THEY'RE DEMANDING TO BE LET OFF THE SHIP.
YOU NEED TO GET HERE RIGHT NOW!
AT A TIME LIKE THIS...
...WELL, YOU HEARD IT.
WHAT SHALL WE DO, LT. REED?
YOU HANDLE IT.
I'M NOT GOOD WITH PETIT BOURGEOIS EGOTISTS.
REST · R
CLAMOR
CLAMOR

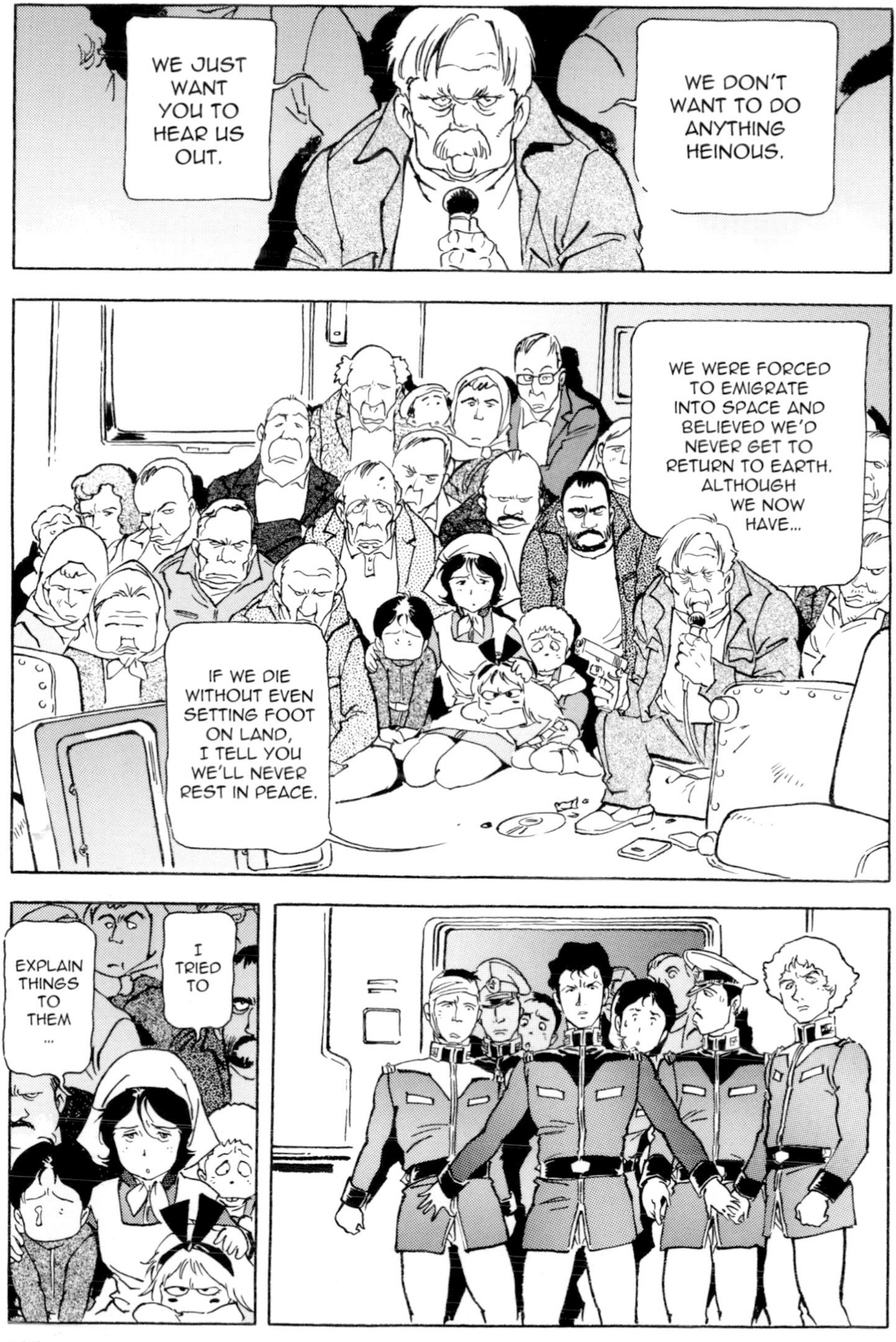
WE DON'T WANT TO DO ANYTHING HEINOUS.
WE JUST WANT YOU TO HEAR US OUT.
WE WERE FORCED TO EMIGRATE INTO SPACE AND BELIEVED WE'D NEVER GET TO RETURN TO EARTH. ALTHOUGH WE NOW HAVE...
IF WE DIE WITHOUT EVEN SETTING FOOT ON LAND, I TELL YOU WE'LL NEVER REST IN PEACE.
I TRIED TO
EXPLAIN THINGS TO THEM ...

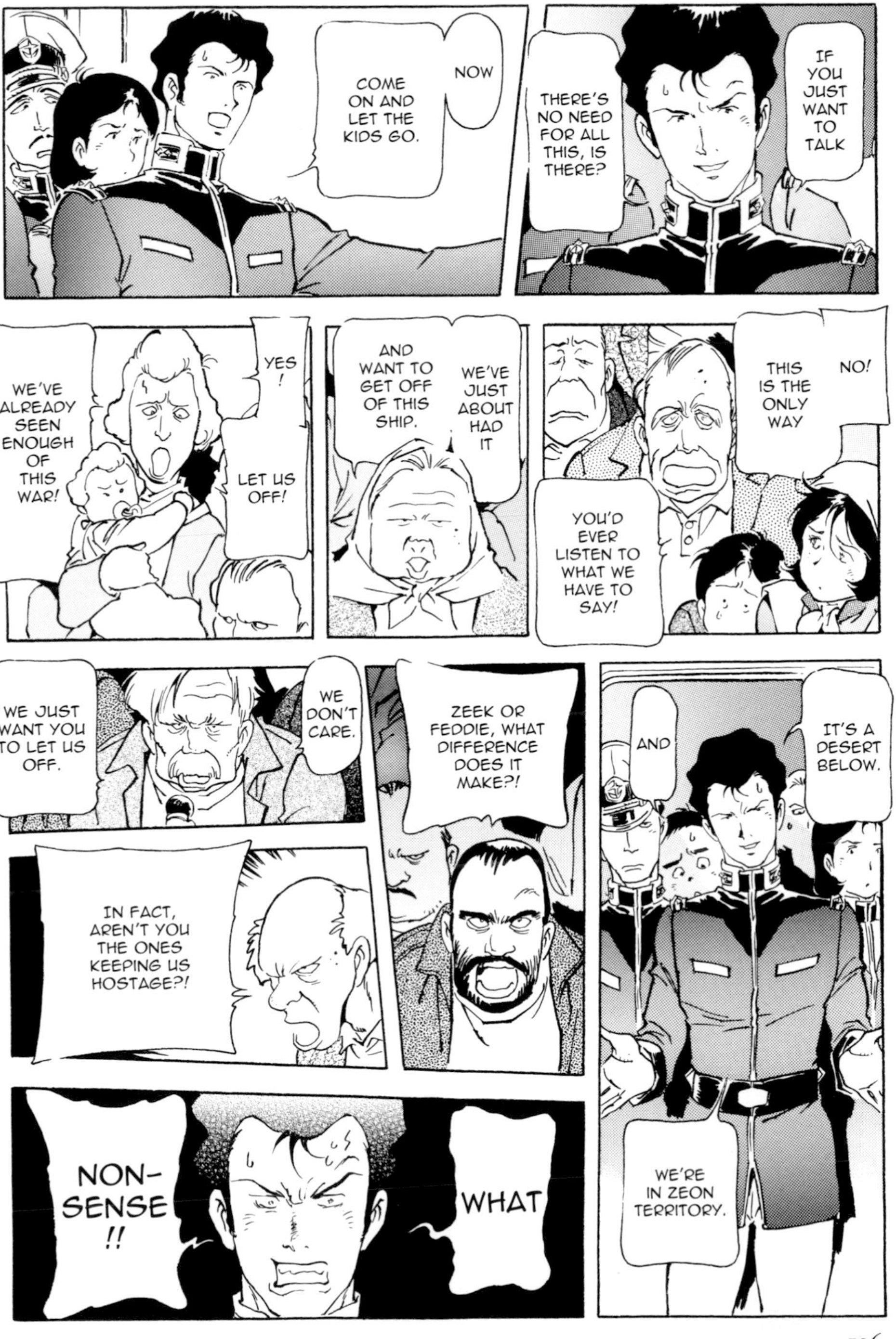
IF YOU JUST WANT TO TALK
THERE'S NO NEED FOR ALL THIS, IS THERE?
NOW
COME ON AND LET THE KIDS GO.
NO!
THIS IS THE ONLY WAY
YOU'D EVER LISTEN TO WHAT WE HAVE TO SAY!
WE'VE JUST ABOUT HAD IT
AND WANT TO GET OFF OF THIS SHIP.
YES!
LET US OFF!
WE'VE ALREADY SEEN ENOUGH OF THIS WAR!
IT'S A DESERT BELOW.
AND
WE'RE IN ZEON TERRITORY.
ZEEK OR FEDDIE, WHAT DIFFERENCE DOES IT MAKE?!
WE DON'T CARE.
WE JUST WANT YOU TO LET US OFF.
IN FACT, AREN'T YOU THE ONES KEEPING US HOSTAGE?!
WHAT
NON-SENSE!!

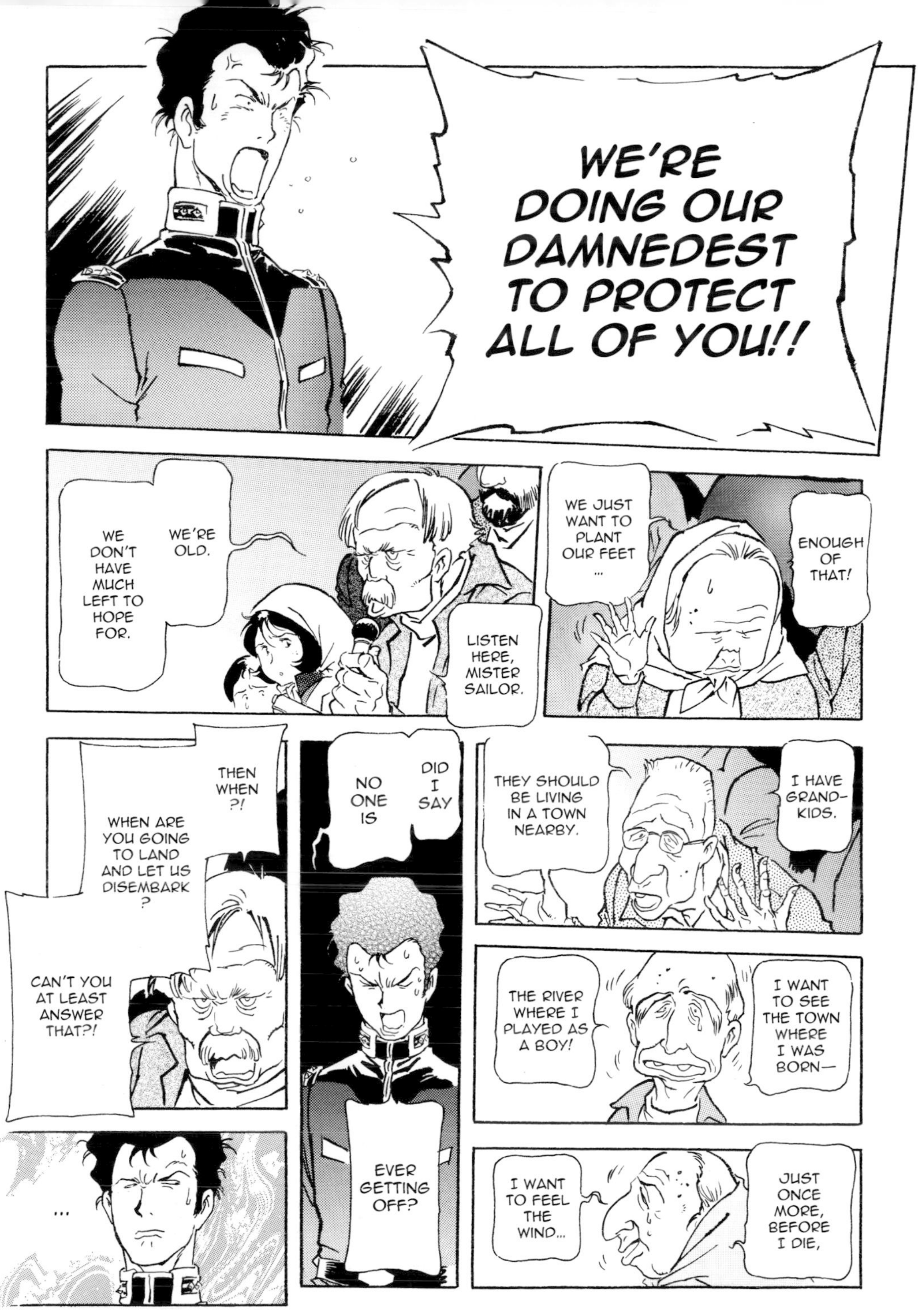
WE'RE DOING OUR DAMNEDEST TO PROTECT ALL OF YOU!!
ENOUGH OF THAT!
WE JUST WANT TO PLANT OUR FEET ...
LISTEN HERE, MISTER SAILOR.
WE'RE OLD.
WE DON'T HAVE MUCH LEFT TO HOPE FOR.
I HAVE GRAND-KIDS.
THEY SHOULD BE LIVING IN A TOWN NEARBY.
I WANT TO SEE THE TOWN WHERE I WAS BORN—
THE RIVER WHERE I PLAYED AS A BOY!
JUST ONCE MORE, BEFORE I DIE,
I WANT TO FEEL THE WIND...
DID I SAY
NO ONE IS
EVER GETTING OFF?
THEN WHEN ?!
WHEN ARE YOU GOING TO LAND AND LET US DISEMBARK ?
CAN'T YOU AT LEAST ANSWER THAT?!
...

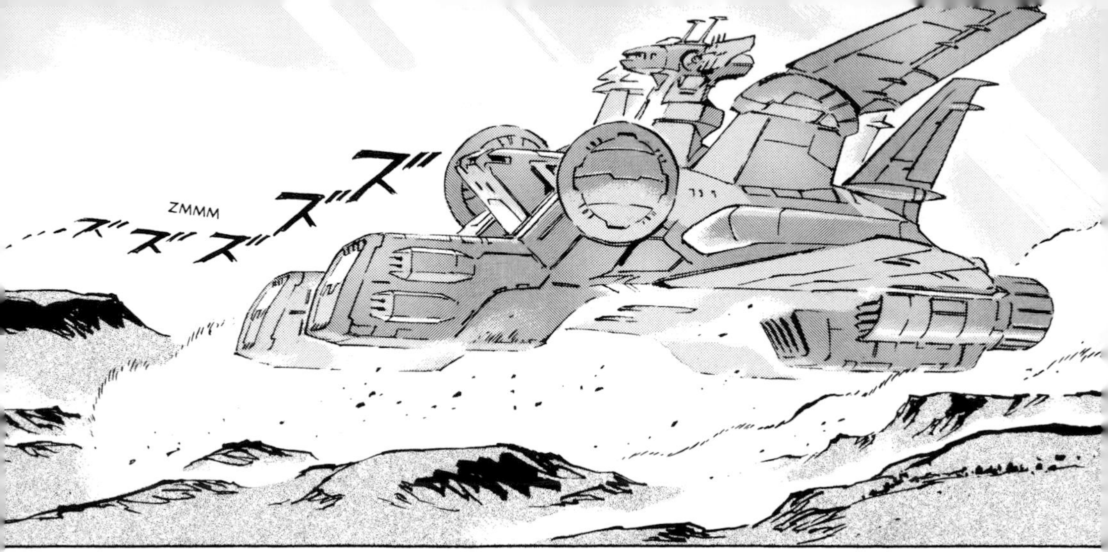
ズズズズズ
ZMMM

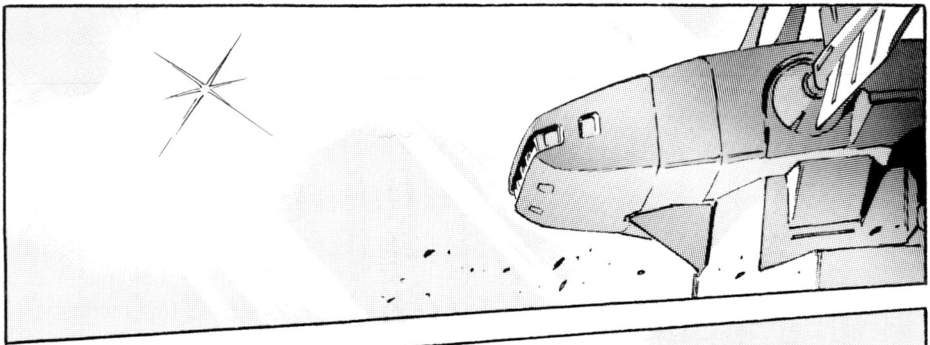

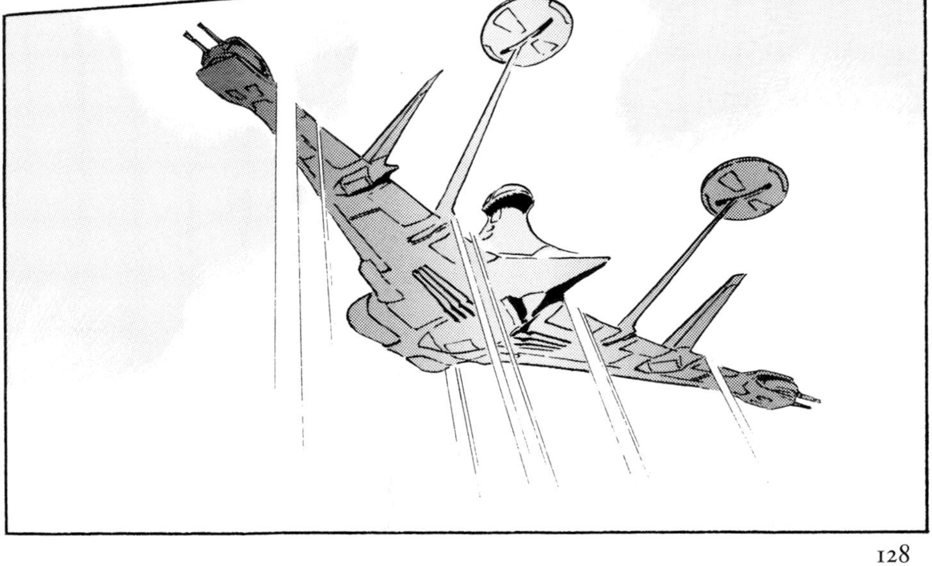

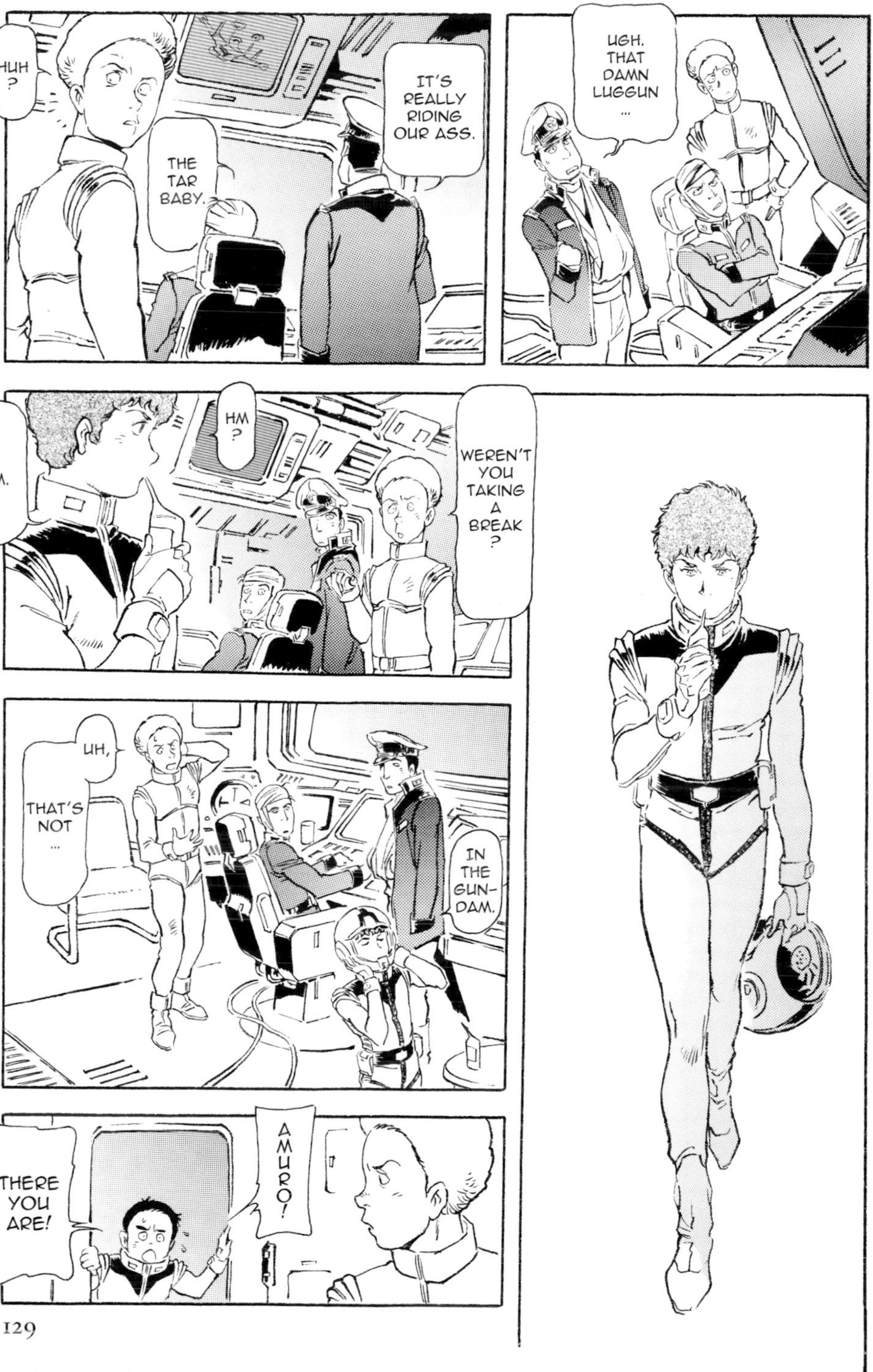
UGH. THAT DAMN LUGGUN ...
IT'S REALLY RIDING OUR ASS.
THE TAR BABY.
HUH?
WEREN'T YOU TAKING A BREAK?
HM?
I AM.
UH,
THAT'S NOT ...
IN THE GUN-DAM.
AMURO!
THERE YOU ARE!

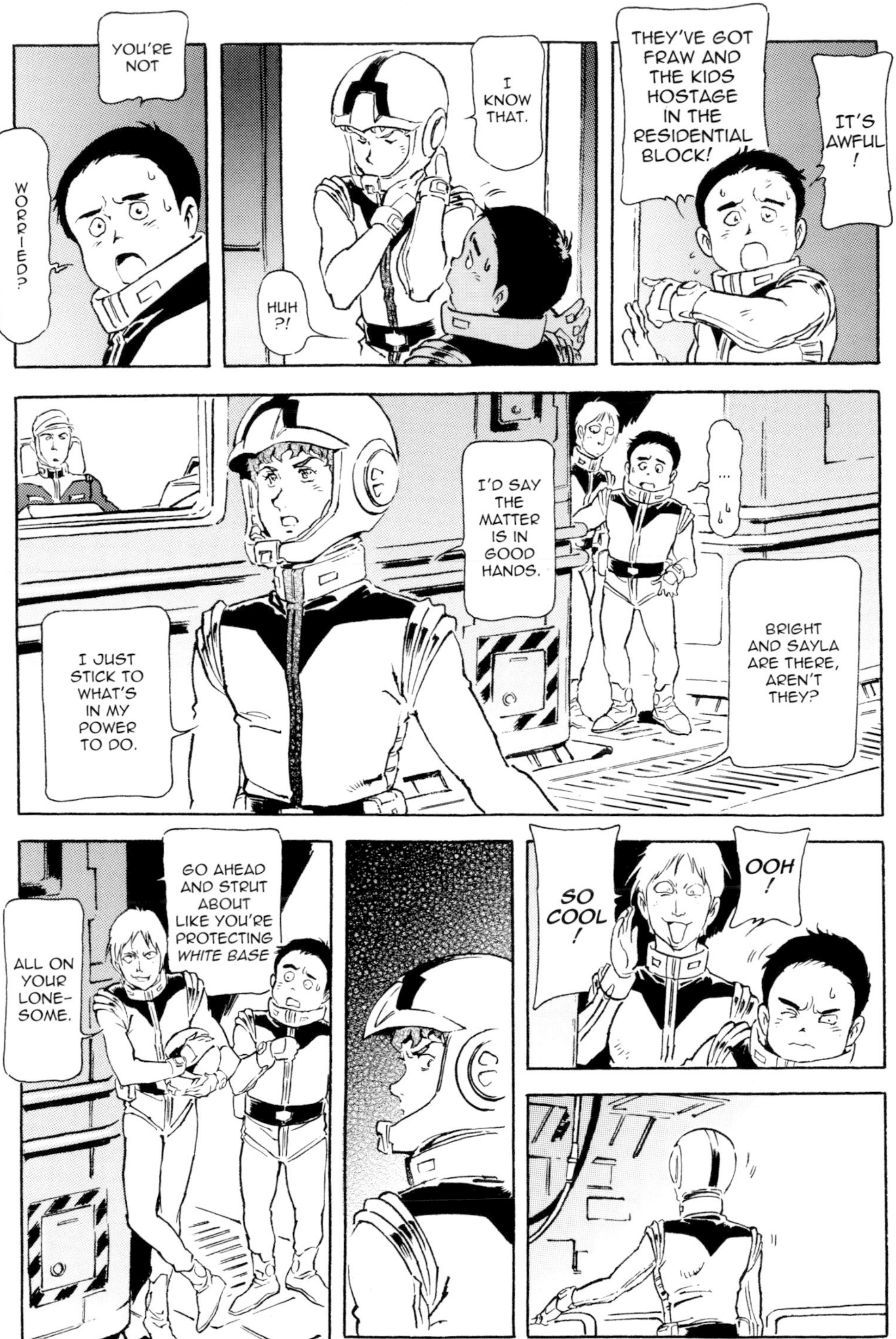
THEY'VE GOT FRAW AND THE KIDS HOSTAGE IN THE RESIDENTIAL BLOCK!
IT'S AWFUL!
I KNOW THAT.
HUH?!
YOU'RE NOT WORRIED?
...
BRIGHT AND SAYLA ARE THERE, AREN'T THEY?
I'D SAY THE MATTER IS IN GOOD HANDS.
I JUST STICK TO WHAT'S IN MY POWER TO DO.
OOH!
SO COOL!
GO AHEAD AND STRUT ABOUT LIKE YOU'RE PROTECTING *WHITE BASE*
ALL ON YOUR LONESOME.

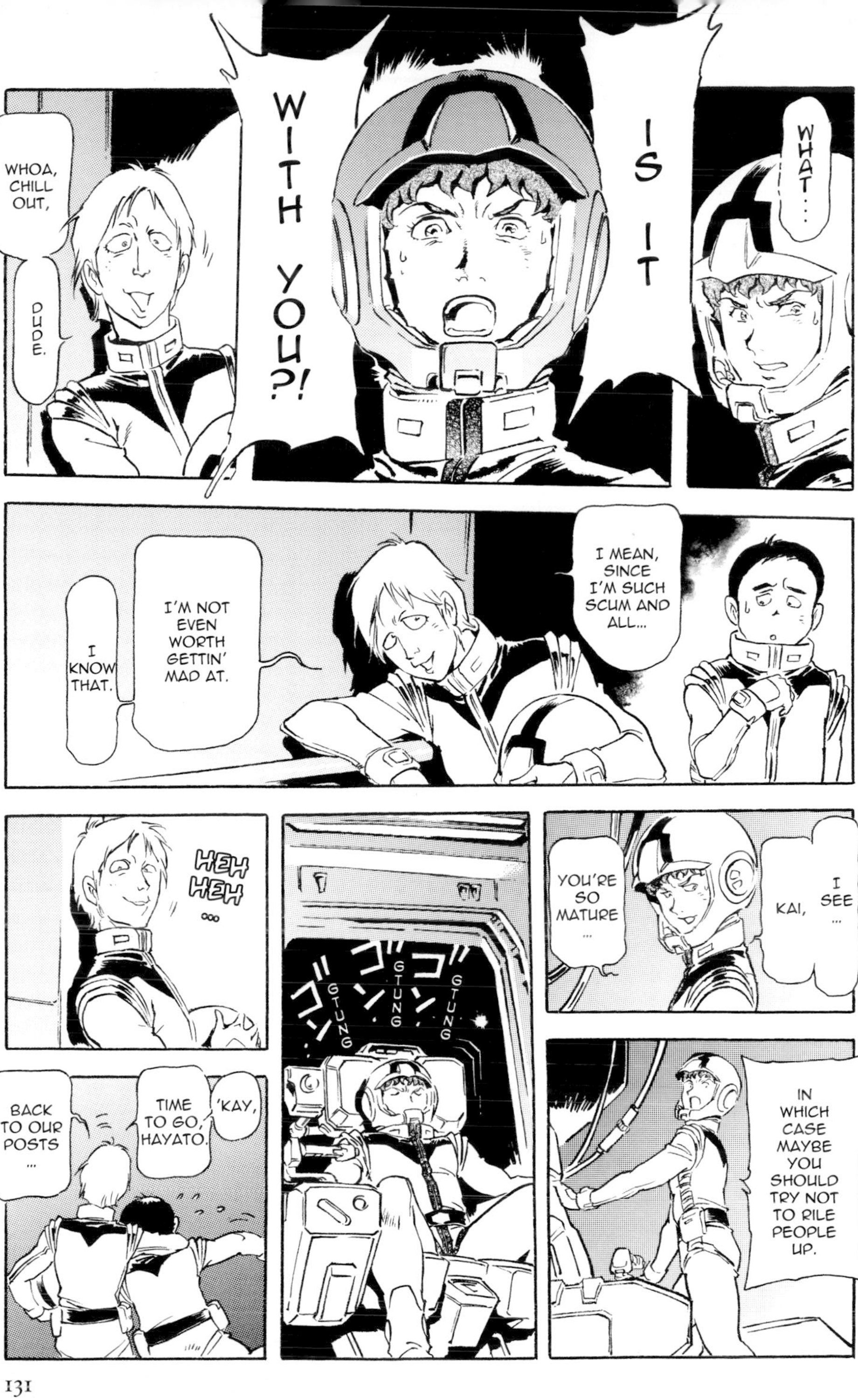
WHAT...
IS IT WITH YOU?!
WHOA, CHILL OUT,
DUDE.
I MEAN, SINCE I'M SUCH SCUM AND ALL...
I'M NOT EVEN WORTH GETTIN' MAD AT.
I KNOW THAT.
I SEE...
KAI,
YOU'RE SO MATURE...
IN WHICH CASE MAYBE YOU SHOULD TRY NOT TO RILE PEOPLE UP.
GTUNG
GTUNG
GTUNG
HEH HEH...
'KAY,
TIME TO GO, HAYATO.
BACK TO OUR POSTS...

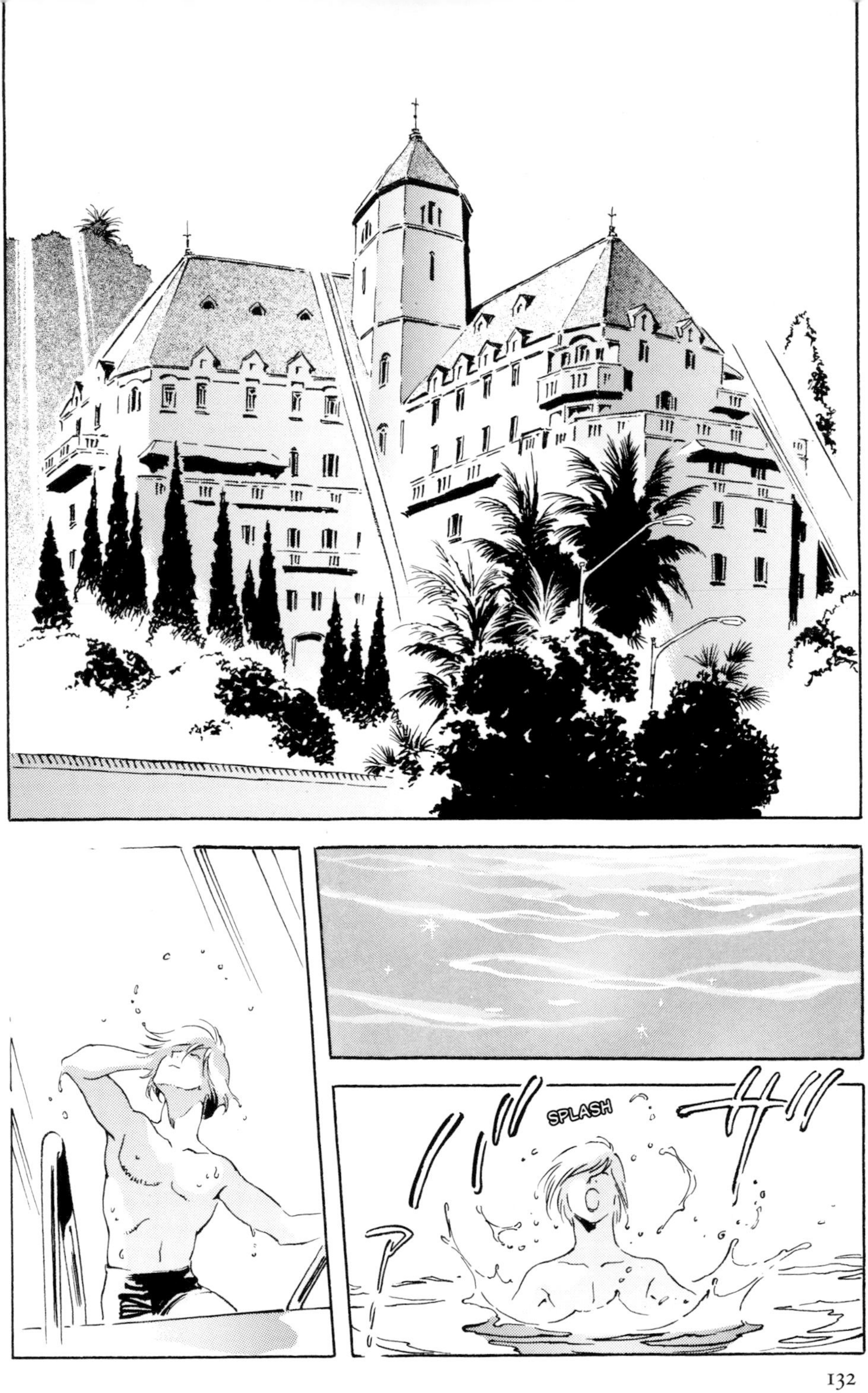
SPLASH

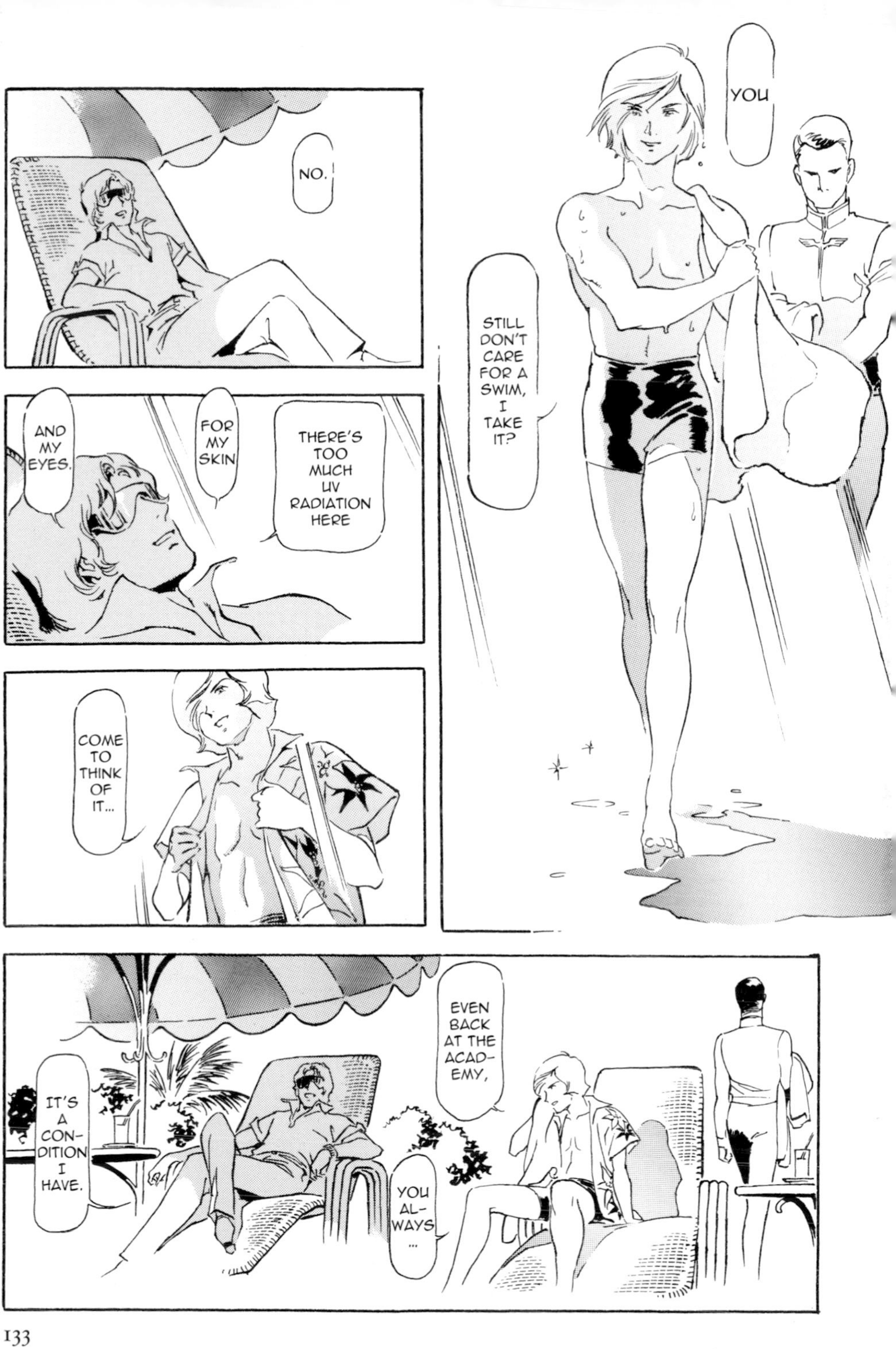
YOU
STILL DON'T CARE FOR A SWIM, I TAKE IT?
NO.
THERE'S TOO MUCH UV RADIATION HERE
FOR MY SKIN
AND MY EYES.
COME TO THINK OF IT...
EVEN BACK AT THE ACADEMY,
YOU ALWAYS...
IT'S A CONDITION I HAVE.

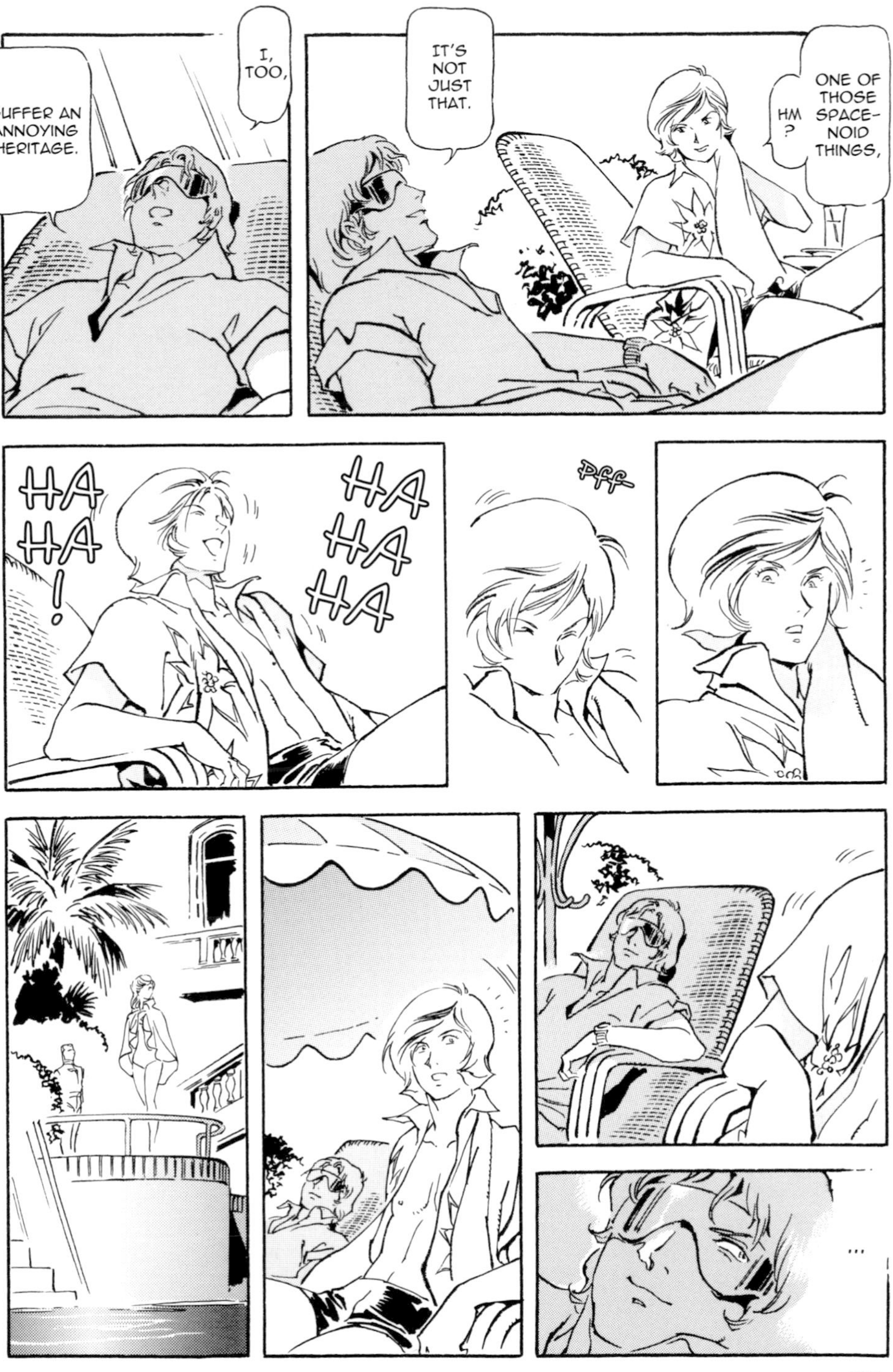
ONE OF THOSE SPACE-NOID THINGS,
HM ?
IT'S NOT JUST THAT.
I, TOO,
SUFFER AN ANNOYING HERITAGE.
Pff-
HA HA HA HA
HA HA!
...

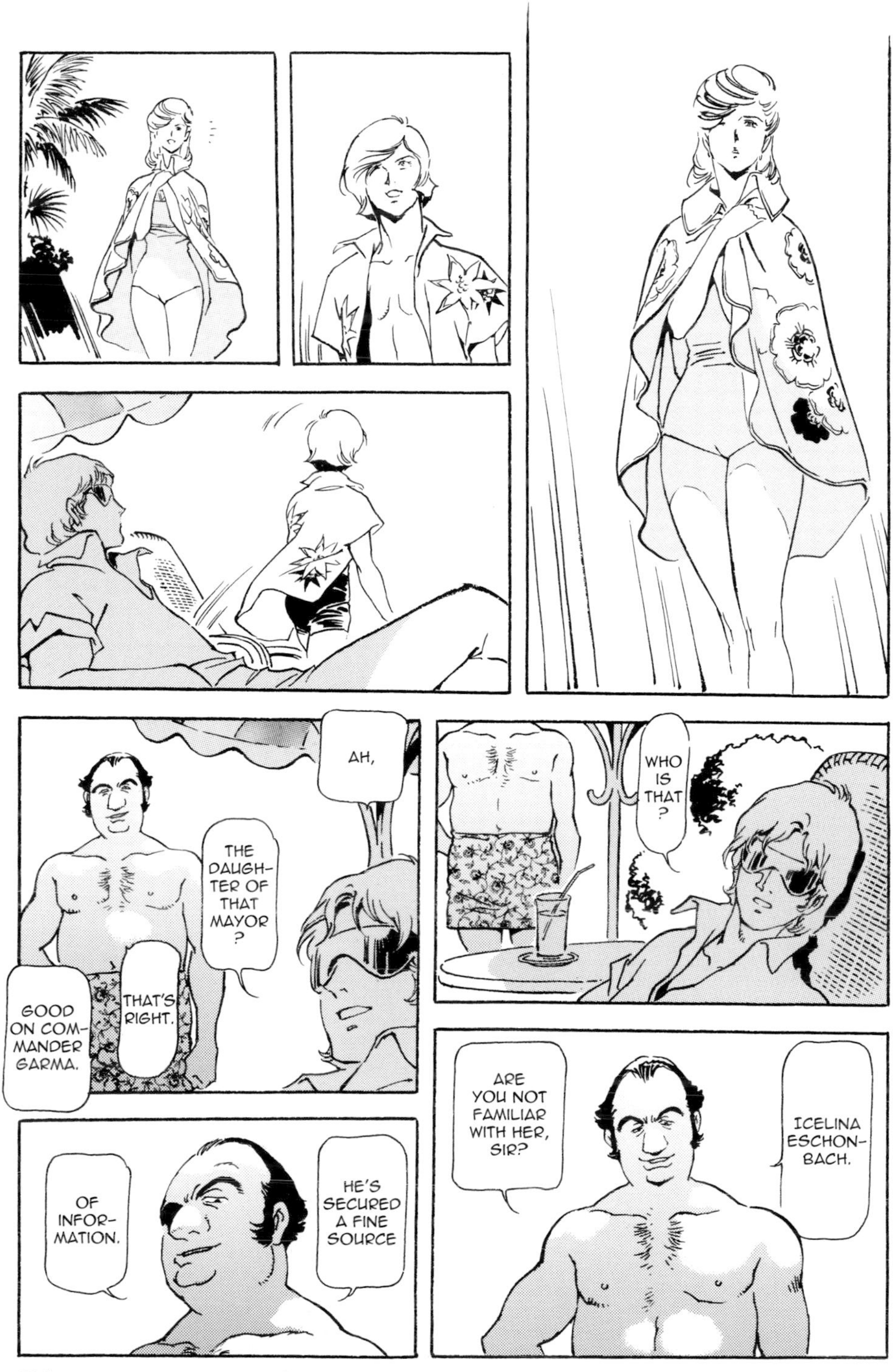
WHO IS THAT?
AH,
THE DAUGHTER OF THAT MAYOR?
THAT'S RIGHT.
GOOD ON COMMANDER GARMA.
ICELINA ESCHONBACH.
ARE YOU NOT FAMILIAR WITH HER, SIR?
HE'S SECURED A FINE SOURCE
OF INFORMATION.

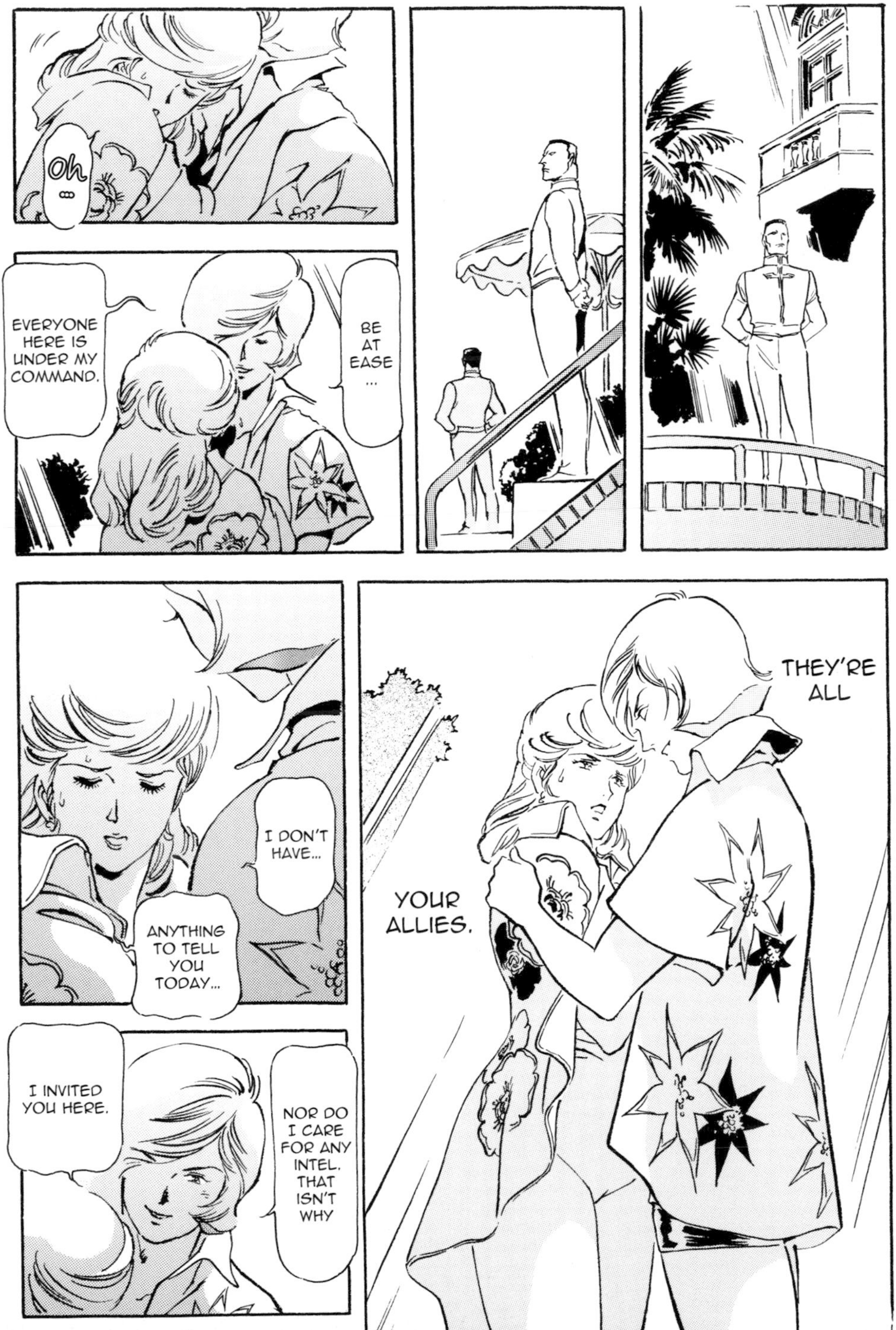
Oh...
BE AT EASE...
EVERYONE HERE IS UNDER MY COMMAND.
THEY'RE ALL
YOUR ALLIES.
I DON'T HAVE...
ANYTHING TO TELL YOU TODAY...
NOR DO I CARE FOR ANY INTEL. THAT ISN'T WHY
I INVITED YOU HERE.

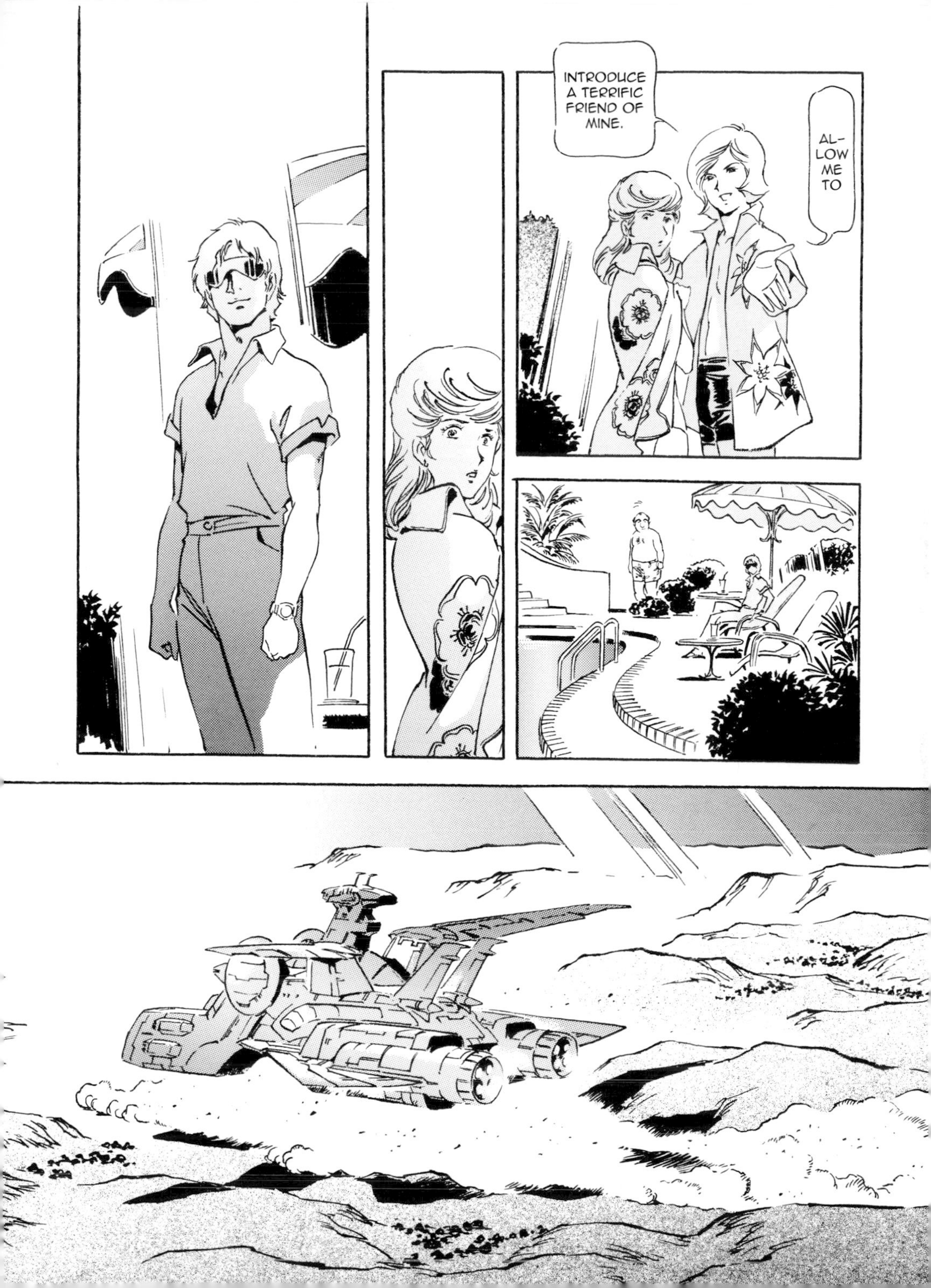
AL-LOW ME TO
INTRODUCE A TERRIFIC FRIEND OF MINE.

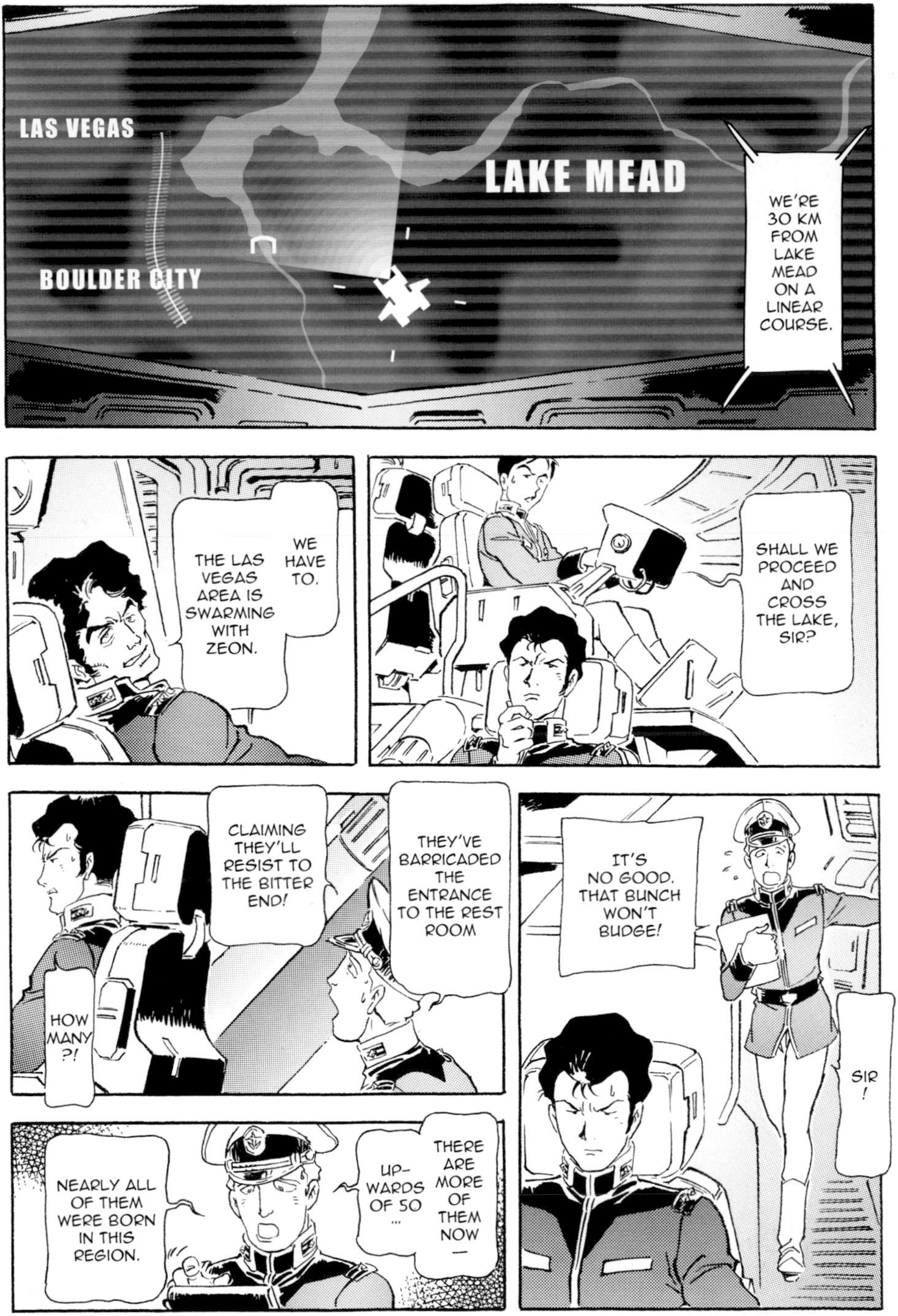

WE'RE 30 KM FROM LAKE MEAD ON A LINEAR COURSE.
LAKE MEAD
LAS VEGAS
BOULDER CITY
SHALL WE PROCEED AND CROSS THE LAKE, SIR?
WE HAVE TO.
THE LAS VEGAS AREA IS SWARMING WITH ZEON.
SIR!
IT'S NO GOOD. THAT BUNCH WON'T BUDGE!
THEY'VE BARRICADED THE ENTRANCE TO THE REST ROOM
CLAIMING THEY'LL RESIST TO THE BITTER END!
HOW MANY?!
THERE ARE MORE OF THEM NOW—
UP-WARDS OF 50...
NEARLY ALL OF THEM WERE BORN IN THIS REGION.

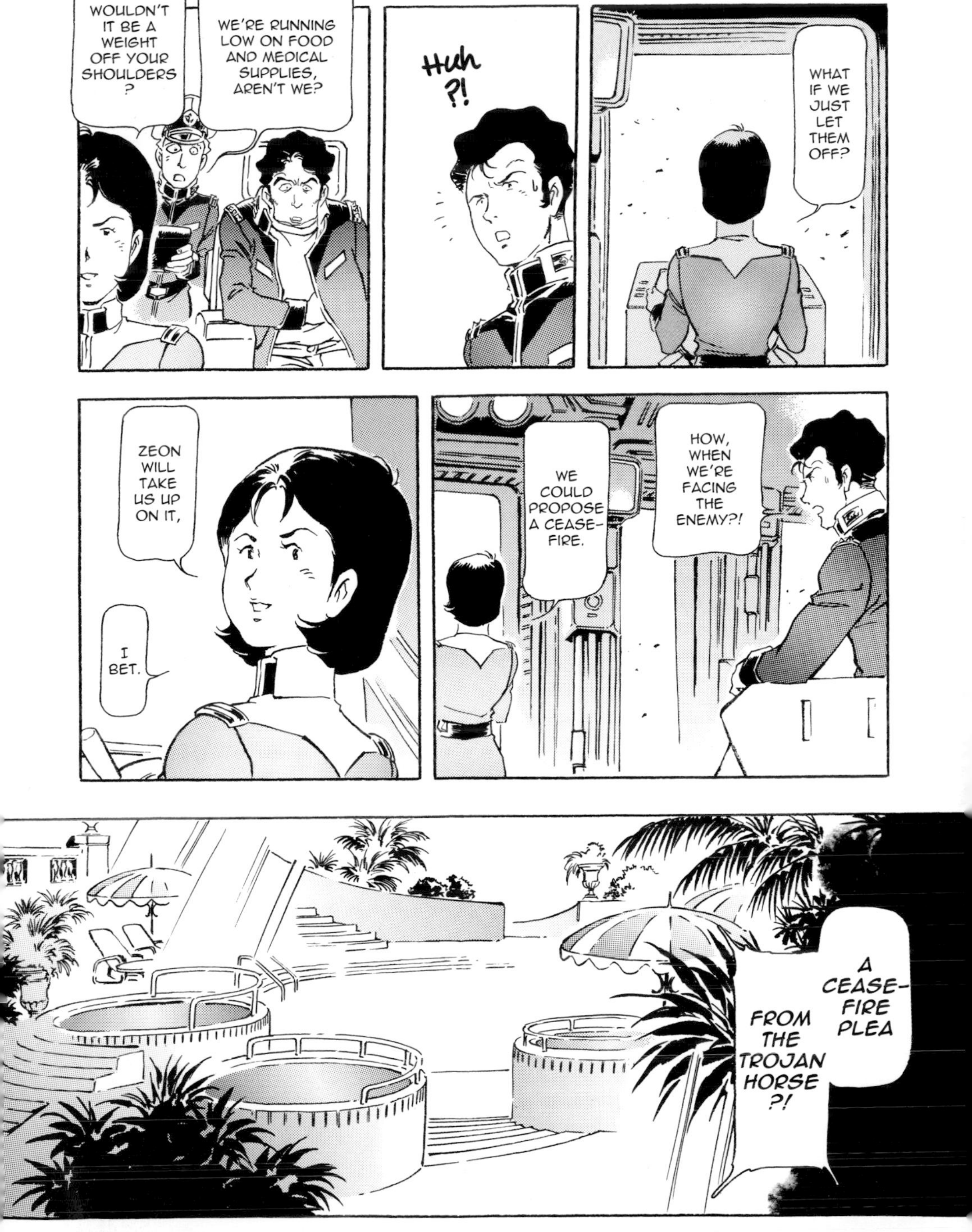
WHAT IF WE JUST LET THEM OFF?
Huh ?!
WE'RE RUNNING LOW ON FOOD AND MEDICAL SUPPLIES, AREN'T WE?
WOULDN'T IT BE A WEIGHT OFF YOUR SHOULDERS?
HOW, WHEN WE'RE FACING THE ENEMY?!
WE COULD PROPOSE A CEASE-FIRE.
ZEON WILL TAKE US UP ON IT,
I BET.
A CEASE-FIRE PLEA
FROM THE TROJAN HORSE?!

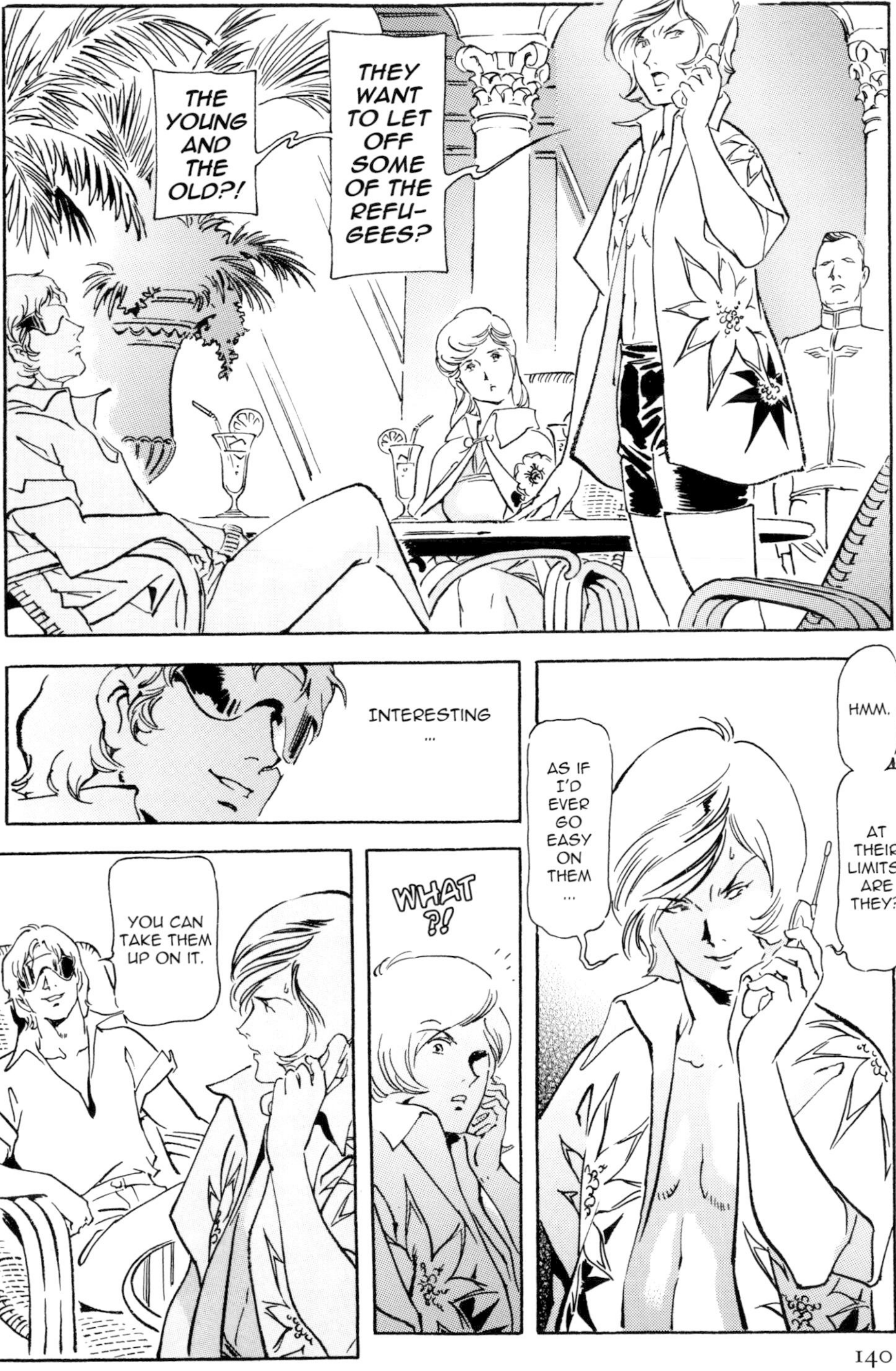
THEY WANT TO LET OFF SOME OF THE REFU-GEES?
THE YOUNG AND THE OLD?!
HMM.
AT THEIR LIMITS, ARE THEY?
AS IF I'D EVER GO EASY ON THEM ...
INTERESTING ...
WHAT?!
YOU CAN TAKE THEM UP ON IT.

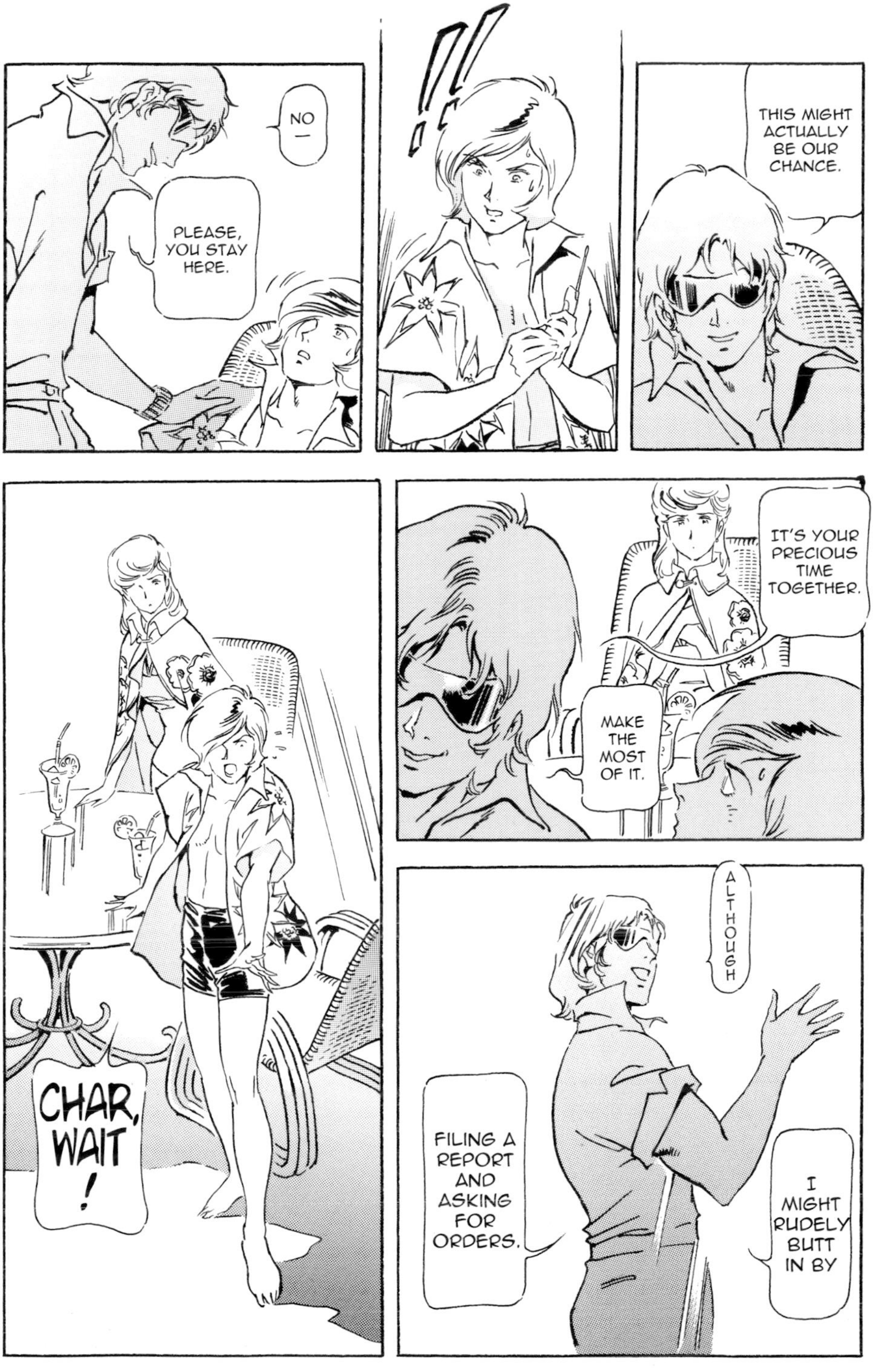
THIS MIGHT ACTUALLY BE OUR CHANCE.
!!
NO —
PLEASE, YOU STAY HERE.
IT'S YOUR PRECIOUS TIME TOGETHER.
MAKE THE MOST OF IT.
ALTHOUGH
I MIGHT RUDELY BUTT IN BY
FILING A REPORT AND ASKING FOR ORDERS.
CHAR, WAIT!

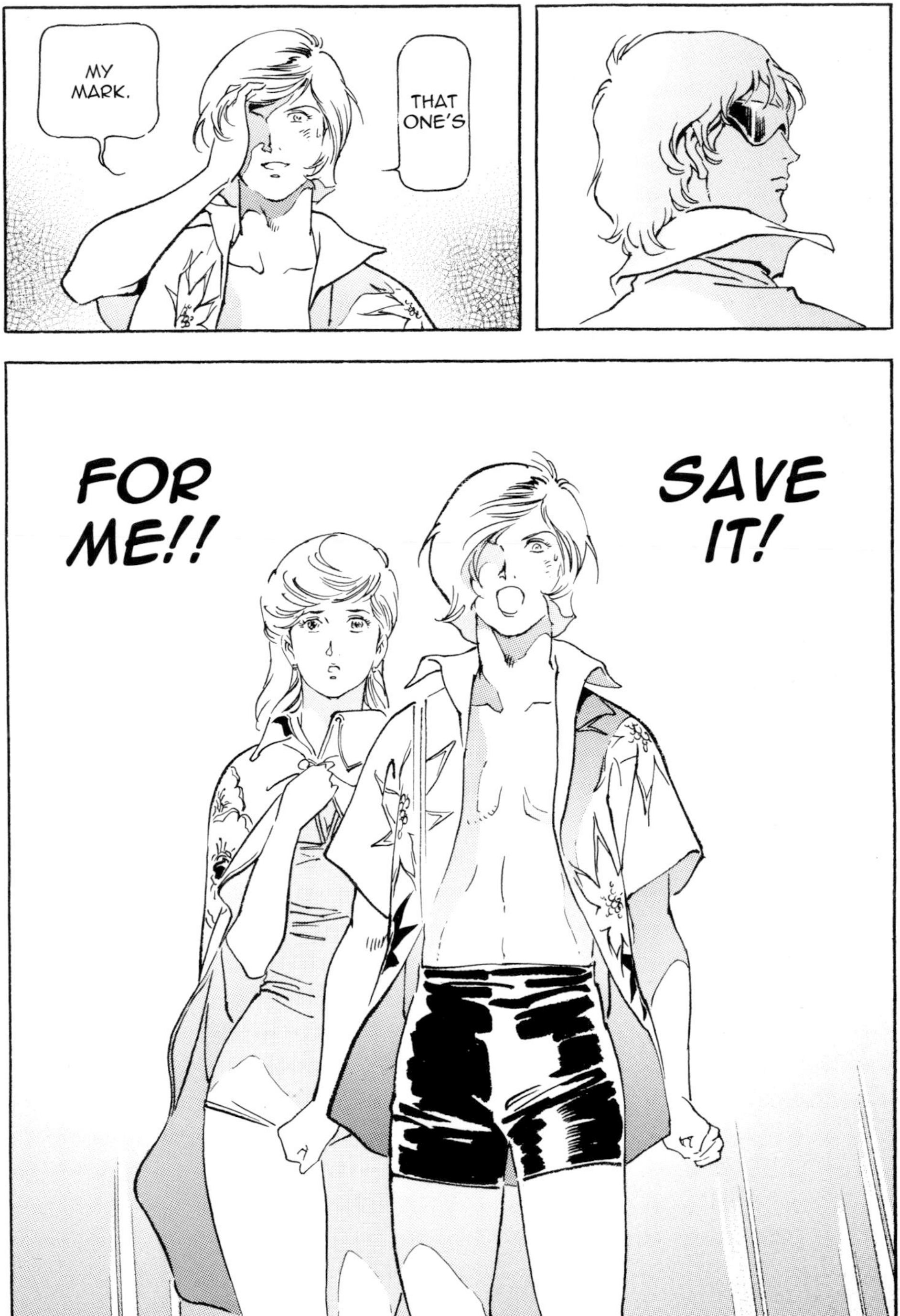
THAT ONE'S
MY MARK.
SAVE IT!
FOR ME!!

SECTION
IV

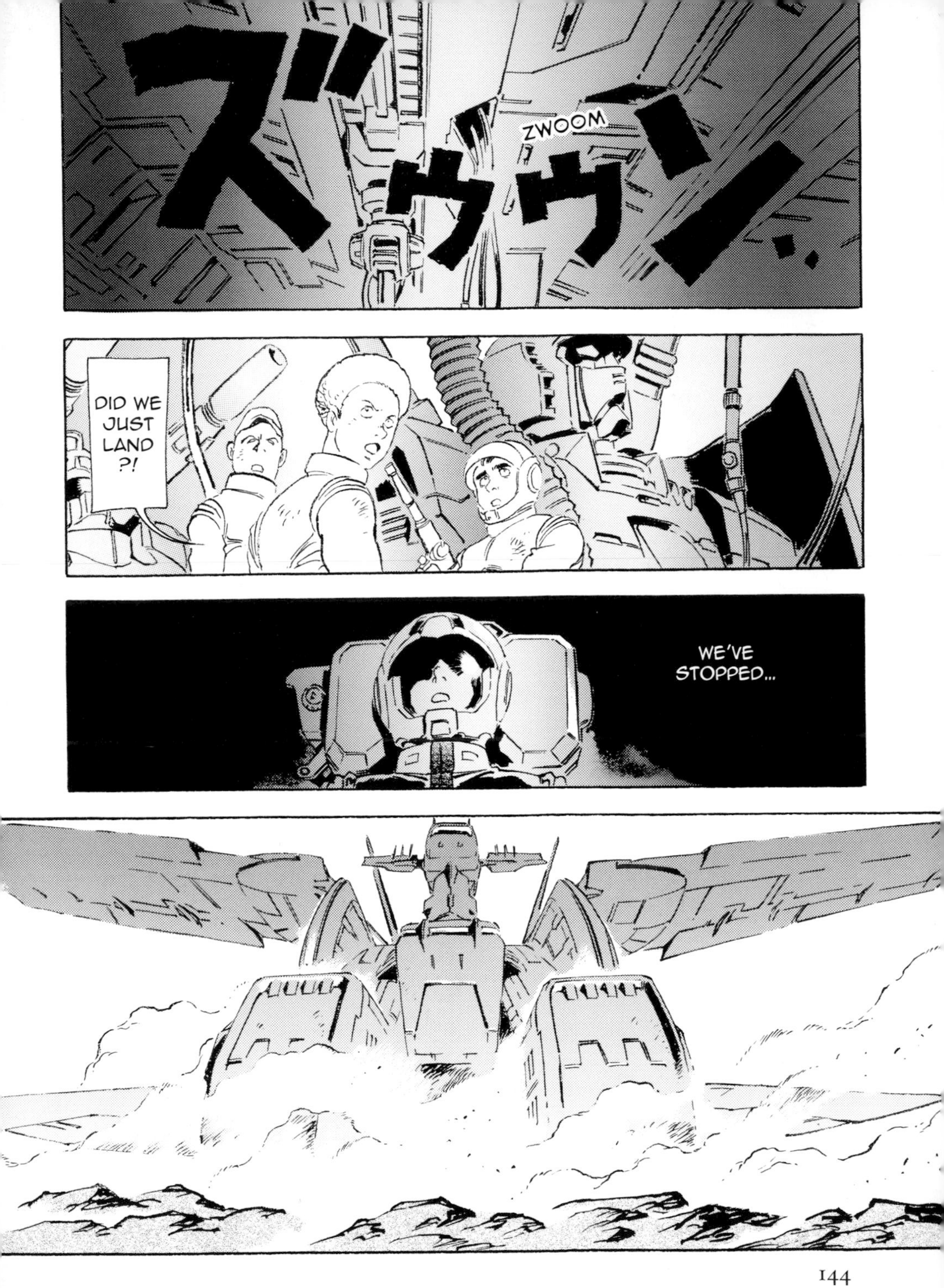
ズヴウン..
ZWOOM
DID WE JUST LAND ?!
WE'VE STOPPED...

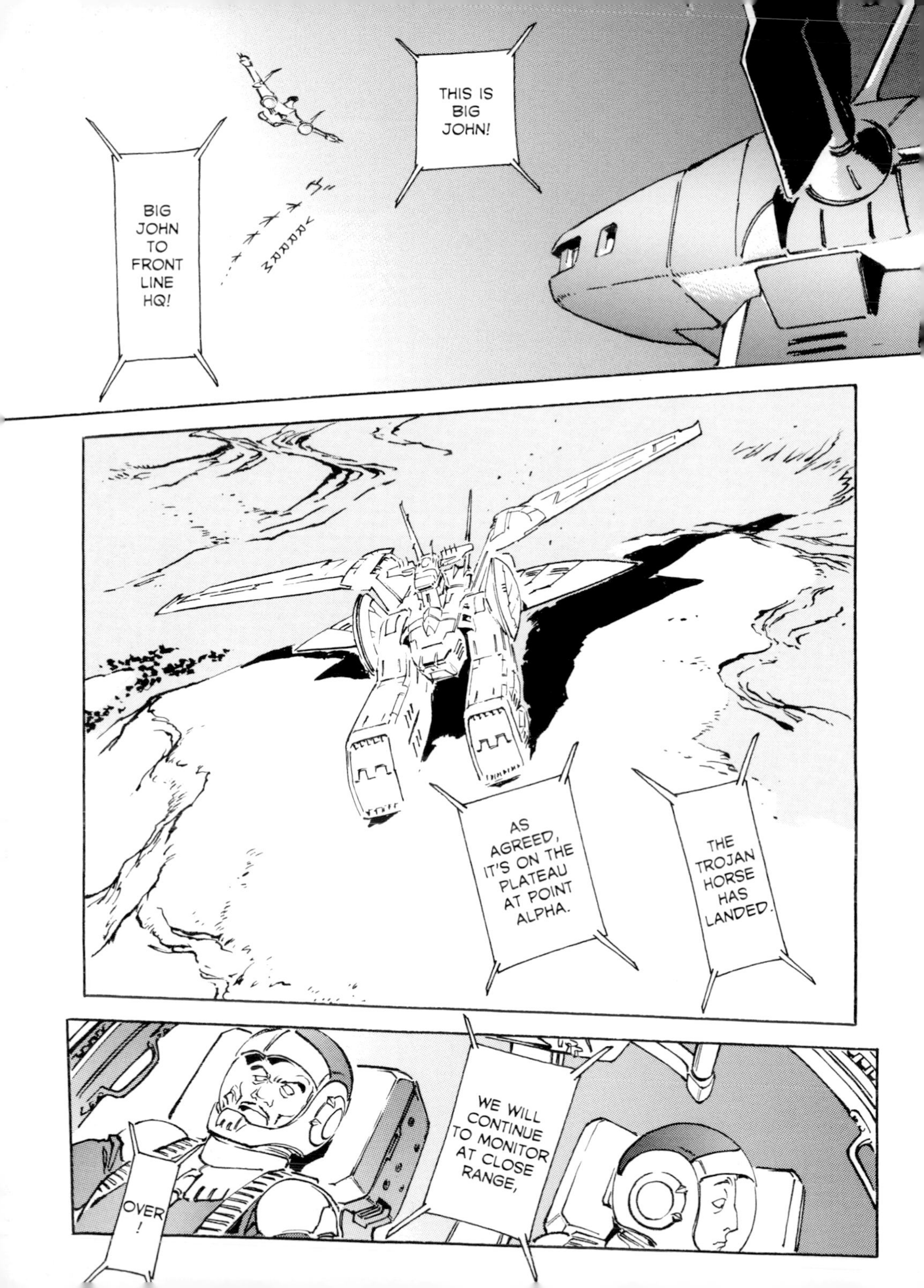
THIS IS BIG JOHN!
BIG JOHN TO FRONT LINE HQ!
THE TROJAN HORSE HAS LANDED.
AS AGREED, IT'S ON THE PLATEAU AT POINT ALPHA.
WE WILL CONTINUE TO MONITOR AT CLOSE RANGE,
OVER!

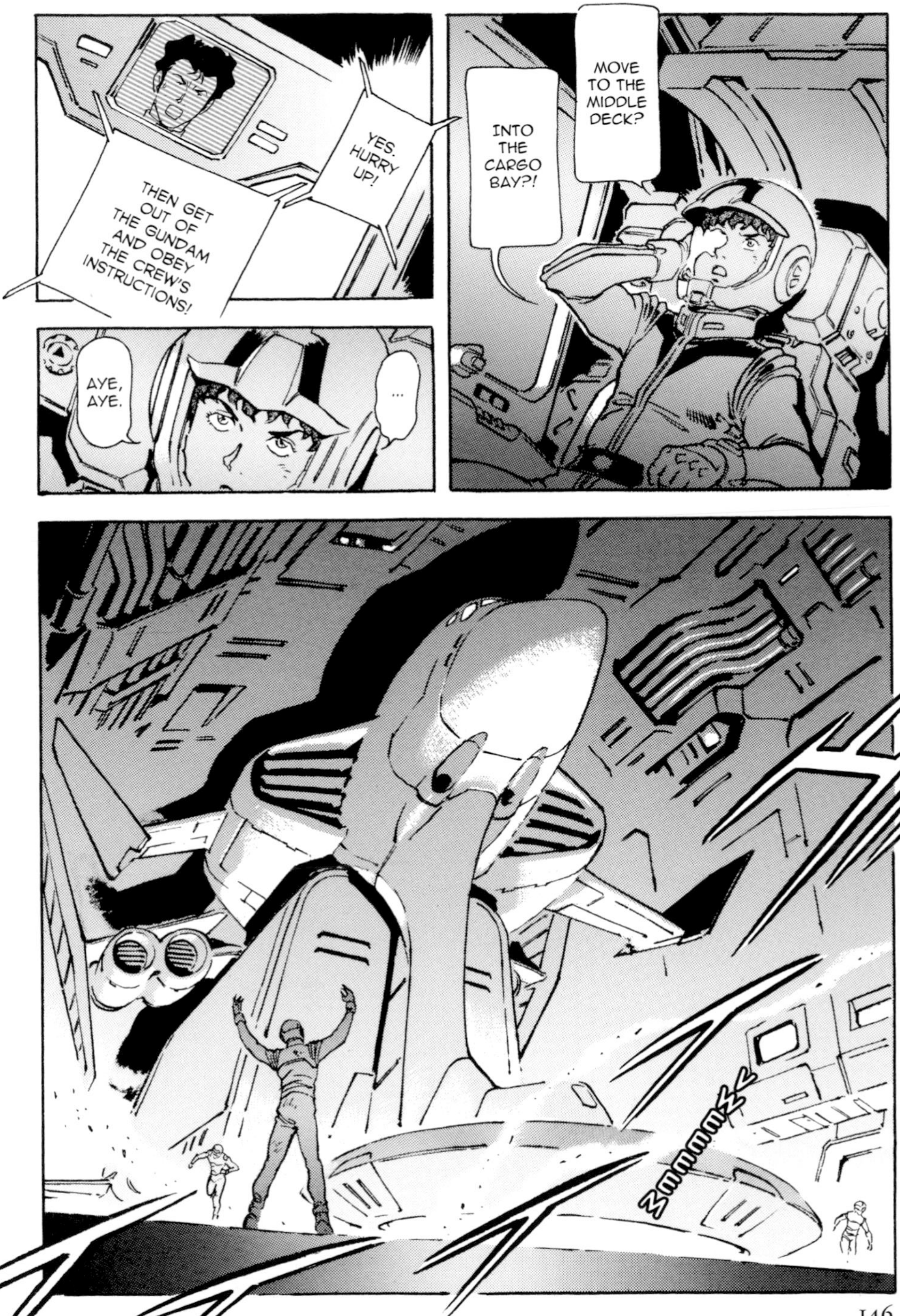
MOVE TO THE MIDDLE DECK?
INTO THE CARGO BAY?!
YES. HURRY UP!
THEN GET OUT OF THE GUNDAM AND OBEY THE CREW'S INSTRUCTIONS!
...
AYE, AYE.

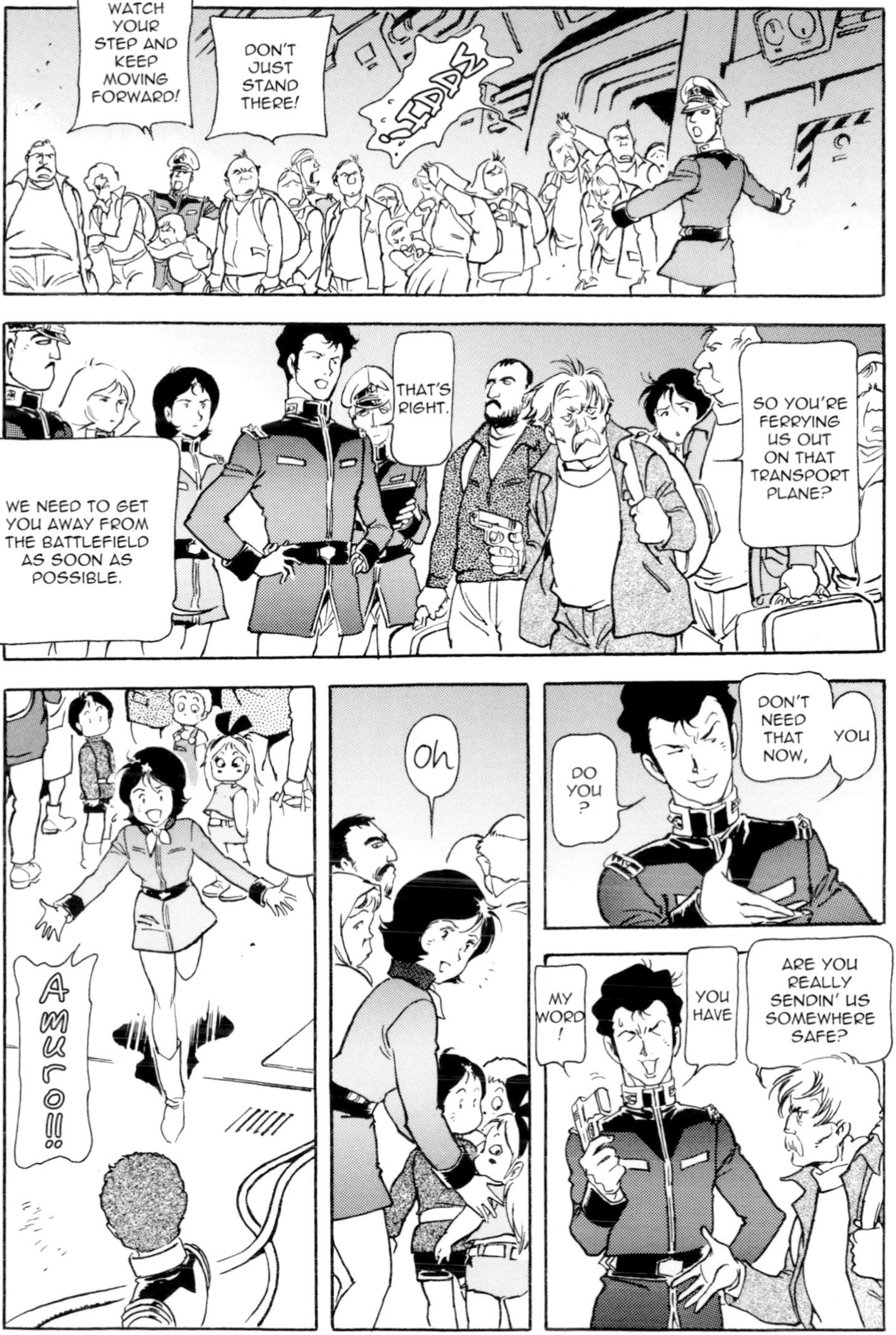
DON'T JUST STAND THERE!
WATCH YOUR STEP AND KEEP MOVING FORWARD!
SO YOU'RE FERRYING US OUT ON THAT TRANSPORT PLANE?
THAT'S RIGHT.
WE NEED TO GET YOU AWAY FROM THE BATTLEFIELD AS SOON AS POSSIBLE.
YOU
DON'T NEED THAT NOW,
DO YOU?
ARE YOU REALLY SENDIN' US SOMEWHERE SAFE?
YOU HAVE
MY WORD!
Oh
Amuro!!

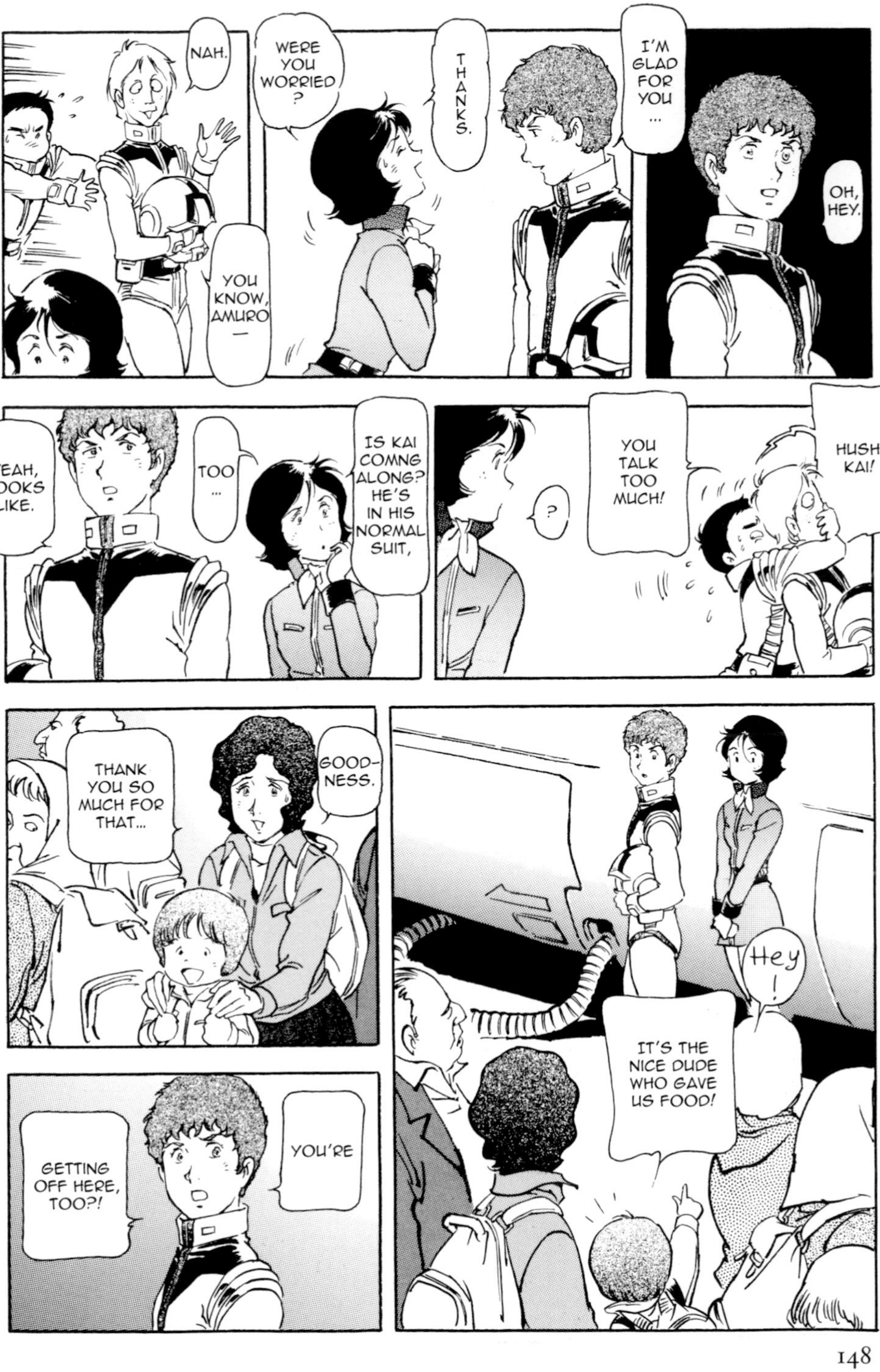
OH, HEY.
I'M GLAD FOR YOU ...
THANKS.
WERE YOU WORRIED?
NAH.
YOU KNOW, AMURO —
HUSH, KAI!
YOU TALK TOO MUCH!
?
IS KAI COMNG ALONG? HE'S IN HIS NORMAL SUIT,
TOO ...
YEAH, LOOKS LIKE.
Hey!
IT'S THE NICE DUDE WHO GAVE US FOOD!
GOOD-NESS.
THANK YOU SO MUCH FOR THAT...
YOU'RE
GETTING OFF HERE, TOO?!

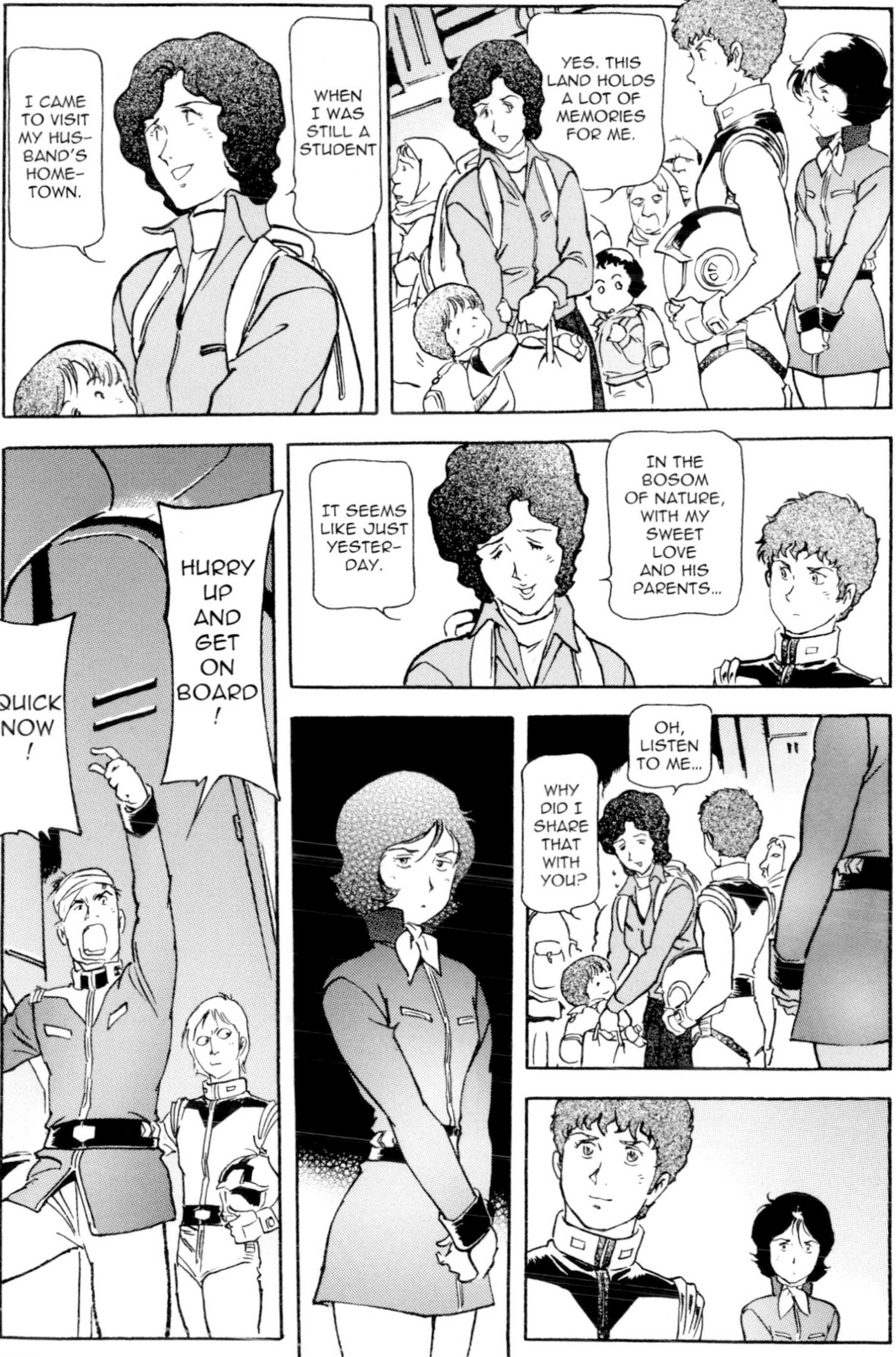
YES. THIS LAND HOLDS A LOT OF MEMORIES FOR ME.
WHEN I WAS STILL A STUDENT
I CAME TO VISIT MY HUS-BAND'S HOME-TOWN.
IN THE BOSOM OF NATURE, WITH MY SWEET LOVE AND HIS PARENTS...
IT SEEMS LIKE JUST YESTER-DAY.
OH, LISTEN TO ME...
WHY DID I SHARE THAT WITH YOU?
HURRY UP AND GET ON BOARD!
QUICK NOW!

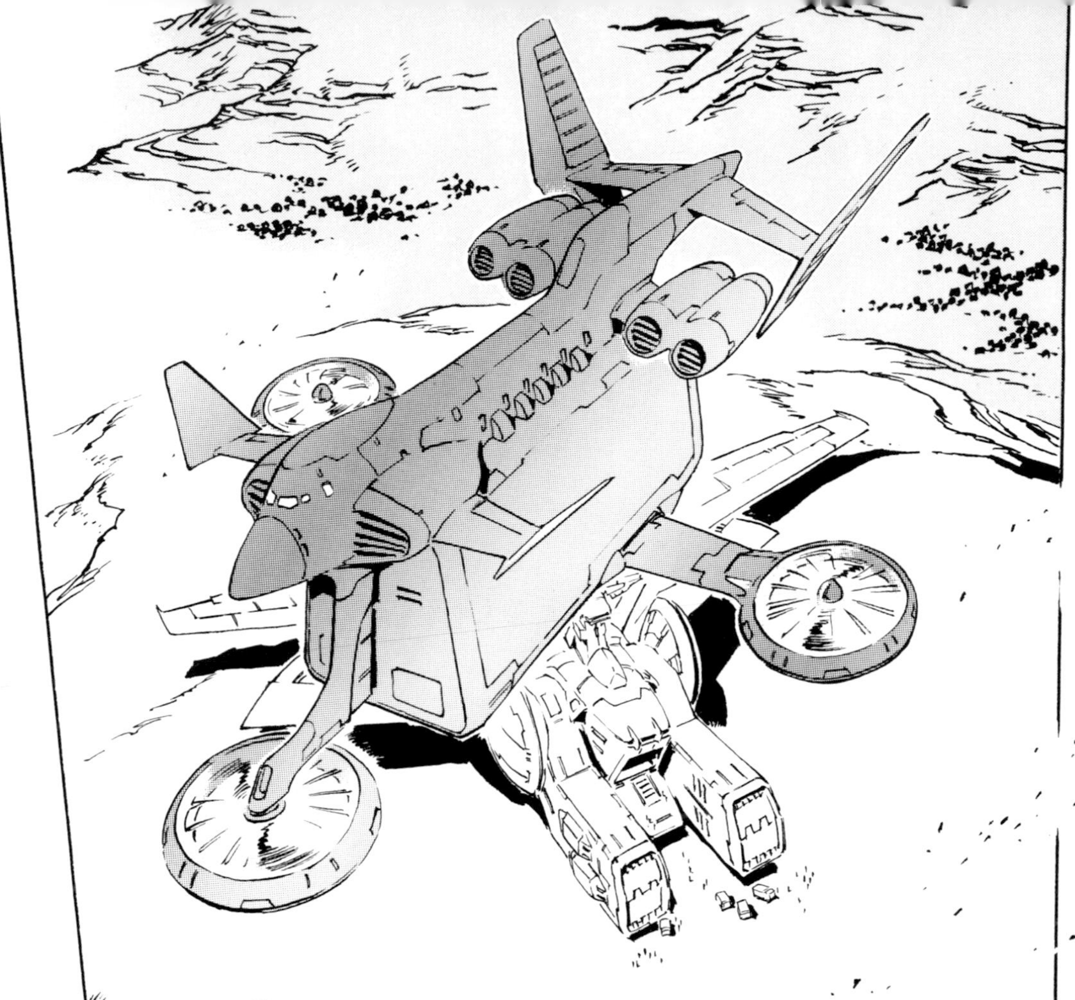

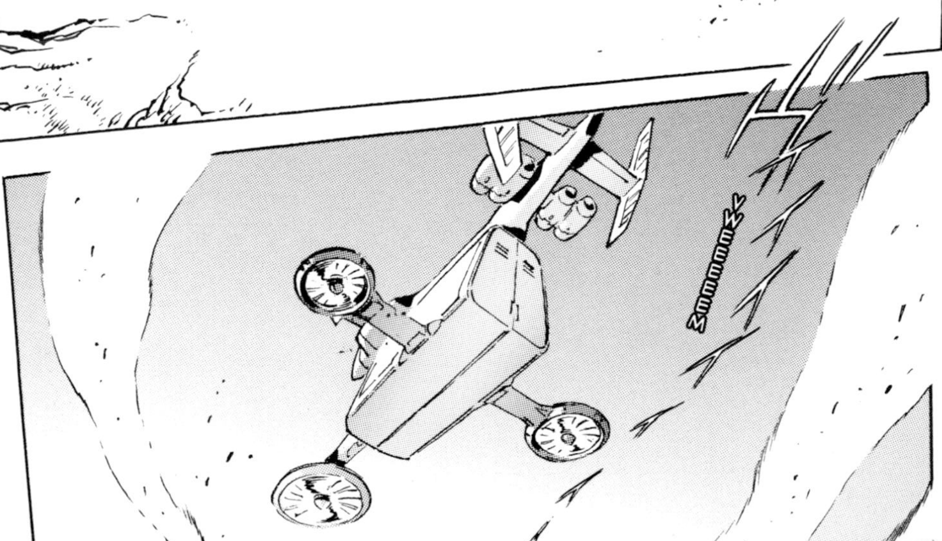
ヒュイイイイ
Zwmmmmmm

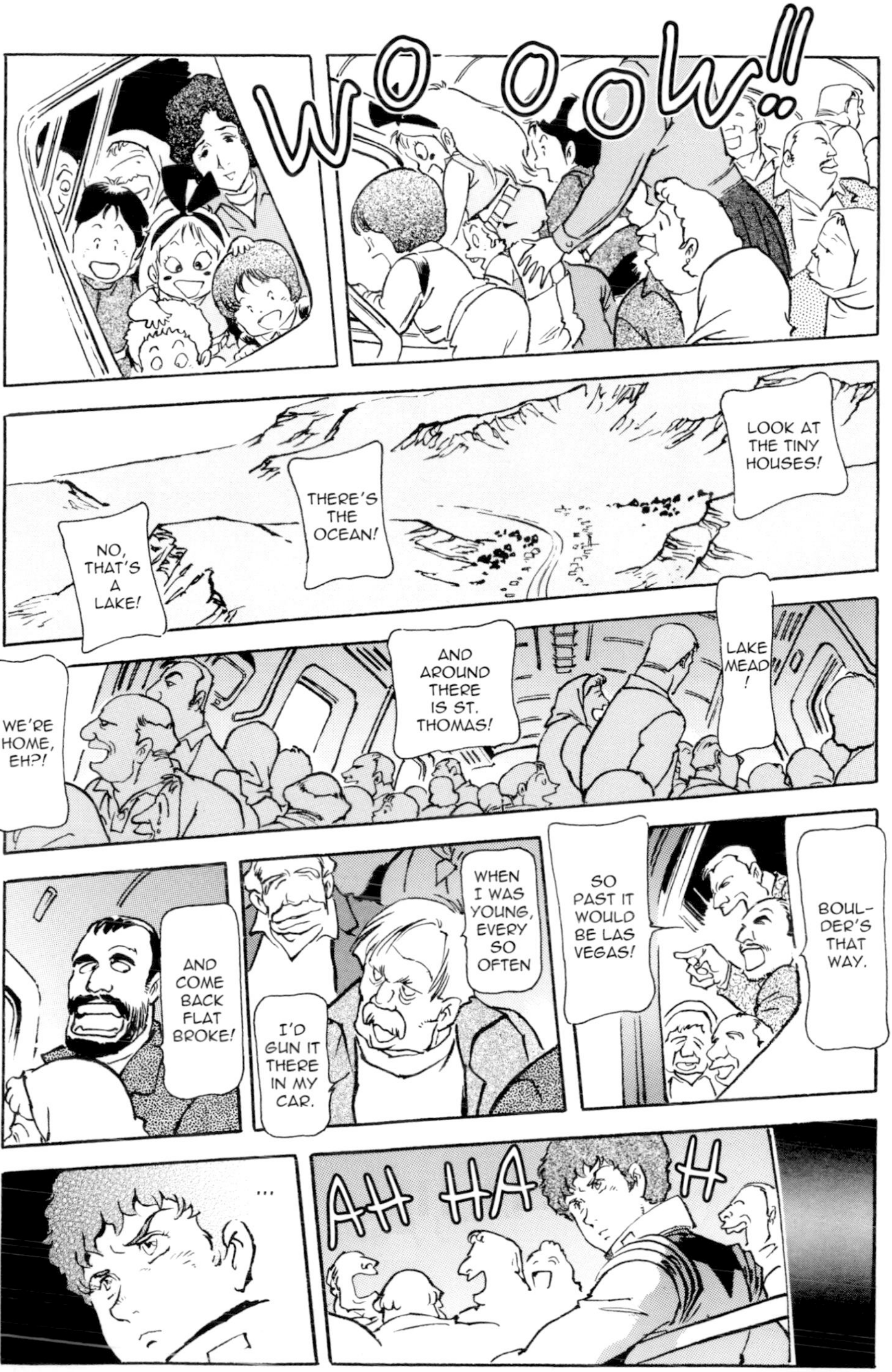
WOOOOW!!
LOOK AT THE TINY HOUSES!
THERE'S THE OCEAN!
NO, THAT'S A LAKE!
LAKE MEAD!
AND AROUND THERE IS ST. THOMAS!
WE'RE HOME, EH?!
BOULDER'S THAT WAY.
SO PAST IT WOULD BE LAS VEGAS!
WHEN I WAS YOUNG, EVERY SO OFTEN
I'D GUN IT THERE IN MY CAR.
AND COME BACK FLAT BROKE!
AH HA HA H
...

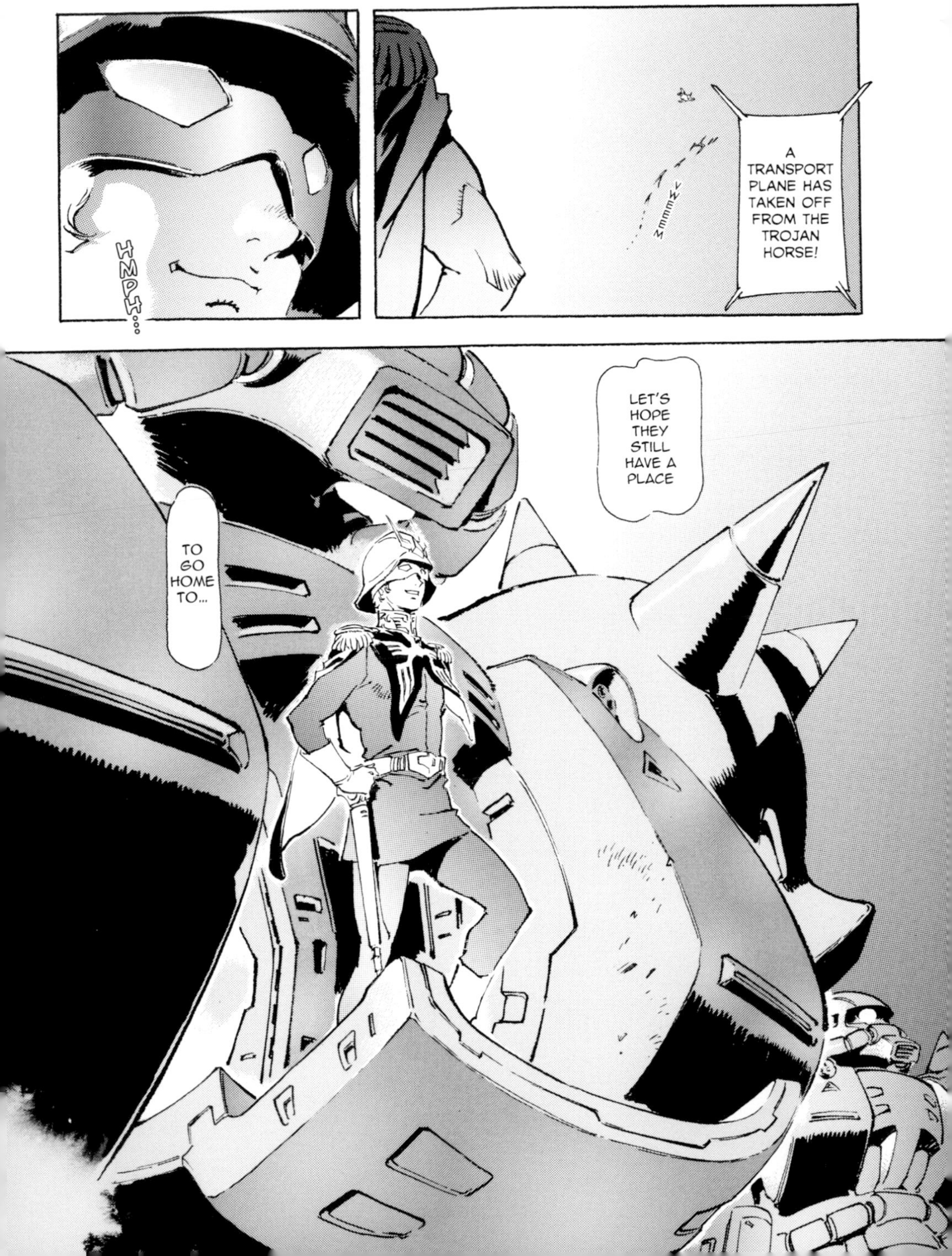
A TRANSPORT PLANE HAS TAKEN OFF FROM THE TROJAN HORSE!
VWEEEM
HMPH...
LET'S HOPE THEY STILL HAVE A PLACE
TO GO HOME TO...

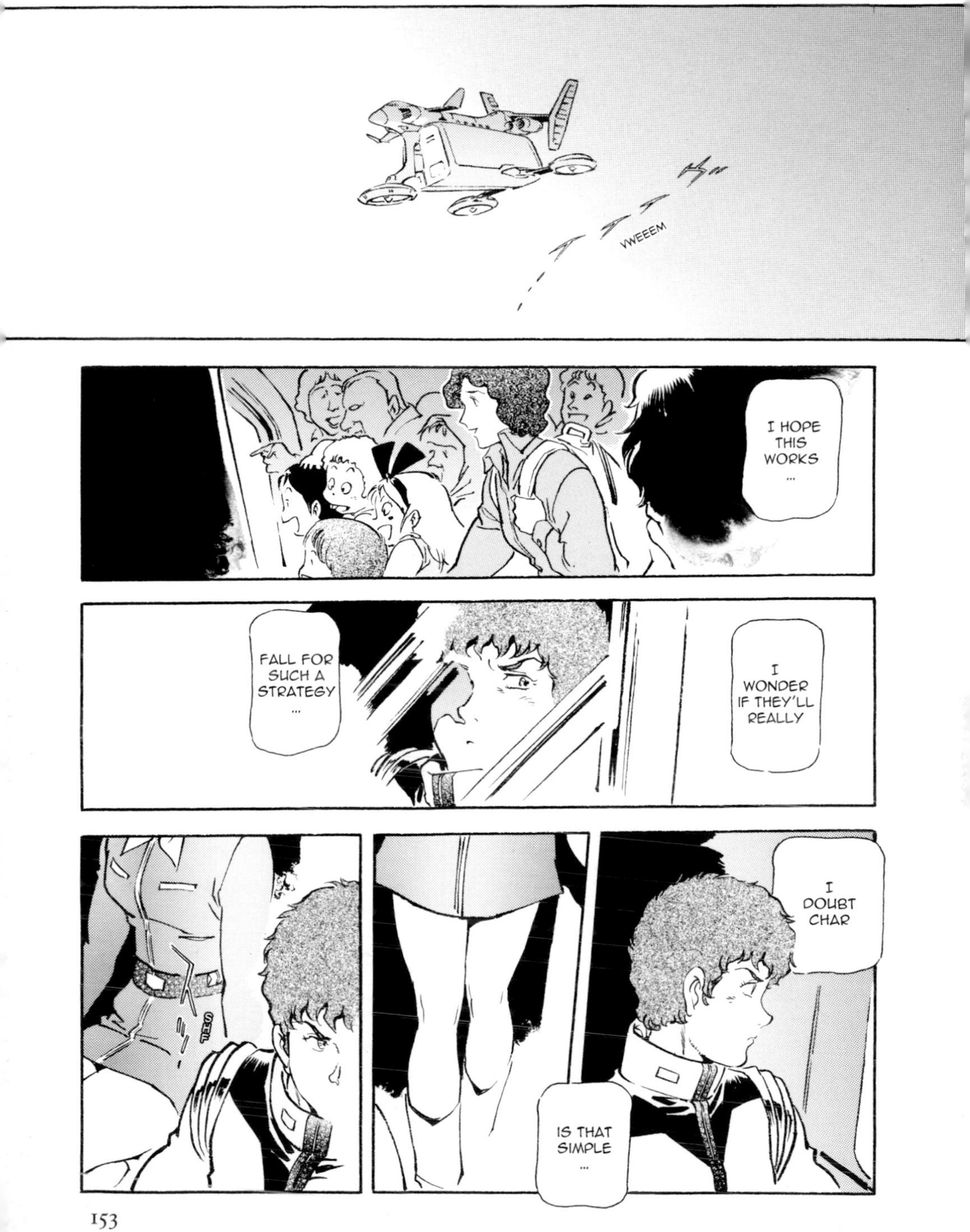
VWEEEM
I HOPE THIS WORKS ...
I WONDER IF THEY'LL REALLY
FALL FOR SUCH A STRATEGY ...
I DOUBT CHAR
IS THAT SIMPLE ...
SHF

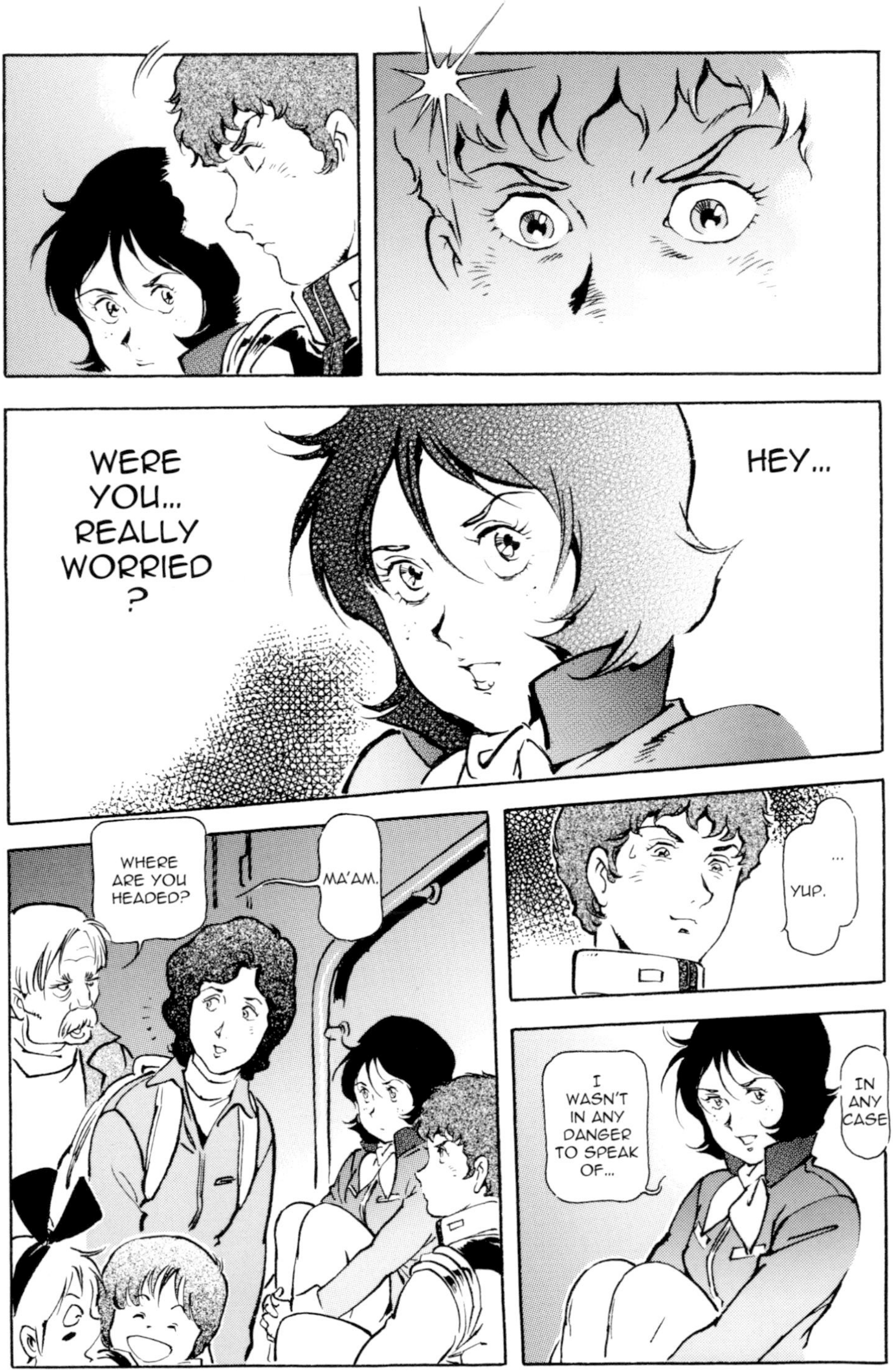
HEY...
WERE YOU... REALLY WORRIED?
... YUP.
IN ANY CASE
I WASN'T IN ANY DANGER TO SPEAK OF...
MA'AM.
WHERE ARE YOU HEADED?

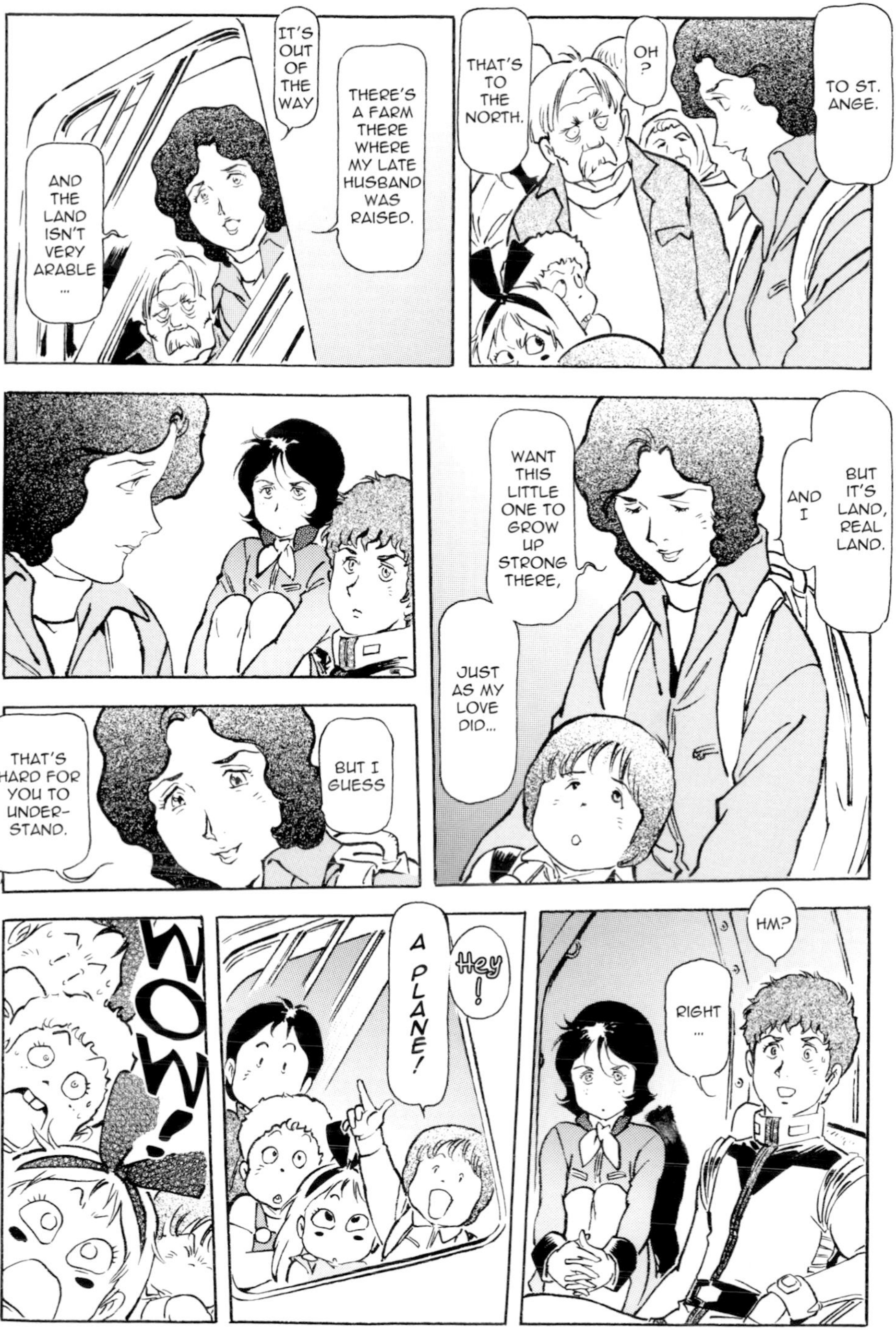
TO ST. ANGE.
OH?
THAT'S TO THE NORTH.
THERE'S A FARM THERE WHERE MY LATE HUSBAND WAS RAISED.
IT'S OUT OF THE WAY
AND THE LAND ISN'T VERY ARABLE ...
BUT IT'S LAND, REAL LAND.
AND I
WANT THIS LITTLE ONE TO GROW UP STRONG THERE,
JUST AS MY LOVE DID...
BUT I GUESS
THAT'S HARD FOR YOU TO UNDERSTAND.
HM?
RIGHT ...
Hey!
A PLANE!
WOW!

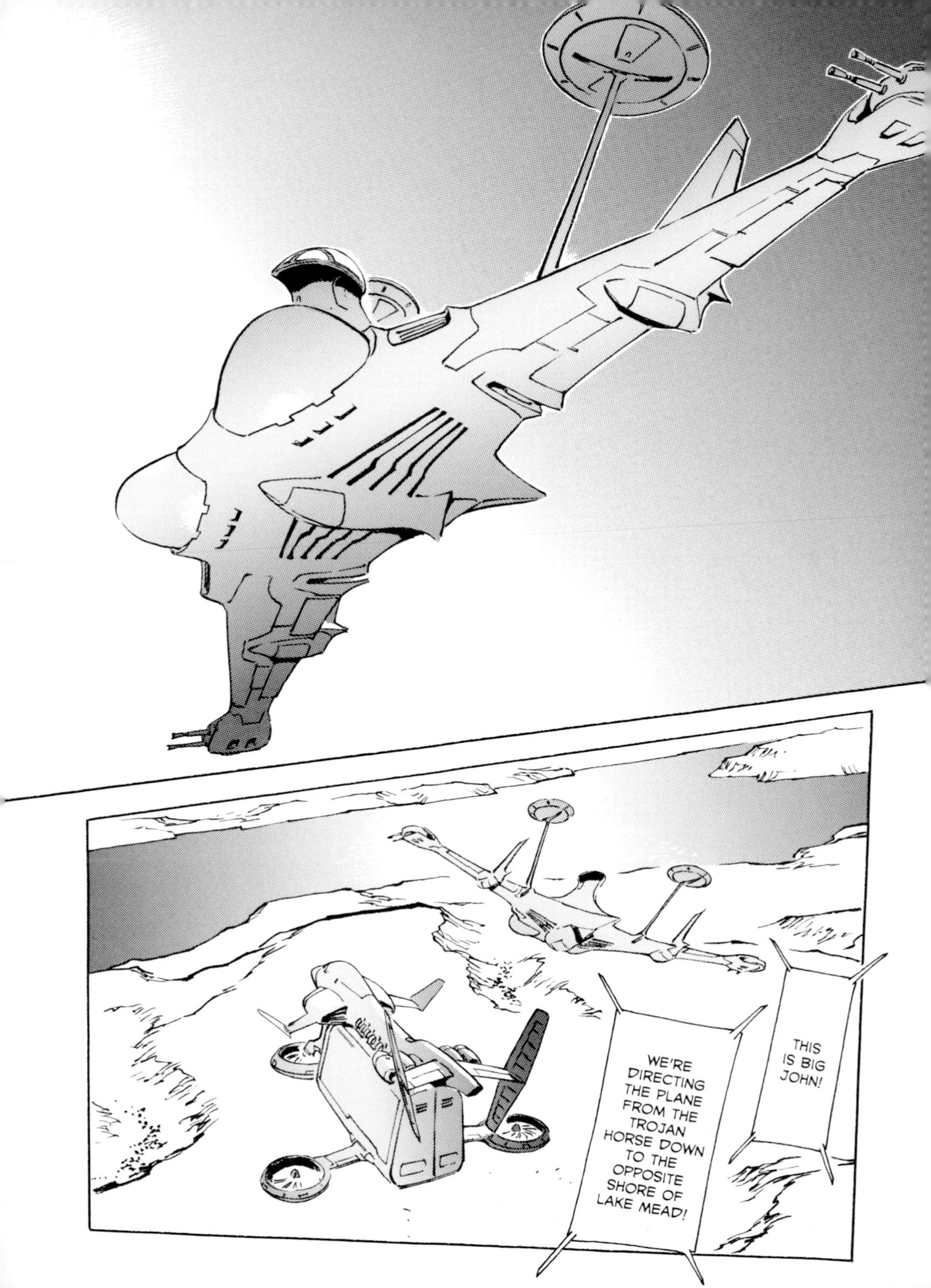
THIS IS BIG JOHN!
WE'RE DIRECTING THE PLANE FROM THE TROJAN HORSE DOWN TO THE OPPOSITE SHORE OF LAKE MEAD!

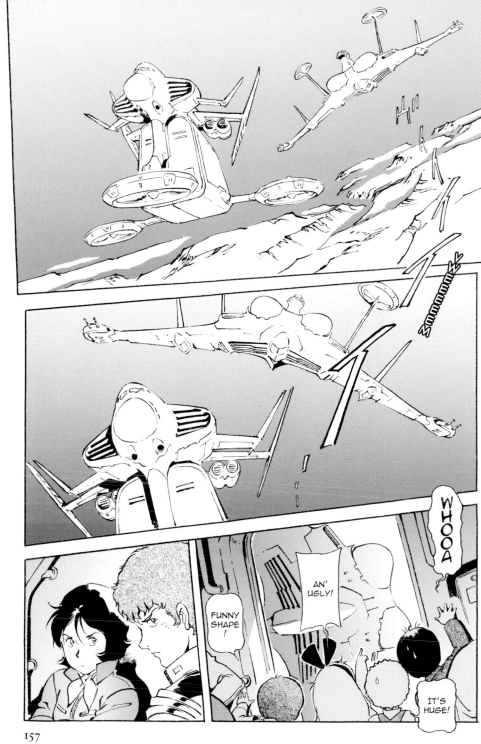

FUNNY
SHAPE
!

AN'
UGLY!

WHOOA

IT'S
HUGE!

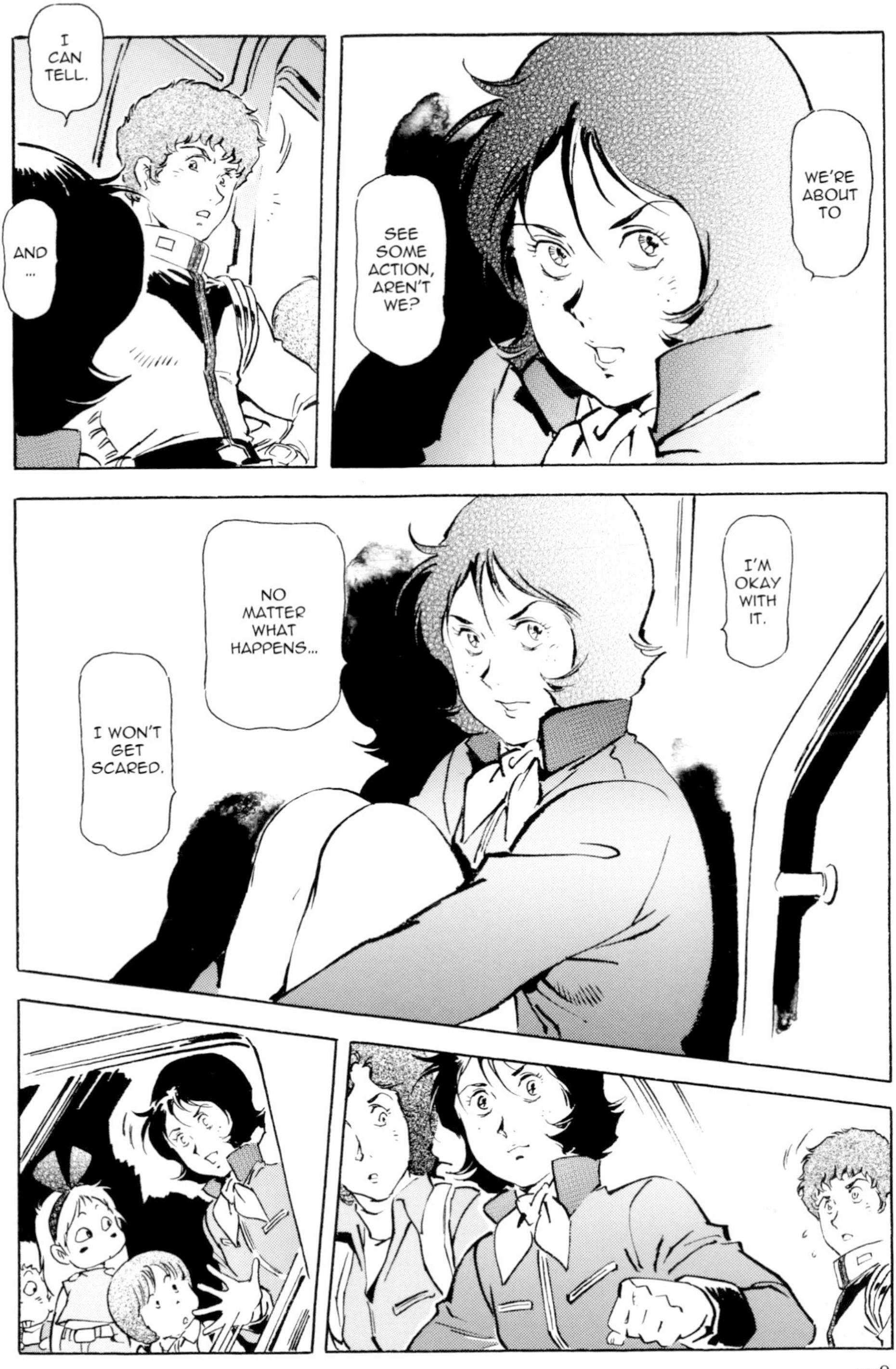
WE'RE ABOUT TO
SEE SOME ACTION, AREN'T WE?
I CAN TELL.
AND ...
I'M OKAY WITH IT.
NO MATTER WHAT HAPPENS...
I WON'T GET SCARED.

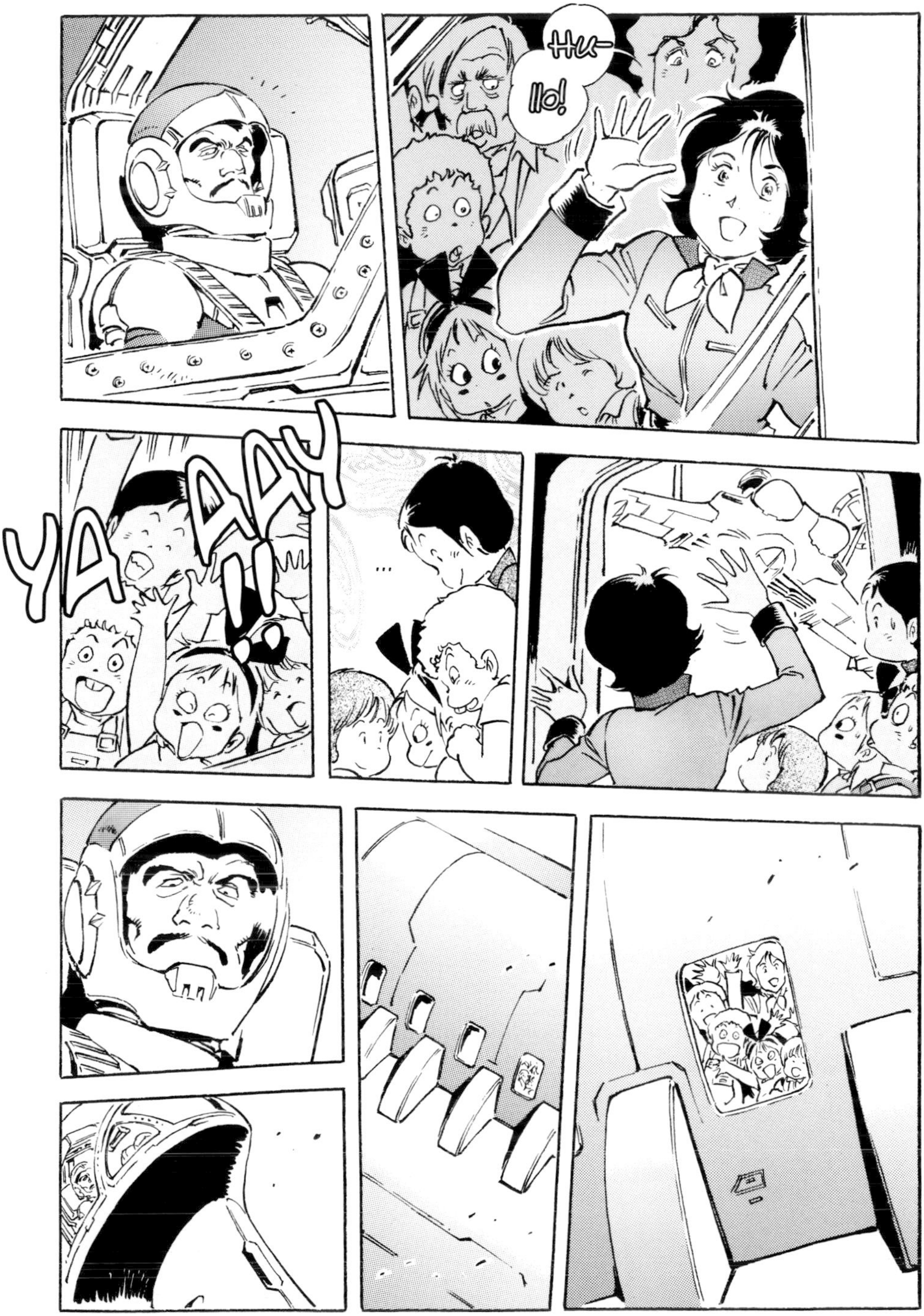
HU-
llo!
...
YA AAY !!

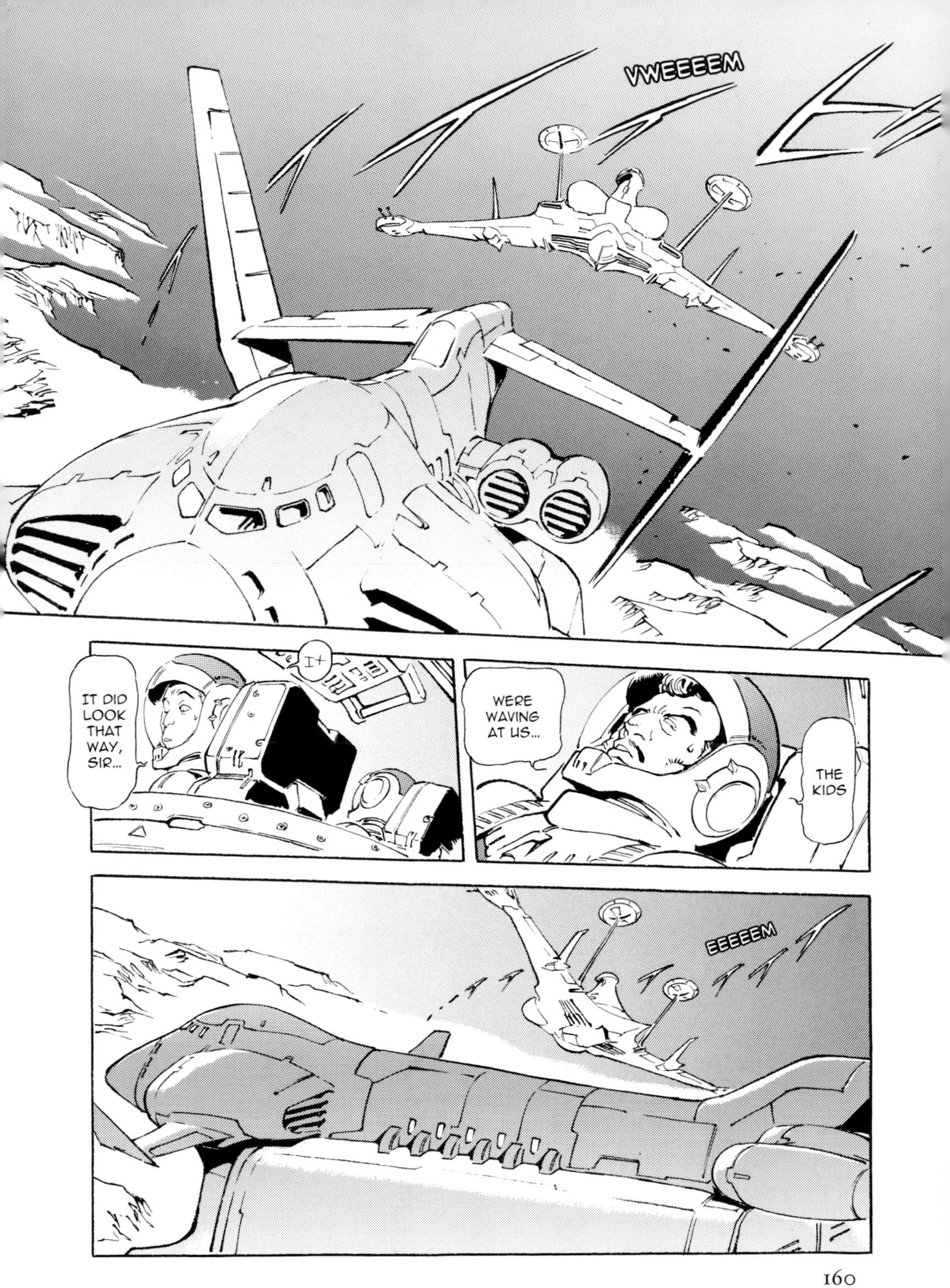
VWEEEEM
THE KIDS
WERE WAVING AT US...
IT DID LOOK THAT WAY, SIR...
EEEEEM

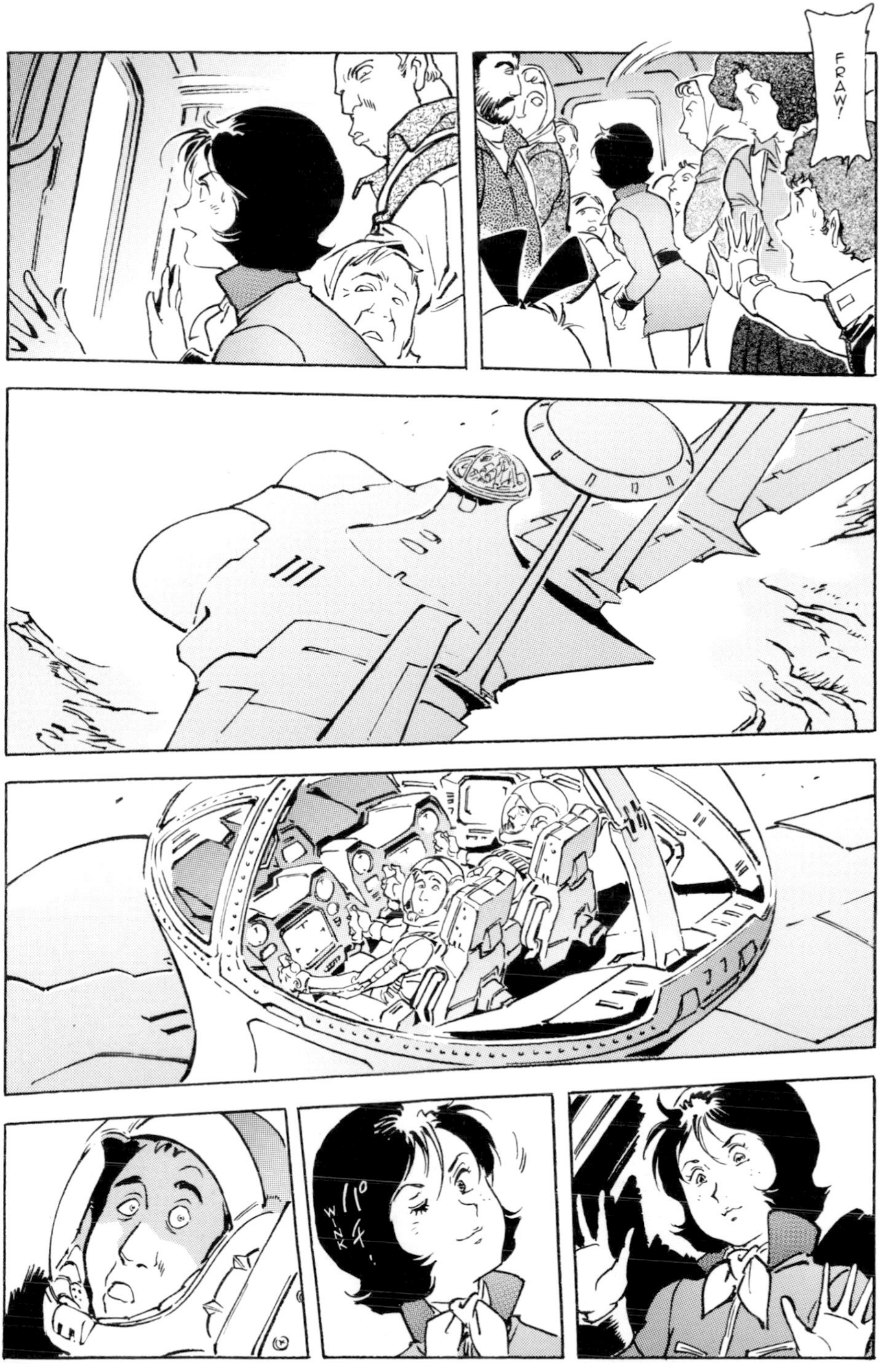
FRAW!
パチ!
WINK

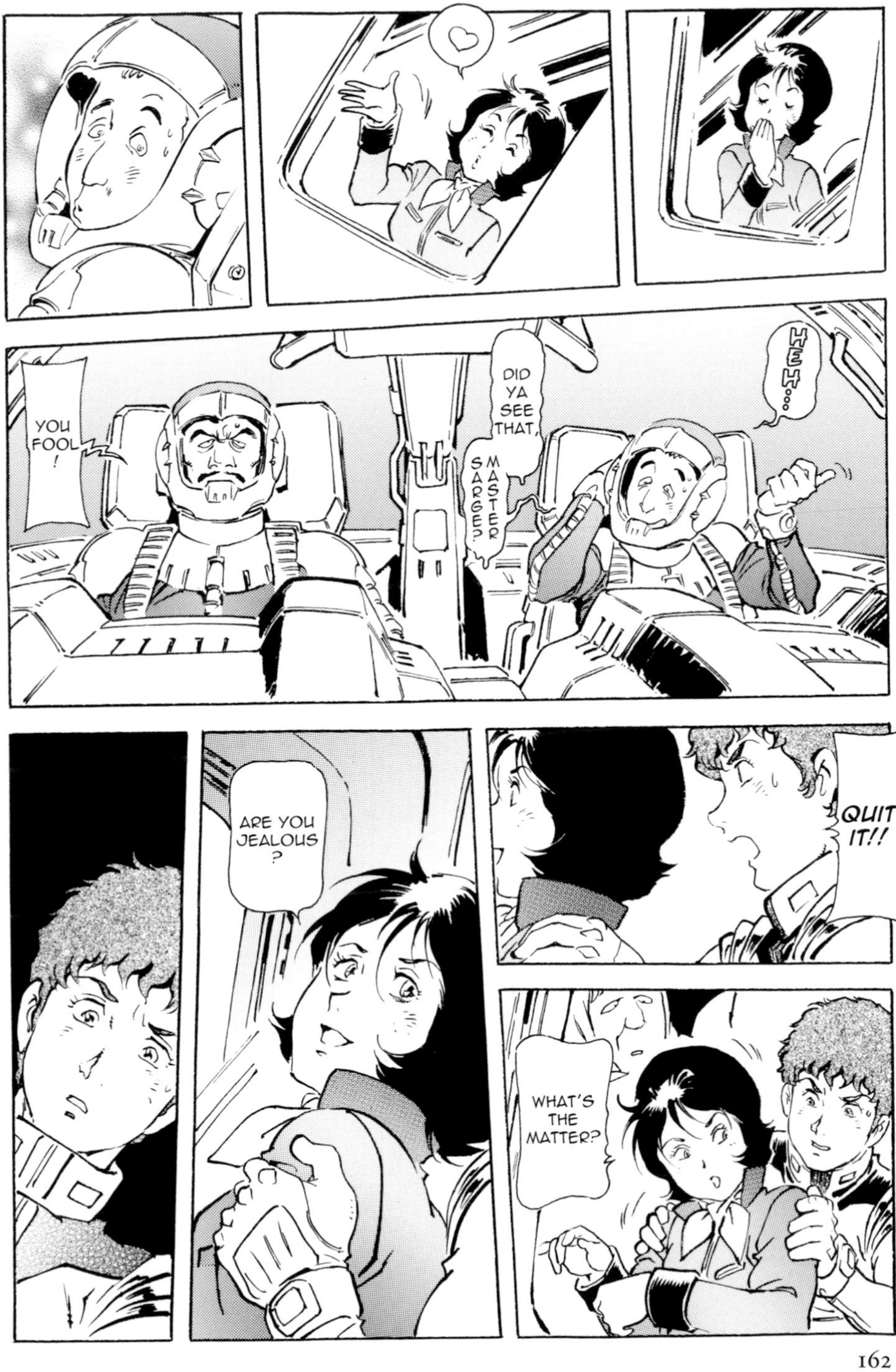
HEH...
DID YA SEE THAT, MASTER SARGE?
YOU FOOL!
QUIT IT!!
WHAT'S THE MATTER?
ARE YOU JEALOUS?

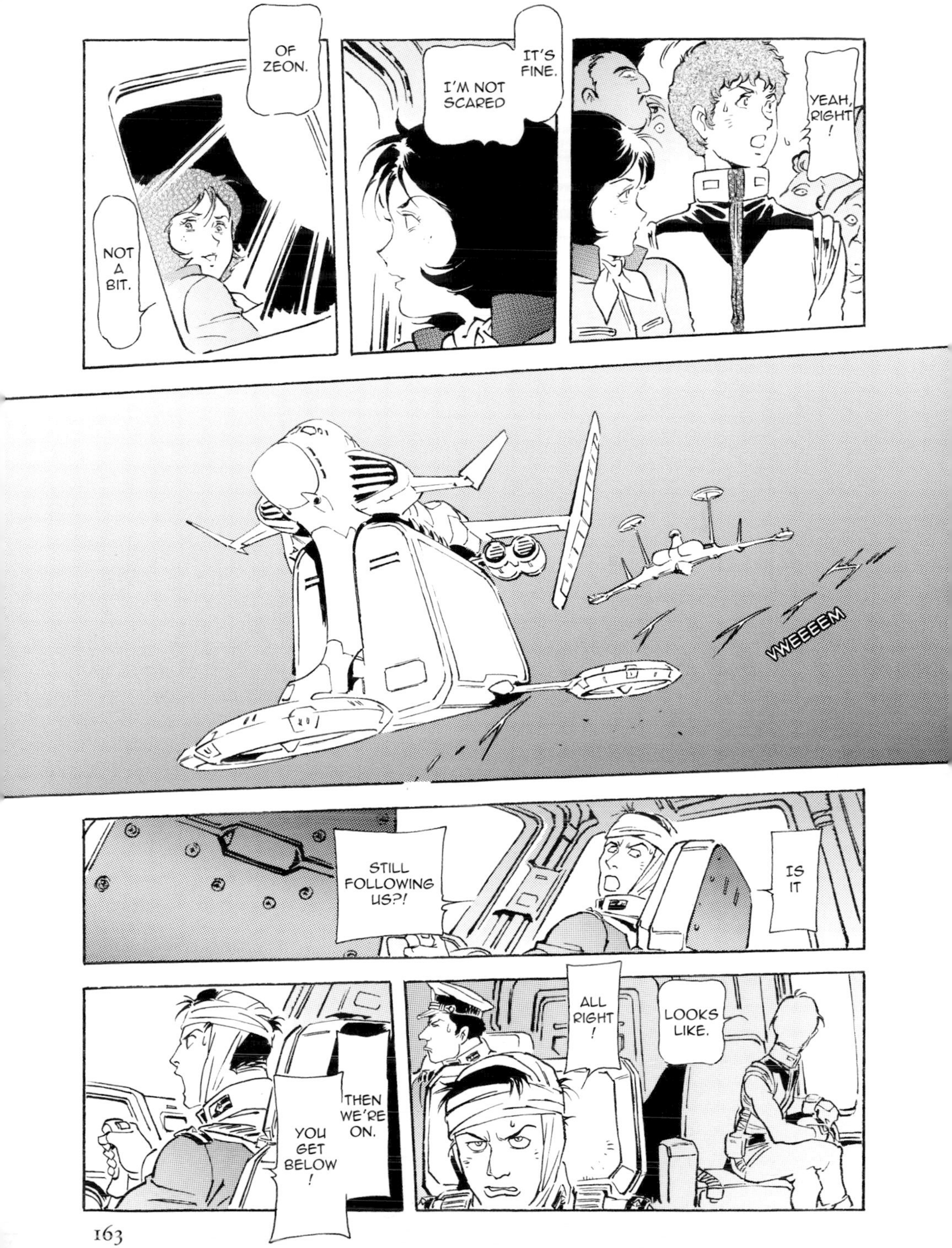
YEAH, RIGHT!
IT'S FINE.
I'M NOT SCARED
OF ZEON.
NOT A BIT.
VWEEEEM
IS IT
STILL FOLLOWING US?!
LOOKS LIKE.
ALL RIGHT!
THEN WE'RE ON.
YOU GET BELOW!

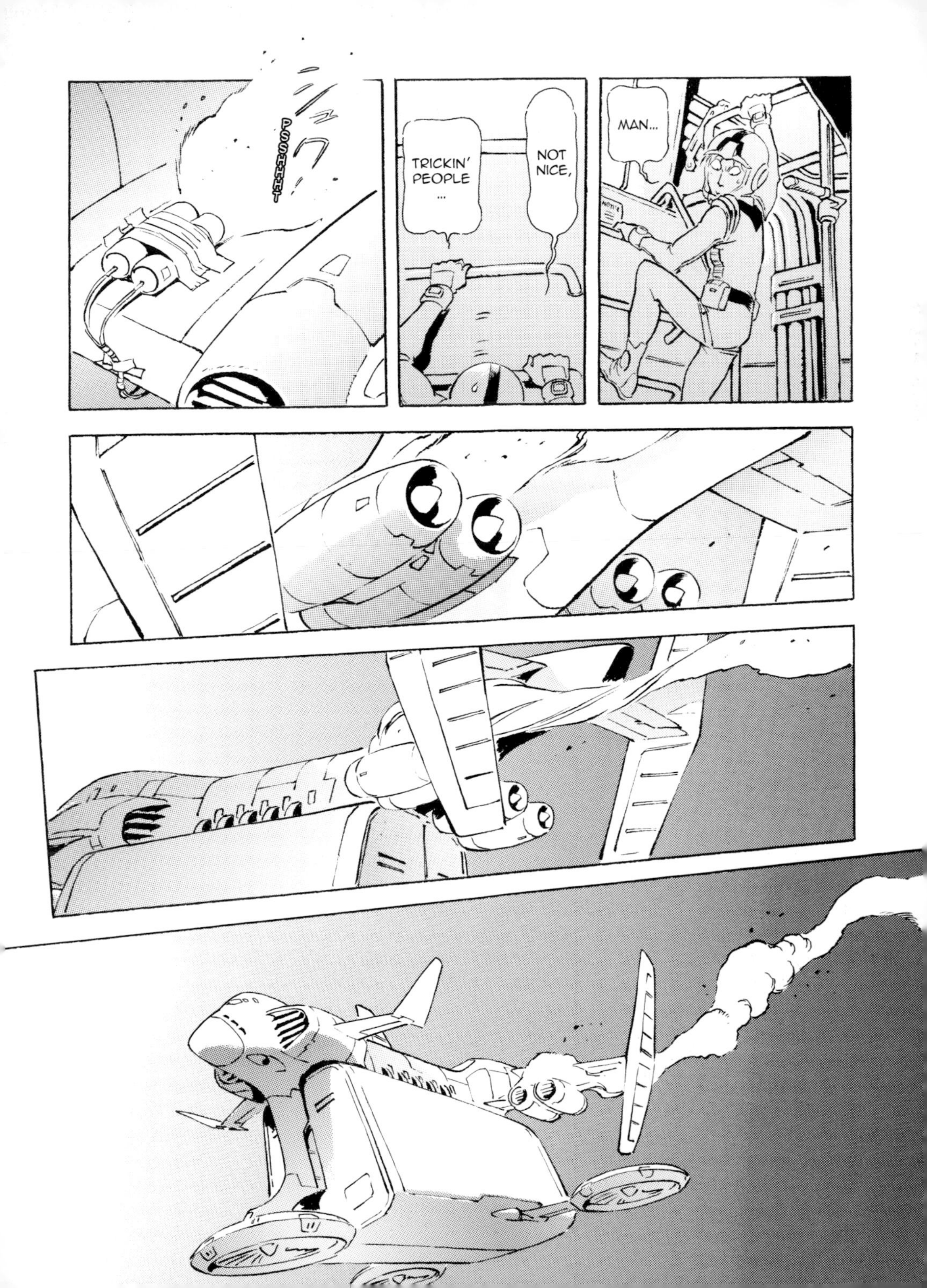
MAN...
NOT NICE,
TRICKIN' PEOPLE ...
PSSHHHT

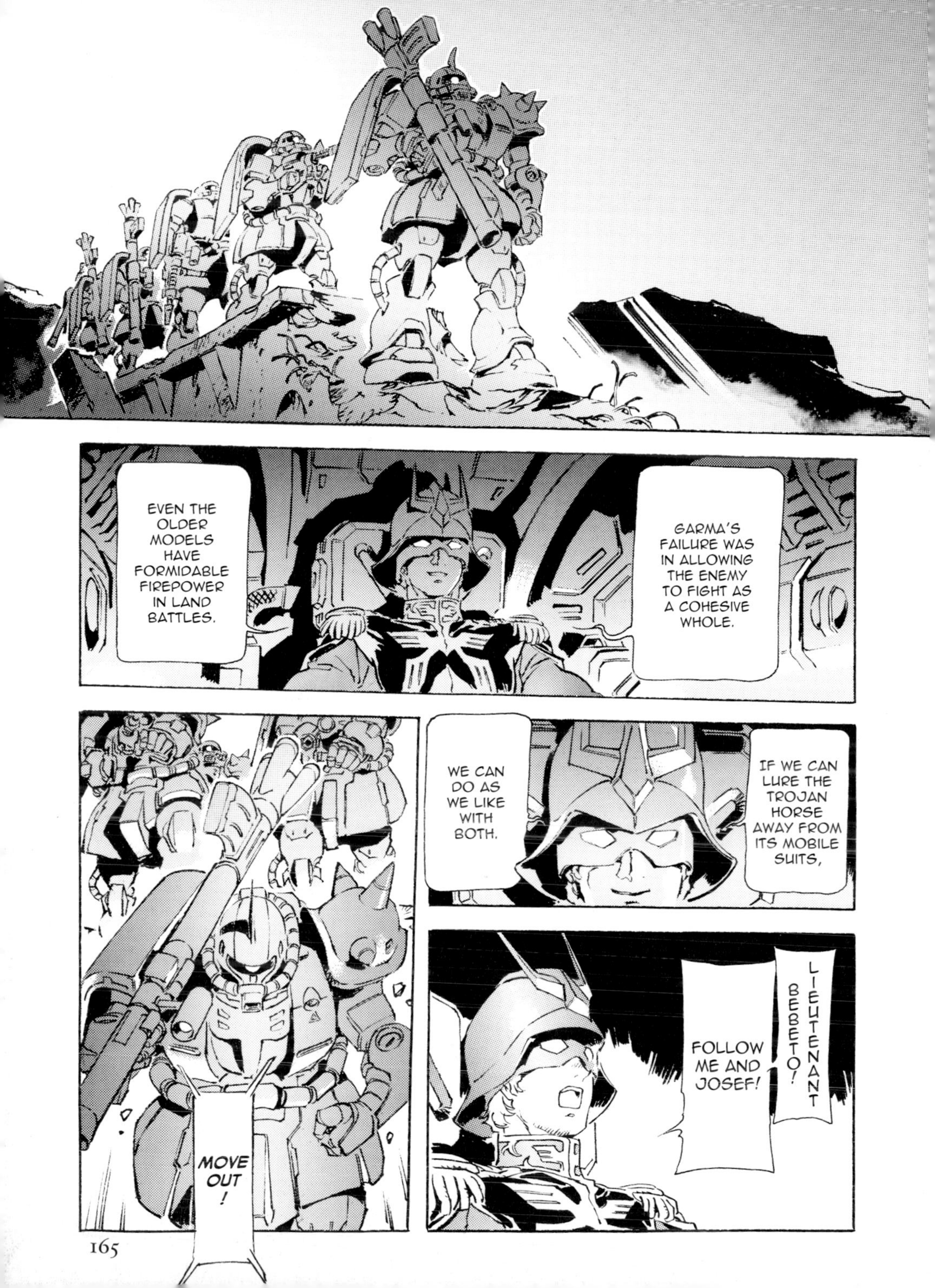
GARMA'S FAILURE WAS IN ALLOWING THE ENEMY TO FIGHT AS A COHESIVE WHOLE.
EVEN THE OLDER MODELS HAVE FORMIDABLE FIREPOWER IN LAND BATTLES.
IF WE CAN LURE THE TROJAN HORSE AWAY FROM ITS MOBILE SUITS,
WE CAN DO AS WE LIKE WITH BOTH.
LIEUTENANT BEBETO!
FOLLOW ME AND JOSEF!
MOVE OUT!

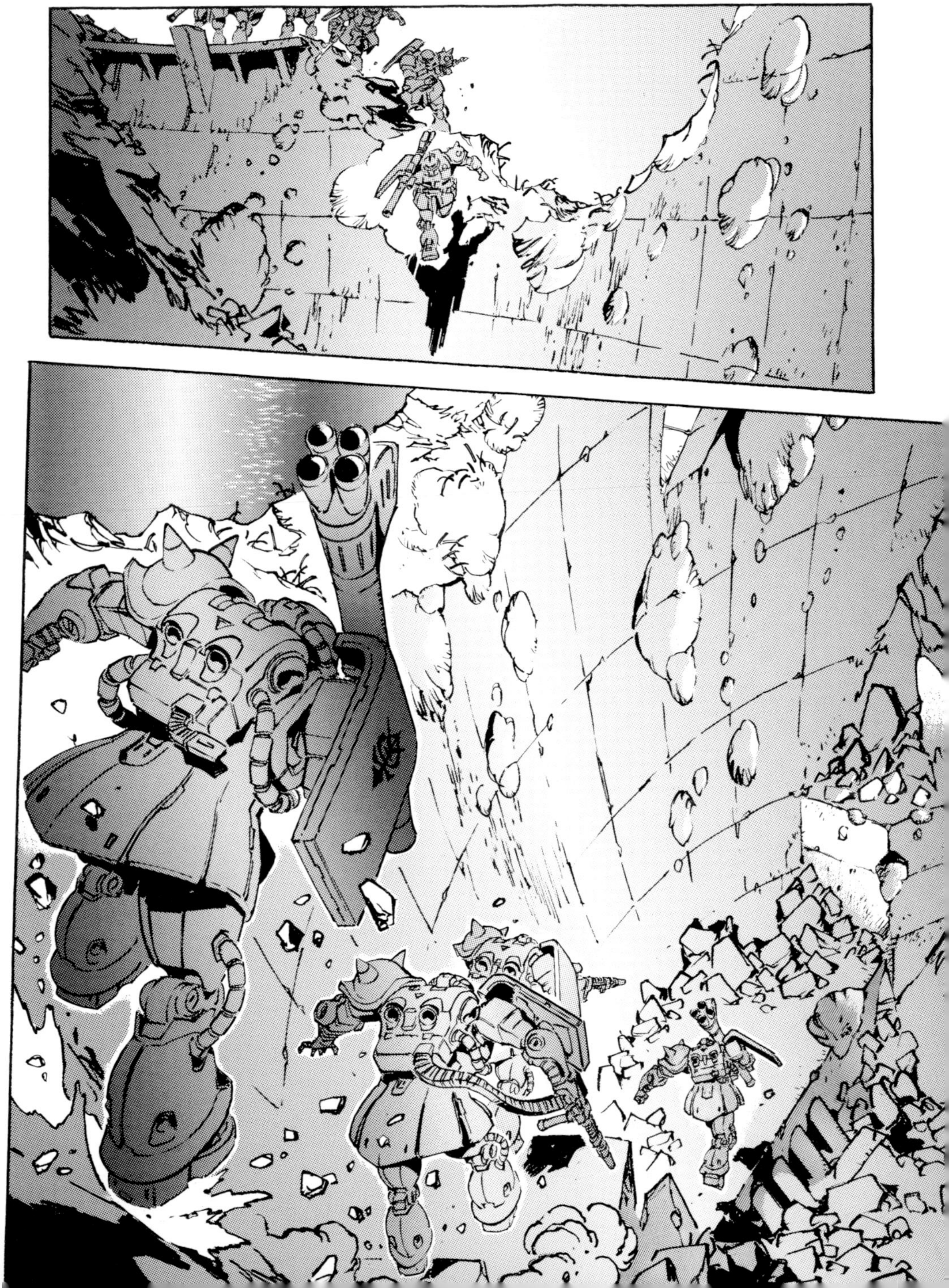

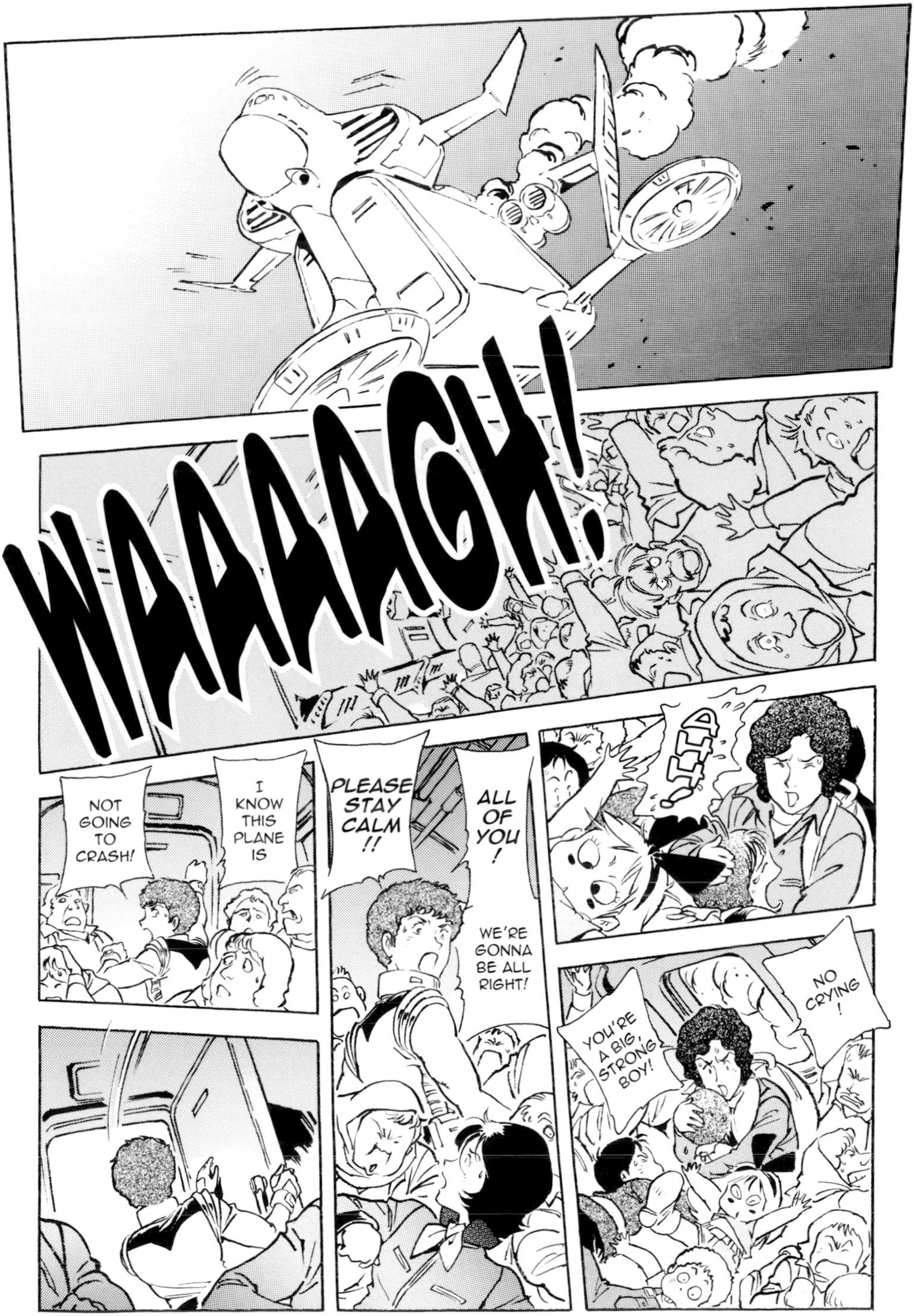
WAAAGH!
AH!!
NO CRYING!
YOU'RE A BIG, STRONG BOY!
PLEASE STAY CALM!!
ALL OF YOU!
WE'RE GONNA BE ALL RIGHT!
I KNOW THIS PLANE IS
NOT GOING TO CRASH!

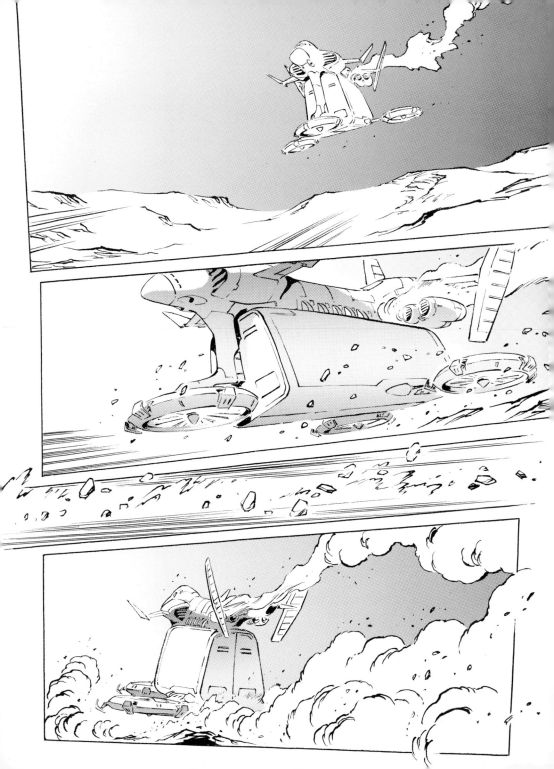

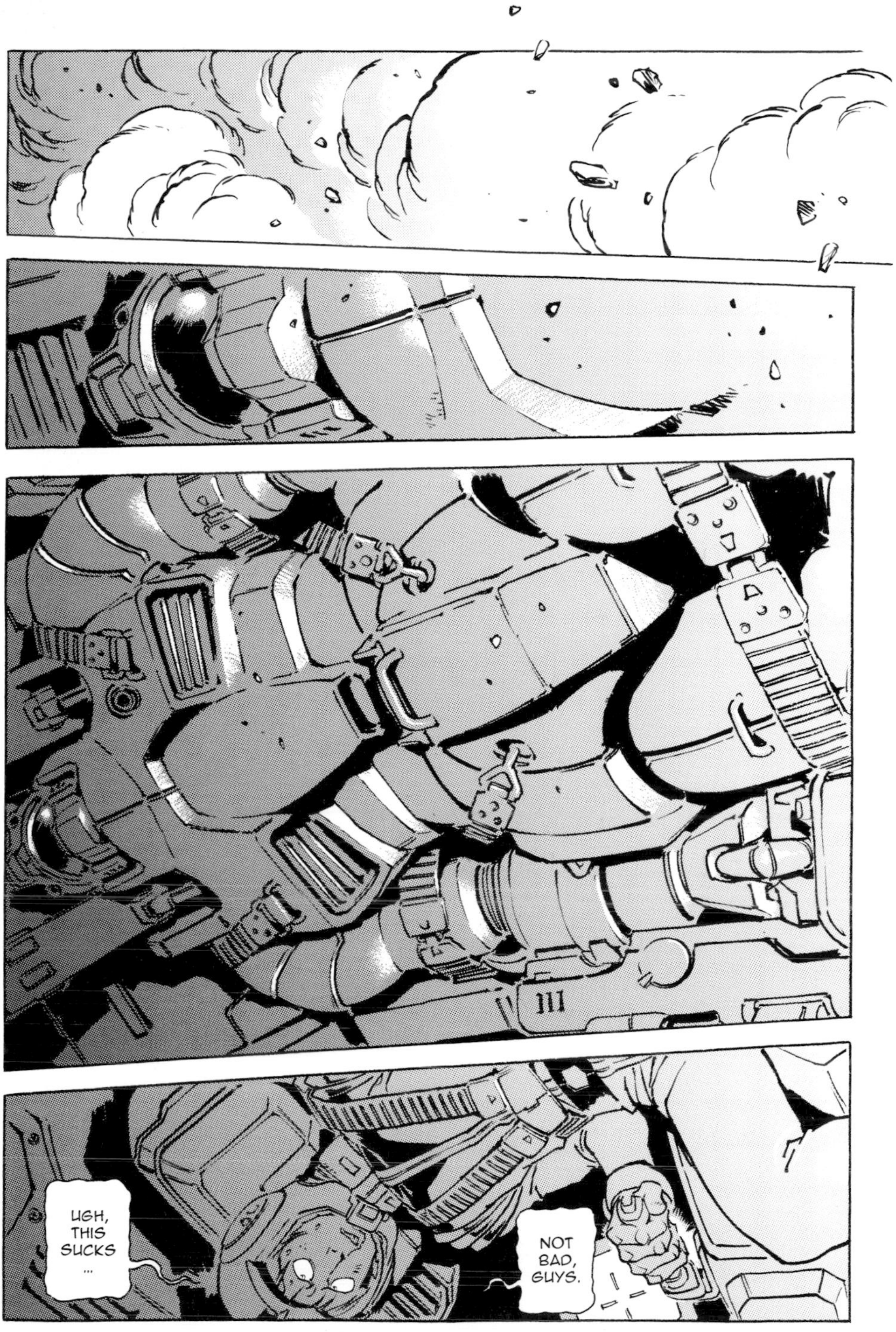
NOT BAD, GUYS.
UGH, THIS SUCKS ...

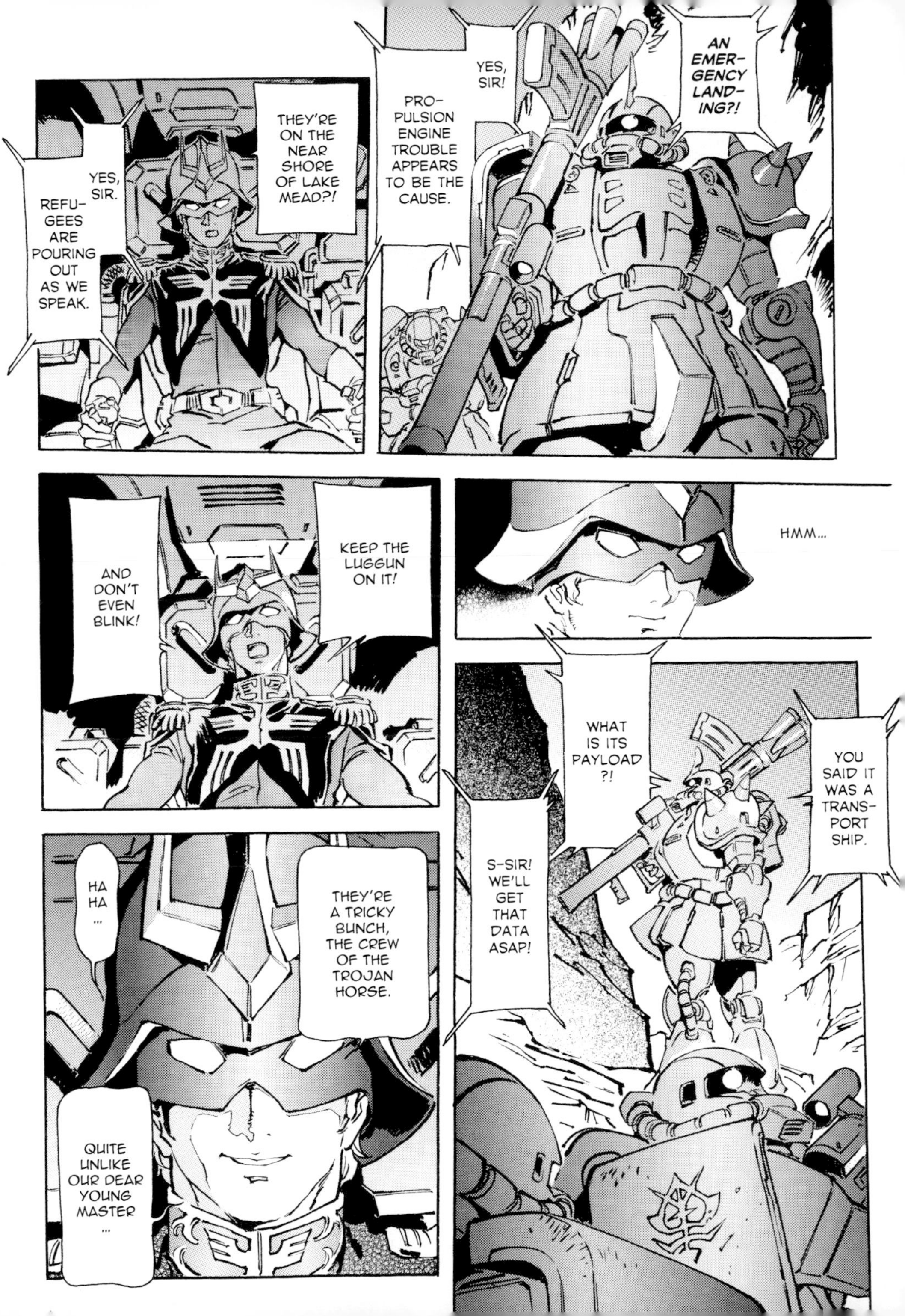
AN EMERGENCY LANDING?!
YES, SIR!
PROPULSION ENGINE TROUBLE APPEARS TO BE THE CAUSE.
THEY'RE ON THE NEAR SHORE OF LAKE MEAD?!
YES, SIR.
REFUGEES ARE POURING OUT AS WE SPEAK.
HMM...
YOU SAID IT WAS A TRANSPORT SHIP.
WHAT IS ITS PAYLOAD?!
S-SIR! WE'LL GET THAT DATA ASAP!
KEEP THE LUGGUN ON IT!
AND DON'T EVEN BLINK!
THEY'RE A TRICKY BUNCH, THE CREW OF THE TROJAN HORSE.
HA HA ...
QUITE UNLIKE OUR DEAR YOUNG MASTER ...

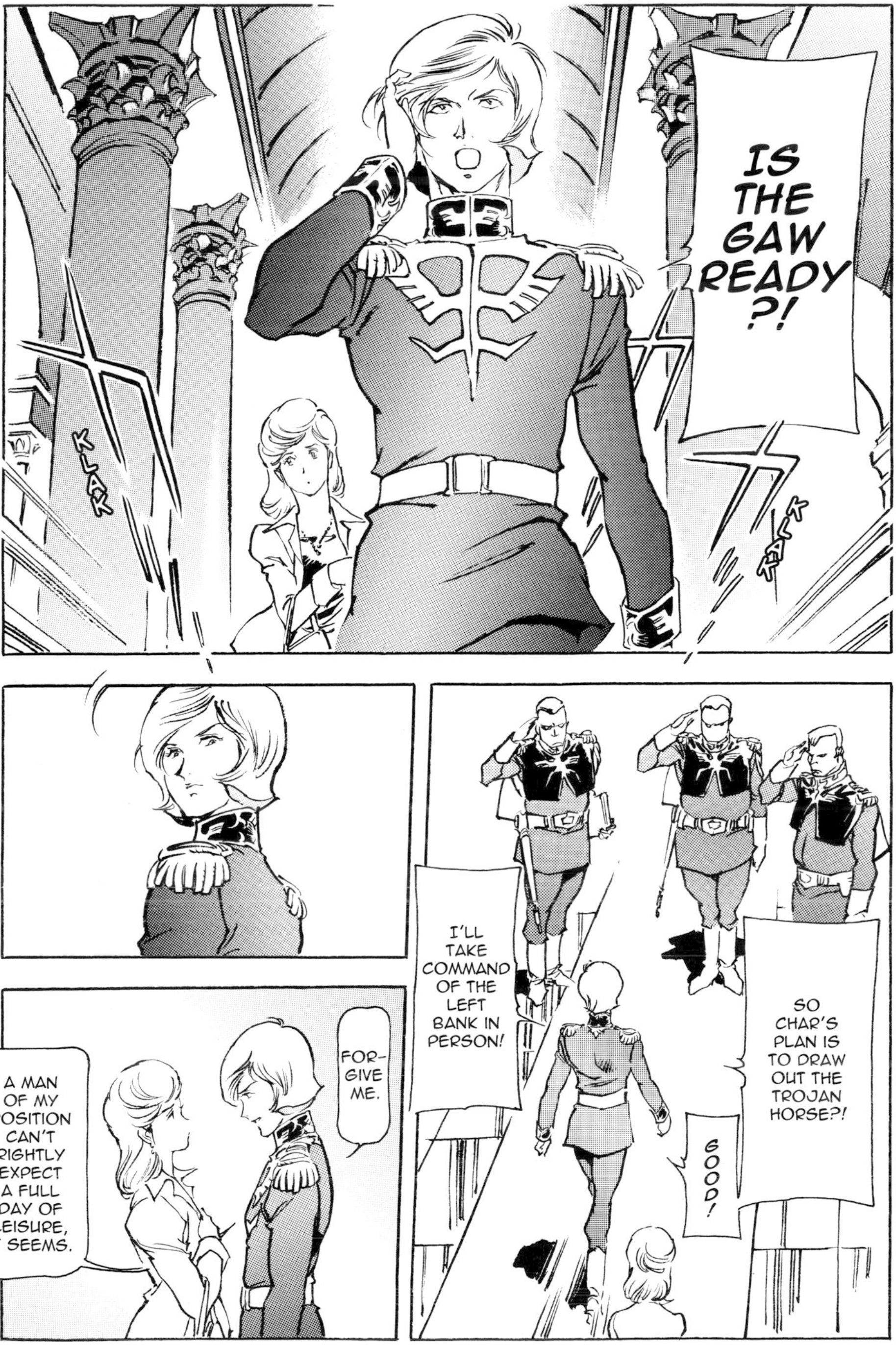
IS THE GAW READY?!
KLAK
KLAK
I'LL TAKE COMMAND OF THE LEFT BANK IN PERSON!
SO CHAR'S PLAN IS TO DRAW OUT THE TROJAN HORSE?!
GOOD!
FOR-GIVE ME.
A MAN OF MY POSITION CAN'T RIGHTLY EXPECT A FULL DAY OF LEISURE, IT SEEMS.

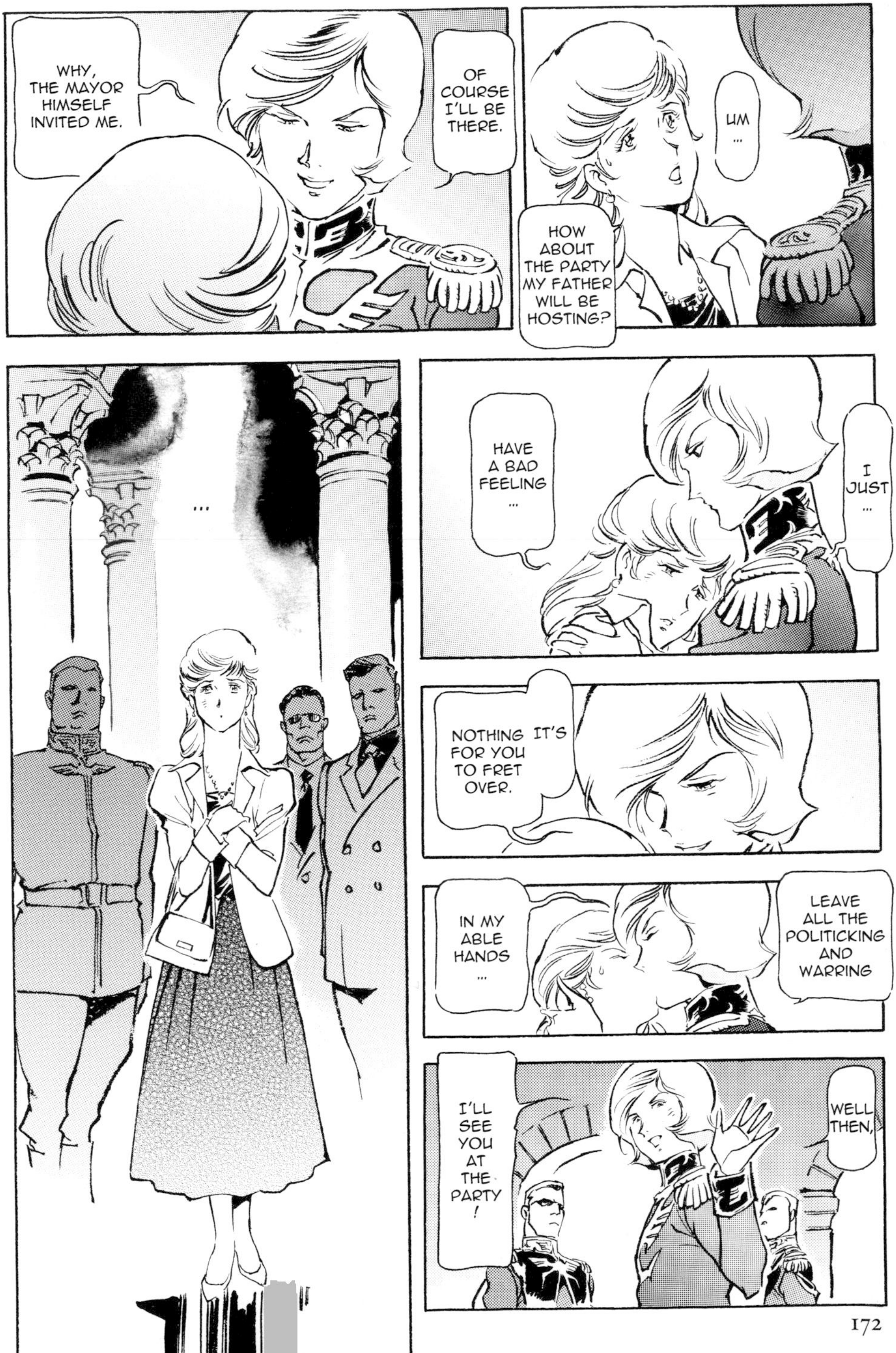
UM ...
HOW ABOUT THE PARTY MY FATHER WILL BE HOSTING?
OF COURSE I'LL BE THERE.
WHY, THE MAYOR HIMSELF INVITED ME.
I JUST ...
HAVE A BAD FEELING ...
IT'S
NOTHING FOR YOU TO FRET OVER.
LEAVE ALL THE POLITICKING AND WARRING
IN MY ABLE HANDS ...
WELL THEN,
I'LL SEE YOU AT THE PARTY!
...

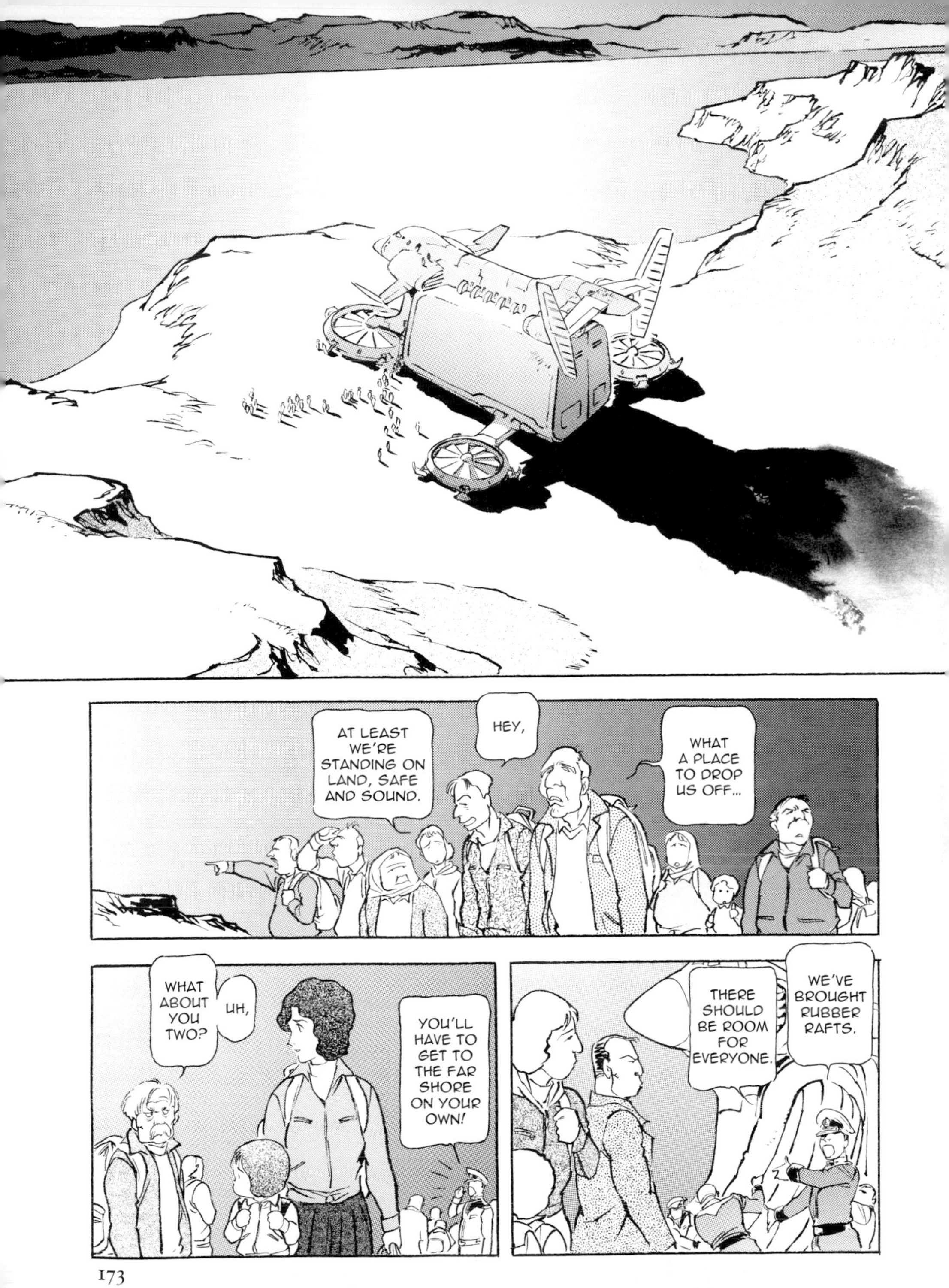
WHAT A PLACE TO DROP US OFF...
HEY,
AT LEAST WE'RE STANDING ON LAND, SAFE AND SOUND.
WE'VE BROUGHT RUBBER RAFTS.
THERE SHOULD BE ROOM FOR EVERYONE.
UH,
WHAT ABOUT YOU TWO?
YOU'LL HAVE TO GET TO THE FAR SHORE ON YOUR OWN!

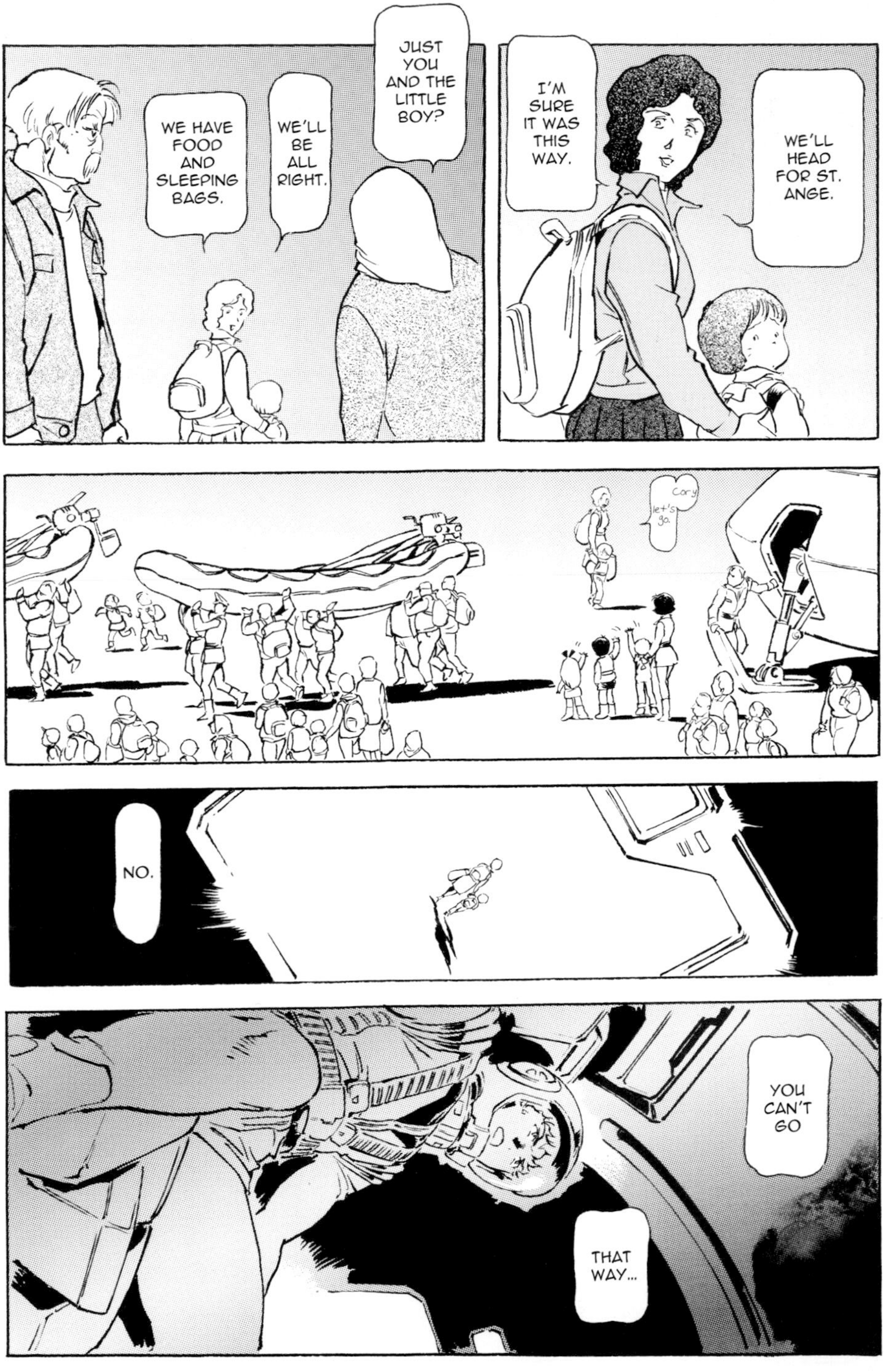
WE'LL HEAD FOR ST. ANGE.
I'M SURE IT WAS THIS WAY.
JUST YOU AND THE LITTLE BOY?
WE'LL BE ALL RIGHT.
WE HAVE FOOD AND SLEEPING BAGS.
Cory let's go.
NO.
YOU CAN'T GO
THAT WAY...

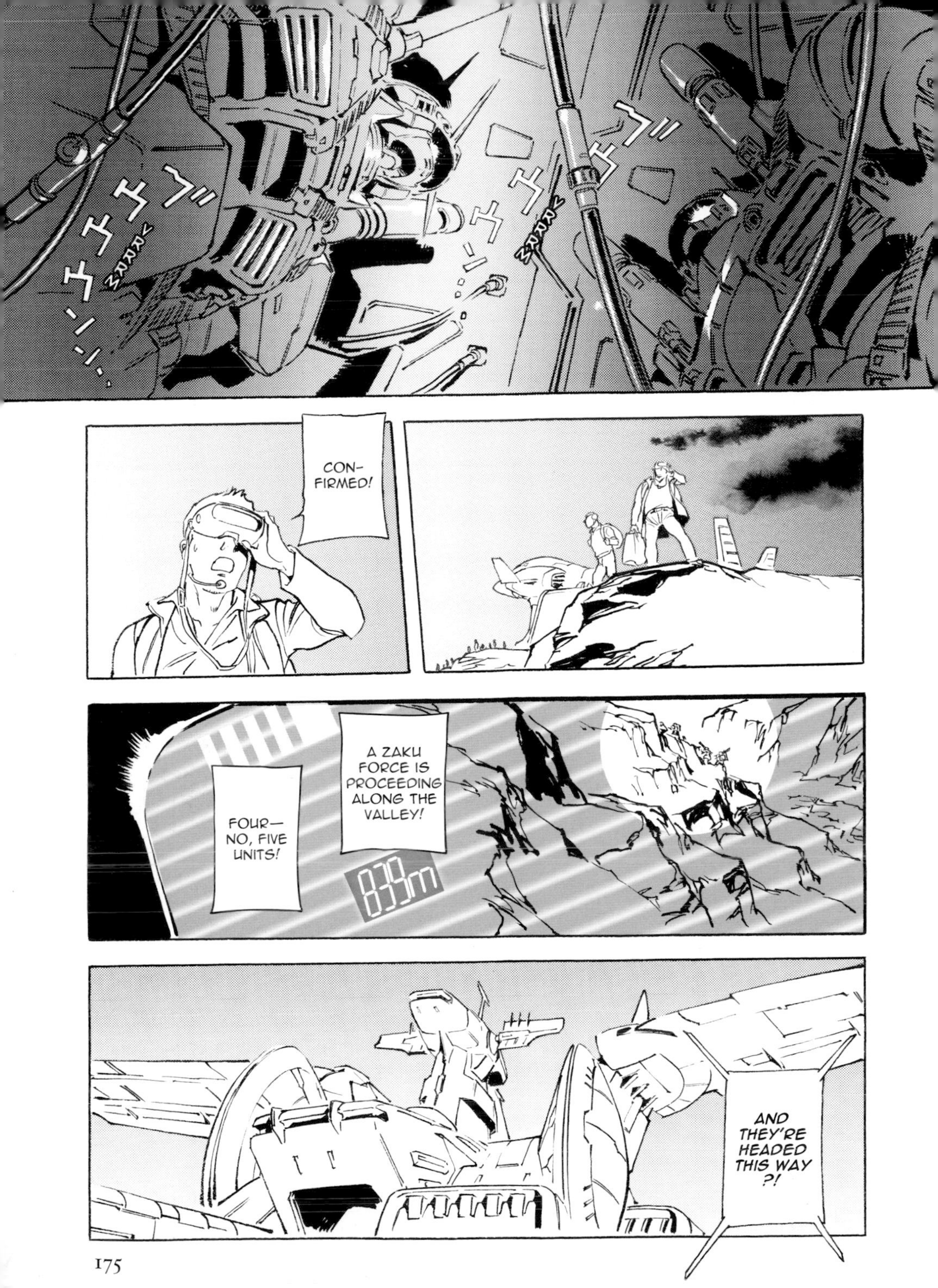
CON-FIRMED!
A ZAKU FORCE IS PROCEEDING ALONG THE VALLEY!
FOUR— NO, FIVE UNITS!
839m
AND THEY'RE HEADED THIS WAY ?!

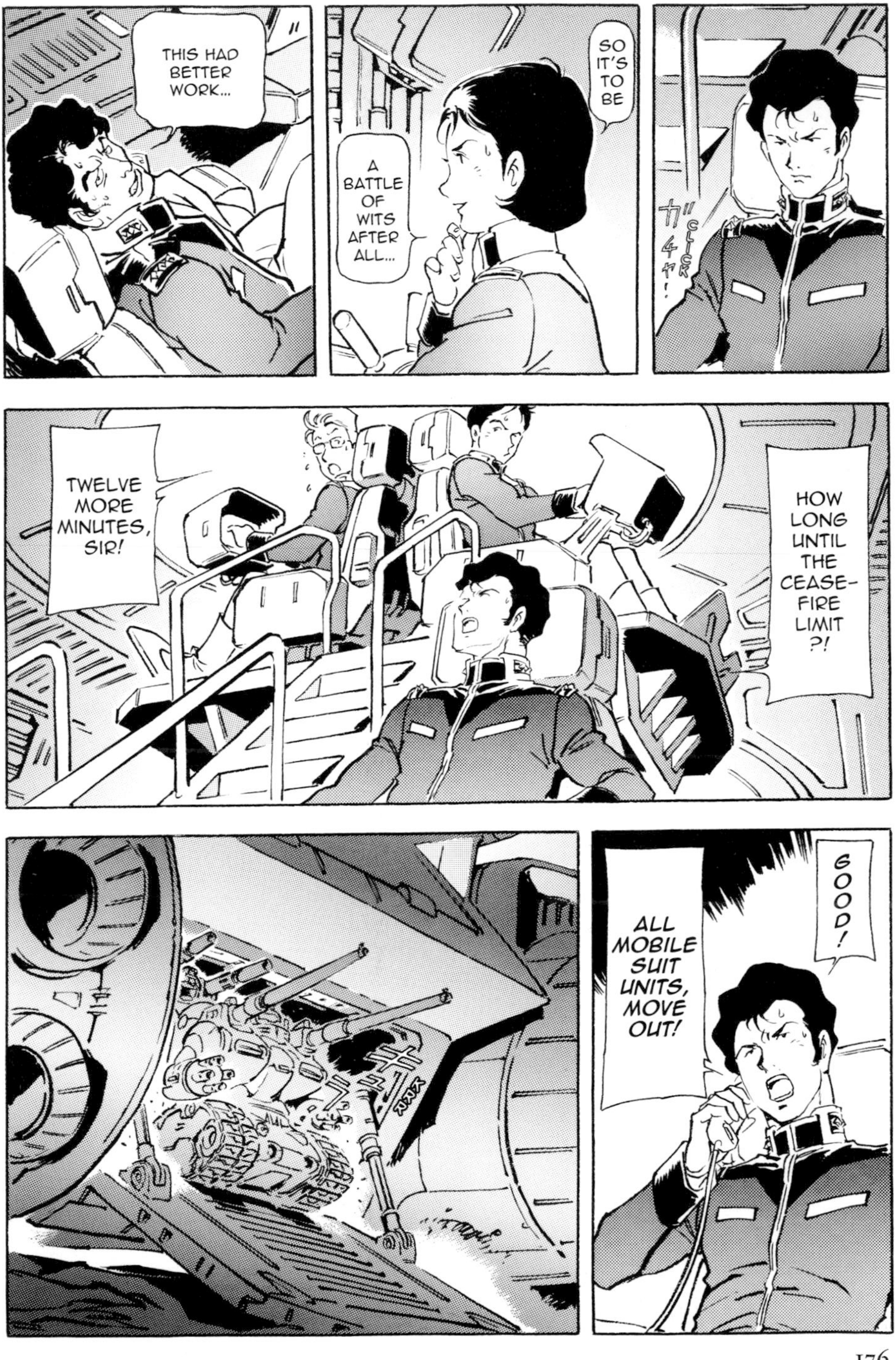
CLICK!
SO IT'S TO BE
A BATTLE OF WITS AFTER ALL...
THIS HAD BETTER WORK...
HOW LONG UNTIL THE CEASE-FIRE LIMIT?!
TWELVE MORE MINUTES, SIR!
GOOD!
ALL MOBILE SUIT UNITS, MOVE OUT!

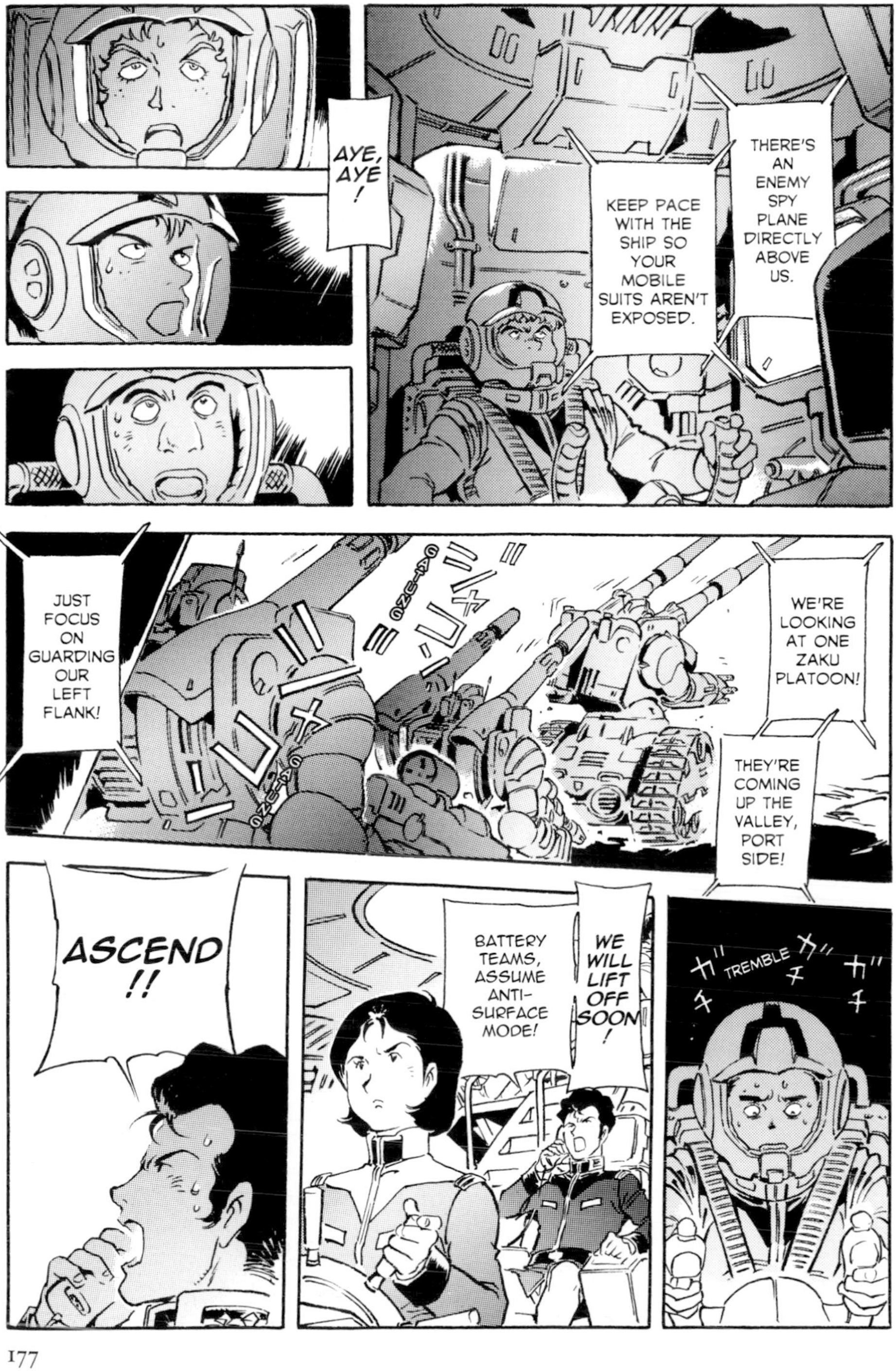
THERE'S AN ENEMY SPY PLANE DIRECTLY ABOVE US.
KEEP PACE WITH THE SHIP SO YOUR MOBILE SUITS AREN'T EXPOSED.
AYE, AYE!
WE'RE LOOKING AT ONE ZAKU PLATOON!
THEY'RE COMING UP THE VALLEY, PORT SIDE!
GA-TUNG
GA-TUNG
JUST FOCUS ON GUARDING OUR LEFT FLANK!
TREMBLE
WE WILL LIFT OFF SOON!
BATTERY TEAMS, ASSUME ANTI-SURFACE MODE!
ASCEND!!

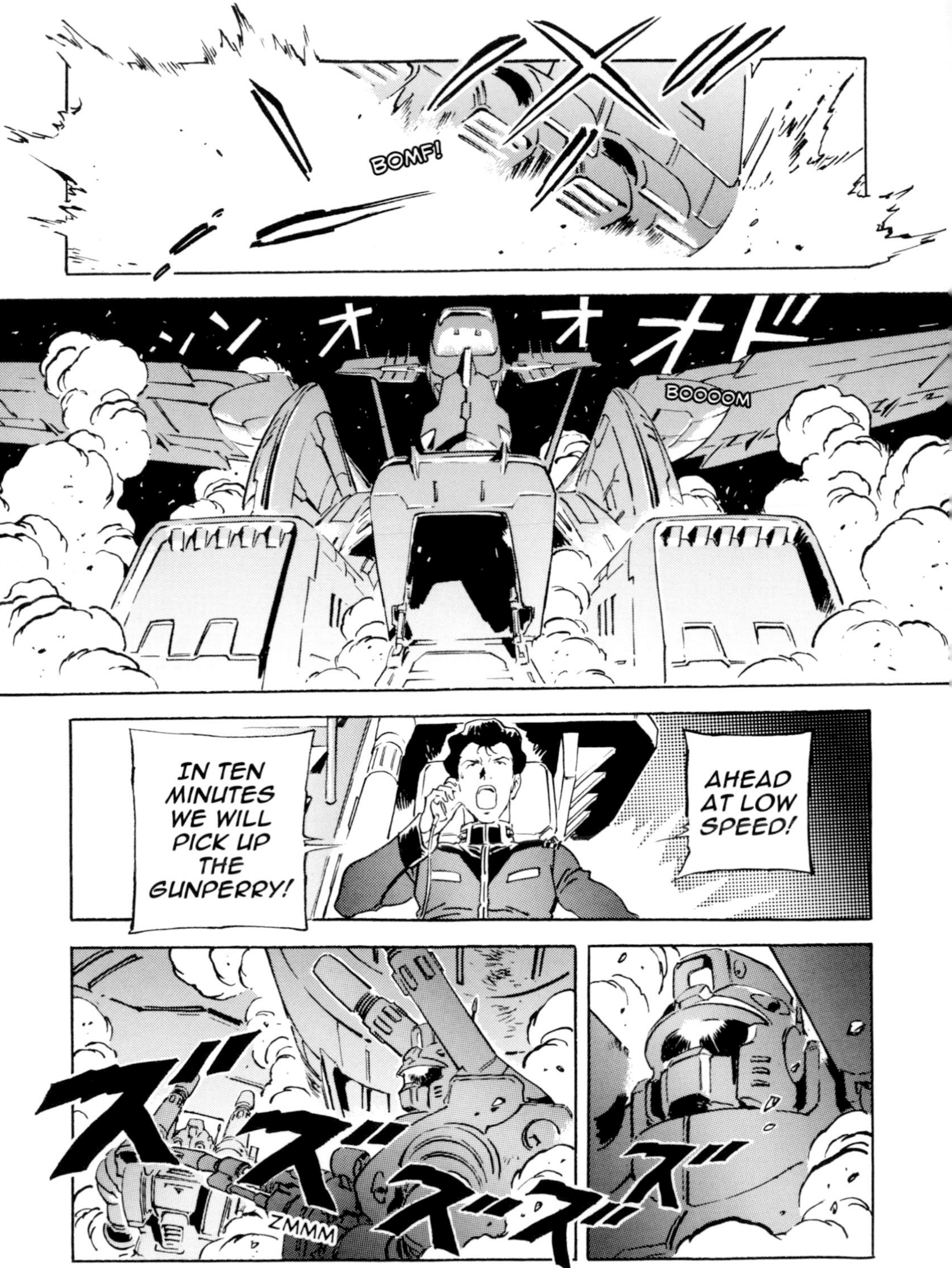
BOMF!
ドオオンッ
BOOOOM
AHEAD AT LOW SPEED!
IN TEN MINUTES WE WILL PICK UP THE GUNPERRY!
ズズズズズズ
ZMMMM

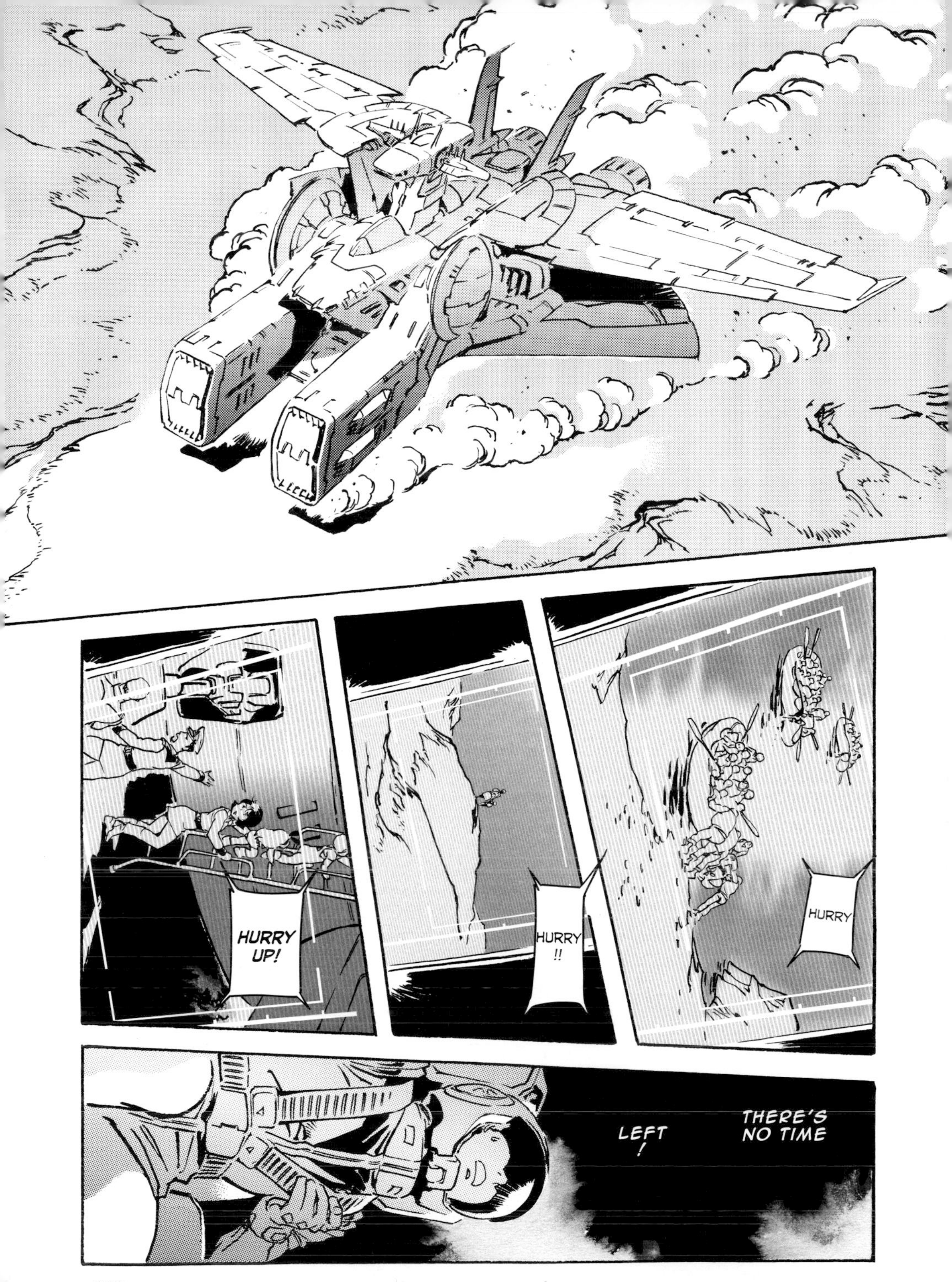
HURRY
HURRY !!
HURRY UP!
THERE'S NO TIME
LEFT !

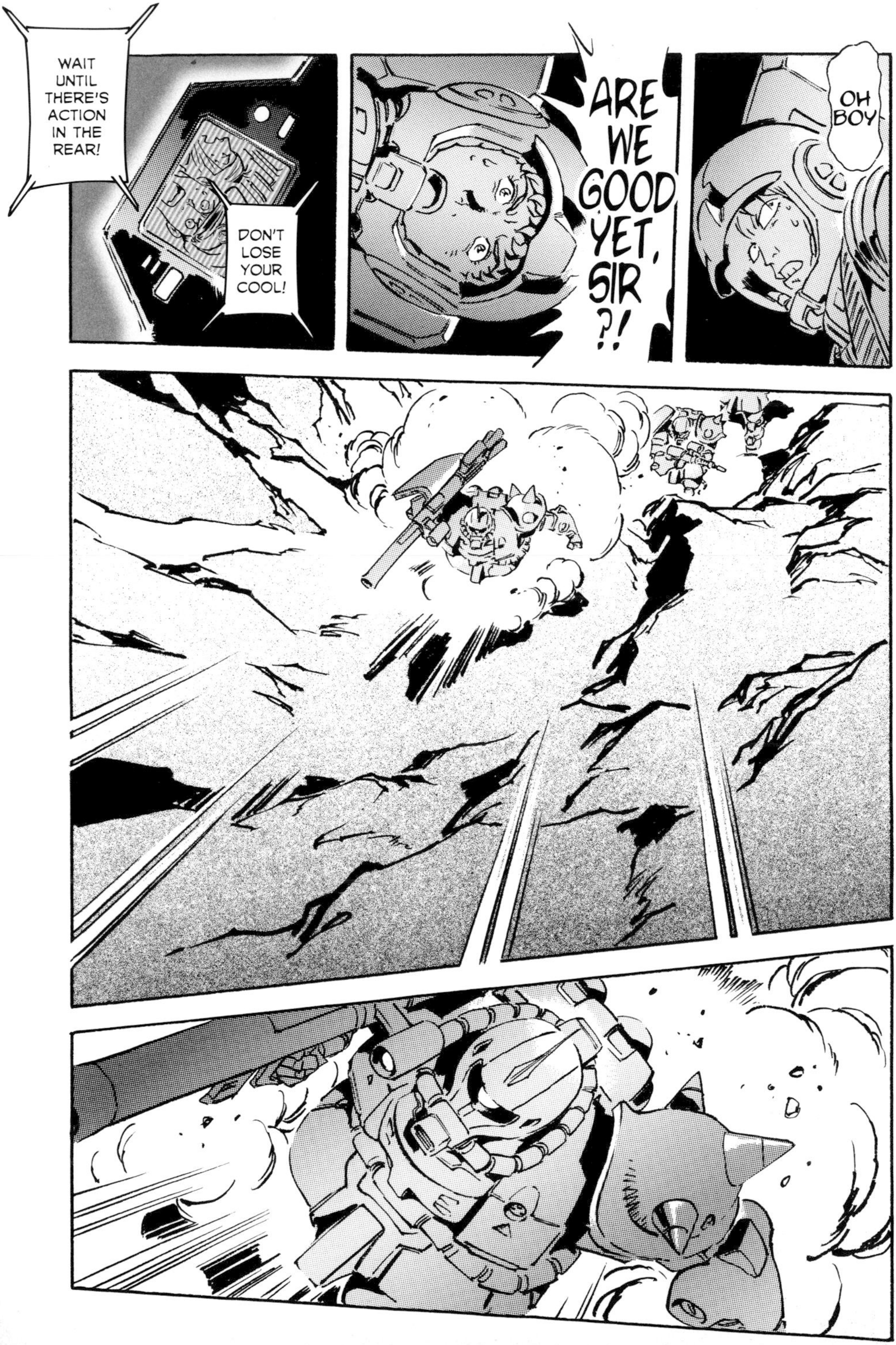
OH BOY
ARE WE GOOD YET, SIR?!
WAIT UNTIL THERE'S ACTION IN THE REAR!
DON'T LOSE YOUR COOL!

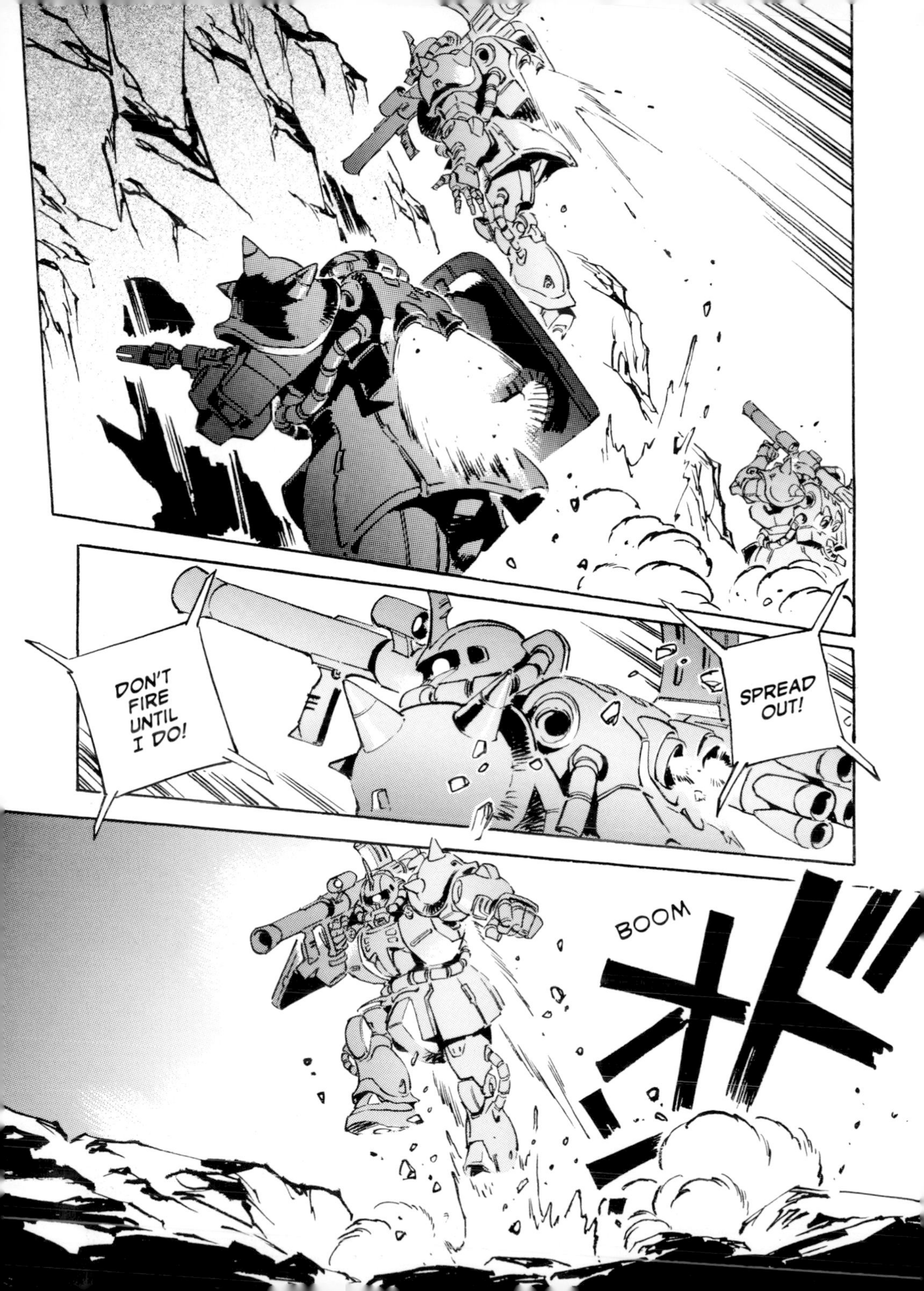
SPREAD OUT!
DON'T FIRE UNTIL I DO!
BOOM

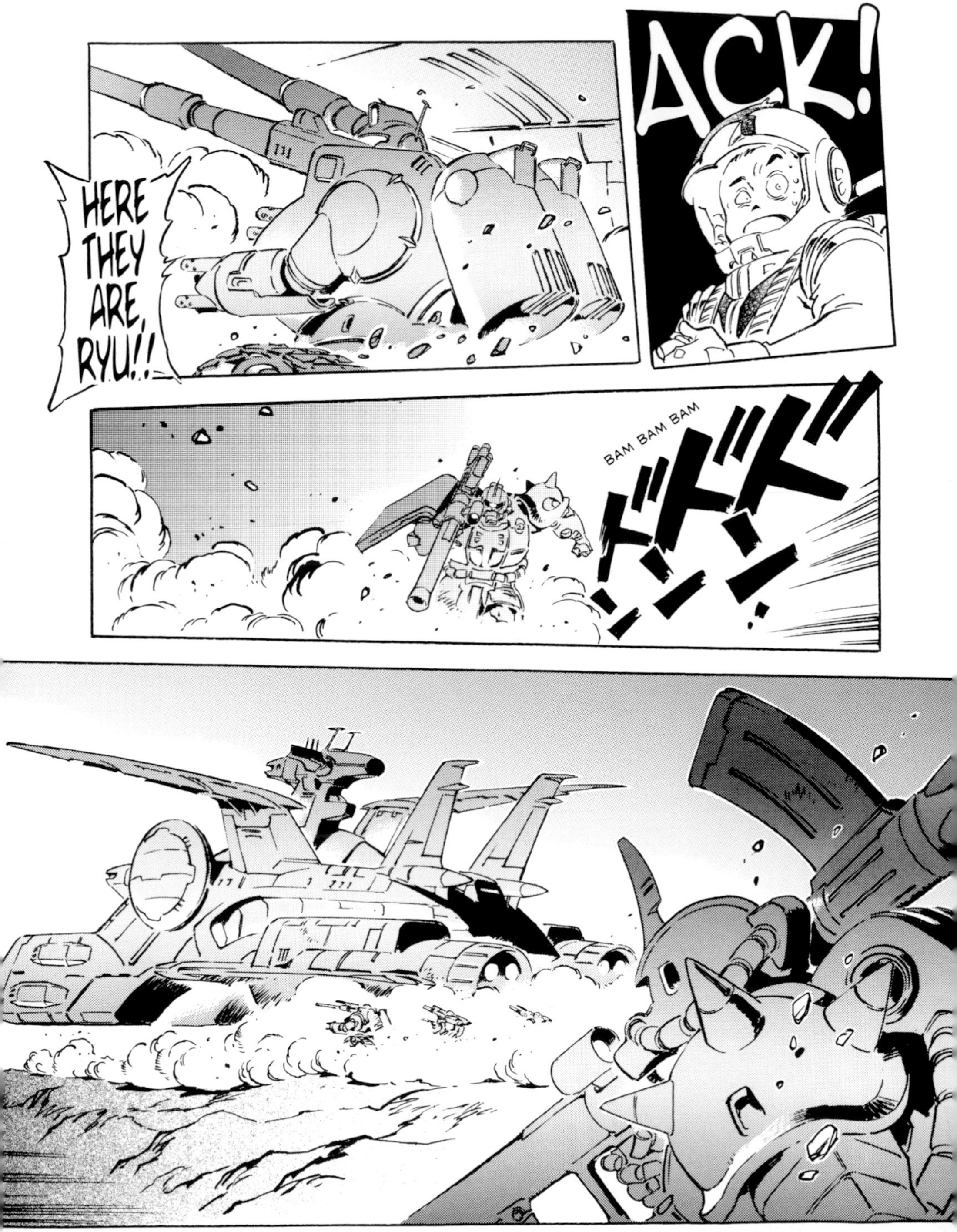
ACK!
HERE THEY ARE, RYU!!
BAM BAM BAM

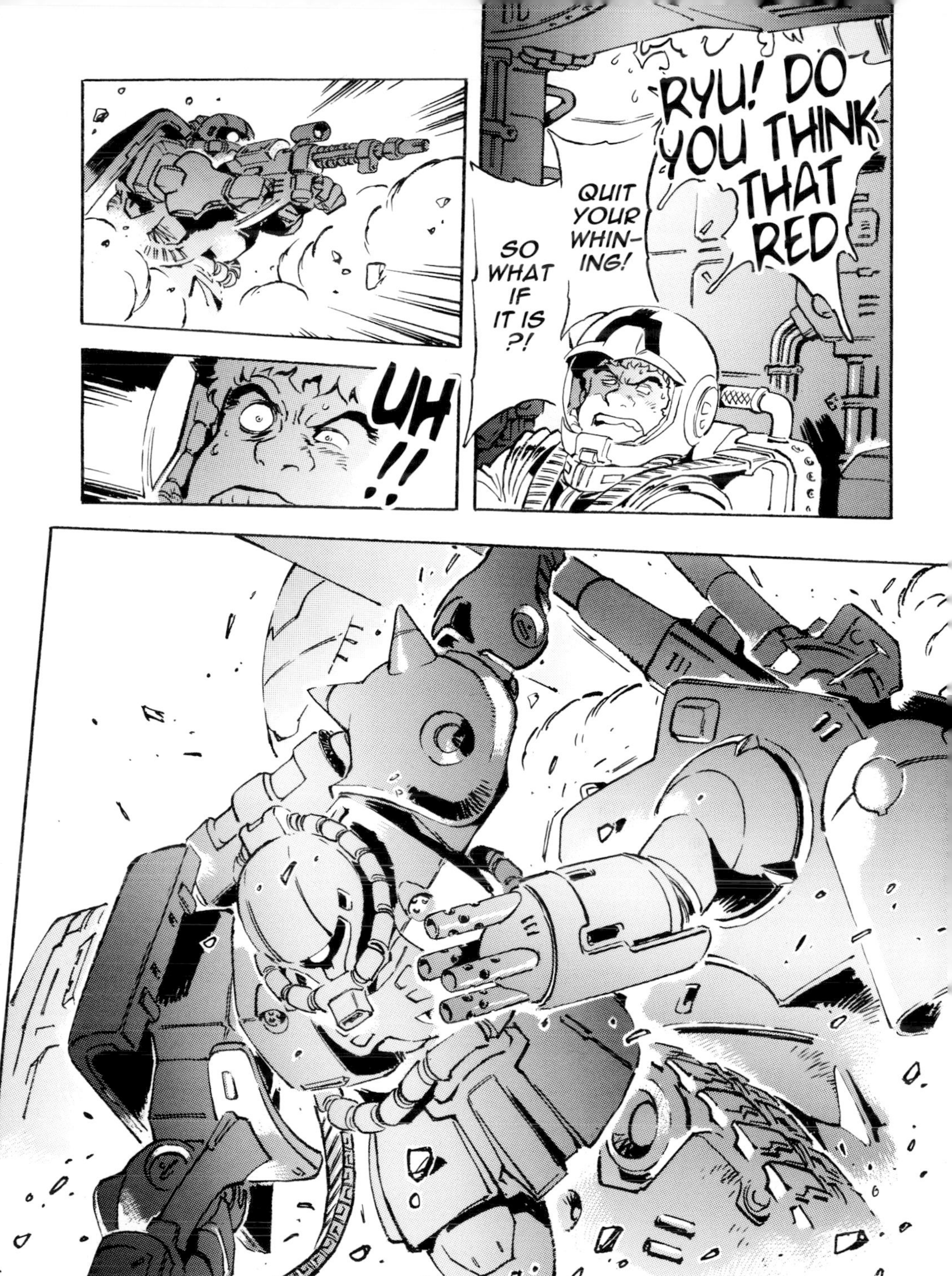
RYU! DO YOU THINK THAT RED
QUIT YOUR WHIN-ING!
SO WHAT IF IT IS ?!
UH !!

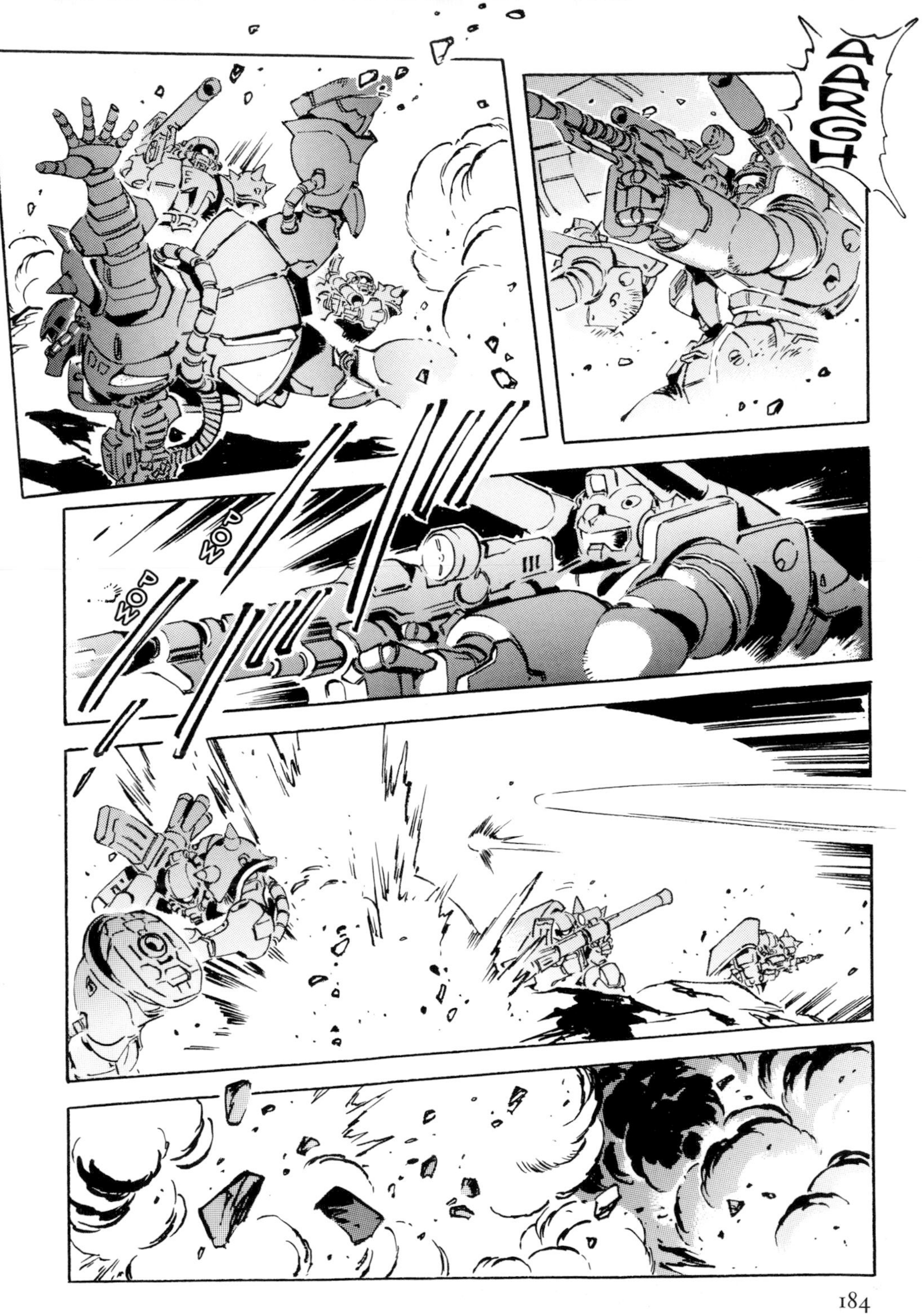
AARGH
POW
POW

IT'S ON!
SOONER THAN PLANNED!
OPEN THE HATCH!
GTUNG
FWEEEE

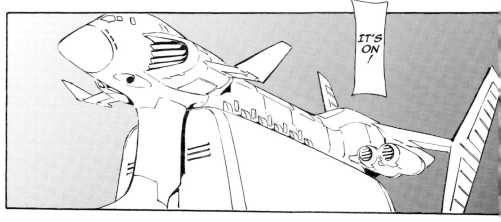

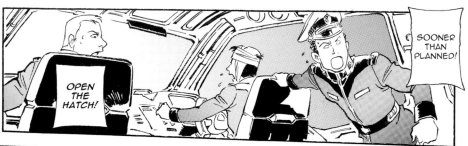

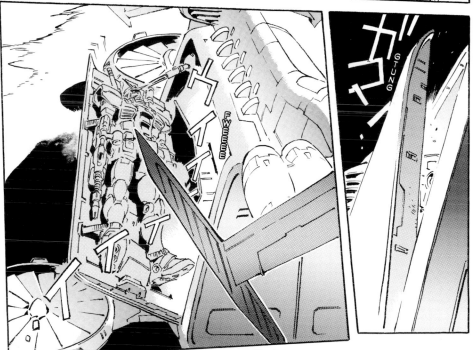

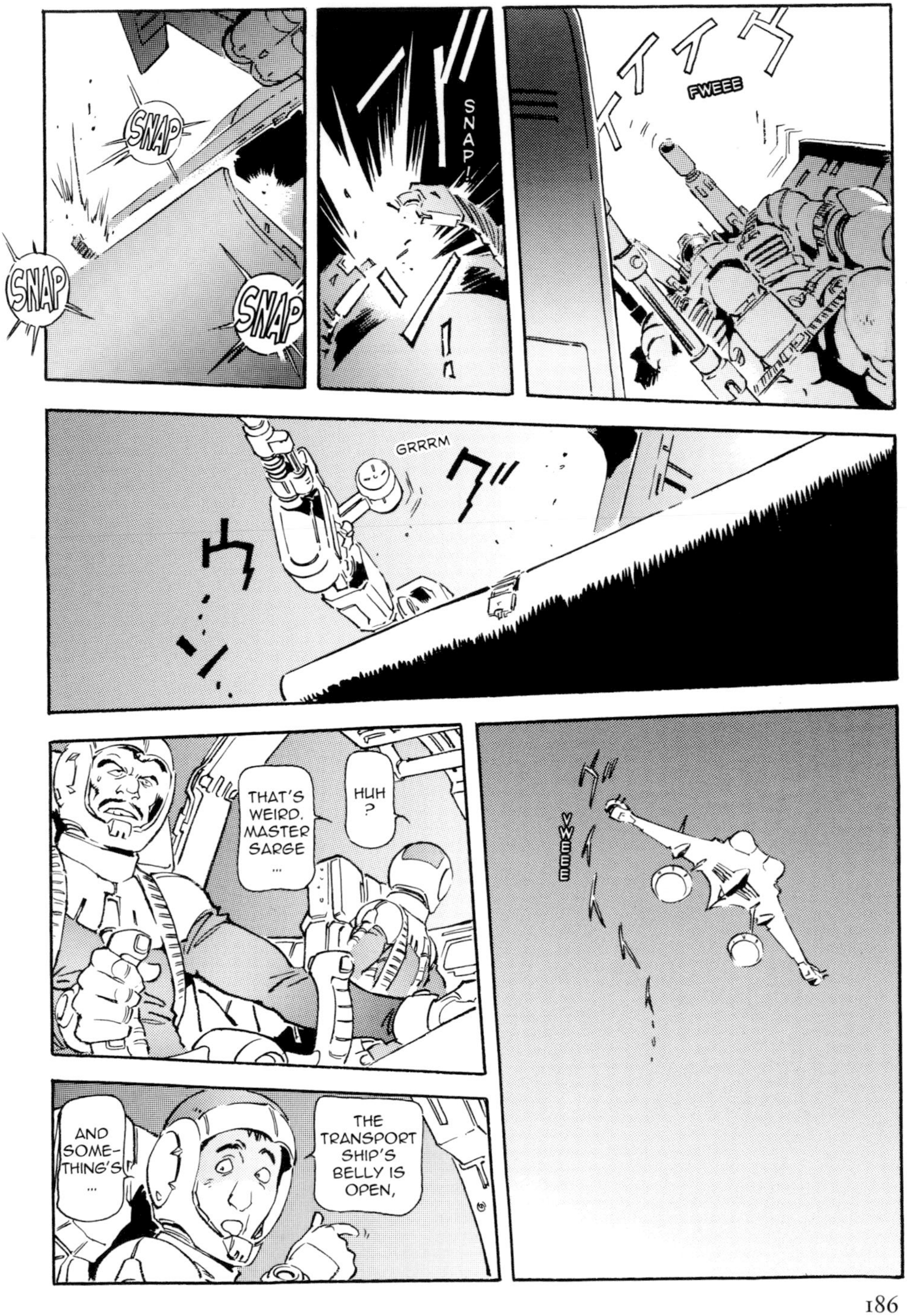
FWEEE
SNAP!
SNAP
SNAP
SNAP
GRRRM
VWEEE
HUH?
THAT'S WEIRD, MASTER SARGE ...
THE TRANSPORT SHIP'S BELLY IS OPEN,
AND SOME-THING'S ...

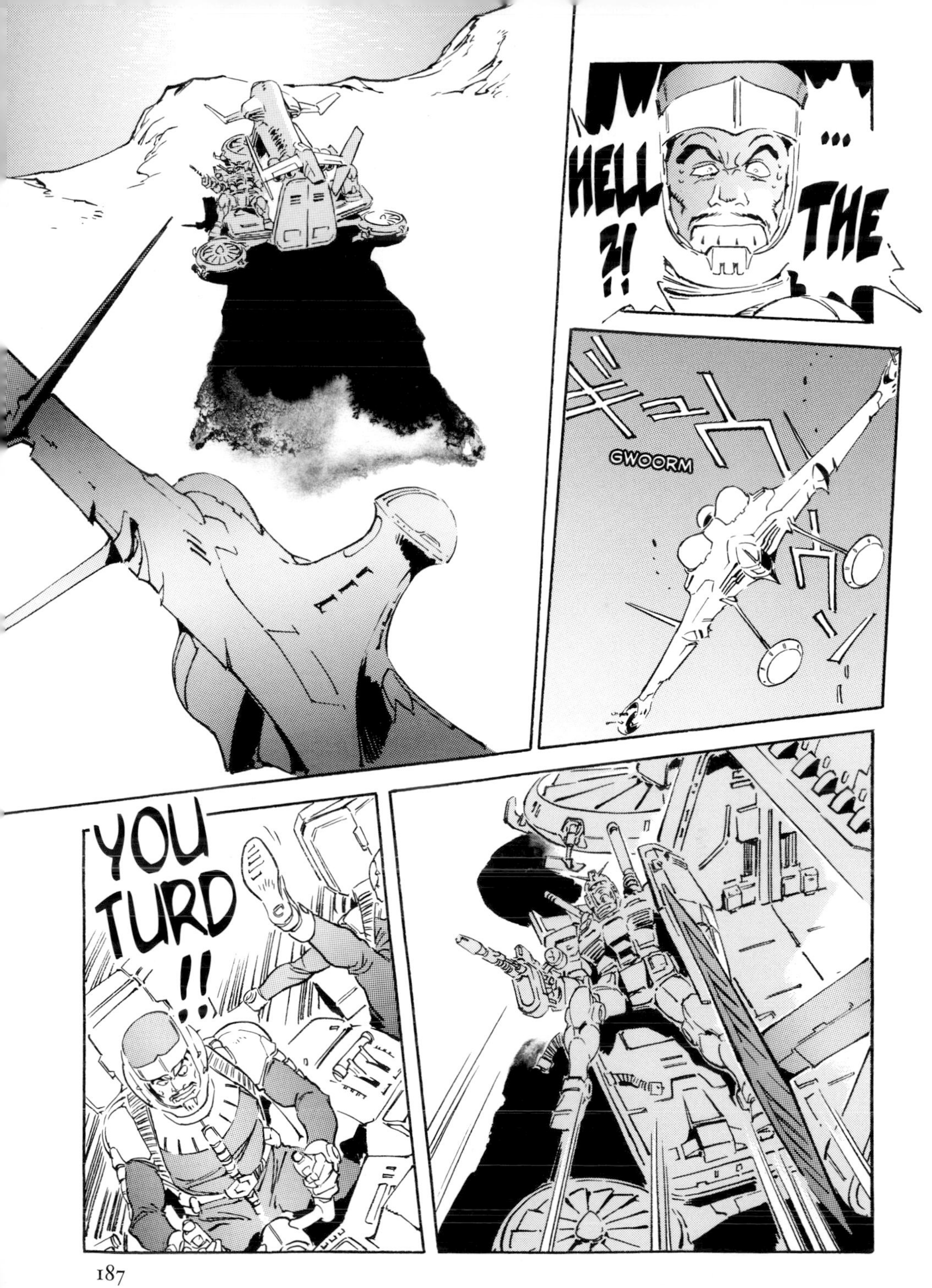
...THE HELL ?!
GWOORM
YOU TURD !!

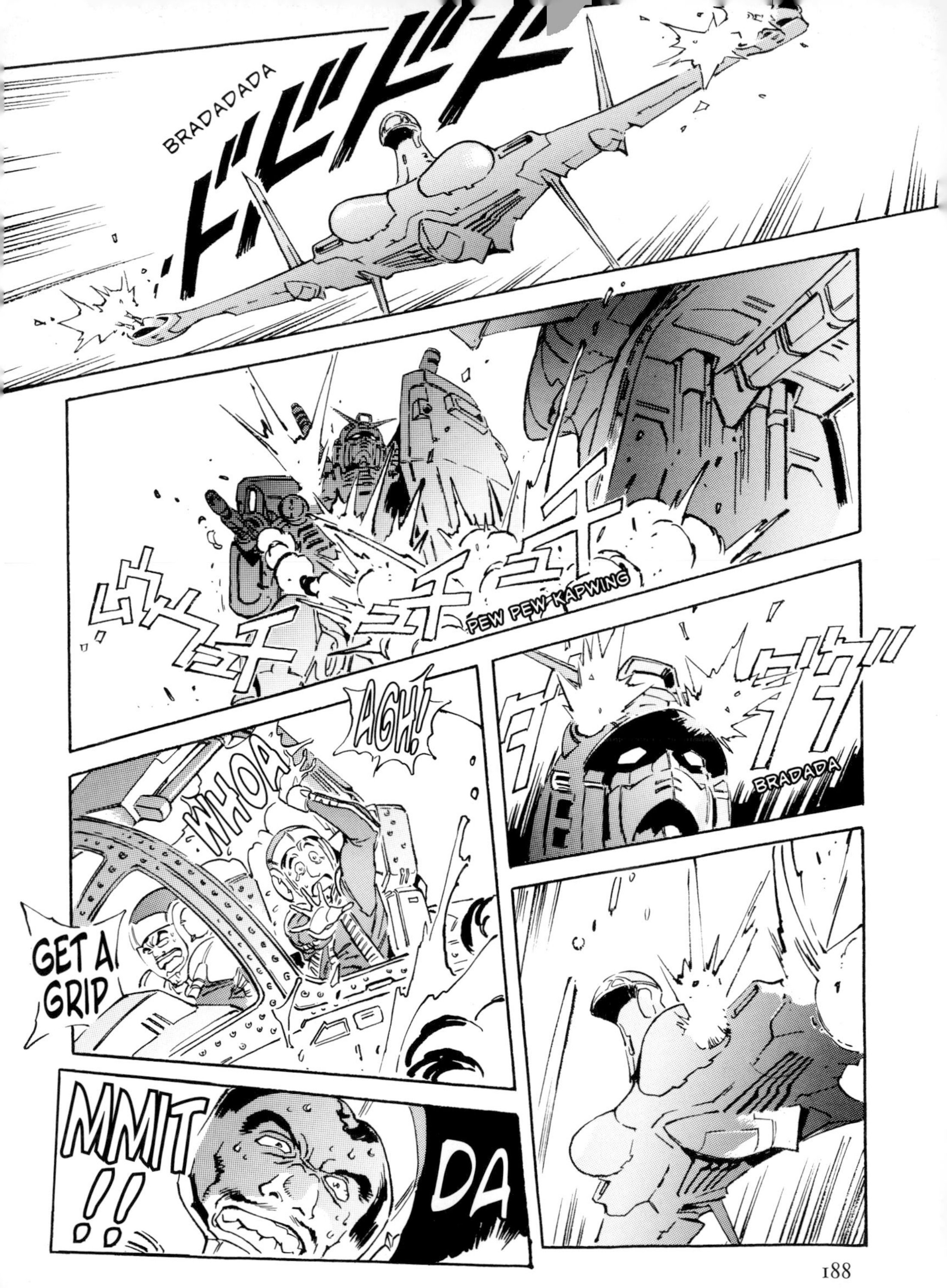
BRADADADA
PEW PEW KAPWING
BRADADA
AGH!
WHOA
GET A GRIP
DA
MMIT !!

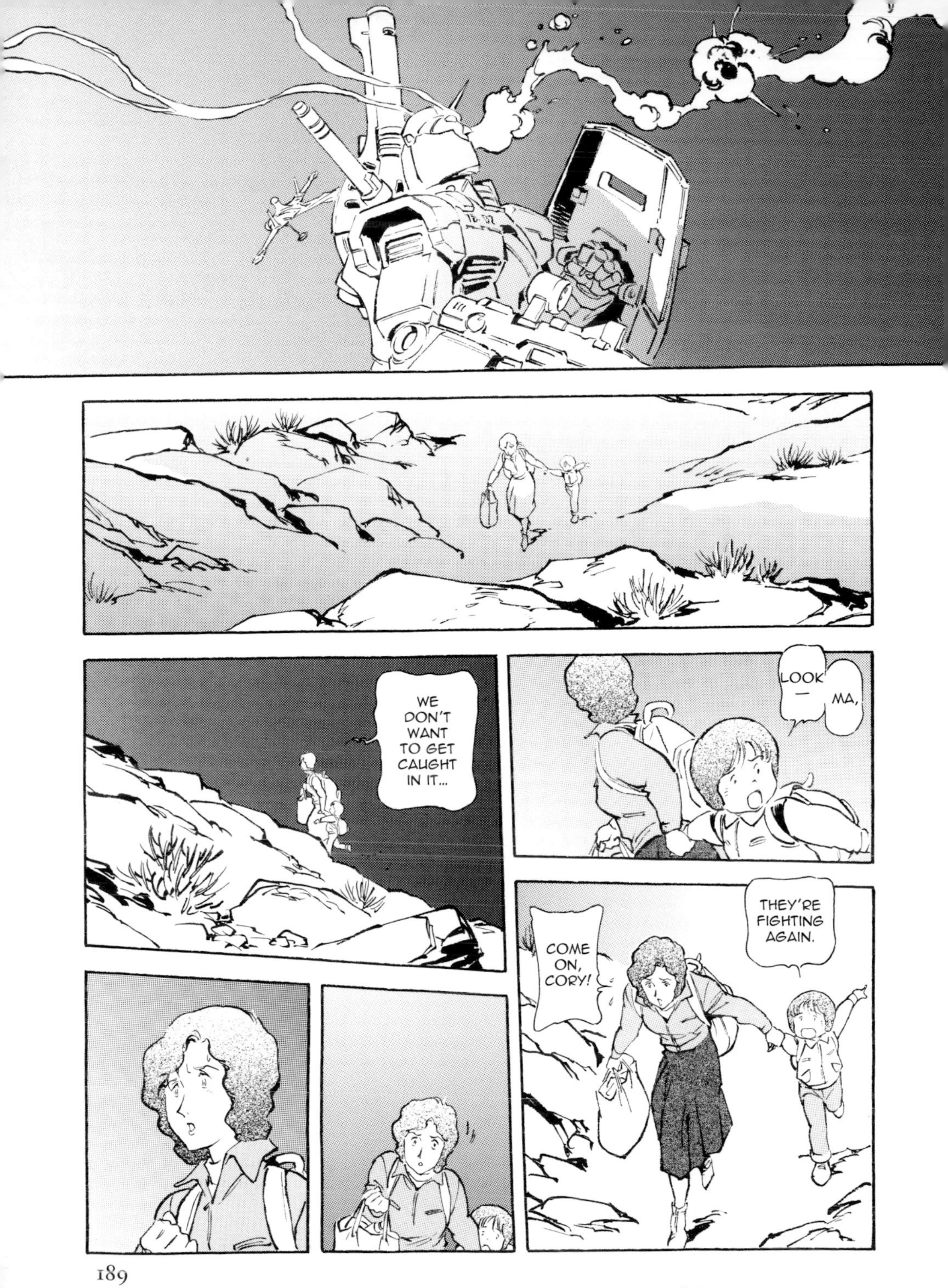
LOOK —
MA,
THEY'RE FIGHTING AGAIN.
COME ON, CORY!
WE DON'T WANT TO GET CAUGHT IN IT...

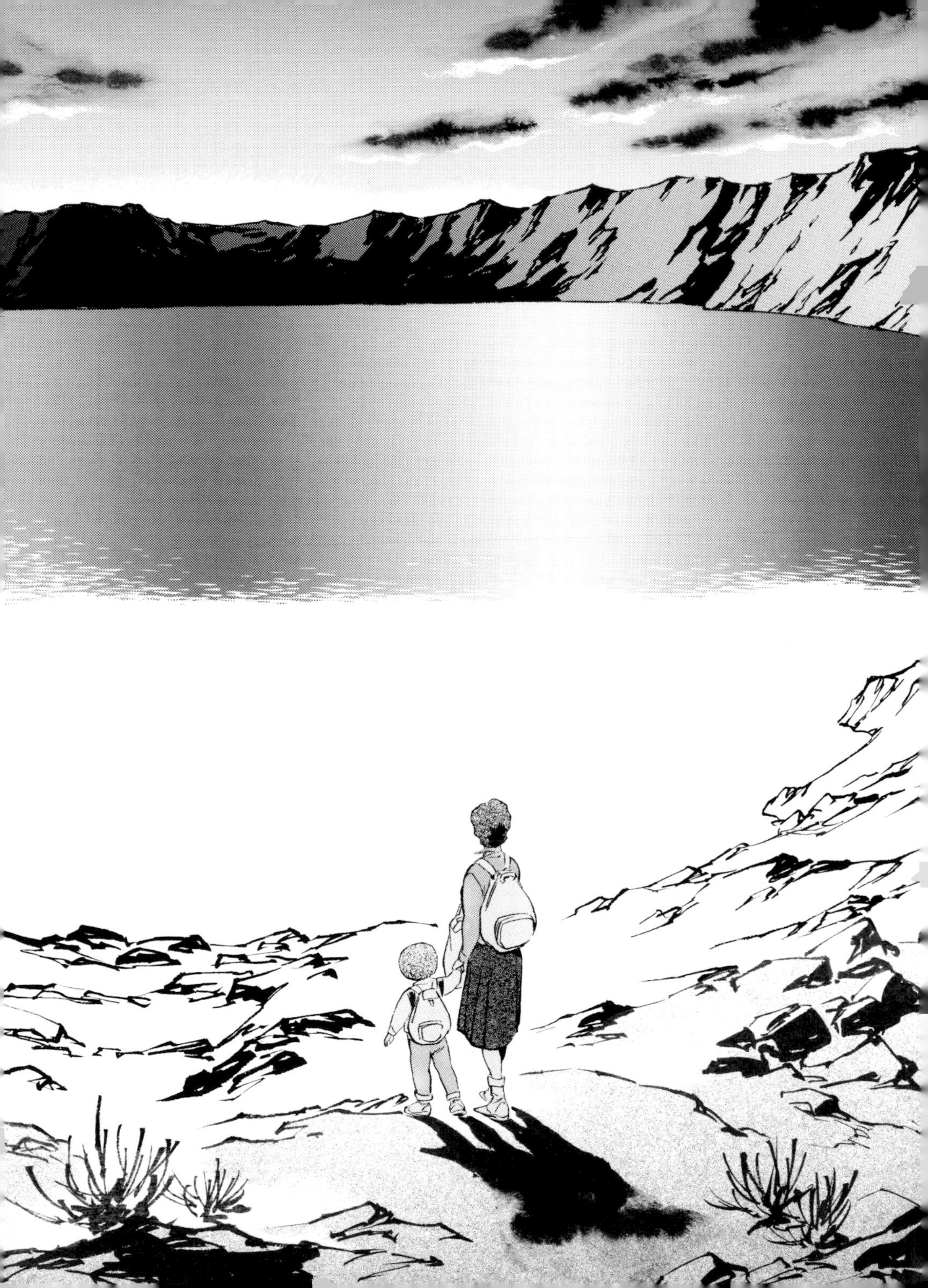

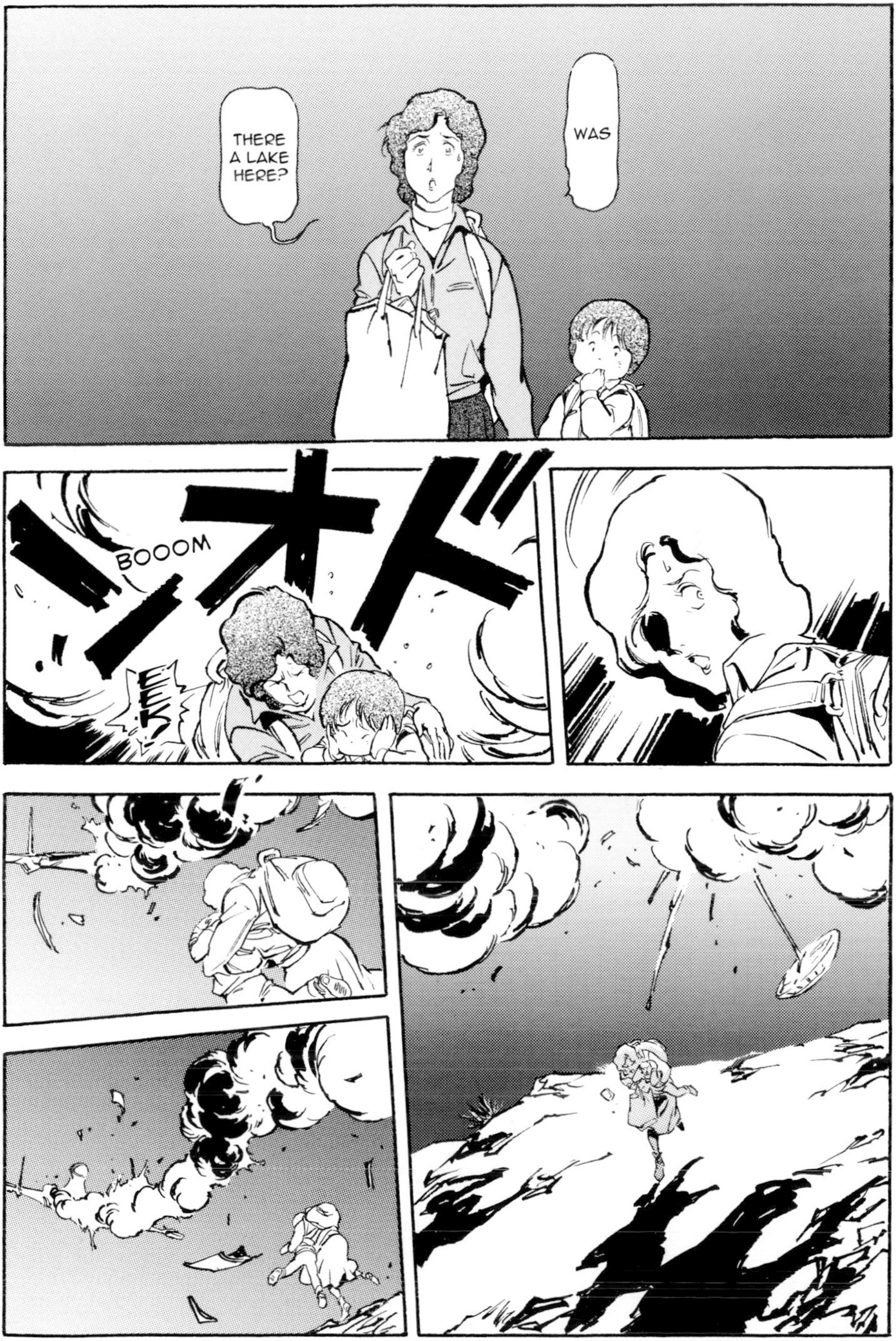
WAS
THERE A LAKE HERE?
ドオン
BOOOM
EEK!

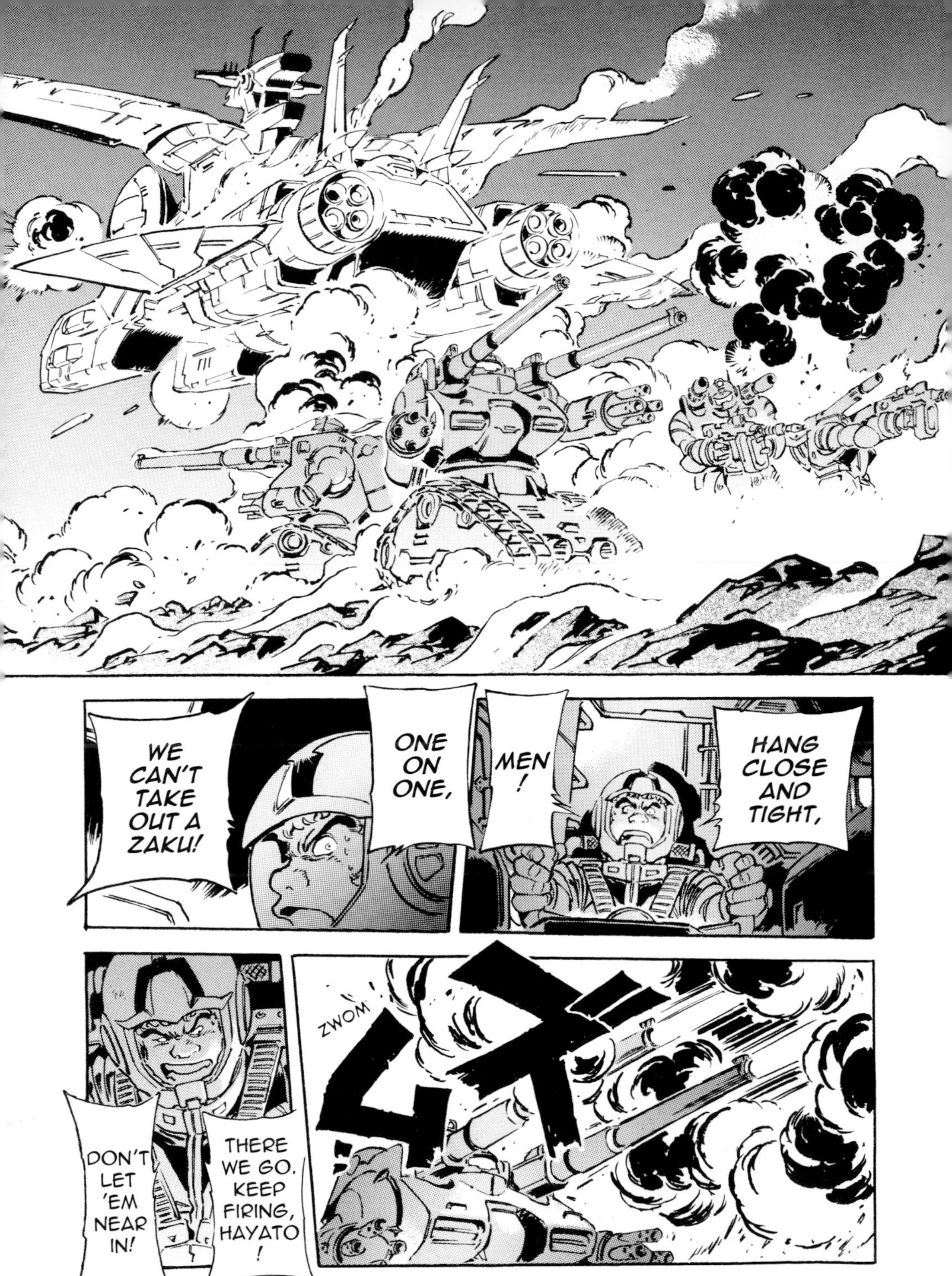
HANG CLOSE AND TIGHT,
MEN!
ONE ON ONE,
WE CAN'T TAKE OUT A ZAKU!
ZWOM
THERE WE GO. KEEP FIRING, HAYATO!
DON'T LET 'EM NEAR IN!

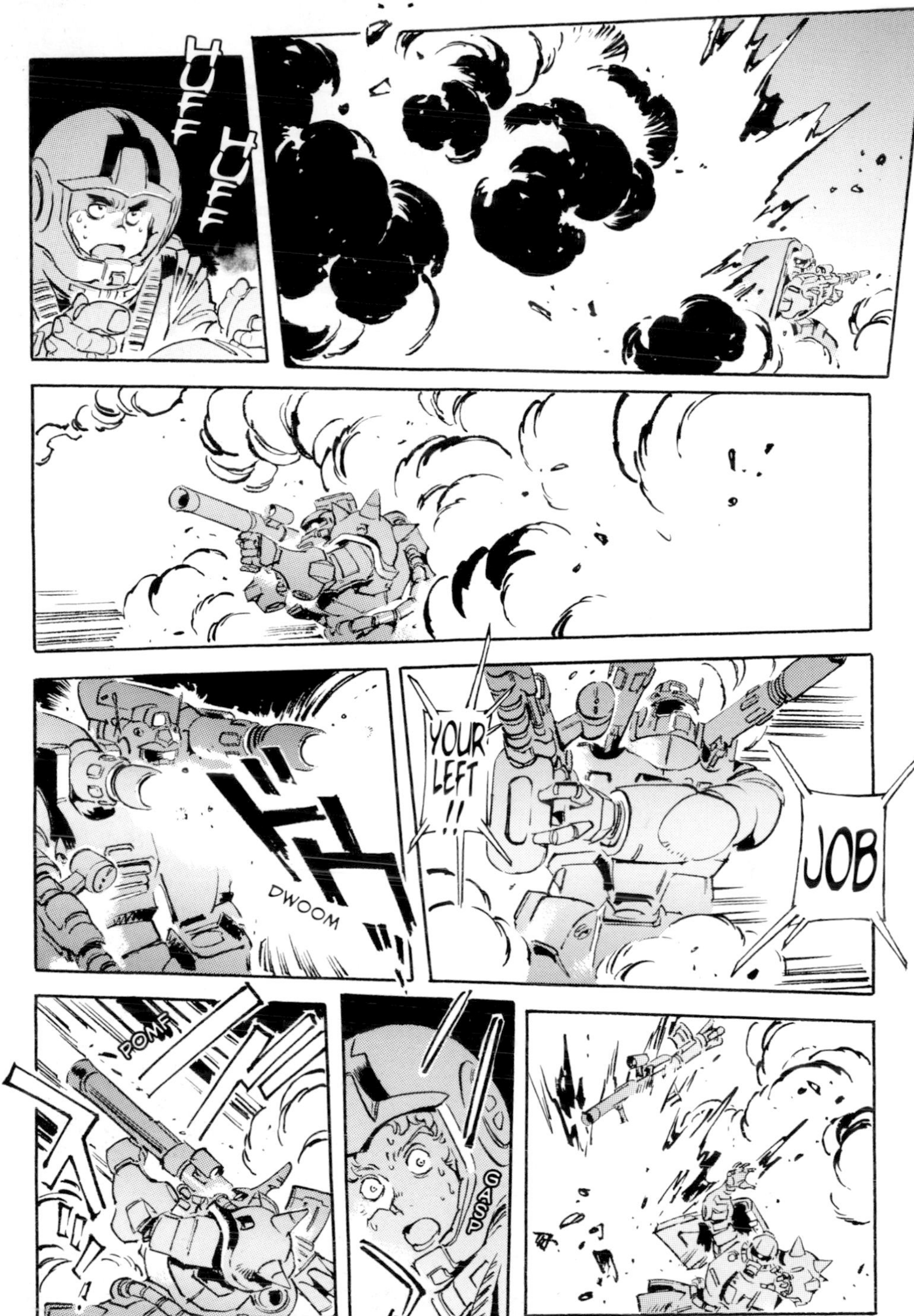
HUFF HUFF
YOUR LEFT!!
JOB
DWOOM
GASP
POMF

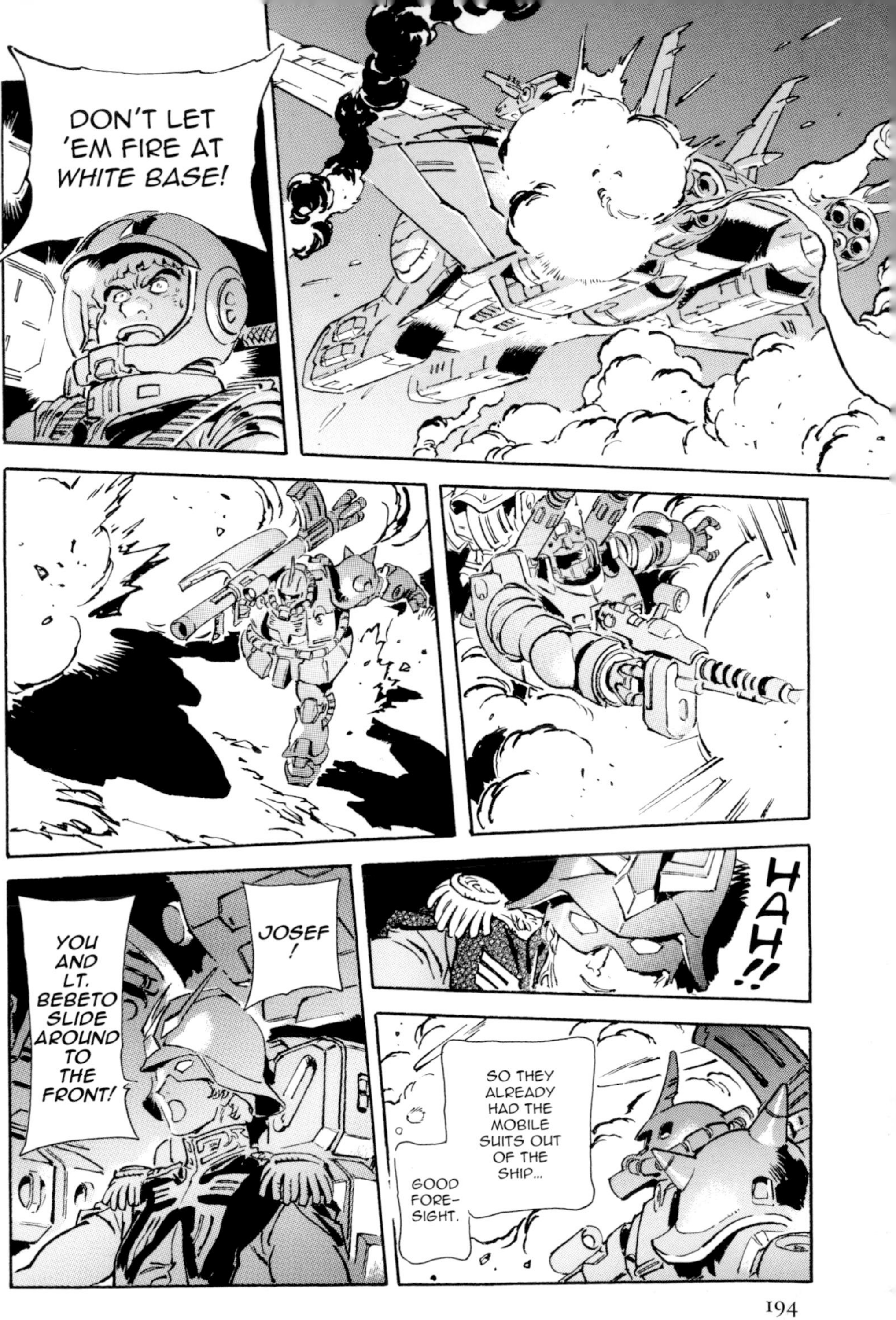
DON'T LET 'EM FIRE AT WHITE BASE!
HAH!!
SO THEY ALREADY HAD THE MOBILE SUITS OUT OF THE SHIP...
GOOD FORE-SIGHT.
JOSEF!
YOU AND LT. BEBETO SLIDE AROUND TO THE FRONT!

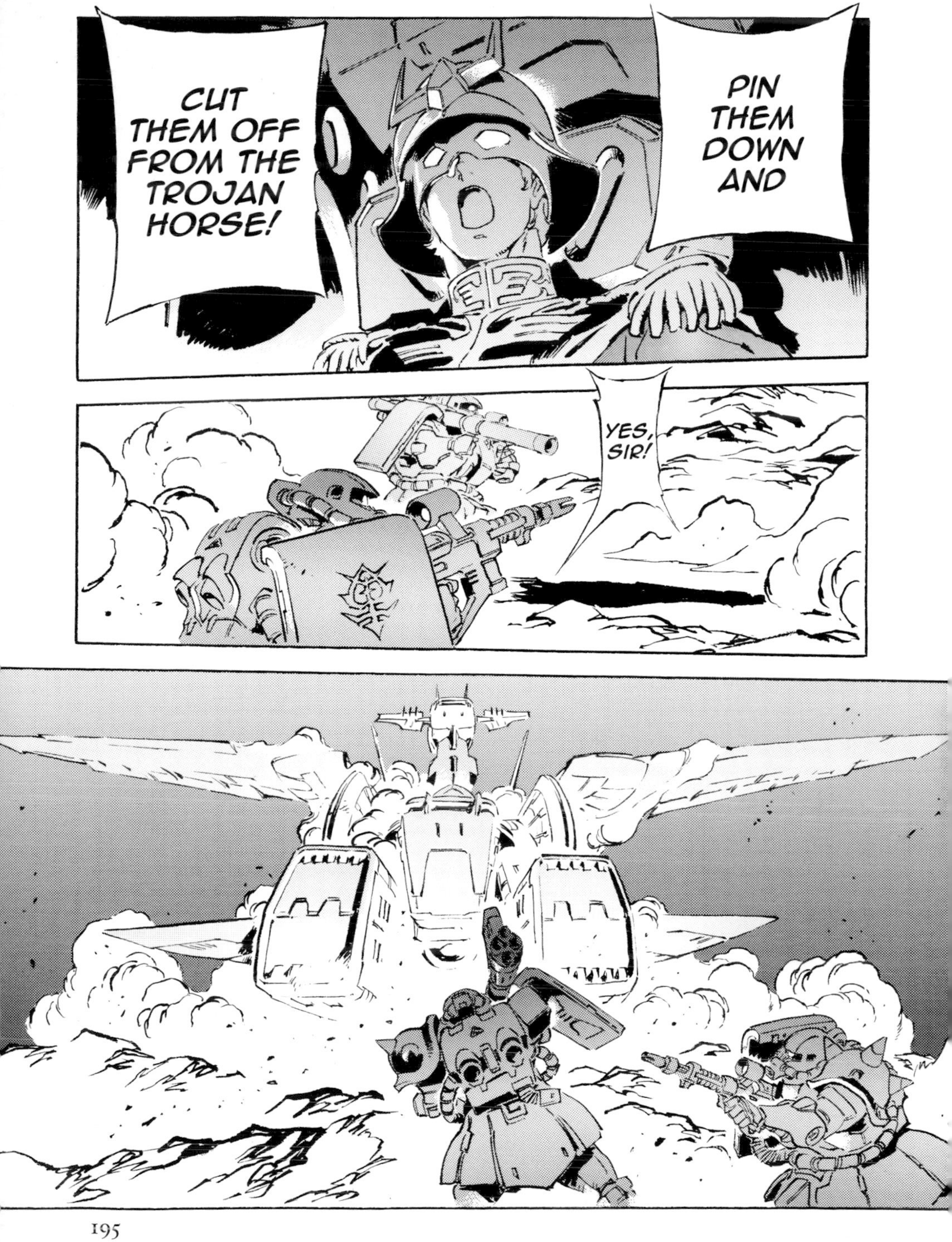
PIN THEM DOWN AND
CUT THEM OFF FROM THE TROJAN HORSE!
YES, SIR!

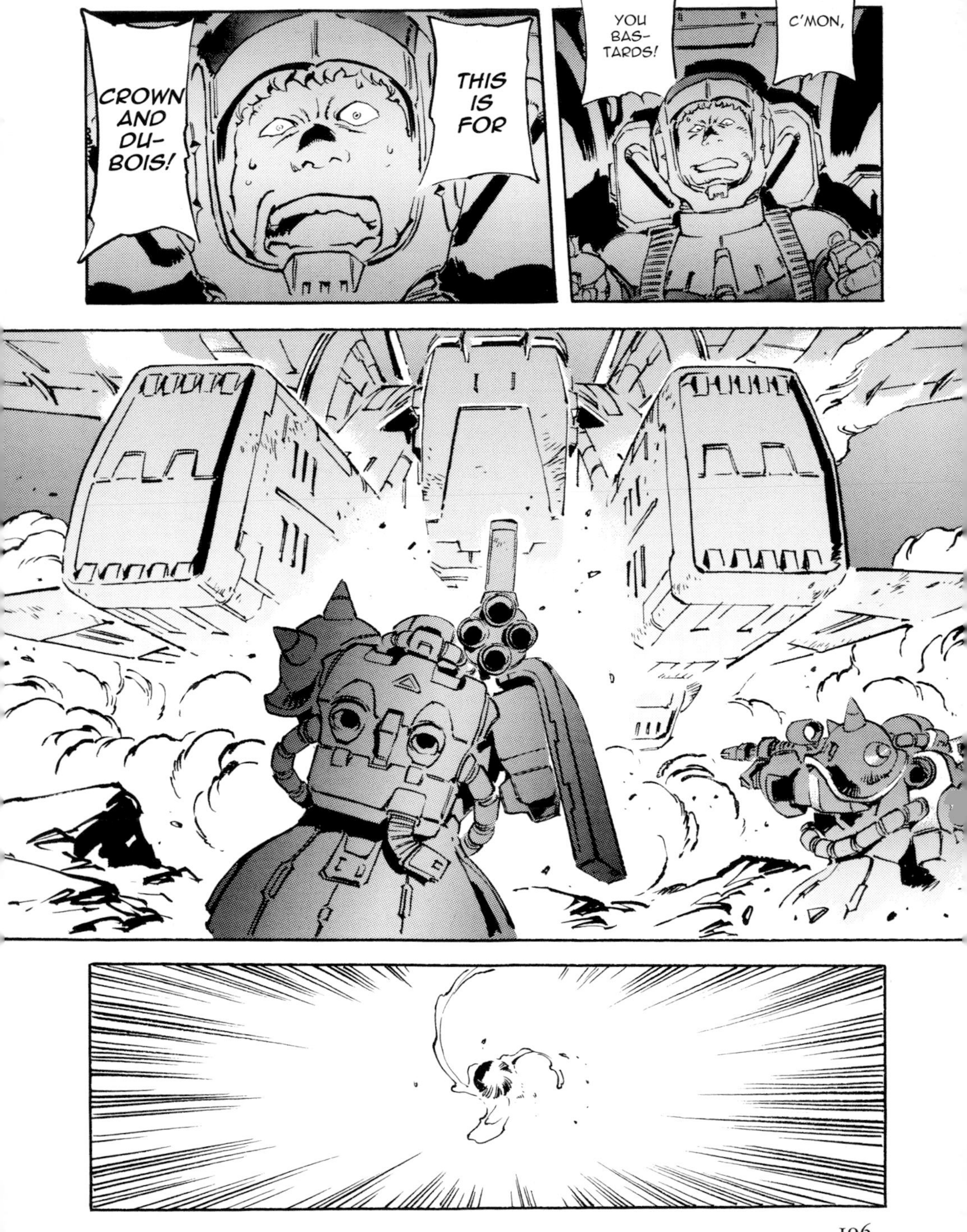
C'MON,
YOU BAS-TARDS!
THIS IS FOR
CROWN AND DU-BOIS!

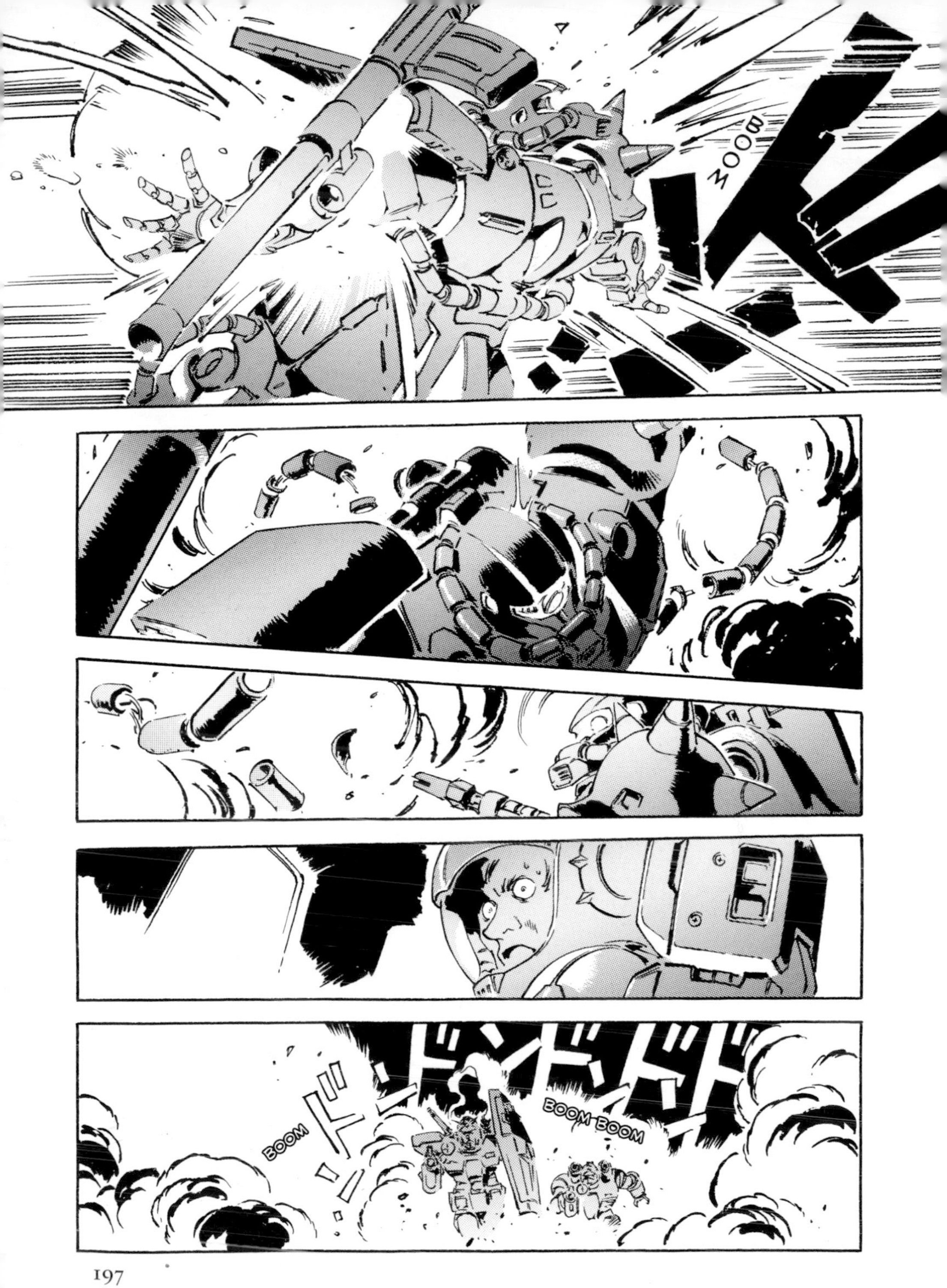
BOOM
BOOM BOOM
BOOM

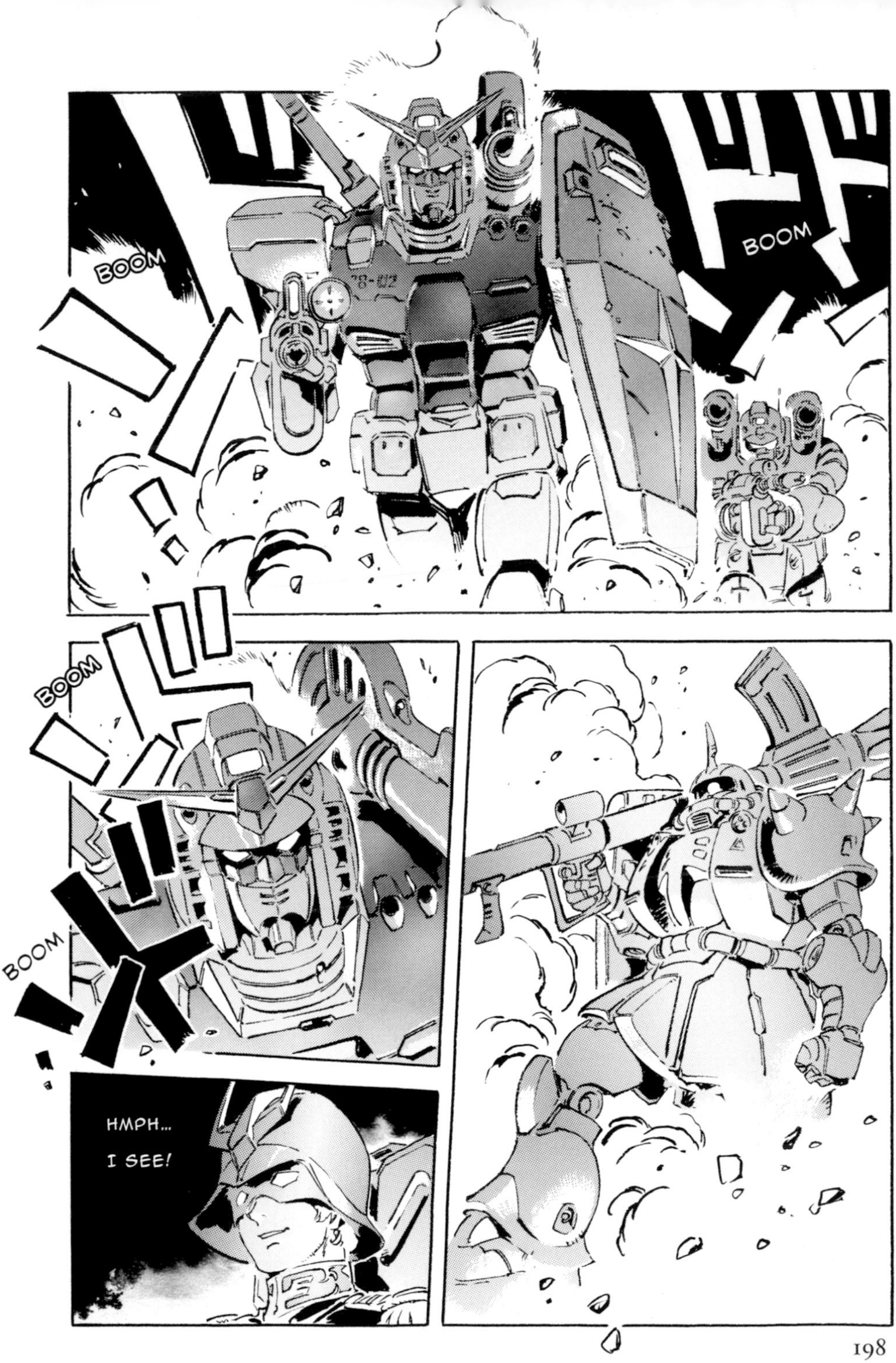
BOOM
BOOM
BOOM
BOOM
HMPH...
I SEE!

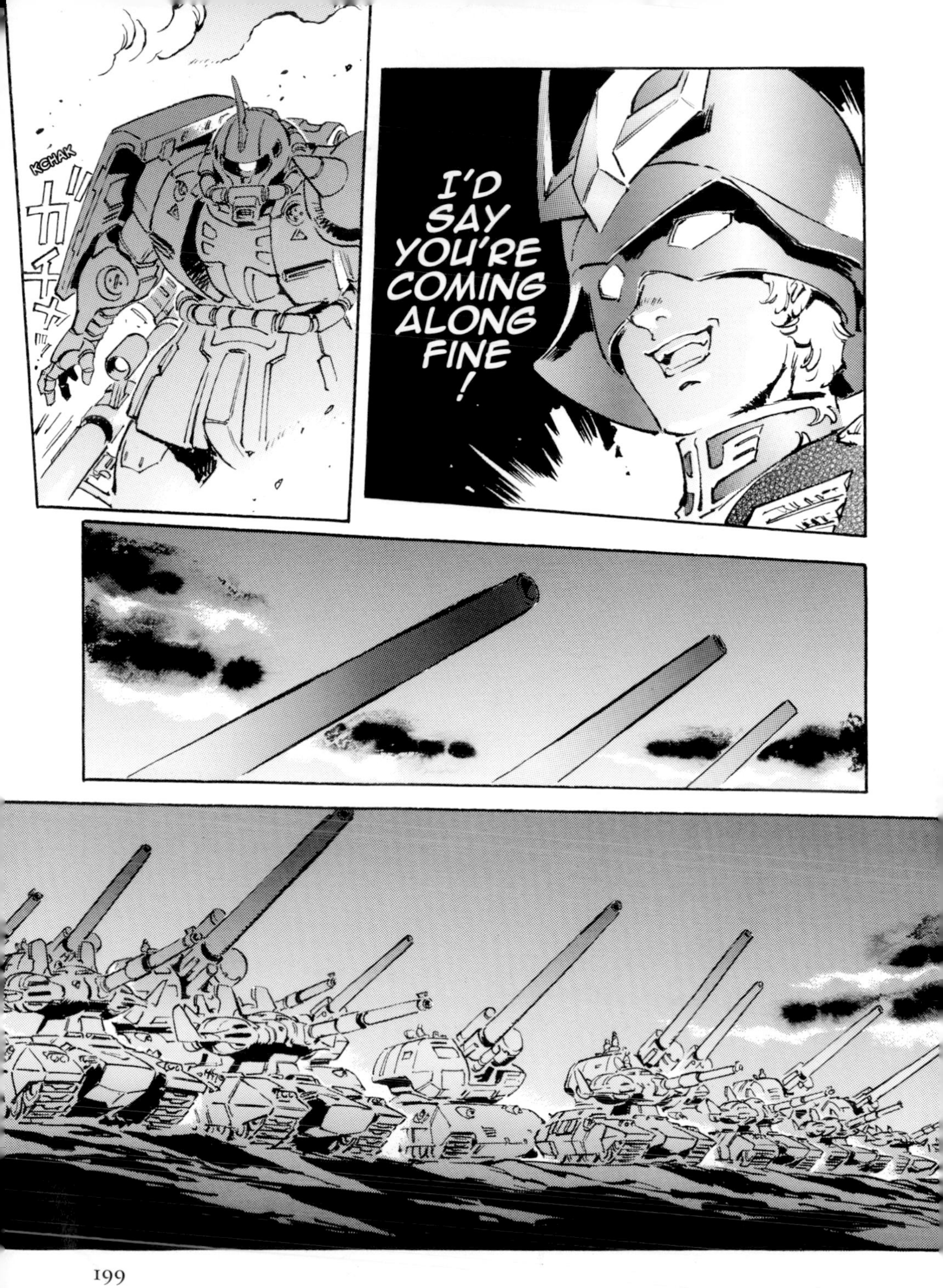
I'D SAY YOU'RE COMING ALONG FINE!
KCHAK

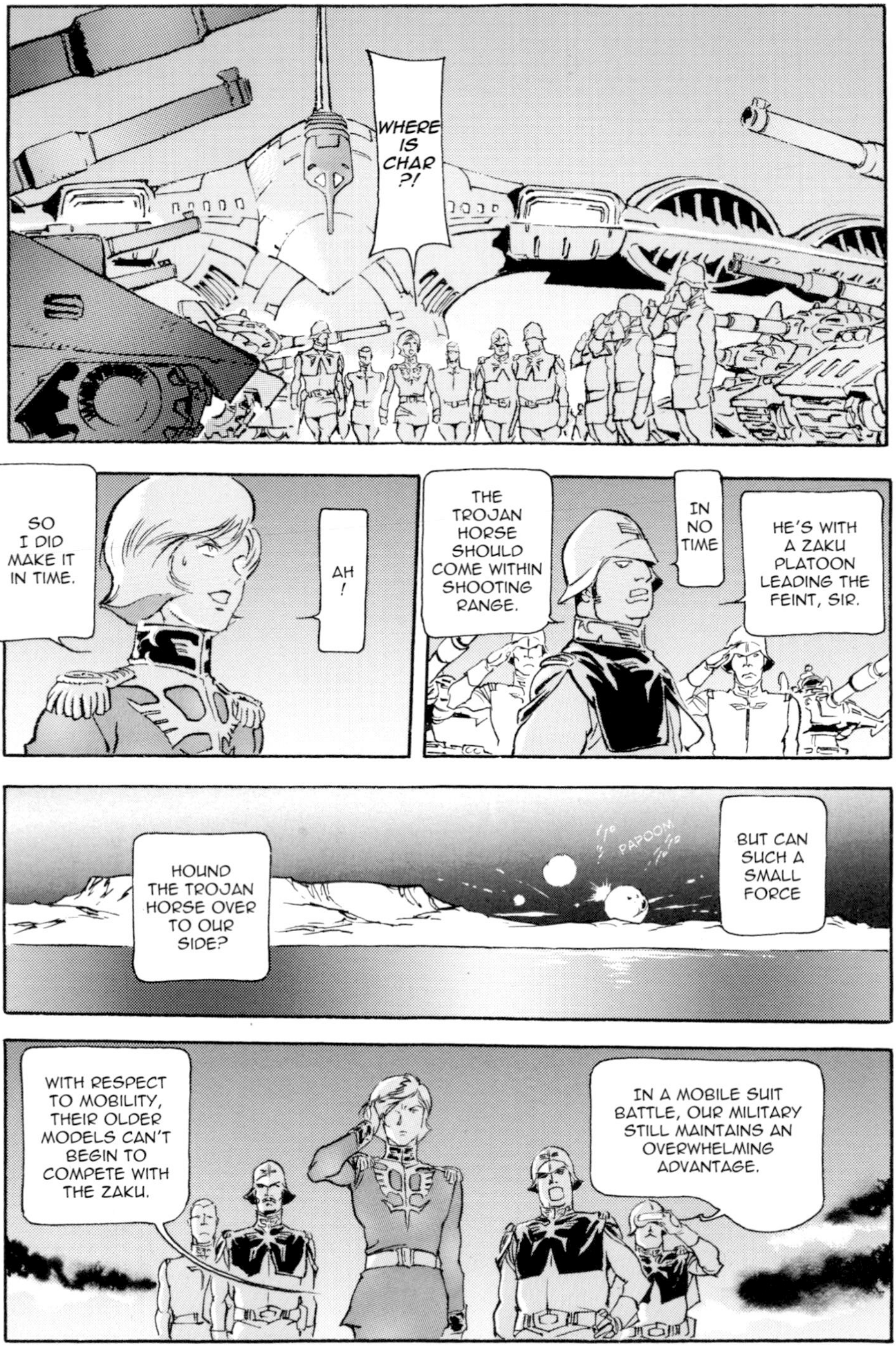
WHERE IS CHAR ?!
HE'S WITH A ZAKU PLATOON LEADING THE FEINT, SIR.
IN NO TIME
THE TROJAN HORSE SHOULD COME WITHIN SHOOTING RANGE.
AH!
SO I DID MAKE IT IN TIME.
BUT CAN SUCH A SMALL FORCE
PAPOOM
HOUND THE TROJAN HORSE OVER TO OUR SIDE?
IN A MOBILE SUIT BATTLE, OUR MILITARY STILL MAINTAINS AN OVERWHELMING ADVANTAGE.
WITH RESPECT TO MOBILITY, THEIR OLDER MODELS CAN'T BEGIN TO COMPETE WITH THE ZAKU.

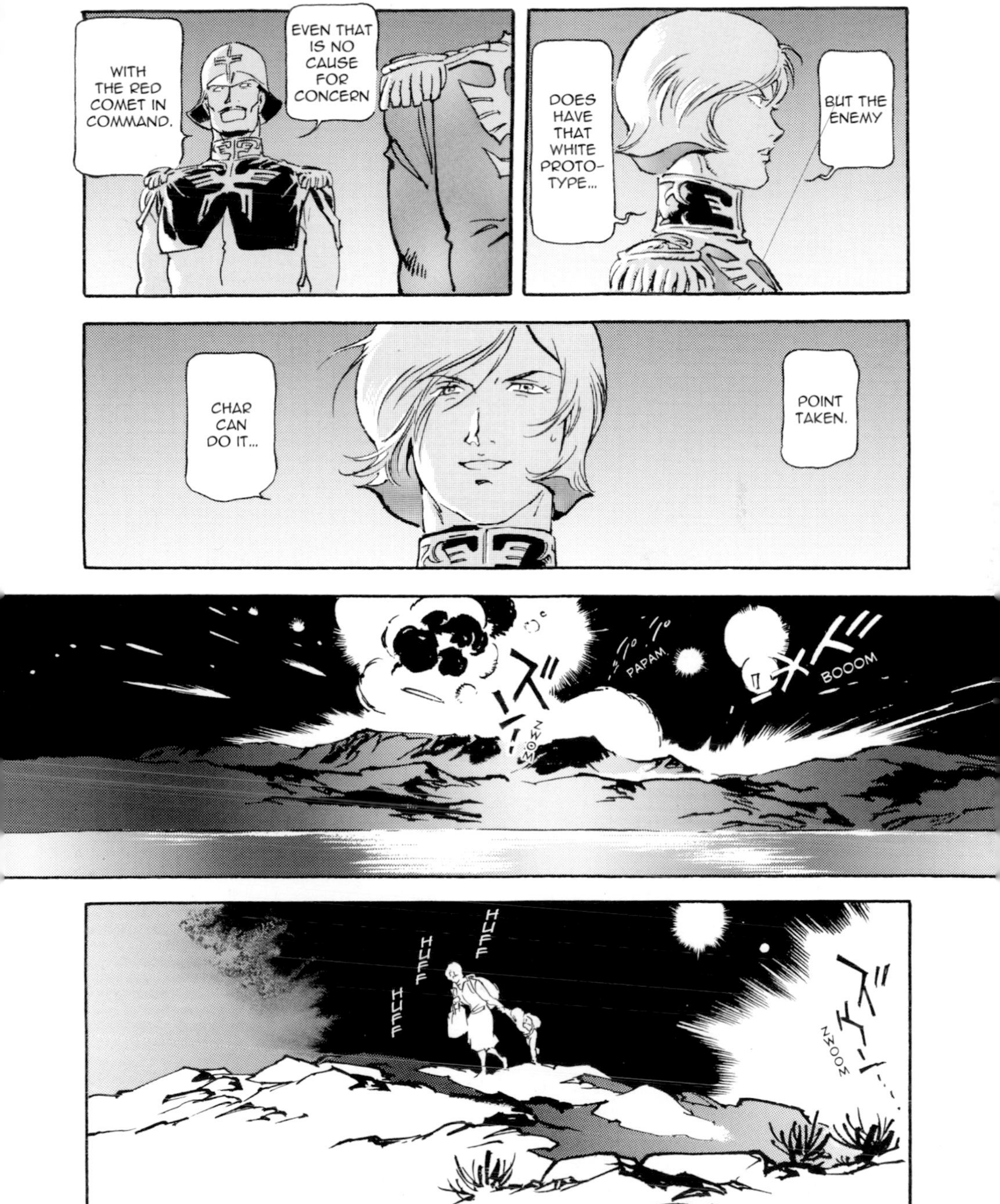
BUT THE ENEMY
DOES HAVE THAT WHITE PROTO-TYPE...
EVEN THAT IS NO CAUSE FOR CONCERN
WITH THE RED COMET IN COMMAND.
POINT TAKEN.
CHAR CAN DO IT...
BOOOM
PAPAM
ZWOOM
HUFF
HUFF
HUFF
ZWOOM

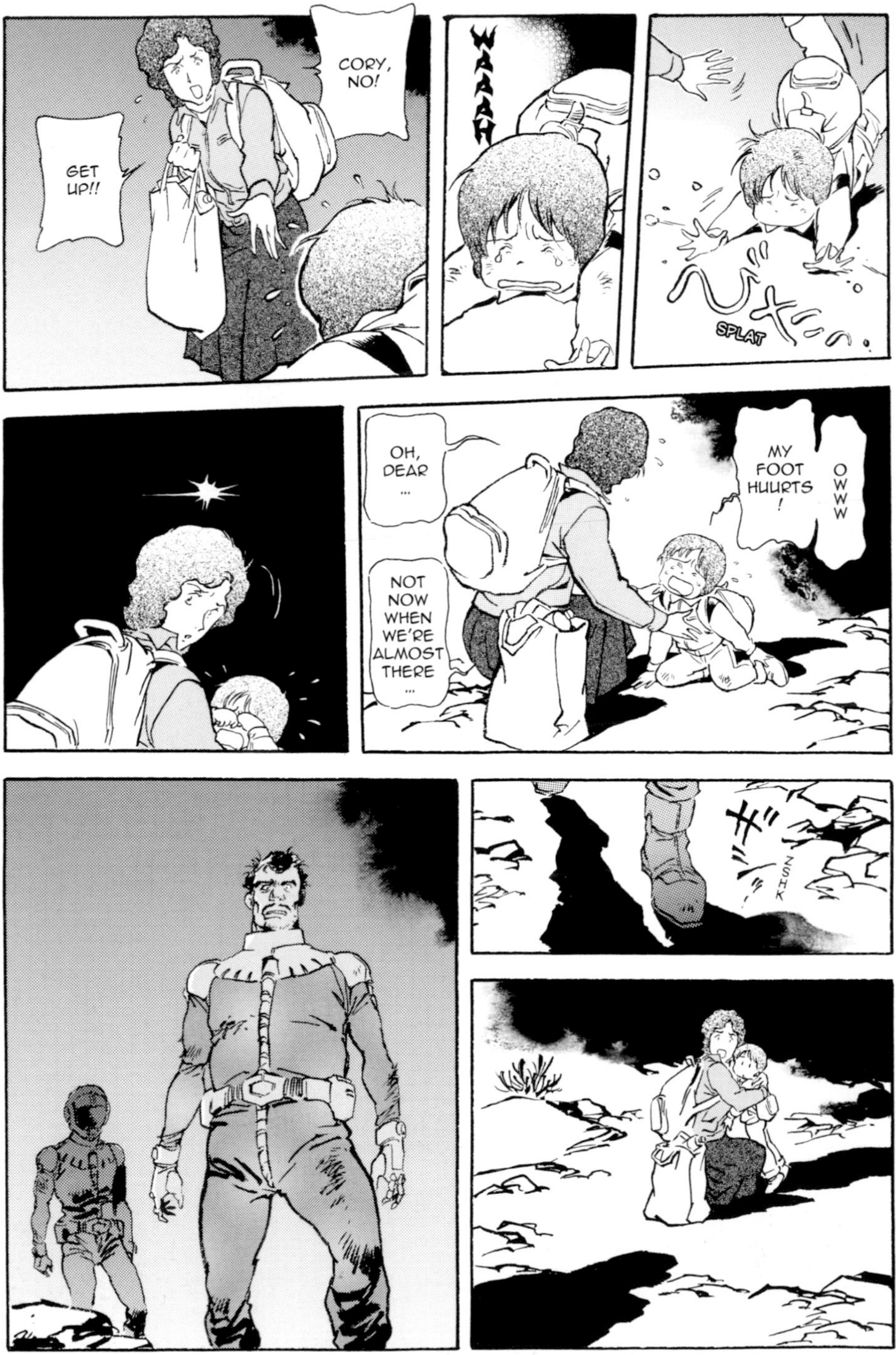
SPLAT
WAAAH
CORY, NO!
GET UP!!
OWWW
MY FOOT HUURTS!
OH, DEAR...
NOT NOW WHEN WE'RE ALMOST THERE...
ZSHK

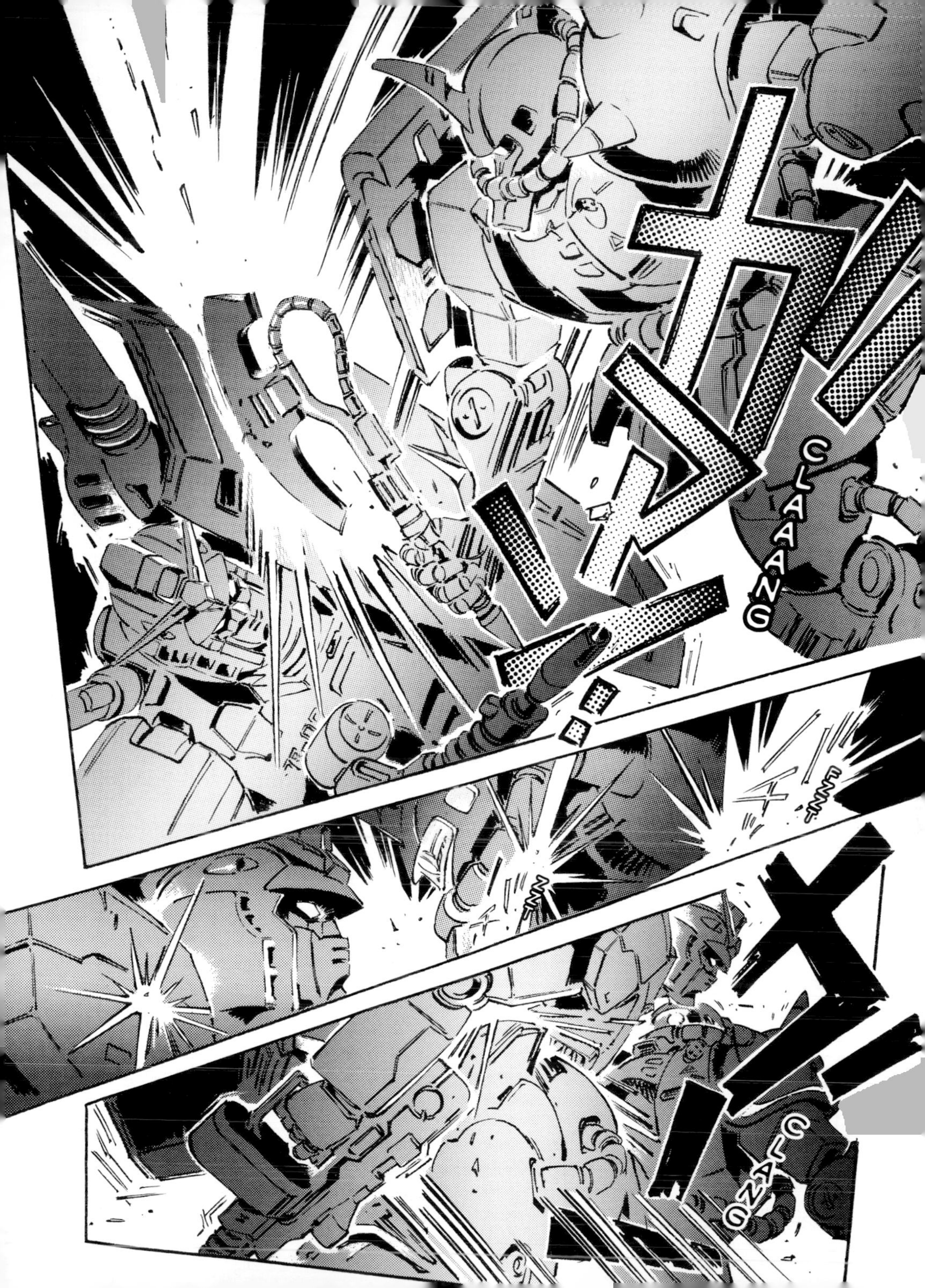
CLAAANG
CLANG

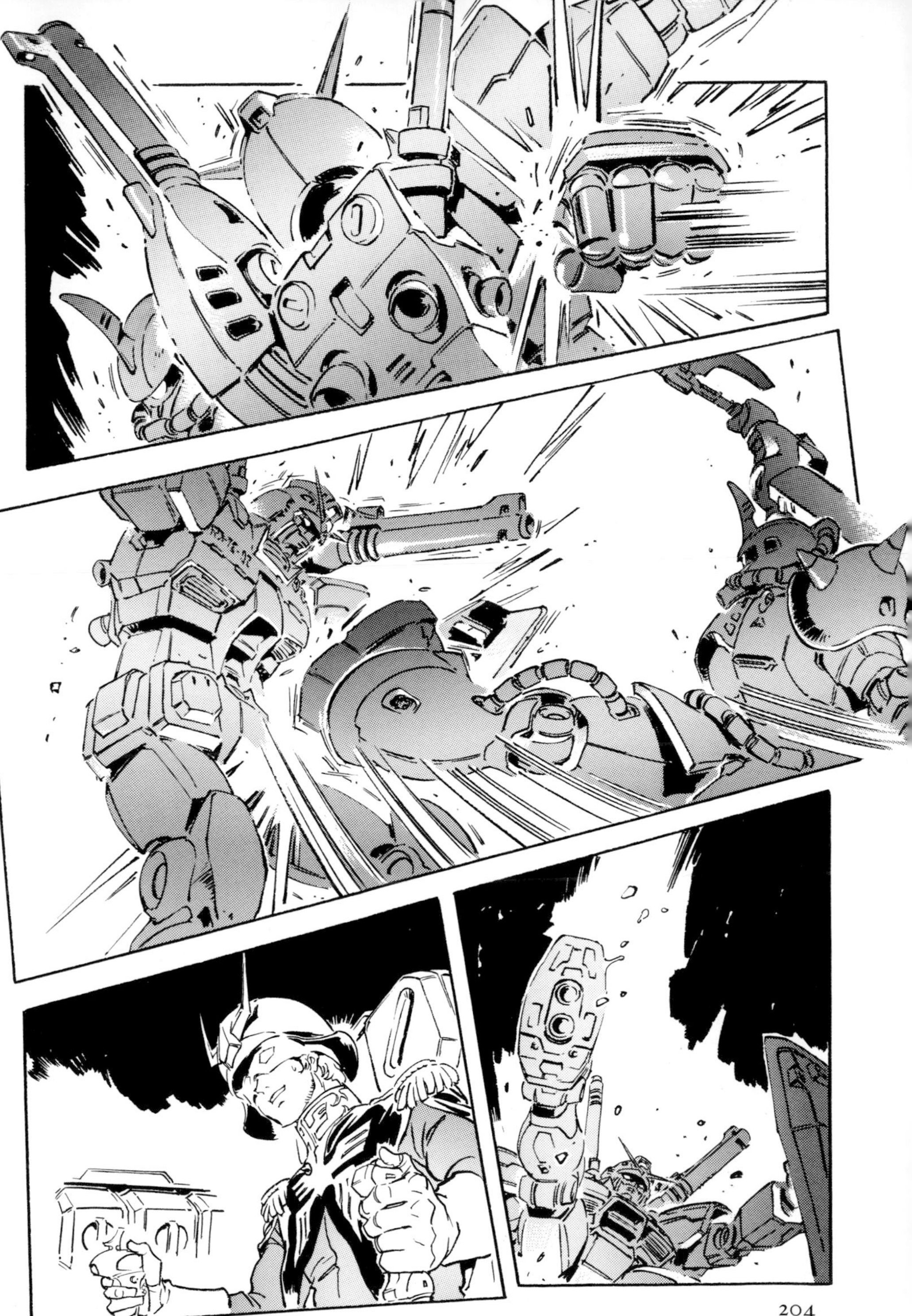

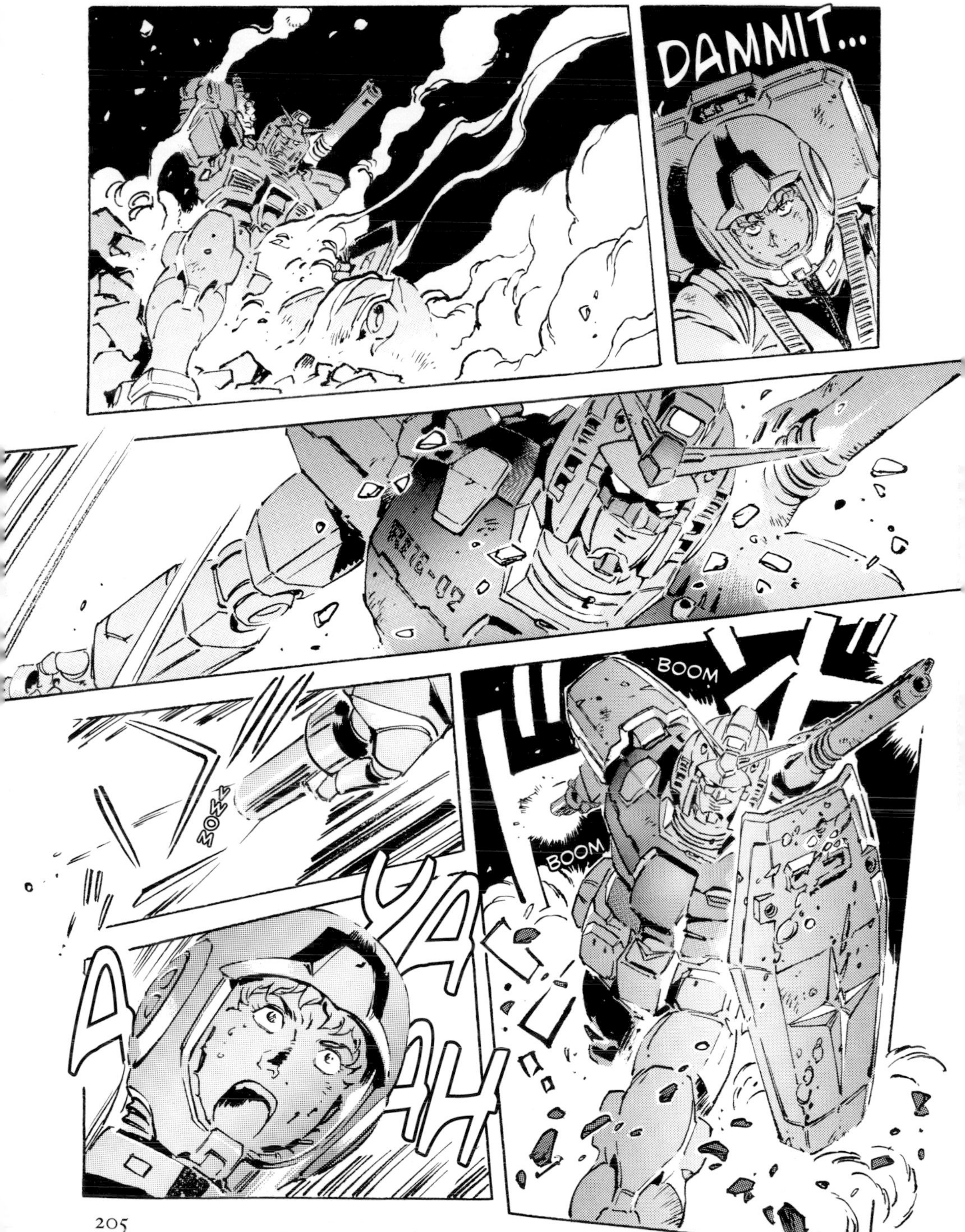
DAMMIT...
BOOM
BOOM

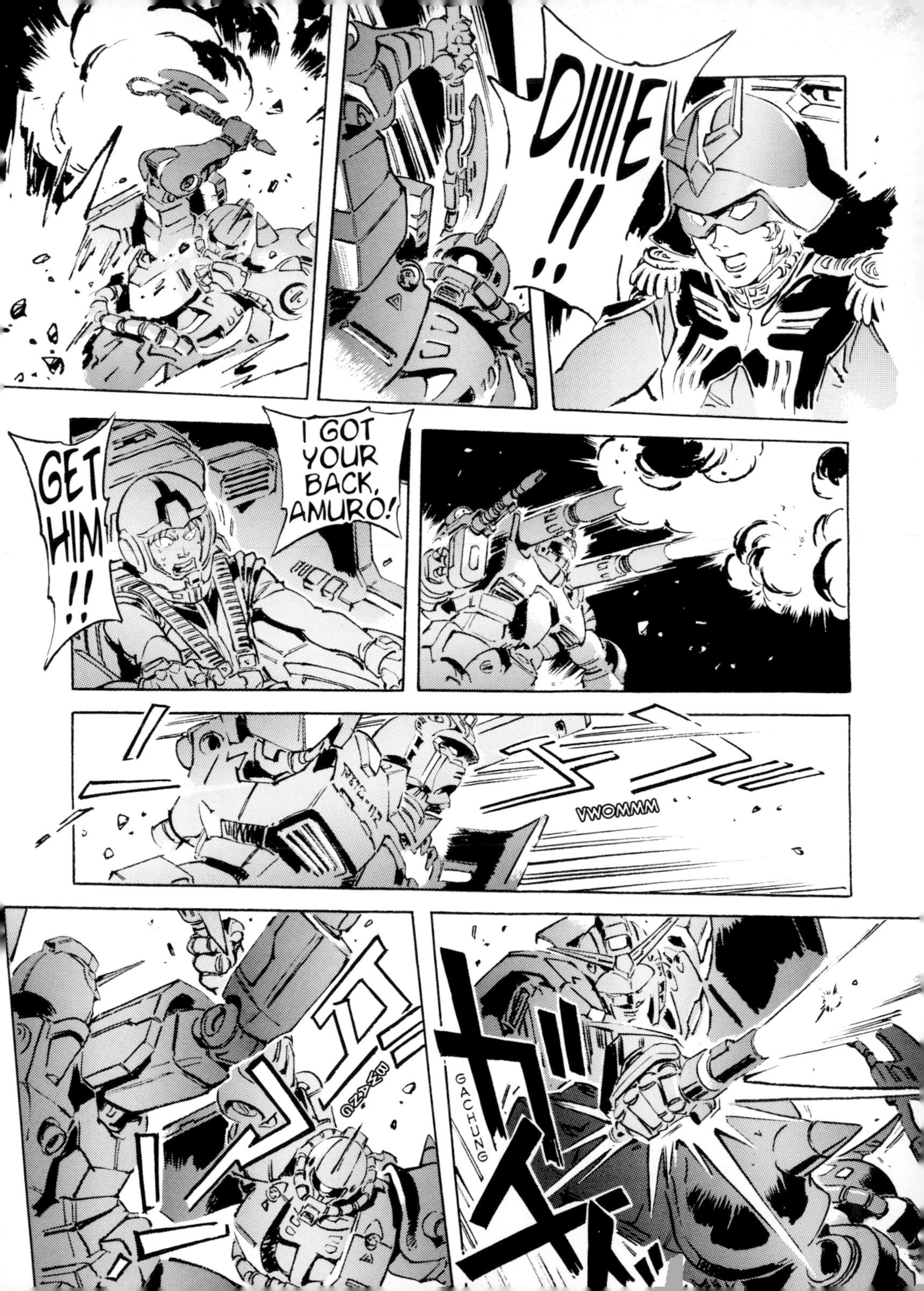
DIIIIE!!!!
I GOT YOUR BACK, AMURO!
GET HIM!!
VWOMMM
GACHUNG
GZASH

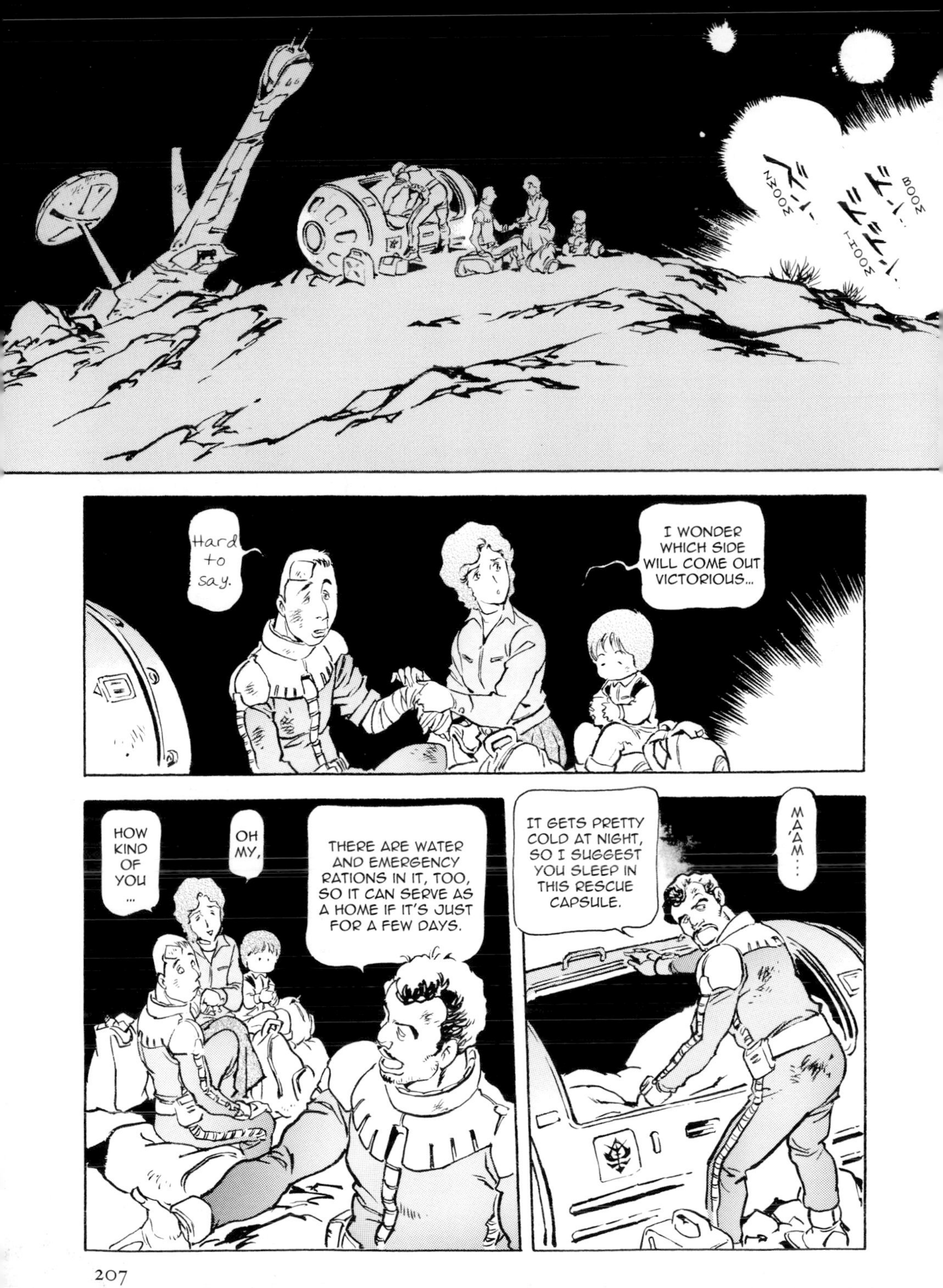
BOOM
THOOM
NWOOM
I WONDER WHICH SIDE WILL COME OUT VICTORIOUS...
Hard to say.
MA'AM...
IT GETS PRETTY COLD AT NIGHT, SO I SUGGEST YOU SLEEP IN THIS RESCUE CAPSULE.
THERE ARE WATER AND EMERGENCY RATIONS IN IT, TOO, SO IT CAN SERVE AS A HOME IF IT'S JUST FOR A FEW DAYS.
OH MY,
HOW KIND OF YOU ...

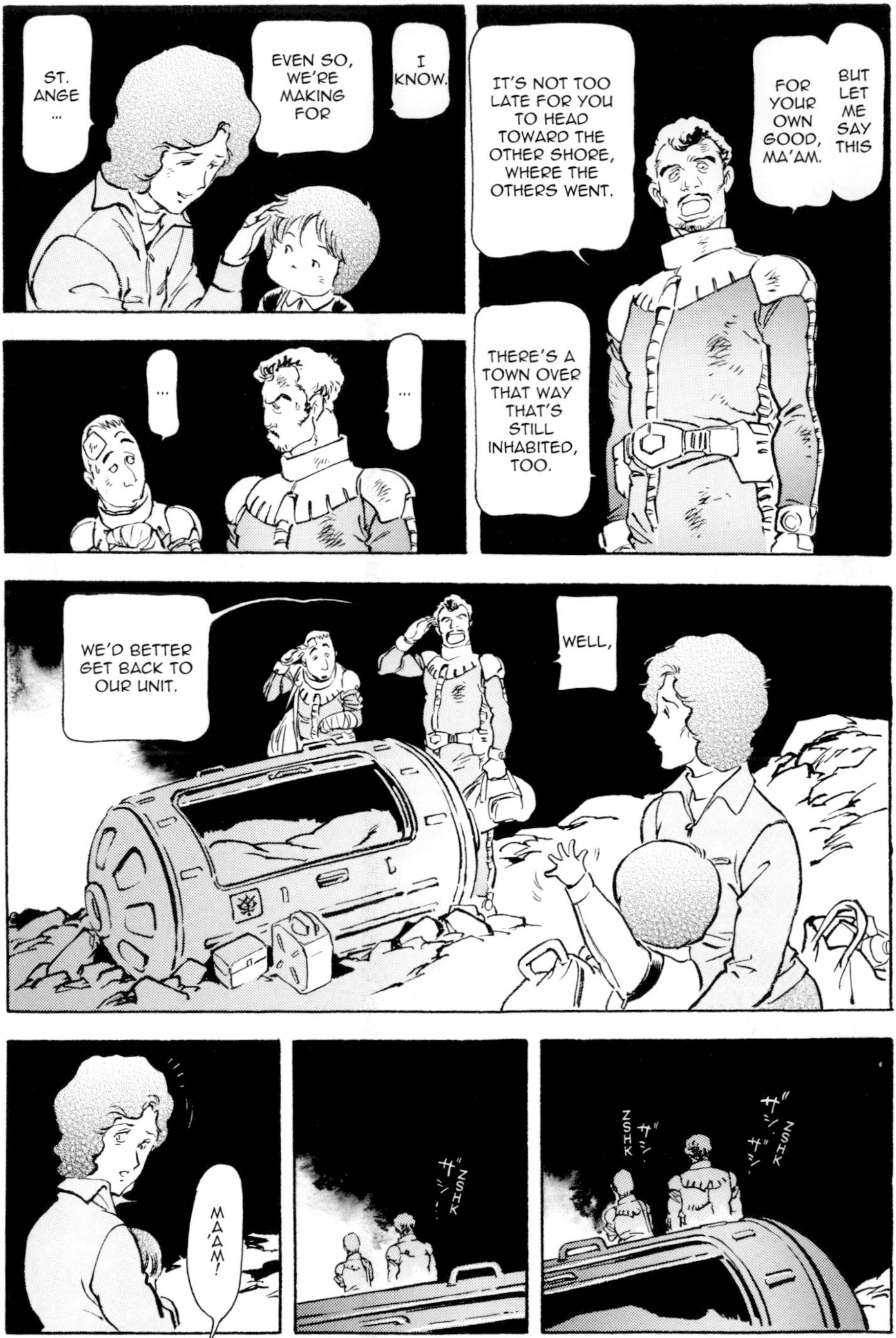
BUT LET ME SAY THIS
FOR YOUR OWN GOOD, MA'AM.
IT'S NOT TOO LATE FOR YOU TO HEAD TOWARD THE OTHER SHORE, WHERE THE OTHERS WENT.
THERE'S A TOWN OVER THAT WAY THAT'S STILL INHABITED, TOO.
I KNOW.
EVEN SO, WE'RE MAKING FOR
ST. ANGE ...
...
...
WELL,
WE'D BETTER GET BACK TO OUR UNIT.
ザッ ZSHK
ザッ ザッ
ZSHK
ザッ ZSHK
MA'AM!

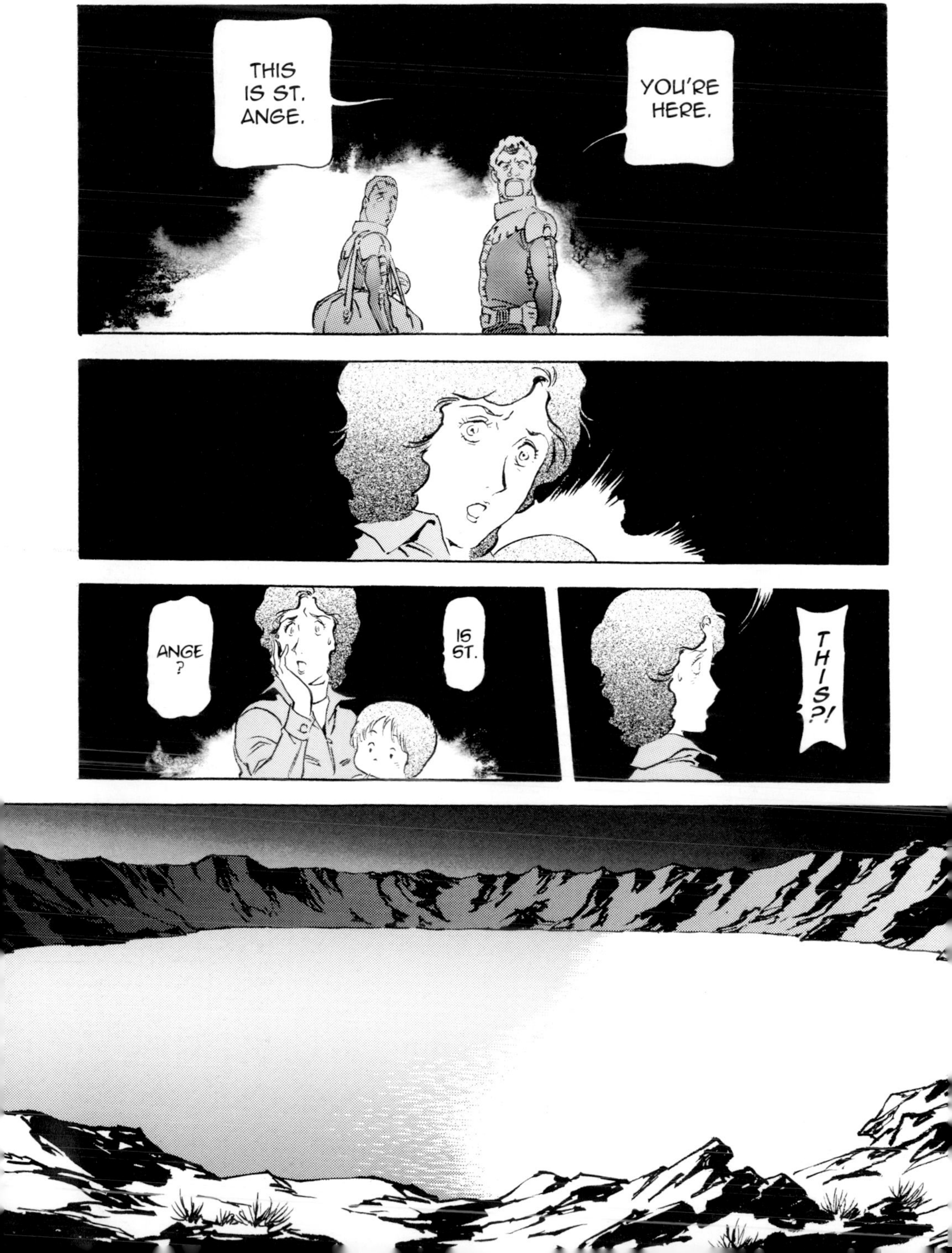
YOU'RE HERE.
THIS IS ST. ANGE.
THIS?!
IS ST.
ANGE?

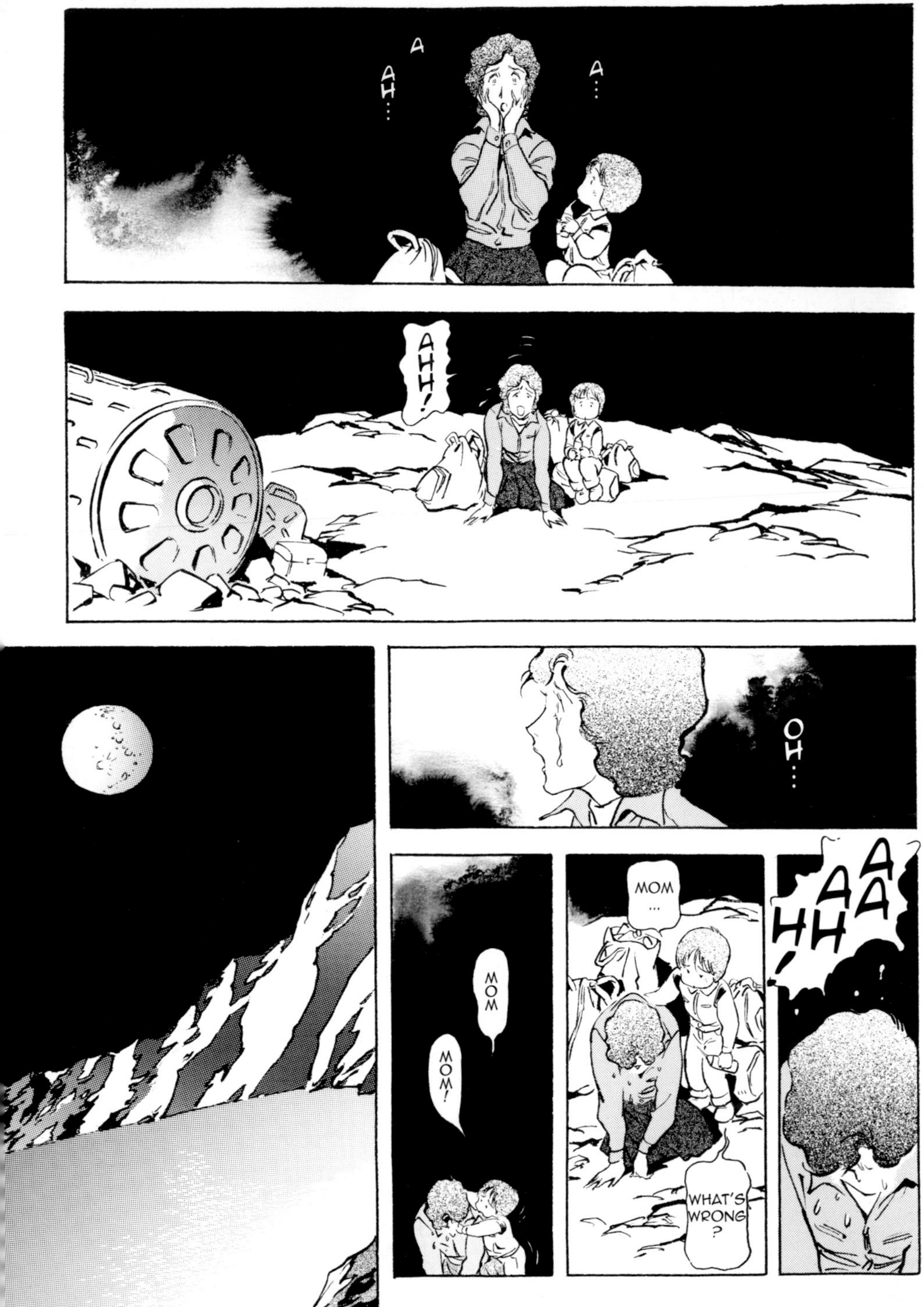
A...
A
AH...
AHH!
OH...
AAAAHH!
MOM...
WHAT'S WRONG?
MOM
MOM!

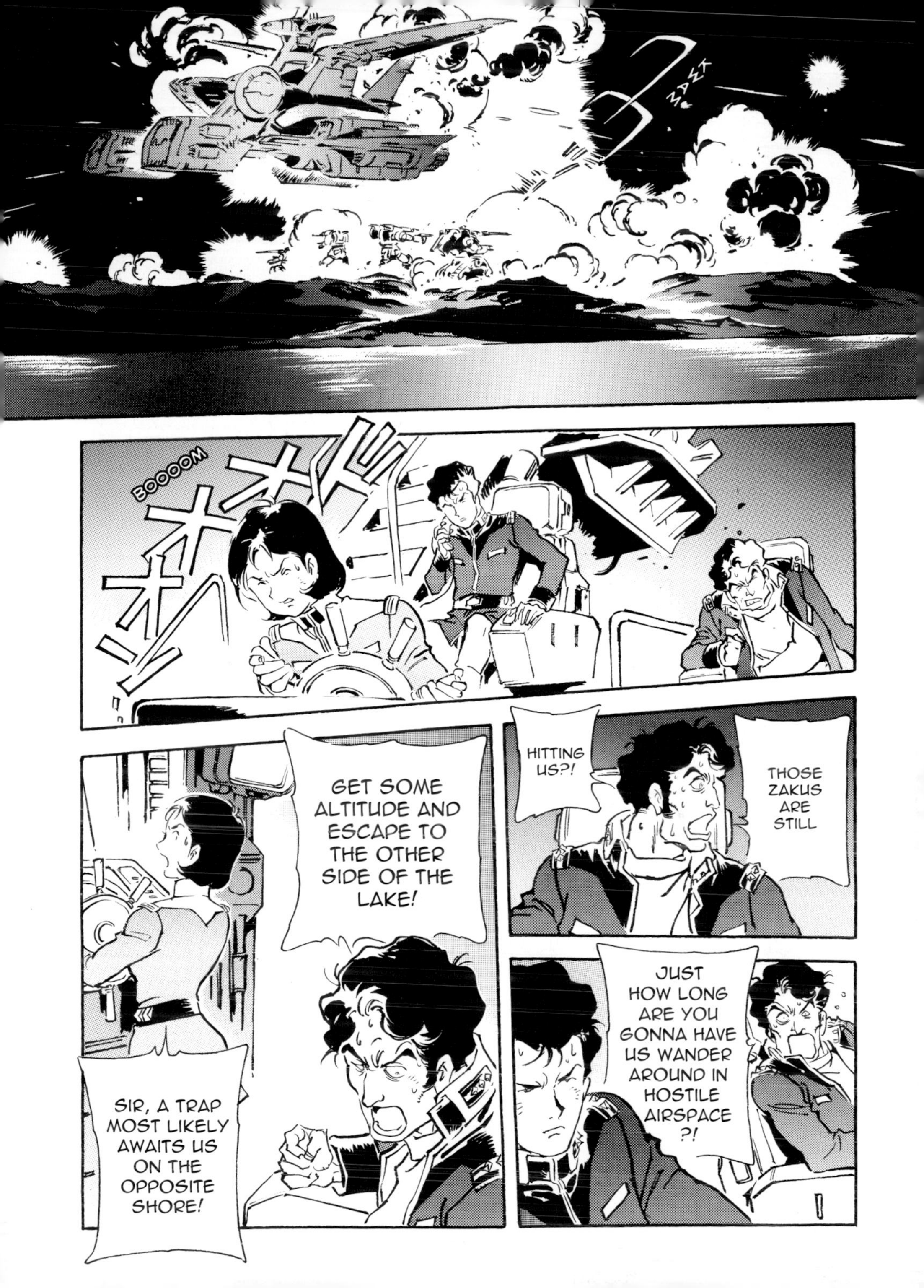
ZPEK
BOOOOM
THOSE ZAKUS ARE STILL
HITTING US?!
JUST HOW LONG ARE YOU GONNA HAVE US WANDER AROUND IN HOSTILE AIRSPACE ?!
GET SOME ALTITUDE AND ESCAPE TO THE OTHER SIDE OF THE LAKE!
SIR, A TRAP MOST LIKELY AWAITS US ON THE OPPOSITE SHORE!

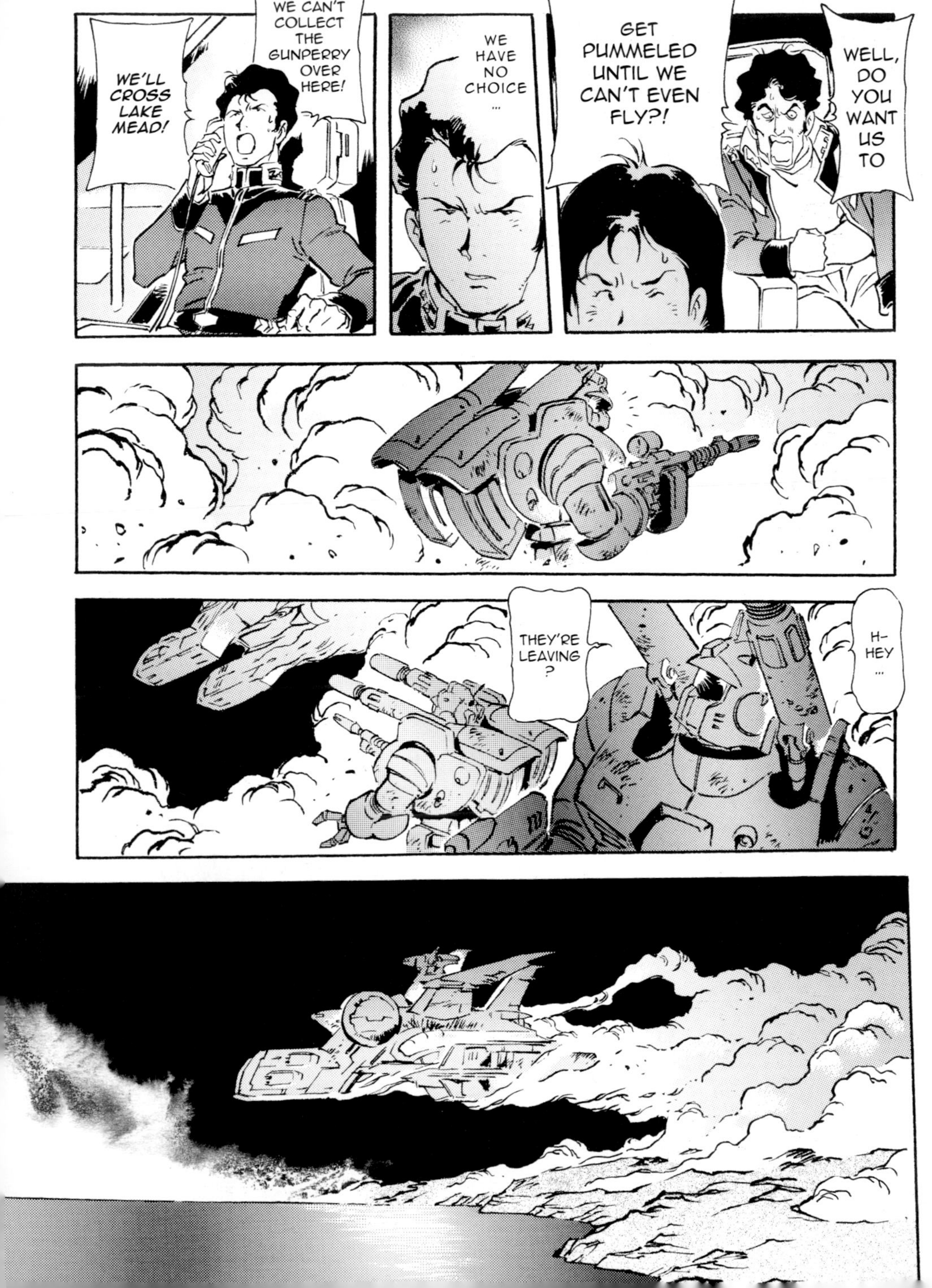
WELL, DO YOU WANT US TO
GET PUMMELED UNTIL WE CAN'T EVEN FLY?!
WE HAVE NO CHOICE ...
WE CAN'T COLLECT THE GUNPERRY OVER HERE!
WE'LL CROSS LAKE MEAD!
H-HEY ...
THEY'RE LEAVING ?

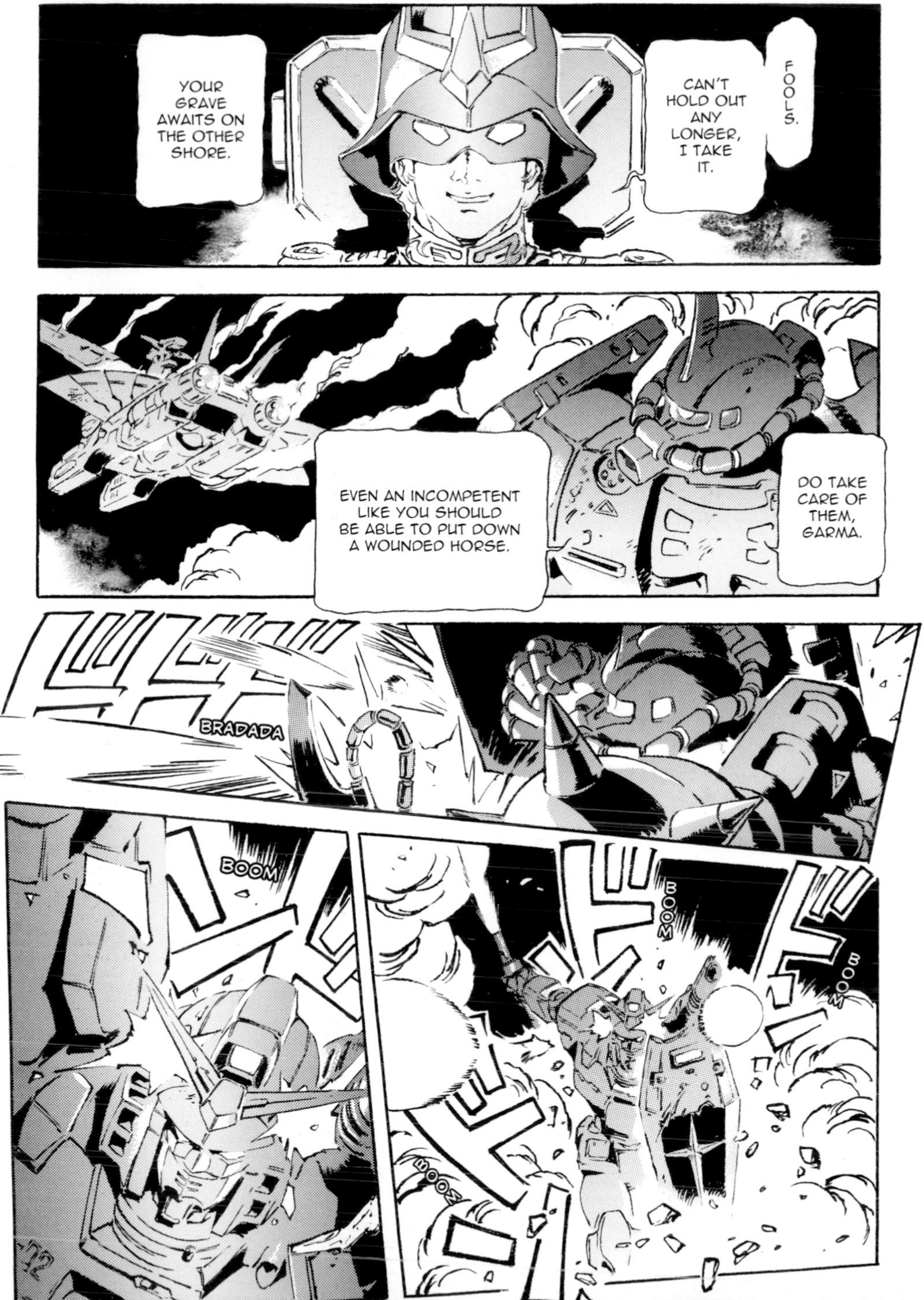
FOOLS.
CAN'T HOLD OUT ANY LONGER, I TAKE IT.
YOUR GRAVE AWAITS ON THE OTHER SHORE.
DO TAKE CARE OF THEM, GARMA.
EVEN AN INCOMPETENT LIKE YOU SHOULD BE ABLE TO PUT DOWN A WOUNDED HORSE.
BRADADA
BOOM
BOOM
BOOM
BOOM

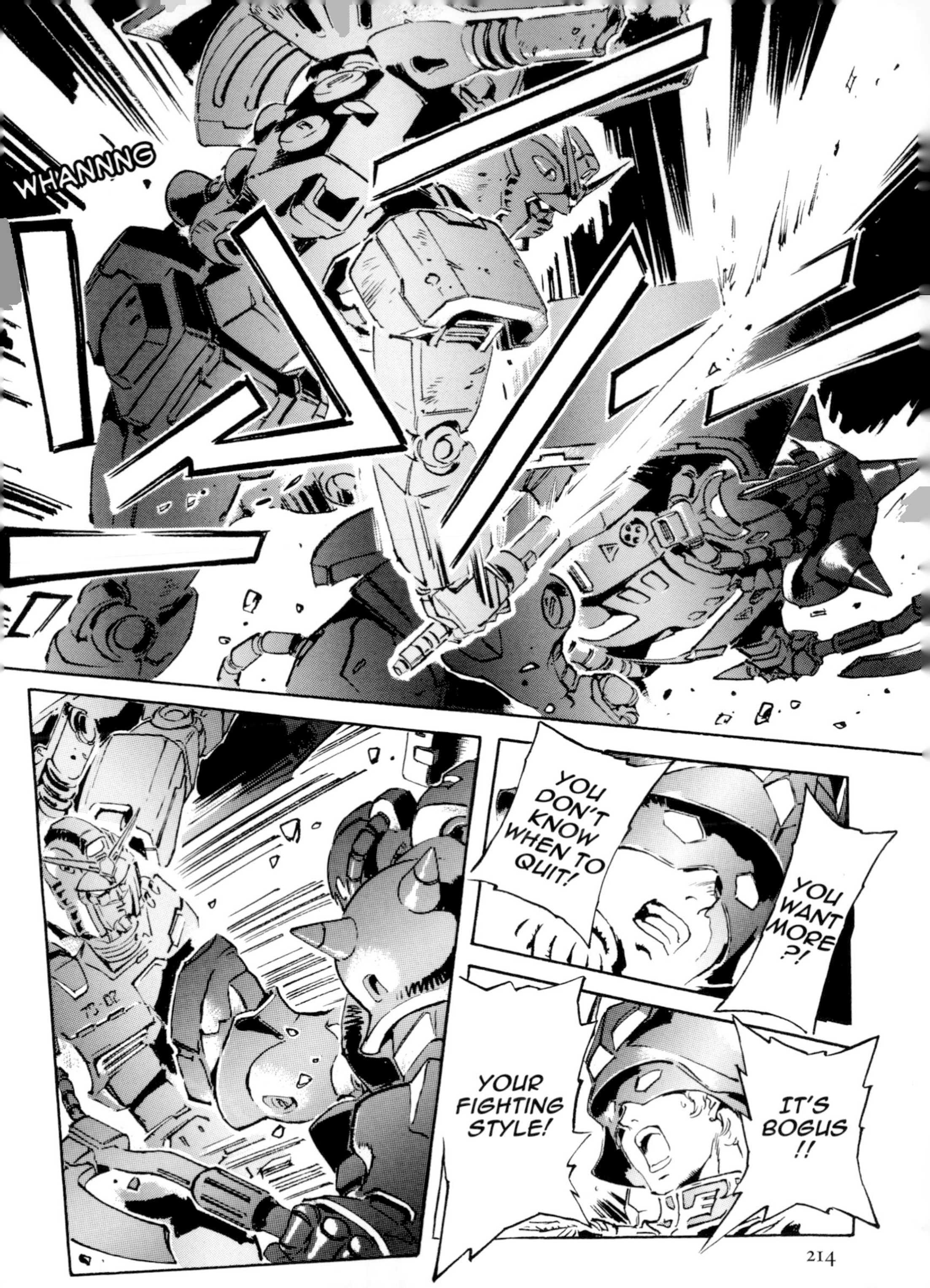
WHANNNG
YOU WANT MORE?!
YOU DON'T KNOW WHEN TO QUIT!
IT'S BOGUS!!
YOUR FIGHTING STYLE!

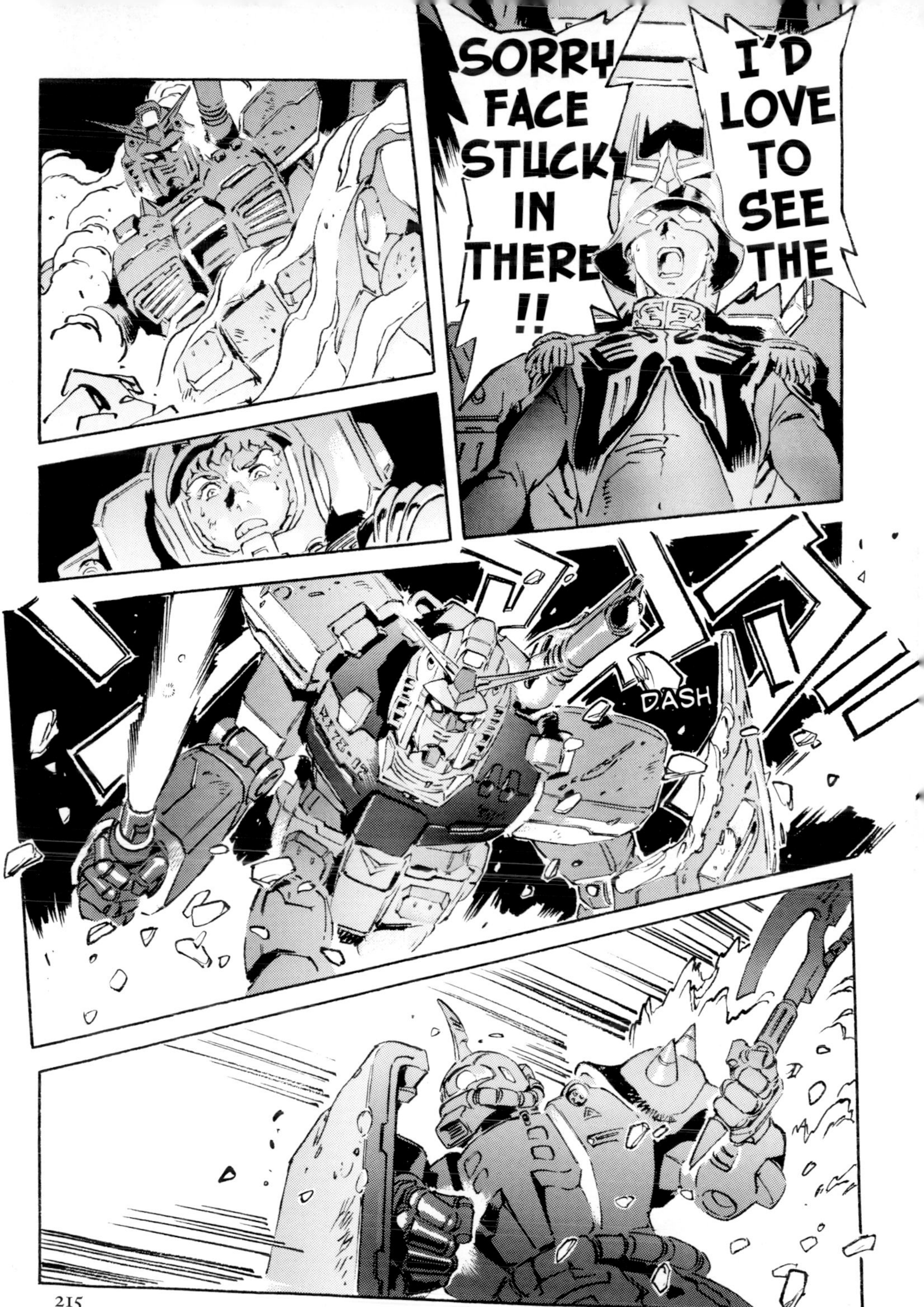
I'D LOVE TO SEE THE
SORRY FACE STUCK IN THERE!!
DASH

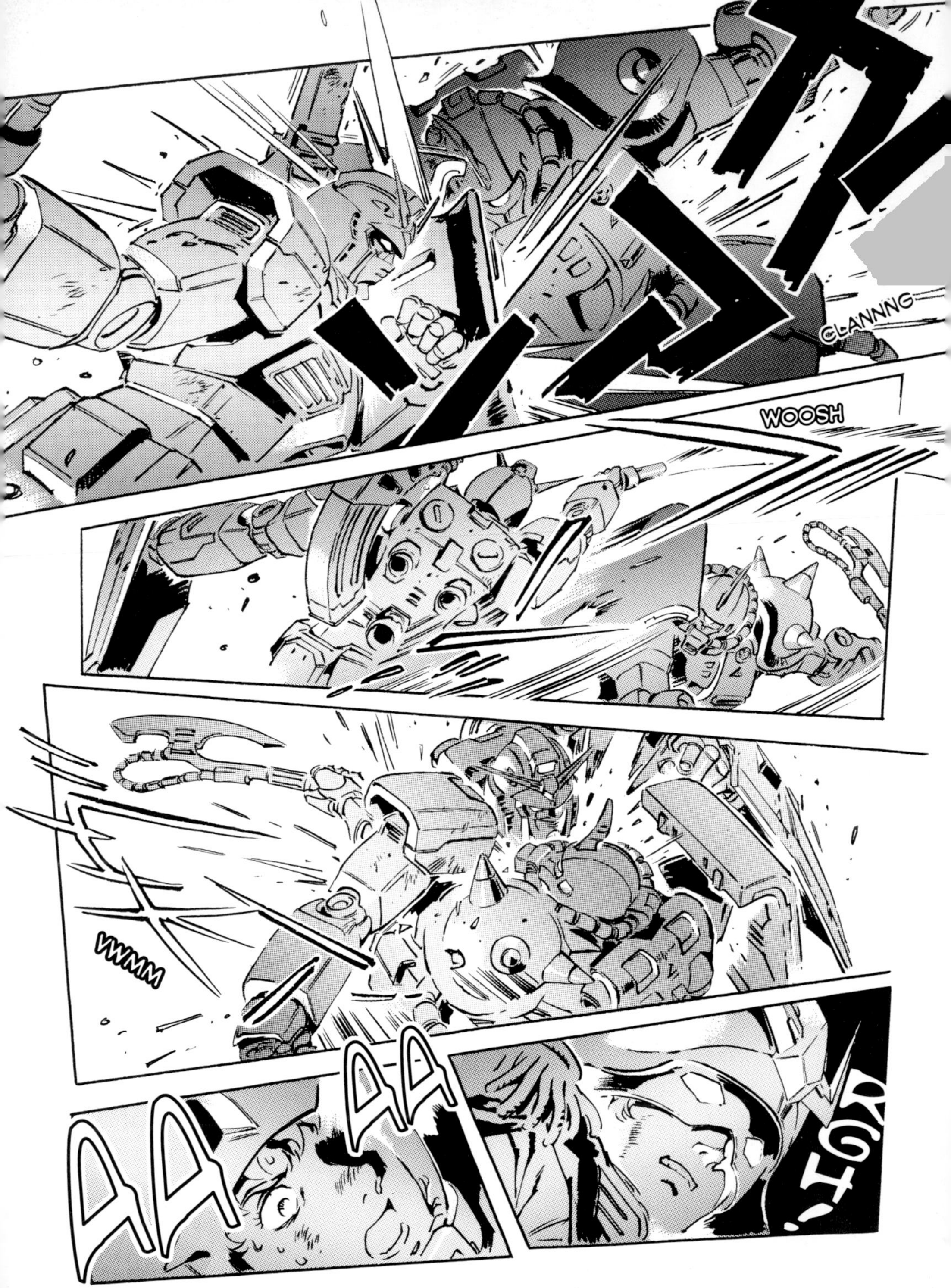
CLANNNG
WOOSH
VWMM
AAAA

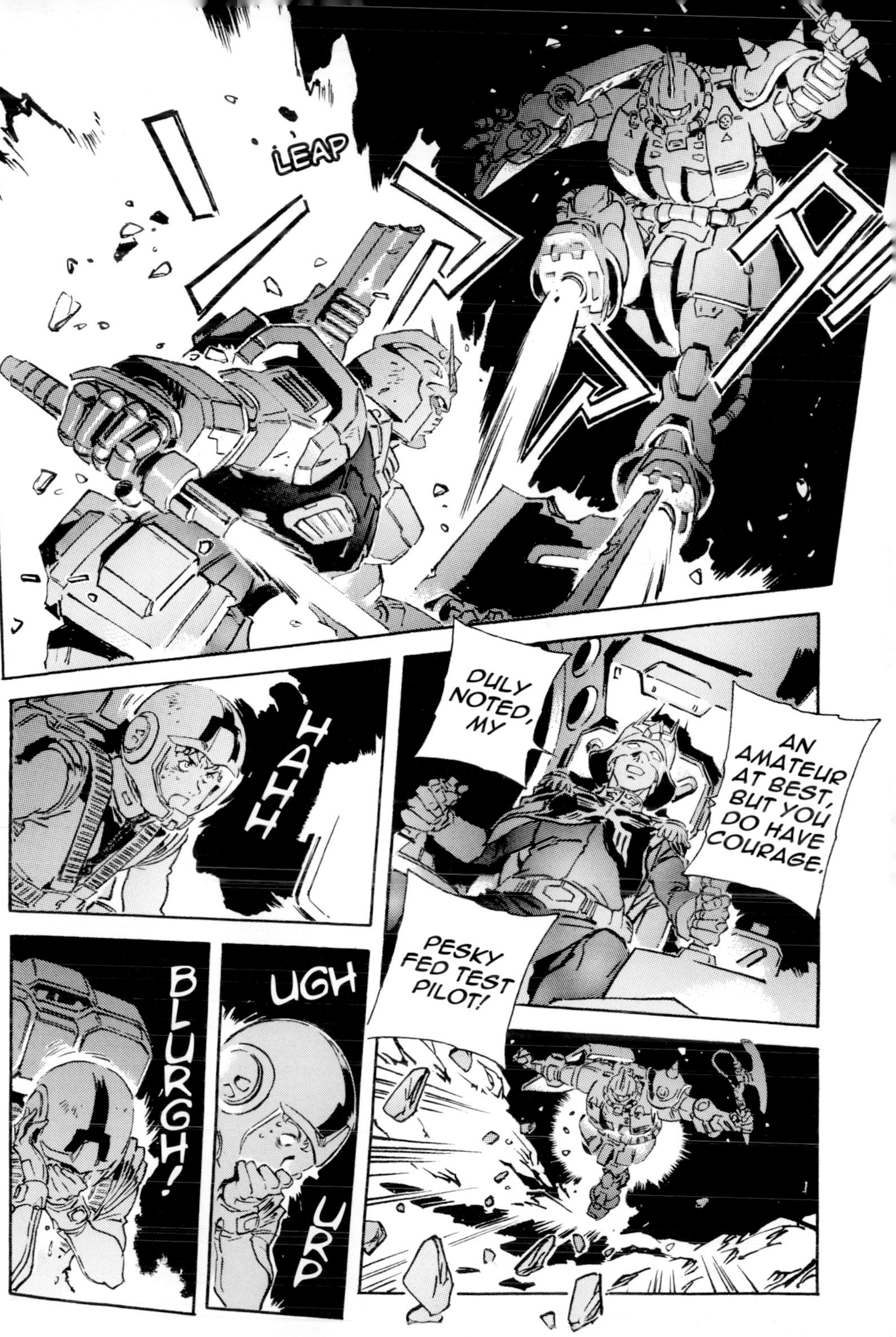
LEAP
AN AMATEUR AT BEST, BUT YOU DO HAVE COURAGE.
DULY NOTED, MY
PESKY FED TEST PILOT!
HAHHH
UGH
URP
BLURGH!

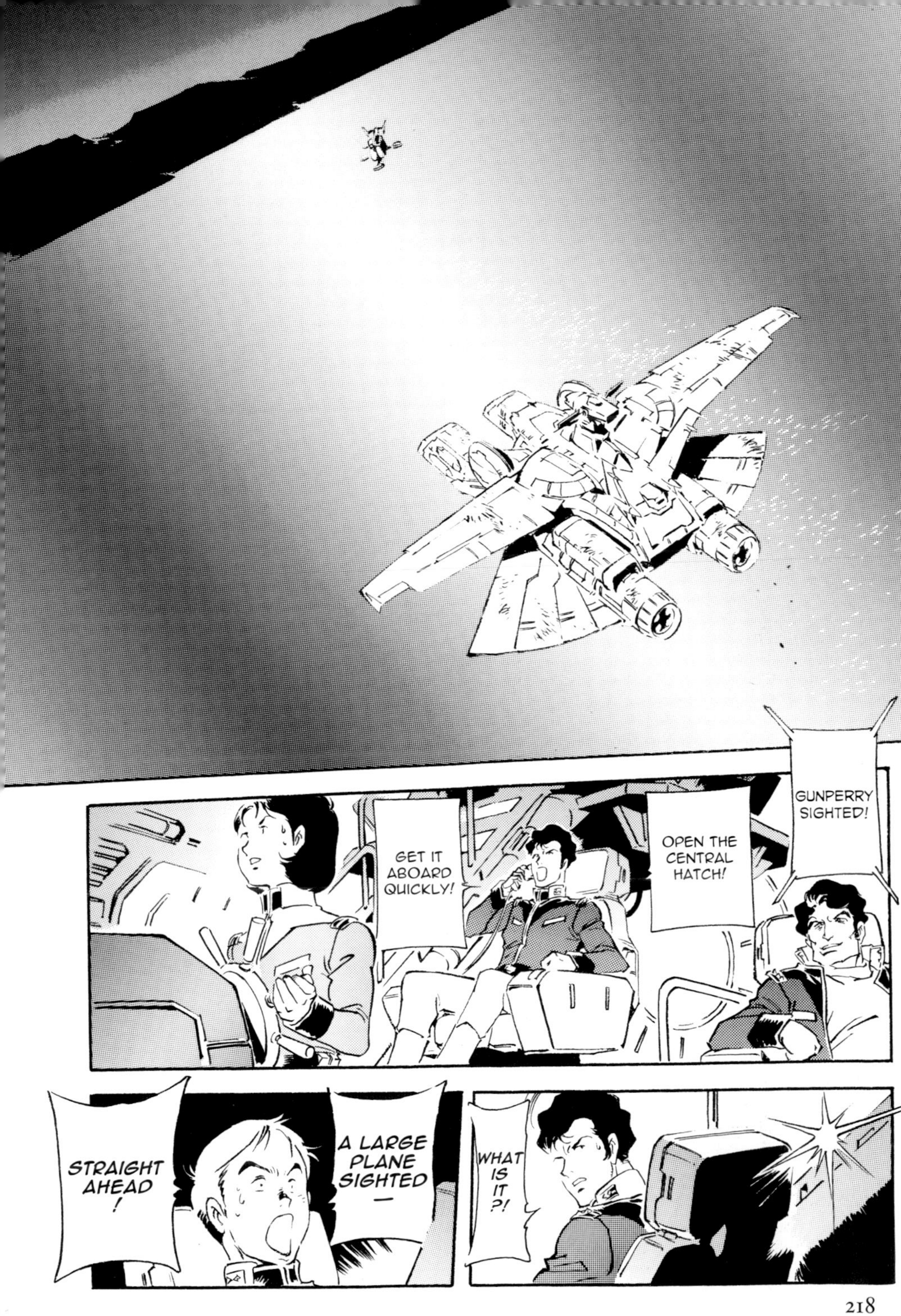
GUNPERRY SIGHTED!
OPEN THE CENTRAL HATCH!
GET IT ABOARD QUICKLY!
WHAT IS IT ?!
A LARGE PLANE SIGHTED —
STRAIGHT AHEAD !

THE GAW ?!
NO —
ANOTHER TYPE!
A MEDEA!

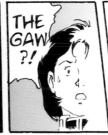

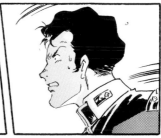

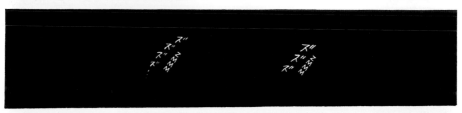

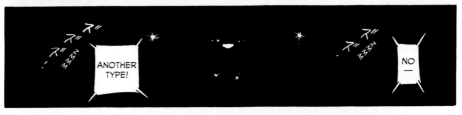

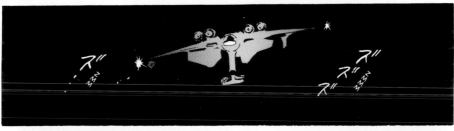

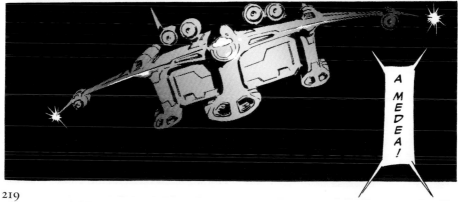

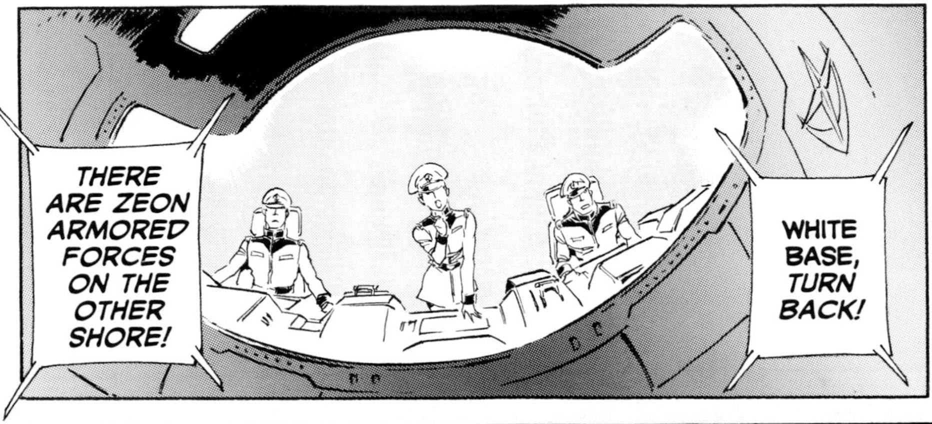
WHITE BASE, TURN BACK!
THERE ARE ZEON ARMORED FORCES ON THE OTHER SHORE!

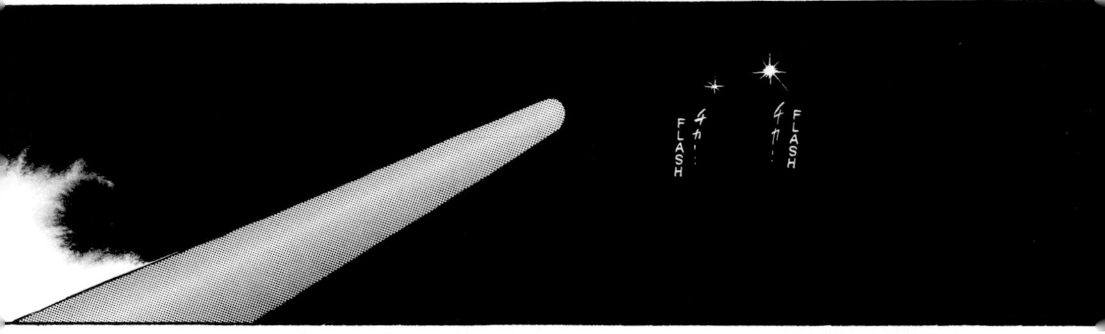
FLASH
FLASH

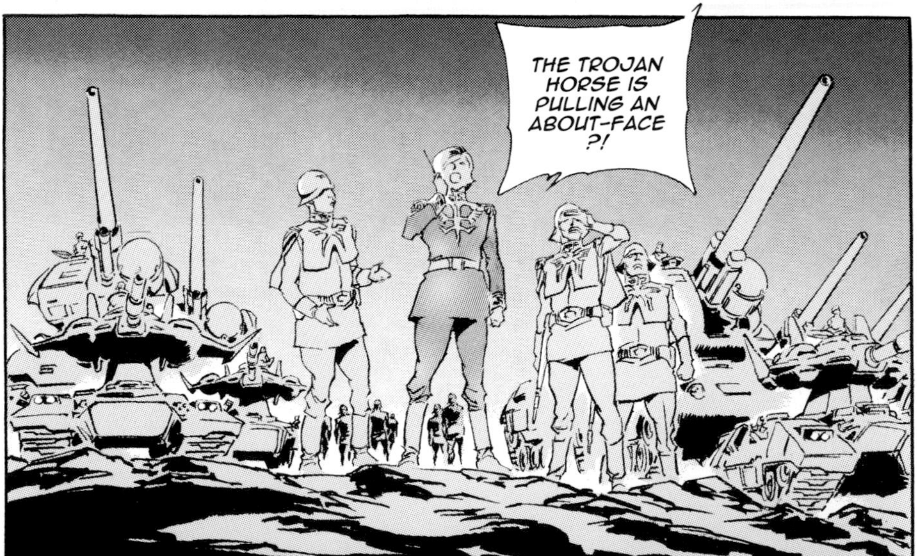
THE TROJAN HORSE IS PULLING AN ABOUT-FACE?!

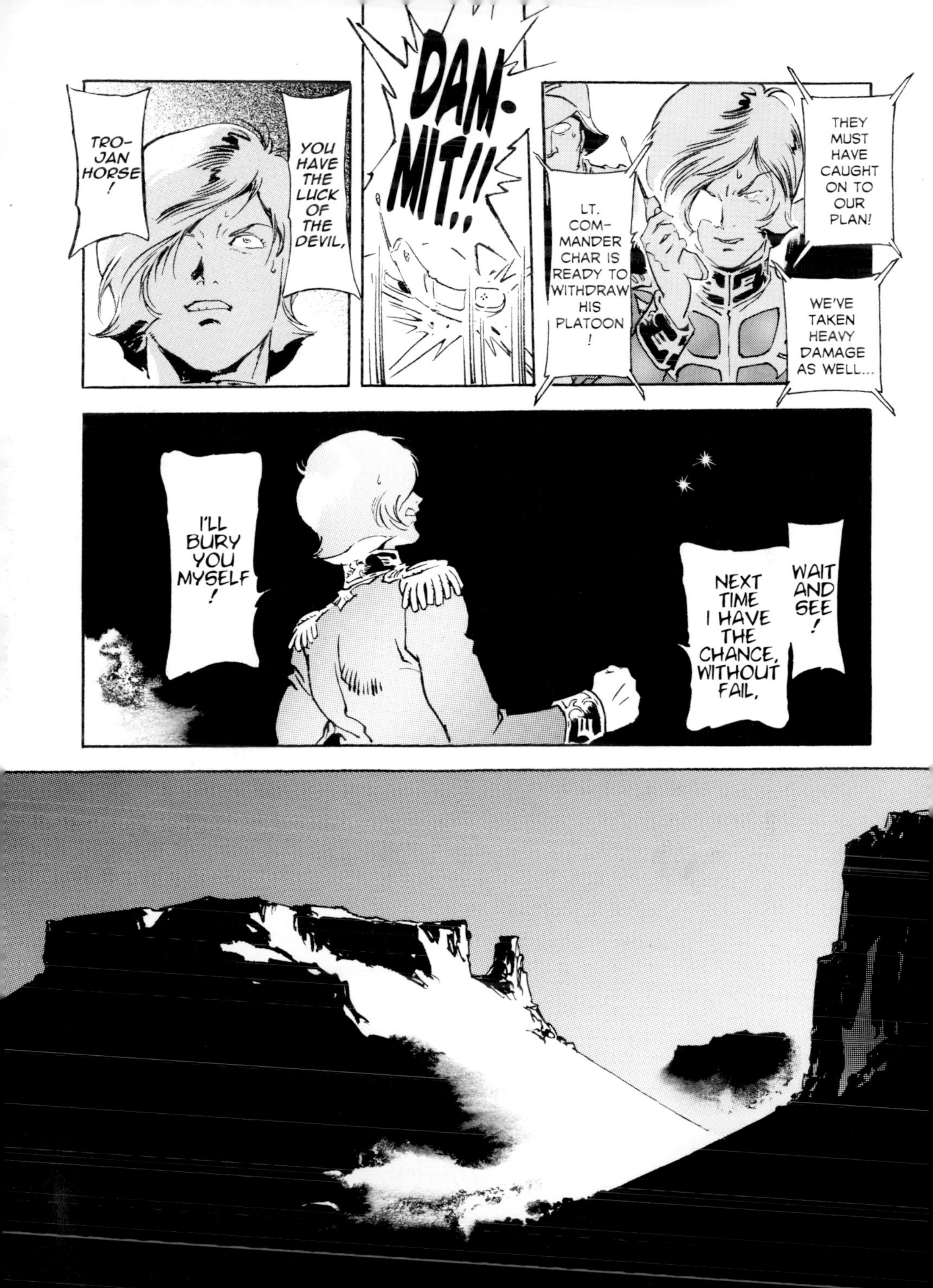
THEY MUST HAVE CAUGHT ON TO OUR PLAN!
WE'VE TAKEN HEAVY DAMAGE AS WELL...
LT. COMMANDER CHAR IS READY TO WITHDRAW HIS PLATOON!
DAMMIT!!
YOU HAVE THE LUCK OF THE DEVIL,
TROJAN HORSE!
WAIT AND SEE!
NEXT TIME I HAVE THE CHANCE, WITHOUT FAIL,
I'LL BURY YOU MYSELF!

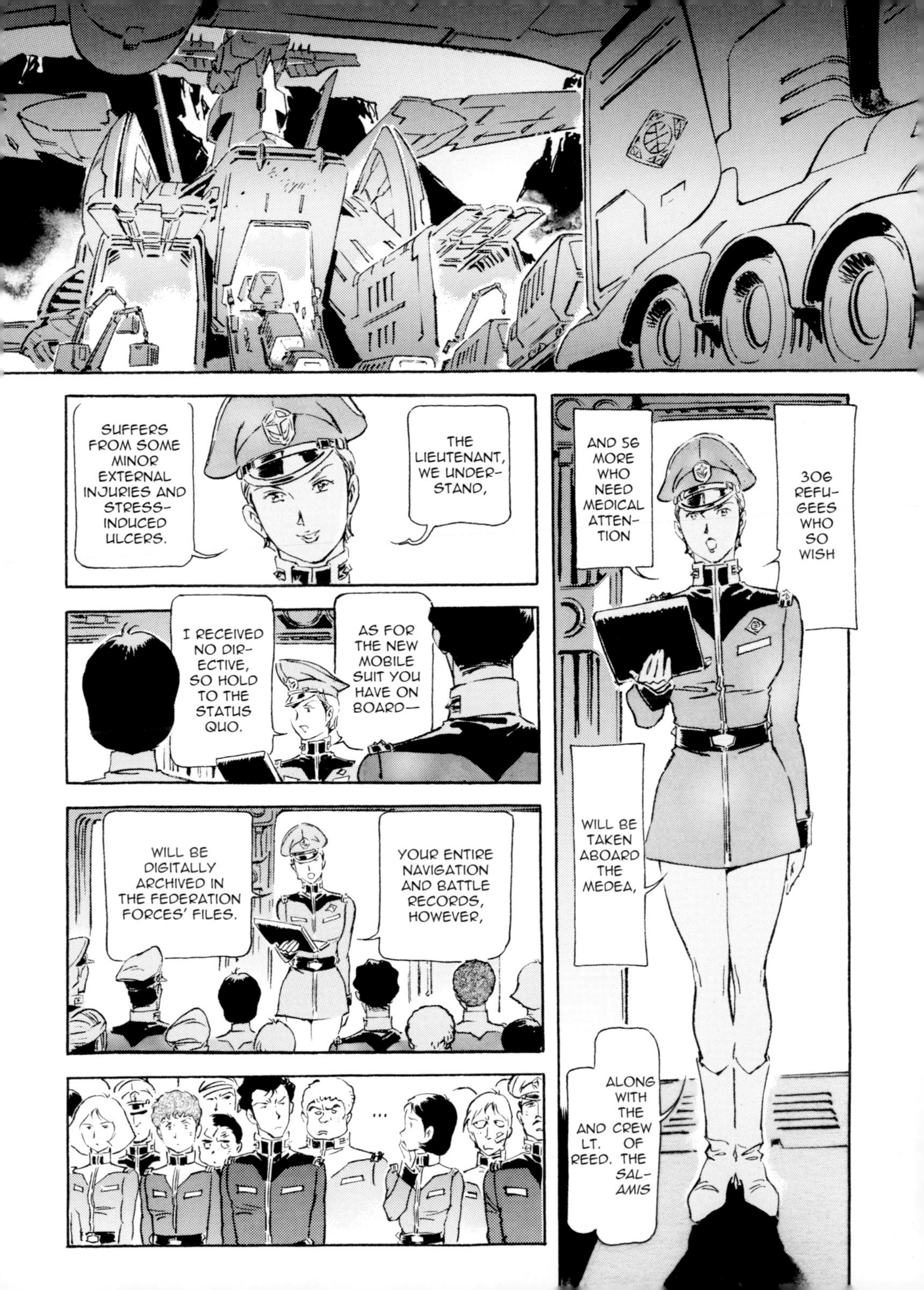
306 REFUGEES WHO SO WISH
AND 56 MORE WHO NEED MEDICAL ATTENTION
WILL BE TAKEN ABOARD THE MEDEA,
ALONG WITH THE CREW OF THE *SALAMIS*
AND LT. REED.
THE LIEUTENANT, WE UNDERSTAND,
SUFFERS FROM SOME MINOR EXTERNAL INJURIES AND STRESS-INDUCED ULCERS.
AS FOR THE NEW MOBILE SUIT YOU HAVE ON BOARD—
I RECEIVED NO DIRECTIVE, SO HOLD TO THE STATUS QUO.
YOUR ENTIRE NAVIGATION AND BATTLE RECORDS, HOWEVER,
WILL BE DIGITALLY ARCHIVED IN THE FEDERATION FORCES' FILES.
...

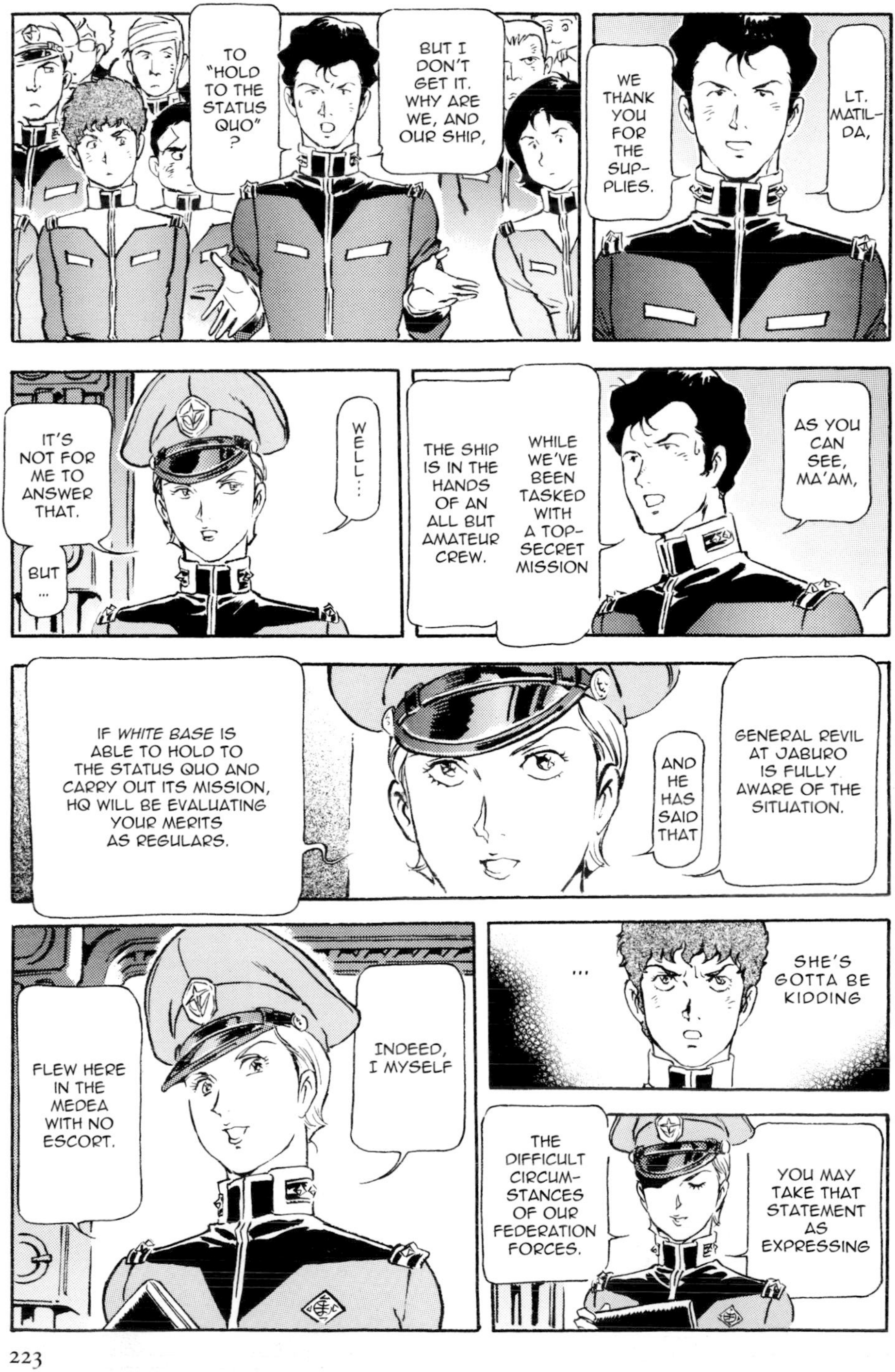
LT. MATILDA,
WE THANK YOU FOR THE SUPPLIES.
BUT I DON'T GET IT. WHY ARE WE, AND OUR SHIP,
TO "HOLD TO THE STATUS QUO"?
AS YOU CAN SEE, MA'AM,
WHILE WE'VE BEEN TASKED WITH A TOP-SECRET MISSION
THE SHIP IS IN THE HANDS OF AN ALL BUT AMATEUR CREW.
WELL...
IT'S NOT FOR ME TO ANSWER THAT.
BUT ...
GENERAL REVIL AT JABURO IS FULLY AWARE OF THE SITUATION.
AND HE HAS SAID THAT
IF *WHITE BASE* IS ABLE TO HOLD TO THE STATUS QUO AND CARRY OUT ITS MISSION, HQ WILL BE EVALUATING YOUR MERITS AS REGULARS.
SHE'S GOTTA BE KIDDING
...
YOU MAY TAKE THAT STATEMENT AS EXPRESSING
THE DIFFICULT CIRCUMSTANCES OF OUR FEDERATION FORCES.
INDEED, I MYSELF
FLEW HERE IN THE MEDEA WITH NO ESCORT.

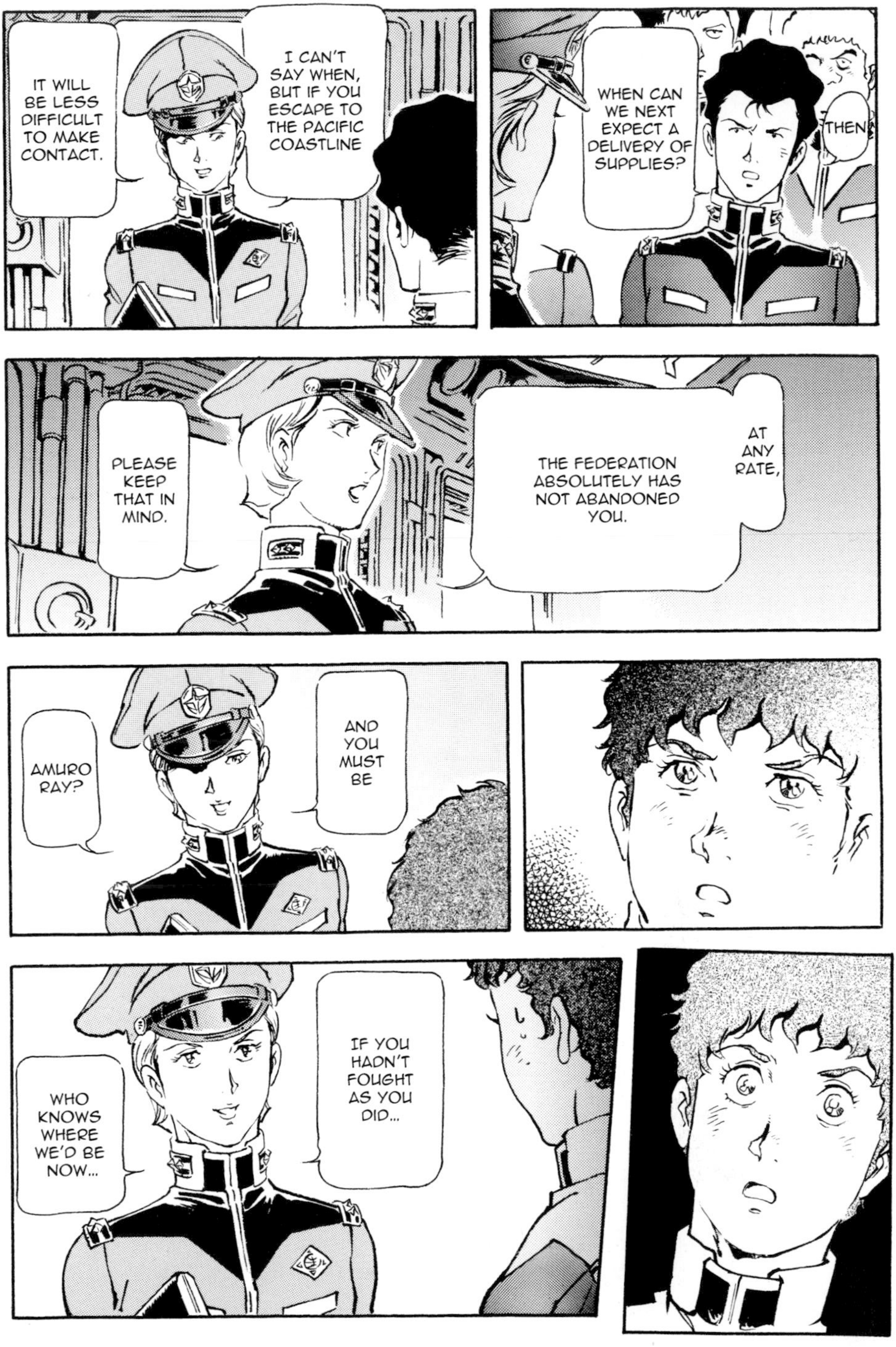
THEN
WHEN CAN WE NEXT EXPECT A DELIVERY OF SUPPLIES?
I CAN'T SAY WHEN, BUT IF YOU ESCAPE TO THE PACIFIC COASTLINE
IT WILL BE LESS DIFFICULT TO MAKE CONTACT.
AT ANY RATE,
THE FEDERATION ABSOLUTELY HAS NOT ABANDONED YOU.
PLEASE KEEP THAT IN MIND.
AND YOU MUST BE
AMURO RAY?
IF YOU HADN'T FOUGHT AS YOU DID...
WHO KNOWS WHERE WE'D BE NOW...

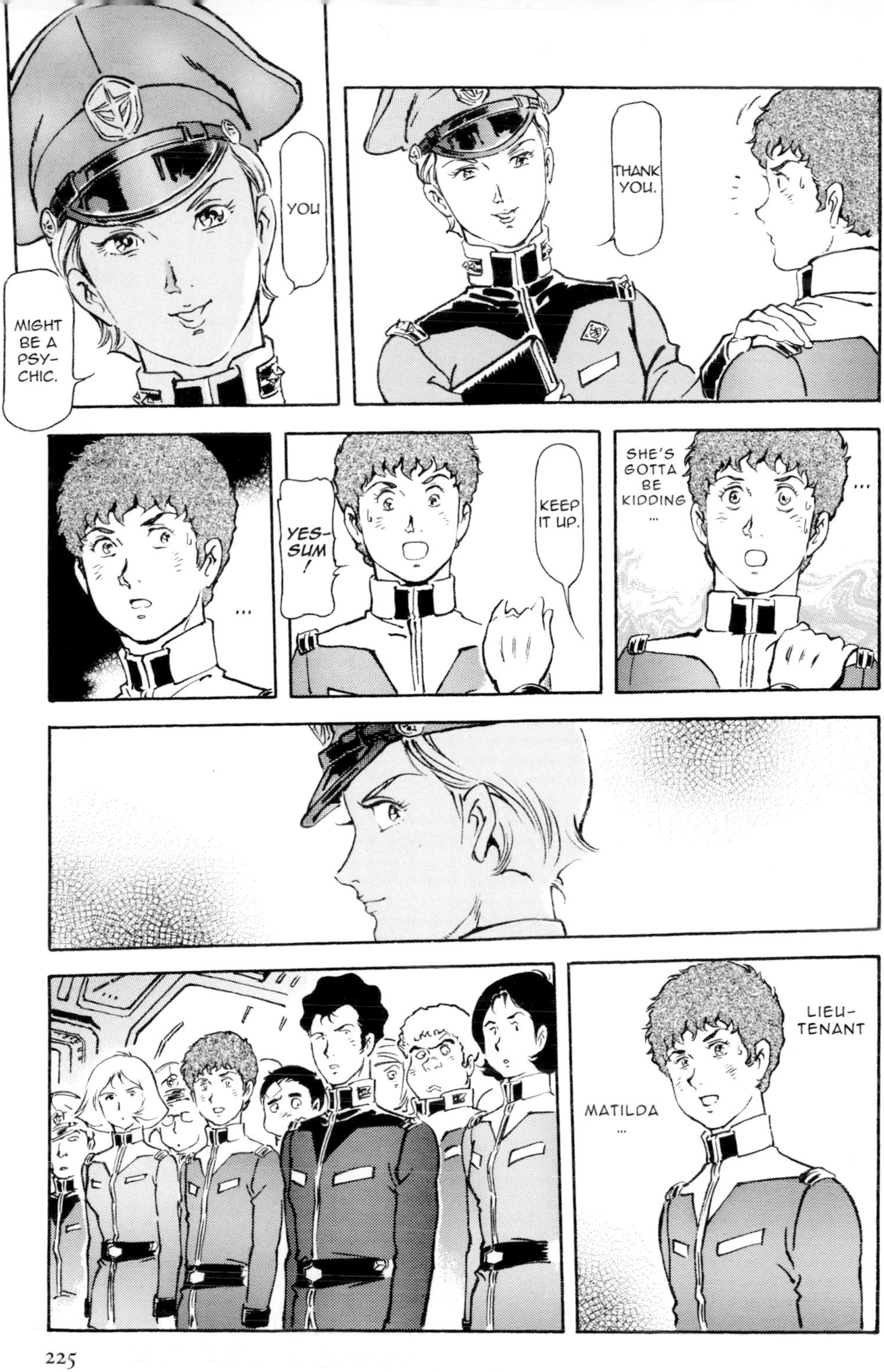
THANK YOU.
YOU
MIGHT BE A PSY-CHIC.
SHE'S GOTTA BE KIDDING ...
...
KEEP IT UP.
YES-SUM!
...
LIEU-TENANT
MATILDA ...

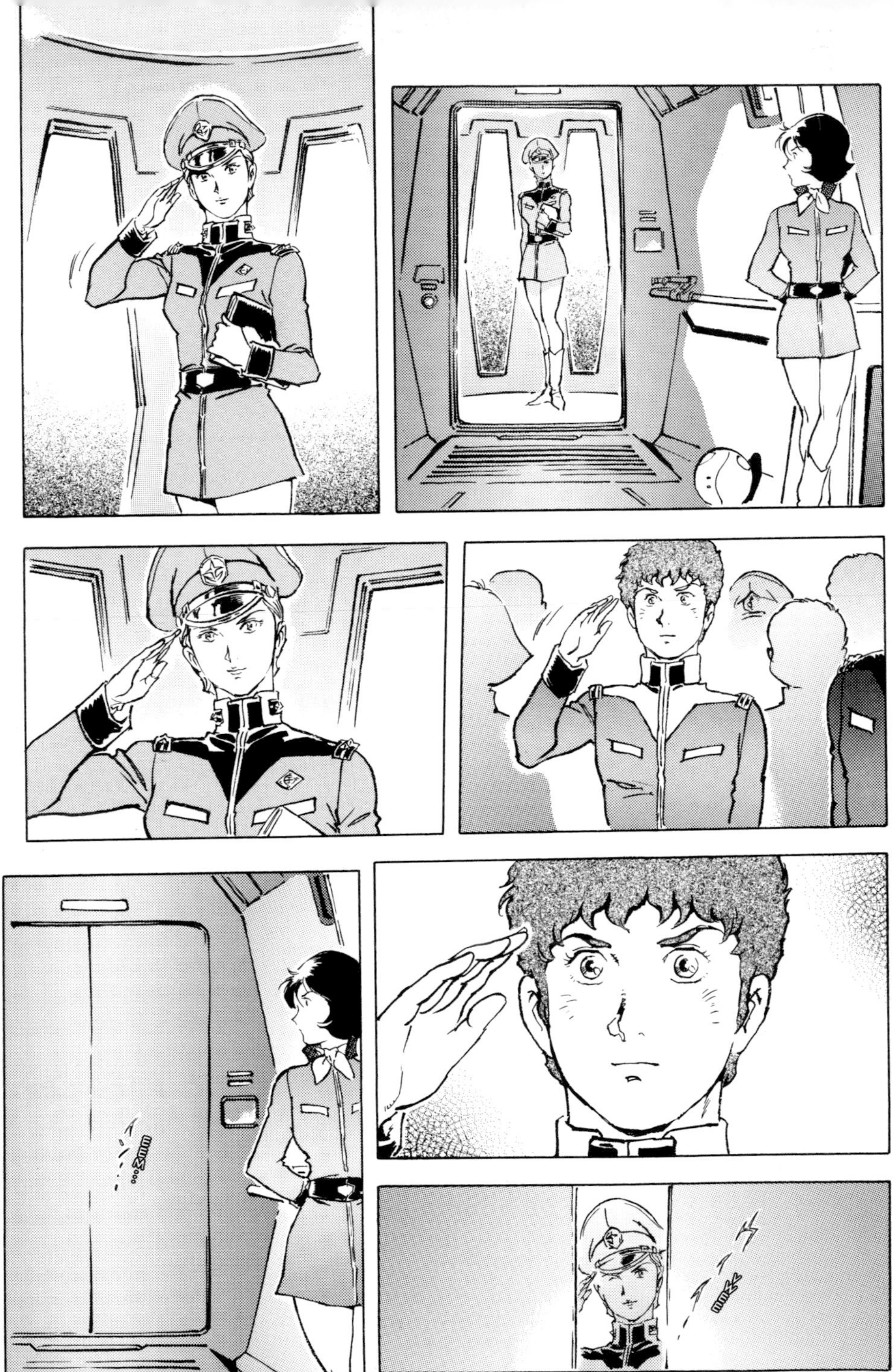

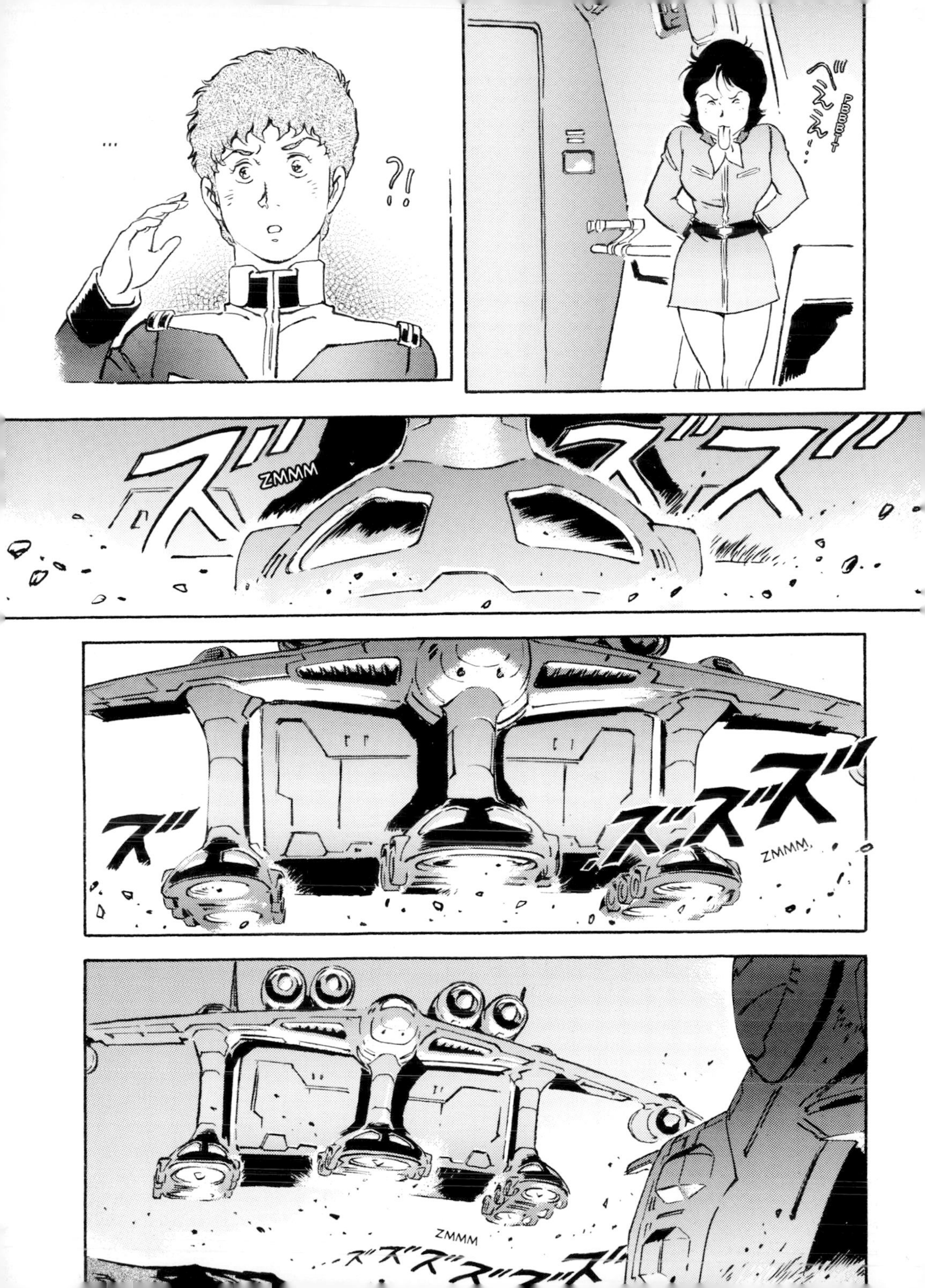
PBBBBTT
…
?!
ズ
ZMMM
ズズズ
ズズズズ
ZMMM
ZMMM
ズズズズズズズ

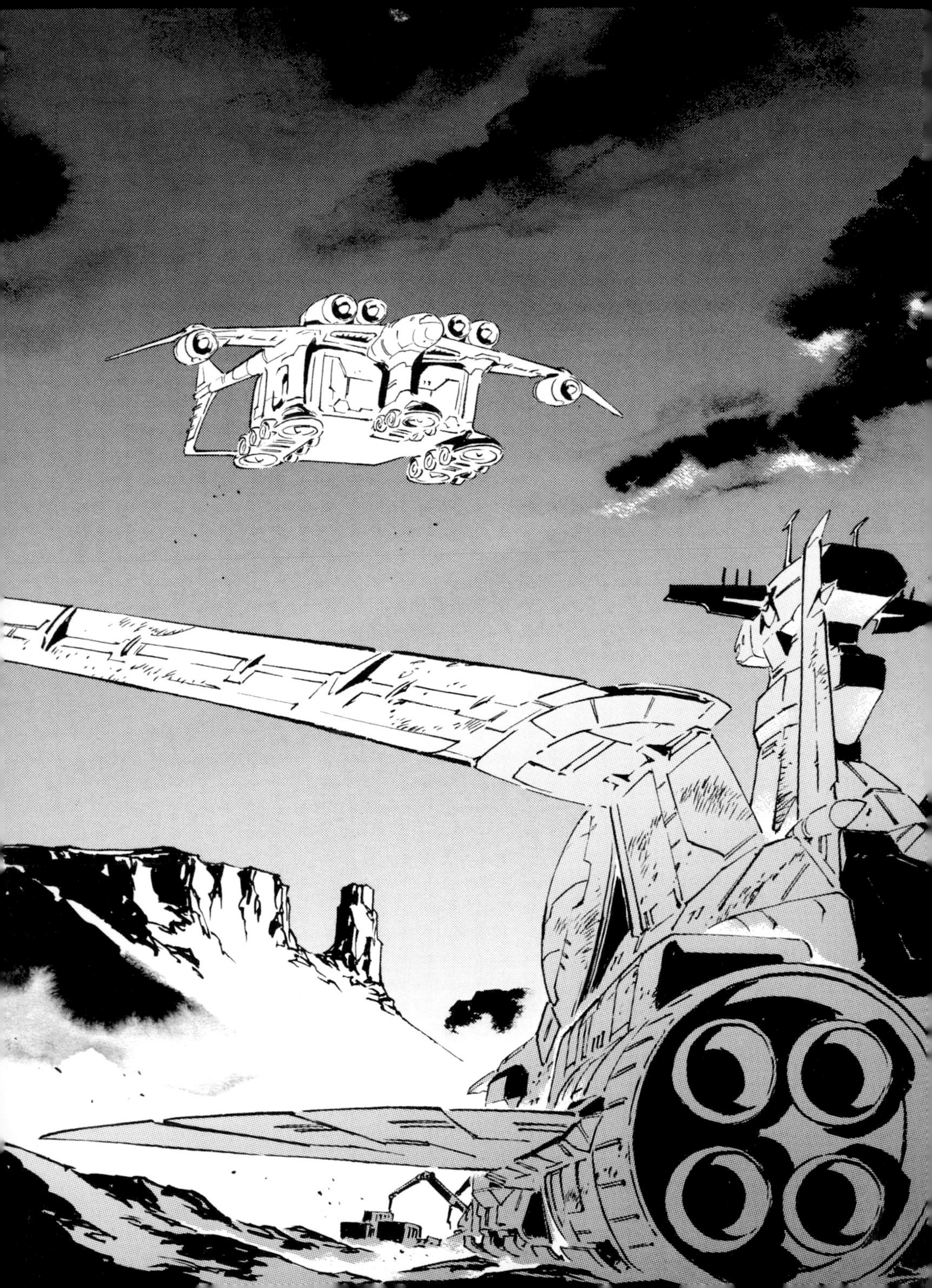

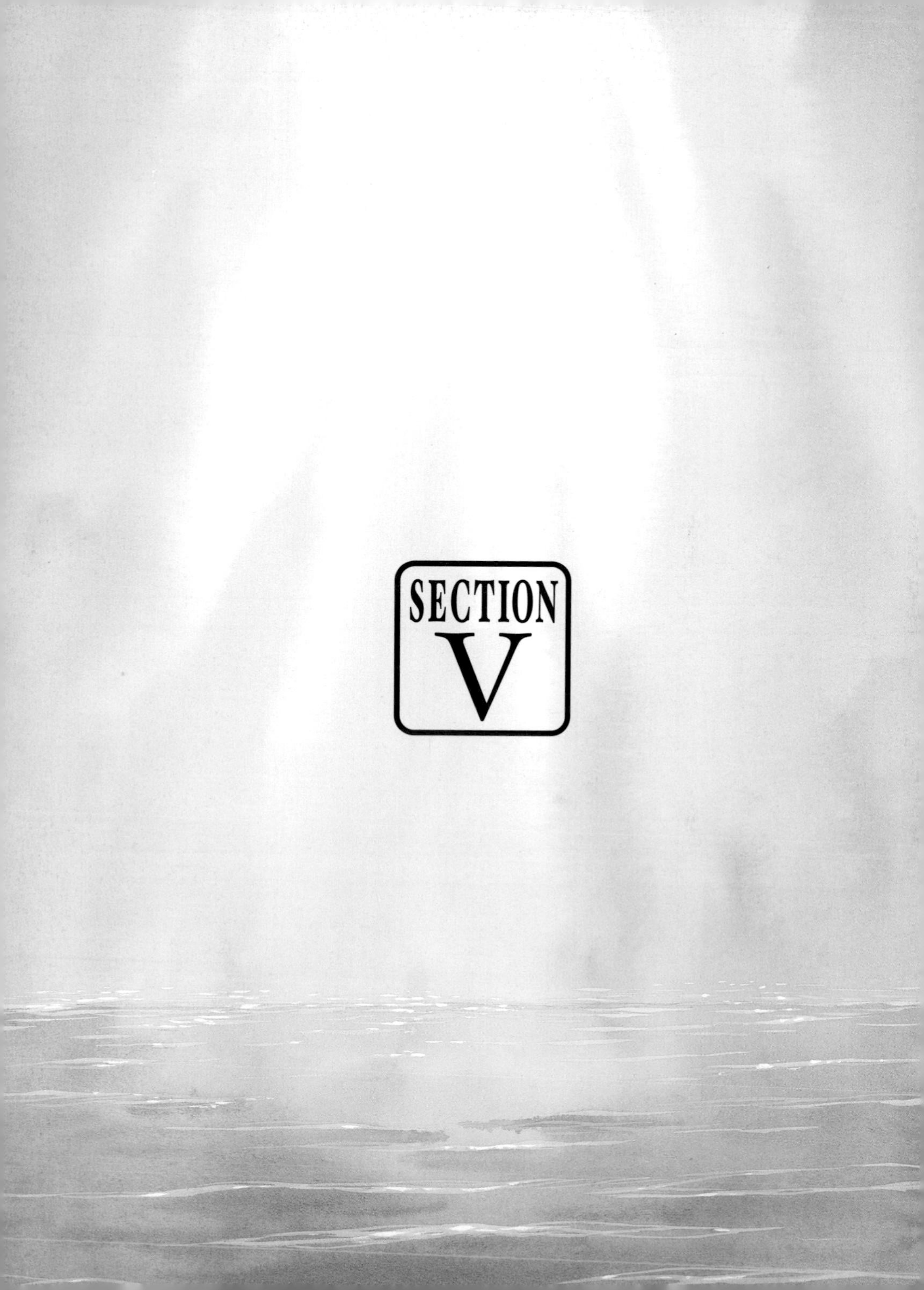

SECTION V

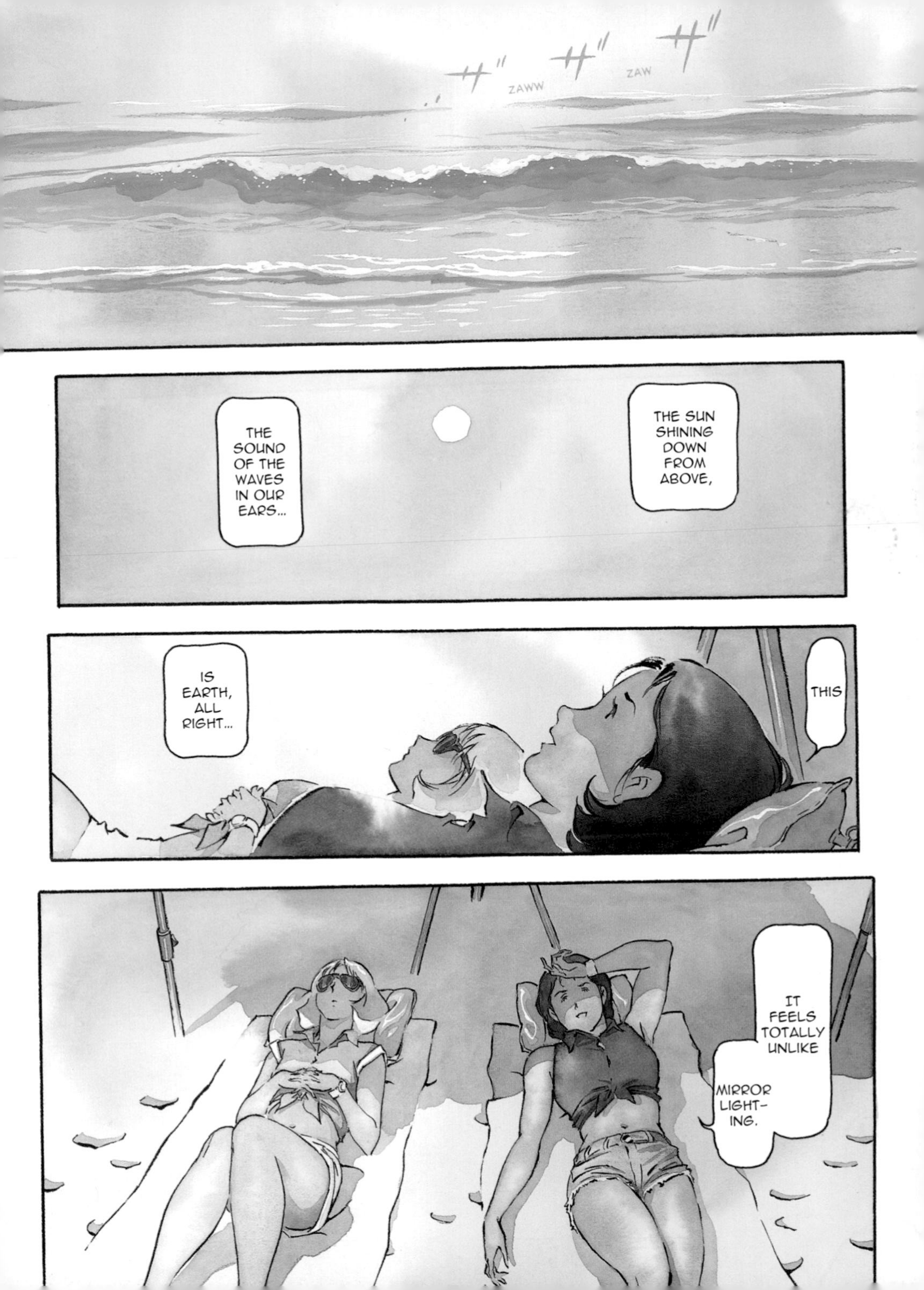
ZAW
ZAWW
THE SUN SHINING DOWN FROM ABOVE,
THE SOUND OF THE WAVES IN OUR EARS...
THIS
IS EARTH, ALL RIGHT...
IT FEELS TOTALLY UNLIKE
MIRROR LIGHTING.

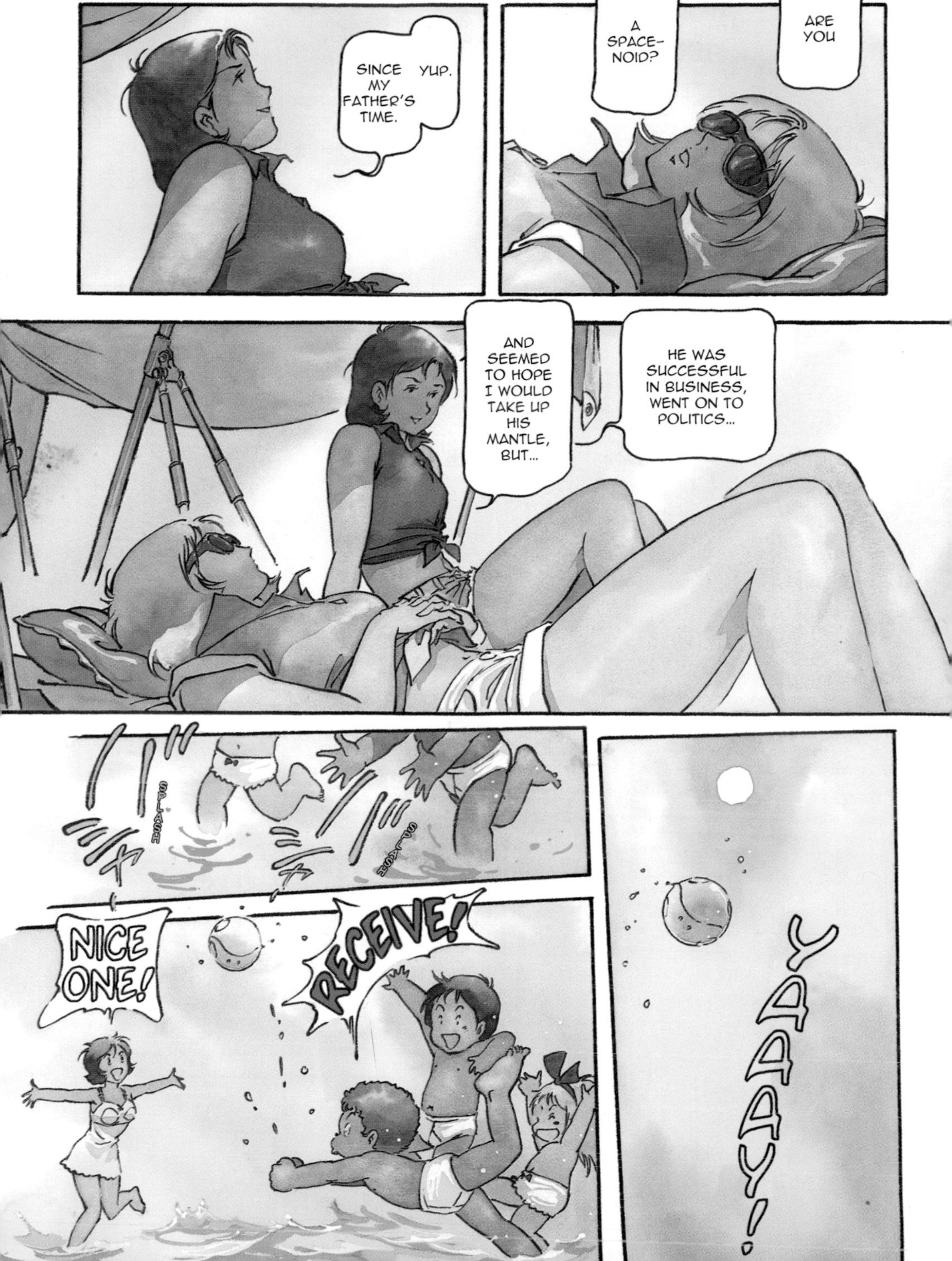
ARE YOU
A SPACE-NOID?
YUP.
SINCE MY FATHER'S TIME.
HE WAS SUCCESSFUL IN BUSINESS, WENT ON TO POLITICS...
AND SEEMED TO HOPE I WOULD TAKE UP HIS MANTLE, BUT...
YAAAY!
SPLASH
SPLASH
RECEIVE!
NICE ONE!

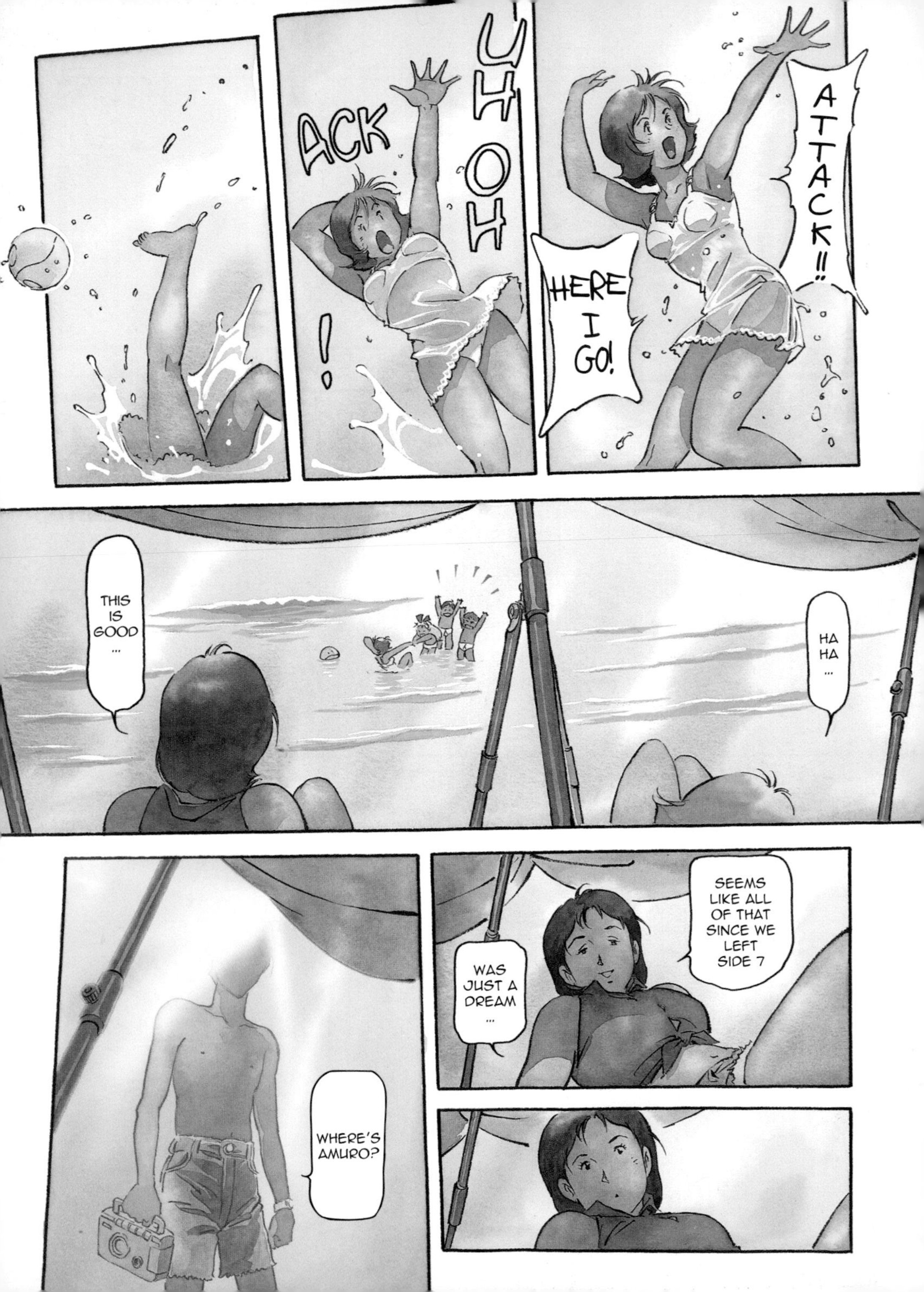
ATTACK!!
HERE I GO!
UH OH
ACK
!
HA HA ...
THIS IS GOOD ...
SEEMS LIKE ALL OF THAT SINCE WE LEFT SIDE 7
WAS JUST A DREAM ...
WHERE'S AMURO?

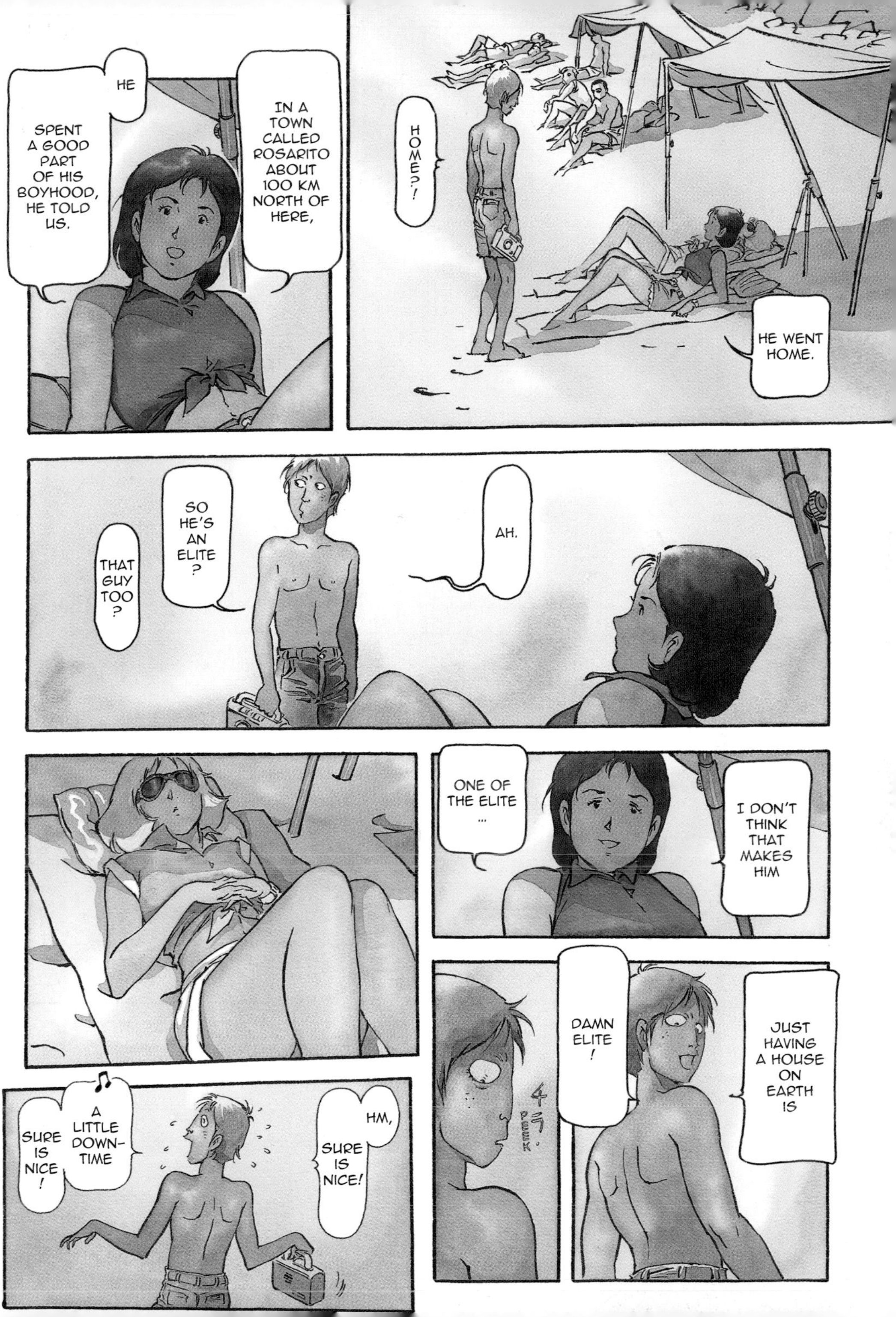
HE WENT HOME.
HOME?!
IN A TOWN CALLED ROSARITO ABOUT 100 KM NORTH OF HERE,
HE
SPENT A GOOD PART OF HIS BOYHOOD, HE TOLD US.
AH.
SO HE'S AN ELITE?
THAT GUY TOO?
I DON'T THINK THAT MAKES HIM
ONE OF THE ELITE ...
JUST HAVING A HOUSE ON EARTH IS
DAMN ELITE!
PEEEK
HM, SURE IS NICE!
♪ A LITTLE DOWN-TIME
SURE IS NICE!

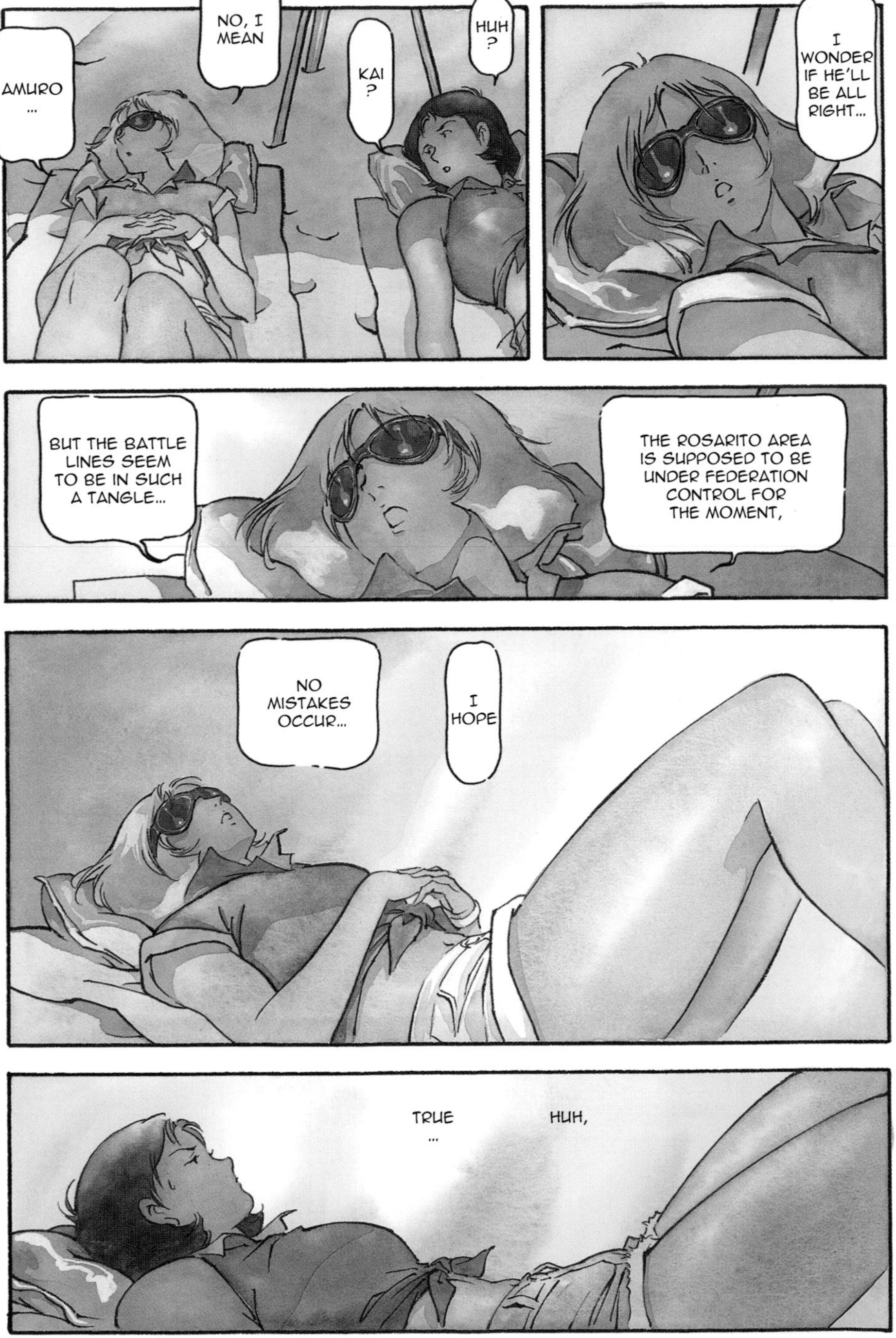
I WONDER IF HE'LL BE ALL RIGHT...
HUH ?
KAI ?
NO, I MEAN
AMURO ...
THE ROSARITO AREA IS SUPPOSED TO BE UNDER FEDERATION CONTROL FOR THE MOMENT,
BUT THE BATTLE LINES SEEM TO BE IN SUCH A TANGLE...
I HOPE
NO MISTAKES OCCUR...
HUH,
TRUE ...

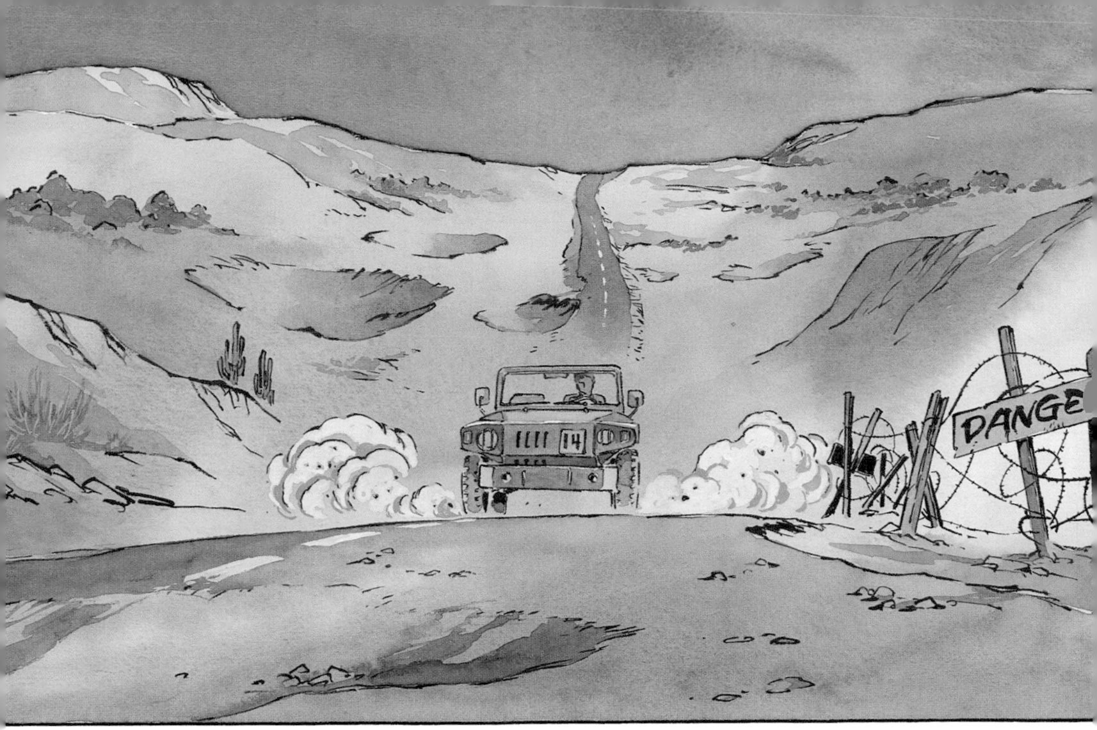
DANGE
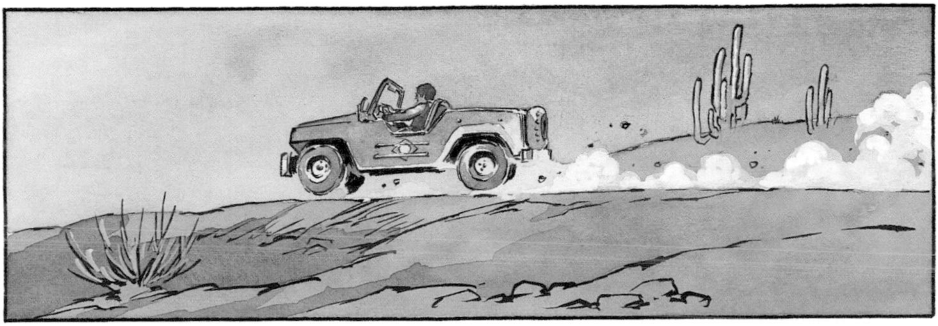
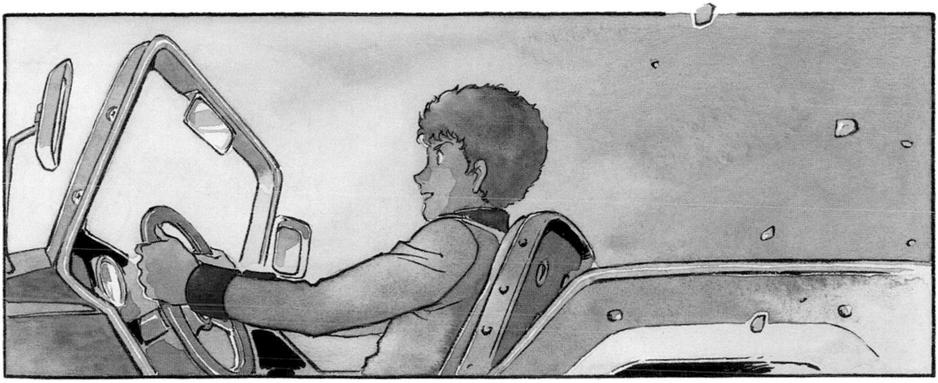

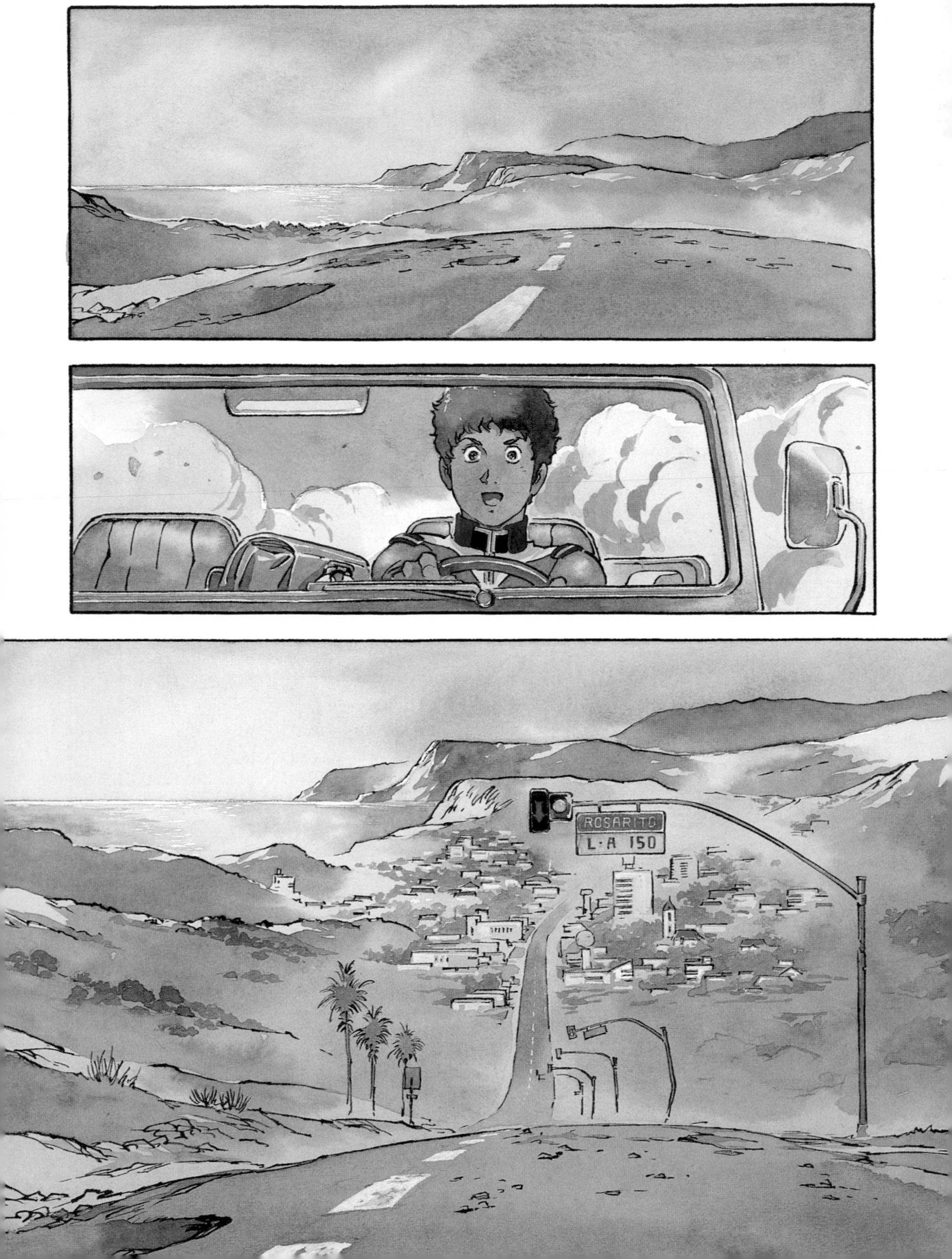
ROSARITO
L·A 150

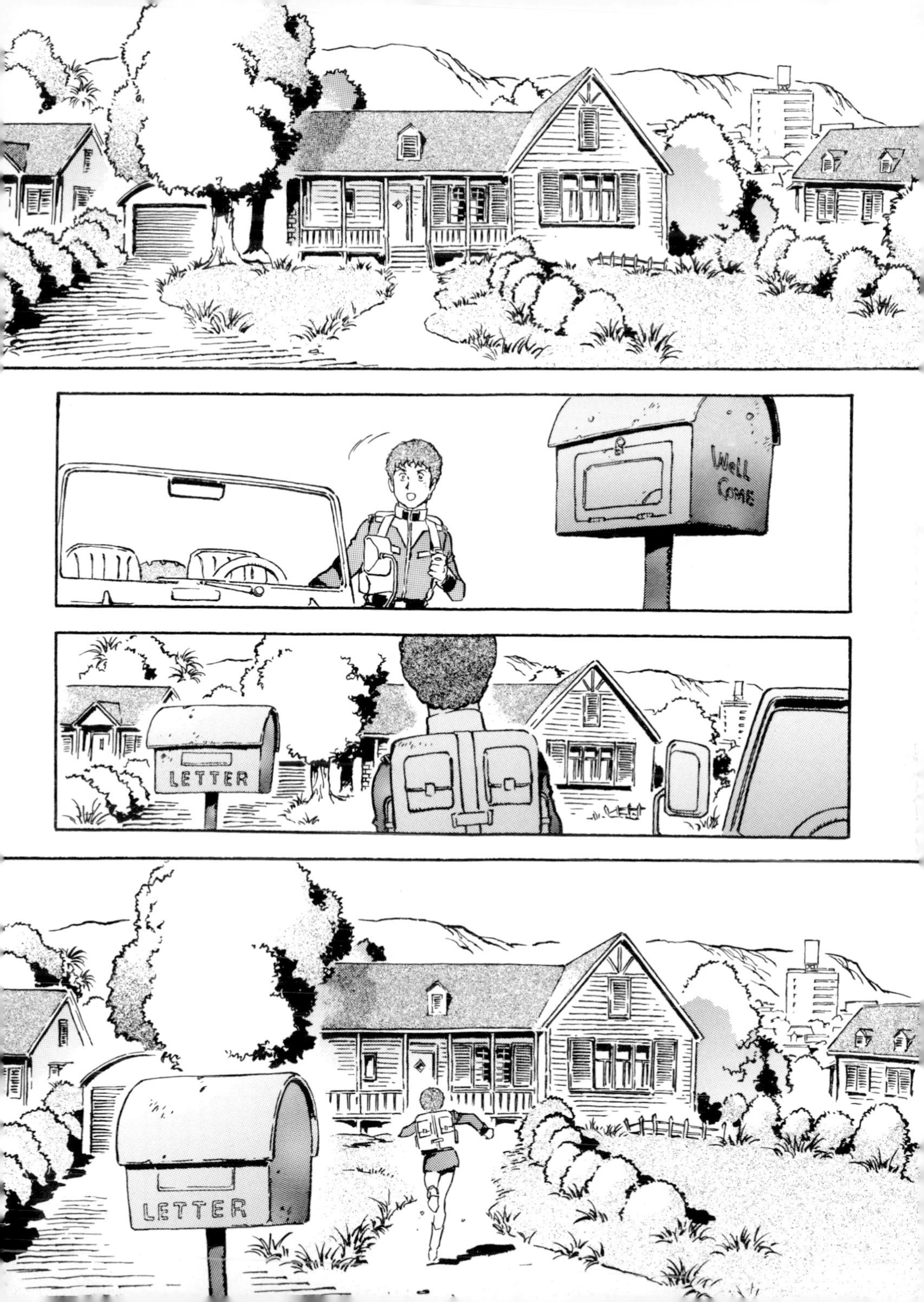
WeLL COME
LETTER
LETTER

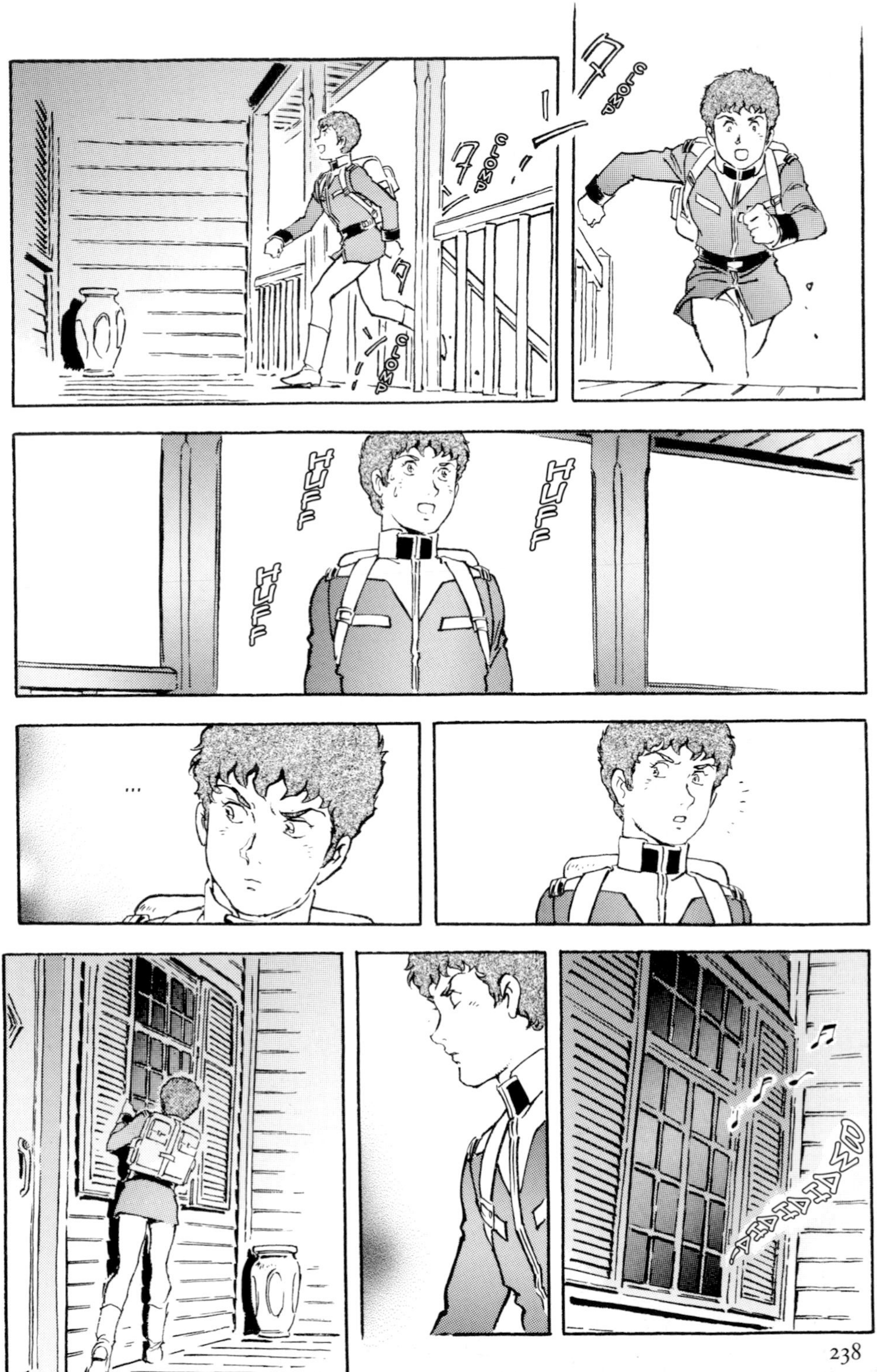
CLOMP
CLOMP
CLOMP
HUFF
HUFF
HUFF
...

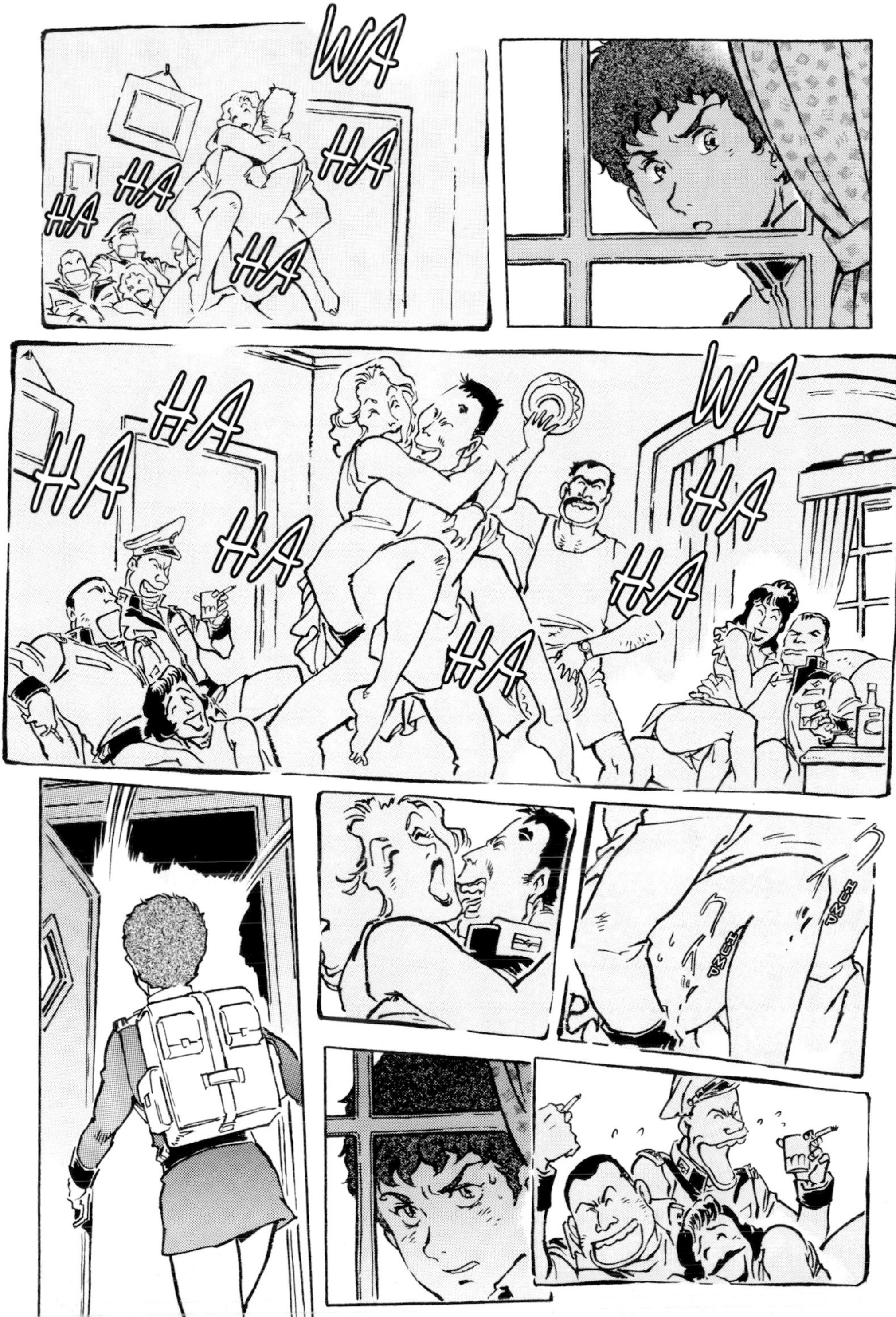
WA
HA
HA
HA
HA
WA
HA
HA
HA
HA
HA
HA
HA

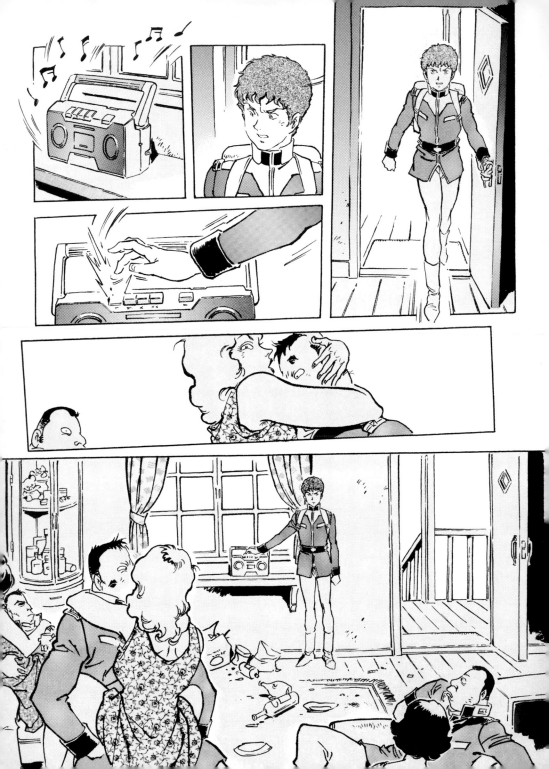

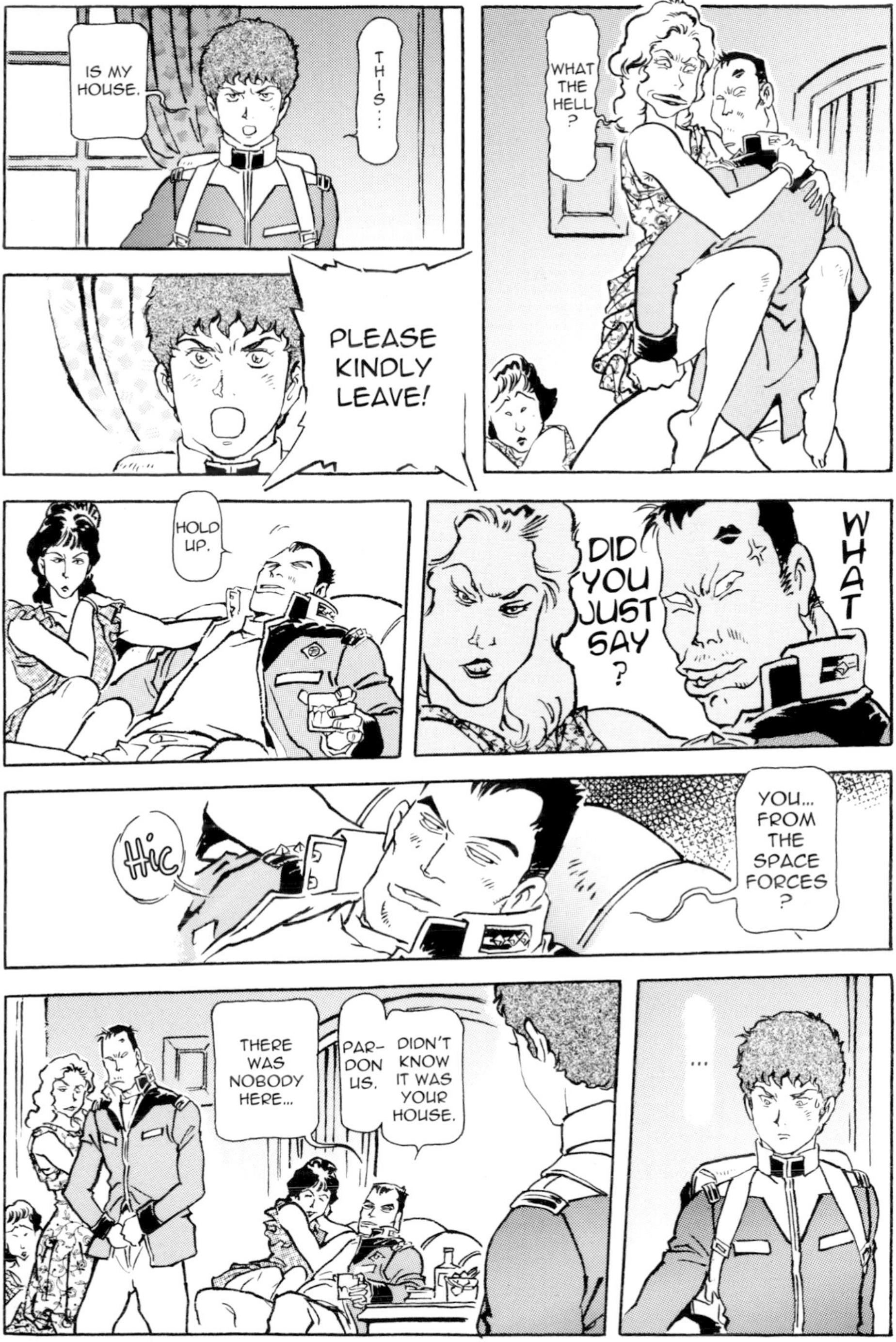
WHAT THE HELL?
THIS...
IS MY HOUSE.
PLEASE KINDLY LEAVE!
WHAT
DID YOU JUST SAY?
HOLD UP.
YOU... FROM THE SPACE FORCES?
Hic
...
DIDN'T KNOW IT WAS YOUR HOUSE.
PARDON US.
THERE WAS NOBODY HERE...

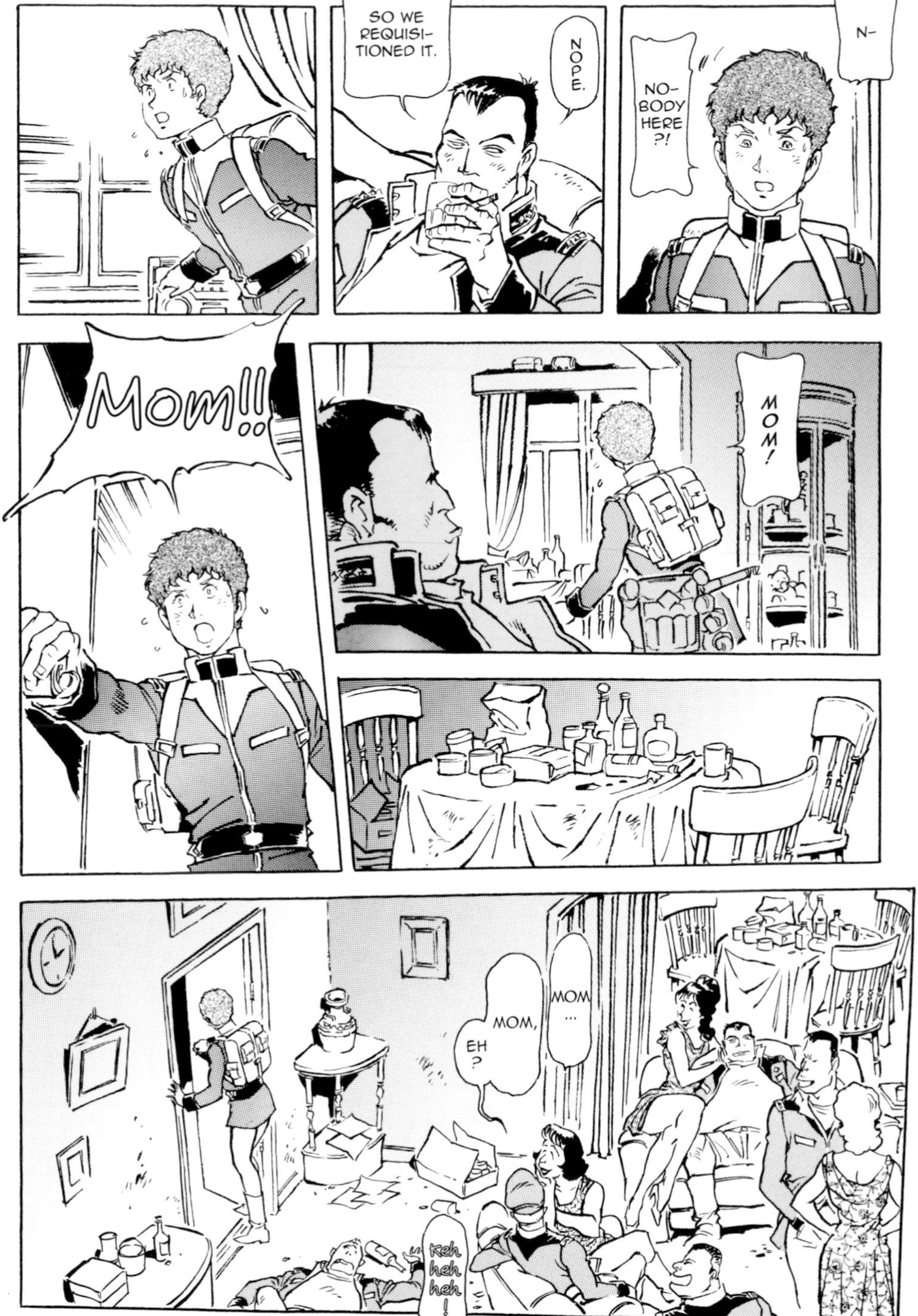
N-
NO-BODY HERE?!
NOPE.
SO WE REQUISITIONED IT.
MOM!
Mom!!
MOM...
MOM, EH?
Keh heh heh!

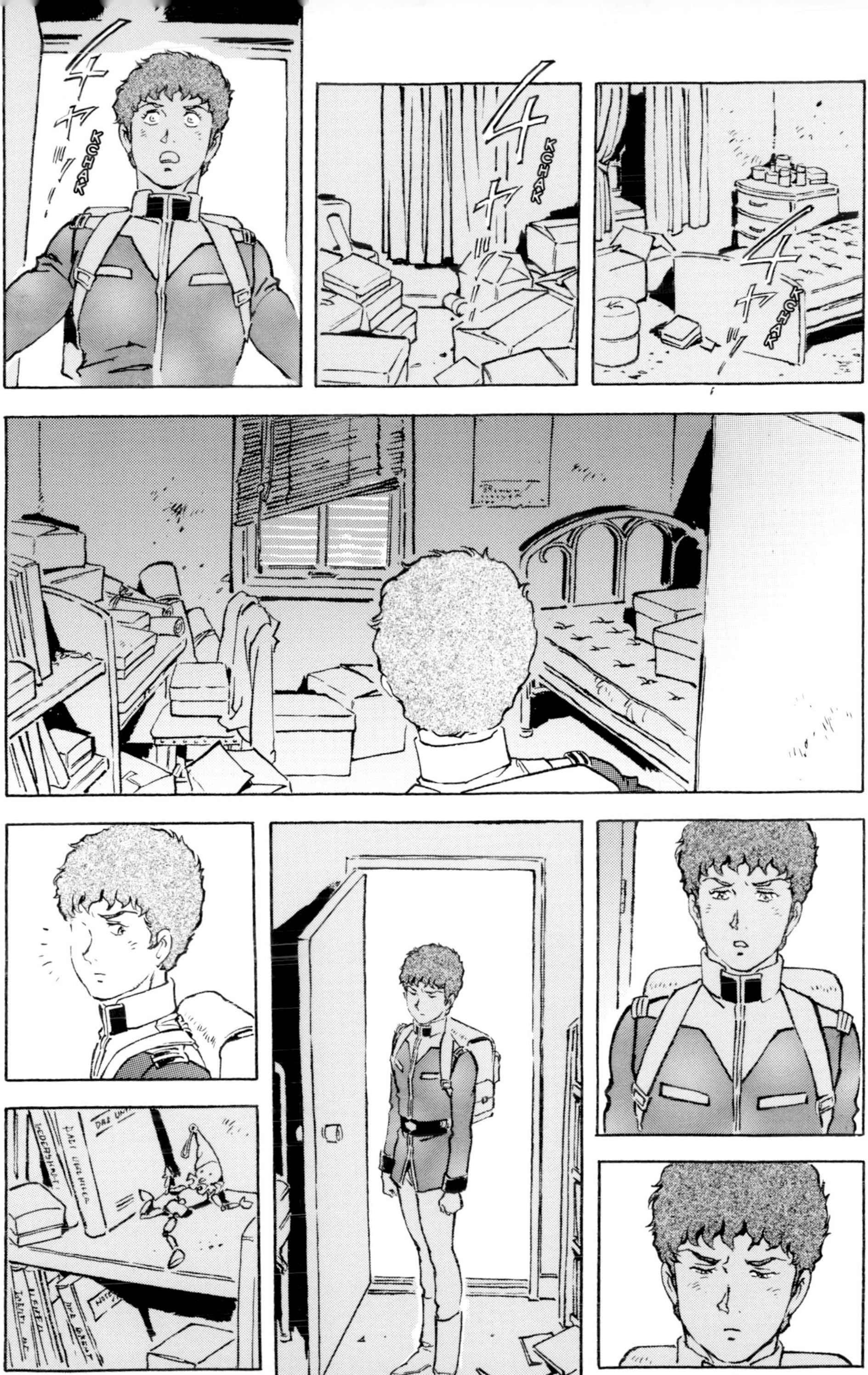
KCHAK
KCHAK
KCHAK

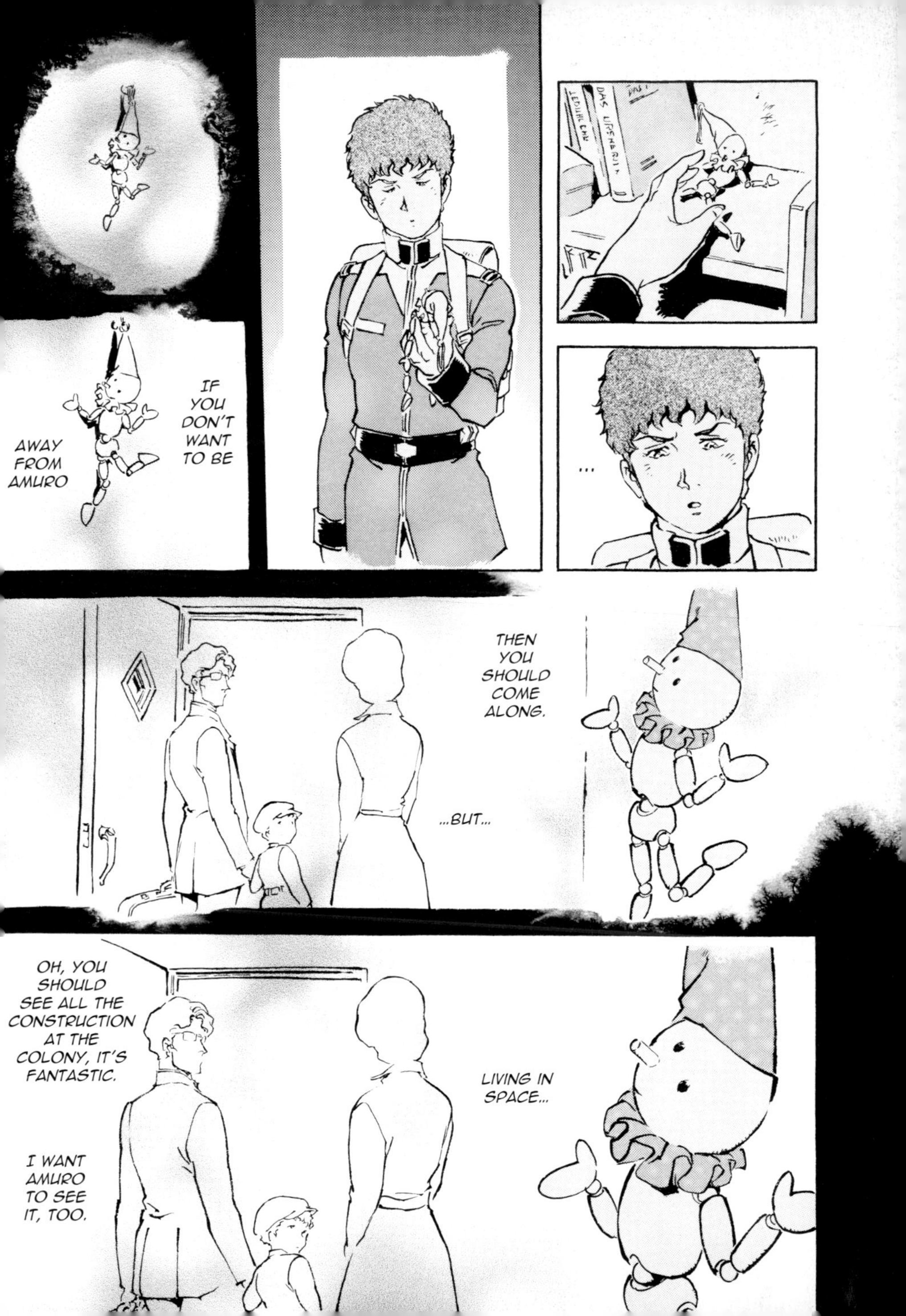
...
IF YOU DON'T WANT TO BE
AWAY FROM AMURO
THEN YOU SHOULD COME ALONG.
...BUT...
LIVING IN SPACE...
OH, YOU SHOULD SEE ALL THE CONSTRUCTION AT THE COLONY, IT'S FANTASTIC.
I WANT AMURO TO SEE IT, TOO.

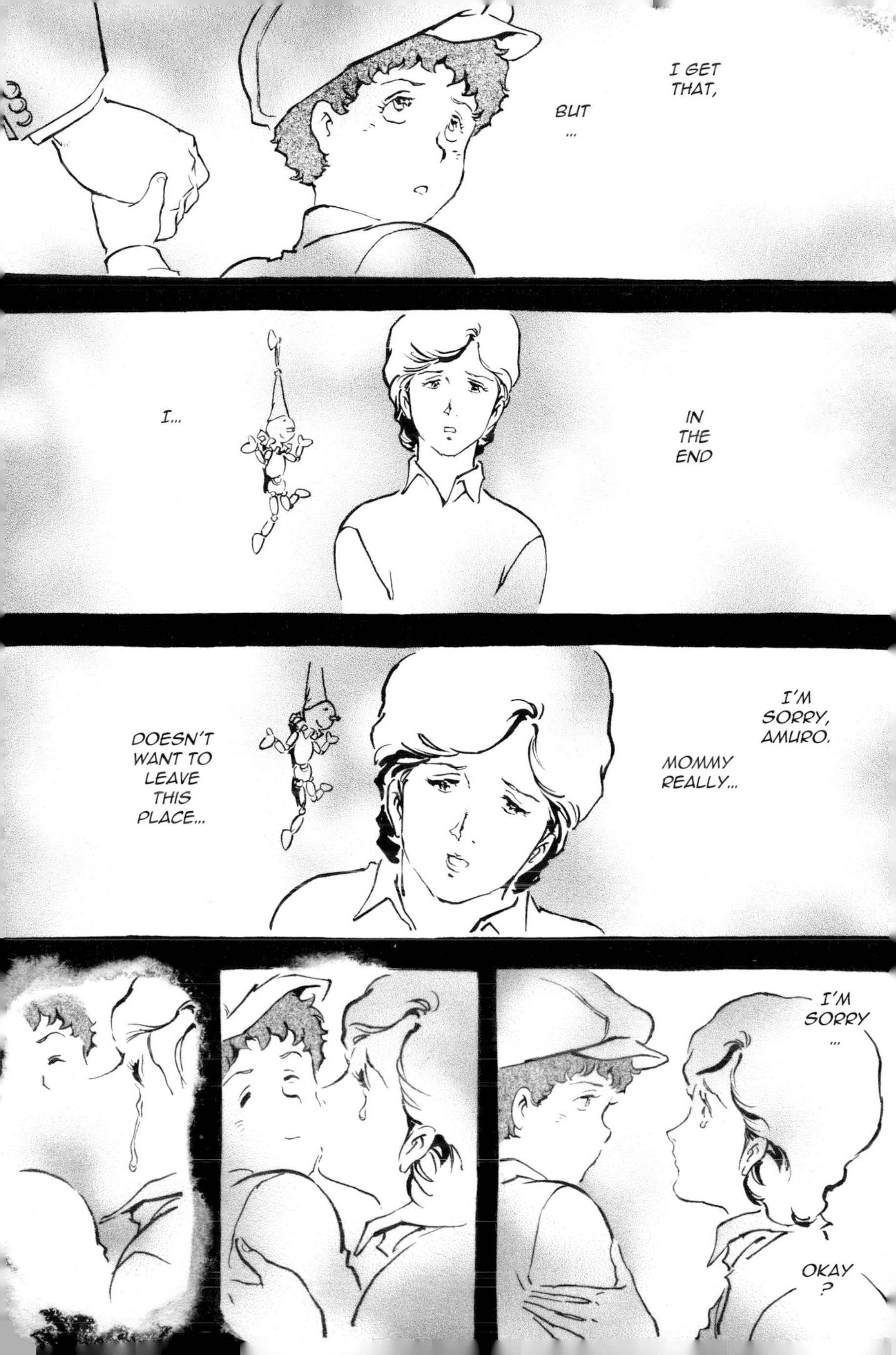
I GET THAT,
BUT ...
IN THE END
I...
I'M SORRY, AMURO.
MOMMY REALLY...
DOESN'T WANT TO LEAVE THIS PLACE...
I'M SORRY ...
OKAY ?

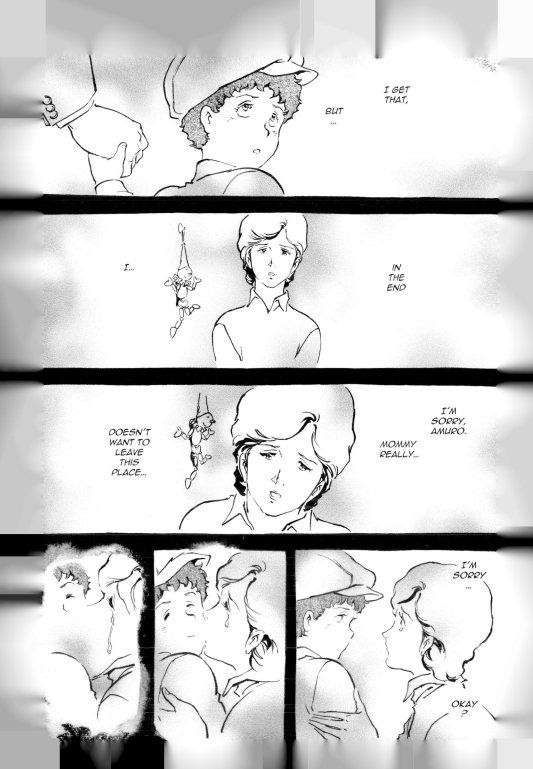

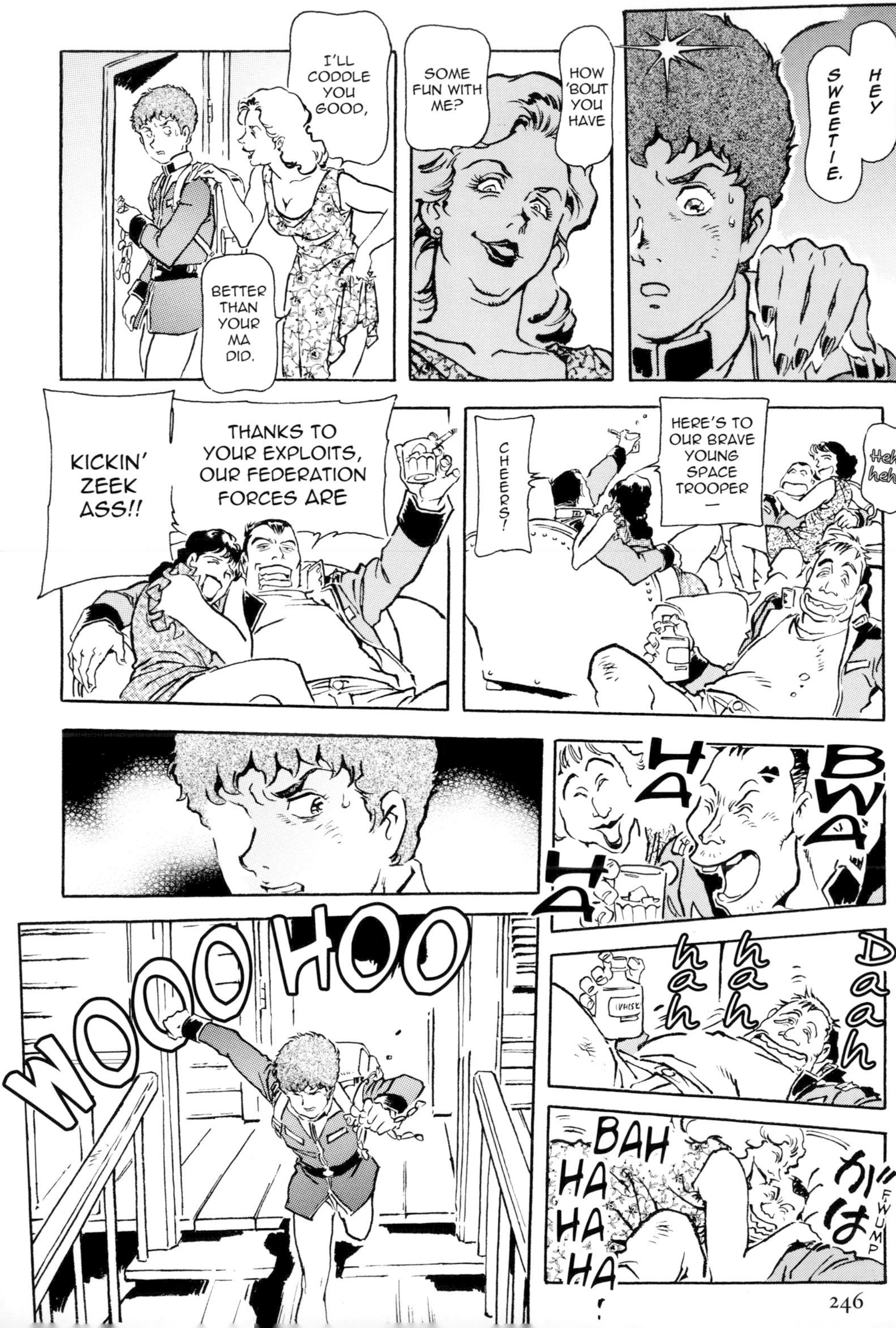

HEY SWEETIE.
HOW 'BOUT YOU HAVE
SOME FUN WITH ME?
I'LL CODDLE YOU GOOD,
BETTER THAN YOUR MA DID.
Heh heh
HERE'S TO OUR BRAVE YOUNG SPACE TROOPER —
CHEERS!
THANKS TO YOUR EXPLOITS, OUR FEDERATION FORCES ARE
KICKIN' ZEEK ASS!!
BWA HA HA
Daah hah hah
がは
FWUMP
BAH HA HA HA!
WOOO HOO

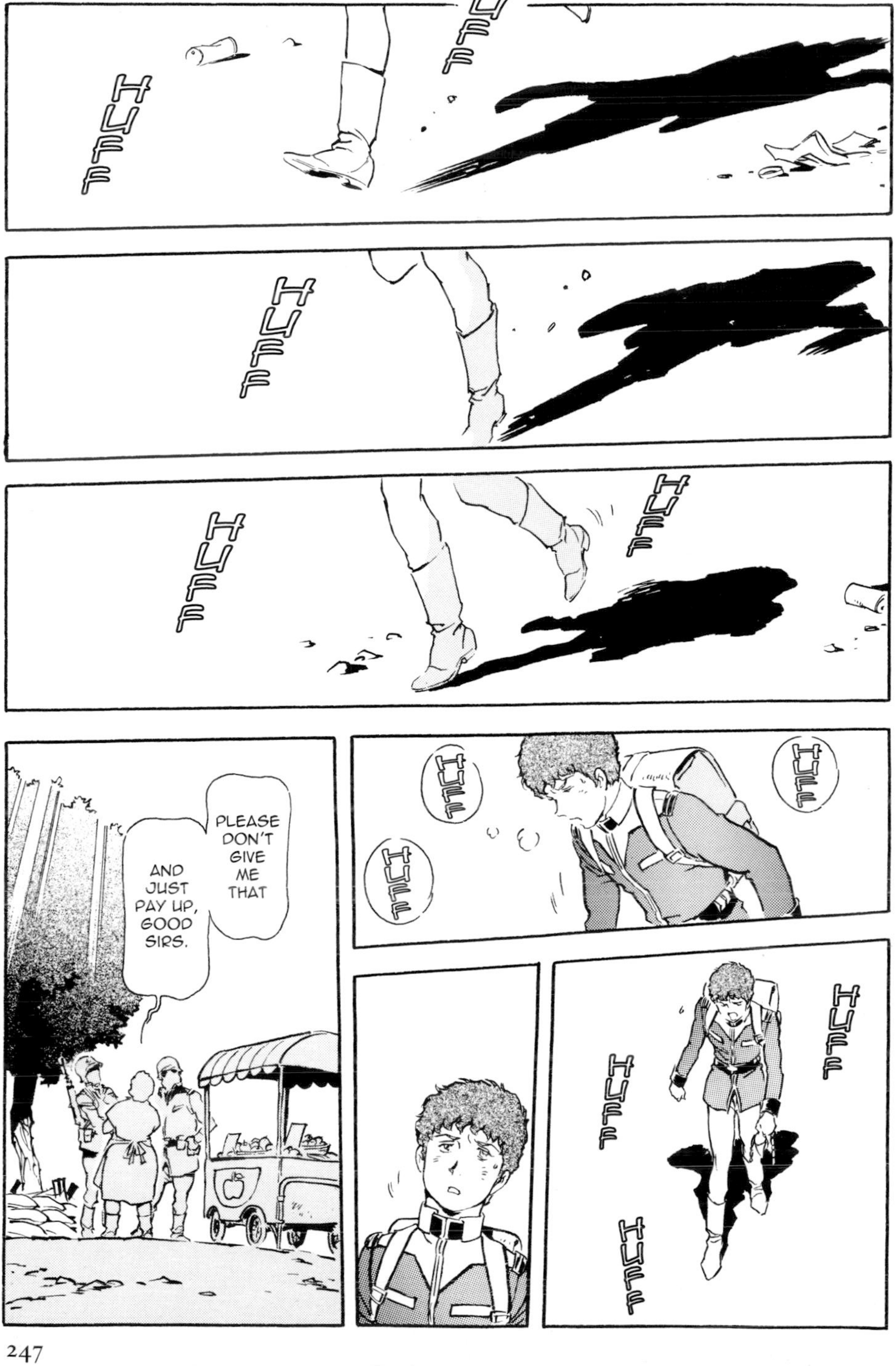
HUFF
HUFF
HUFF
HUFF
HUFF
HUFF
HUFF
HUFF
HUFF
HUFF
HUFF
PLEASE DON'T GIVE ME THAT
AND JUST PAY UP, GOOD SIRS.

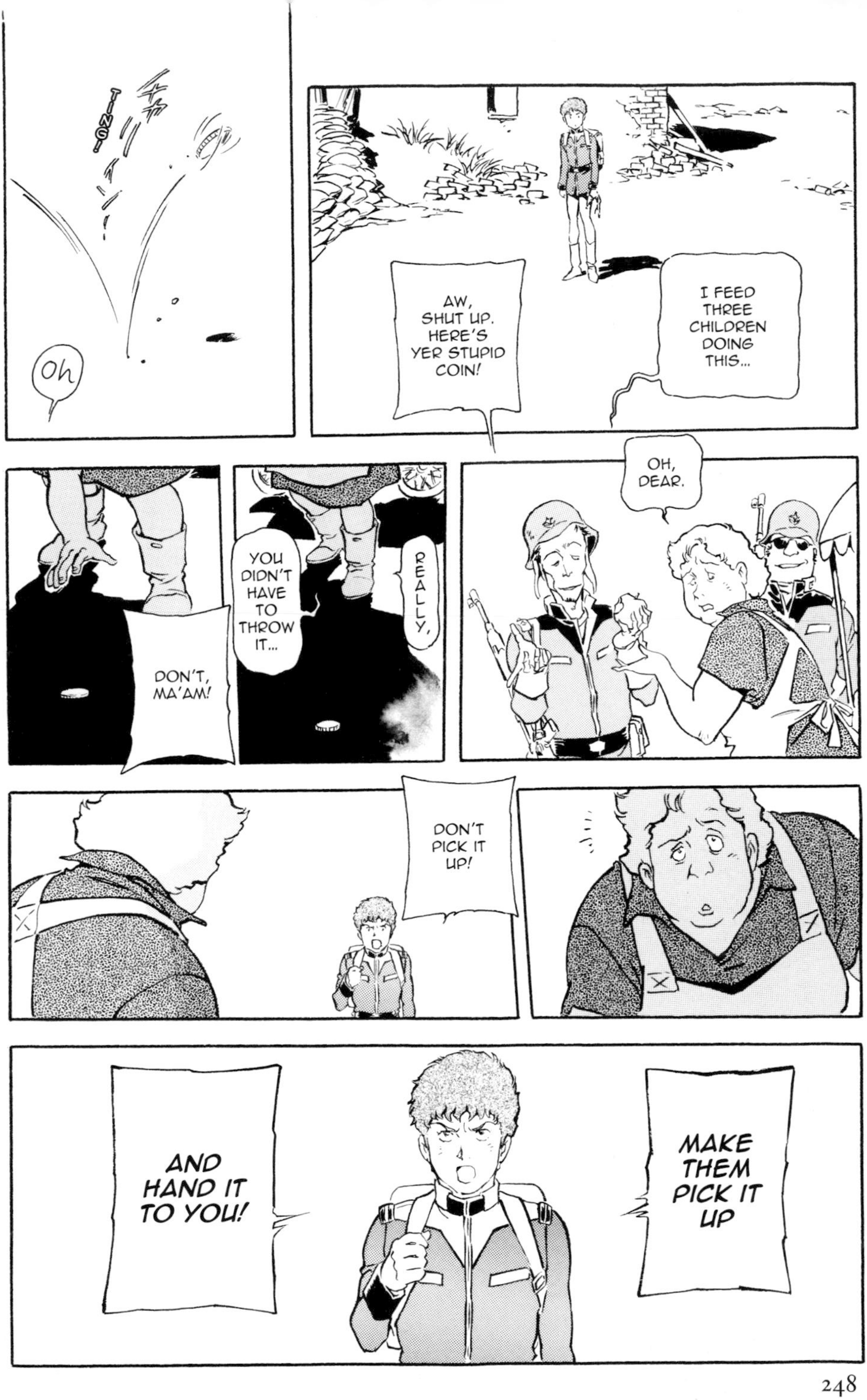
I FEED THREE CHILDREN DOING THIS...
AW, SHUT UP. HERE'S YER STUPID COIN!
TING!
Oh
OH, DEAR.
REALLY,
YOU DIDN'T HAVE TO THROW IT...
DON'T, MA'AM!
DON'T PICK IT UP!
MAKE THEM PICK IT UP
AND HAND IT TO YOU!

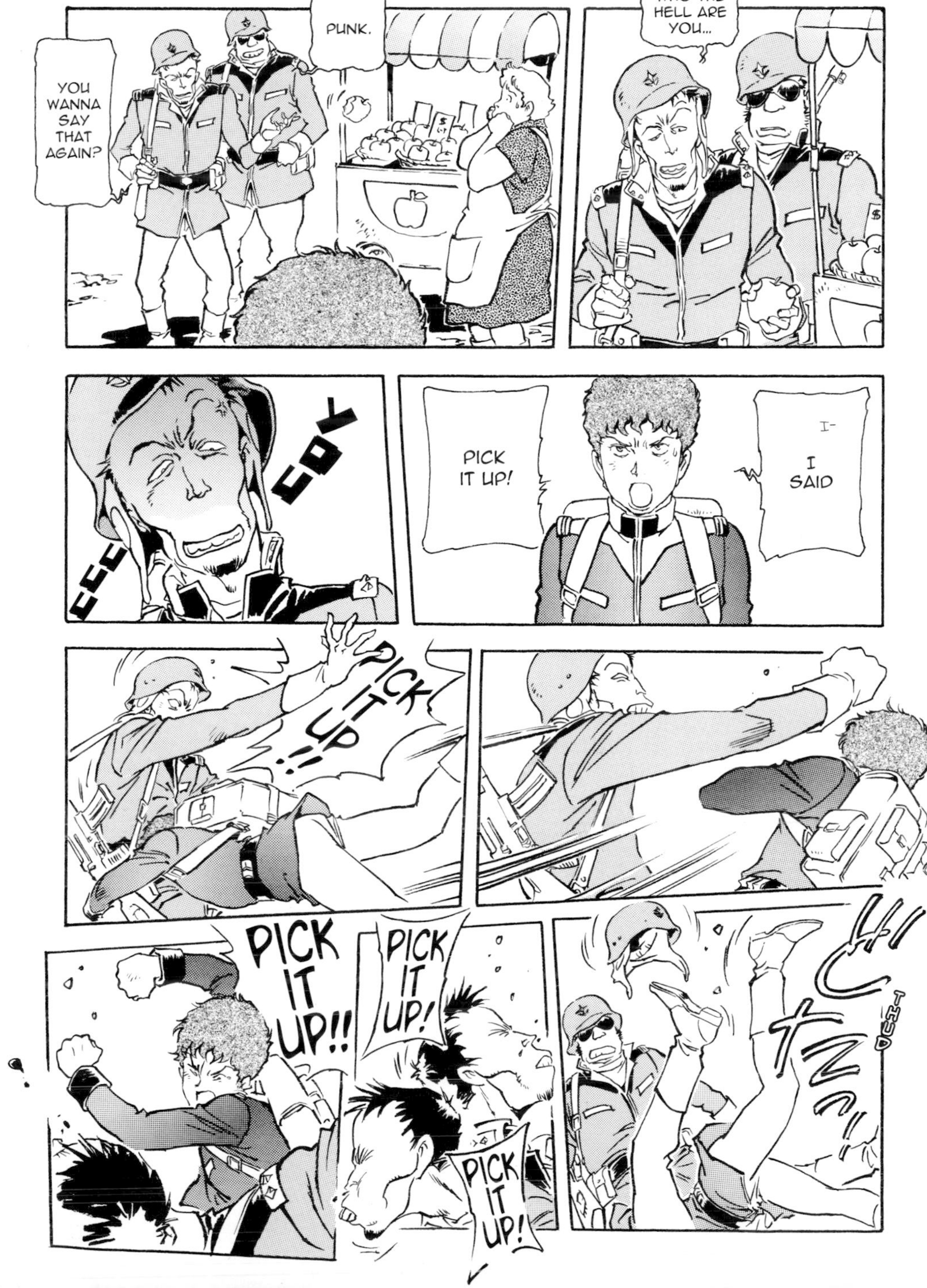
WHO THE HELL ARE YOU...
PUNK.
YOU WANNA SAY THAT AGAIN?
I- I SAID
PICK IT UP!
PICK IT UP!!
THUD
PICK IT UP!!
PICK IT UP!
PICK IT UP!

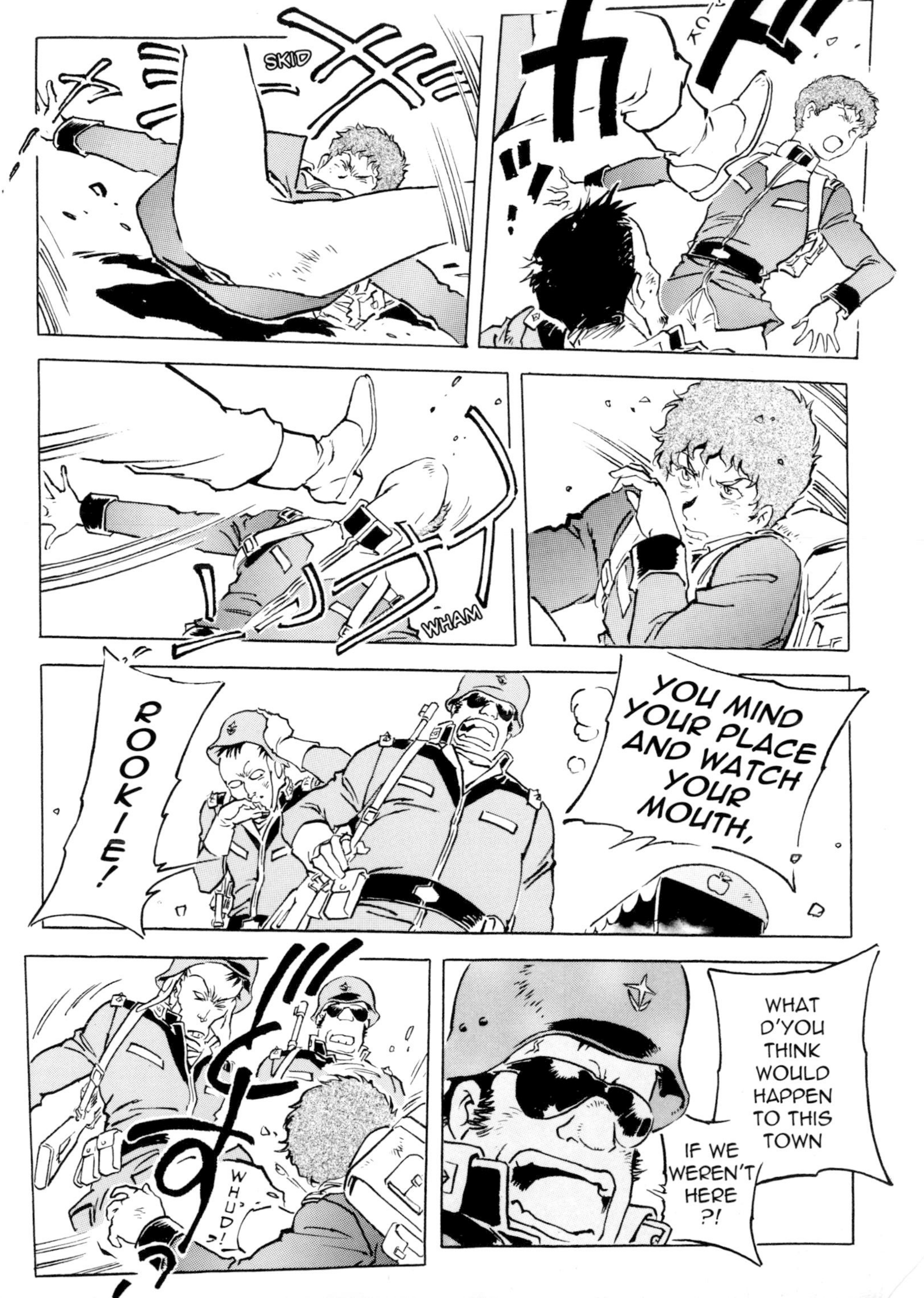
KICK
SKID
WHAM
YOU MIND YOUR PLACE AND WATCH YOUR MOUTH,
ROOKIE!
WHAT D'YOU THINK WOULD HAPPEN TO THIS TOWN
IF WE WEREN'T HERE ?!
WHUD!

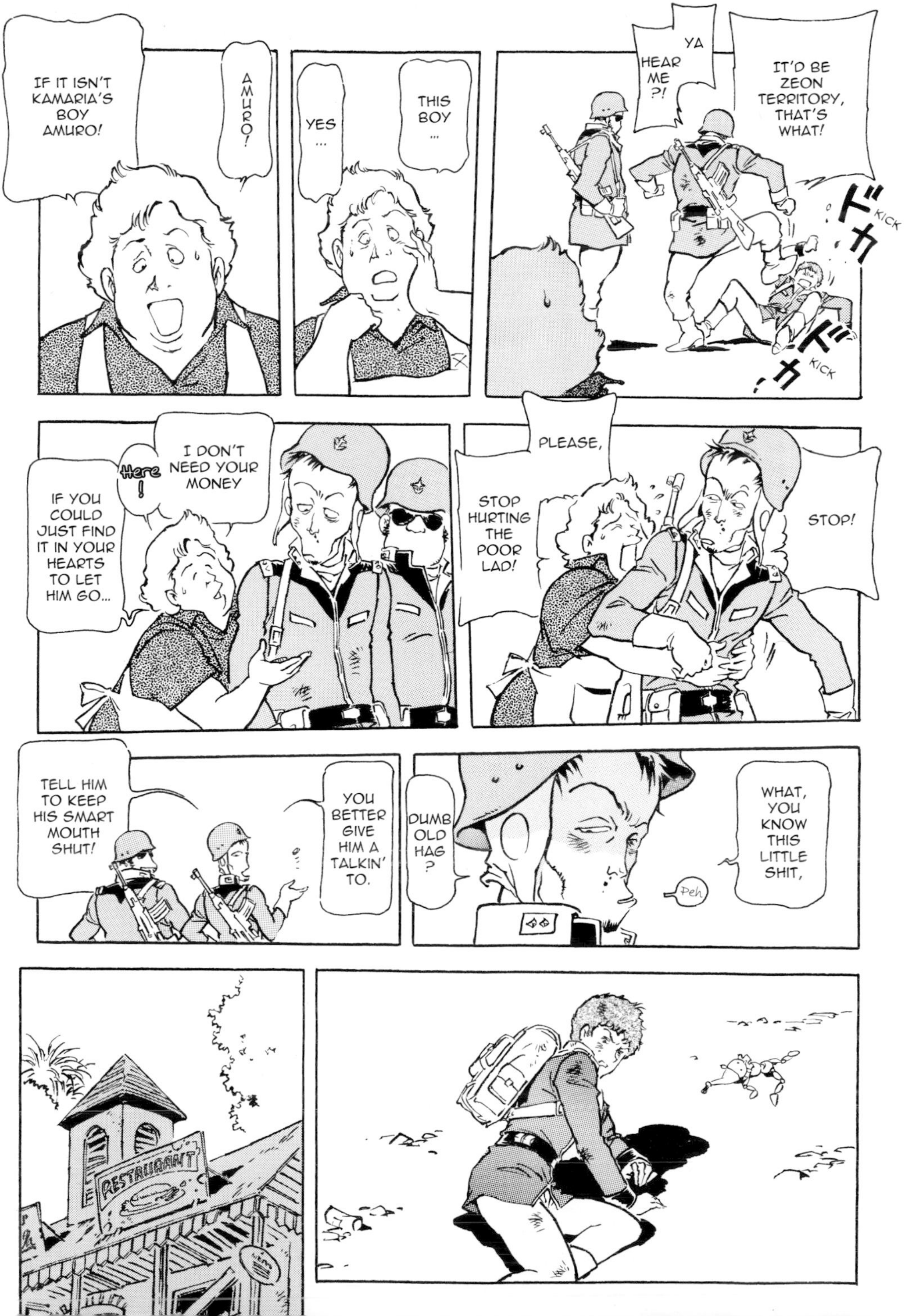
IT'D BE ZEON TERRITORY, THAT'S WHAT!
YA HEAR ME ?!
ドカ
KICK
ドカ
KICK
THIS BOY ...
YES ...
AMURO!
IF IT ISN'T KAMARIA'S BOY AMURO!
STOP!
PLEASE,
STOP HURTING THE POOR LAD!
I DON'T NEED YOUR MONEY
Here!
IF YOU COULD JUST FIND IT IN YOUR HEARTS TO LET HIM GO...
WHAT, YOU KNOW THIS LITTLE SHIT,
Peh
DUMB OLD HAG ?
YOU BETTER GIVE HIM A TALKIN' TO.
TELL HIM TO KEEP HIS SMART MOUTH SHUT!
RESTAURANT

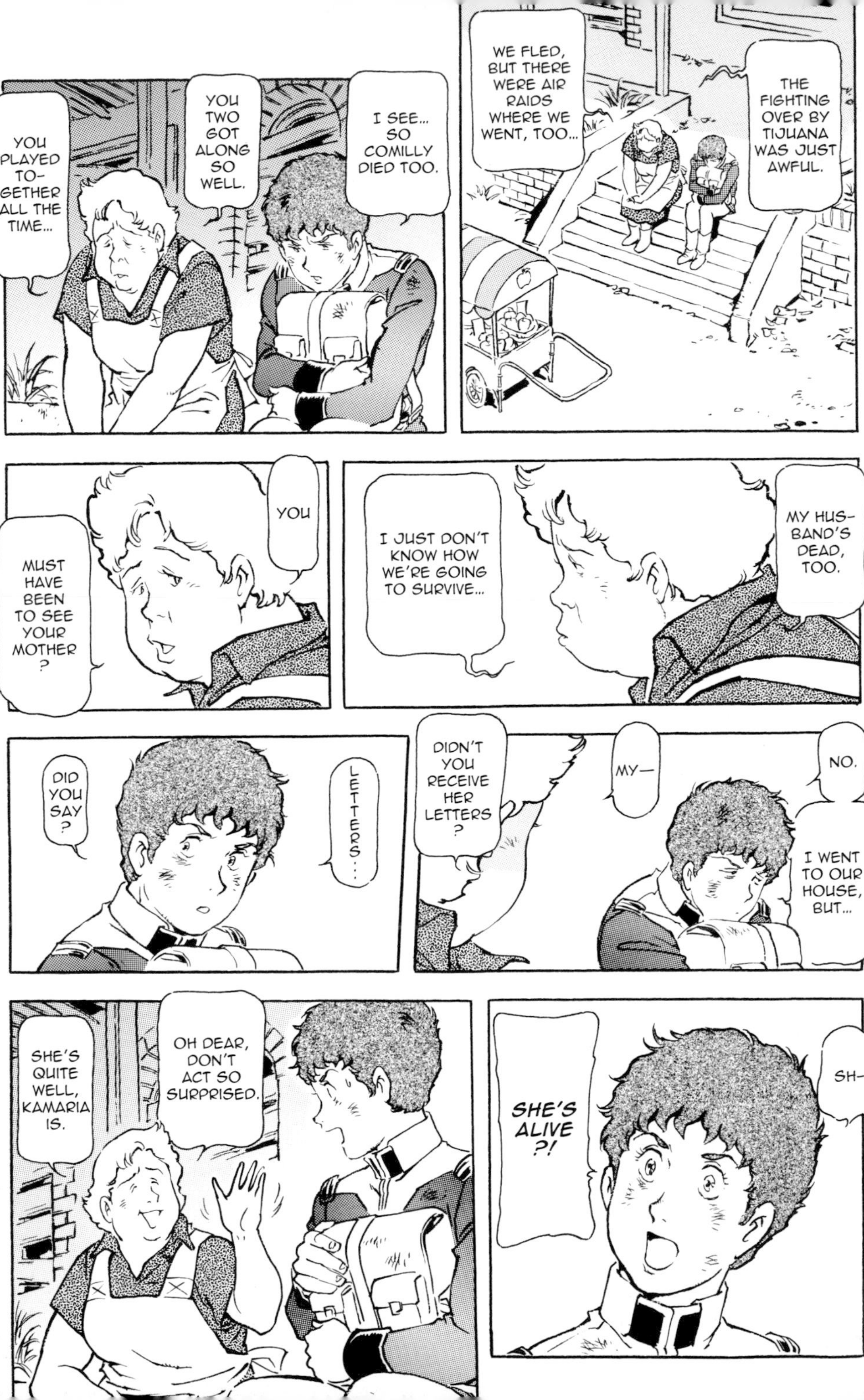
THE FIGHTING OVER BY TIJUANA WAS JUST AWFUL.
WE FLED, BUT THERE WERE AIR RAIDS WHERE WE WENT, TOO...
I SEE... SO COMILLY DIED TOO.
YOU TWO GOT ALONG SO WELL.
YOU PLAYED TO-GETHER ALL THE TIME...
MY HUS-BAND'S DEAD, TOO.
I JUST DON'T KNOW HOW WE'RE GOING TO SURVIVE...
YOU
MUST HAVE BEEN TO SEE YOUR MOTHER?
NO.
I WENT TO OUR HOUSE, BUT...
MY—
DIDN'T YOU RECEIVE HER LETTERS?
LETTERS...
DID YOU SAY?
SH-
SHE'S ALIVE?!
OH DEAR, DON'T ACT SO SURPRISED.
SHE'S QUITE WELL, KAMARIA IS.

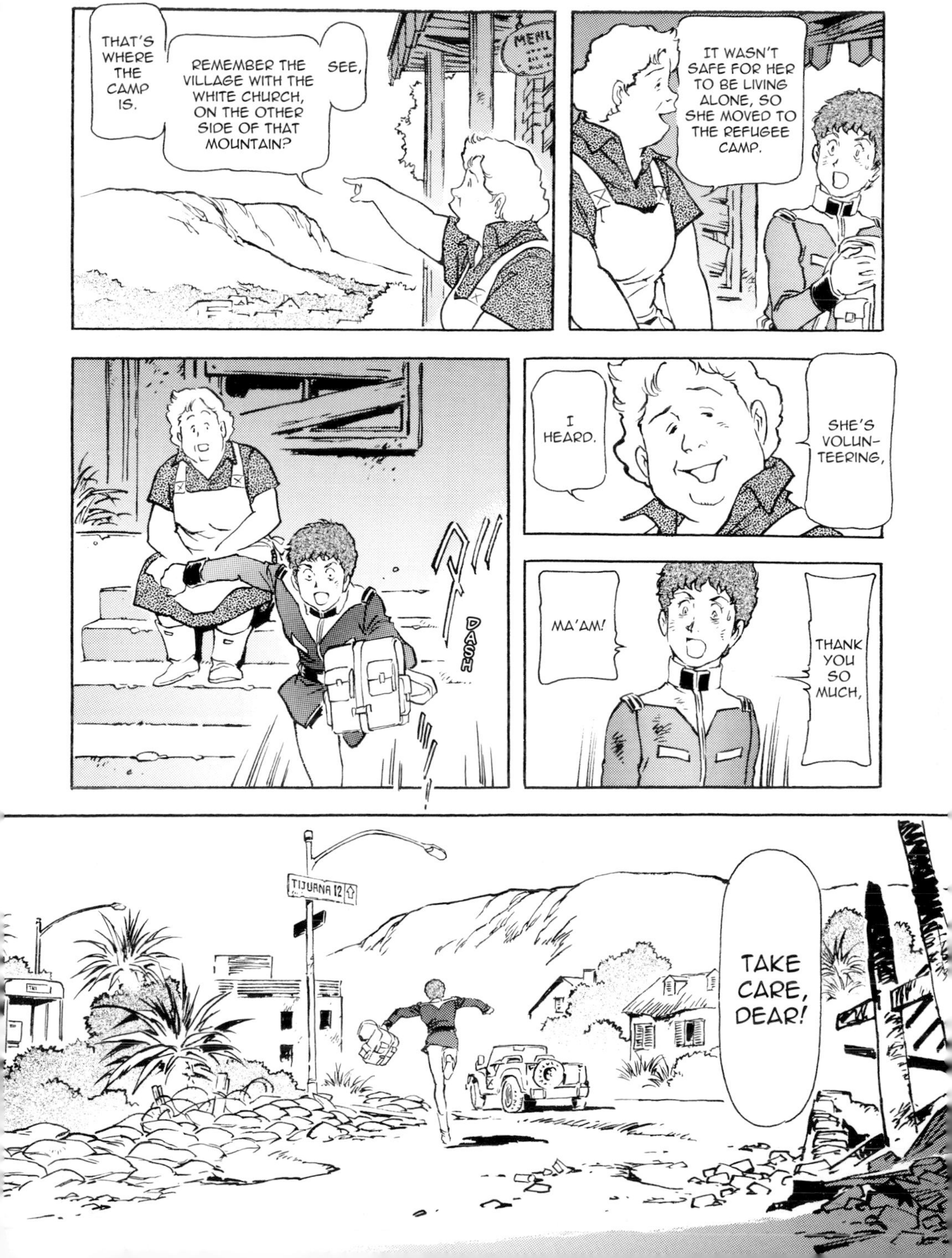
IT WASN'T SAFE FOR HER TO BE LIVING ALONE, SO SHE MOVED TO THE REFUGEE CAMP.
SEE,
REMEMBER THE VILLAGE WITH THE WHITE CHURCH, ON THE OTHER SIDE OF THAT MOUNTAIN?
THAT'S WHERE THE CAMP IS.
SHE'S VOLUNTEERING,
I HEARD.
THANK YOU SO MUCH,
MA'AM!
DASH
TIJUANA 12
TAKE CARE, DEAR!

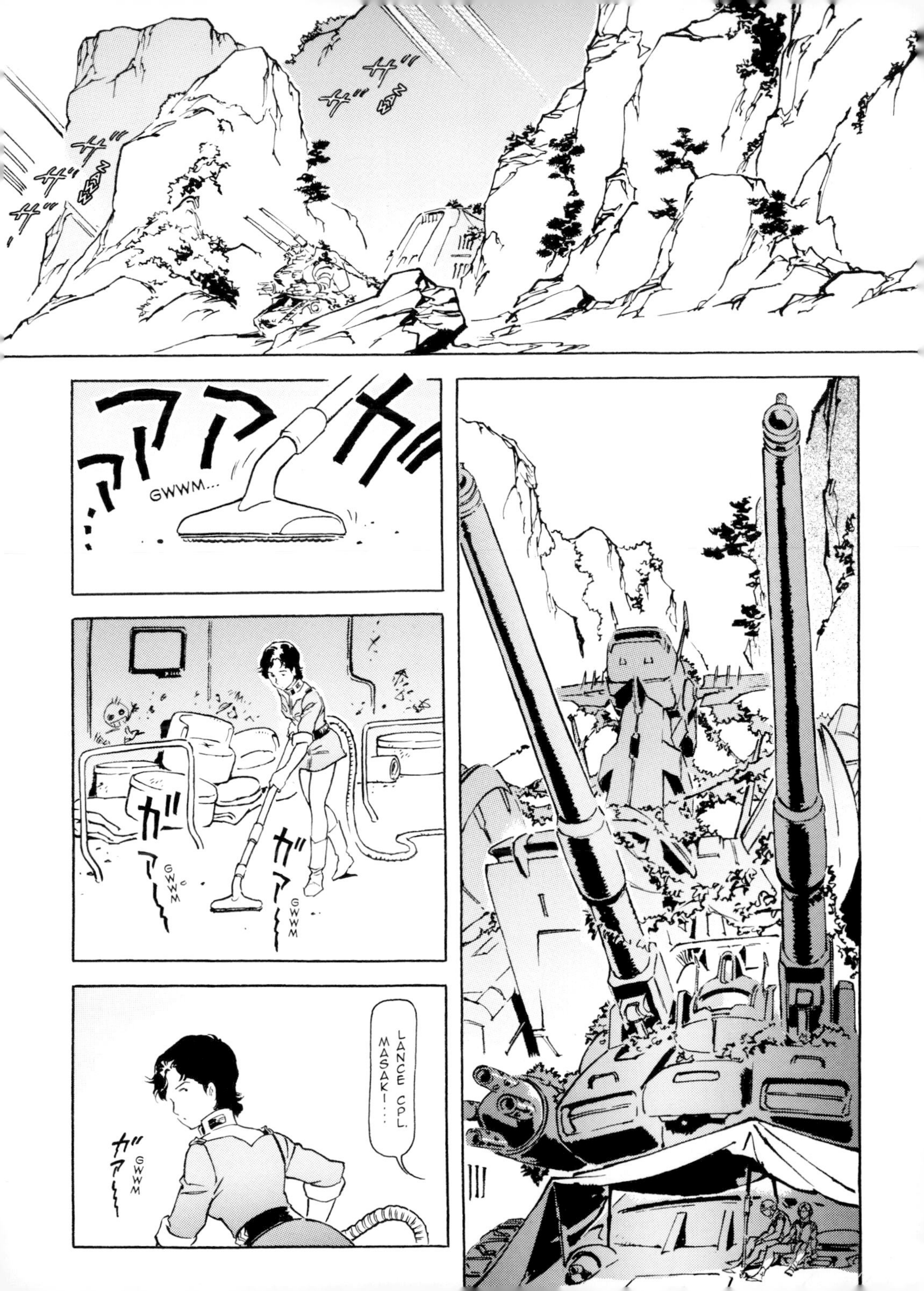
ザ" ザ"
ザ" ザ" ザ"
アアアー…
GWWM…
ガアー
GWWM
ガアー
GWWM
LANCE CPL. MASAKI…
ガアー
GWWM

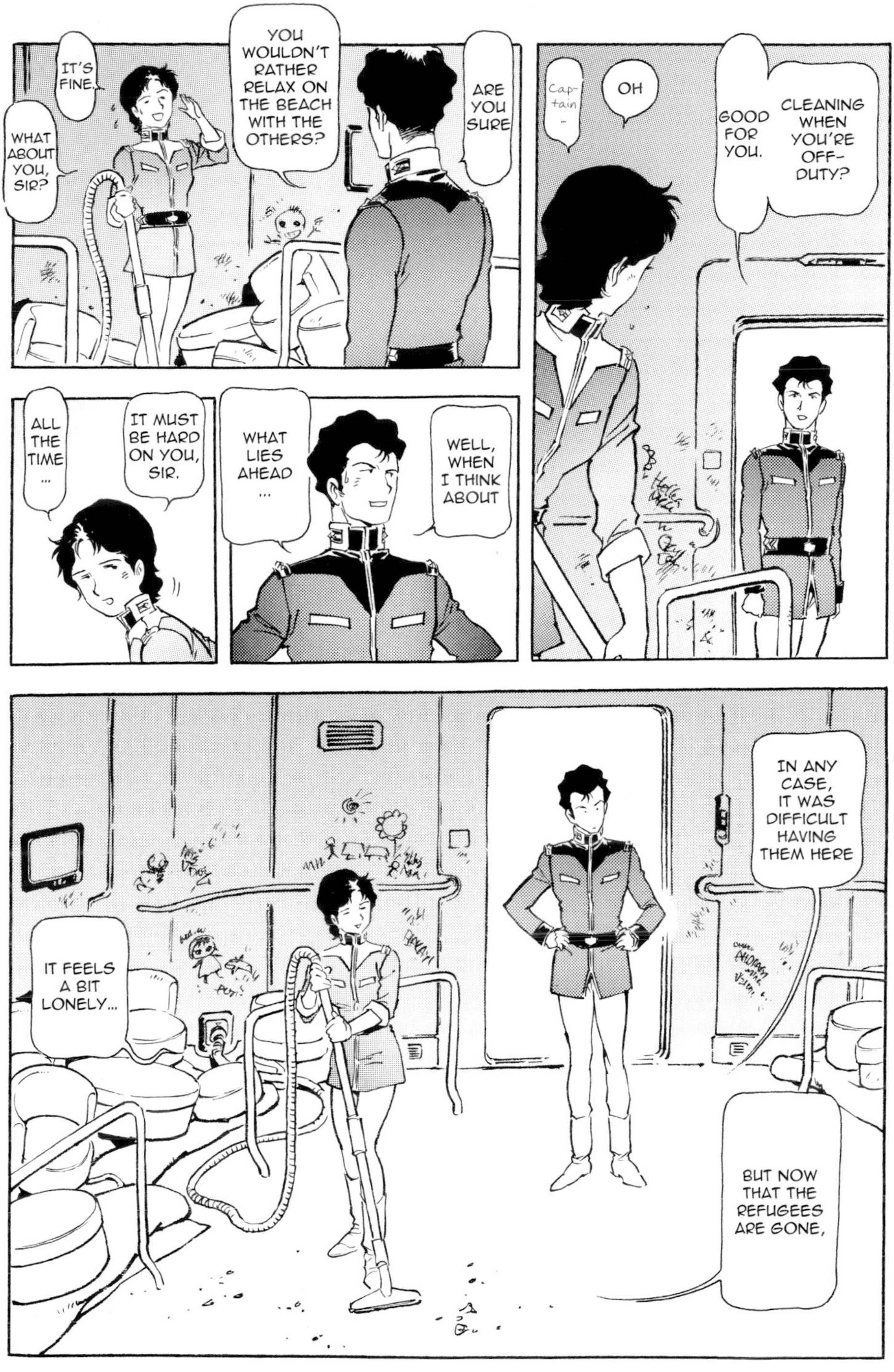
CLEANING WHEN YOU'RE OFF-DUTY?
GOOD FOR YOU.
OH
Cap-tain ...
ARE YOU SURE
YOU WOULDN'T RATHER RELAX ON THE BEACH WITH THE OTHERS?
IT'S FINE.
WHAT ABOUT YOU, SIR?
WELL, WHEN I THINK ABOUT
WHAT LIES AHEAD ...
IT MUST BE HARD ON YOU, SIR.
ALL THE TIME ...
IN ANY CASE, IT WAS DIFFICULT HAVING THEM HERE
BUT NOW THAT THE REFUGEES ARE GONE,
IT FEELS A BIT LONELY...

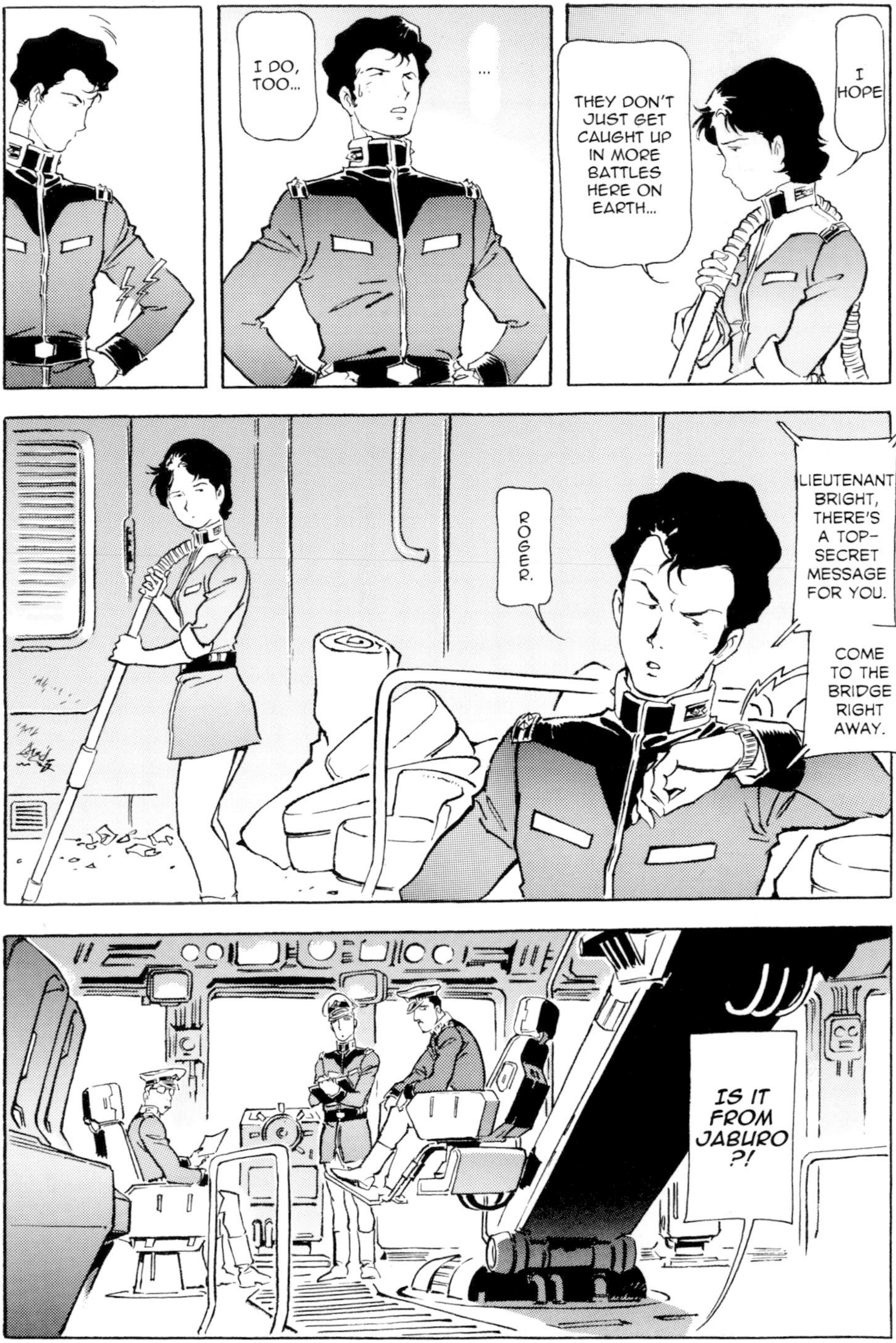
I HOPE
THEY DON'T JUST GET CAUGHT UP IN MORE BATTLES HERE ON EARTH...
...
I DO, TOO...
LIEUTENANT BRIGHT, THERE'S A TOP-SECRET MESSAGE FOR YOU.
COME TO THE BRIDGE RIGHT AWAY.
ROGER.
IS IT FROM JABURO?!

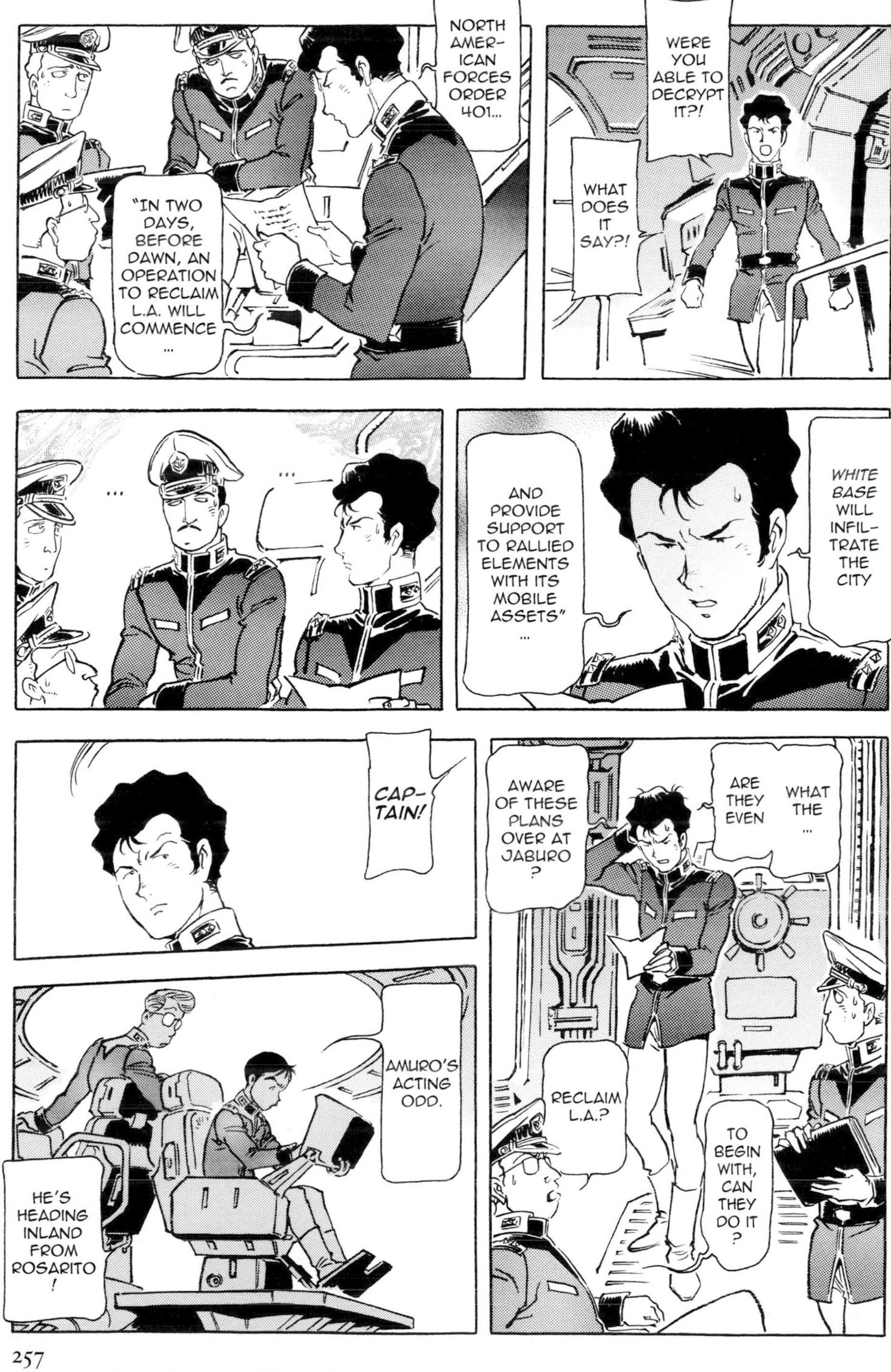
WERE YOU ABLE TO DECRYPT IT?!
WHAT DOES IT SAY?!
NORTH AMERICAN FORCES ORDER 401...
"IN TWO DAYS, BEFORE DAWN, AN OPERATION TO RECLAIM L.A. WILL COMMENCE ...
WHITE BASE WILL INFILTRATE THE CITY
AND PROVIDE SUPPORT TO RALLIED ELEMENTS WITH ITS MOBILE ASSETS" ...
...
...
WHAT THE ...
ARE THEY EVEN AWARE OF THESE PLANS OVER AT JABURO ?
RECLAIM L.A.?
TO BEGIN WITH, CAN THEY DO IT ?
CAPTAIN!
AMURO'S ACTING ODD.
HE'S HEADING INLAND FROM ROSARITO !

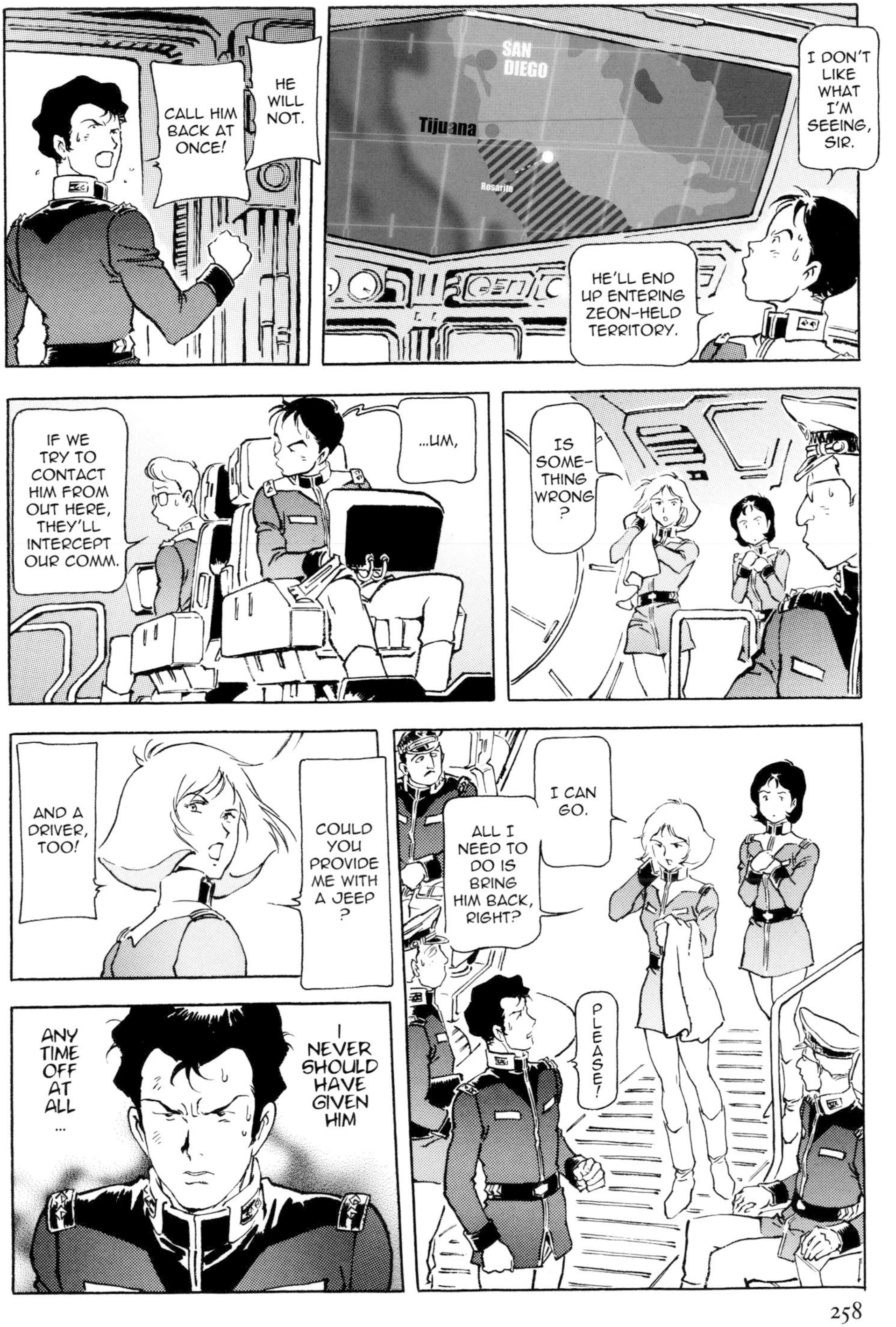
SAN DIEGO
Tijuana
Rosarito
I DON'T LIKE WHAT I'M SEEING, SIR.
HE'LL END UP ENTERING ZEON-HELD TERRITORY.
HE WILL NOT.
CALL HIM BACK AT ONCE!
IS SOME-THING WRONG?
...UM,
IF WE TRY TO CONTACT HIM FROM OUT HERE, THEY'LL INTERCEPT OUR COMM.
I CAN GO.
ALL I NEED TO DO IS BRING HIM BACK, RIGHT?
PLEASE!
COULD YOU PROVIDE ME WITH A JEEP?
AND A DRIVER, TOO!
I NEVER SHOULD HAVE GIVEN HIM
ANY TIME OFF AT ALL ...

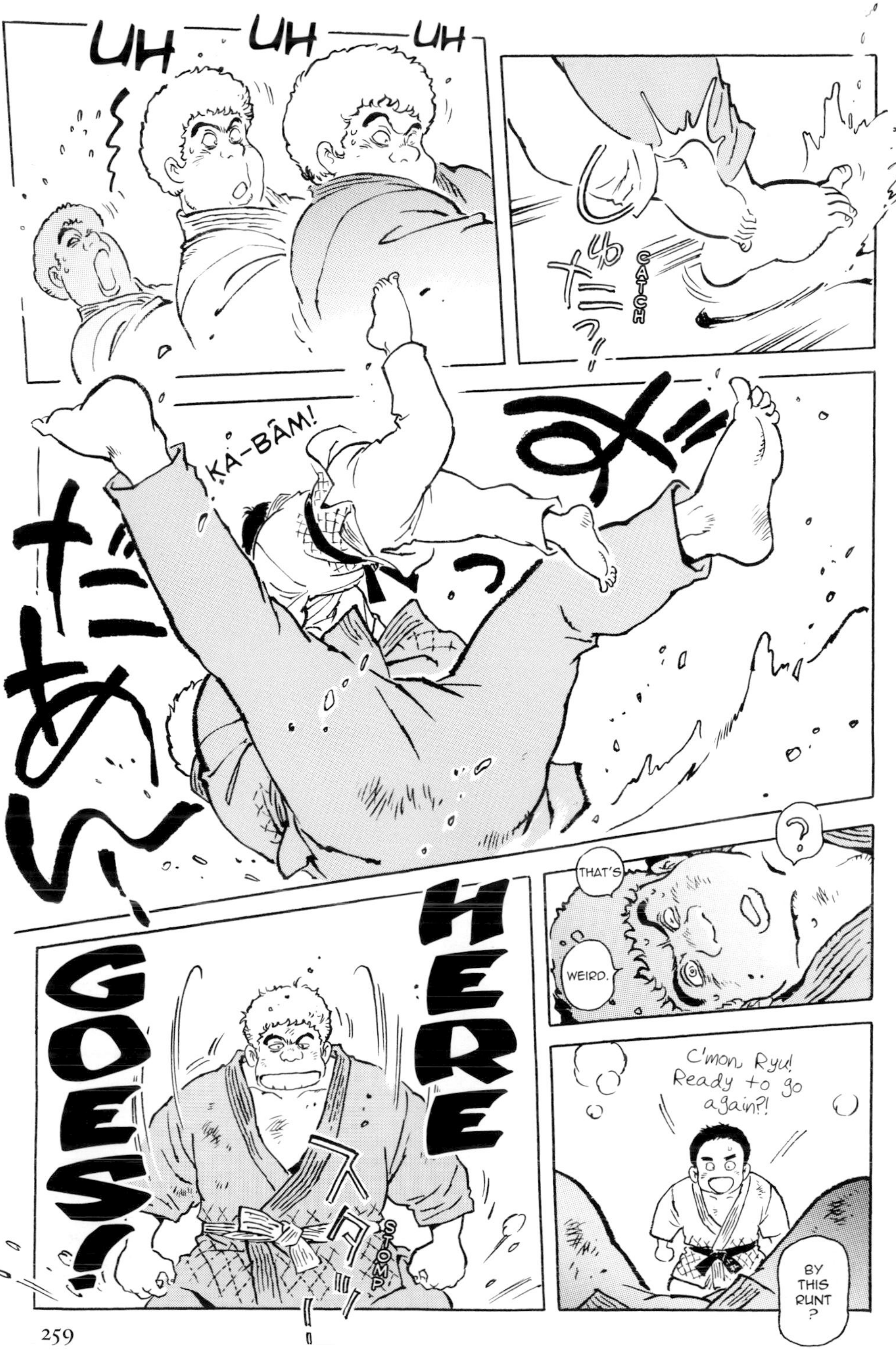
CATCH
UH
UH
UH
KA-BAM!
?
THAT'S
WEIRD.
C'mon, Ryu! Ready to go again?!
BY THIS RUNT?
HERE GOES!
STOMP

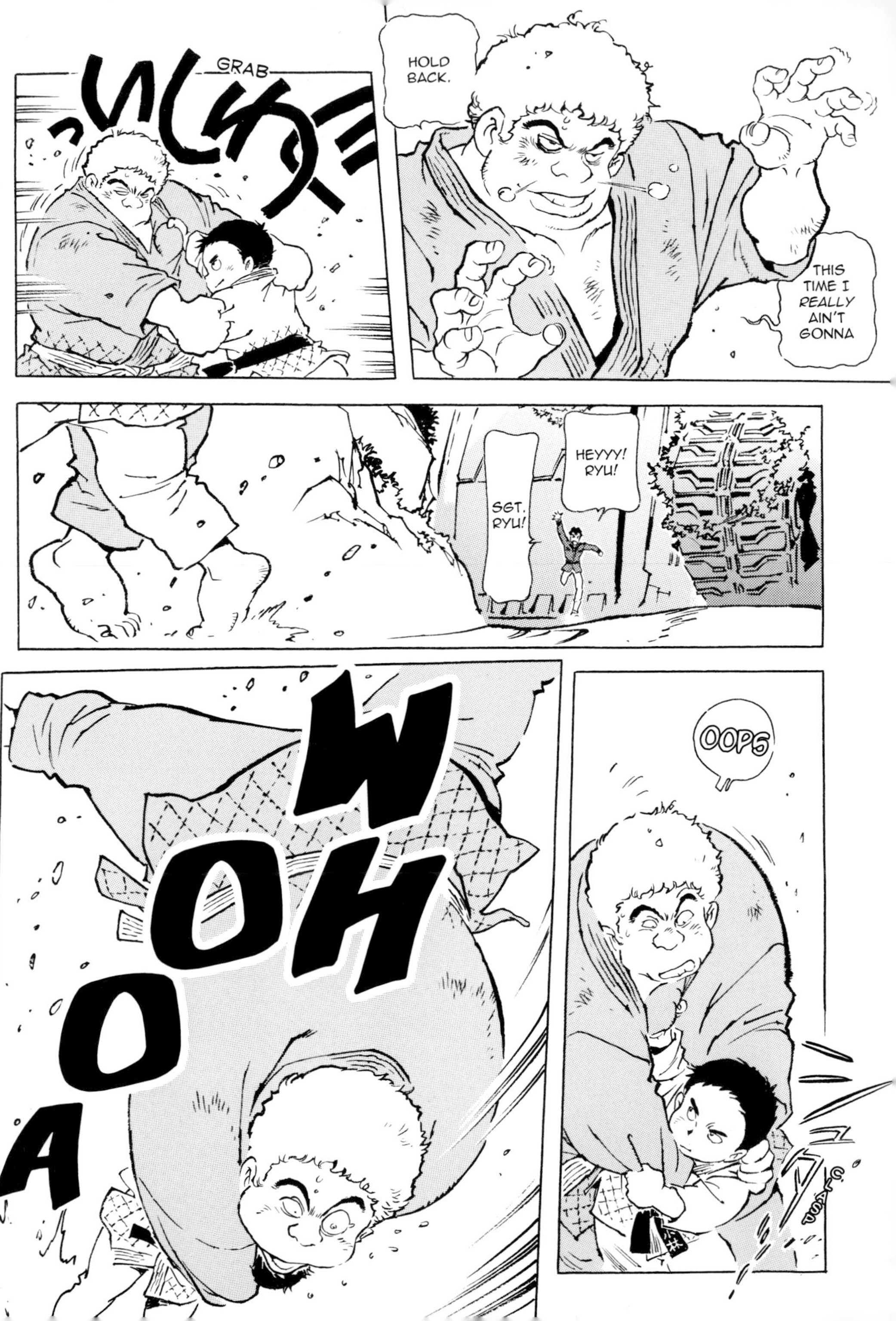

THIS TIME I REALLY AIN'T GONNA
HOLD BACK.
GRAB
HEYYY! RYU!
SGT. RYU!
OOPS
WHOA

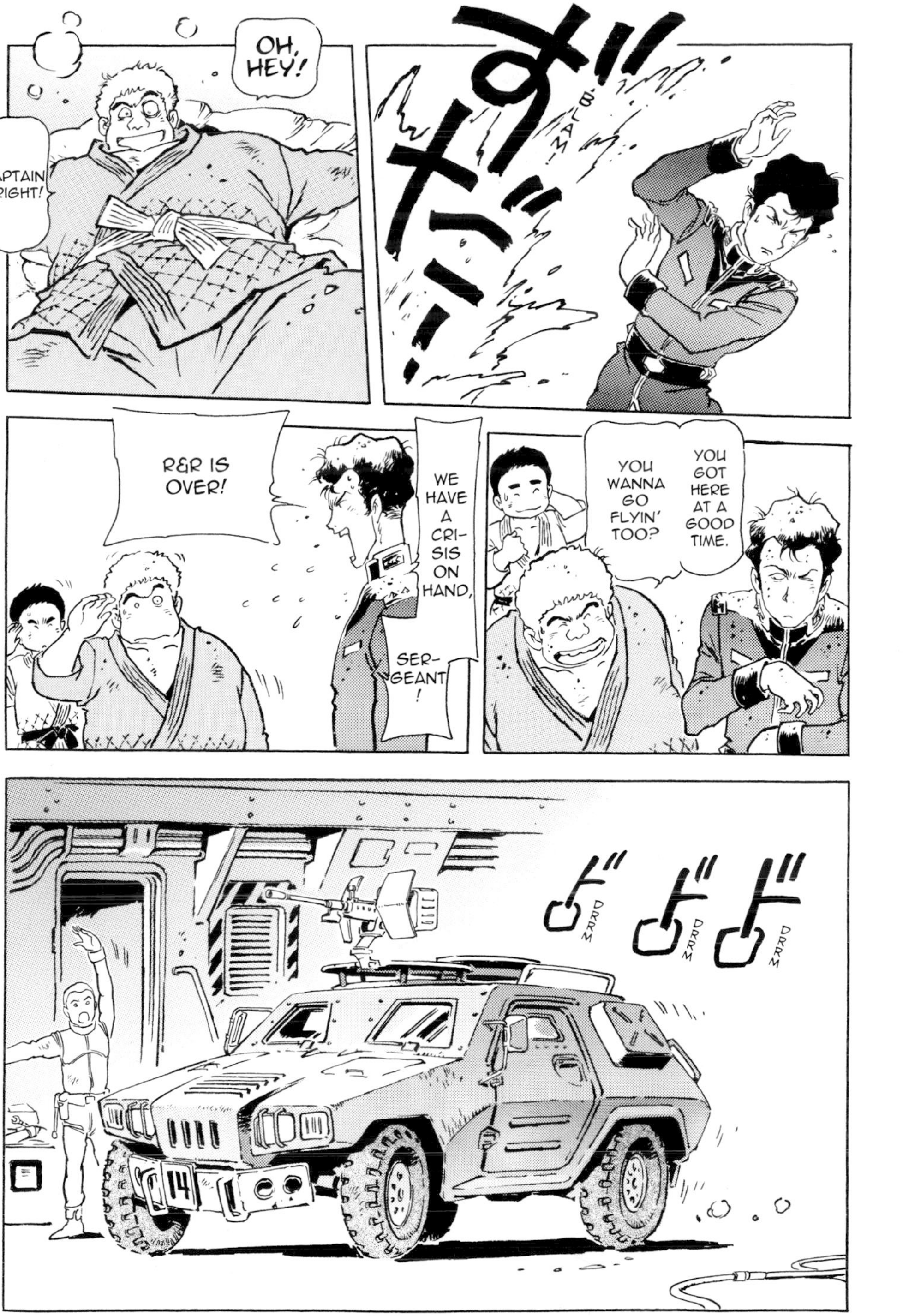
BLAM!
OH, HEY!
CAPTAIN BRIGHT!
YOU GOT HERE AT A GOOD TIME.
YOU WANNA GO FLYIN' TOO?
WE HAVE A CRISIS ON HAND, SERGEANT!
R&R IS OVER!
DRRM
DRRM
DRRM
14

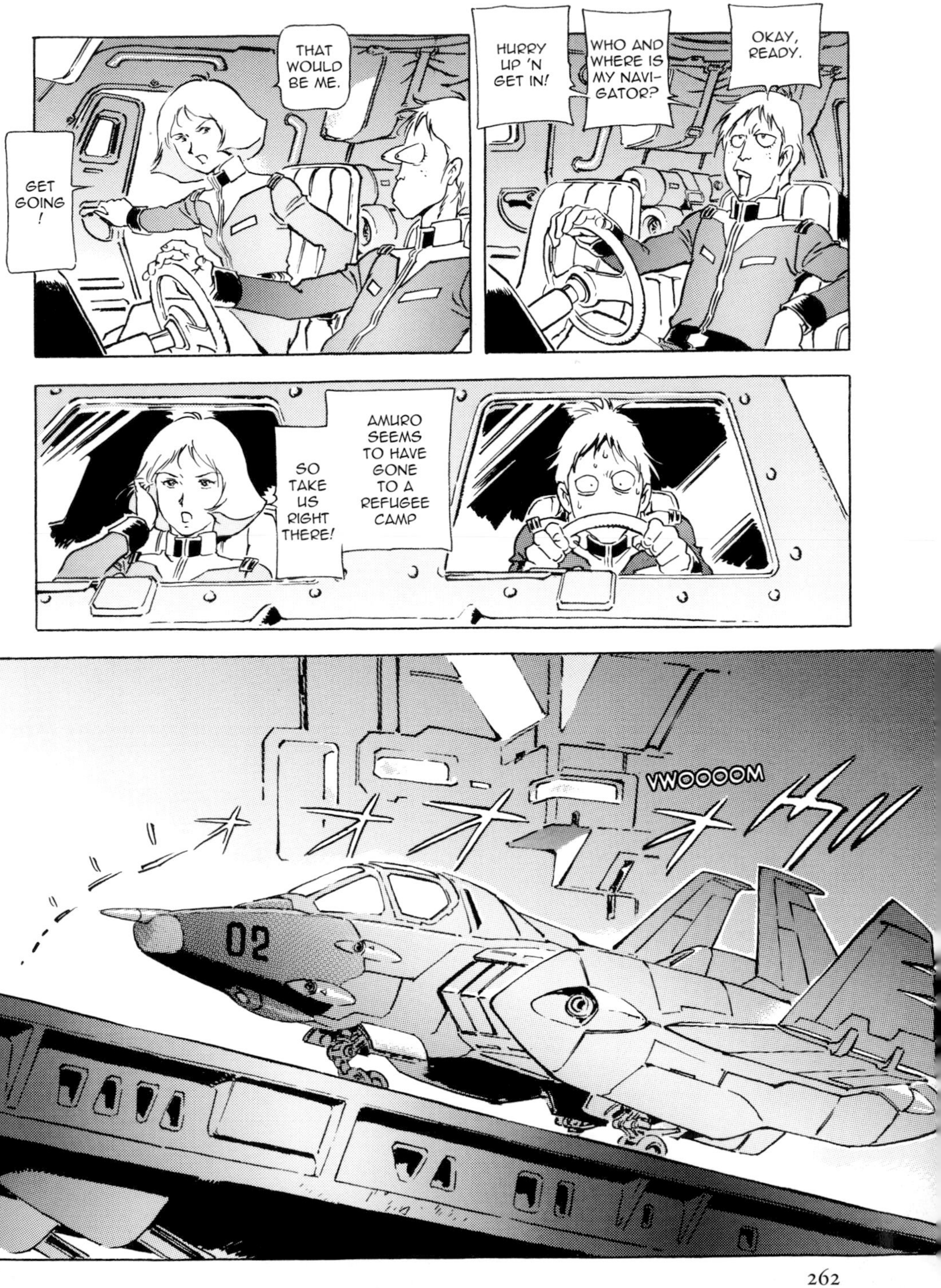
OKAY, READY.
WHO AND WHERE IS MY NAVIGATOR?
HURRY UP 'N GET IN!
THAT WOULD BE ME.
GET GOING!
AMURO SEEMS TO HAVE GONE TO A REFUGEE CAMP
SO TAKE US RIGHT THERE!
VWOOOOM

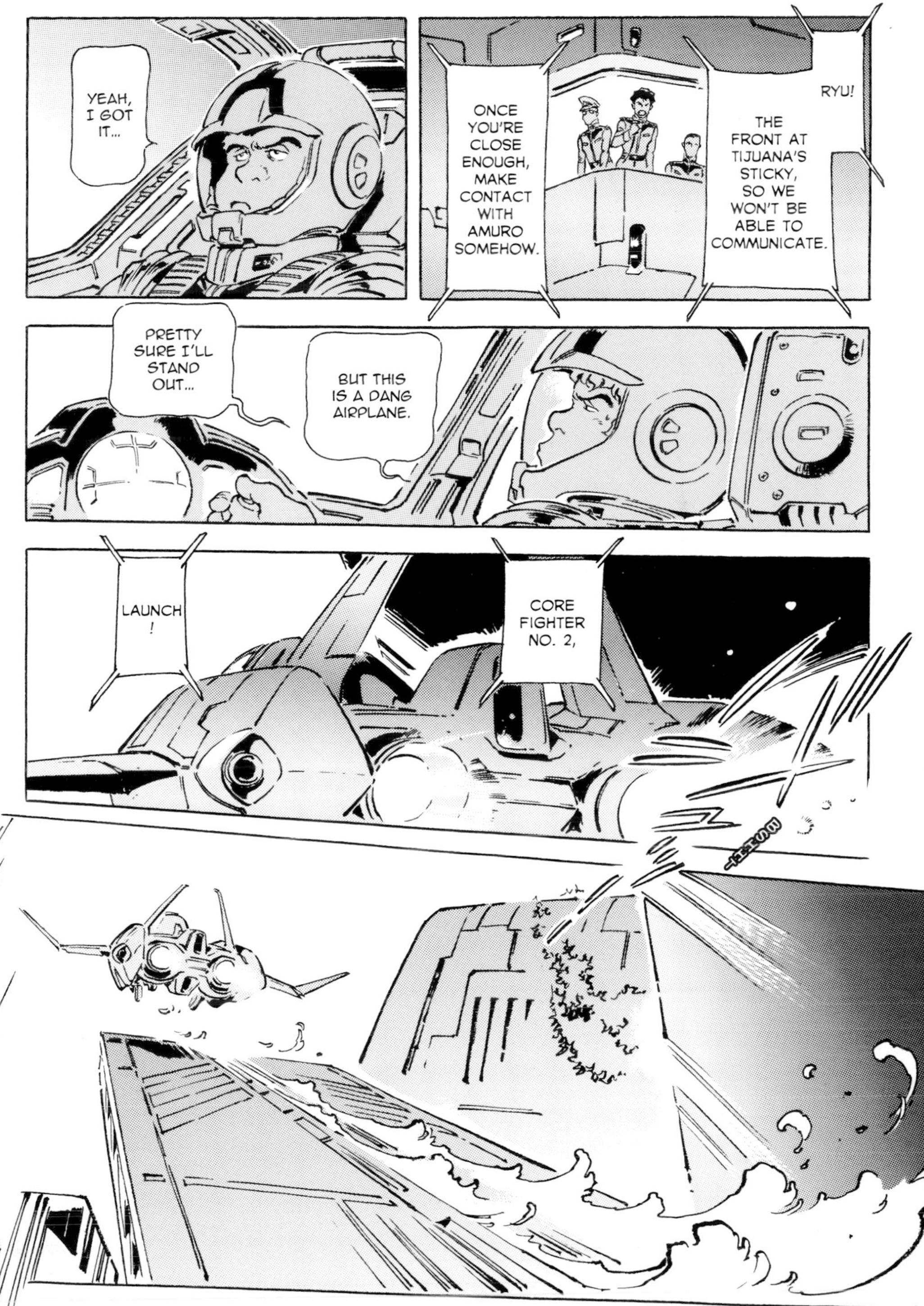
RYU!
THE FRONT AT TIJUANA'S STICKY, SO WE WON'T BE ABLE TO COMMUNICATE.
ONCE YOU'RE CLOSE ENOUGH, MAKE CONTACT WITH AMURO SOMEHOW.
YEAH, I GOT IT...
BUT THIS IS A DANG AIRPLANE.
PRETTY SURE I'LL STAND OUT...
CORE FIGHTER NO. 2,
LAUNCH!

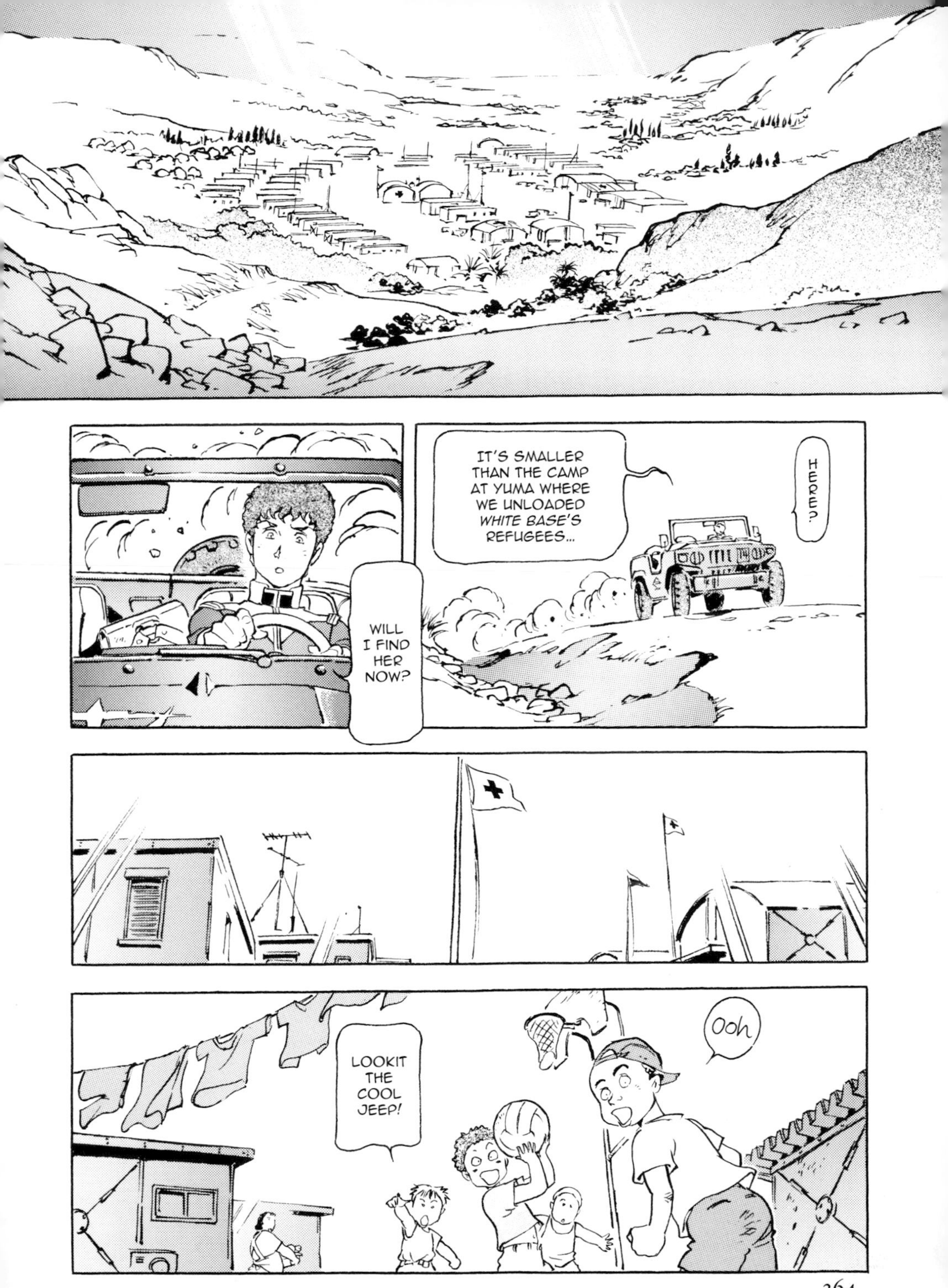
HERE?
IT'S SMALLER THAN THE CAMP AT YUMA WHERE WE UNLOADED *WHITE BASE'S* REFUGEES...
WILL I FIND HER NOW?
Ooh
LOOKIT THE COOL JEEP!

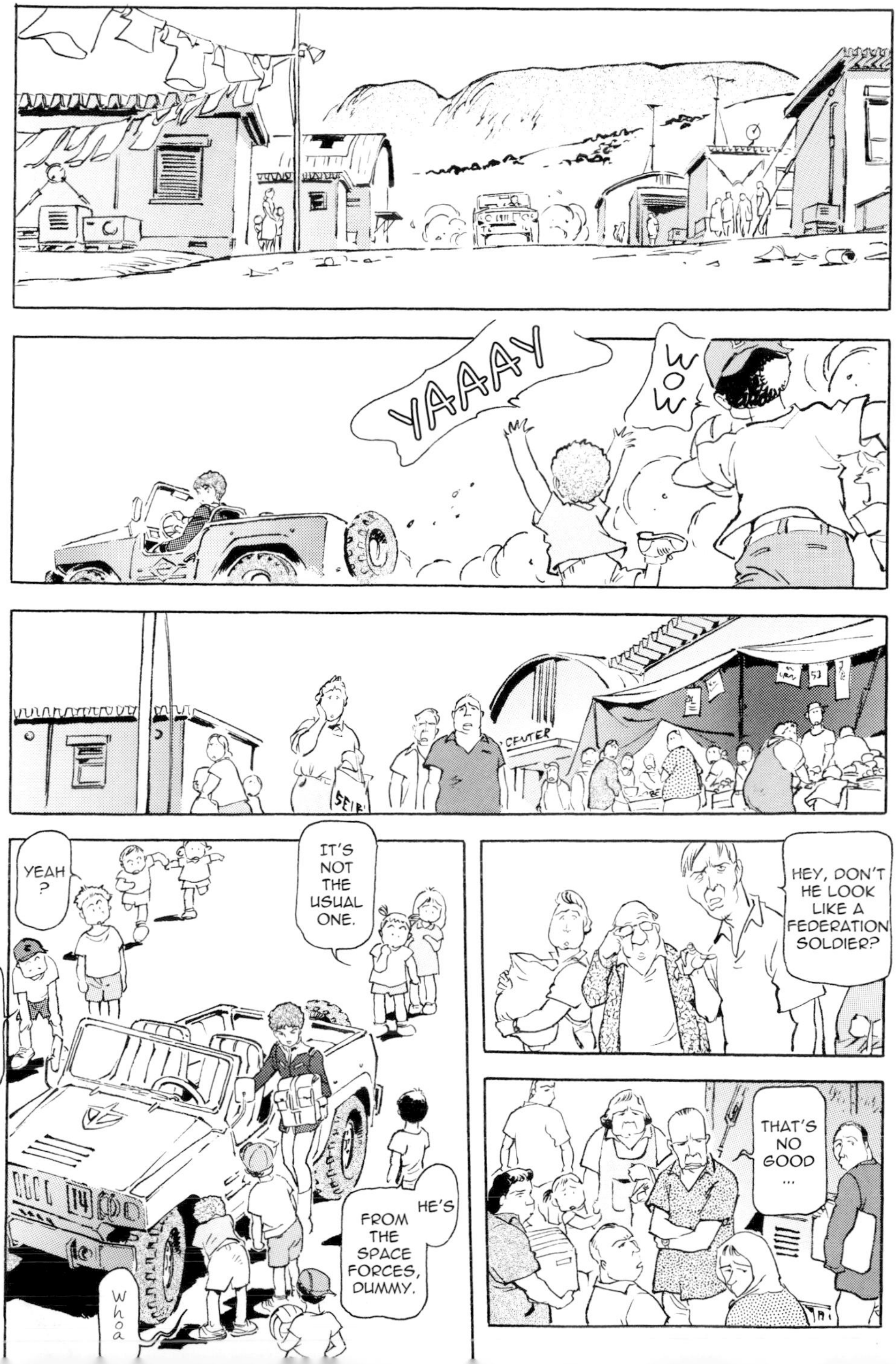
WOW
YAAAY
CENTER
HEY, DON'T HE LOOK LIKE A FEDERATION SOLDIER?
THAT'S NO GOOD ...
IT'S NOT THE USUAL ONE.
YEAH?
COOL!
HE'S FROM THE SPACE FORCES, DUMMY.
Whoa

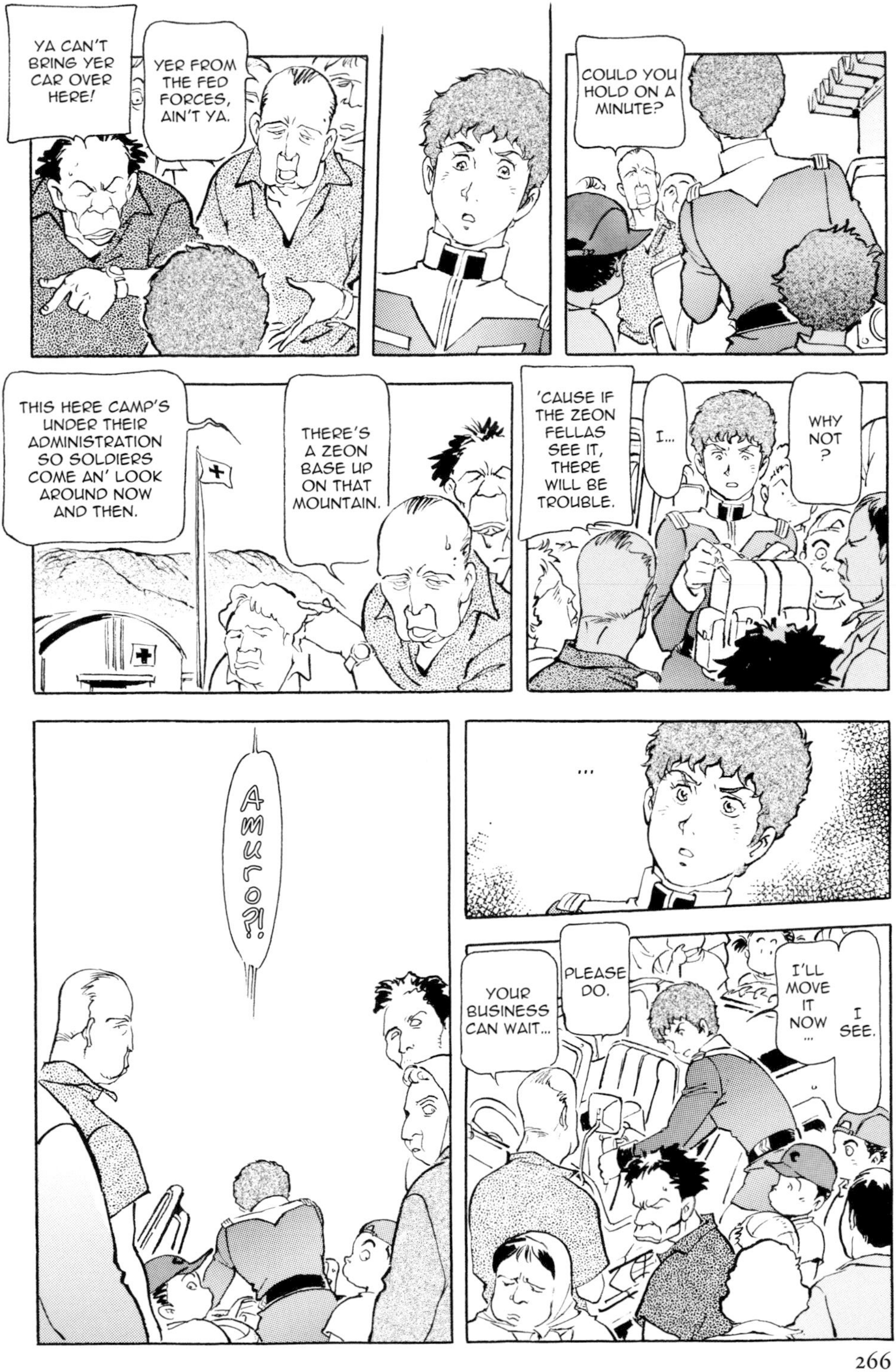
COULD YOU HOLD ON A MINUTE?
YER FROM THE FED FORCES, AIN'T YA.
YA CAN'T BRING YER CAR OVER HERE!
WHY NOT ?
I...
'CAUSE IF THE ZEON FELLAS SEE IT, THERE WILL BE TROUBLE.
THERE'S A ZEON BASE UP ON THAT MOUNTAIN.
THIS HERE CAMP'S UNDER THEIR ADMINISTRATION SO SOLDIERS COME AN' LOOK AROUND NOW AND THEN.
...
I SEE.
I'LL MOVE IT NOW ...
PLEASE DO.
YOUR BUSINESS CAN WAIT...
Amuro?!

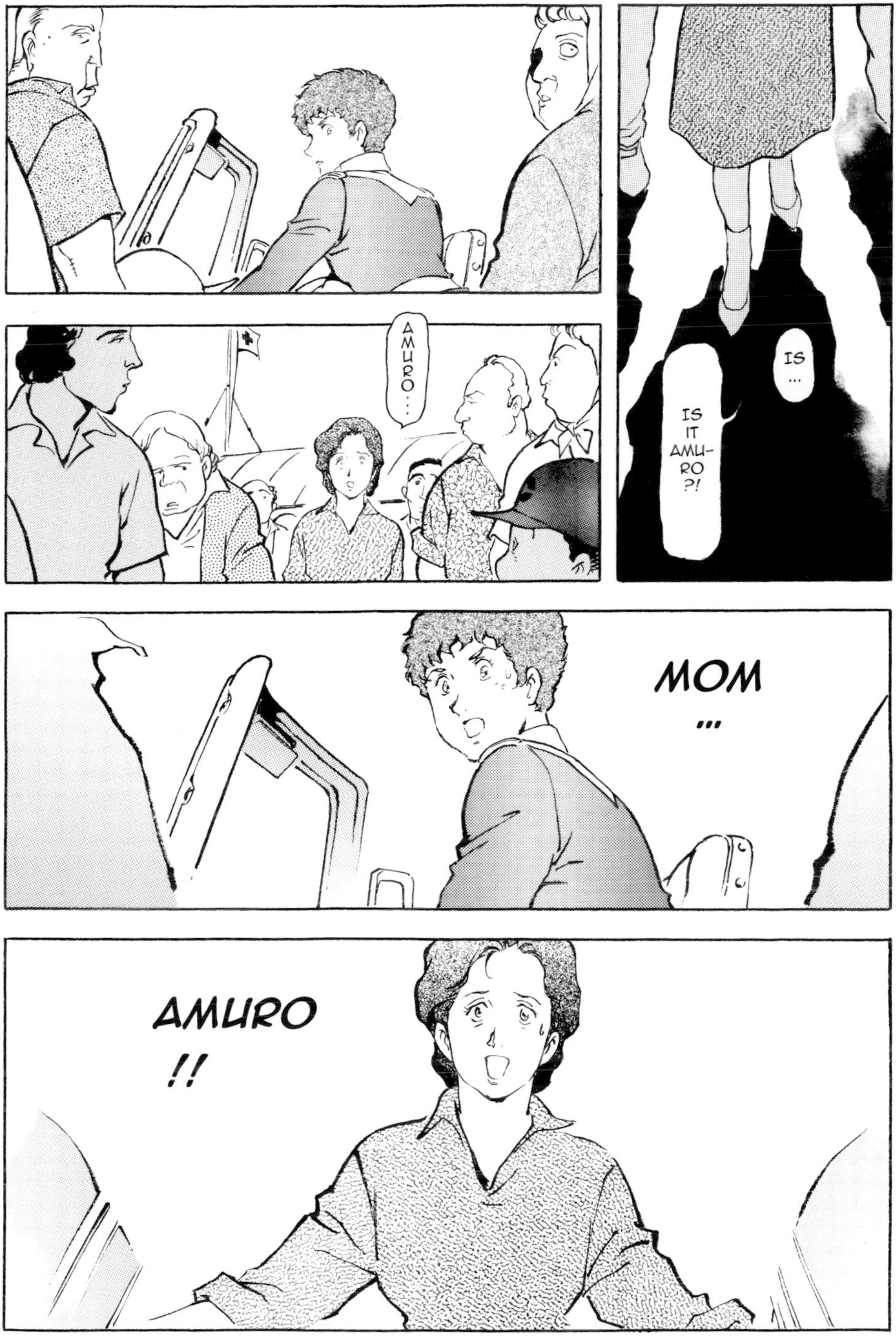
IS ...
IS IT AMU-RO ?!
AMURO...
MOM ...
AMURO !!

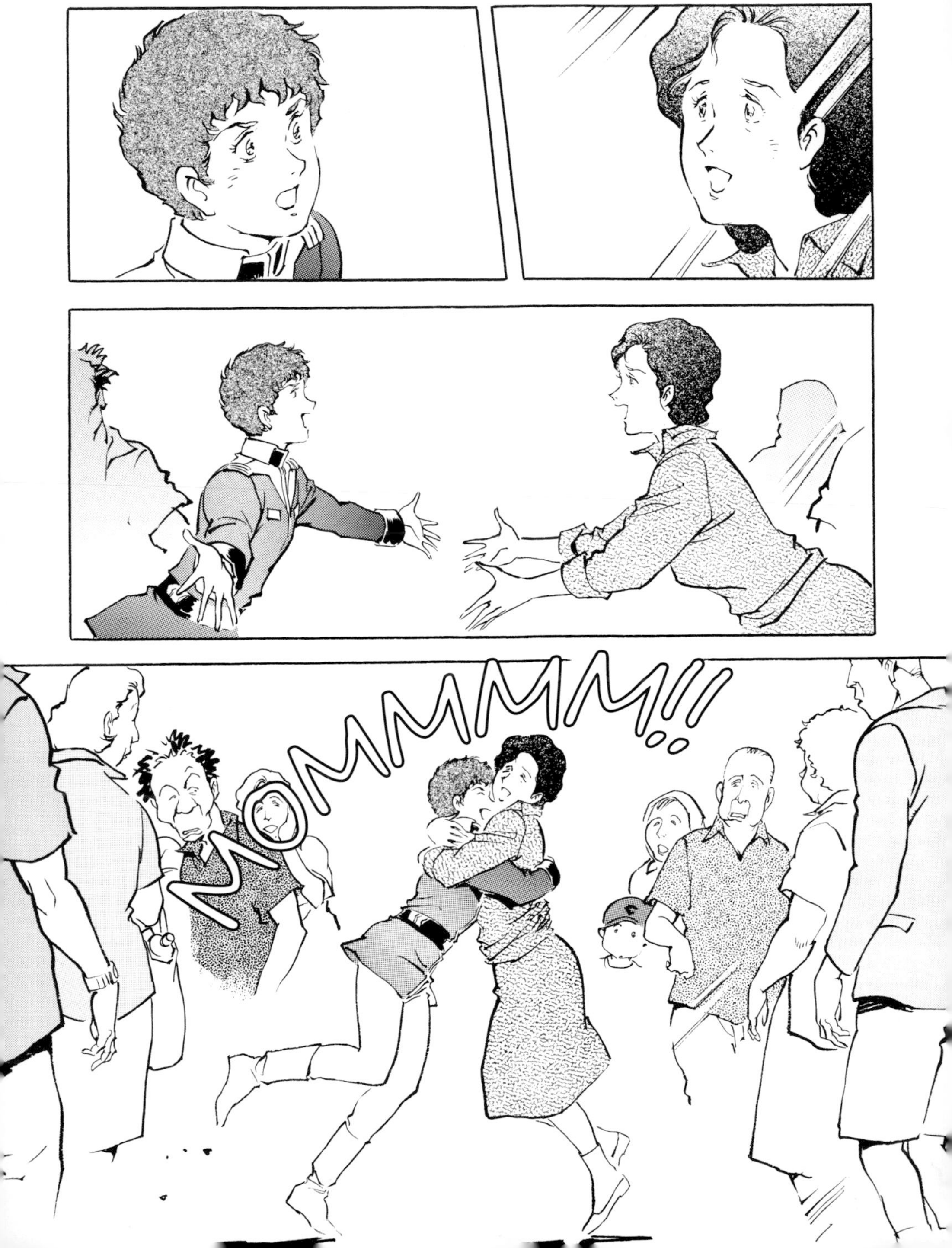
MOMMMMM!!

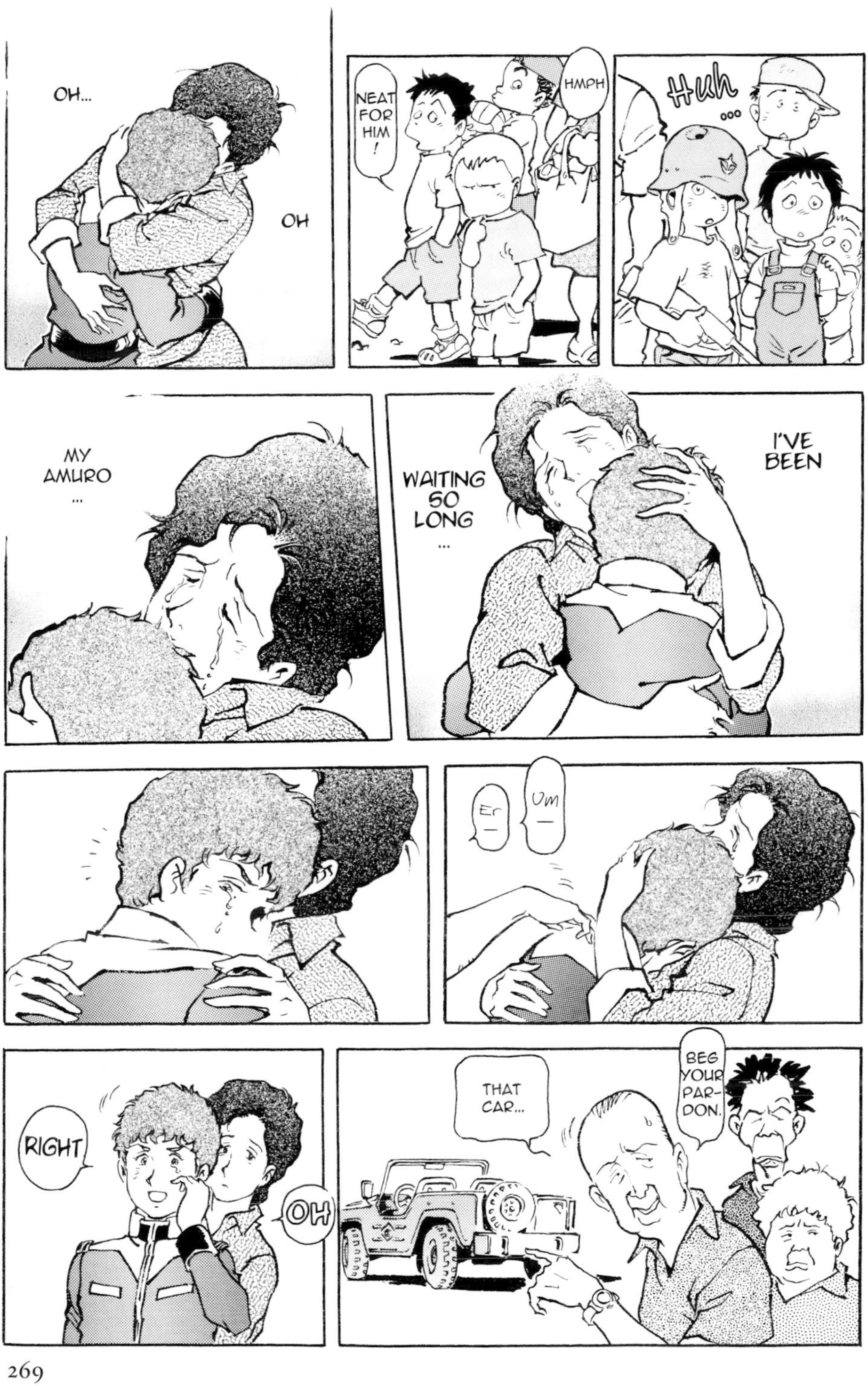
Huh
ooo
HMPH
NEAT FOR HIM!
OH
OH...
I'VE BEEN
WAITING SO LONG ...
MY AMURO ...
Um—
Er—
BEG YOUR PAR-DON.
THAT CAR...
OH
RIGHT

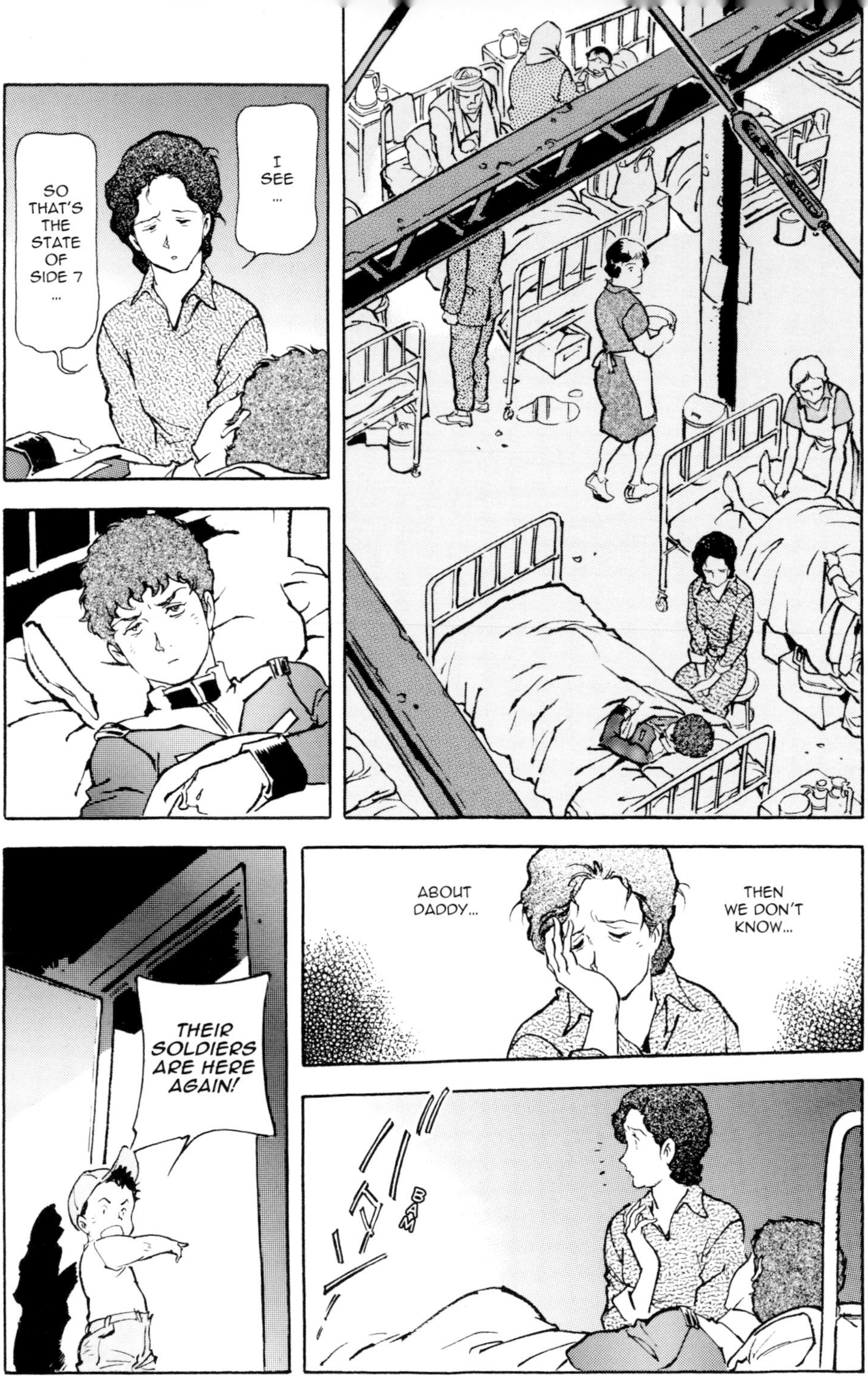
I SEE ...
SO THAT'S THE STATE OF SIDE 7 ...
THEN WE DON'T KNOW...
ABOUT DADDY...
BAM
THEIR SOLDIERS ARE HERE AGAIN!

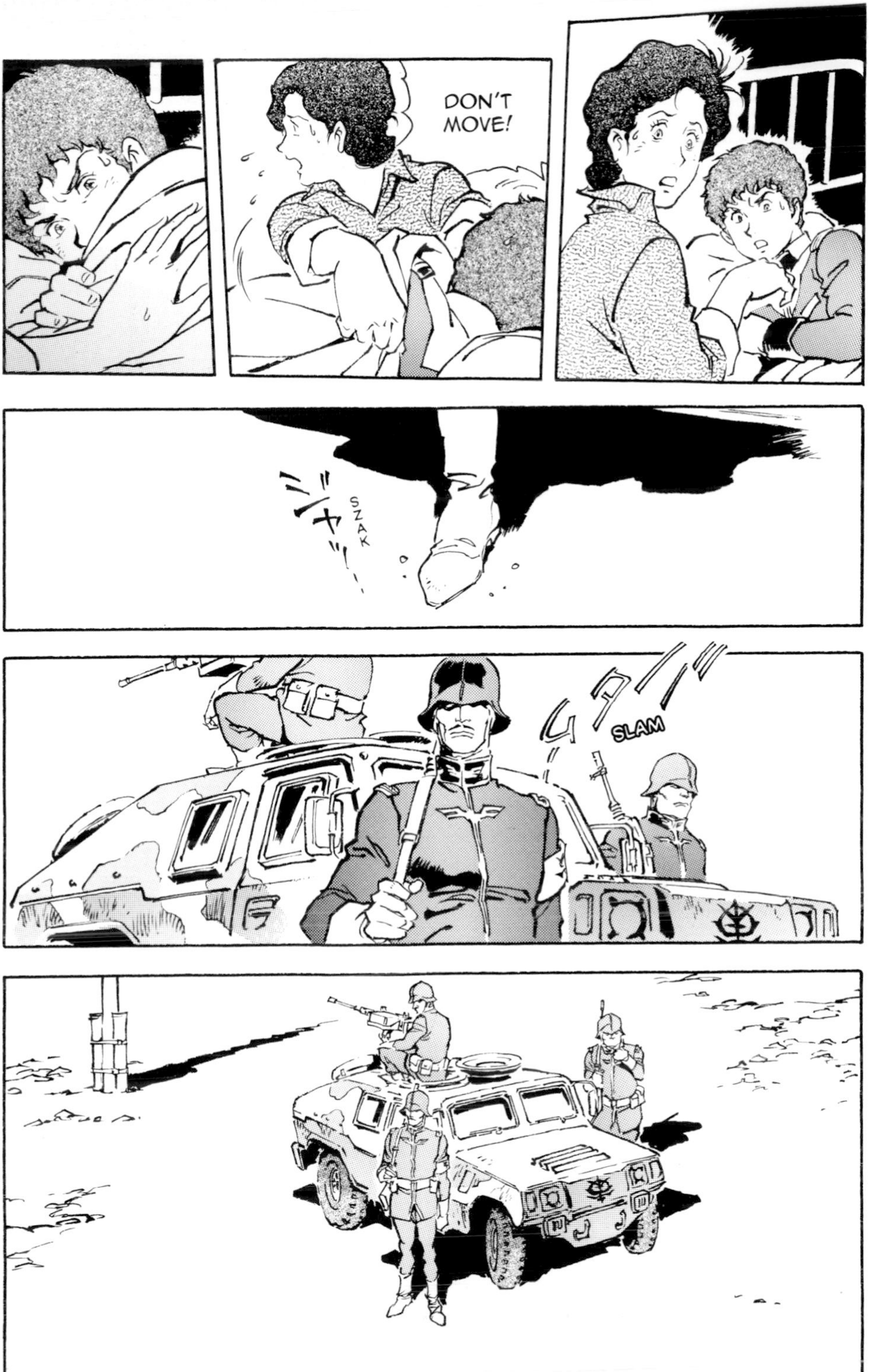
DON'T MOVE!
SZAK
SLAM

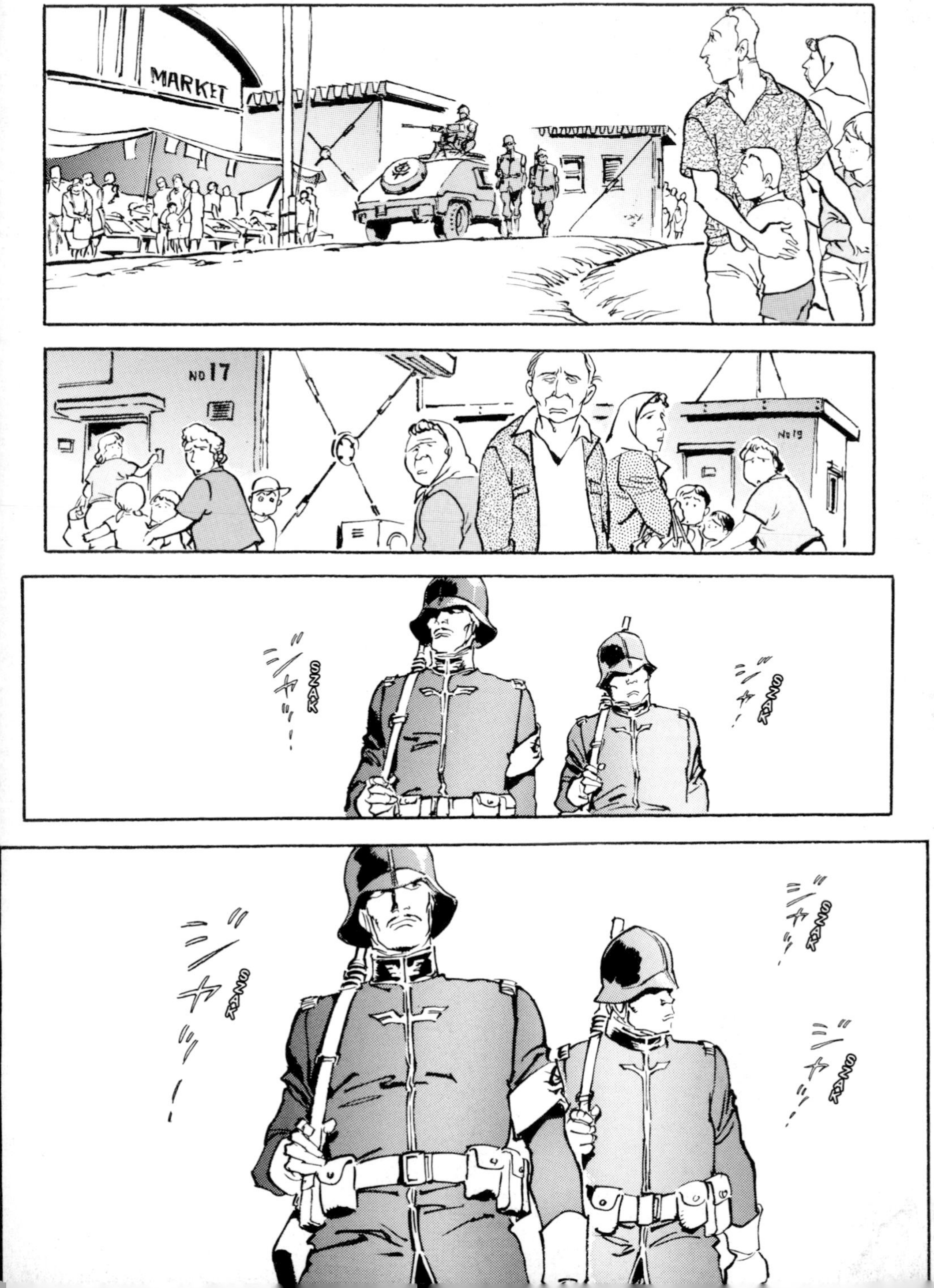
MARKET
No 19
NO 17
ジャ
SZAK
ジャ
SZAK
ジャ
SZAK
ジャ
SZAK
ジャ
SZAK

SECTION VI

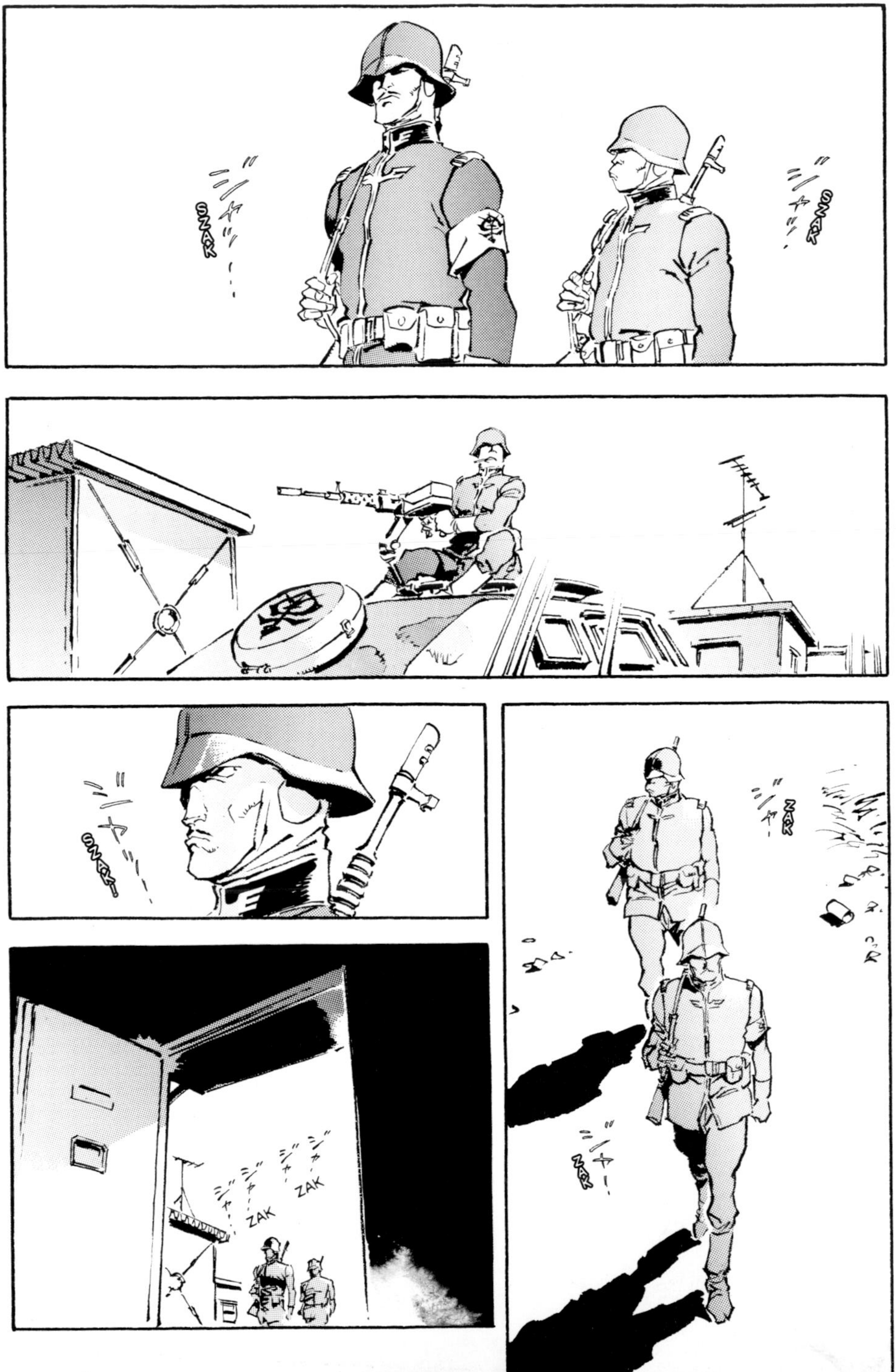
SZAK
SZAK
SNAK!
ZAK
ZAK
ZAK
ZAK

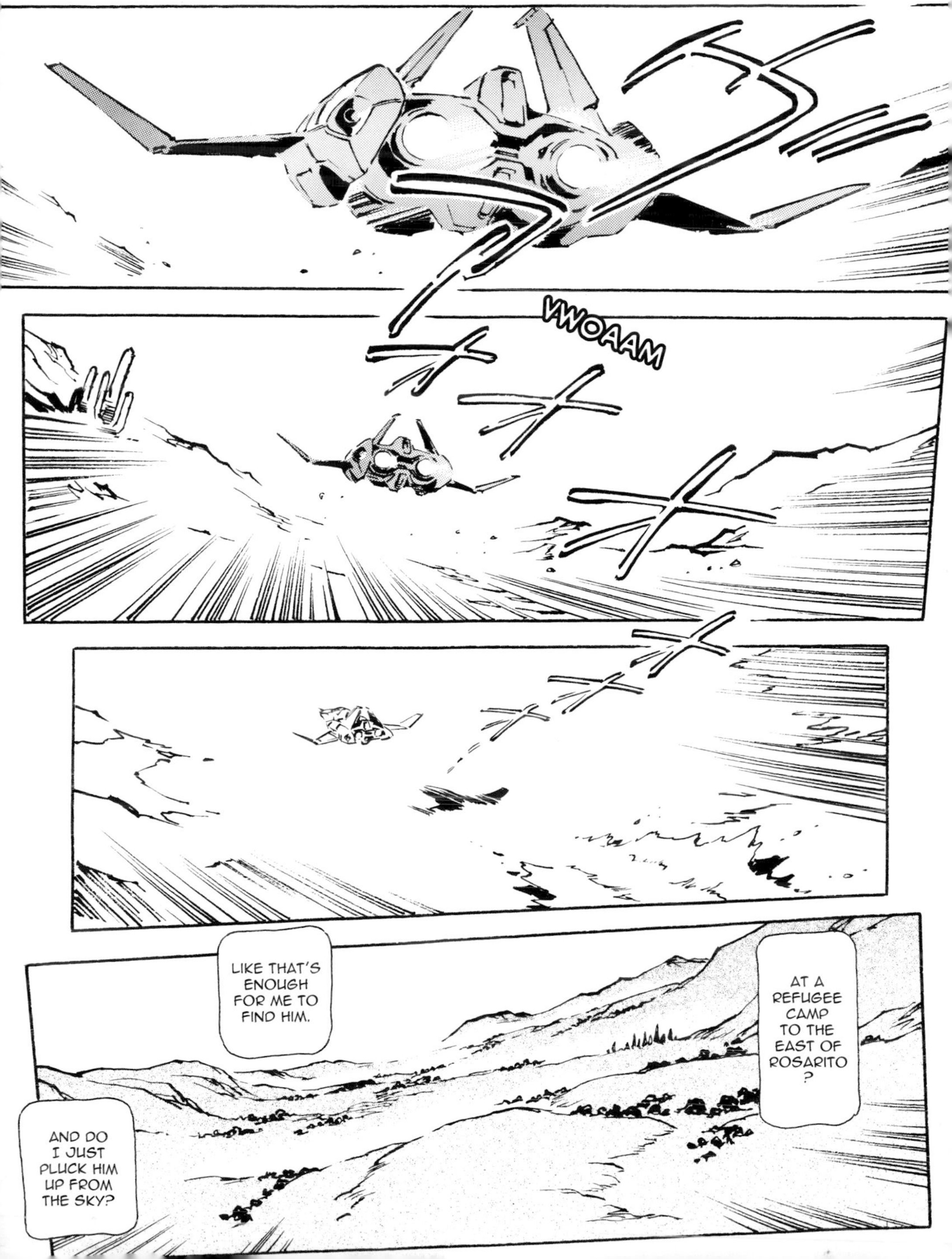
VWOAAM
AT A REFUGEE CAMP TO THE EAST OF ROSARITO?
LIKE THAT'S ENOUGH FOR ME TO FIND HIM.
AND DO I JUST PLUCK HIM UP FROM THE SKY?

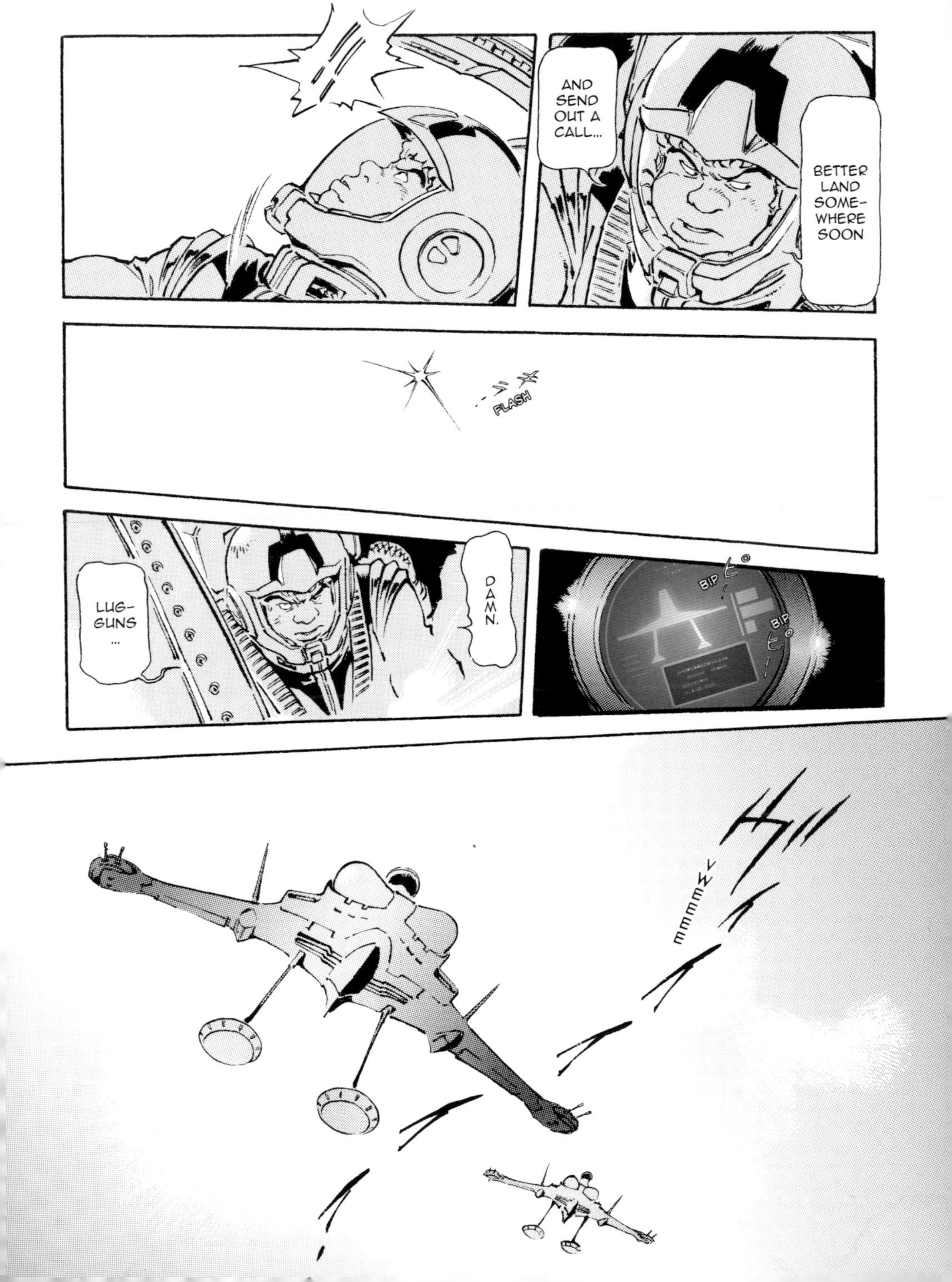
BETTER LAND SOME-WHERE SOON
AND SEND OUT A CALL...
FLASH
BIP
BIP
DAMN.
LUG-GUNS ...
VWEEEEE

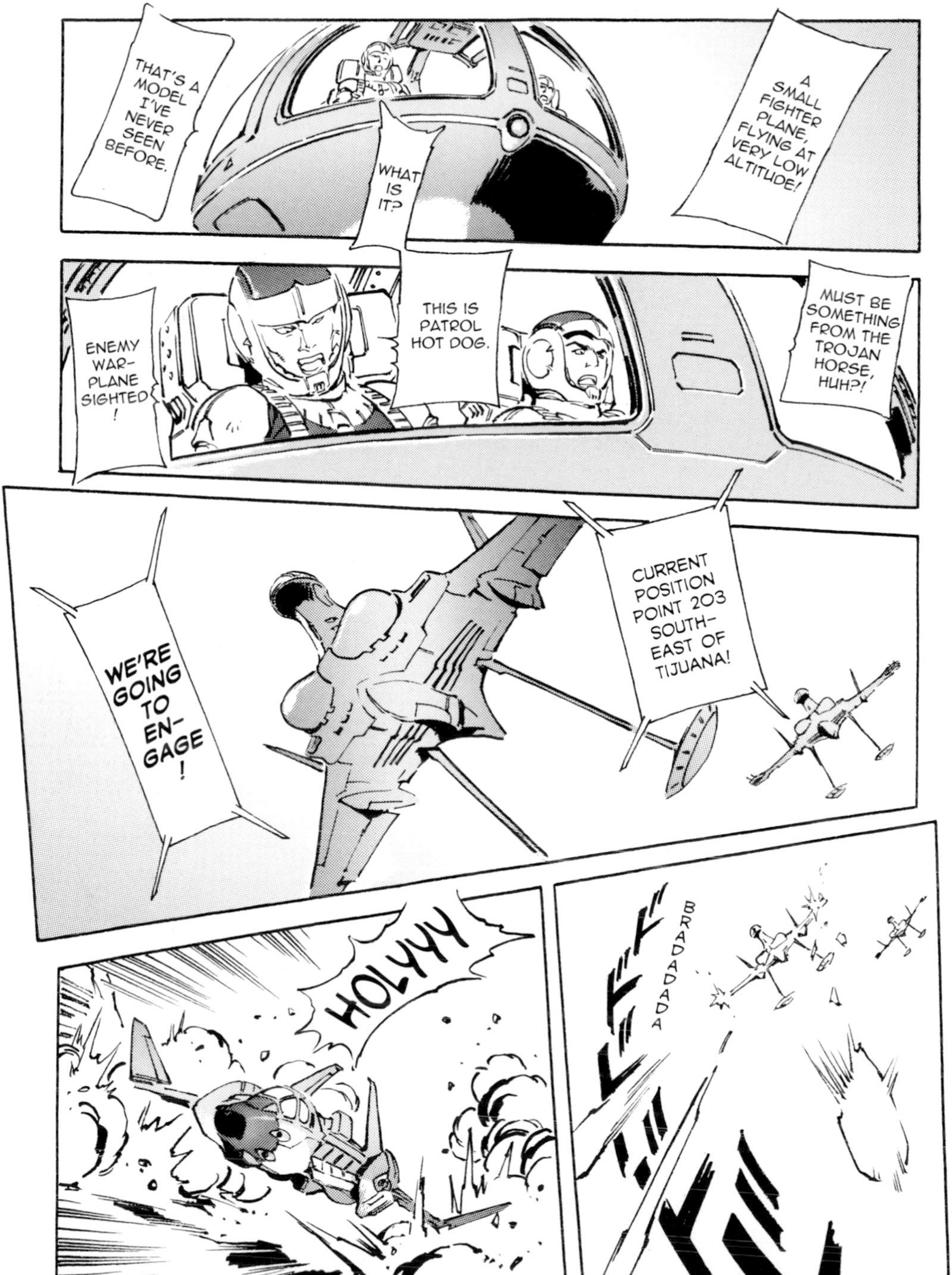
A SMALL FIGHTER PLANE, FLYING AT VERY LOW ALTITUDE!
WHAT IS IT?
THAT'S A MODEL I'VE NEVER SEEN BEFORE.
MUST BE SOMETHING FROM THE TROJAN HORSE, HUH?!
THIS IS PATROL HOT DOG.
ENEMY WAR-PLANE SIGHTED!
CURRENT POSITION POINT 203 SOUTH-EAST OF TIJUANA!
WE'RE GOING TO EN-GAGE!
BRADADADA
HOLYYY

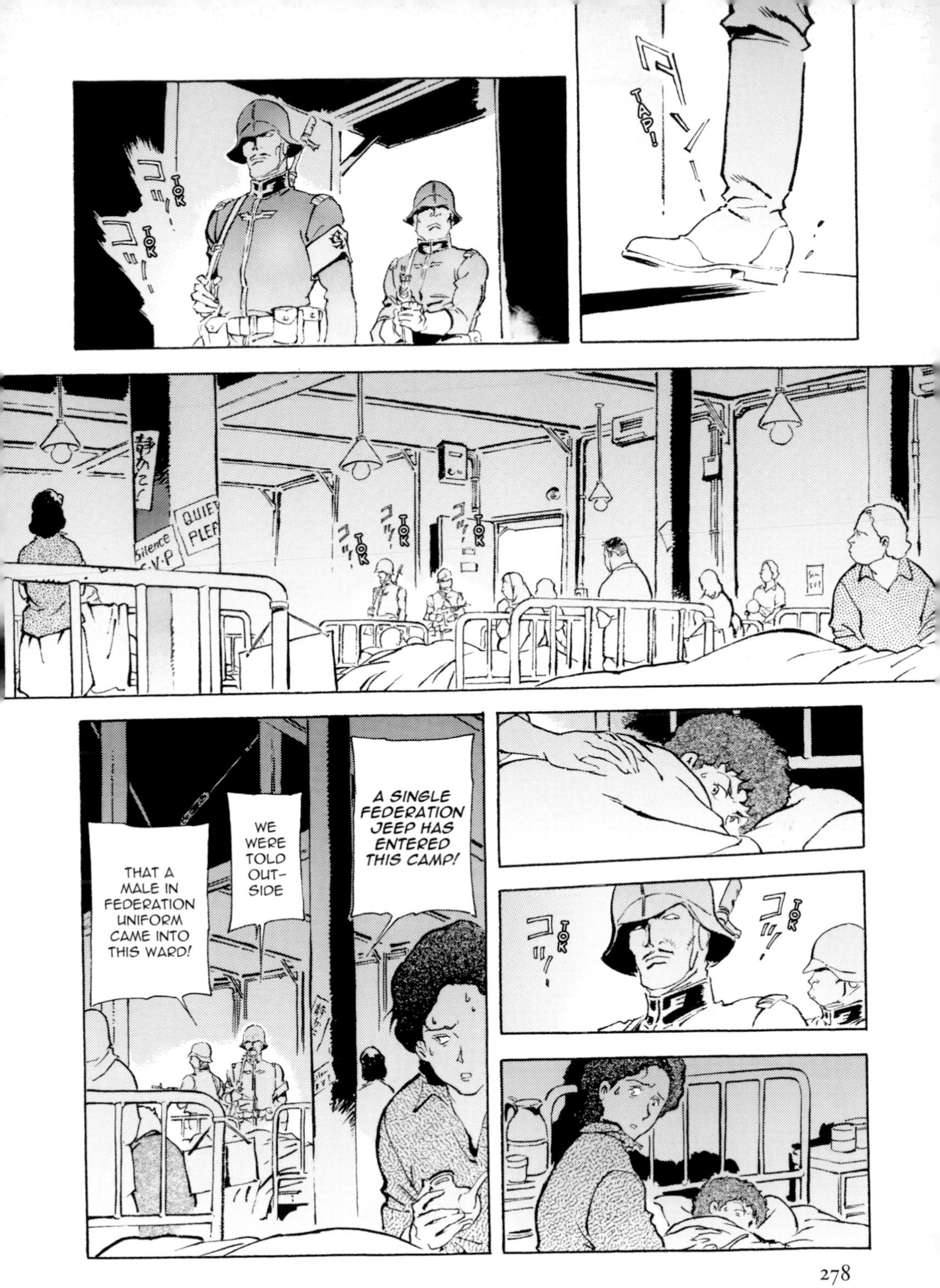
TAP!
TOK
TOK
静かに
QUIET PLEA
Silence S.V.P
TOK
TOK
TOK
TOK
TOK
A SINGLE FEDERATION JEEP HAS ENTERED THIS CAMP!
WE WERE TOLD OUT-SIDE
THAT A MALE IN FEDERATION UNIFORM CAME INTO THIS WARD!

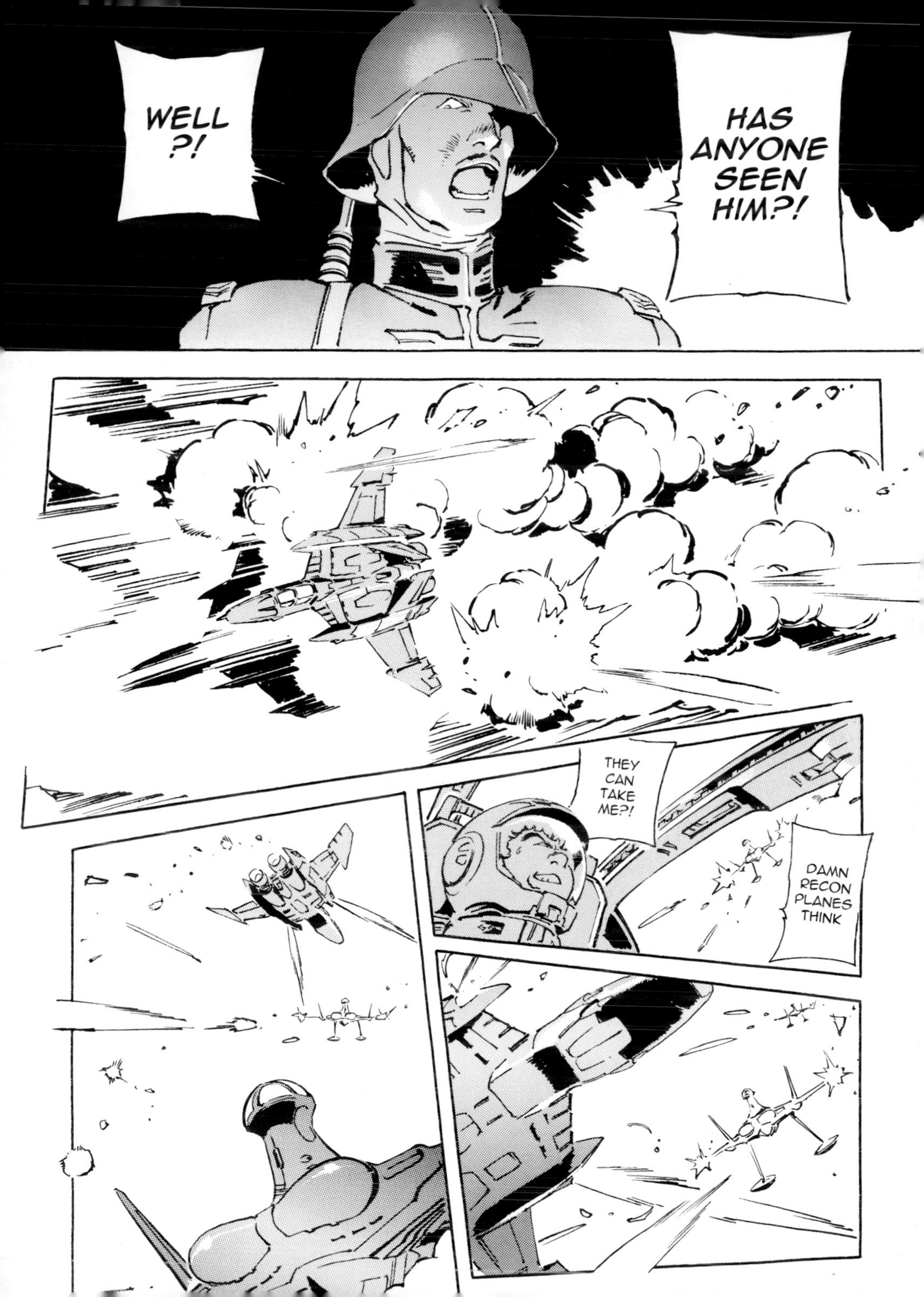
HAS ANYONE SEEN HIM?!
WELL ?!
DAMN RECON PLANES THINK
THEY CAN TAKE ME?!

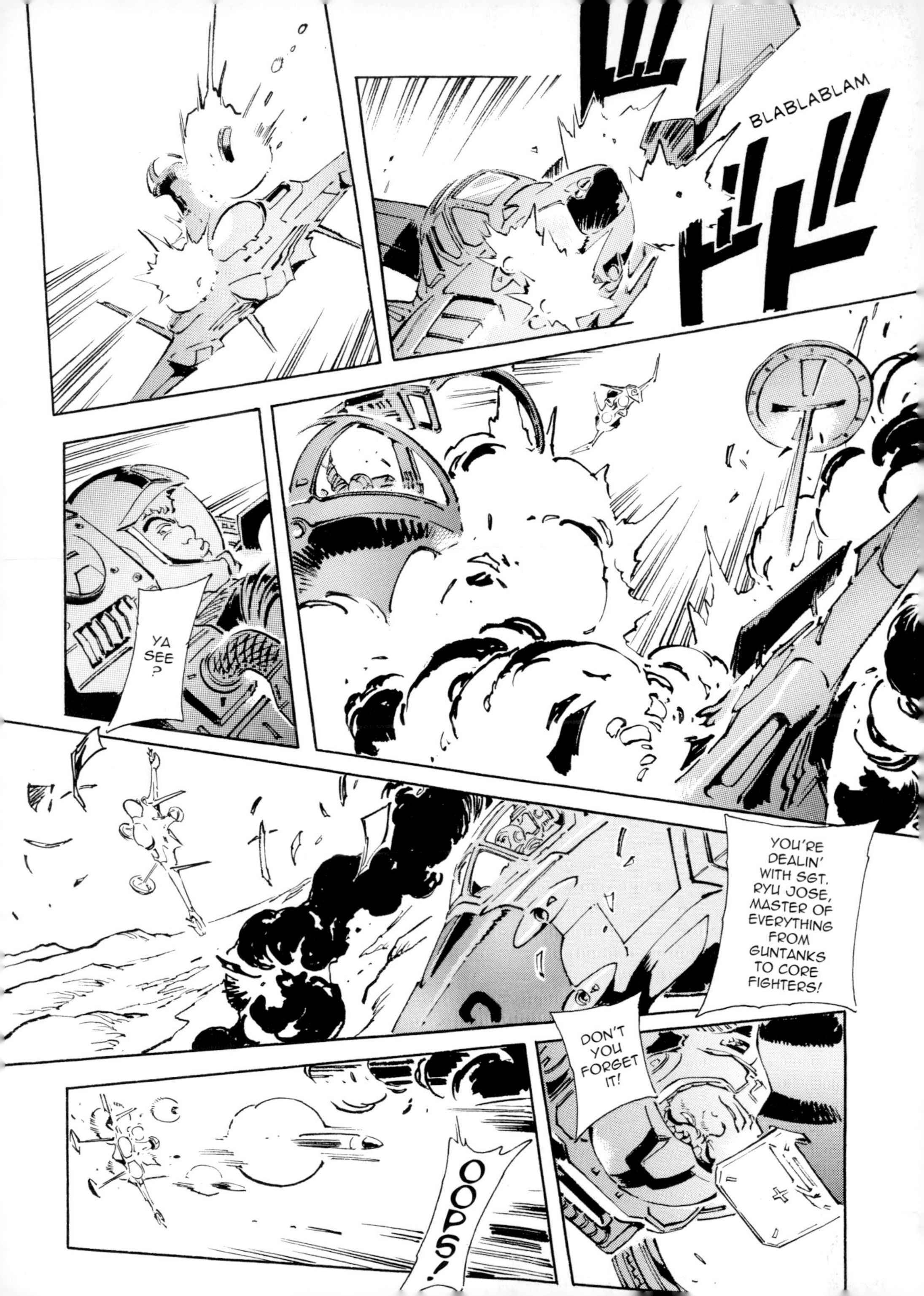
BLABLABLAM
YA SEE?
YOU'RE DEALIN' WITH SGT. RYU JOSE, MASTER OF EVERYTHING FROM GUNTANKS TO CORE FIGHTERS!
DON'T YOU FORGET IT!
OOPS!

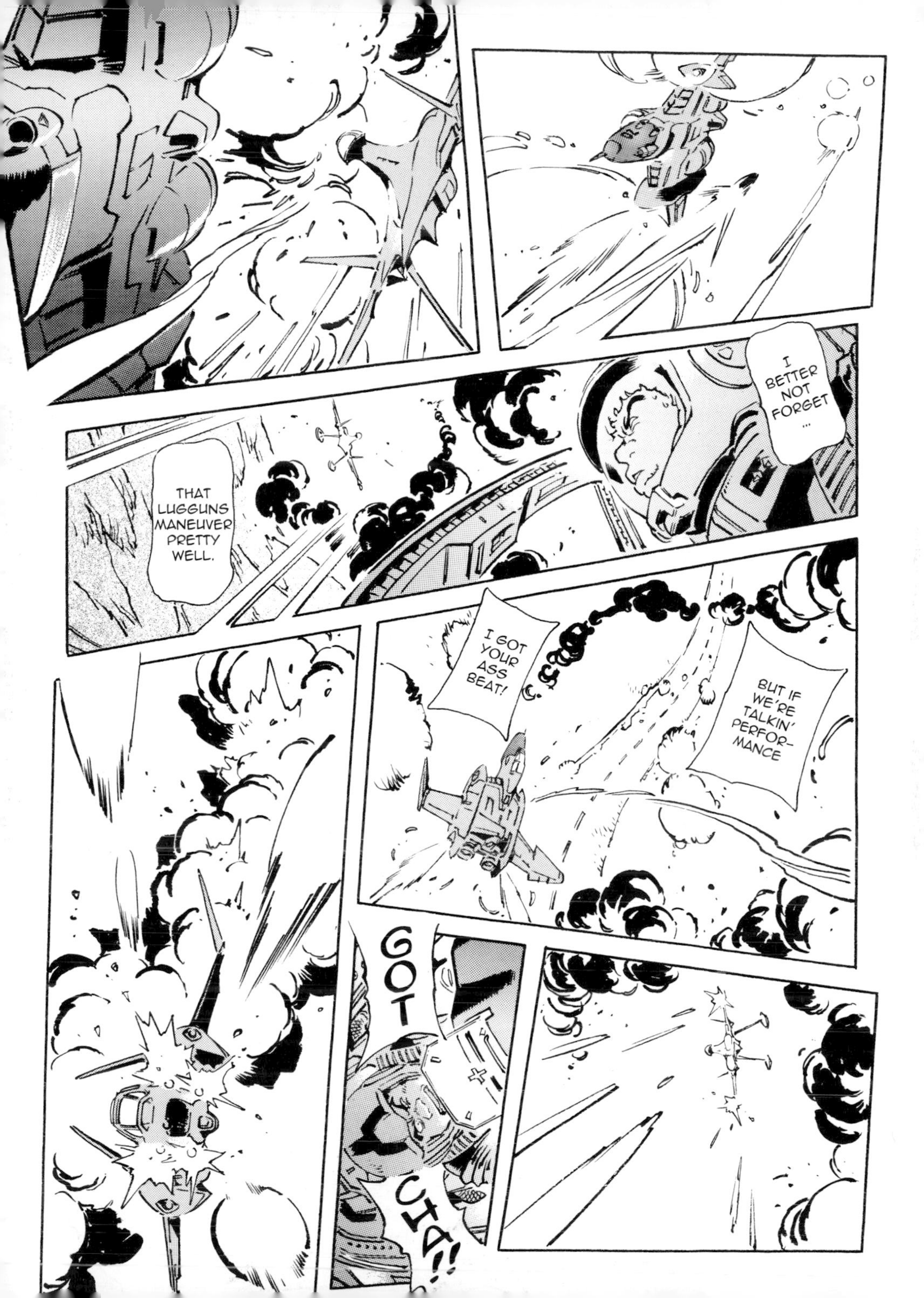
I BETTER NOT FORGET ...
THAT LUGGUNS MANEUVER PRETTY WELL.
BUT IF WE'RE TALKIN' PERFORMANCE
I GOT YOUR ASS BEAT!
GOT CHA!!

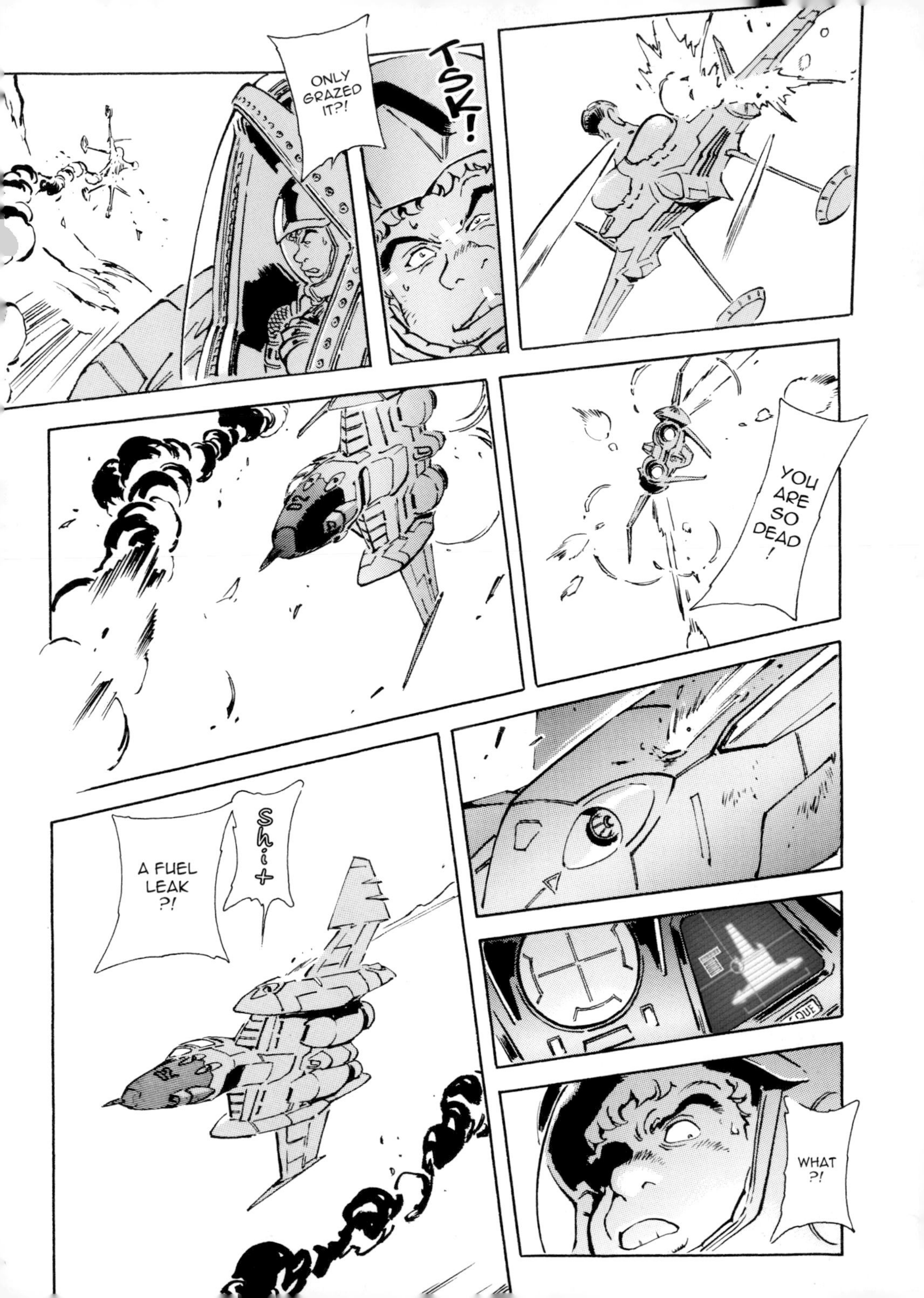
TSK!
ONLY GRAZED IT?!
YOU ARE SO DEAD!
WHAT?!
Shit
A FUEL LEAK?!

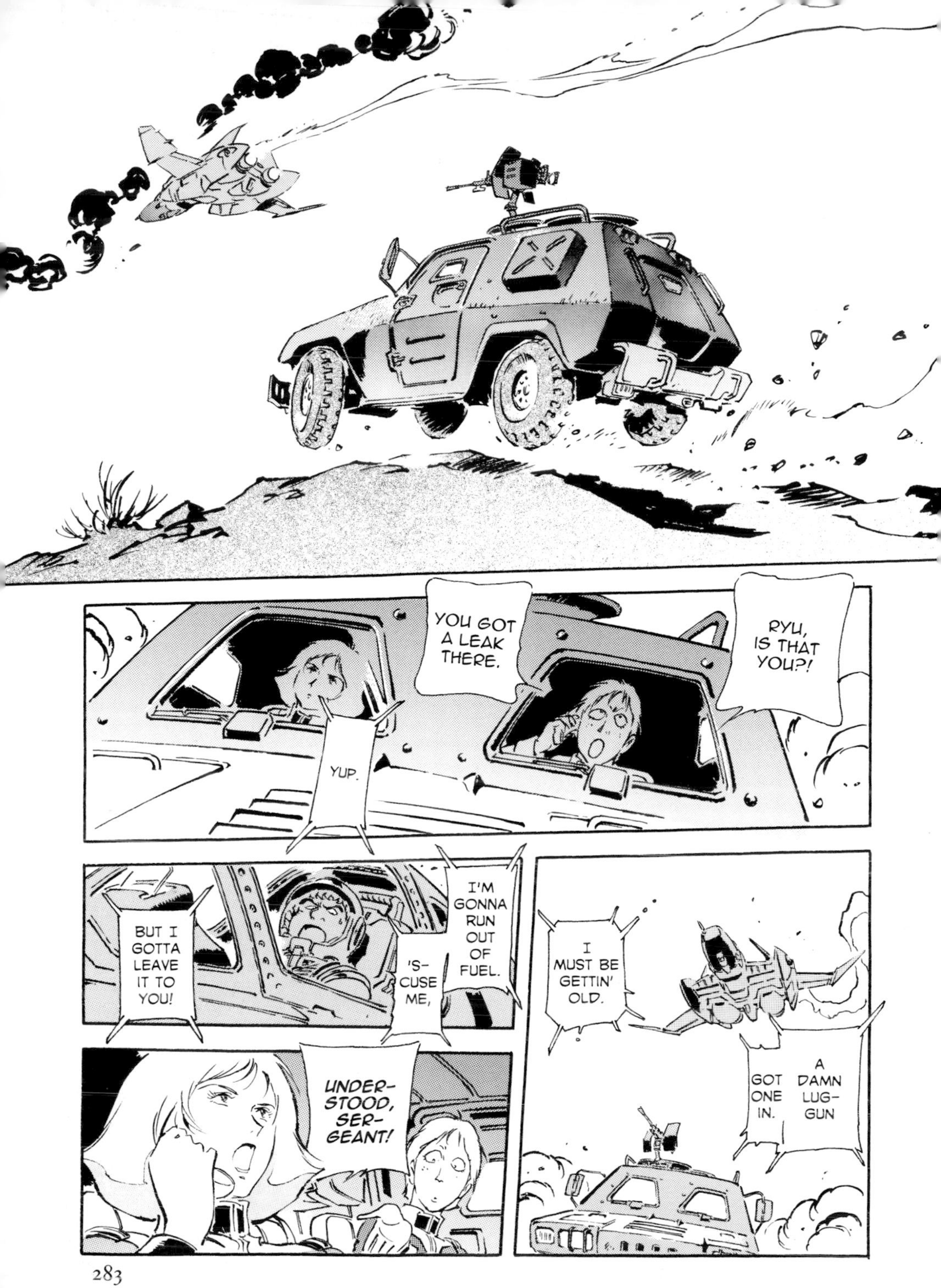
RYU, IS THAT YOU?!
YOU GOT A LEAK THERE.
YUP.
I MUST BE GETTIN' OLD.
A DAMN LUG-GUN
GOT ONE IN.
I'M GONNA RUN OUT OF FUEL.
'S-CUSE ME,
BUT I GOTTA LEAVE IT TO YOU!
UNDER-STOOD, SER-GEANT!

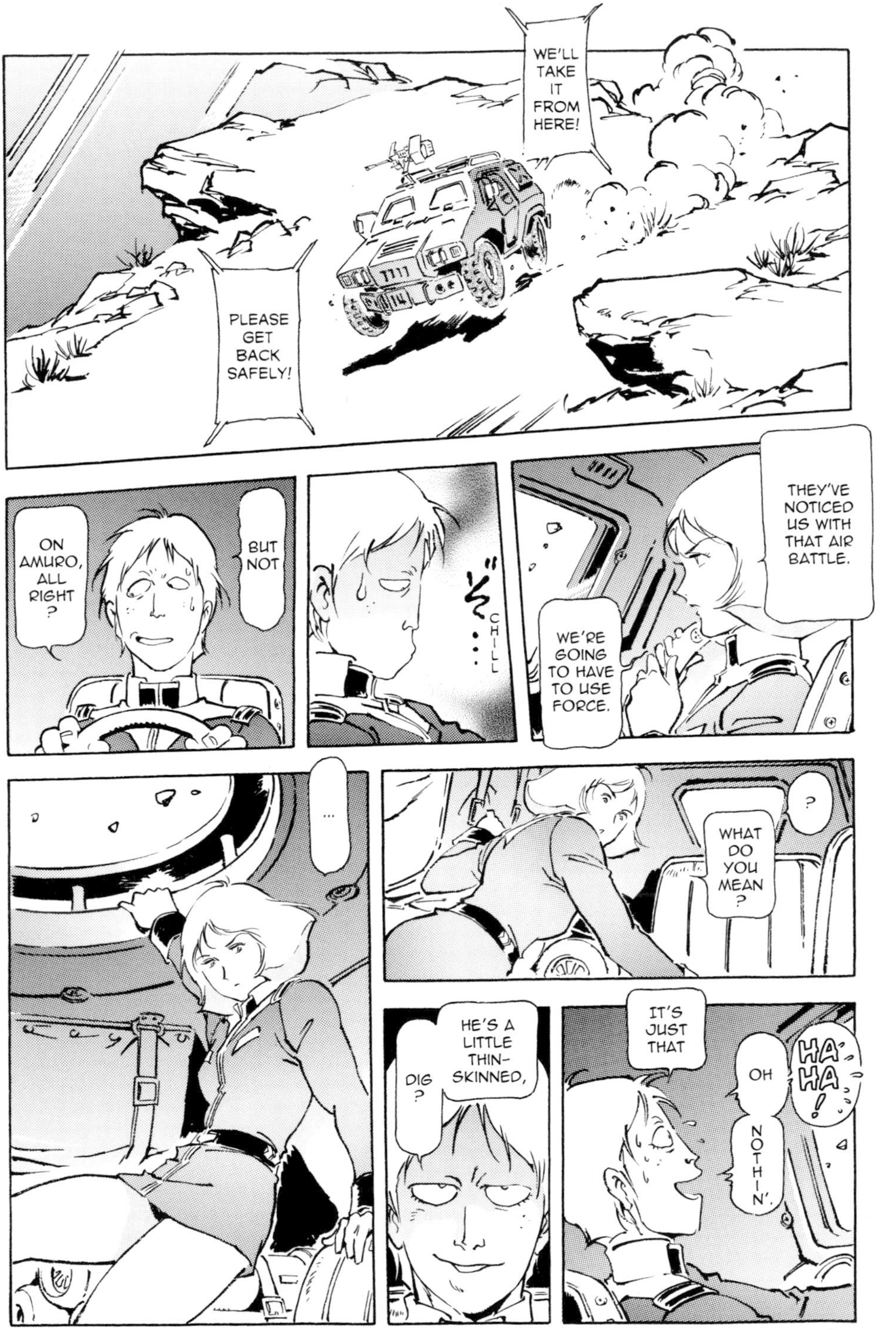
WE'LL TAKE IT FROM HERE!
PLEASE GET BACK SAFELY!
THEY'VE NOTICED US WITH THAT AIR BATTLE.
WE'RE GOING TO HAVE TO USE FORCE.
CHILL...
BUT NOT
ON AMURO, ALL RIGHT?
?
WHAT DO YOU MEAN?
IT'S JUST THAT
HAHA!
OH
NOTHIN'.
HE'S A LITTLE THIN-SKINNED,
DIG?
...

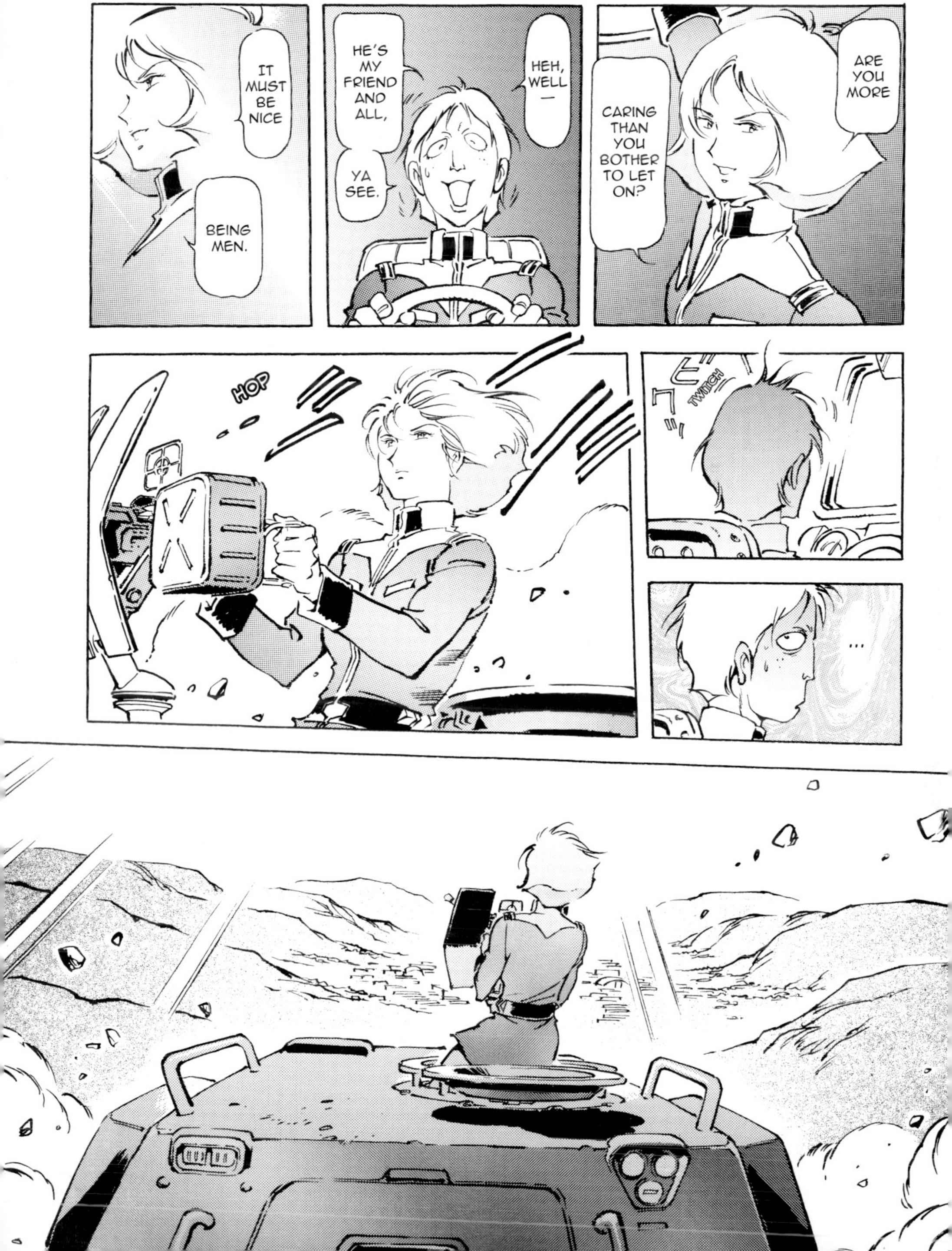
ARE YOU MORE
CARING THAN YOU BOTHER TO LET ON?
HEH, WELL—
HE'S MY FRIEND AND ALL,
YA SEE.
IT MUST BE NICE
BEING MEN.
TWITCH
...
HOP

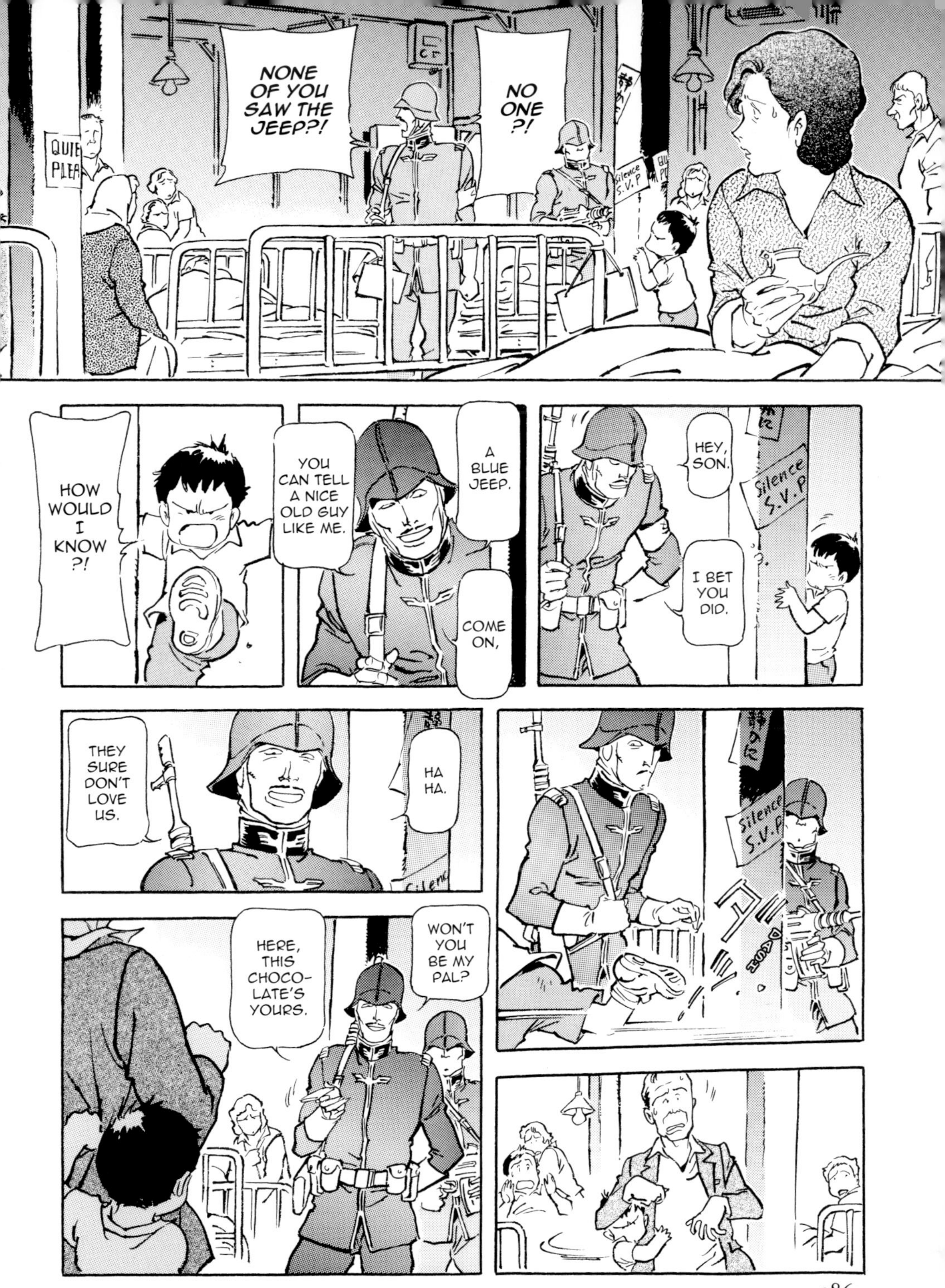
NO ONE ?!
NONE OF YOU SAW THE JEEP?!
Silence S.V.P
HEY, SON.
I BET YOU DID.
A BLUE JEEP.
YOU CAN TELL A NICE OLD GUY LIKE ME.
COME ON,
HOW WOULD I KNOW ?!
Silence S.V.P
HA HA.
THEY SURE DON'T LOVE US.
WON'T YOU BE MY PAL?
HERE, THIS CHOCO-LATE'S YOURS.

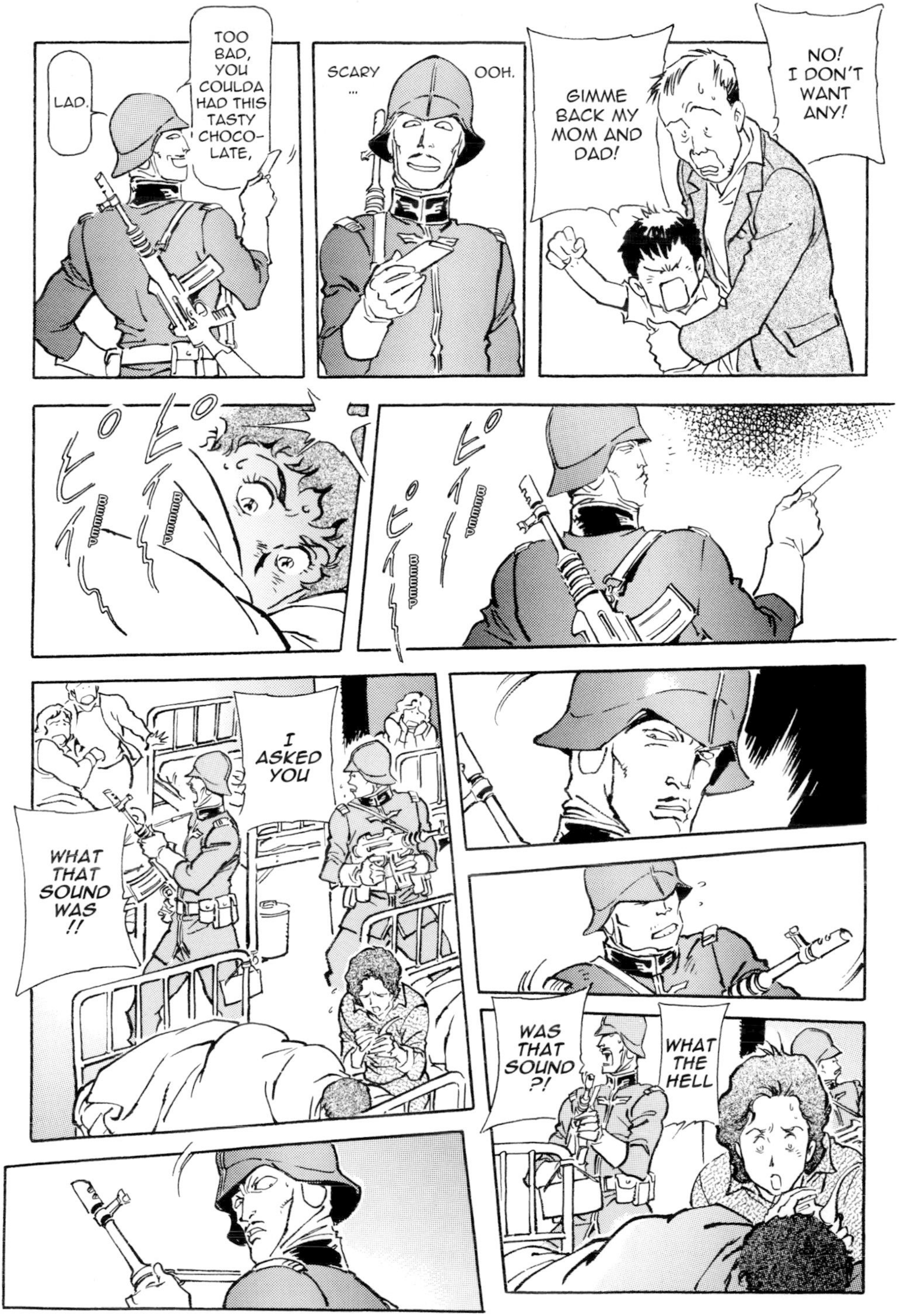
NO! I DON'T WANT ANY!
GIMME BACK MY MOM AND DAD!
OOH.
SCARY ...
TOO BAD, YOU COULDA HAD THIS TASTY CHOCO-LATE,
LAD.
WHAT THE HELL
WAS THAT SOUND ?!
I ASKED YOU
WHAT THAT SOUND WAS !!

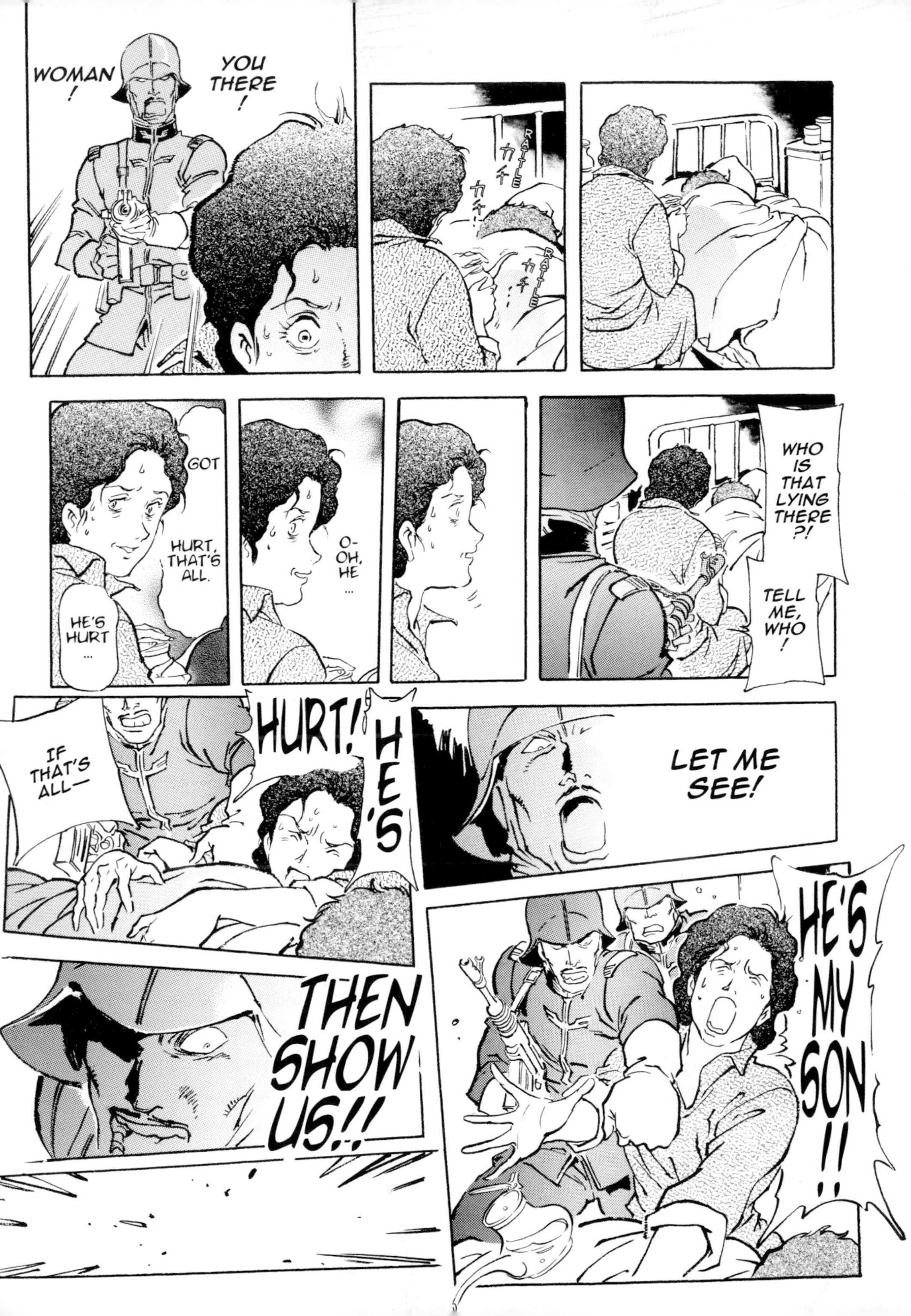
RATTLE
カチ カチ…
RATTLE
カチ…
YOU THERE!
WOMAN!
WHO IS THAT LYING THERE?!
TELL ME, WHO!
O-OH, HE ...
GOT HURT, THAT'S ALL.
HE'S HURT ...
LET ME SEE!
HE'S HURT!
IF THAT'S ALL—
HE'S MY SON!!
THEN SHOW US!!

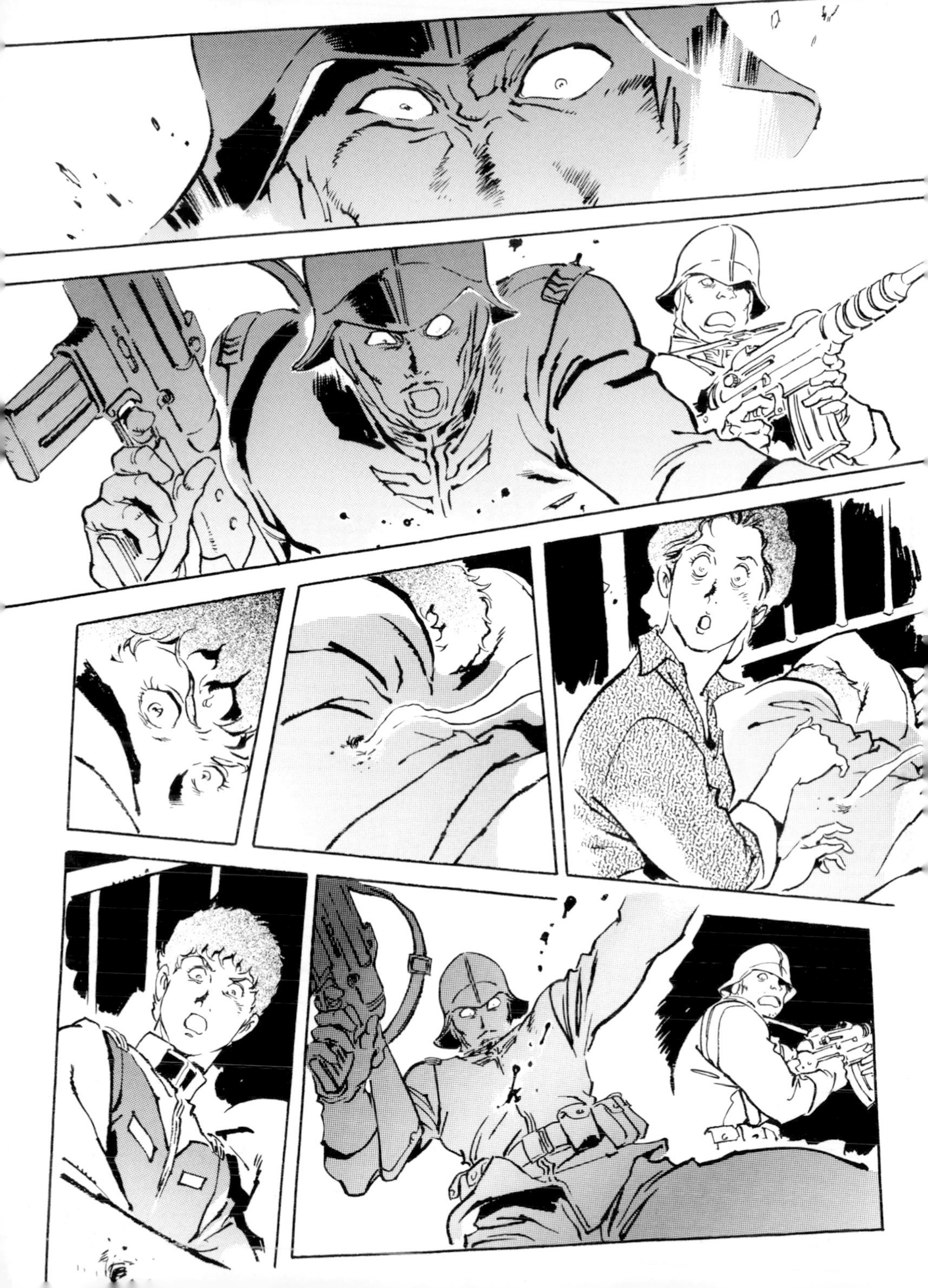

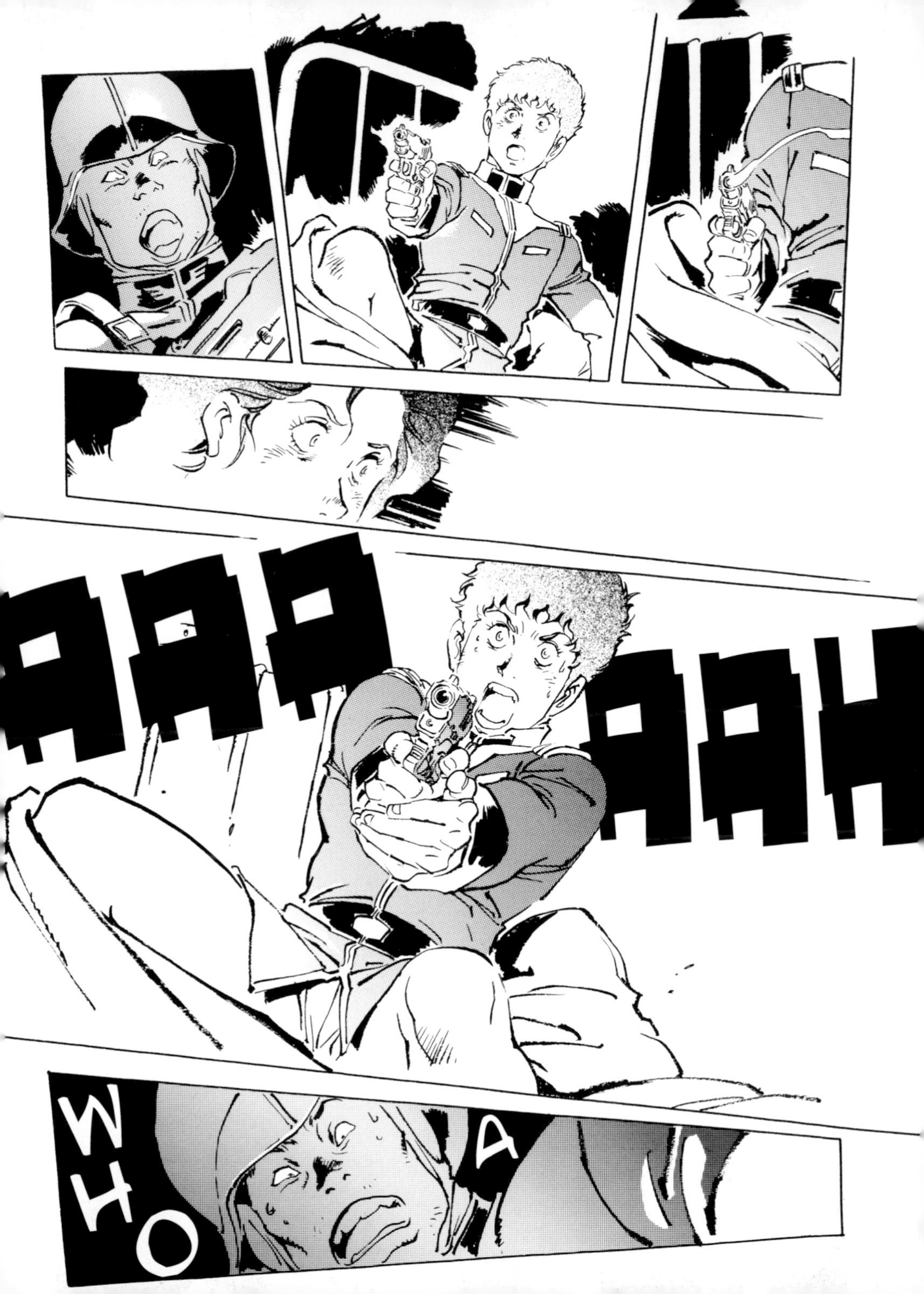
AAA
AAH
WHO
A

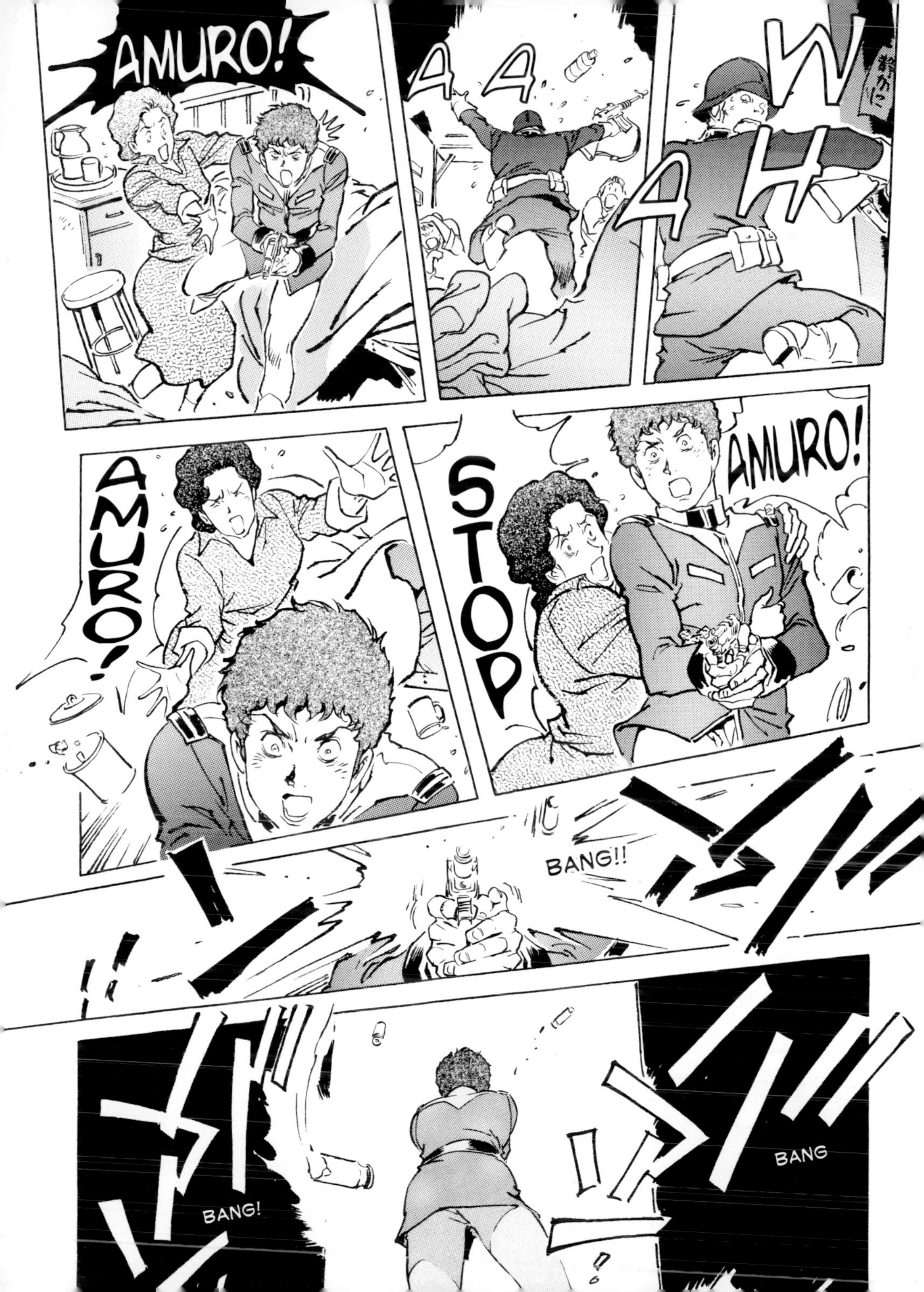

W
A H
A A
AMURO!
AMURO!
STOP
AMURO!
BANG!!
BANG
BANG!

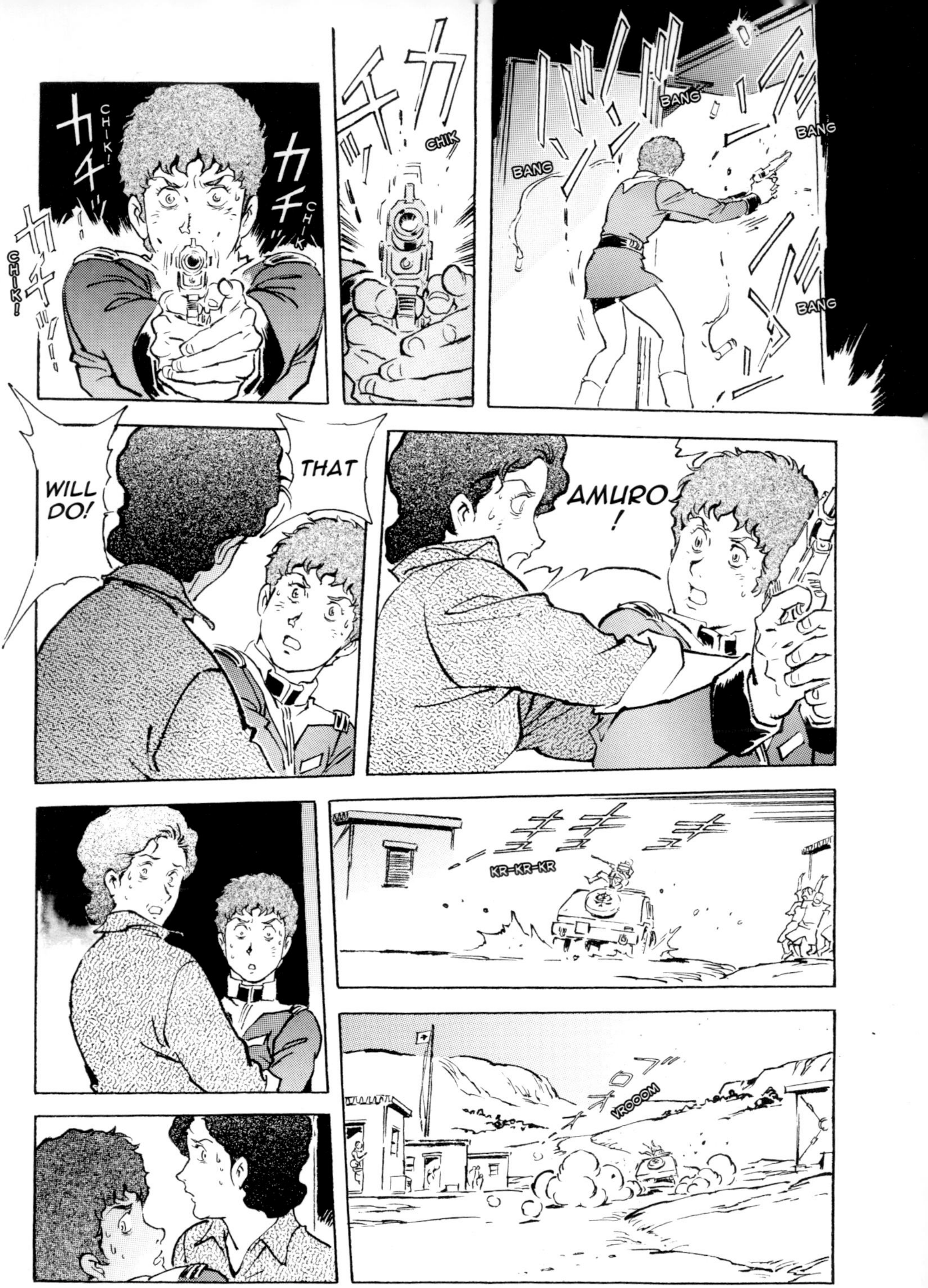
BANG
BANG
BANG
BANG
CHIK
CHIK!
CHIK
CHIK!
AMURO!
THAT WILL DO!
KR-KR-KR
VROOOM

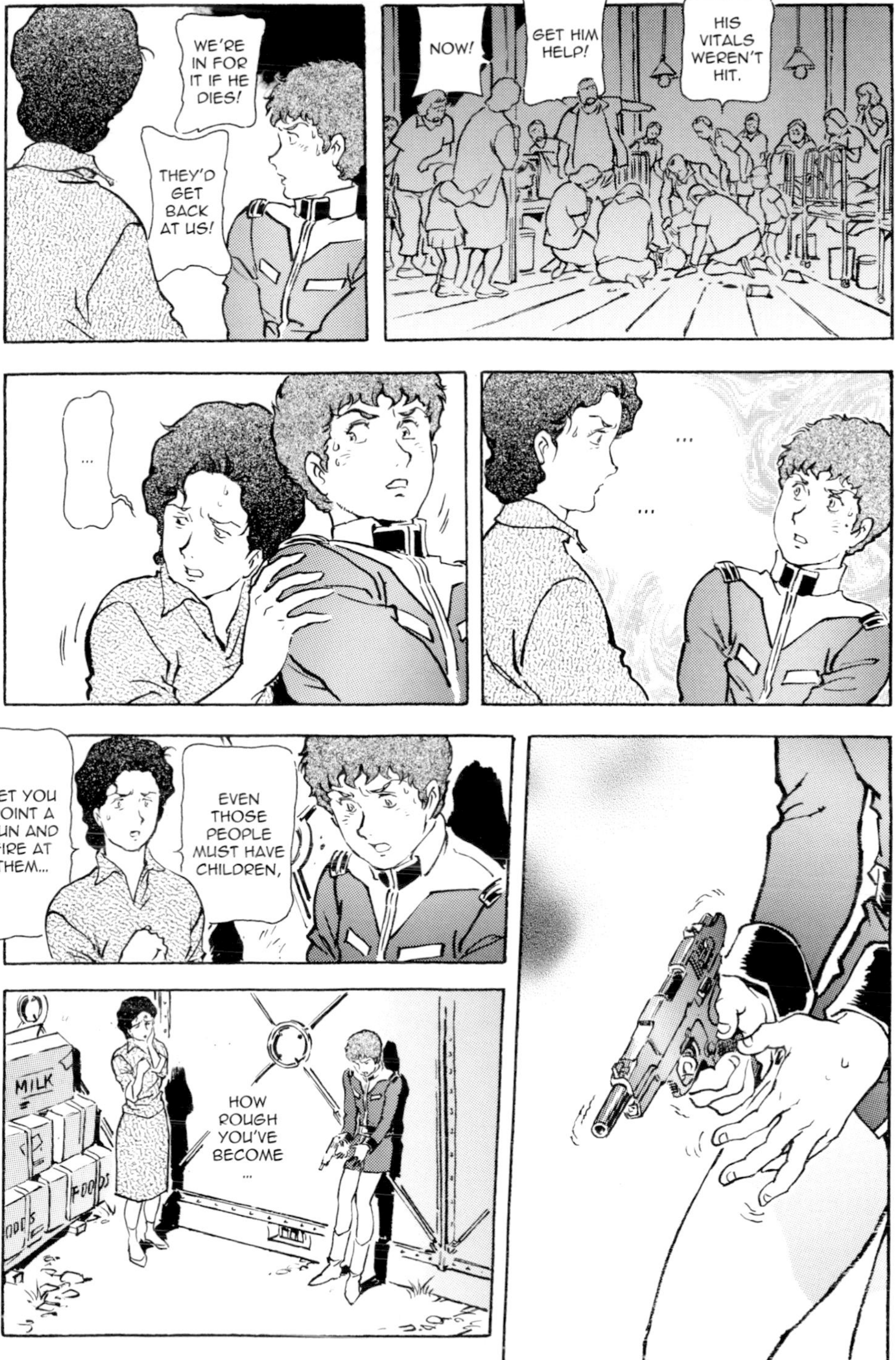
HIS VITALS WEREN'T HIT.
GET HIM HELP!
NOW!
WE'RE IN FOR IT IF HE DIES!
THEY'D GET BACK AT US!
...
...
...
EVEN THOSE PEOPLE MUST HAVE CHILDREN,
YET YOU POINT A GUN AND FIRE AT THEM...
HOW ROUGH YOU'VE BECOME ...
MILK
FOODS
FOODS

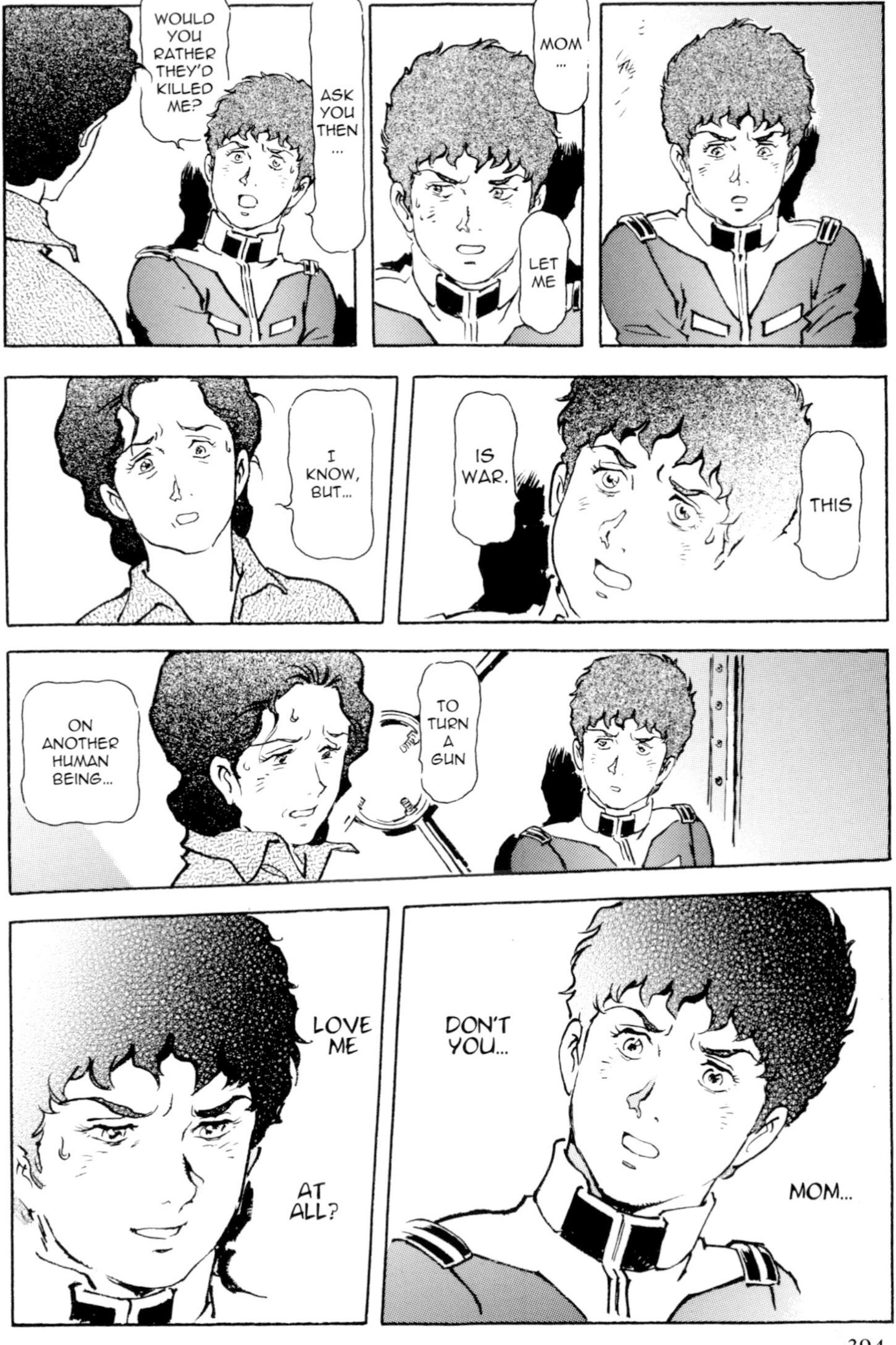
MOM ...
LET ME
ASK YOU THEN ...
WOULD YOU RATHER THEY'D KILLED ME?
THIS
IS WAR.
I KNOW, BUT...
TO TURN A GUN
ON ANOTHER HUMAN BEING...
MOM...
DON'T YOU...
LOVE ME
AT ALL?

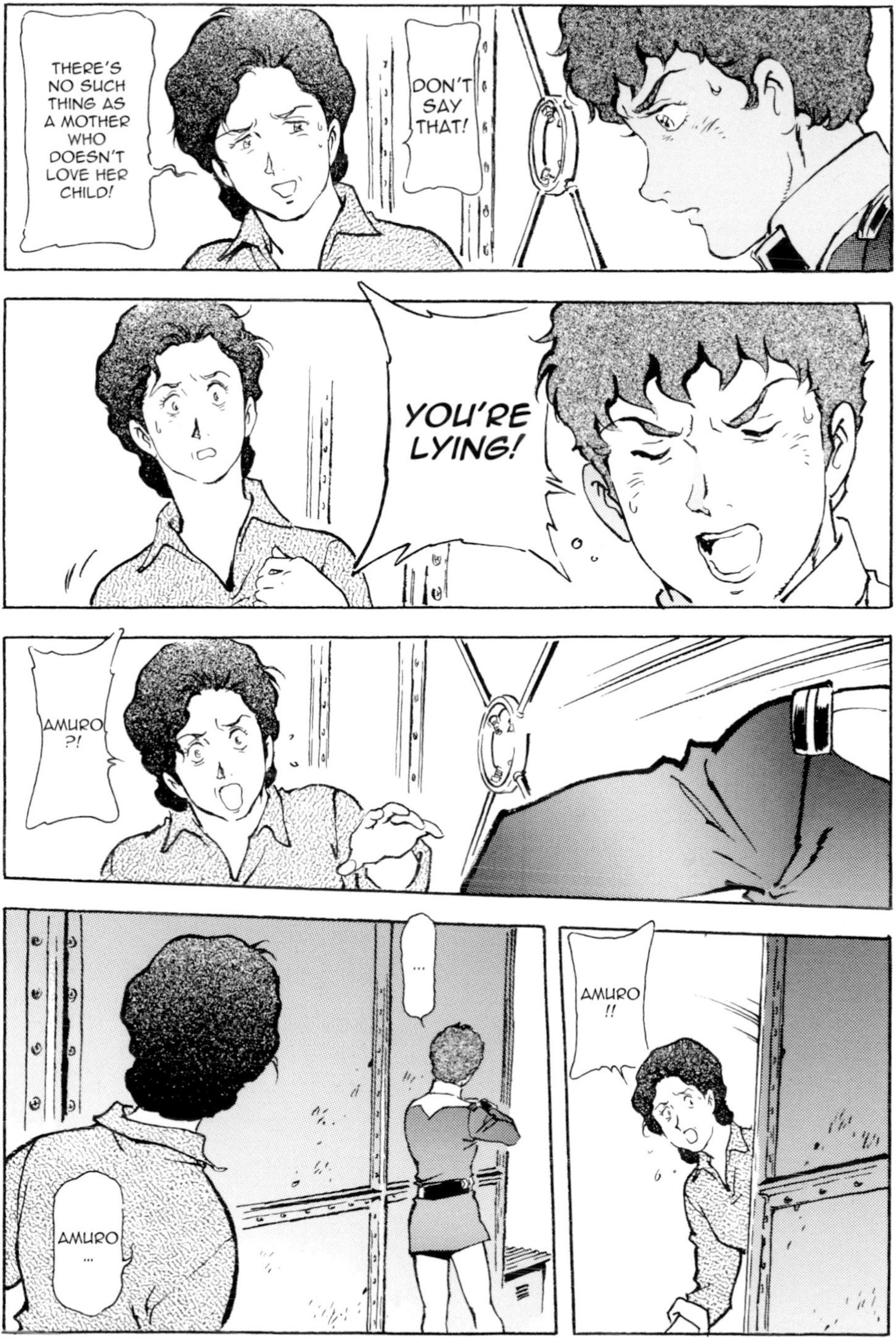
DON'T SAY THAT!
THERE'S NO SUCH THING AS A MOTHER WHO DOESN'T LOVE HER CHILD!
YOU'RE LYING!
AMURO ?!
AMURO !!
...
AMURO ...

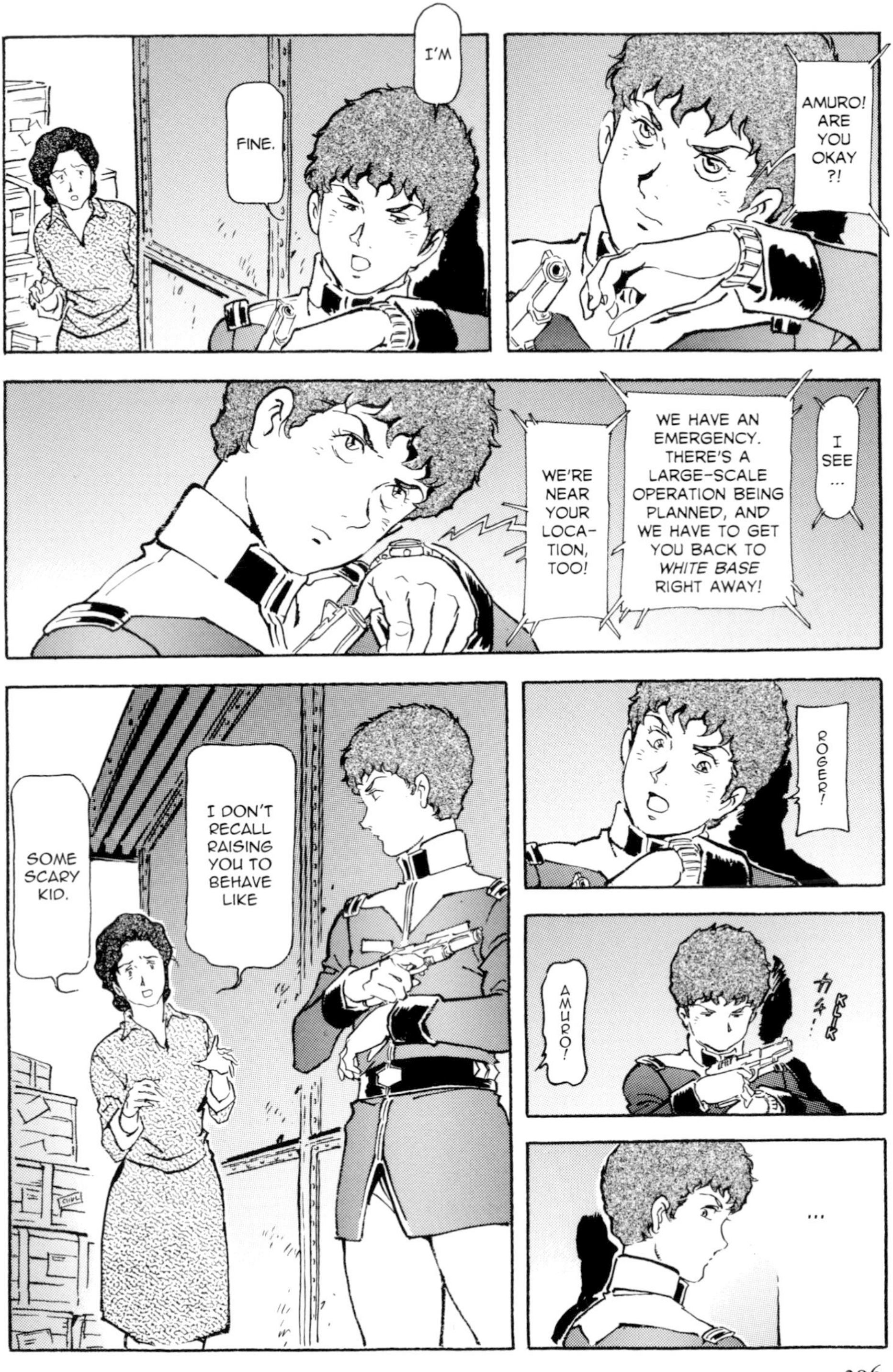
AMURO! ARE YOU OKAY ?!
I'M
FINE.
I SEE ...
WE HAVE AN EMERGENCY. THERE'S A LARGE-SCALE OPERATION BEING PLANNED, AND WE HAVE TO GET YOU BACK TO *WHITE BASE* RIGHT AWAY!
WE'RE NEAR YOUR LOCA-TION, TOO!
ROGER!
AMURO!
KLIK
...
I DON'T RECALL RAISING YOU TO BEHAVE LIKE
SOME SCARY KID.

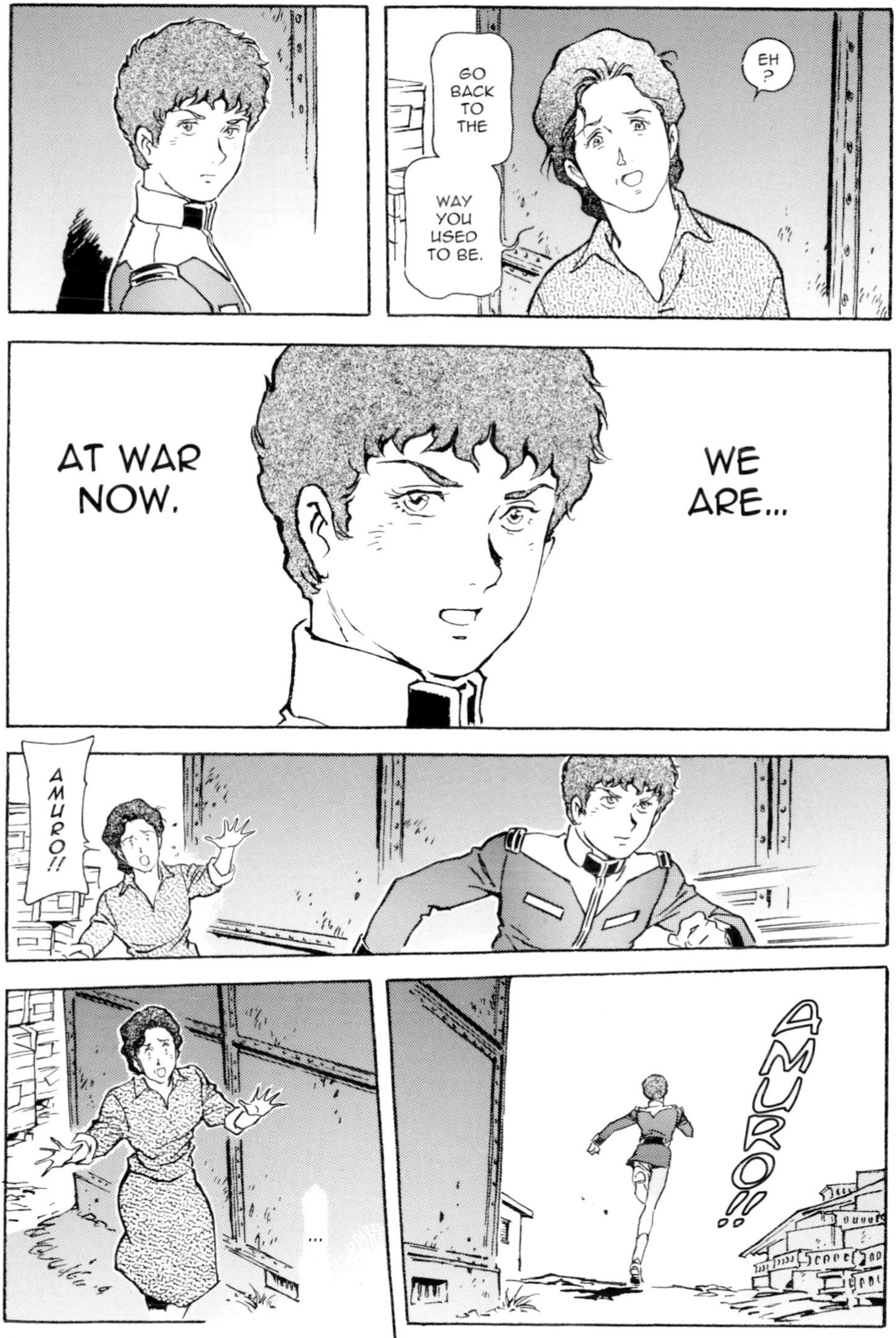
EH?
GO BACK TO THE
WAY YOU USED TO BE.
WE ARE...
AT WAR NOW.
AMURO!!
AMURO!!
...

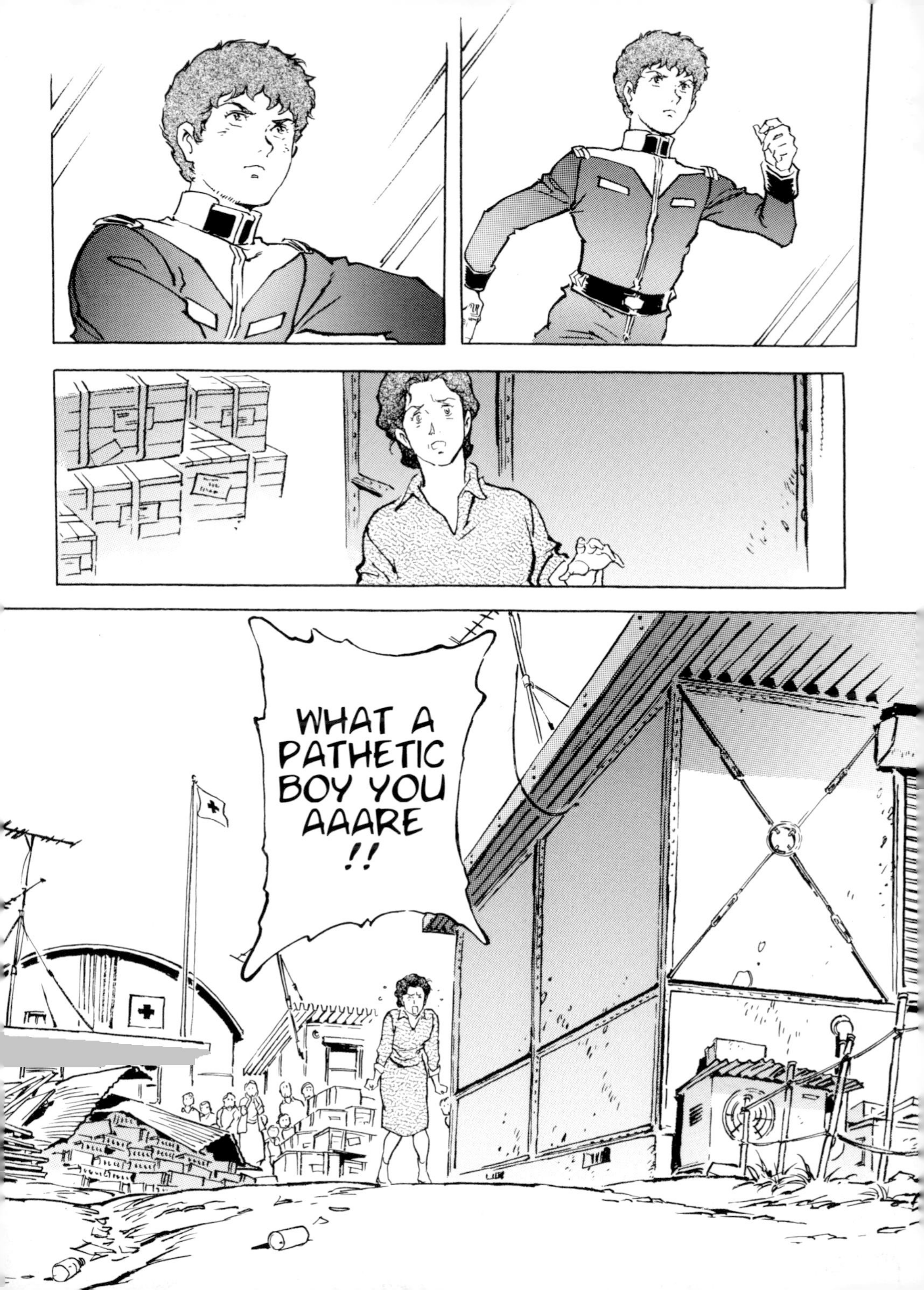
WHAT A PATHETIC BOY YOU AAARE !!

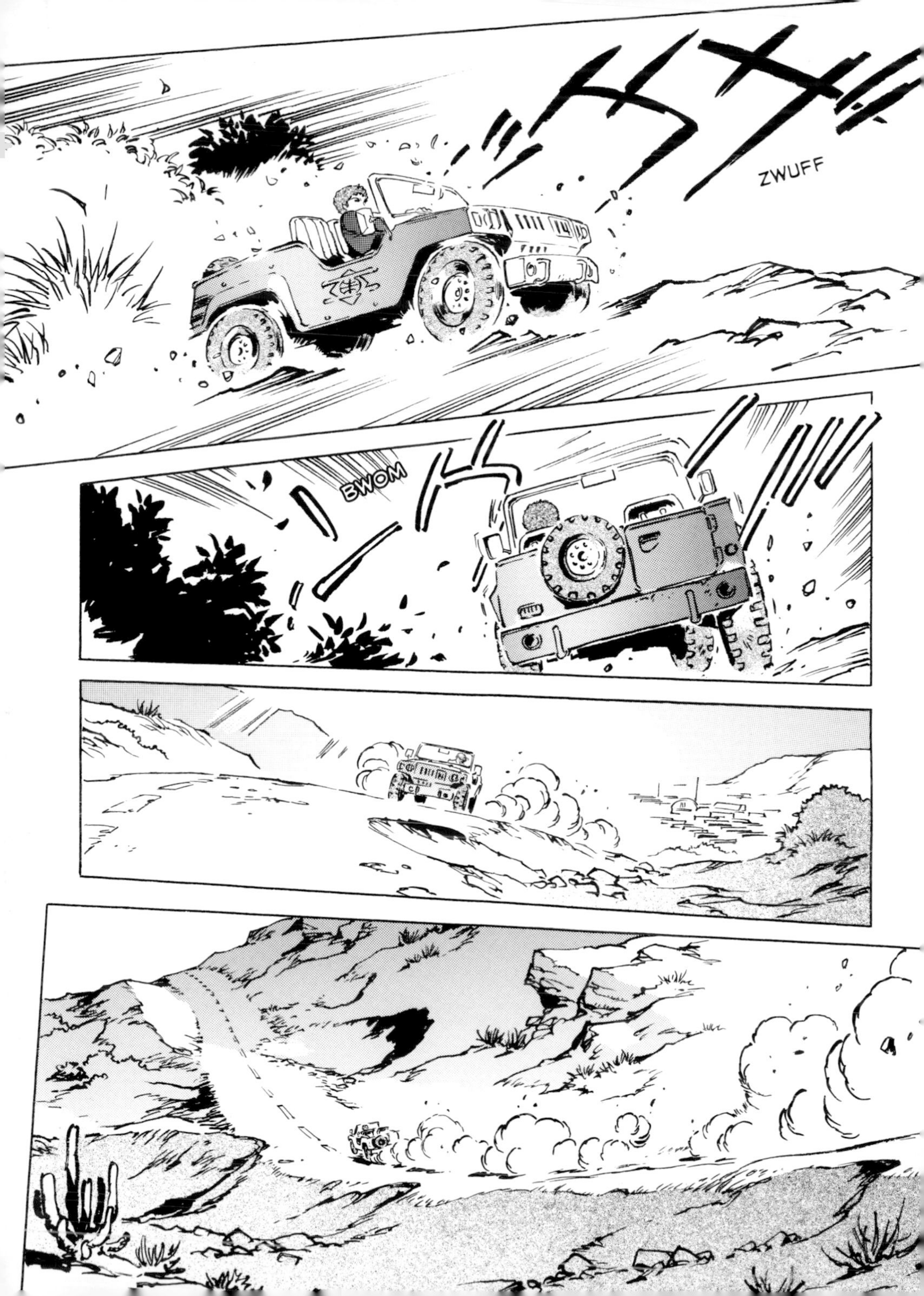
ZWUFF
BWOM

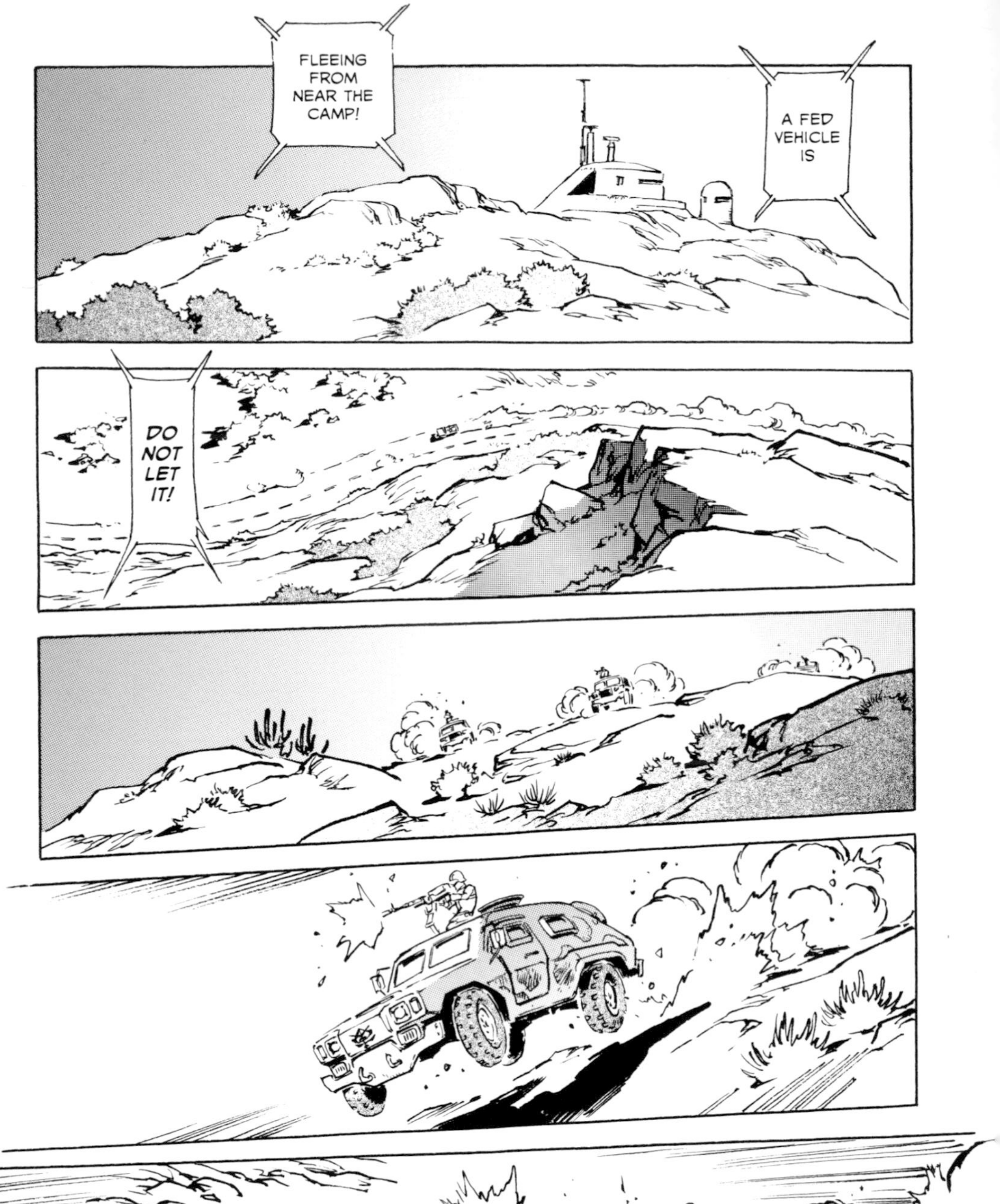
A FED VEHICLE IS
FLEEING FROM NEAR THE CAMP!
DO NOT LET IT!

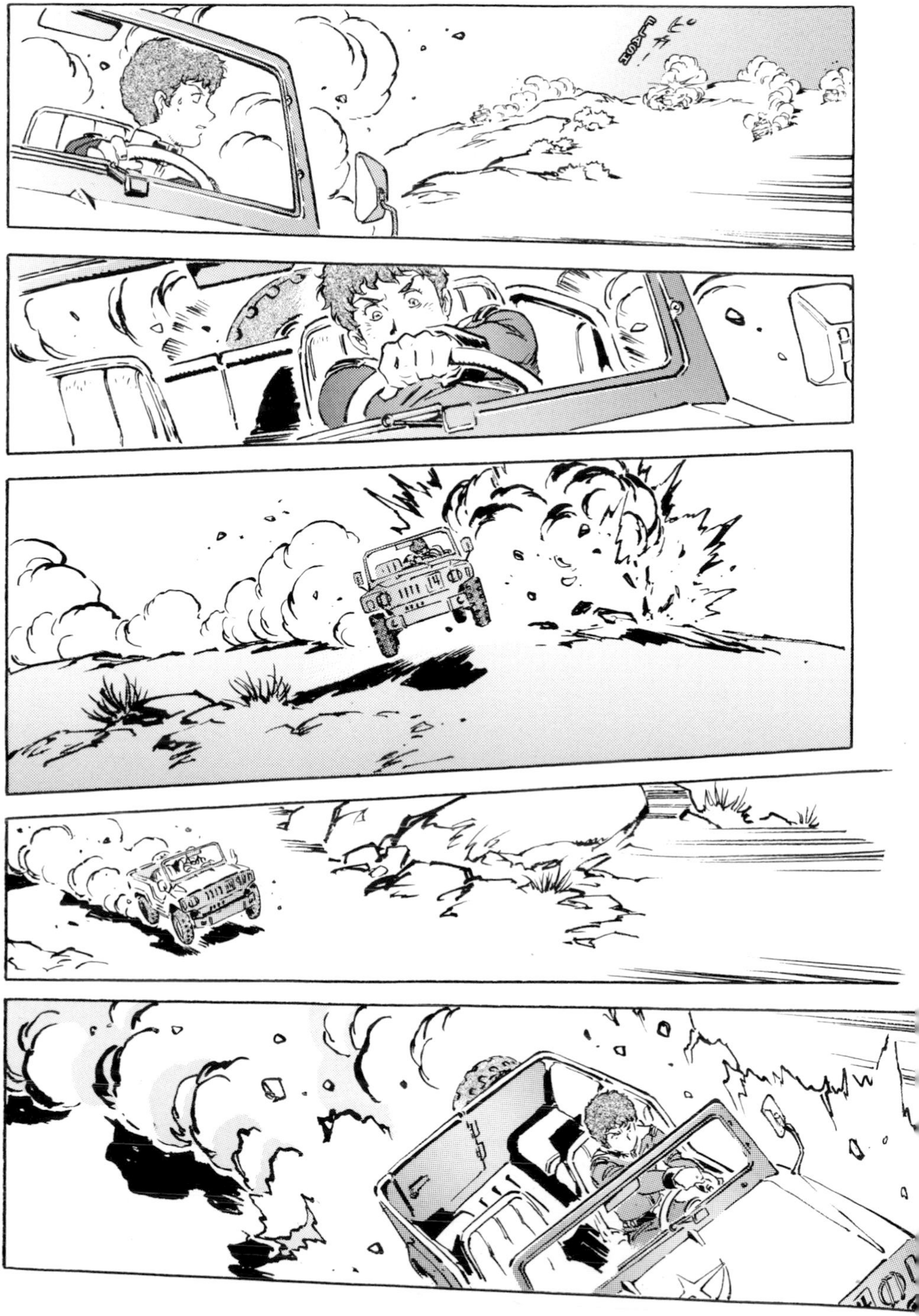
ピカ!
FLASH!

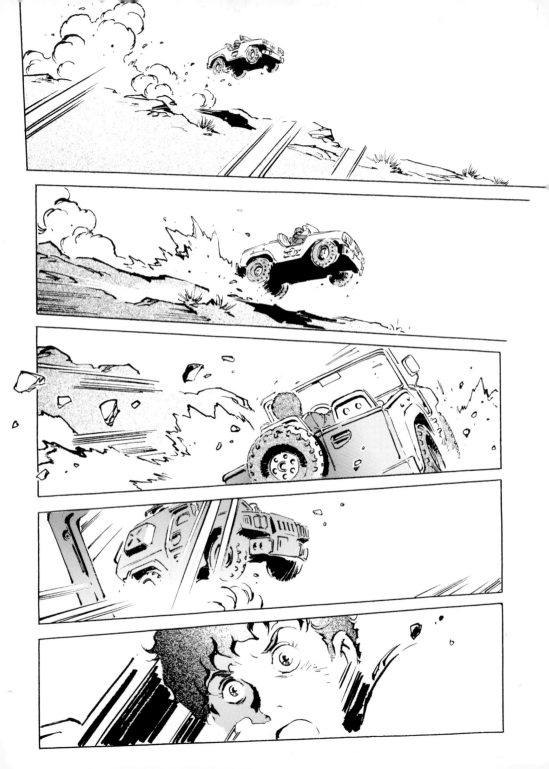

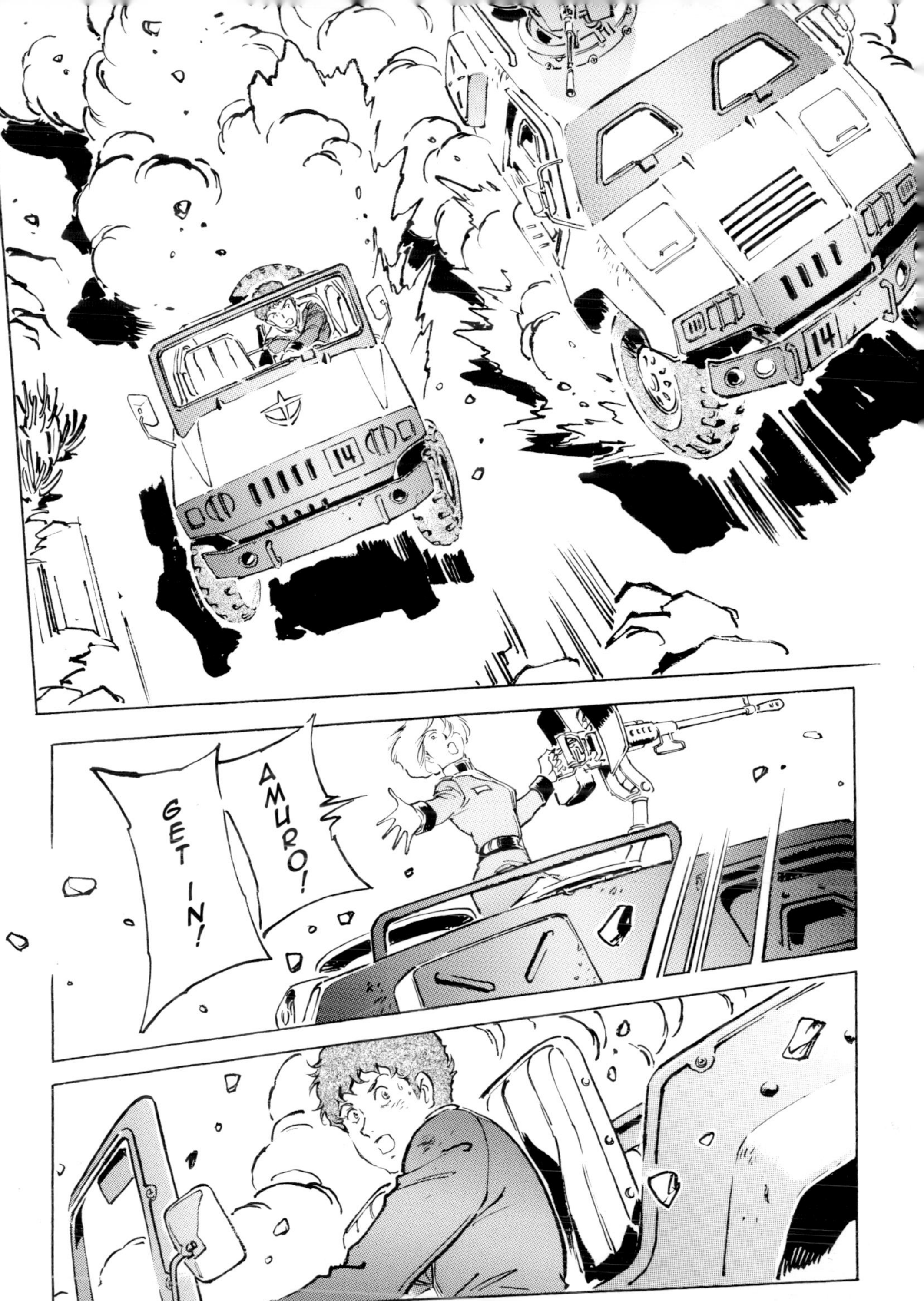
AMURO!
GET IN!

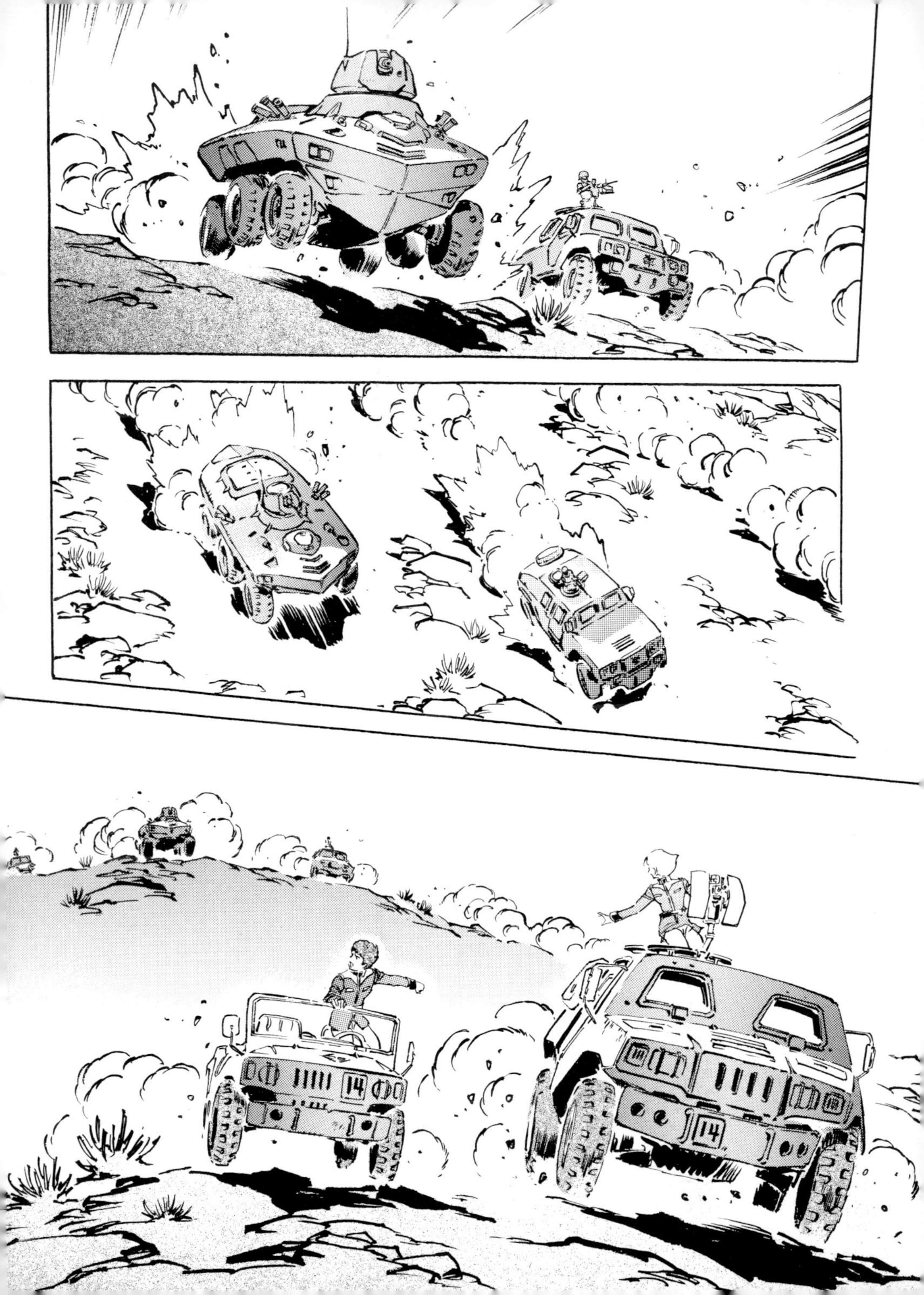
14
14

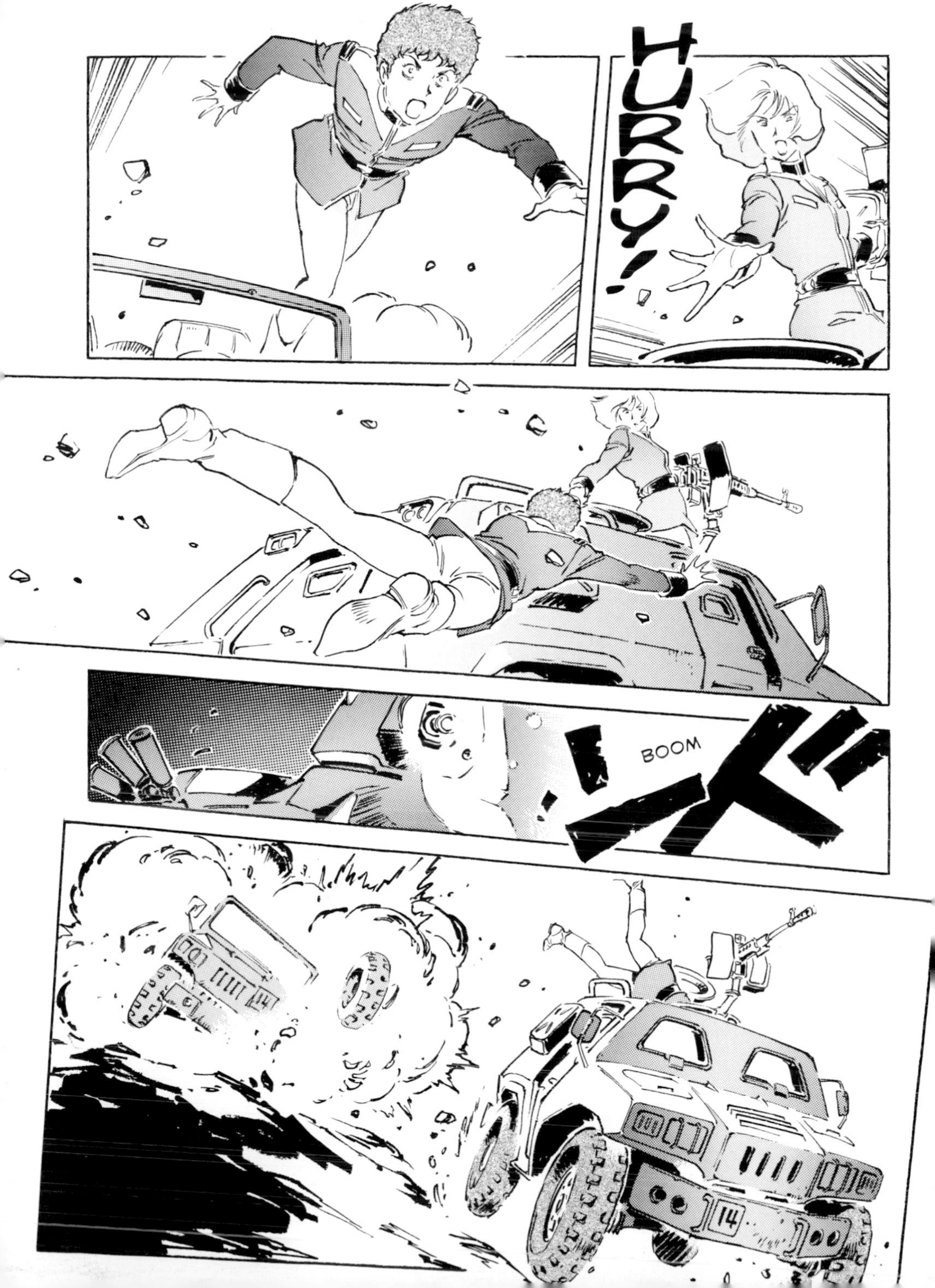
HURRY!
BOOM

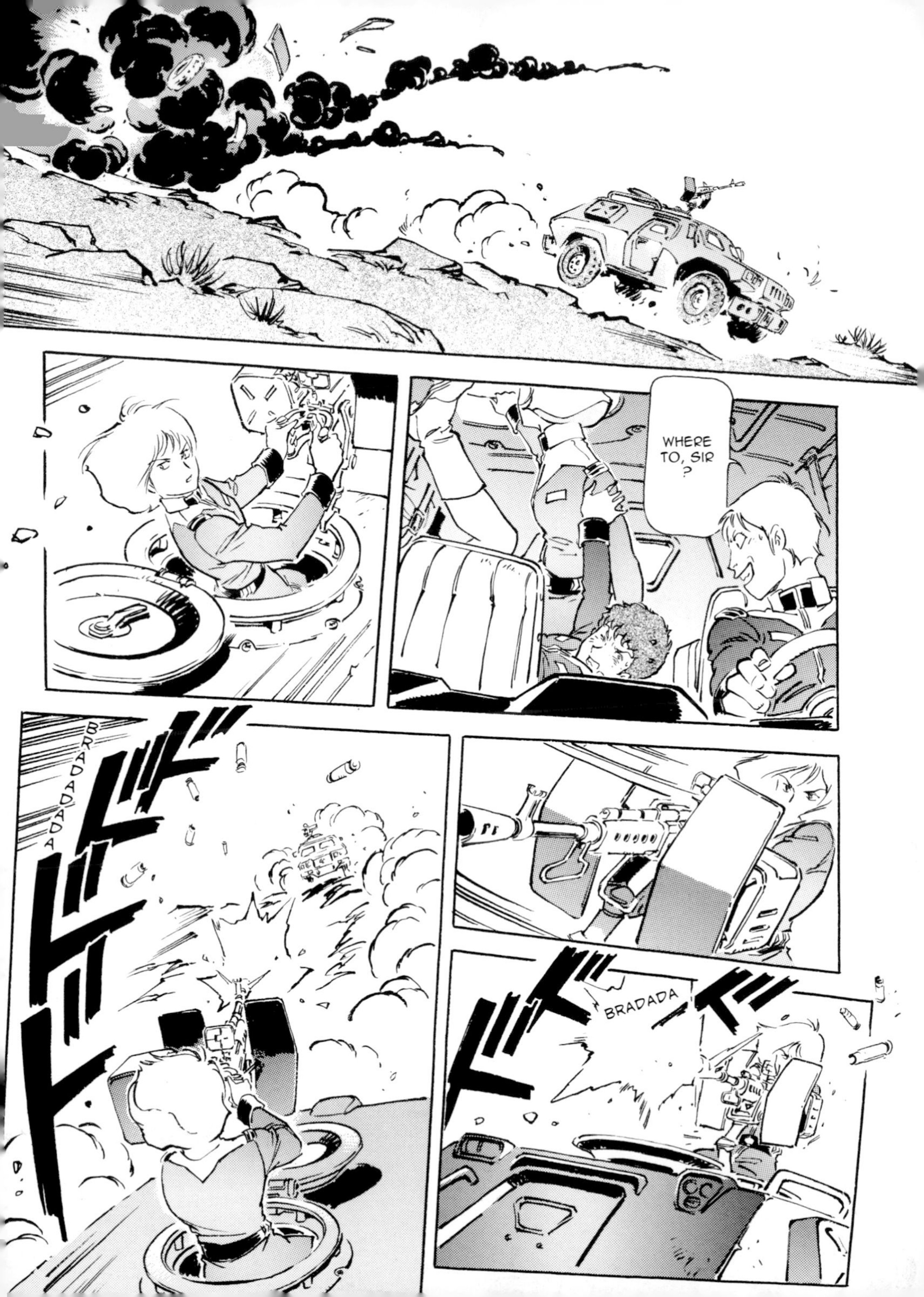
WHERE TO, SIR ?
BRADADA
BRADADADA

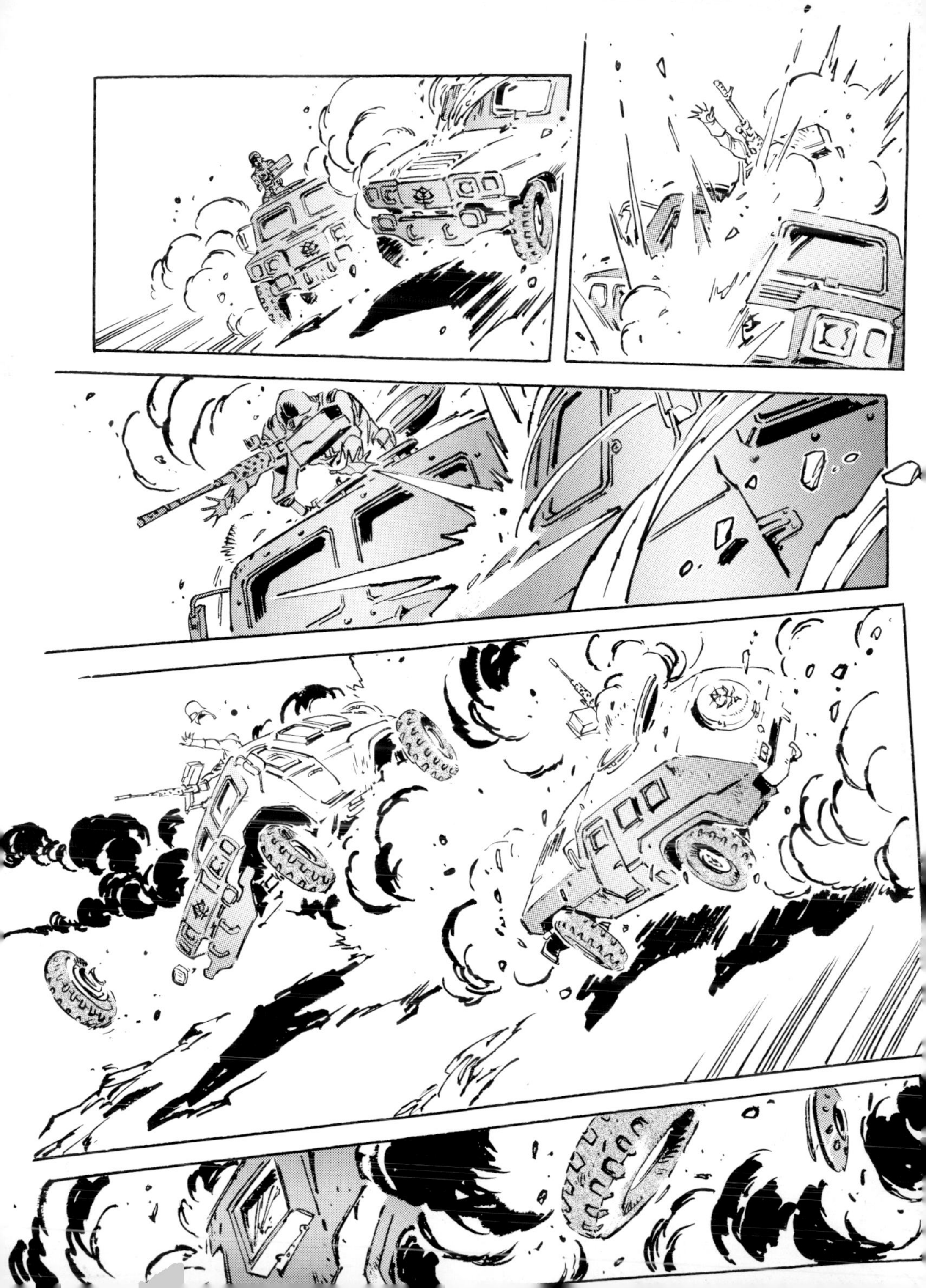

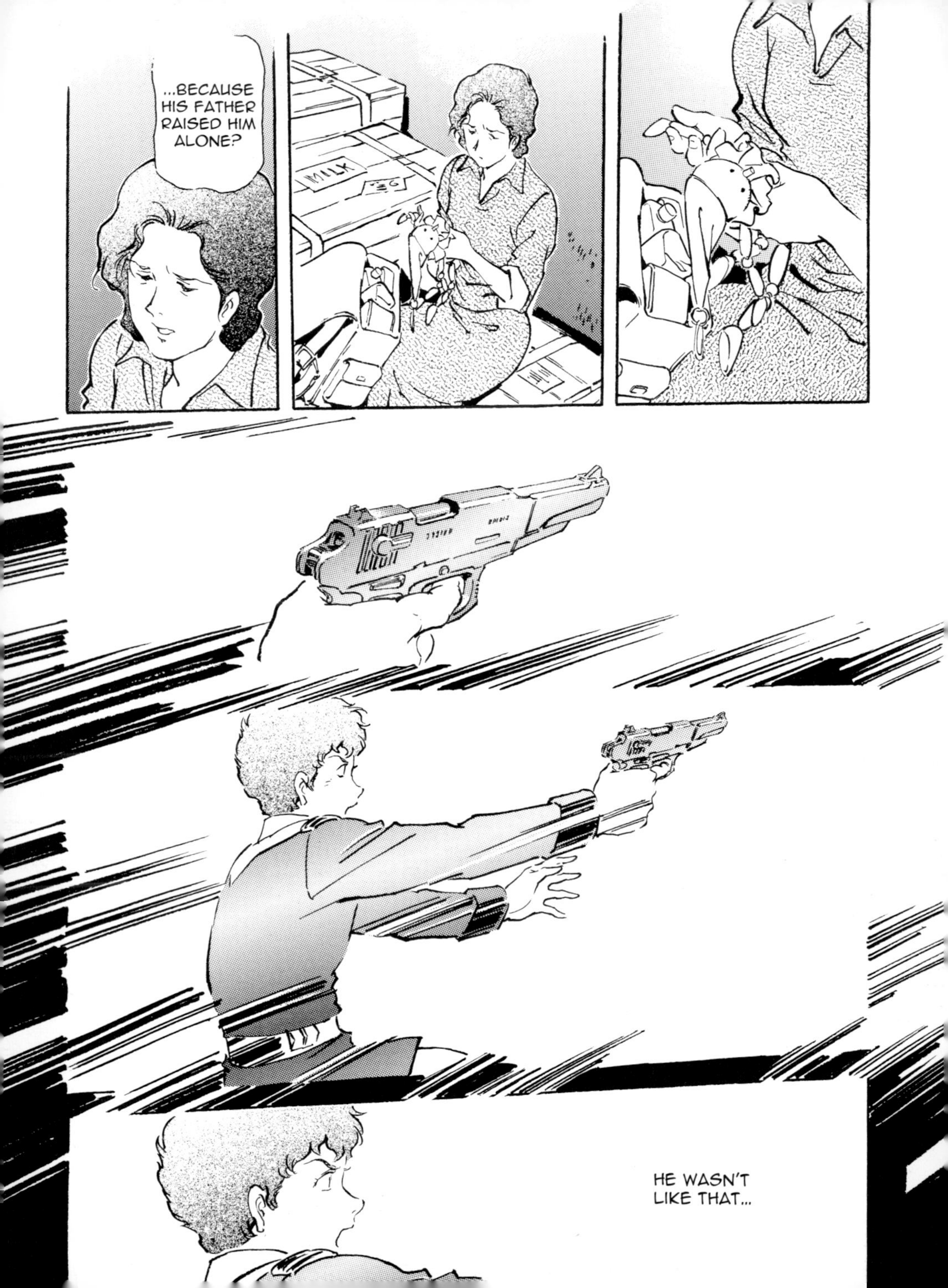
...BECAUSE HIS FATHER RAISED HIM ALONE?
HE WASN'T LIKE THAT...

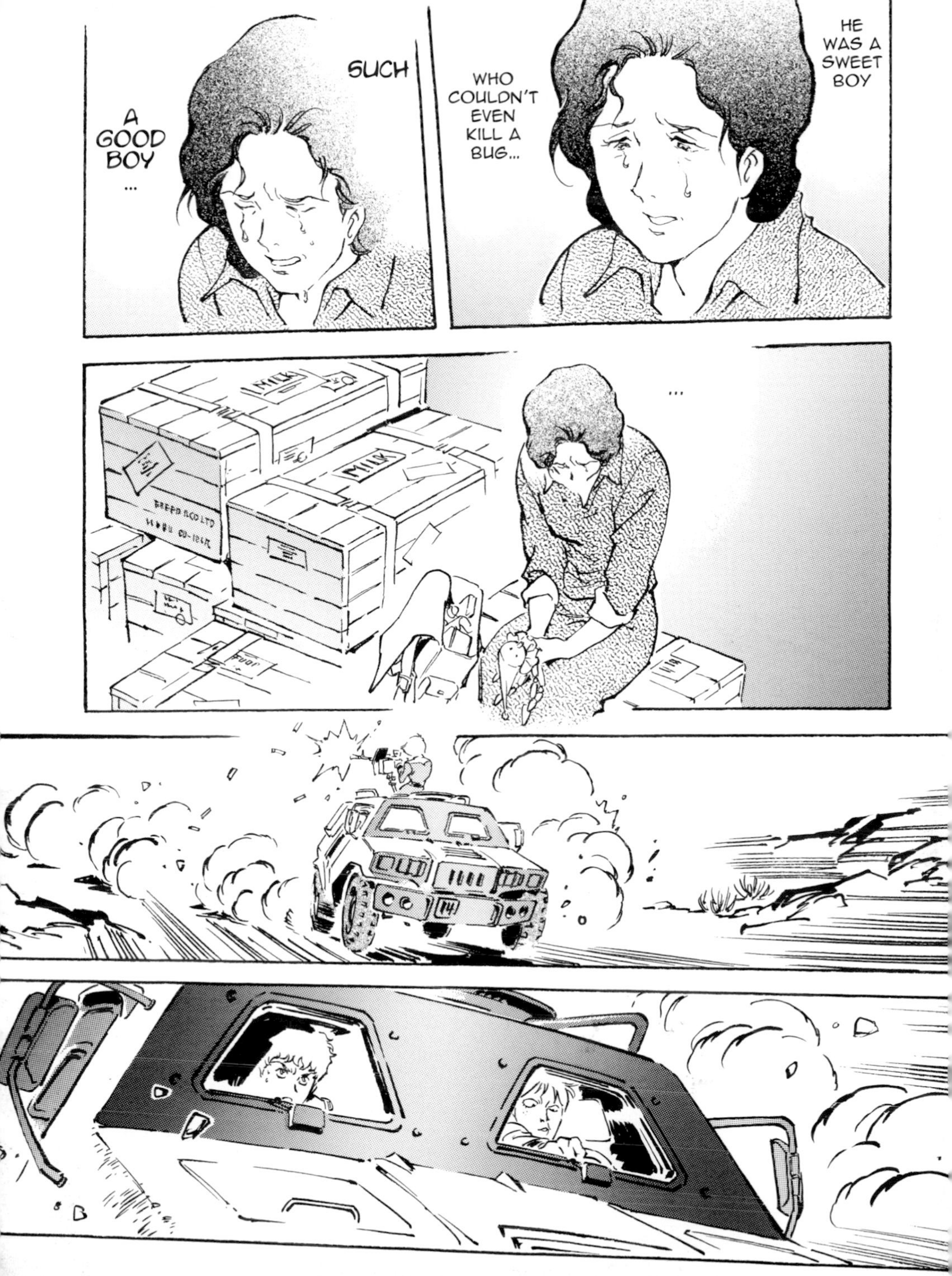
HE WAS A SWEET BOY
WHO COULDN'T EVEN KILL A BUG...
SUCH
A GOOD BOY ...
MILK
MILK
...

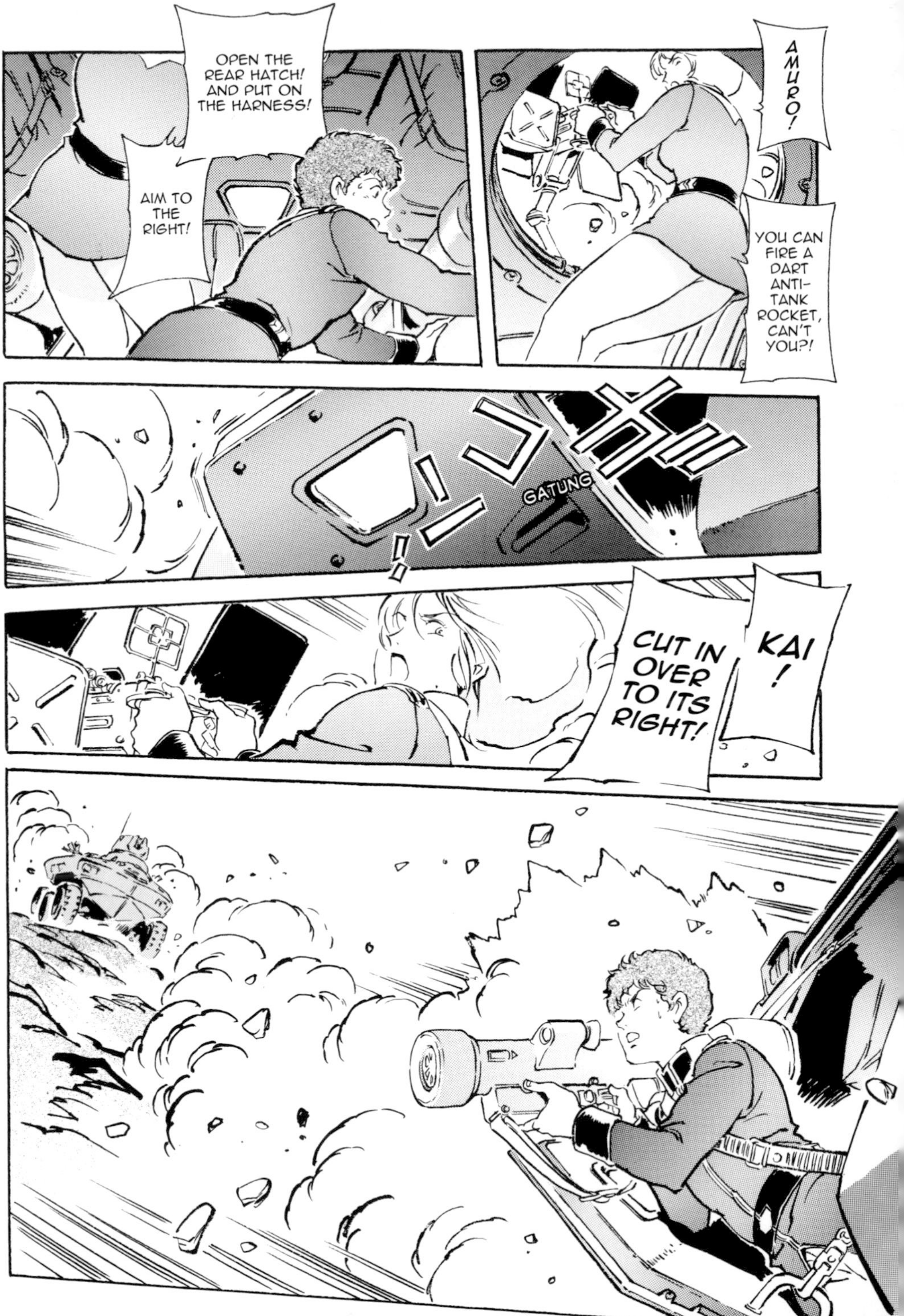
AMURO!
YOU CAN FIRE A DART ANTI-TANK ROCKET, CAN'T YOU?!
OPEN THE REAR HATCH! AND PUT ON THE HARNESS!
AIM TO THE RIGHT!
GATUNG
KAI!
CUT IN OVER TO ITS RIGHT!

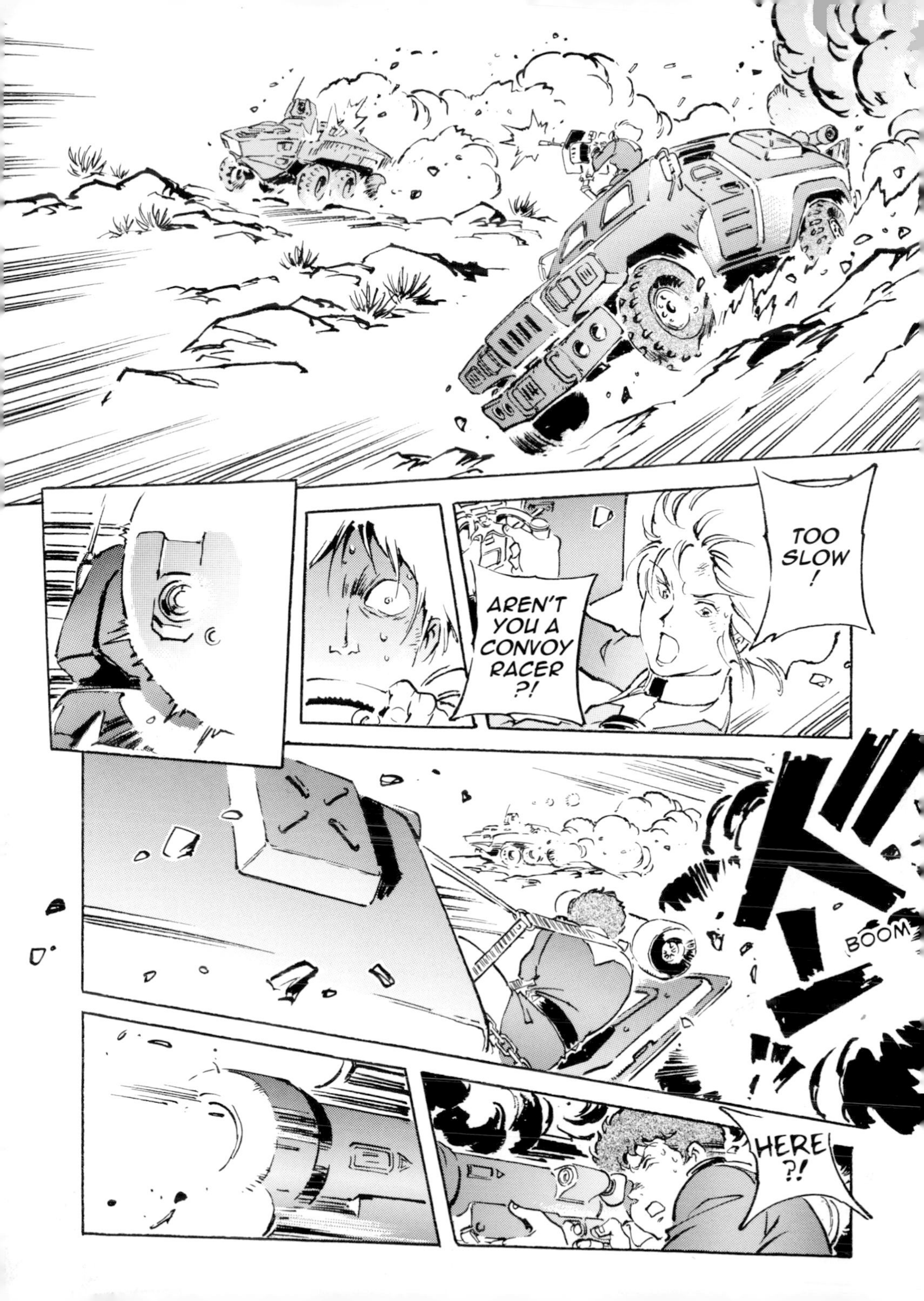
TOO SLOW!
AREN'T YOU A CONVOY RACER?!
BOOM
HERE?!

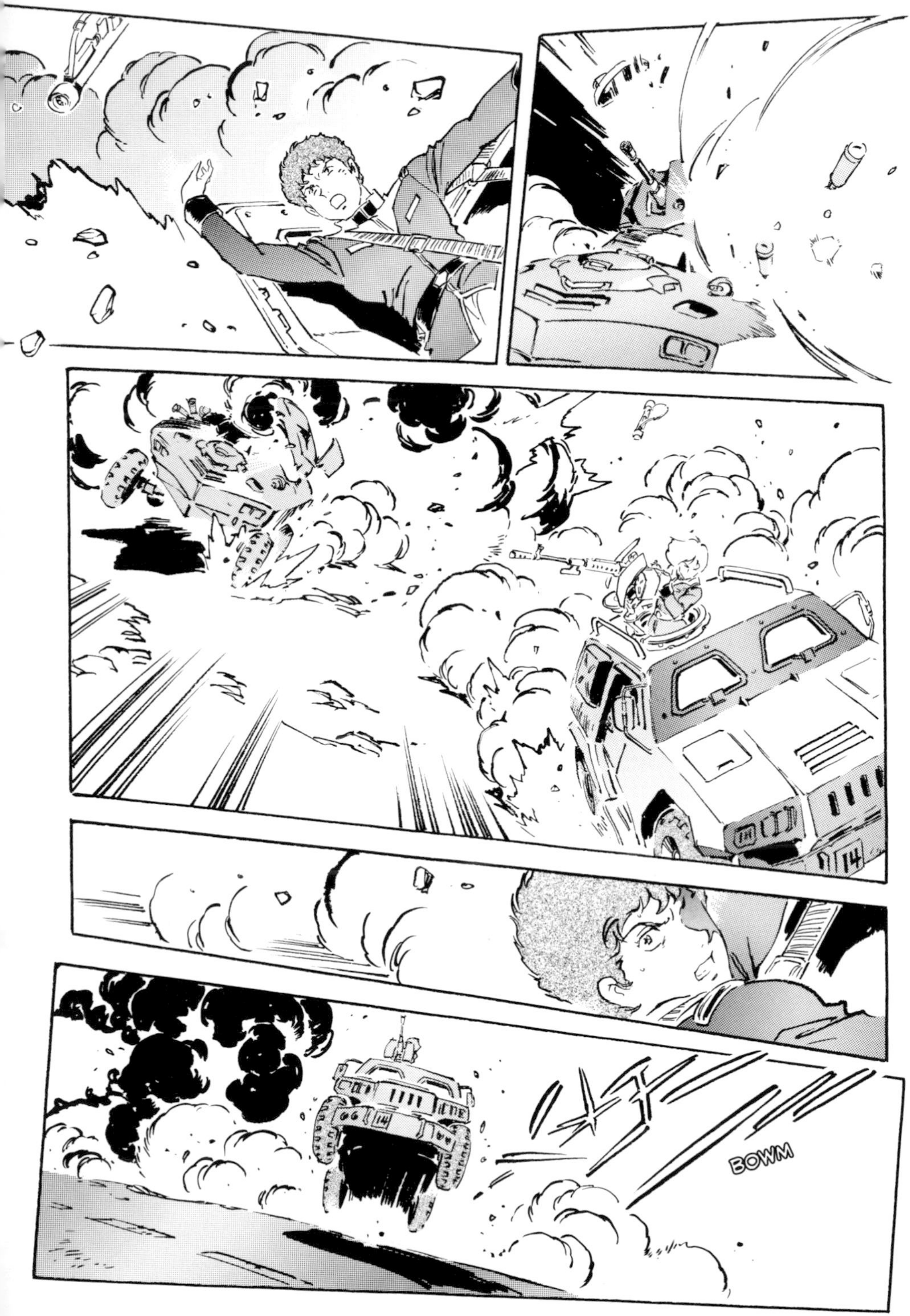
BOWM

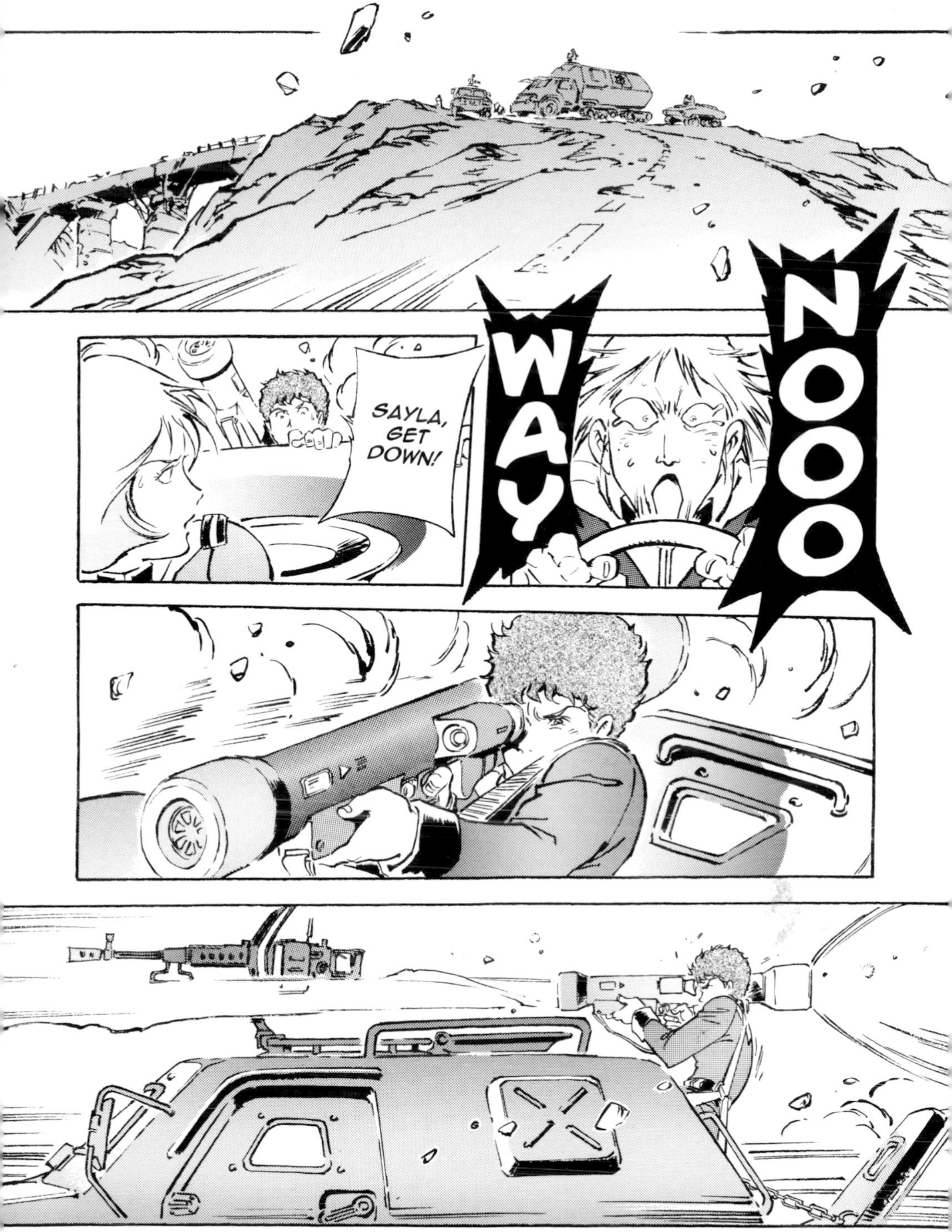
NOOO
WAY
SAYLA, GET DOWN!

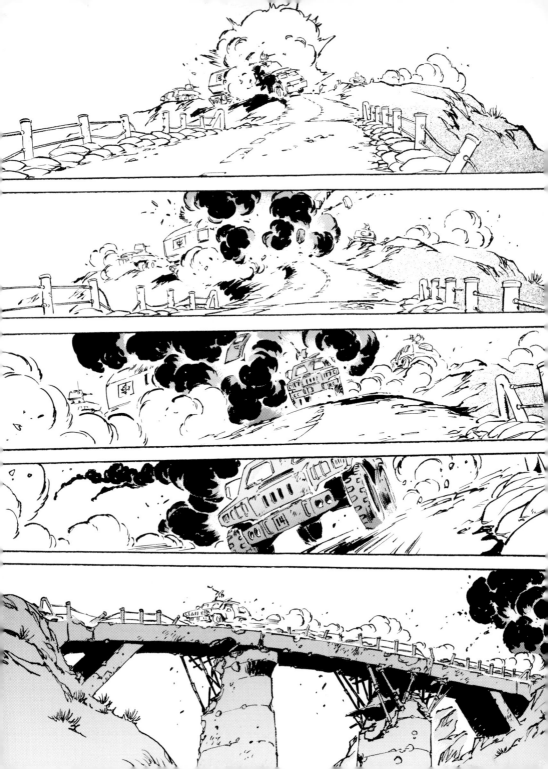

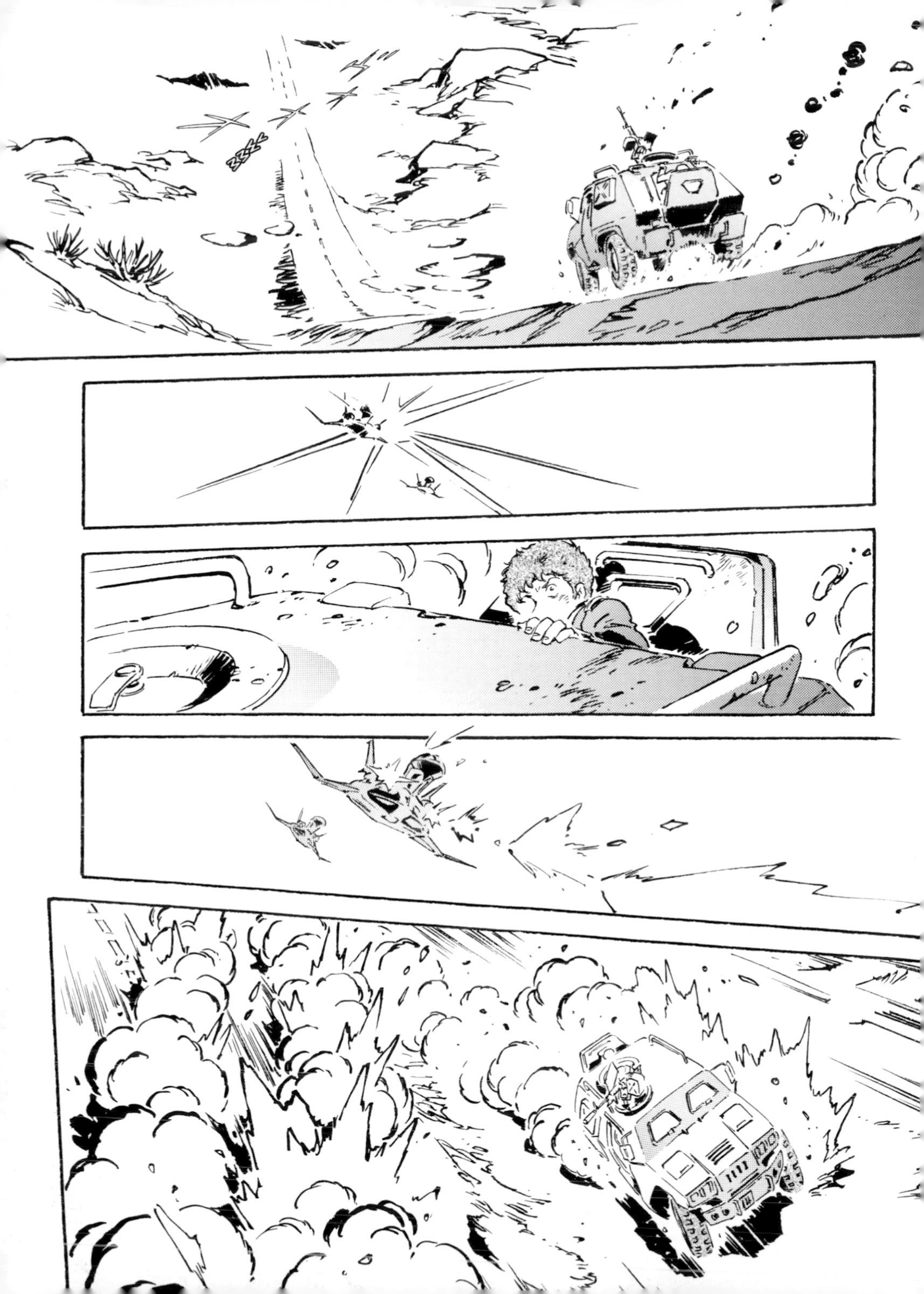

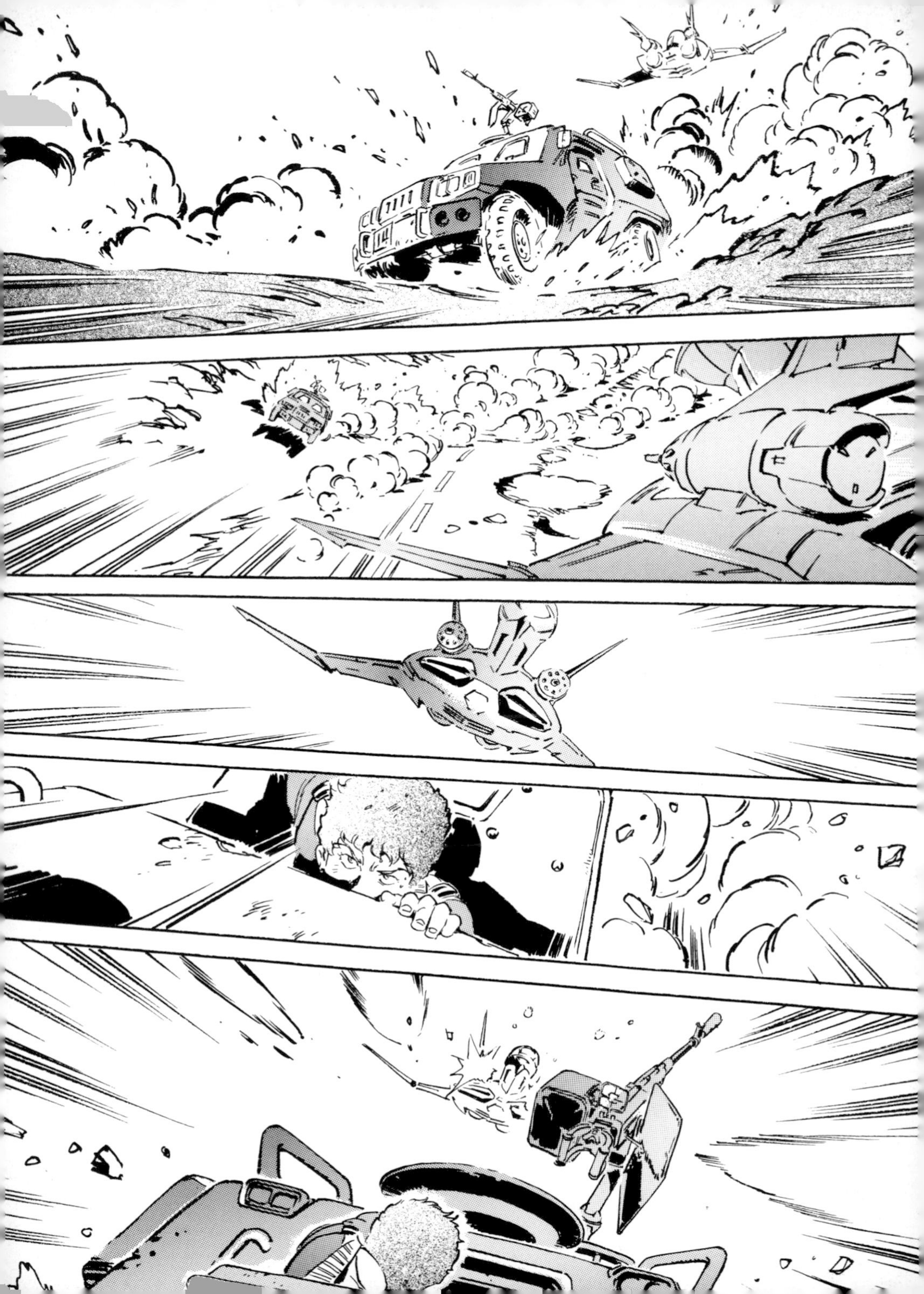

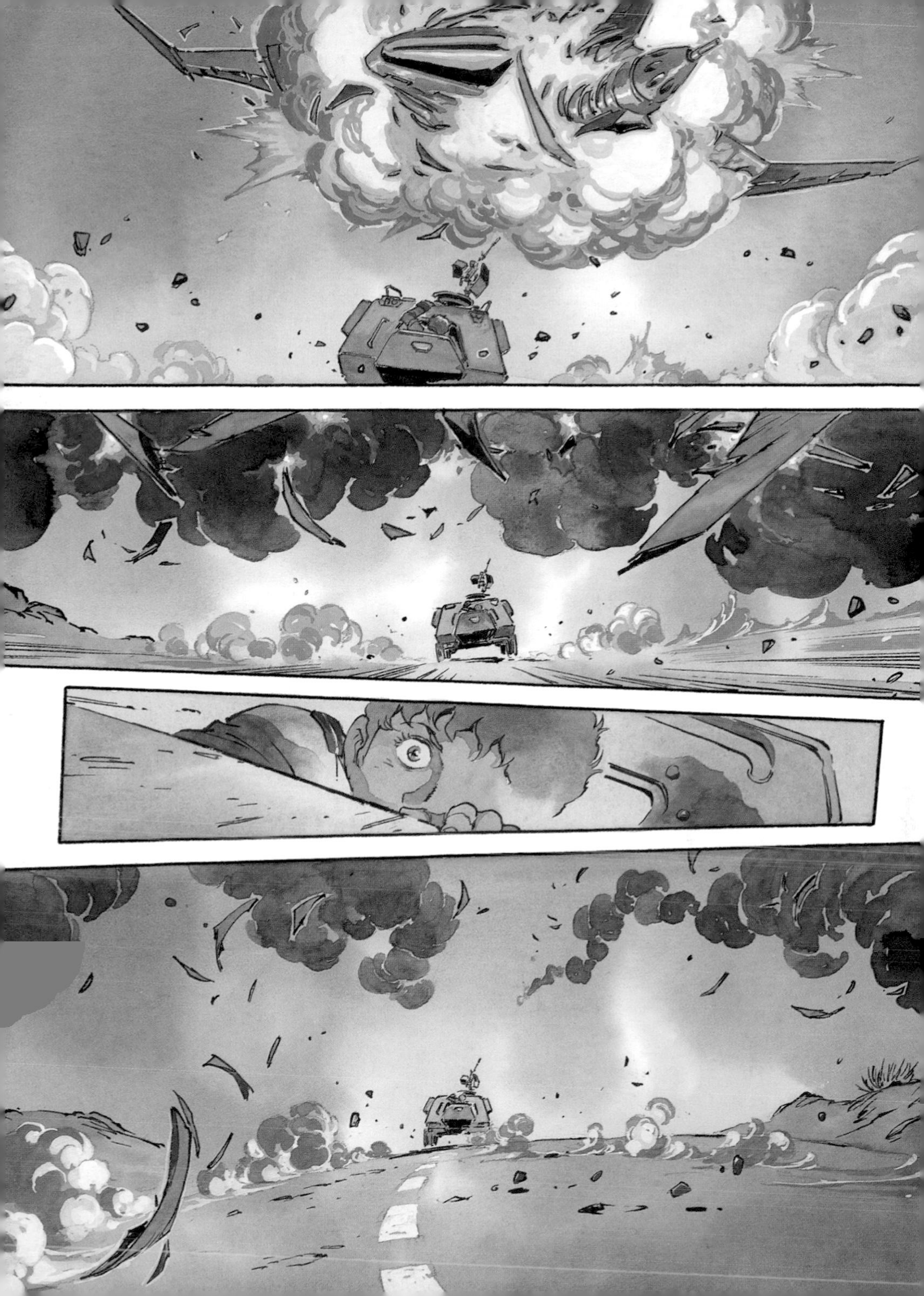

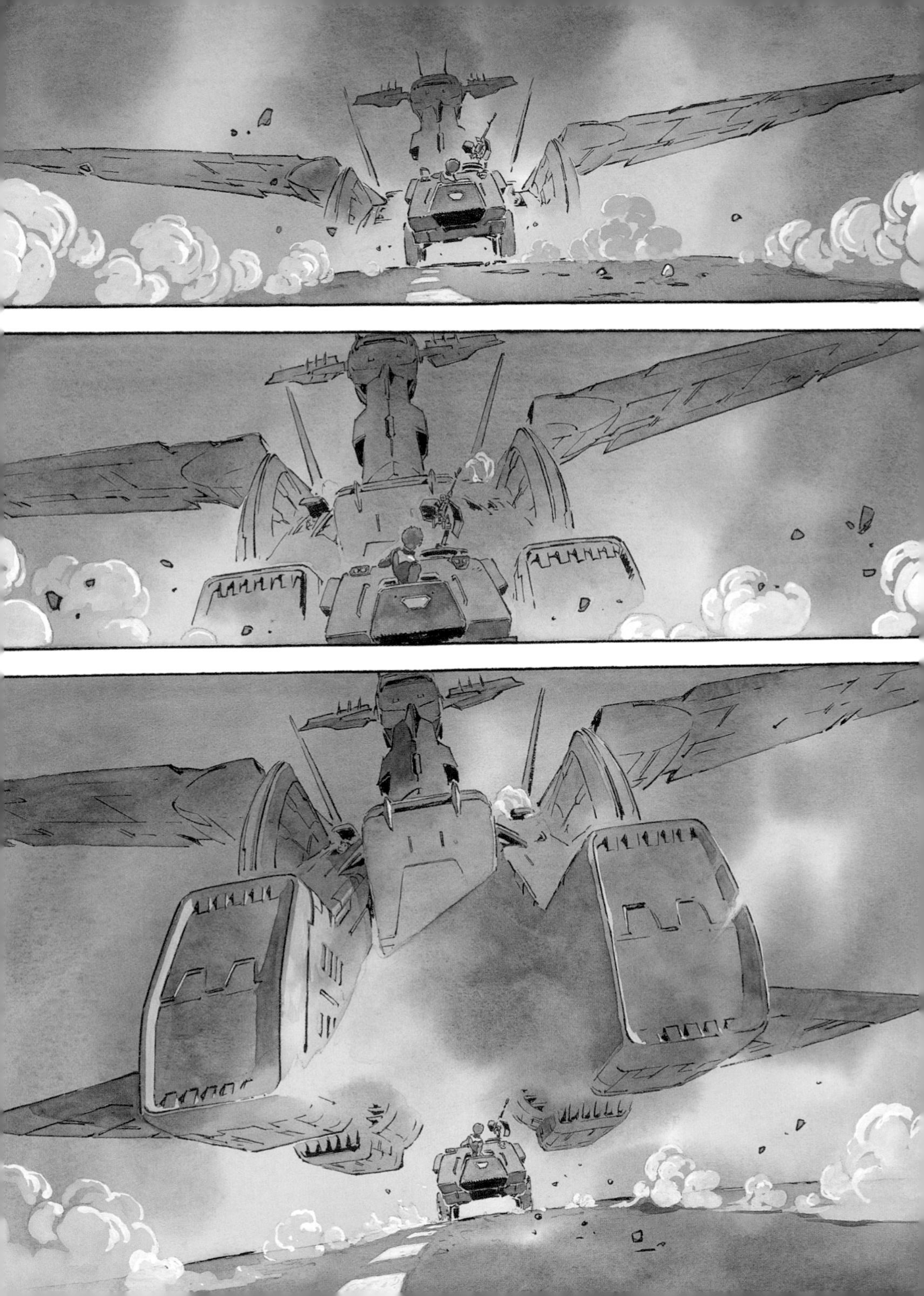

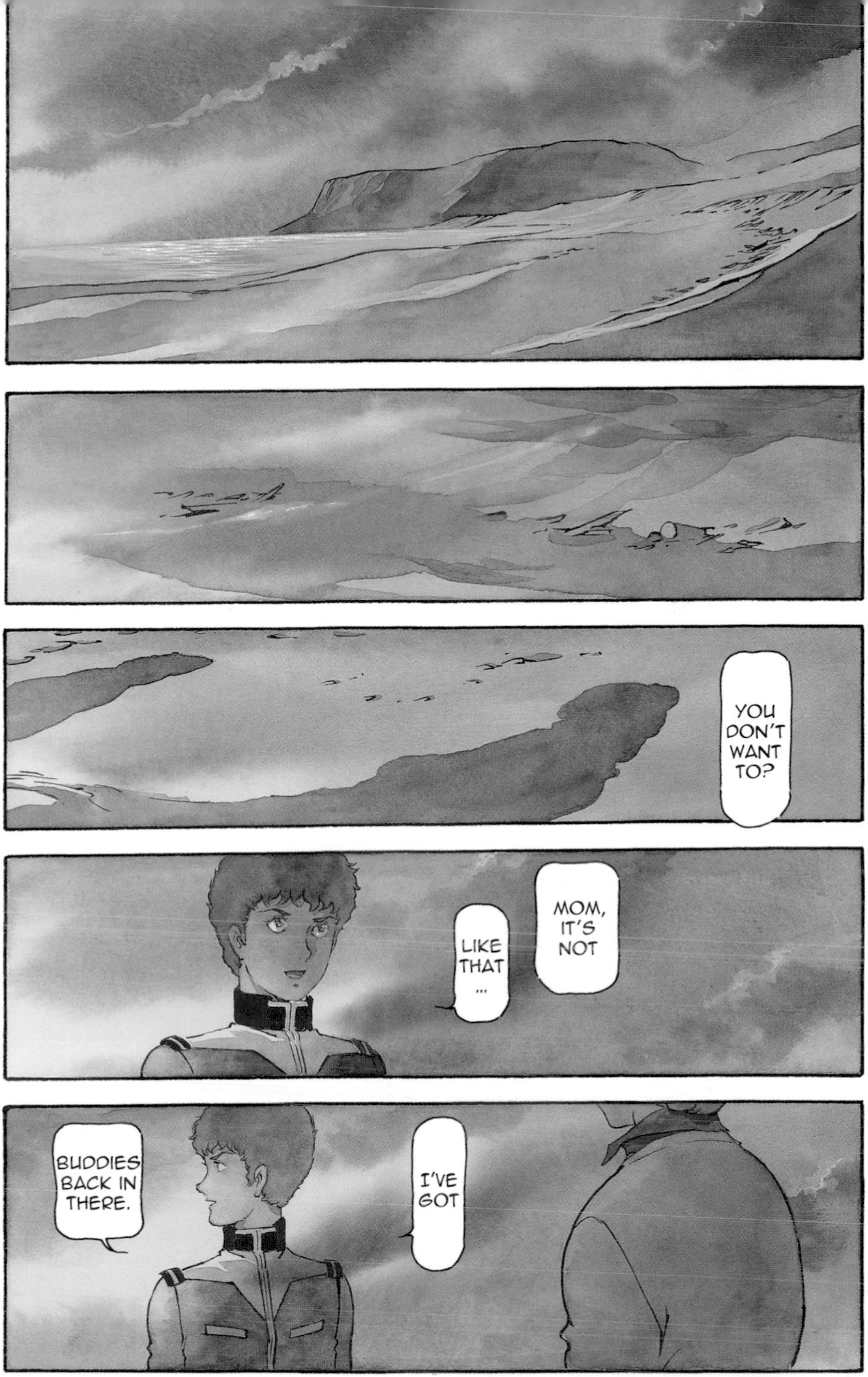
YOU DON'T WANT TO?
MOM, IT'S NOT
LIKE THAT ...
I'VE GOT
BUDDIES BACK IN THERE.

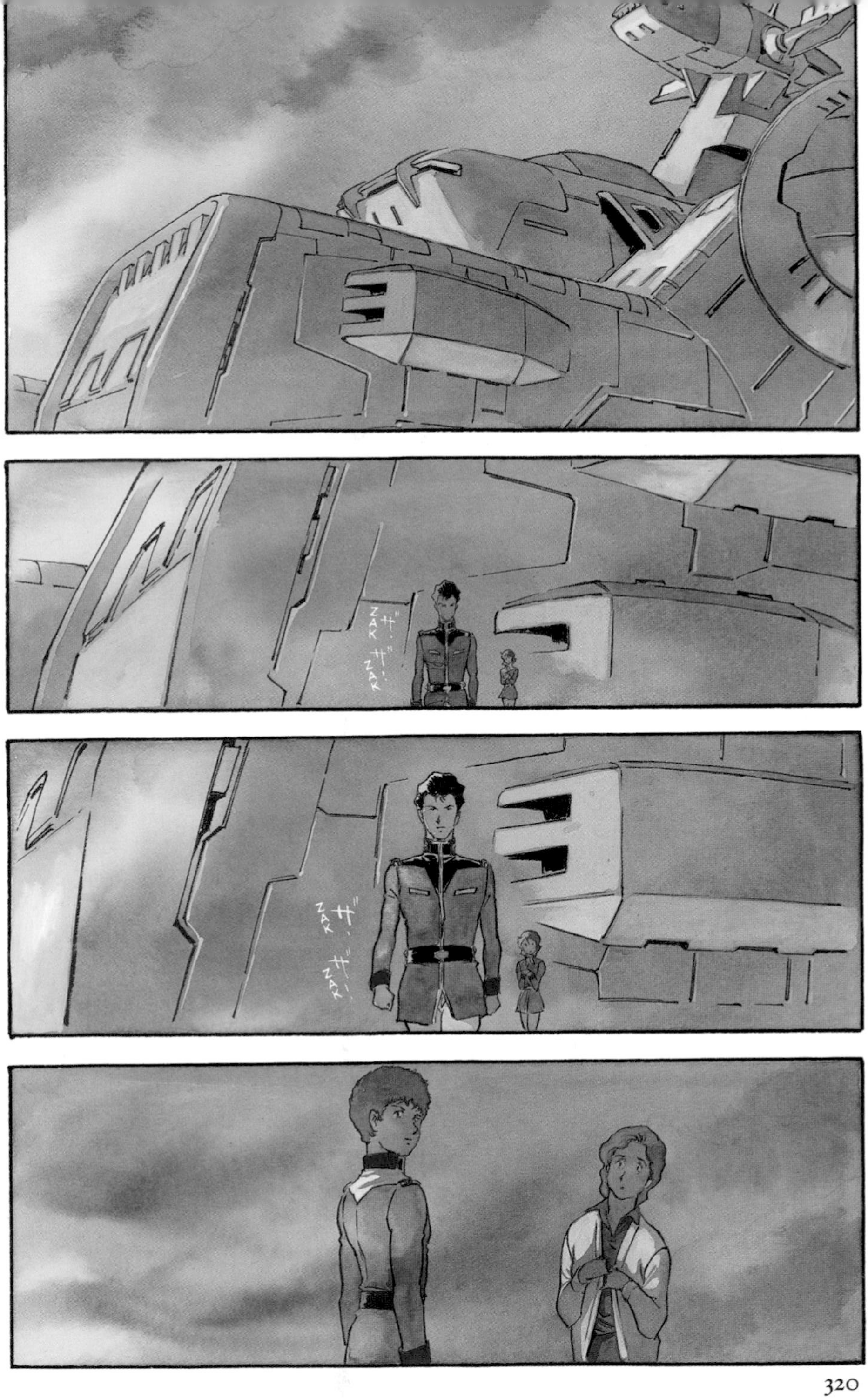
ZAK
ZAK
ZAK
ZAK

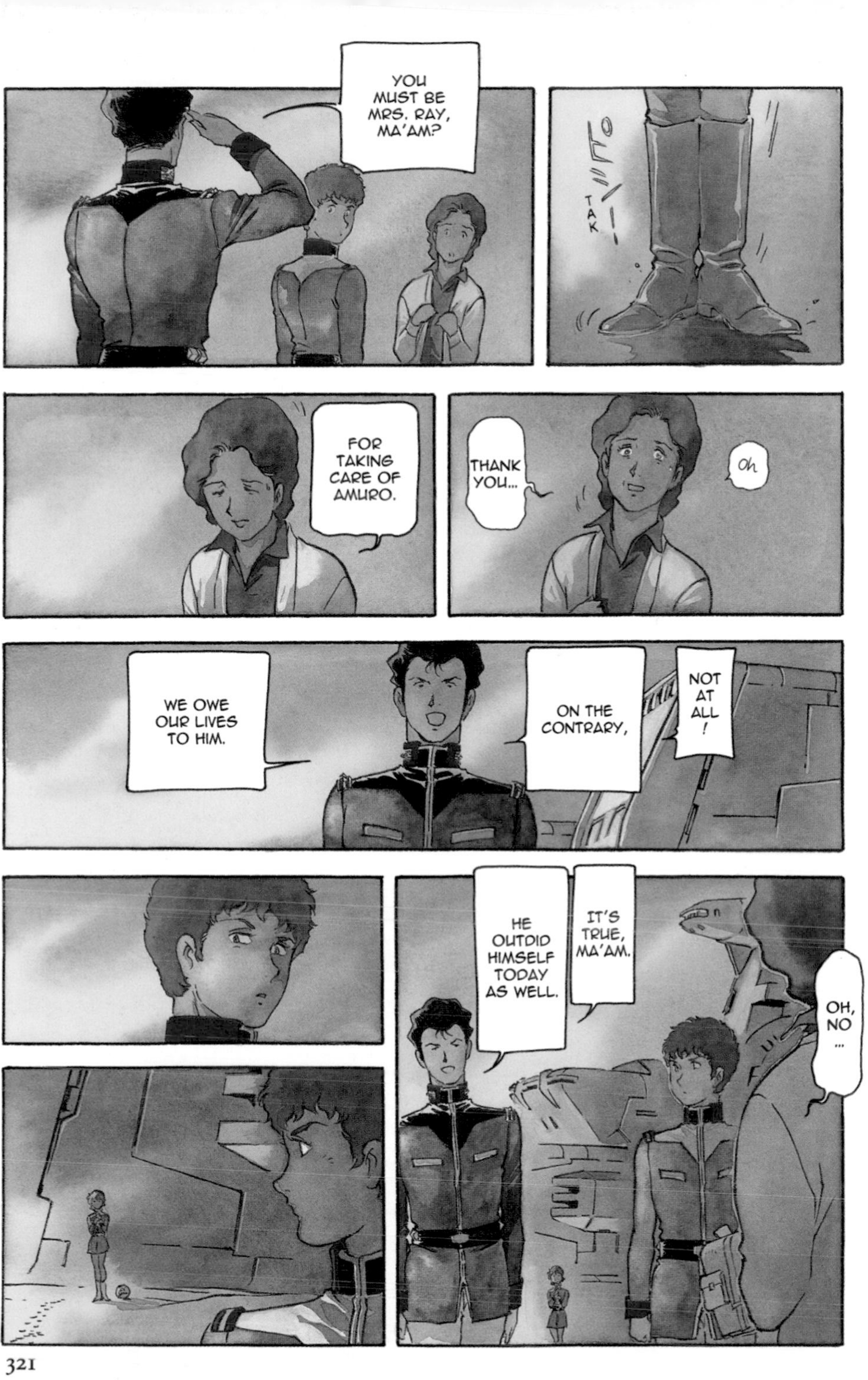

TAK
YOU MUST BE MRS. RAY, MA'AM?
Oh
THANK YOU...
FOR TAKING CARE OF AMURO.
NOT AT ALL!
ON THE CONTRARY,
WE OWE OUR LIVES TO HIM.
IT'S TRUE, MA'AM.
HE OUTDID HIMSELF TODAY AS WELL.
OH, NO ...

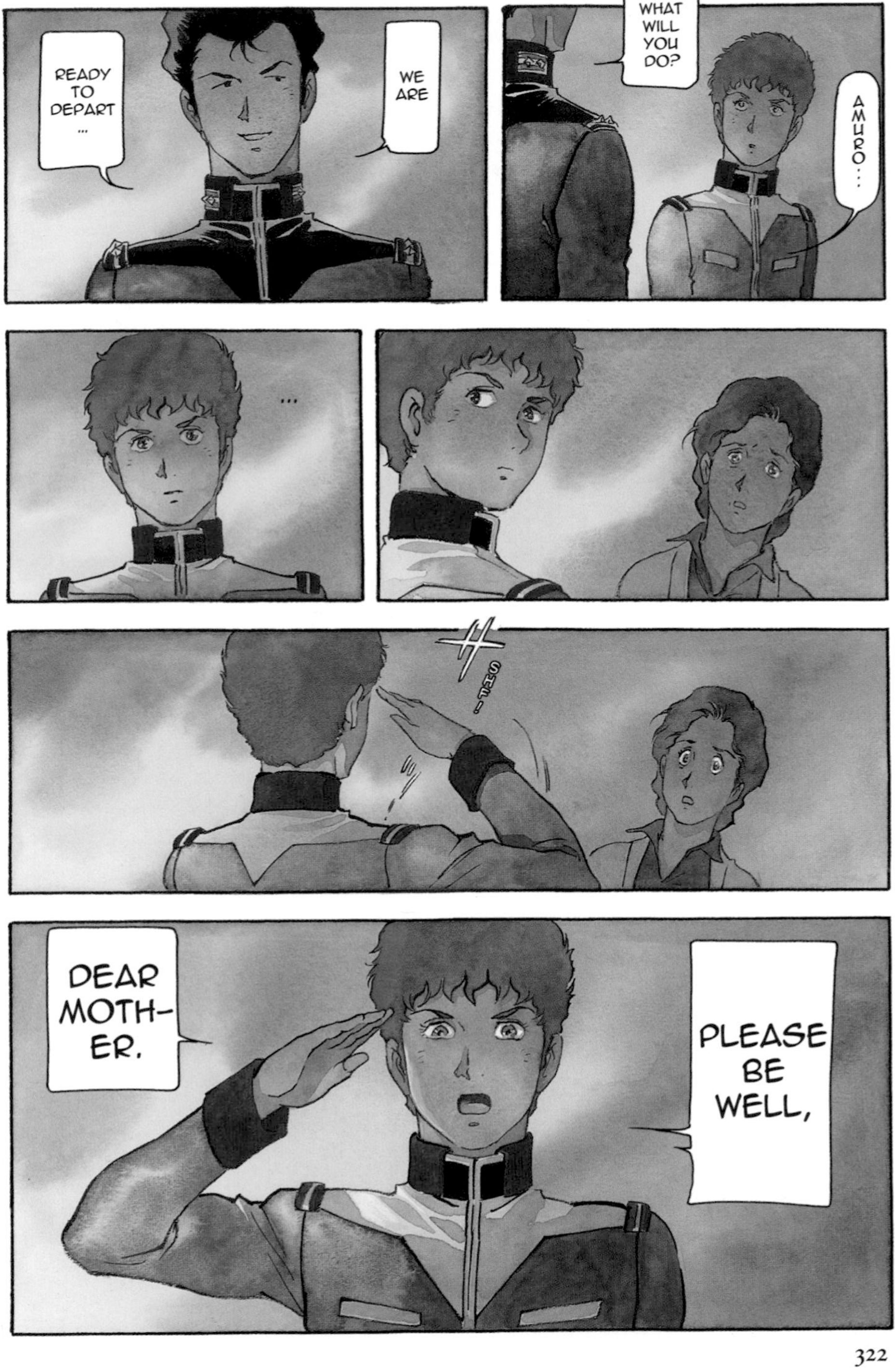
WHAT WILL YOU DO?
AMURO...
WE ARE
READY TO DEPART ...
...
SHF!
PLEASE BE WELL,
DEAR MOTHER.

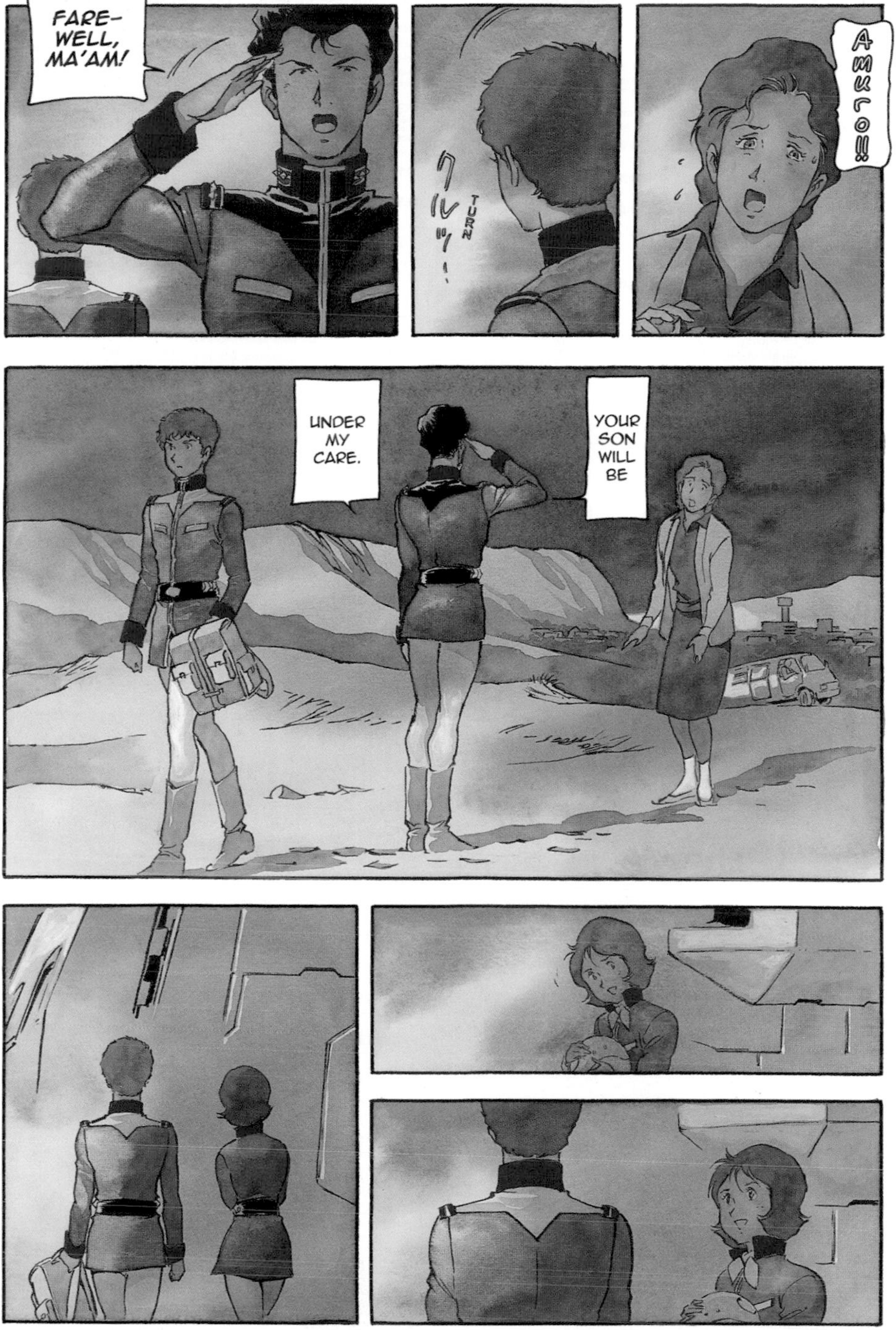
AMURO!!
クルッ
TURN
FARE-WELL, MA'AM!
YOUR SON WILL BE
UNDER MY CARE.

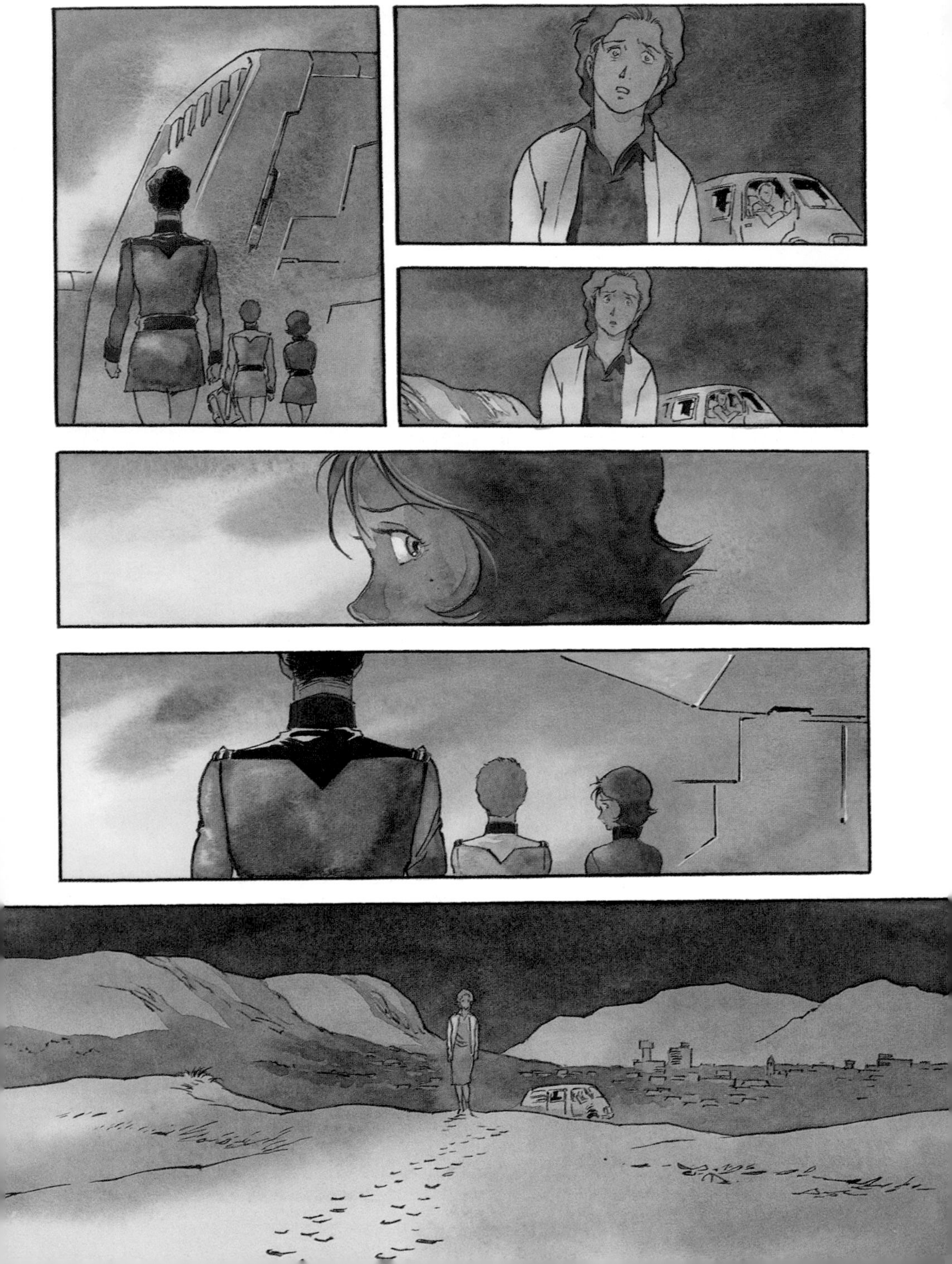

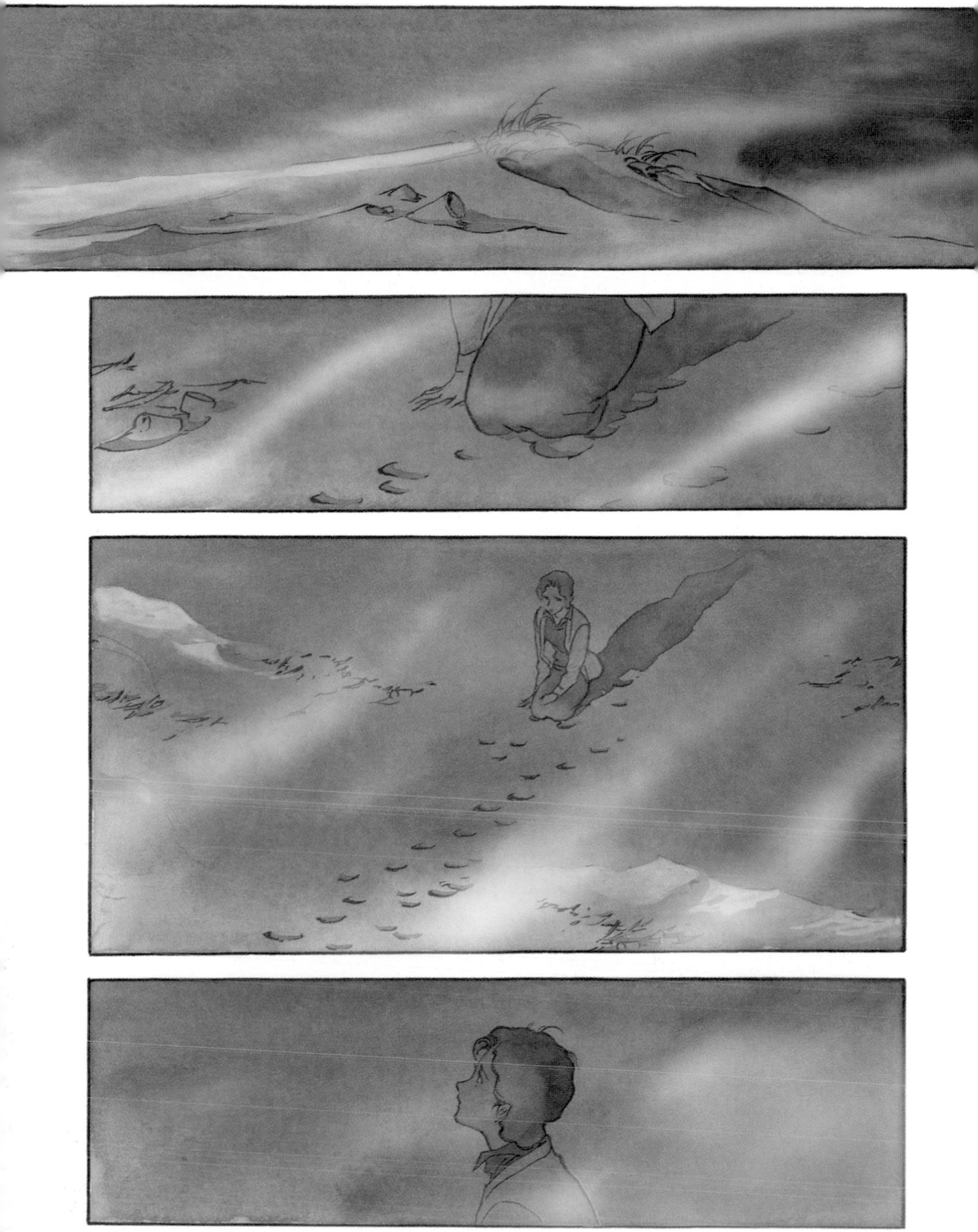

ズズズズ ZMMM

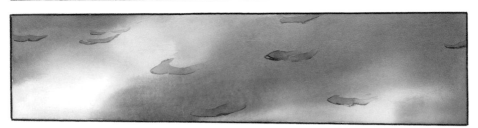

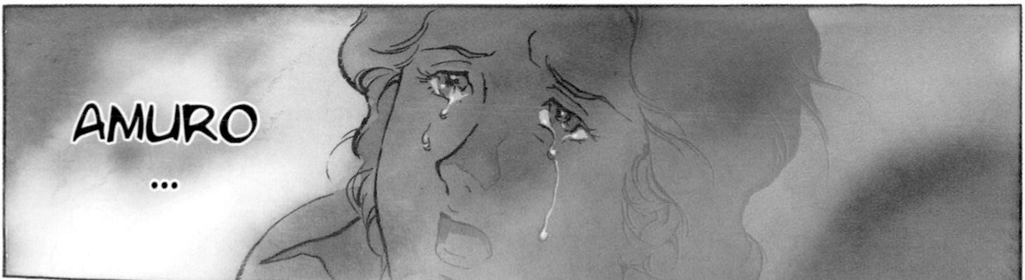
AMURO
...
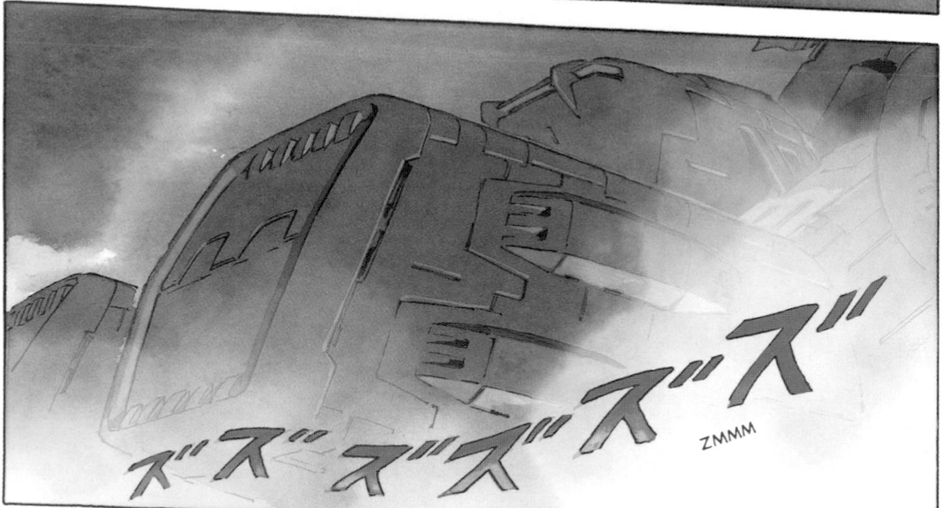
ズズズズズ
ZMMM
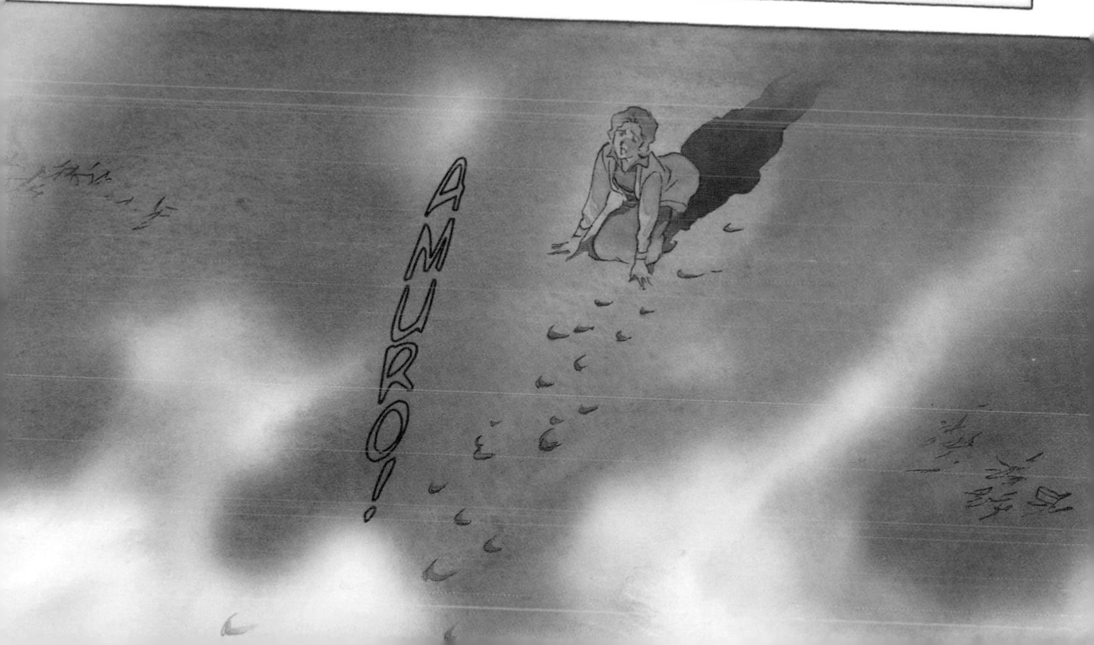
AMURO!

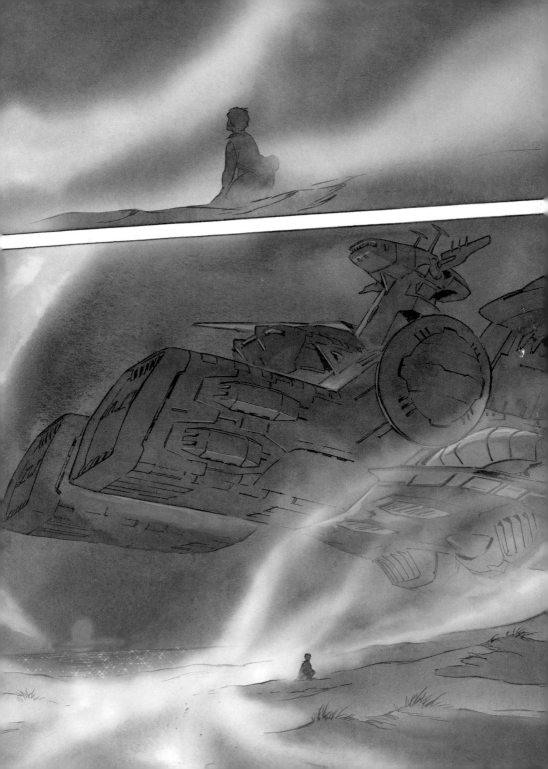

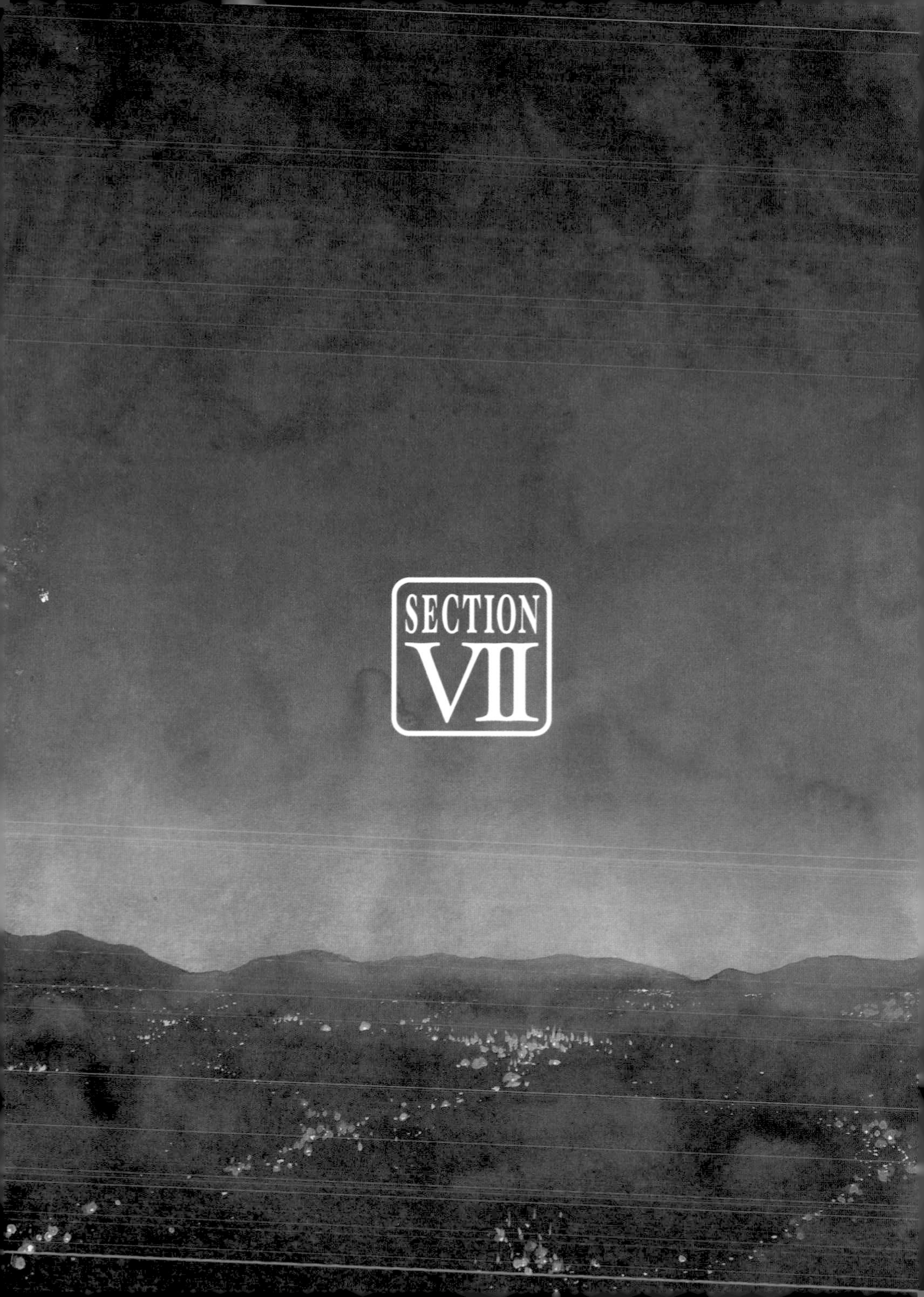

SECTION VII

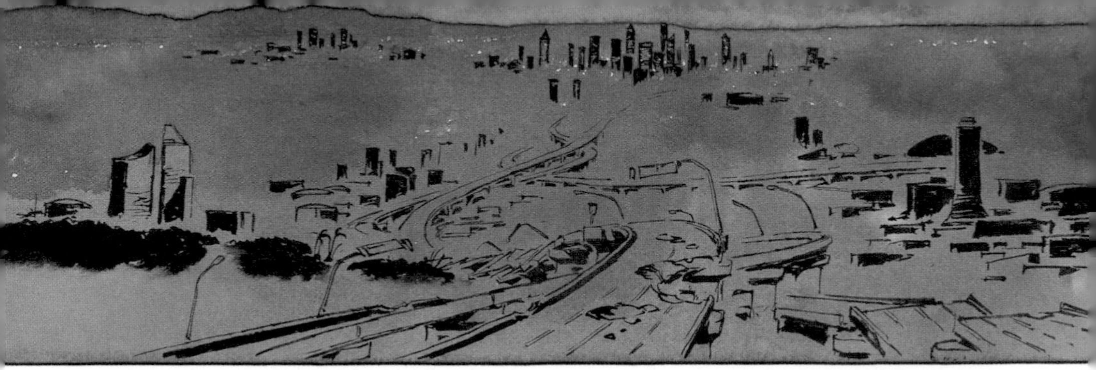

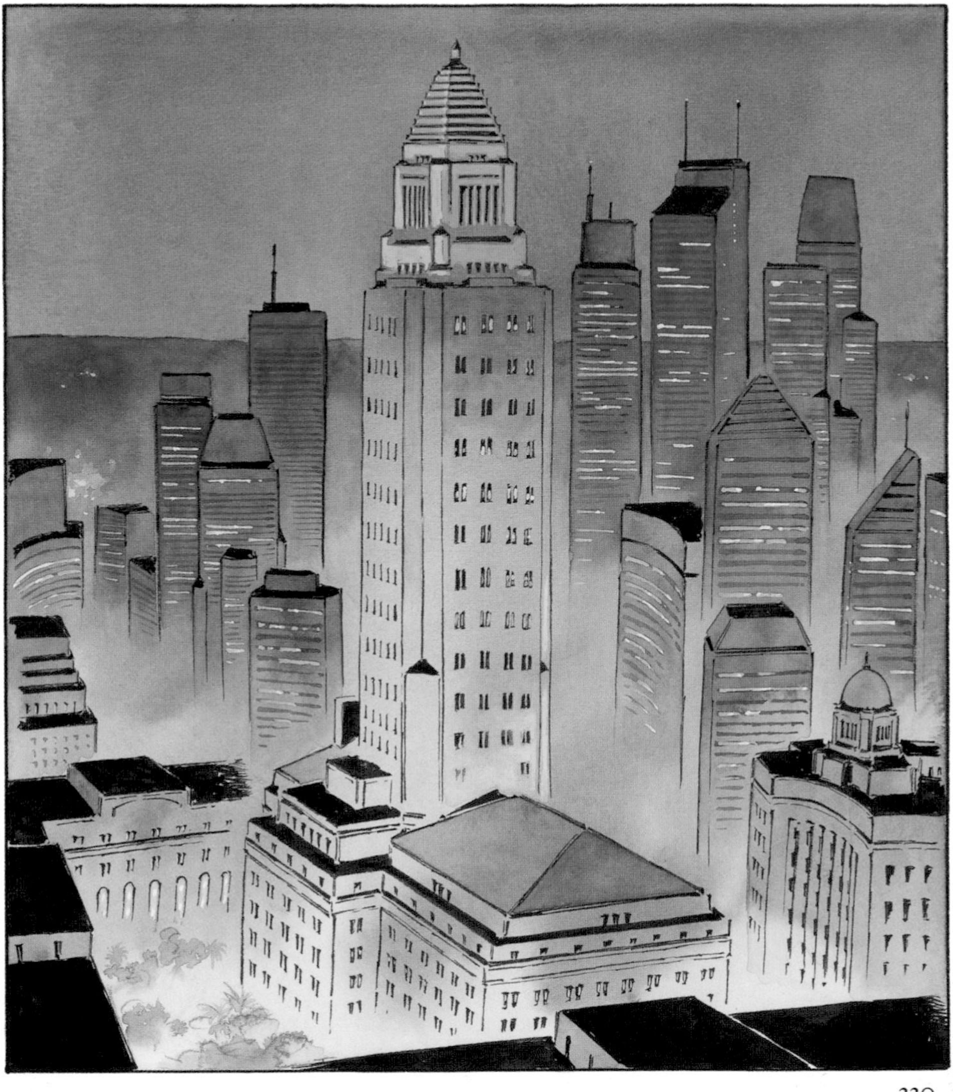

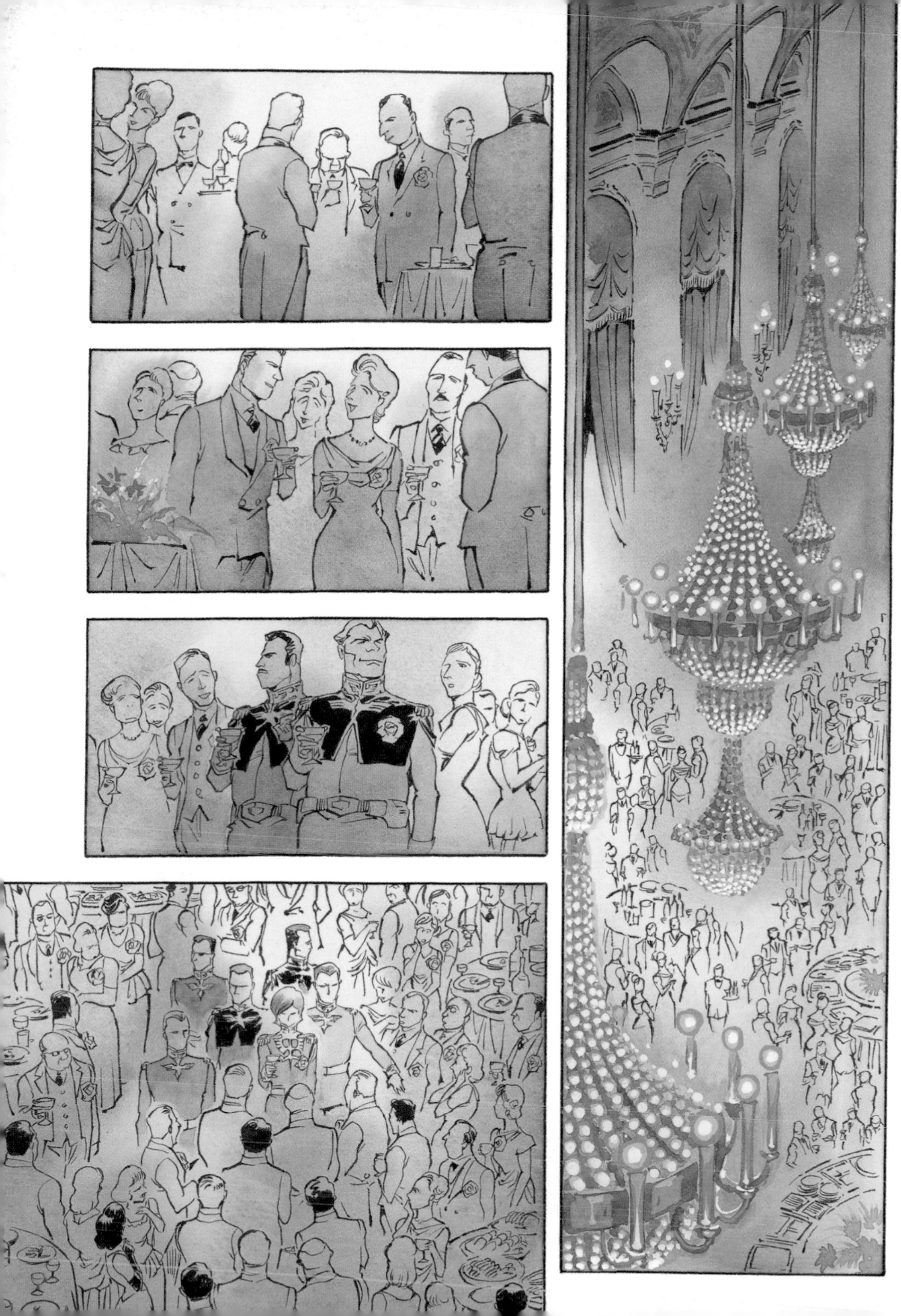

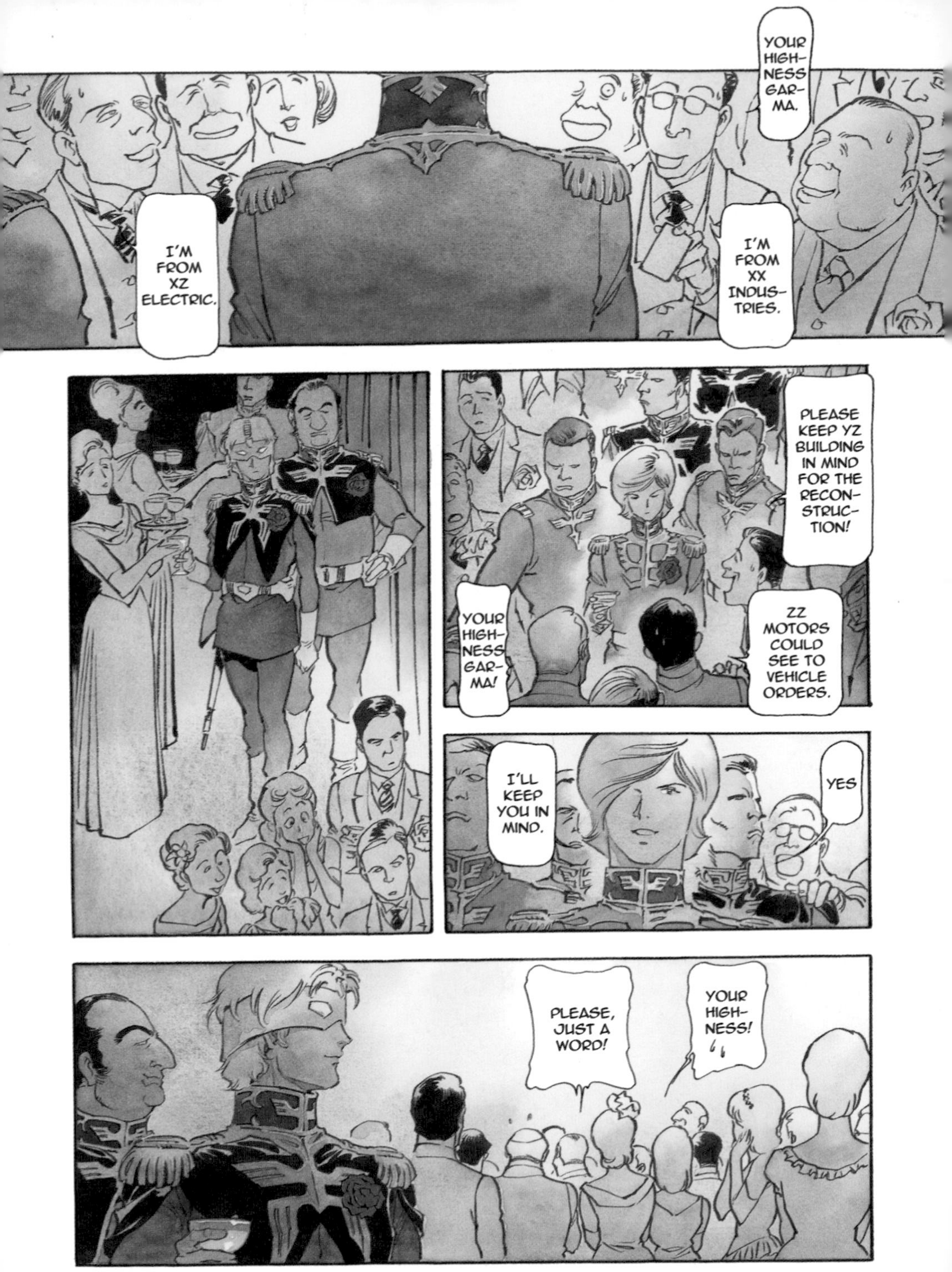
YOUR HIGHNESS GARMA.
I'M FROM XX INDUSTRIES.
I'M FROM XZ ELECTRIC.
PLEASE KEEP YZ BUILDING IN MIND FOR THE RECONSTRUCTION!
ZZ MOTORS COULD SEE TO VEHICLE ORDERS.
YOUR HIGHNESS GARMA!
YES
I'LL KEEP YOU IN MIND.
YOUR HIGHNESS!
PLEASE, JUST A WORD!

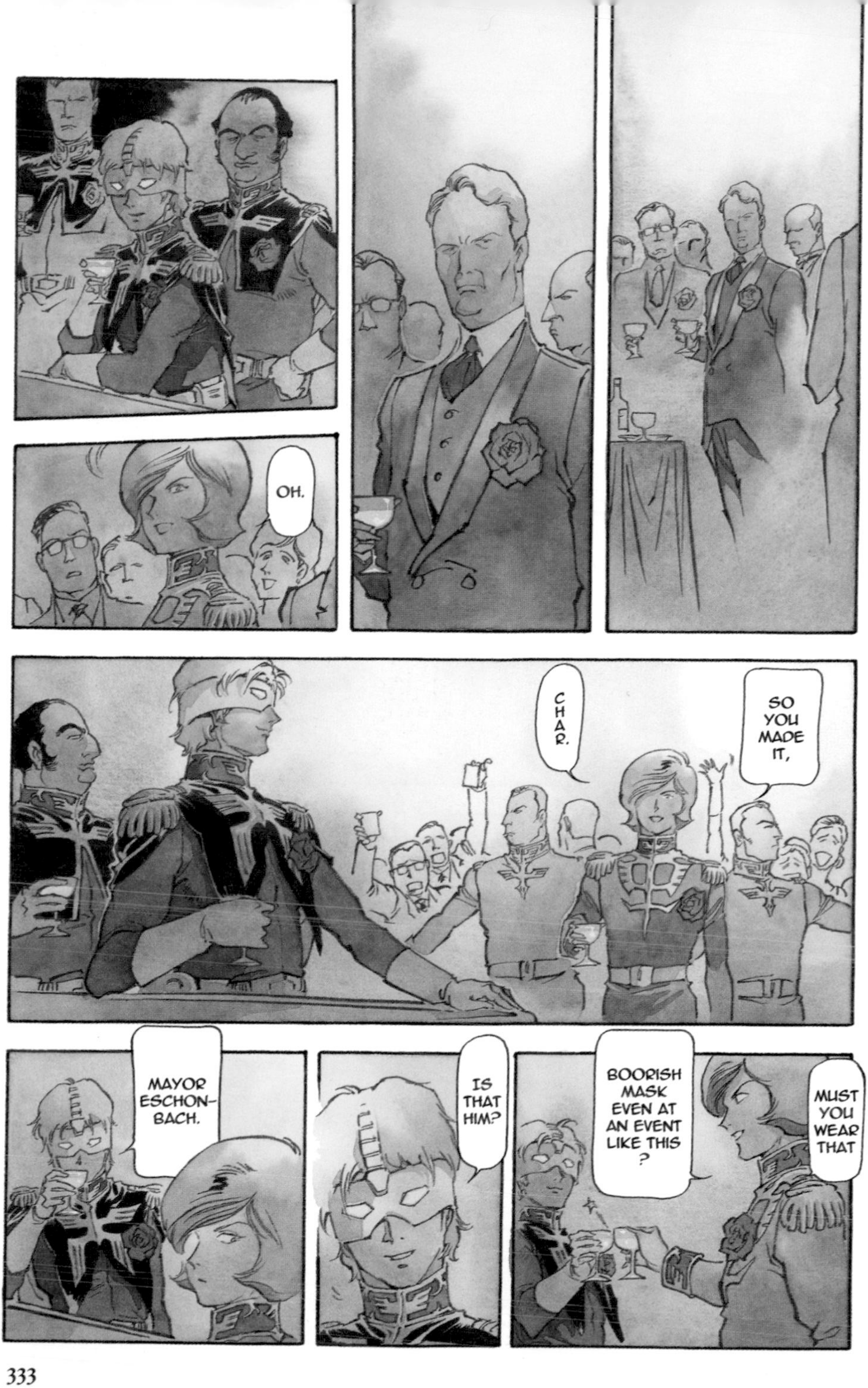
OH.
SO YOU MADE IT,
CHAR.
MUST YOU WEAR THAT
BOORISH MASK EVEN AT AN EVENT LIKE THIS ?
IS THAT HIM?
MAYOR ESCHON-BACH.

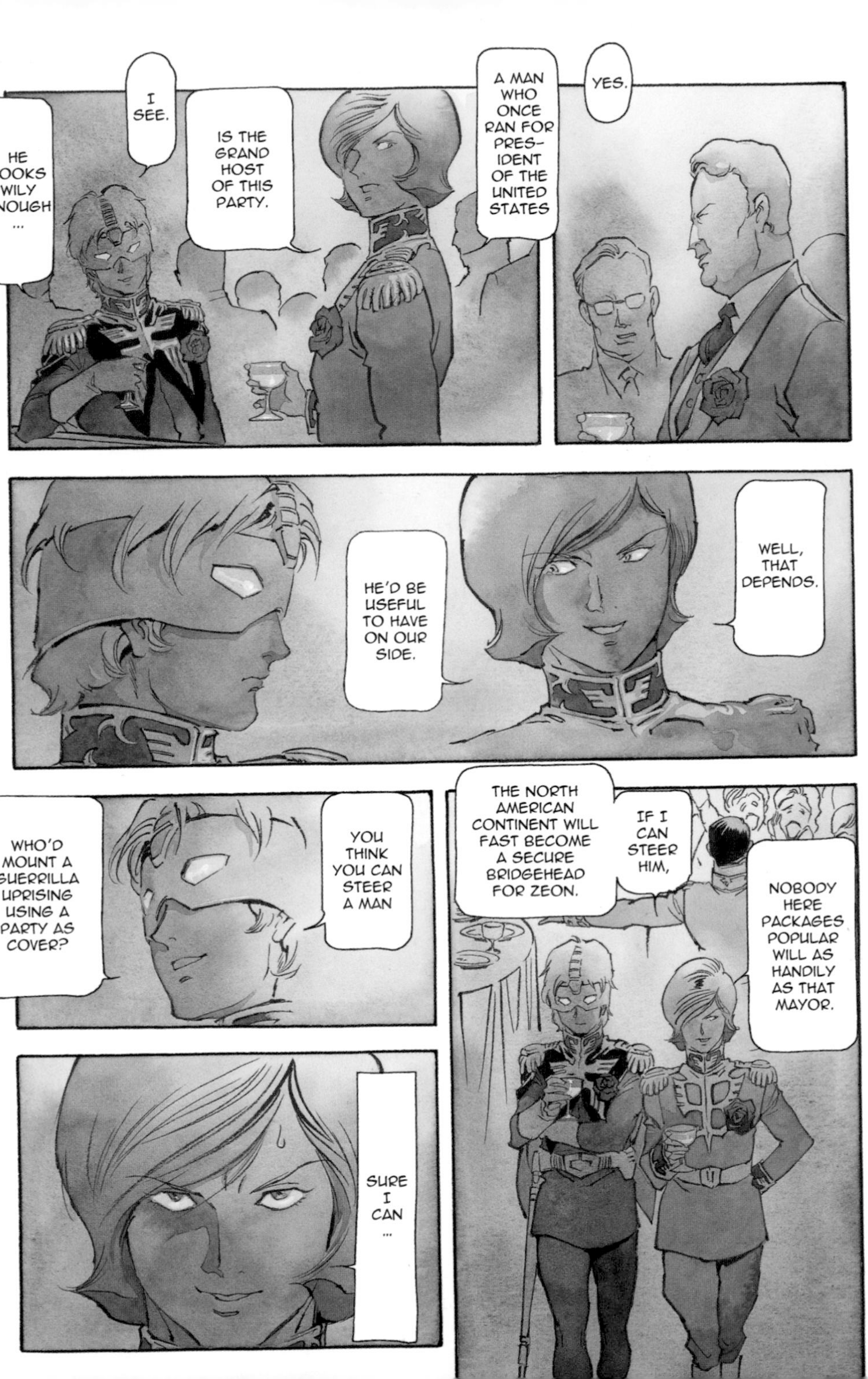
YES.
A MAN WHO ONCE RAN FOR PRES-IDENT OF THE UNITED STATES
IS THE GRAND HOST OF THIS PARTY.
I SEE.
HE LOOKS WILY ENOUGH ...
WELL, THAT DEPENDS.
HE'D BE USEFUL TO HAVE ON OUR SIDE.
IF I CAN STEER HIM,
THE NORTH AMERICAN CONTINENT WILL FAST BECOME A SECURE BRIDGEHEAD FOR ZEON.
NOBODY HERE PACKAGES POPULAR WILL AS HANDILY AS THAT MAYOR.
YOU THINK YOU CAN STEER A MAN
WHO'D MOUNT A GUERRILLA UPRISING USING A PARTY AS COVER?
SURE I CAN ...

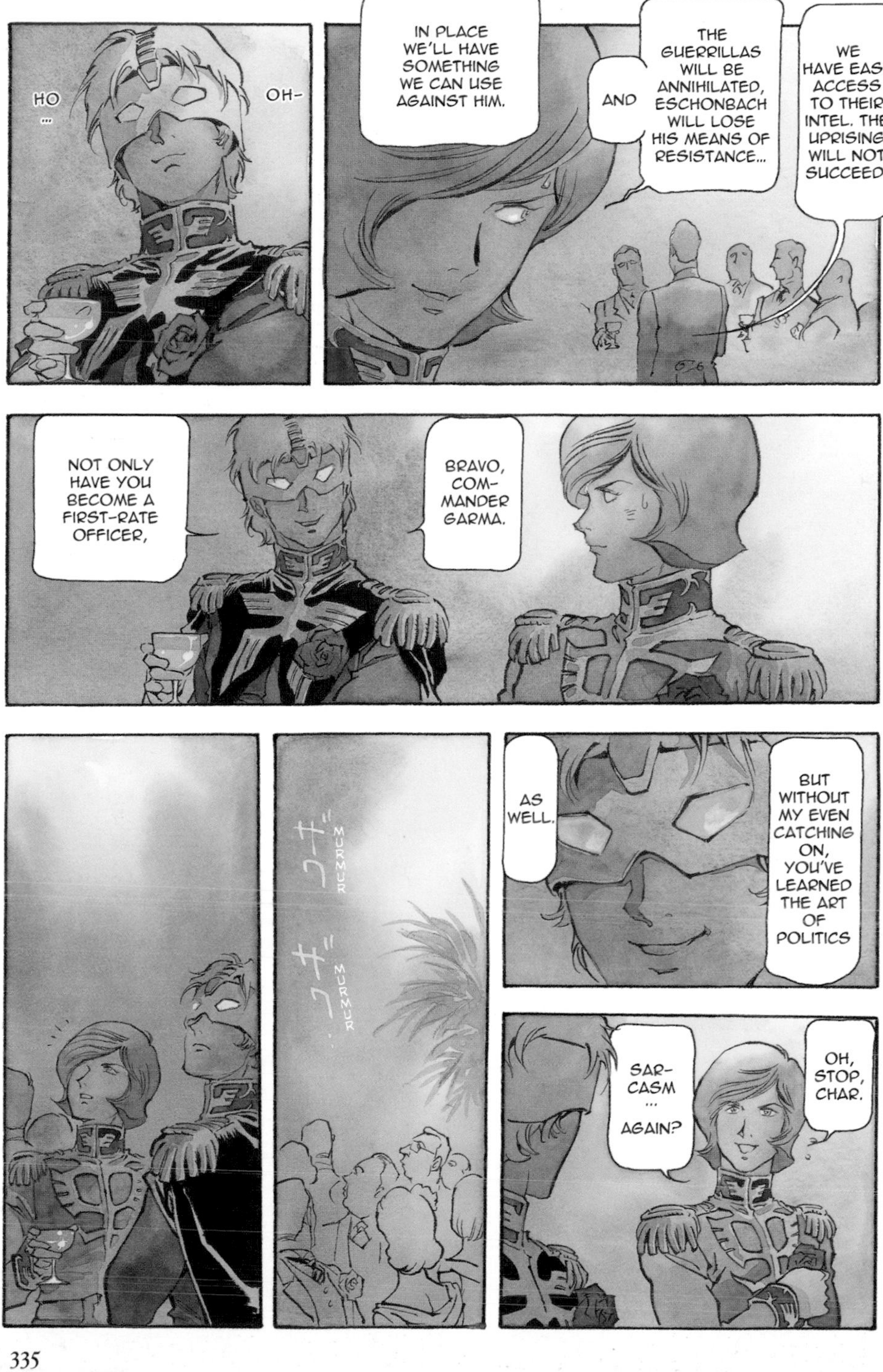
WE HAVE EASY ACCESS TO THEIR INTEL. THE UPRISING WILL NOT SUCCEED.
THE GUERRILLAS WILL BE ANNIHILATED, ESCHONBACH WILL LOSE HIS MEANS OF RESISTANCE...
AND
IN PLACE WE'LL HAVE SOMETHING WE CAN USE AGAINST HIM.
OH-
HO ...
BRAVO, COM-MANDER GARMA.
NOT ONLY HAVE YOU BECOME A FIRST-RATE OFFICER,
BUT WITHOUT MY EVEN CATCHING ON, YOU'VE LEARNED THE ART OF POLITICS
AS WELL.
OH, STOP, CHAR.
SAR-CASM ... AGAIN?
ザワ MURMUR
ザワ MURMUR

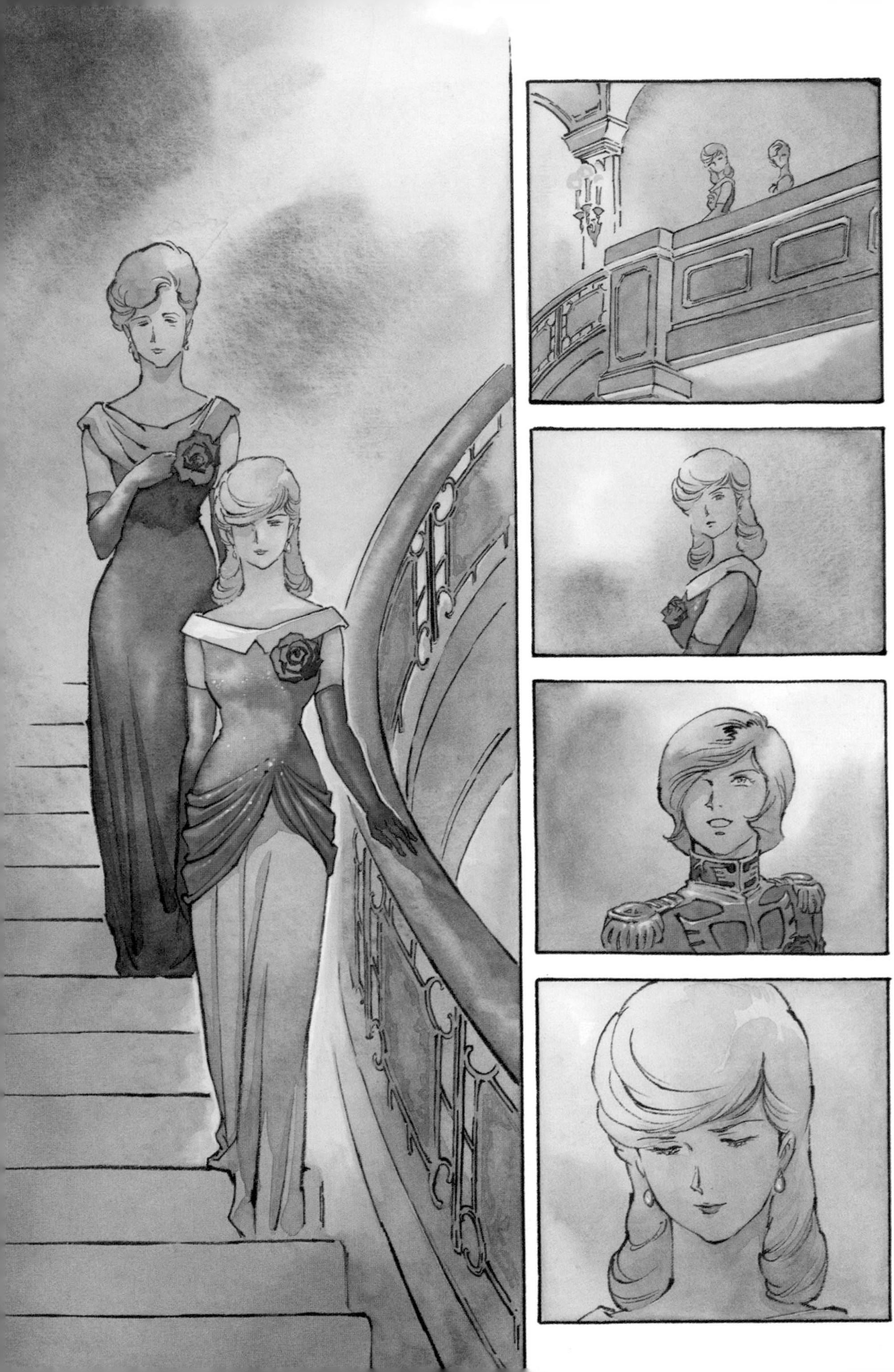

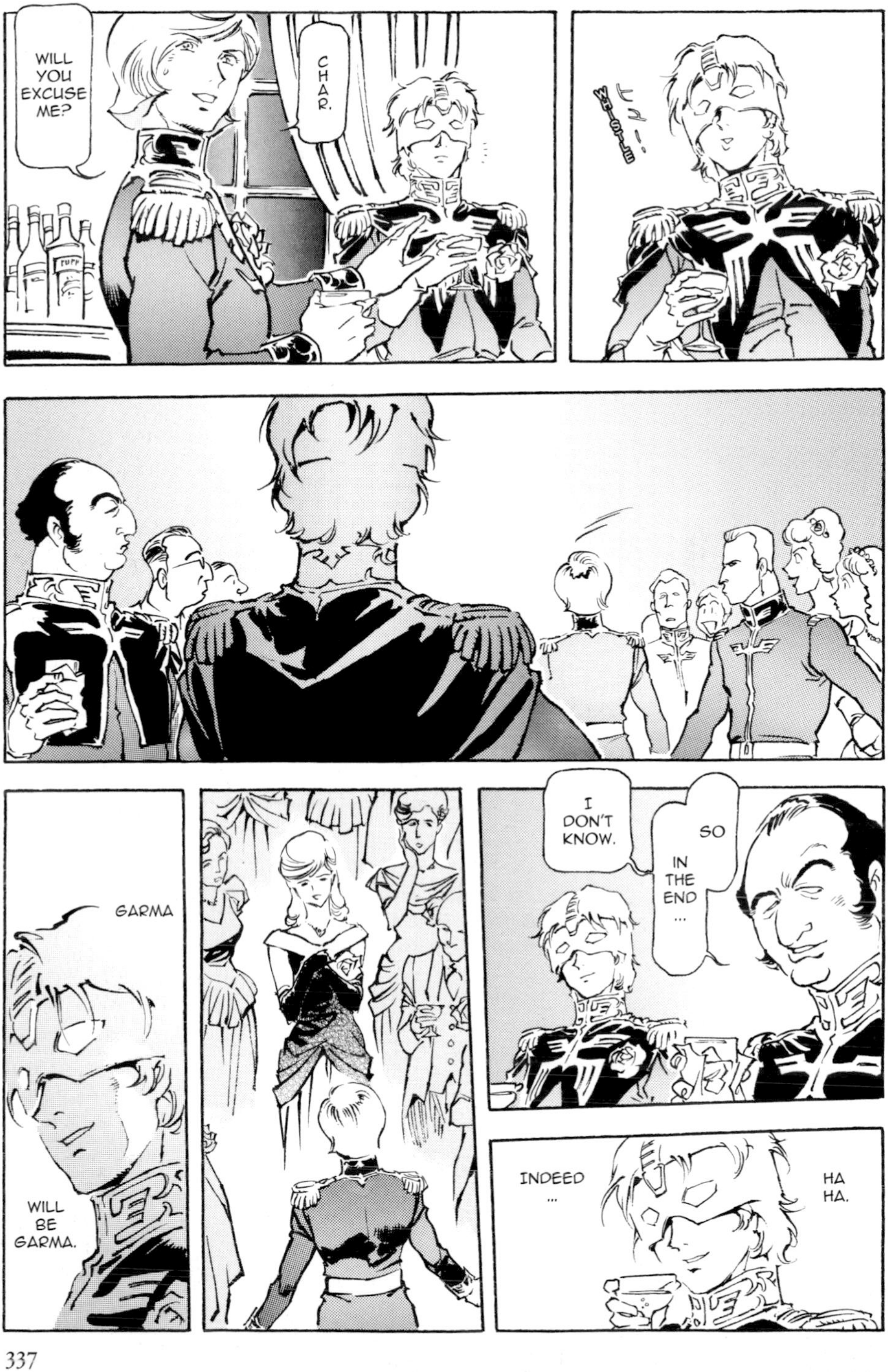
WHISTLE
CHAR.
WILL YOU EXCUSE ME?
SO IN THE END ...
I DON'T KNOW.
HA HA.
INDEED ...
GARMA
WILL BE GARMA.

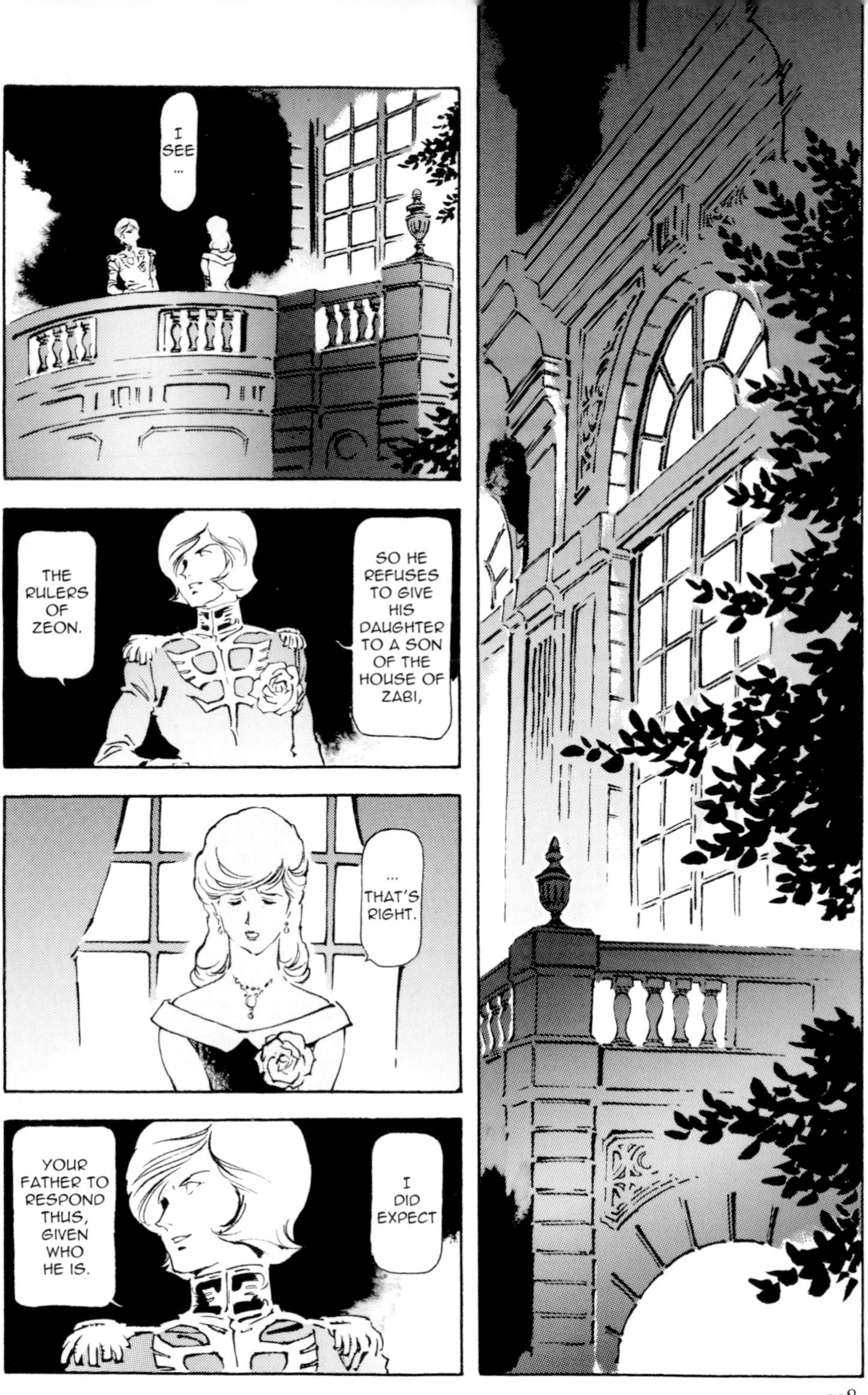
I SEE ...
SO HE REFUSES TO GIVE HIS DAUGHTER TO A SON OF THE HOUSE OF ZABI,
THE RULERS OF ZEON.
... THAT'S RIGHT.
I DID EXPECT
YOUR FATHER TO RESPOND THUS, GIVEN WHO HE IS.

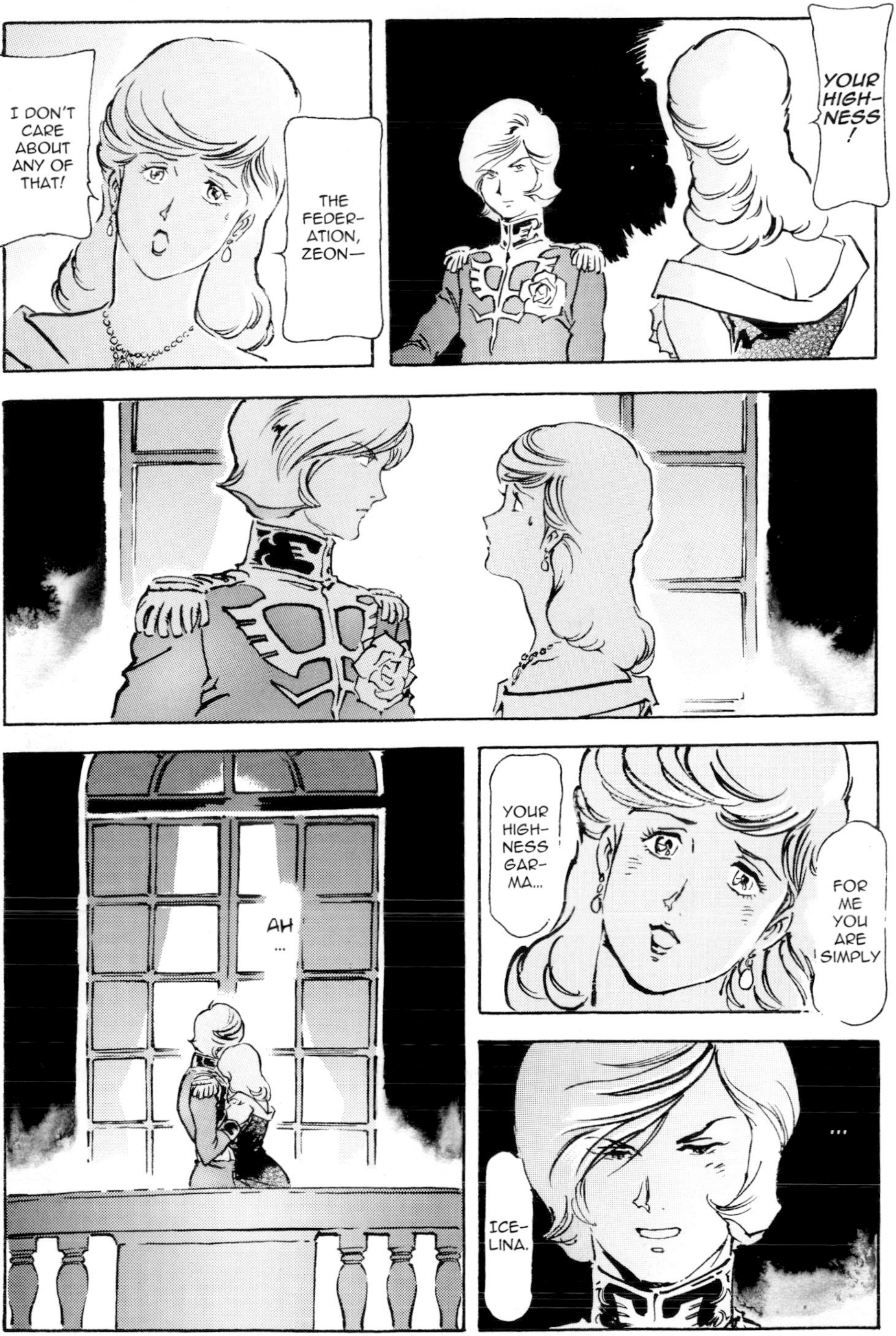
YOUR HIGHNESS!
THE FEDERATION, ZEON—
I DON'T CARE ABOUT ANY OF THAT!
FOR ME YOU ARE SIMPLY
YOUR HIGHNESS GARMA...
...
ICELINA.
AH ...

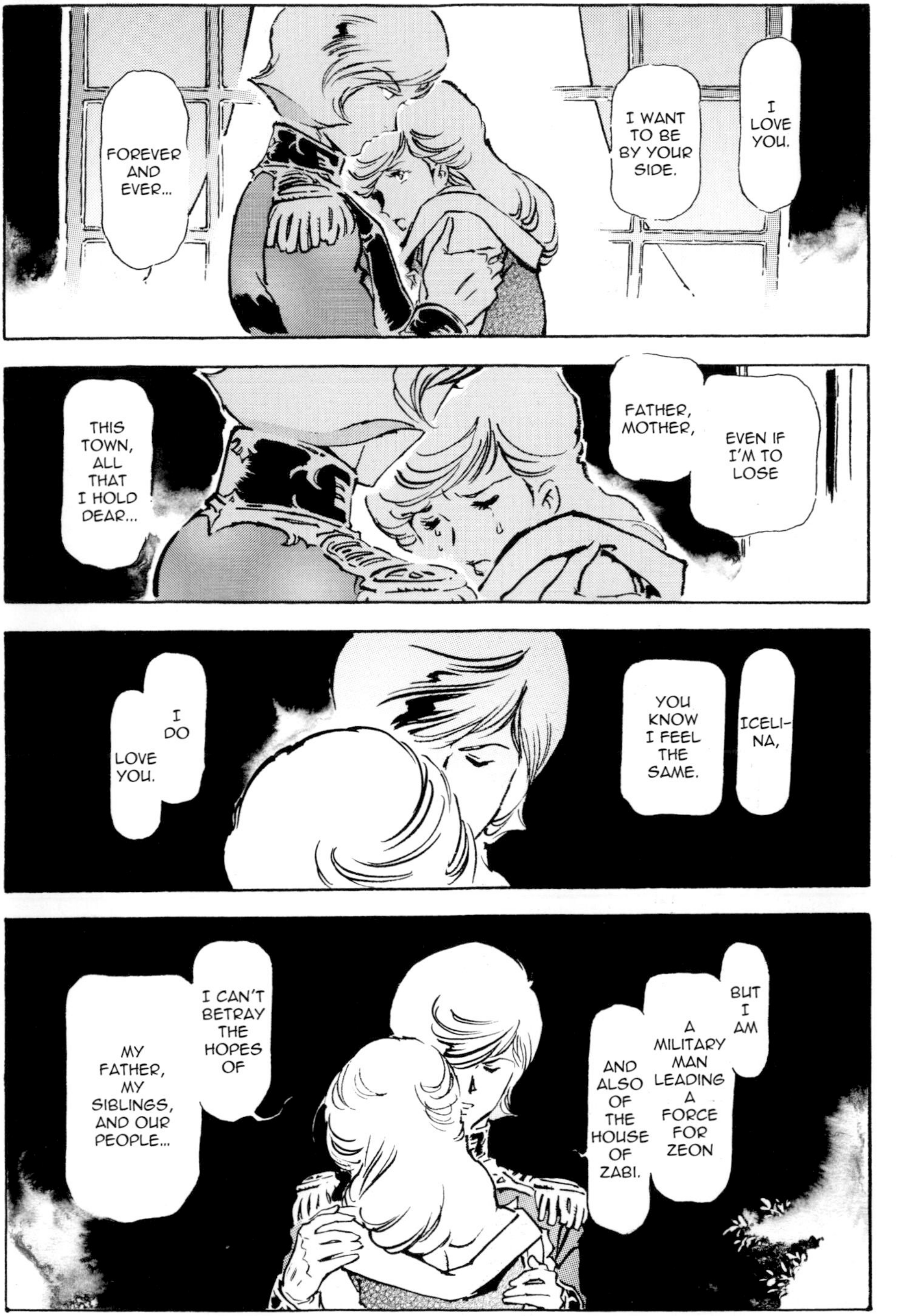
I LOVE YOU.
I WANT TO BE BY YOUR SIDE.
FOREVER AND EVER...
EVEN IF I'M TO LOSE
FATHER, MOTHER,
THIS TOWN, ALL THAT I HOLD DEAR...
ICELI-NA,
YOU KNOW I FEEL THE SAME.
I DO LOVE YOU.
BUT I AM
A MILITARY MAN LEADING A FORCE FOR ZEON
AND ALSO OF THE HOUSE OF ZABI.
I CAN'T BETRAY THE HOPES OF
MY FATHER, MY SIBLINGS, AND OUR PEOPLE...

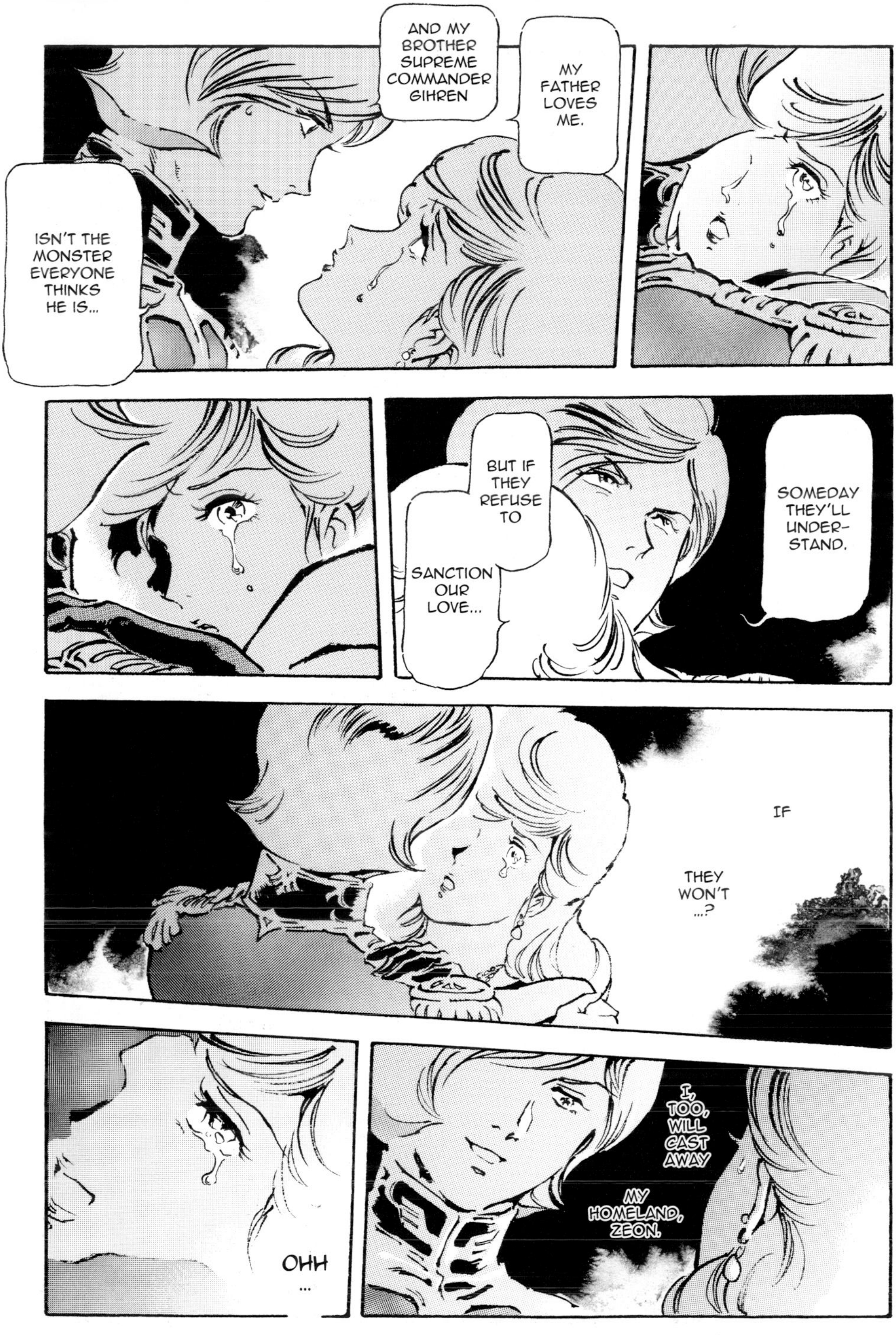
MY FATHER LOVES ME.
AND MY BROTHER SUPREME COMMANDER GIHREN
ISN'T THE MONSTER EVERYONE THINKS HE IS...
SOMEDAY THEY'LL UNDER-STAND.
BUT IF THEY REFUSE TO
SANCTION OUR LOVE...
IF
THEY WON'T ...?
I, TOO, WILL CAST AWAY
MY HOMELAND, ZEON.
OHH ...

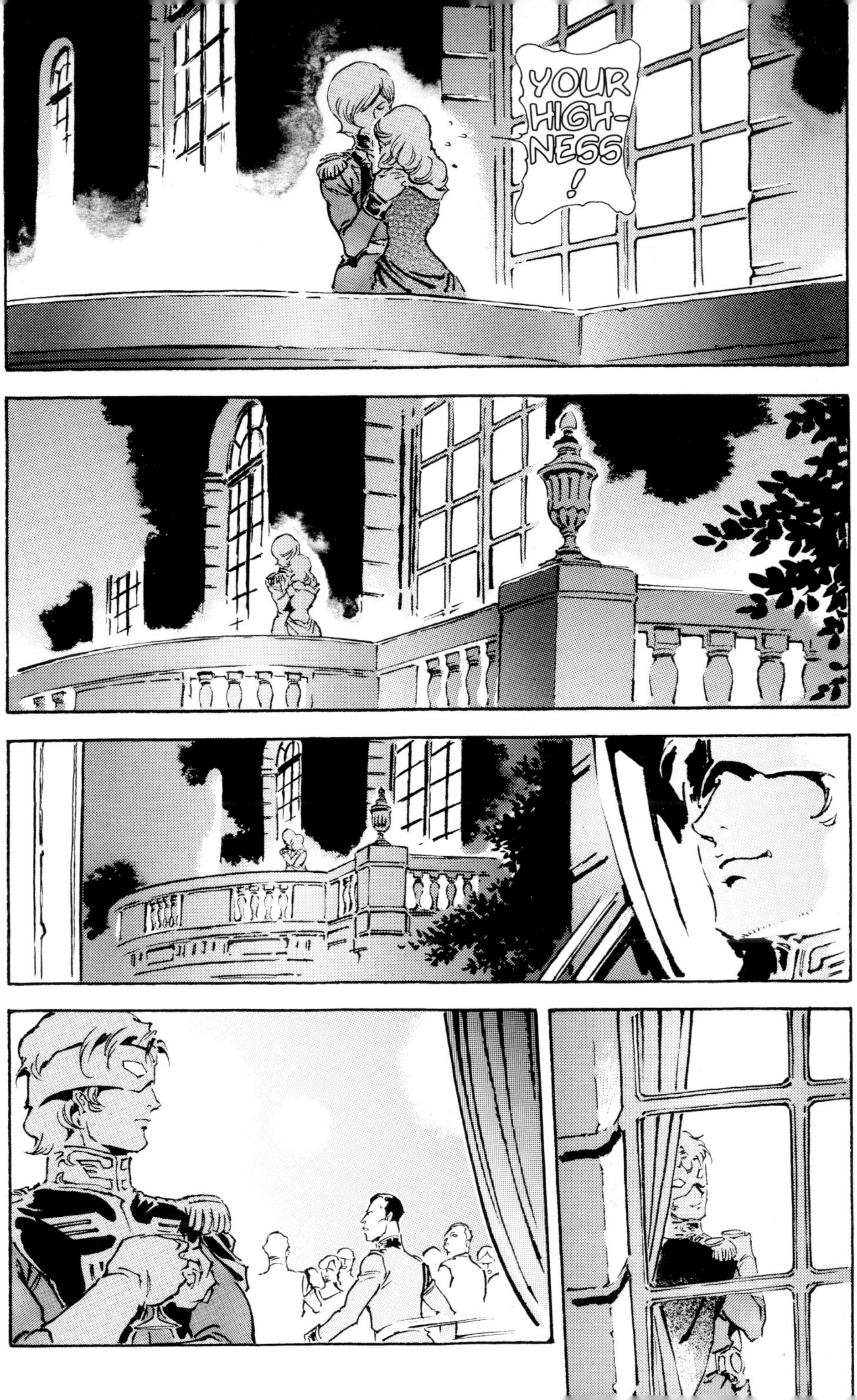
YOUR HIGH-NESS!

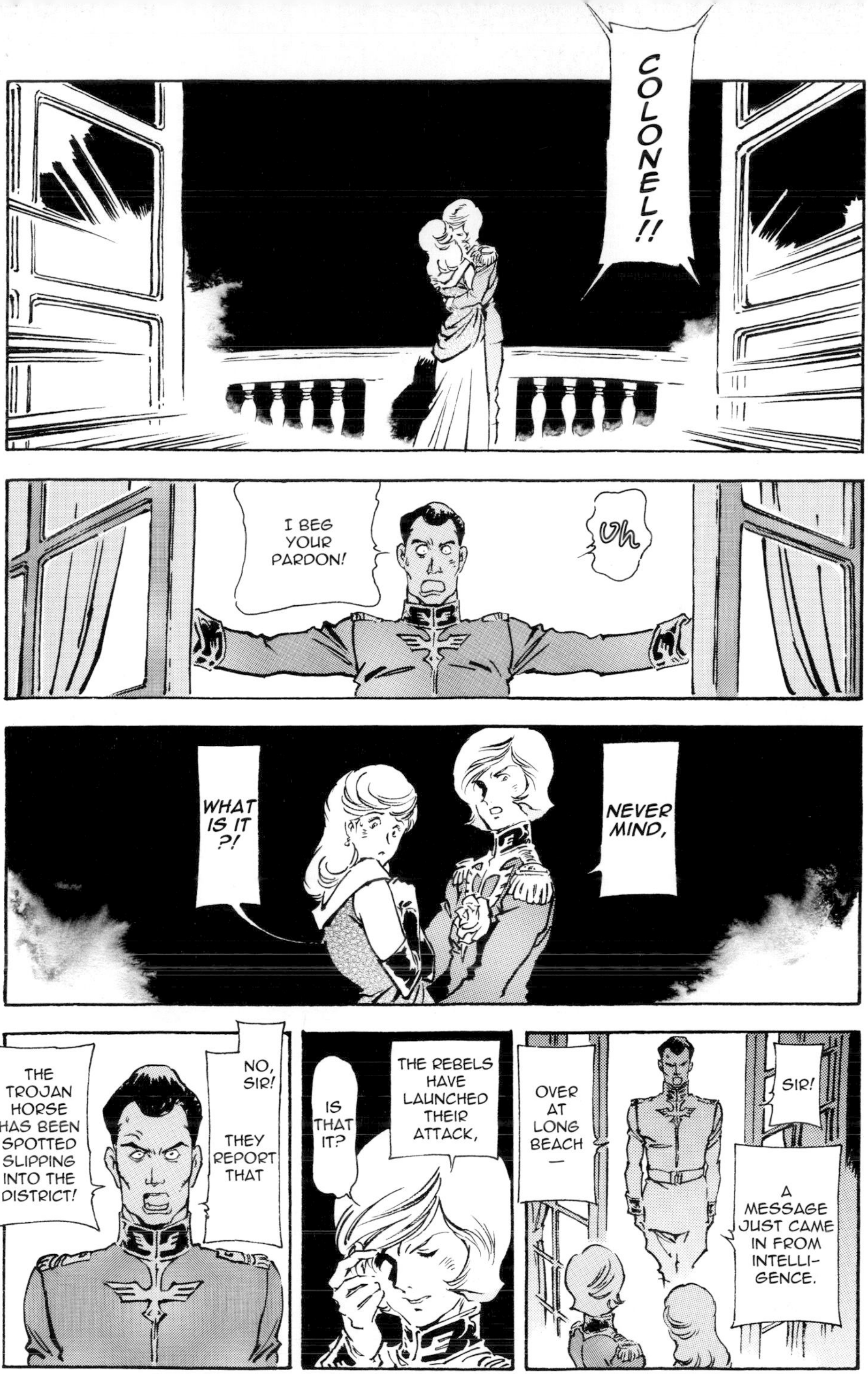
COLONEL!!
Uh
I BEG YOUR PARDON!
NEVER MIND,
WHAT IS IT ?!
SIR!
A MESSAGE JUST CAME IN FROM INTELLI- GENCE.
OVER AT LONG BEACH —
THE REBELS HAVE LAUNCHED THEIR ATTACK,
IS THAT IT?
NO, SIR!
THEY REPORT THAT
THE TROJAN HORSE HAS BEEN SPOTTED SLIPPING INTO THE DISTRICT!

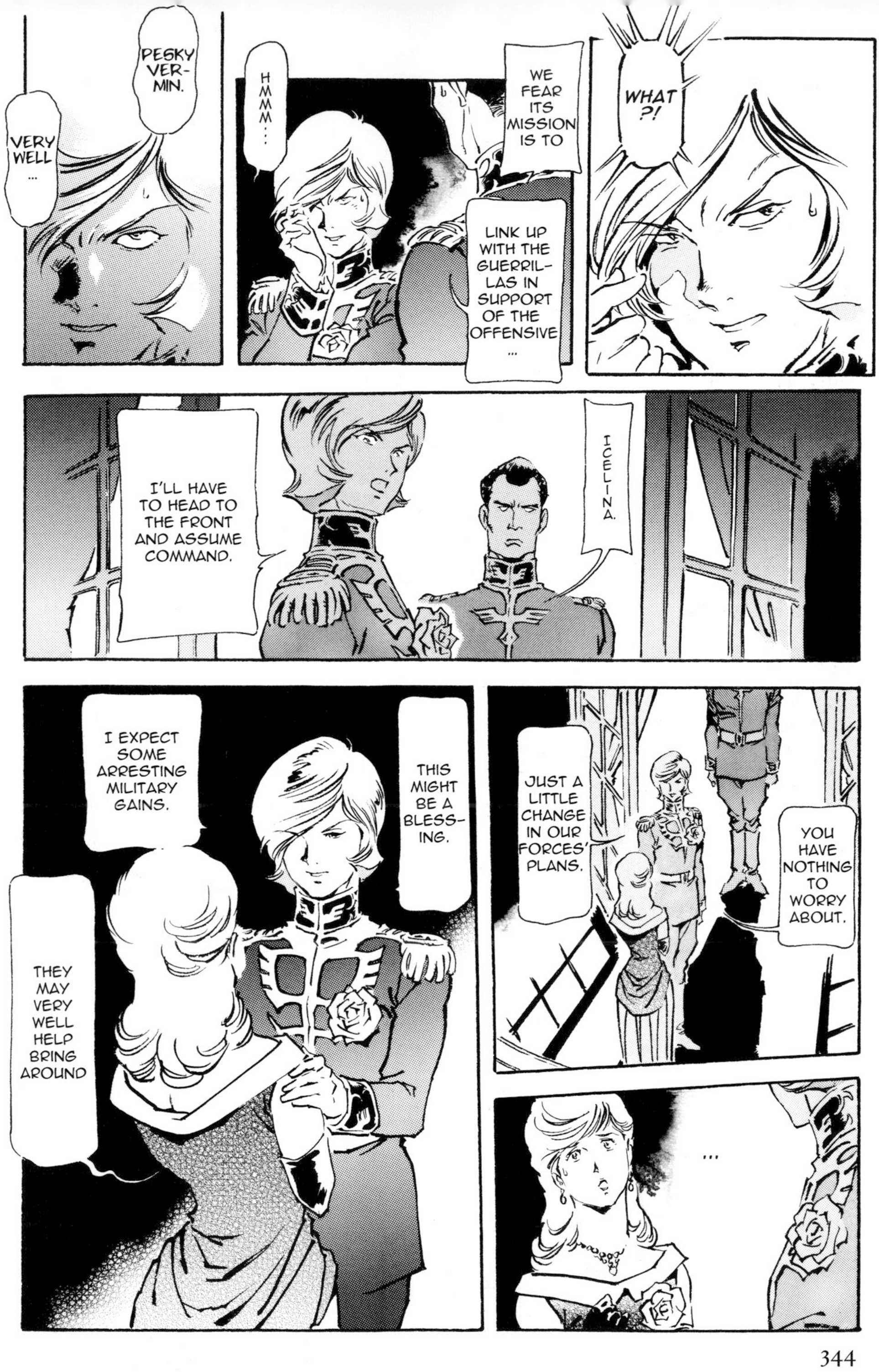
WHAT?!
WE FEAR ITS MISSION IS TO
LINK UP WITH THE GUERRILLAS IN SUPPORT OF THE OFFENSIVE...
HMMM...
PESKY VERMIN.
VERY WELL...
ICELINA.
I'LL HAVE TO HEAD TO THE FRONT AND ASSUME COMMAND.
YOU HAVE NOTHING TO WORRY ABOUT.
JUST A LITTLE CHANGE IN OUR FORCES' PLANS.
...
THIS MIGHT BE A BLESSING.
I EXPECT SOME ARRESTING MILITARY GAINS.
THEY MAY VERY WELL HELP BRING AROUND

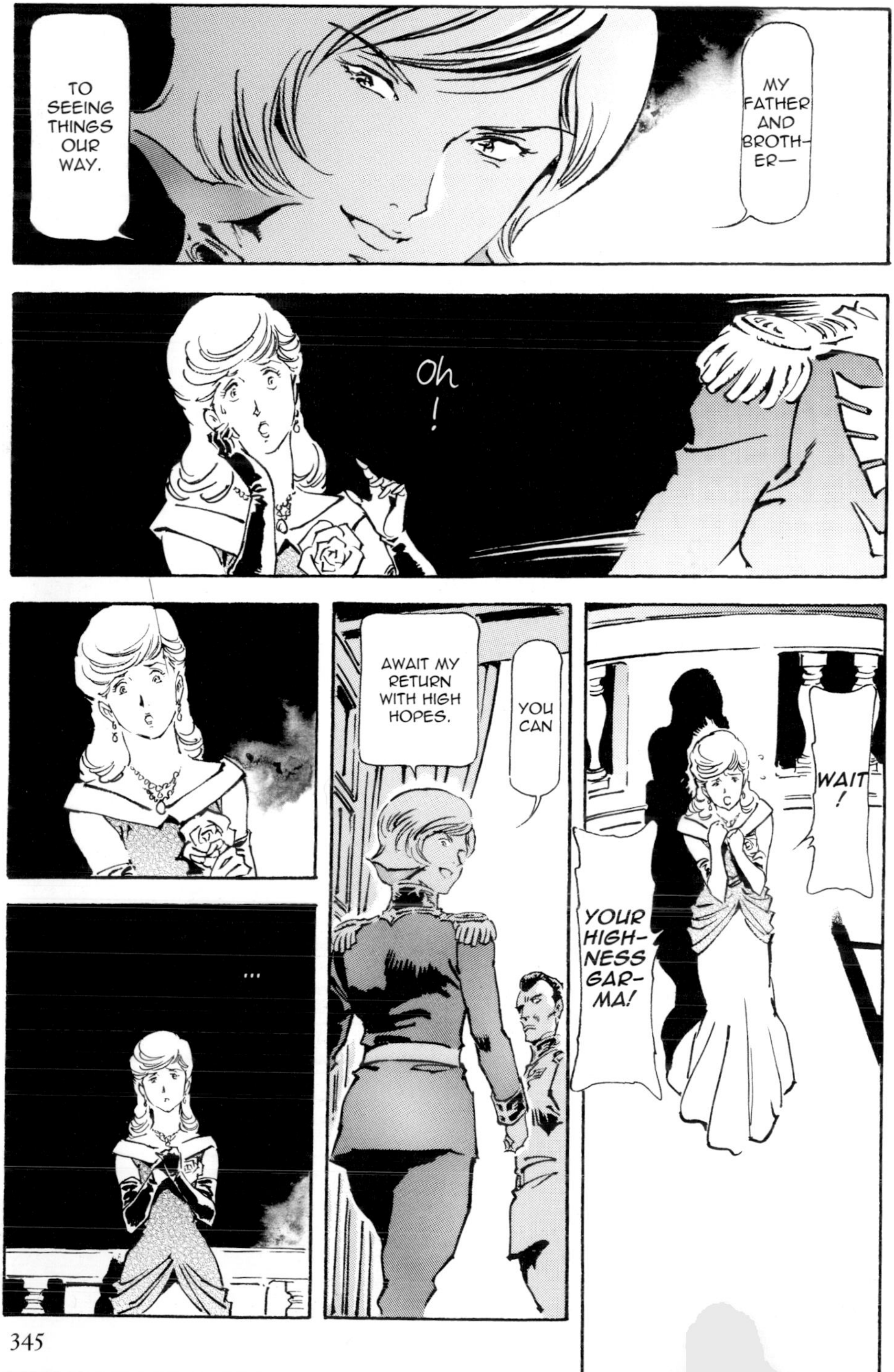
MY FATHER AND BROTH-ER—
TO SEEING THINGS OUR WAY.
Oh!
WAIT!
YOUR HIGH-NESS GAR-MA!
YOU CAN
AWAIT MY RETURN WITH HIGH HOPES.
...

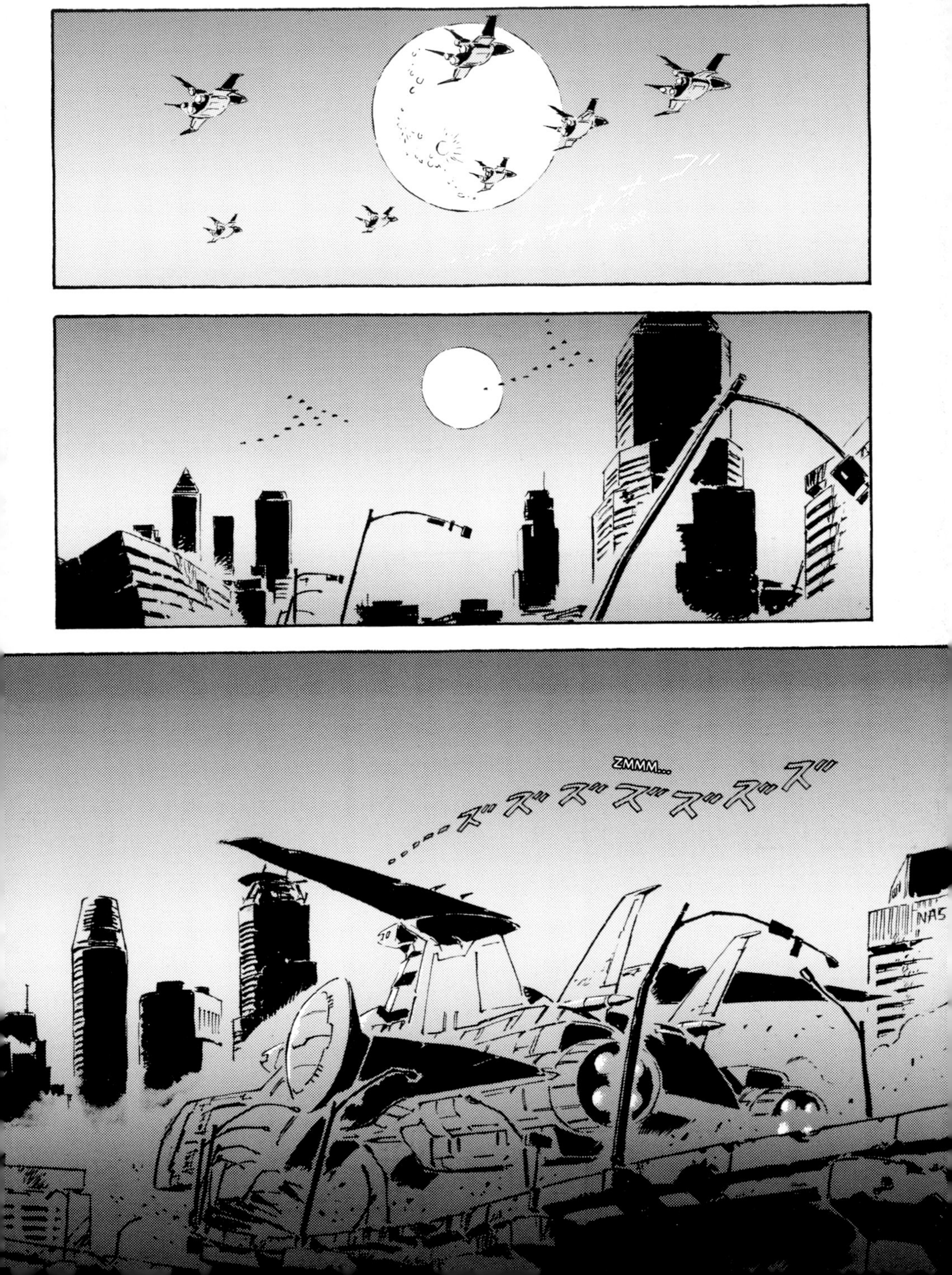
ZMMM...
ズズズズズズ

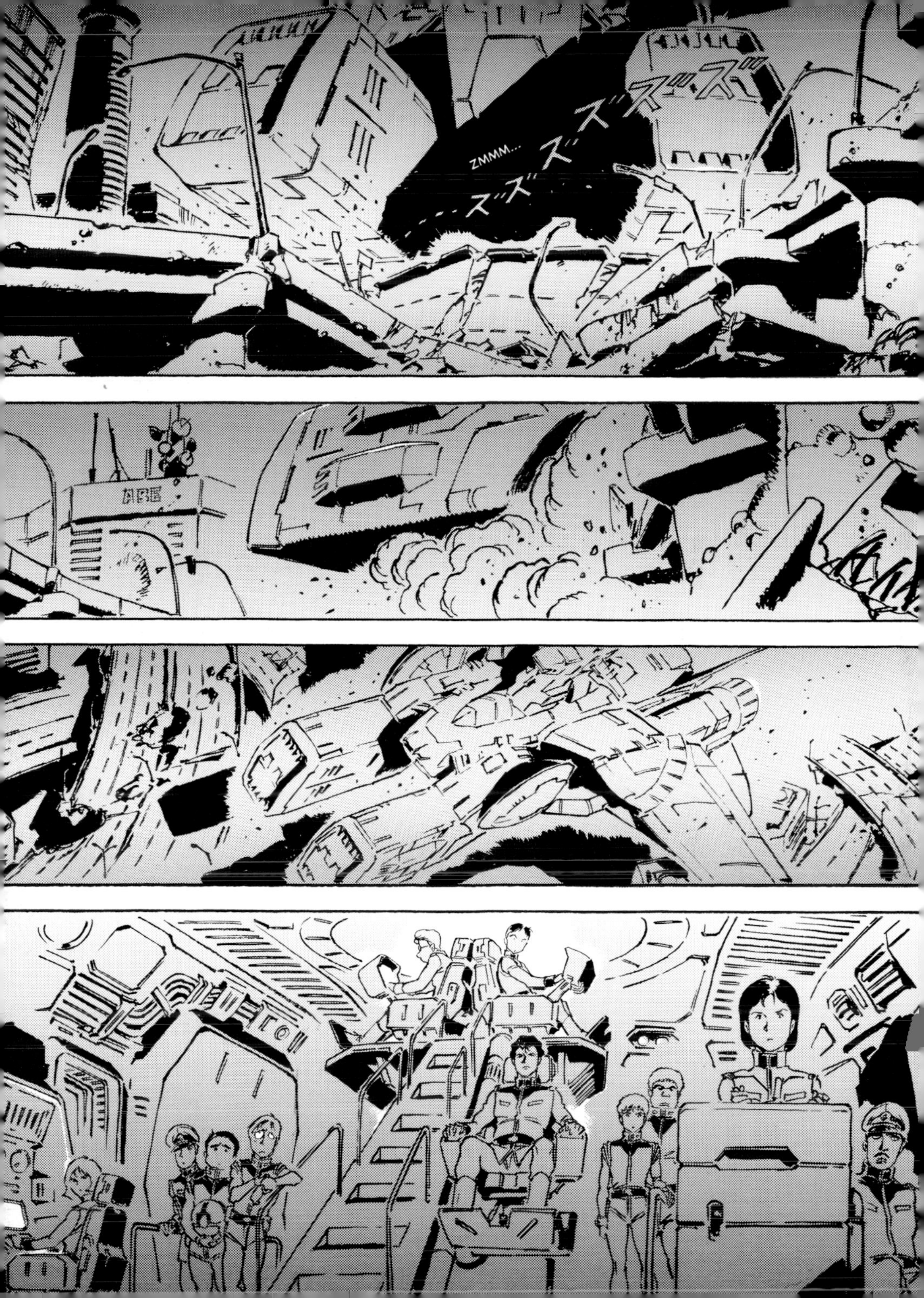
ズズズズズズ
ZMMM...

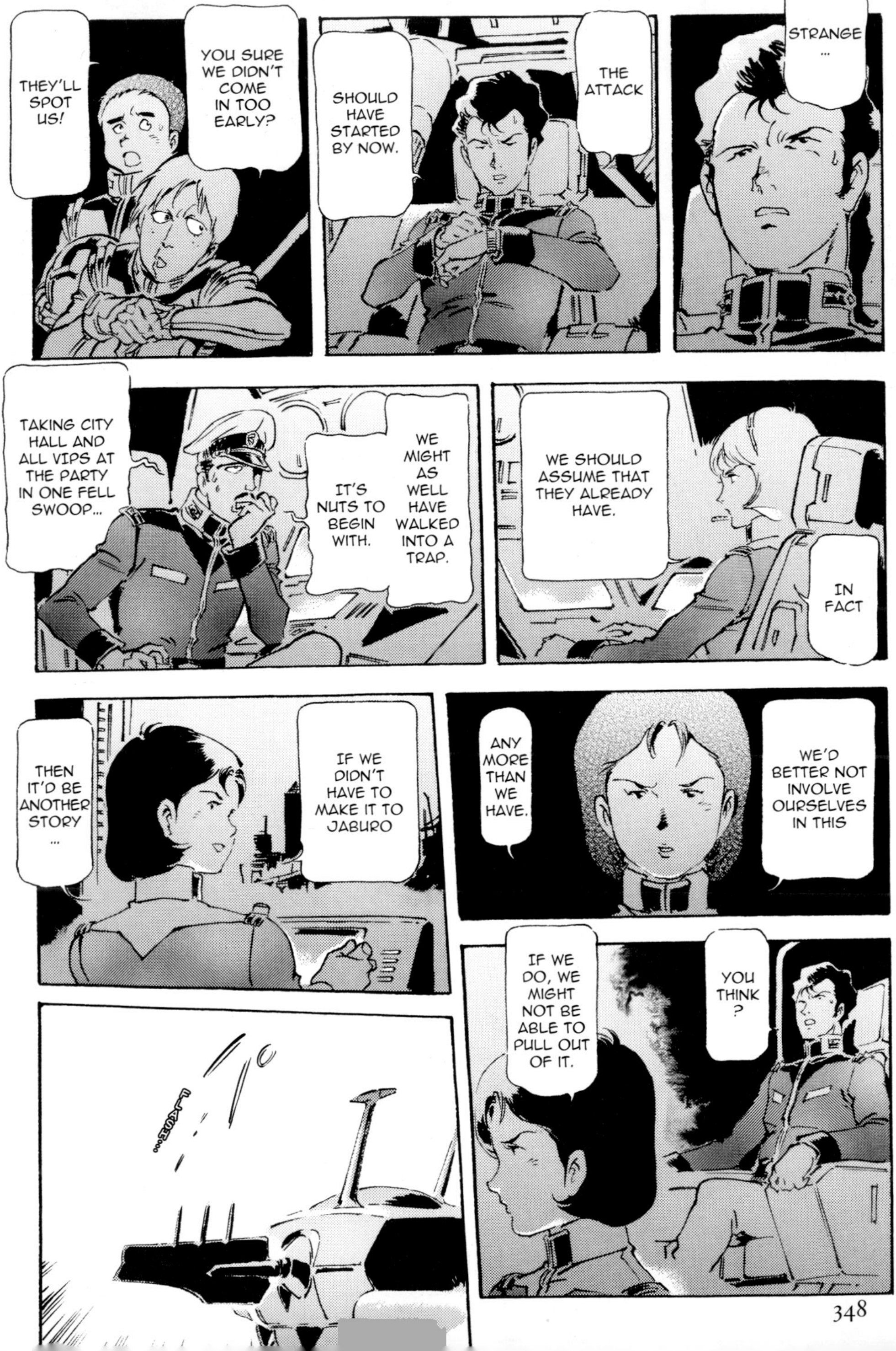
STRANGE ...
THE ATTACK
SHOULD HAVE STARTED BY NOW.
YOU SURE WE DIDN'T COME IN TOO EARLY?
THEY'LL SPOT US!
WE SHOULD ASSUME THAT THEY ALREADY HAVE.
IN FACT
TAKING CITY HALL AND ALL VIPS AT THE PARTY IN ONE FELL SWOOP...
IT'S NUTS TO BEGIN WITH.
WE MIGHT AS WELL HAVE WALKED INTO A TRAP.
WE'D BETTER NOT INVOLVE OURSELVES IN THIS
ANY MORE THAN WE HAVE.
IF WE DIDN'T HAVE TO MAKE IT TO JABURO
THEN IT'D BE ANOTHER STORY ...
YOU THINK ?
IF WE DO, WE MIGHT NOT BE ABLE TO PULL OUT OF IT.
FLASH...

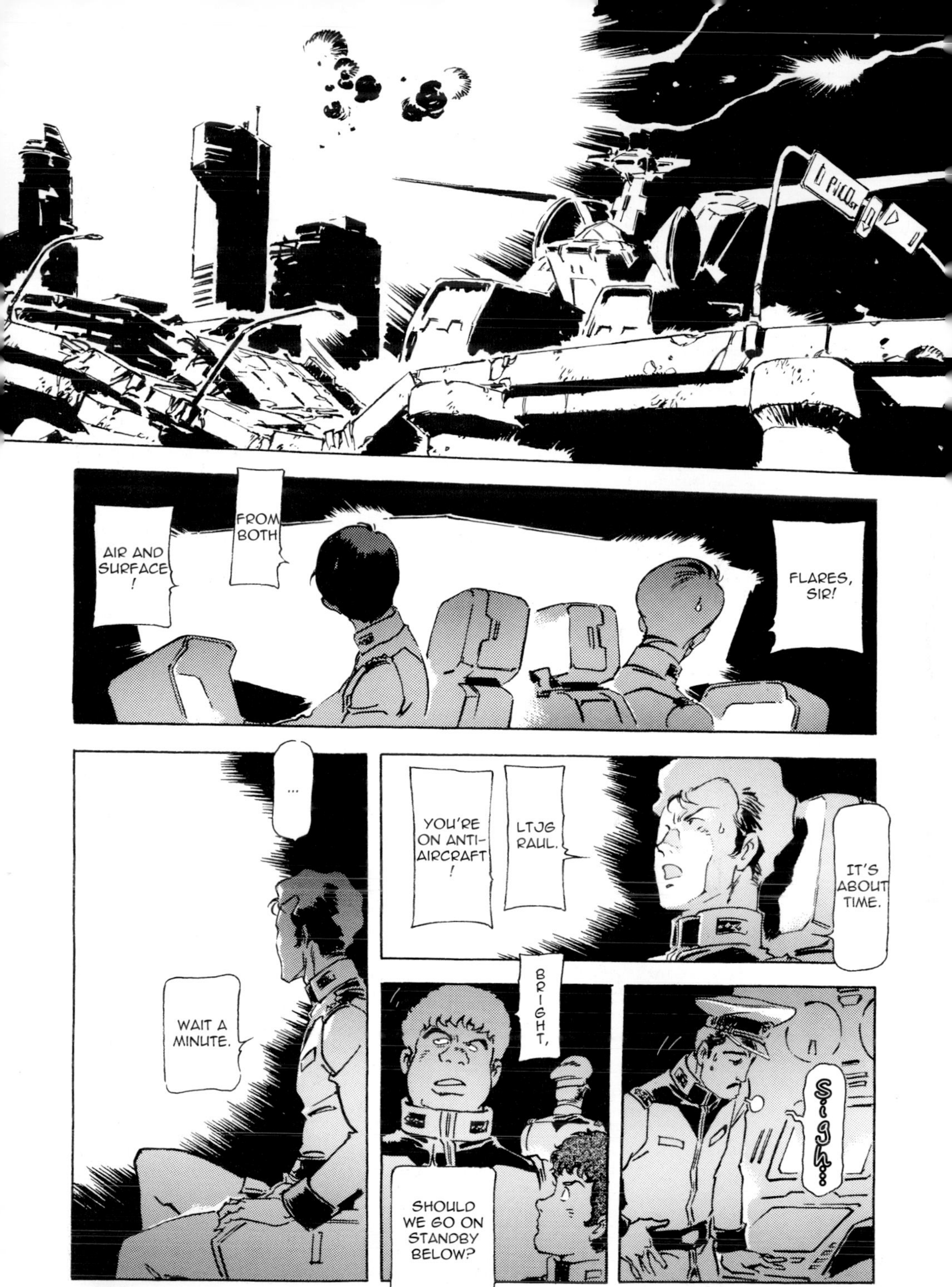
FLARES, SIR!
FROM BOTH
AIR AND SURFACE!
IT'S ABOUT TIME.
LTJG RAUL.
YOU'RE ON ANTI-AIRCRAFT!
Sigh...
BRIGHT,
SHOULD WE GO ON STANDBY BELOW?
...
WAIT A MINUTE.

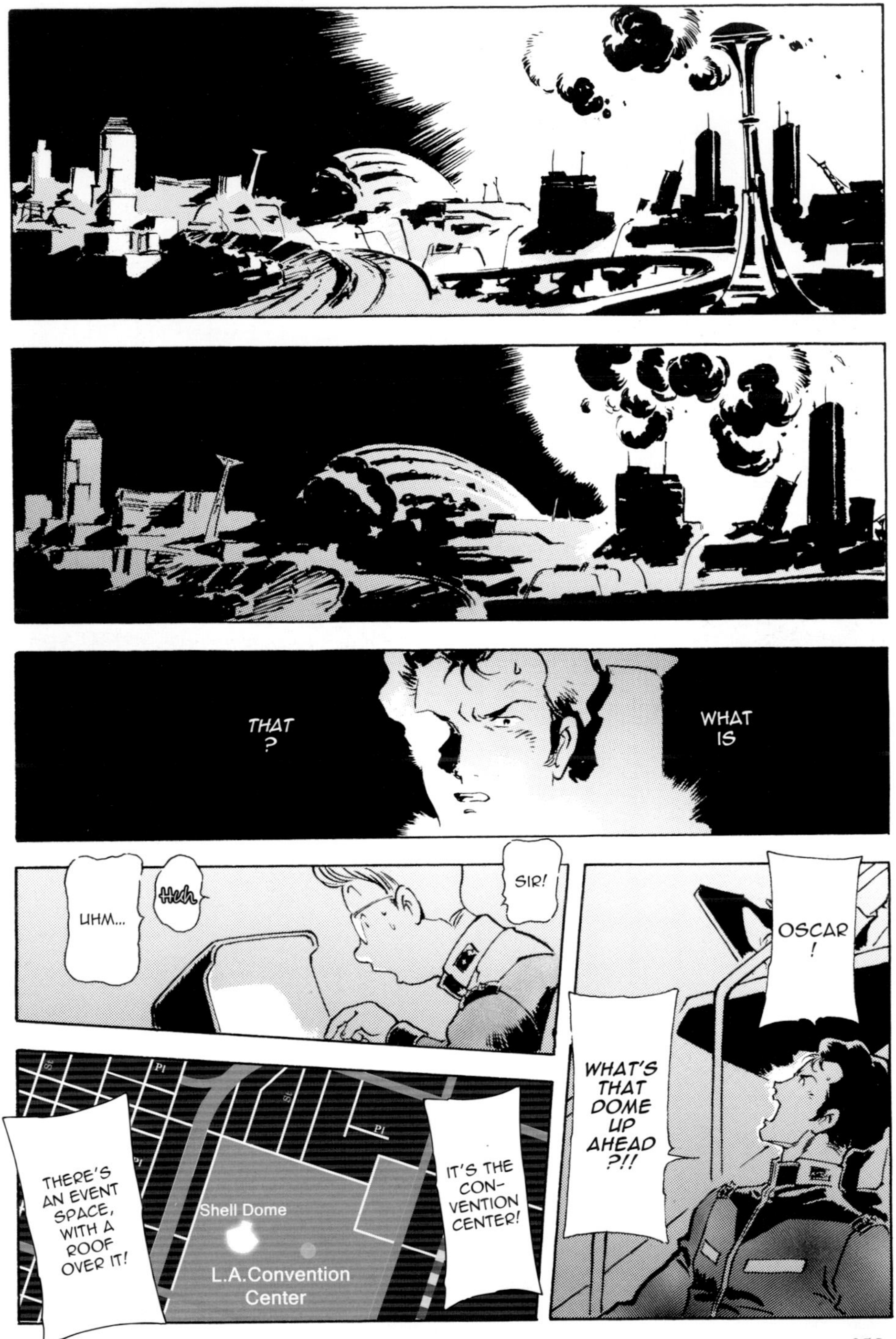
WHAT IS
THAT ?
OSCAR !
WHAT'S THAT DOME UP AHEAD ?!!
SIR!
Huh
UHM...
IT'S THE CON-VENTION CENTER!
THERE'S AN EVENT SPACE, WITH A ROOF OVER IT!
Shell Dome
L.A.Convention Center

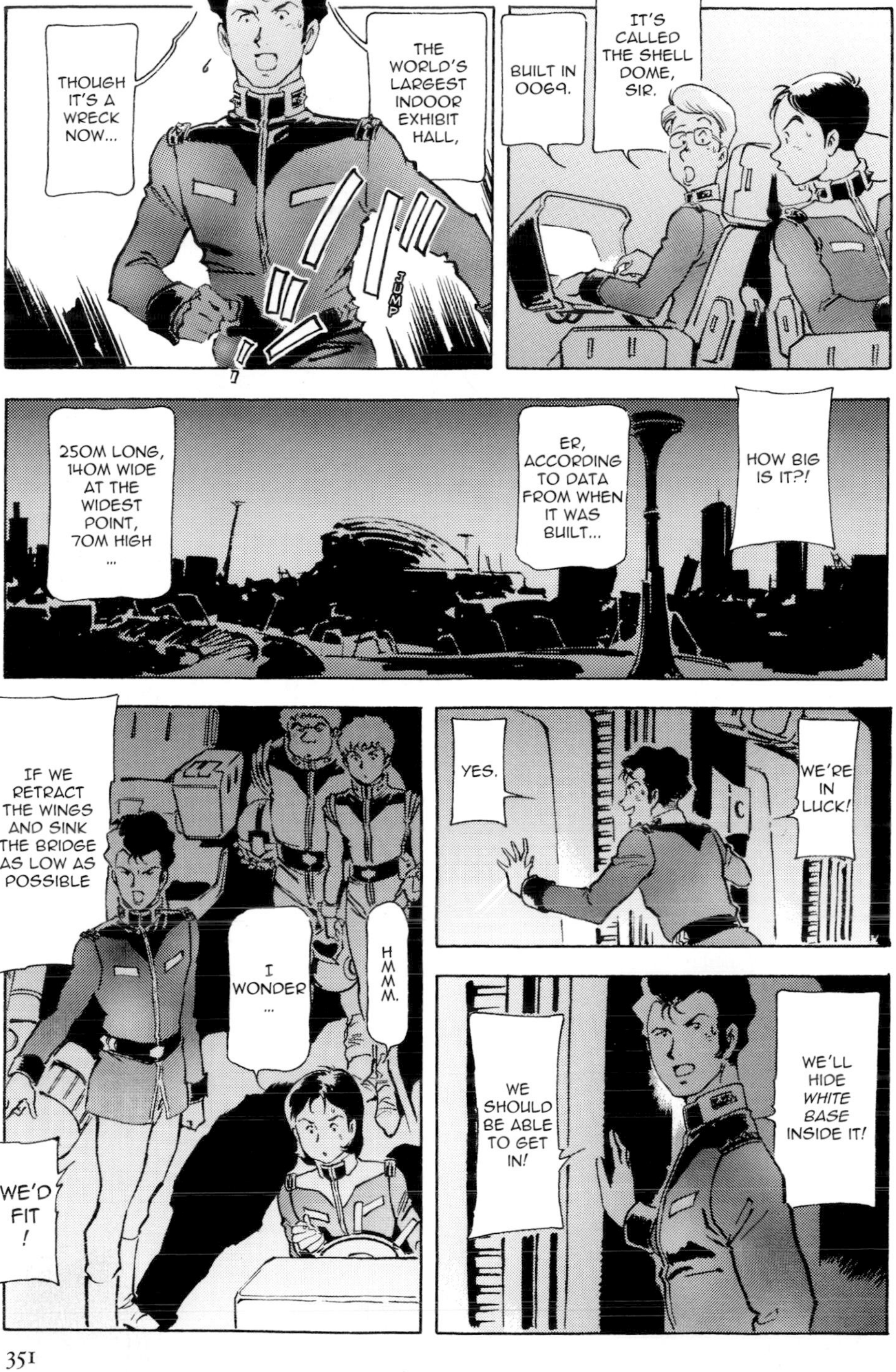
IT'S CALLED THE SHELL DOME, SIR.
BUILT IN 0069.
THE WORLD'S LARGEST INDOOR EXHIBIT HALL,
THOUGH IT'S A WRECK NOW...
JUMP
HOW BIG IS IT?!
ER, ACCORDING TO DATA FROM WHEN IT WAS BUILT...
250M LONG, 140M WIDE AT THE WIDEST POINT, 70M HIGH ...
WE'RE IN LUCK!
YES.
WE'LL HIDE *WHITE BASE* INSIDE IT!
WE SHOULD BE ABLE TO GET IN!
IF WE RETRACT THE WINGS AND SINK THE BRIDGE AS LOW AS POSSIBLE
HMMM.
I WONDER ...
WE'D FIT !

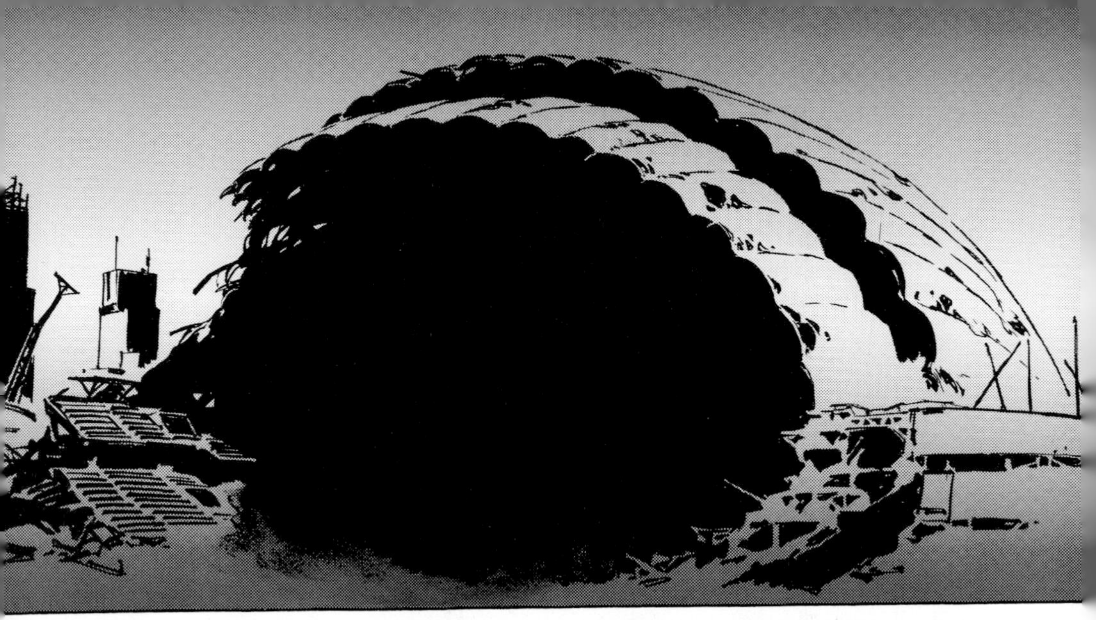

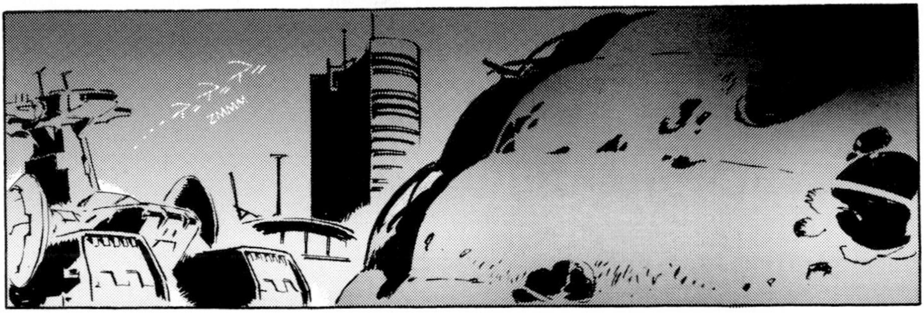
ZMMM

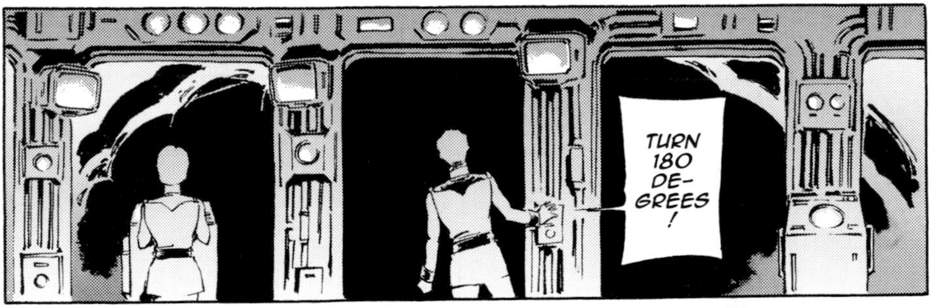
TURN 180 DE- GREES !

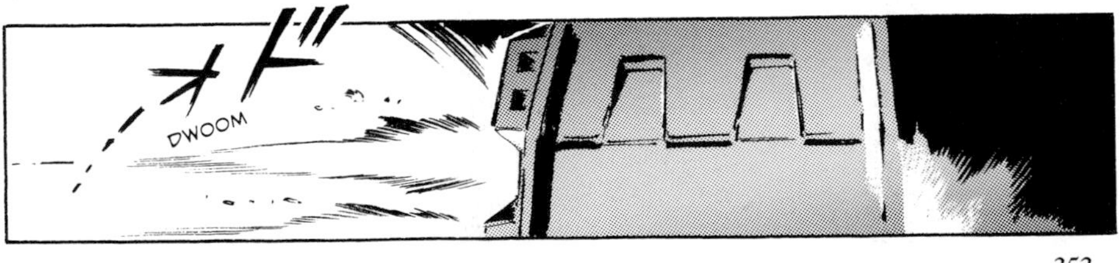
DWOOM

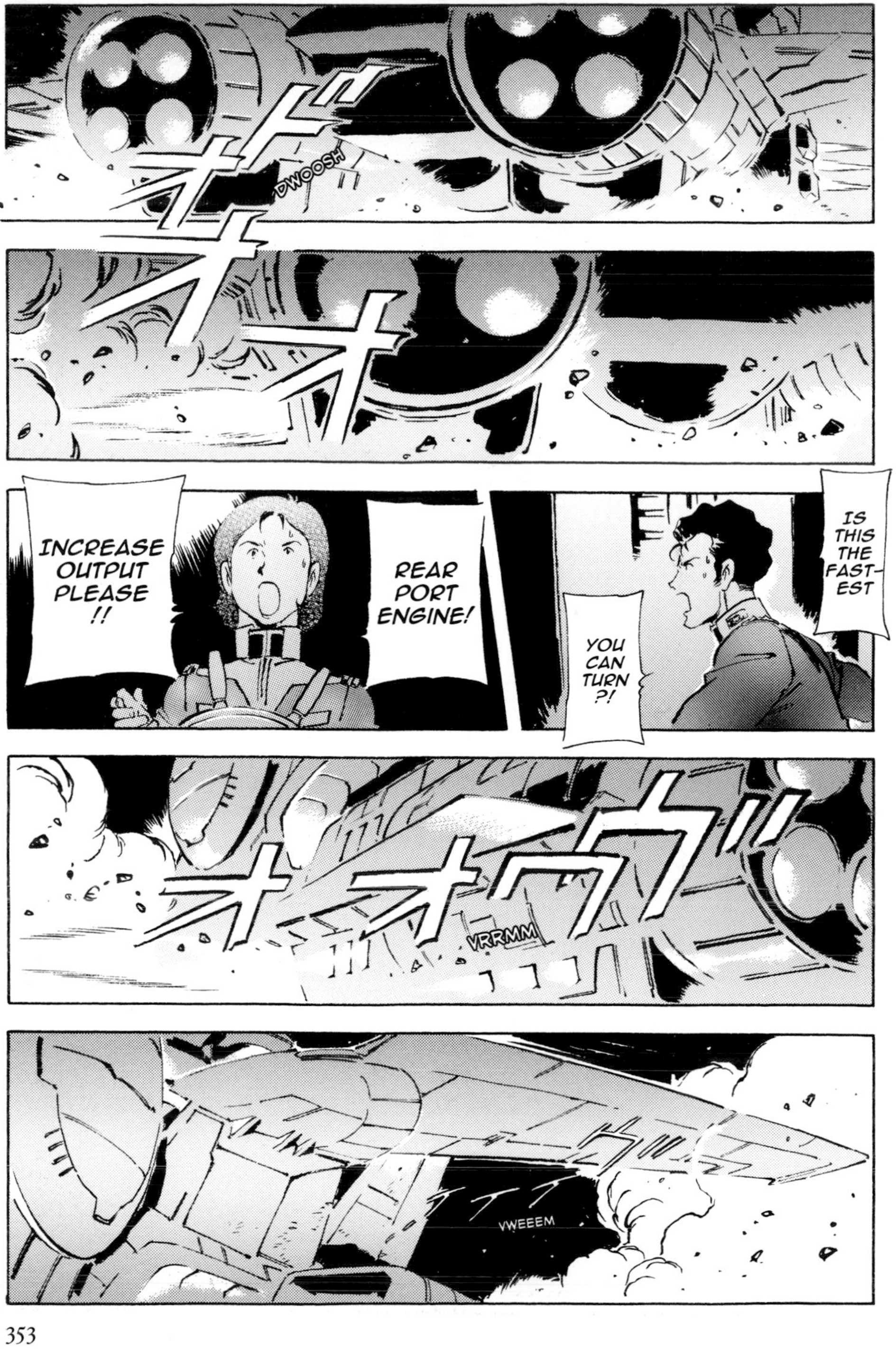
DWOOSH
IS THIS THE FAST-EST
YOU CAN TURN ?!
REAR PORT ENGINE!
INCREASE OUTPUT PLEASE !!
VRRMM
VWEEEM

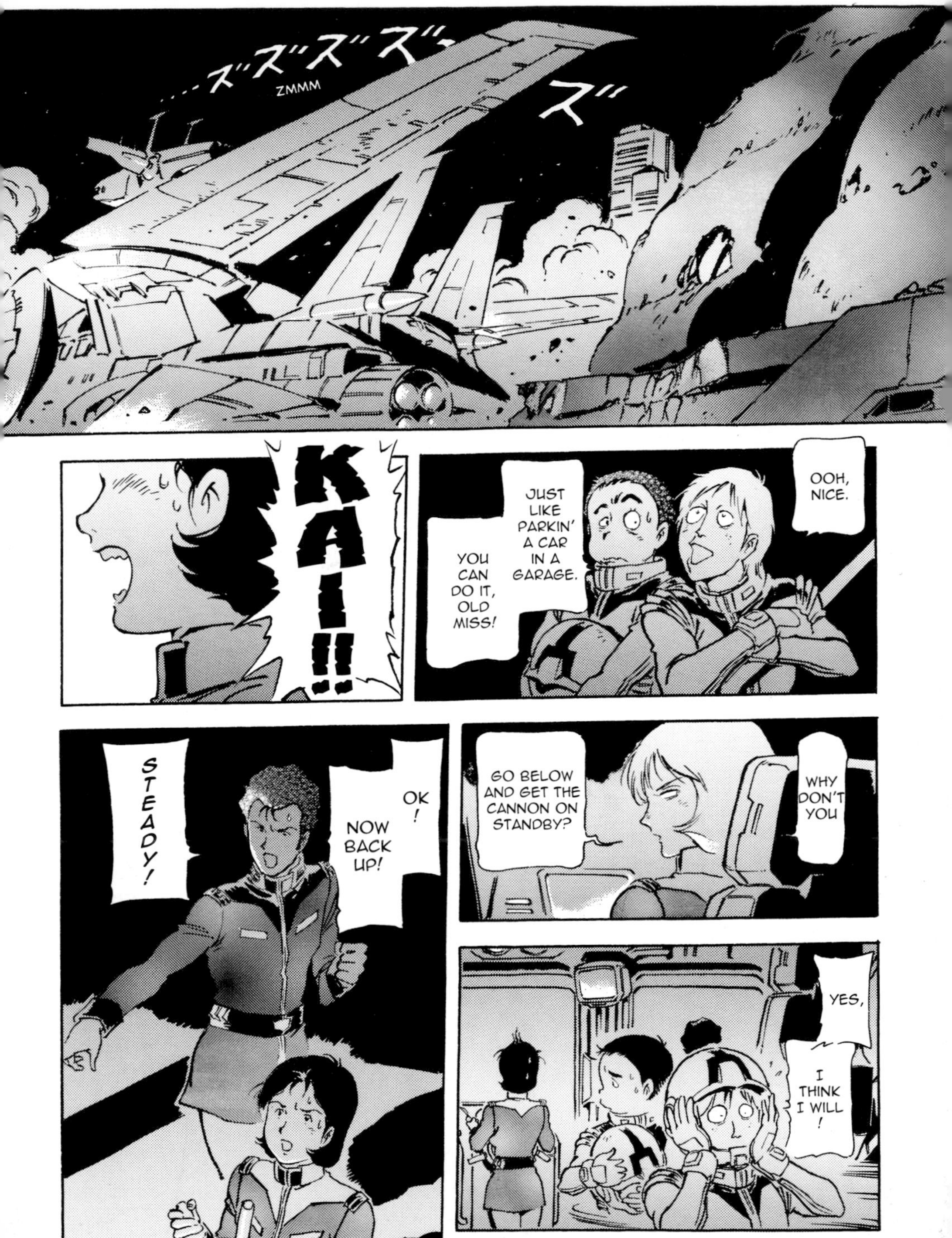
…ズズズズ
ZMMM
ズ
OOH, NICE.
JUST LIKE PARKIN' A CAR IN A GARAGE.
YOU CAN DO IT, OLD MISS!
KAI!!
WHY DON'T YOU
GO BELOW AND GET THE CANNON ON STANDBY?
YES,
I THINK I WILL!
OK!
NOW BACK UP!
STEADY!

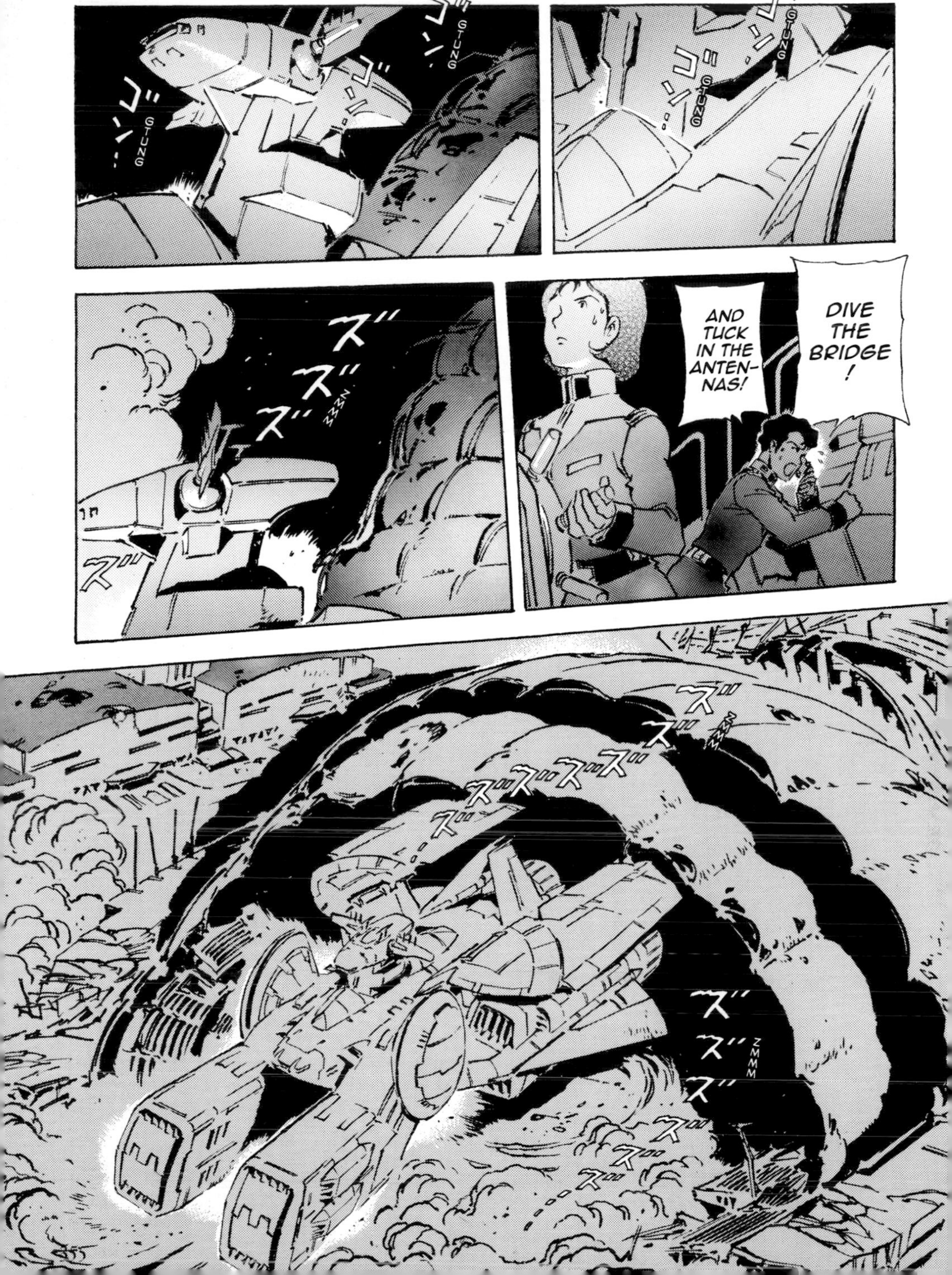
GTUNG
GTUNG
GTUNG
GTUNG
GTUNG
DIVE THE BRIDGE!
AND TUCK IN THE ANTEN-NAS!
ZMMM
ZMMM
ZMMM

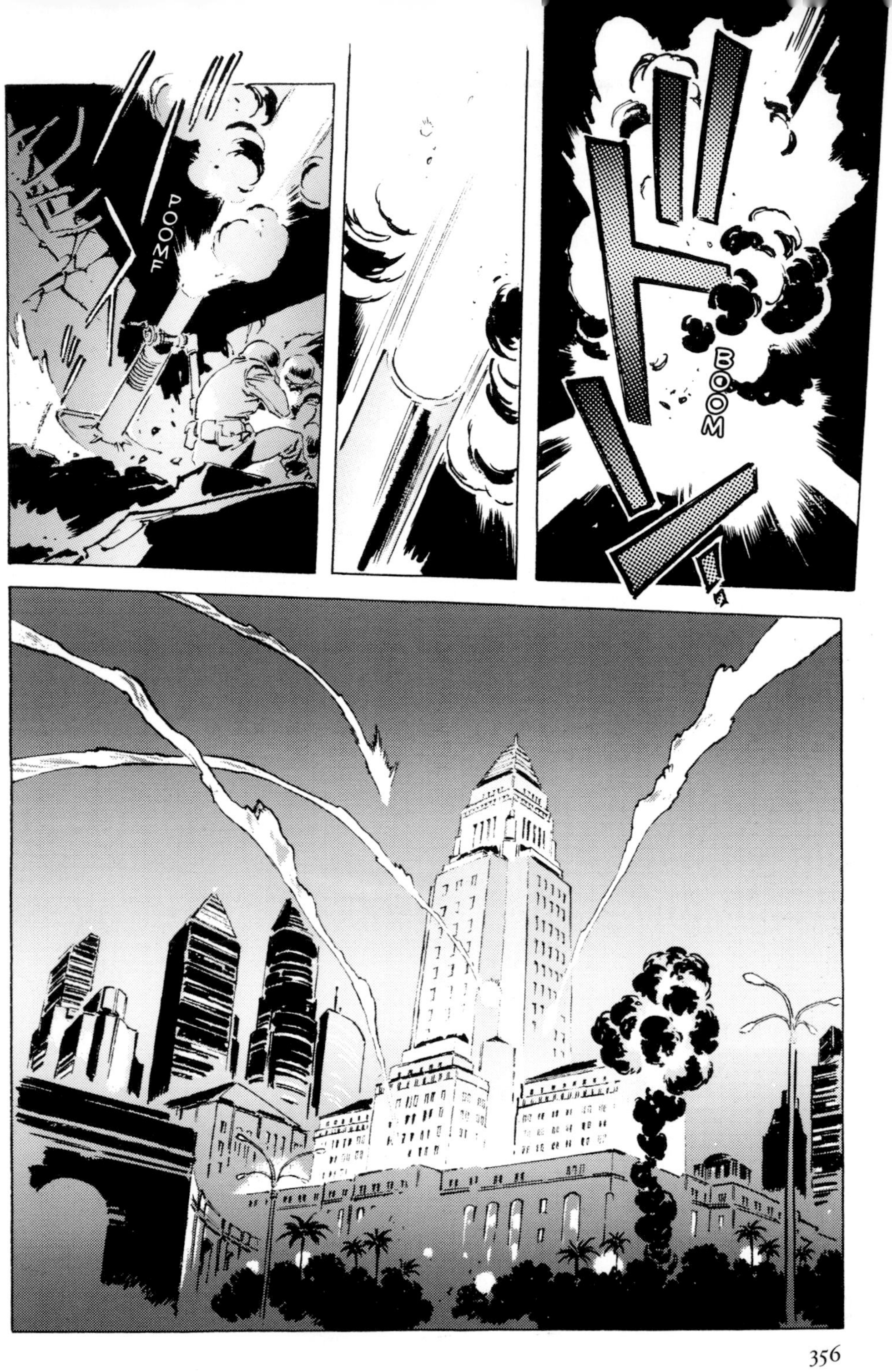
BOOM
POOMF

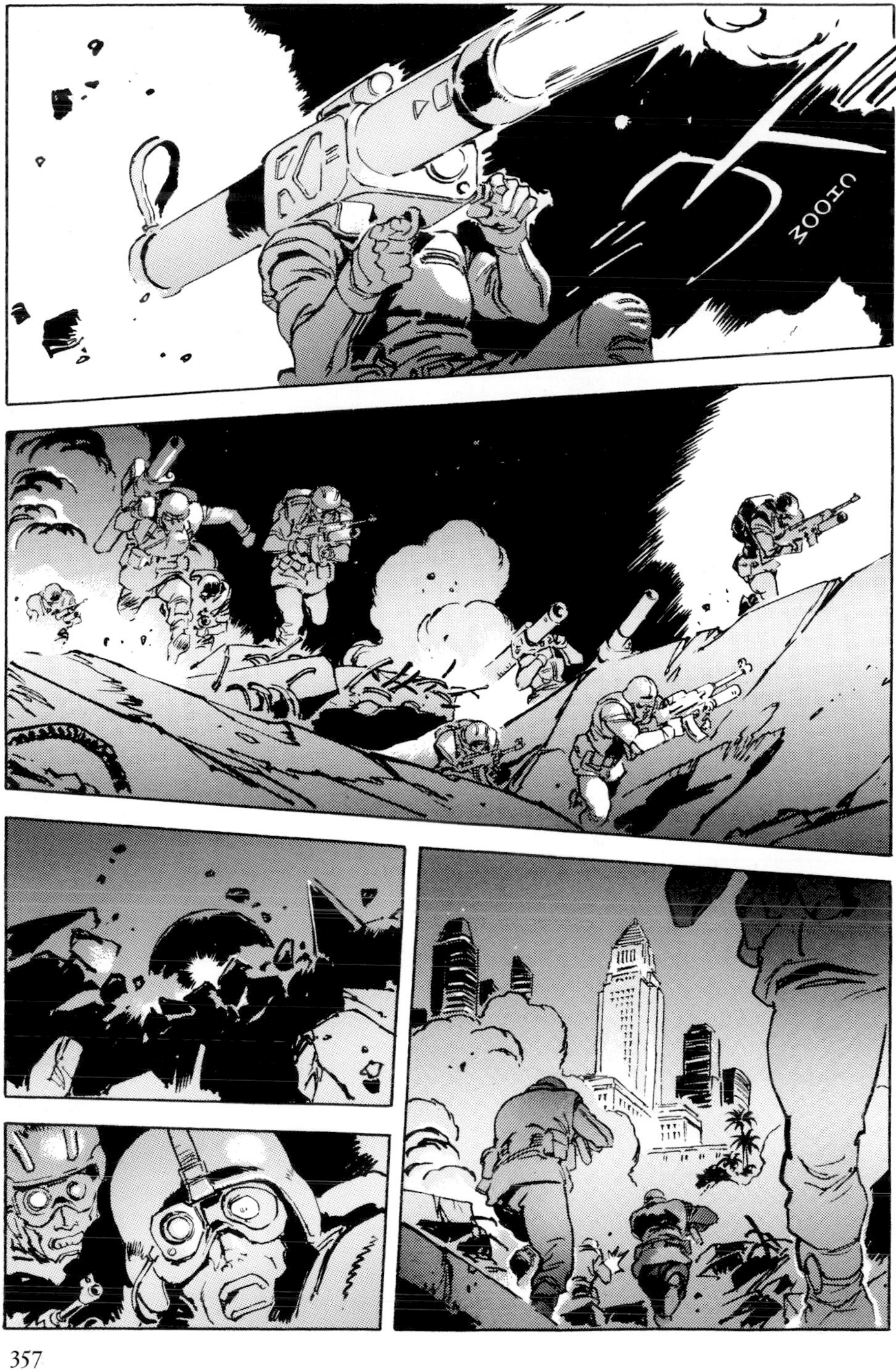
CHOOM

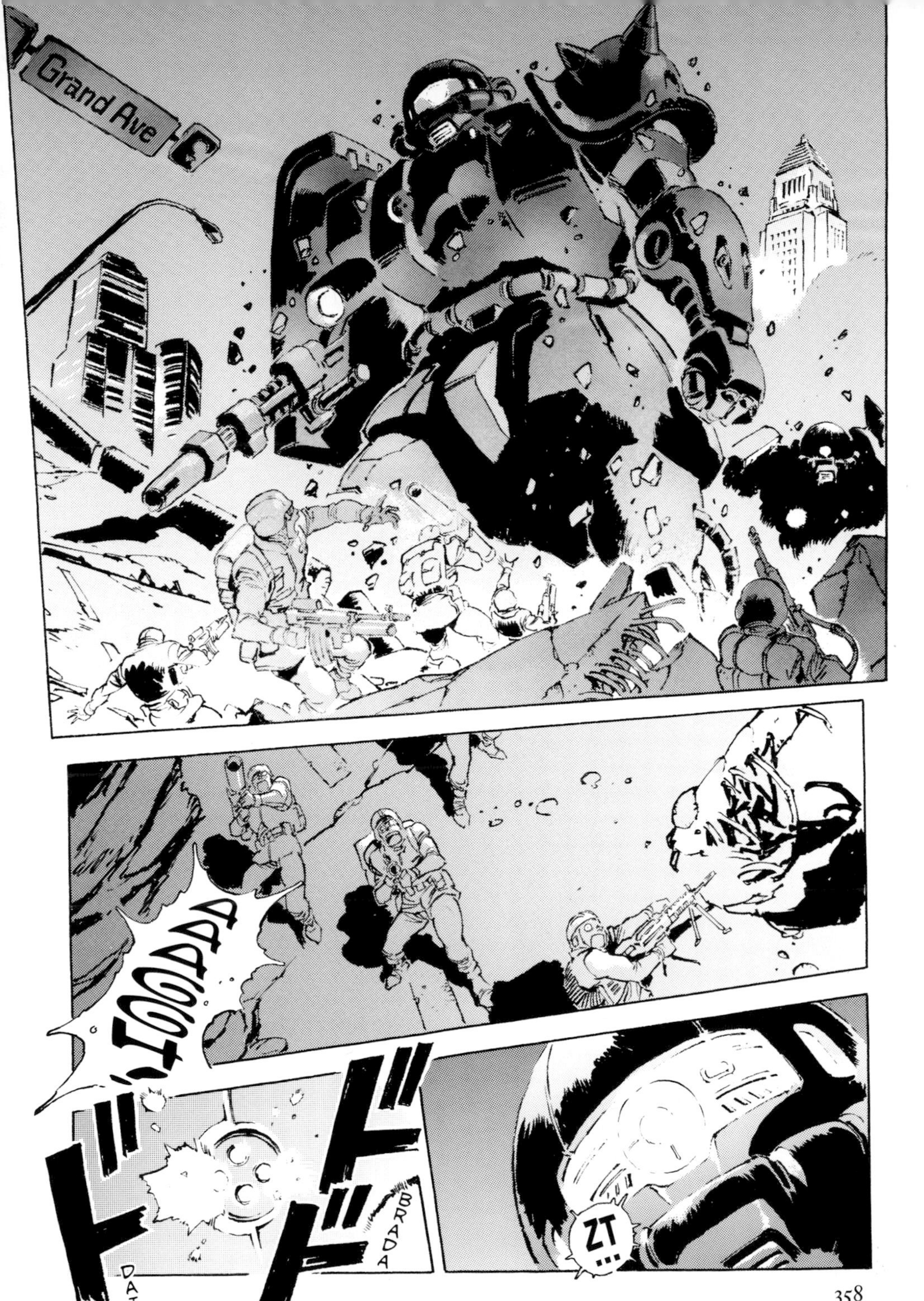

Grand Ave
DDDOOOT!!
ZT...
ドドドド
BRADA
DAT

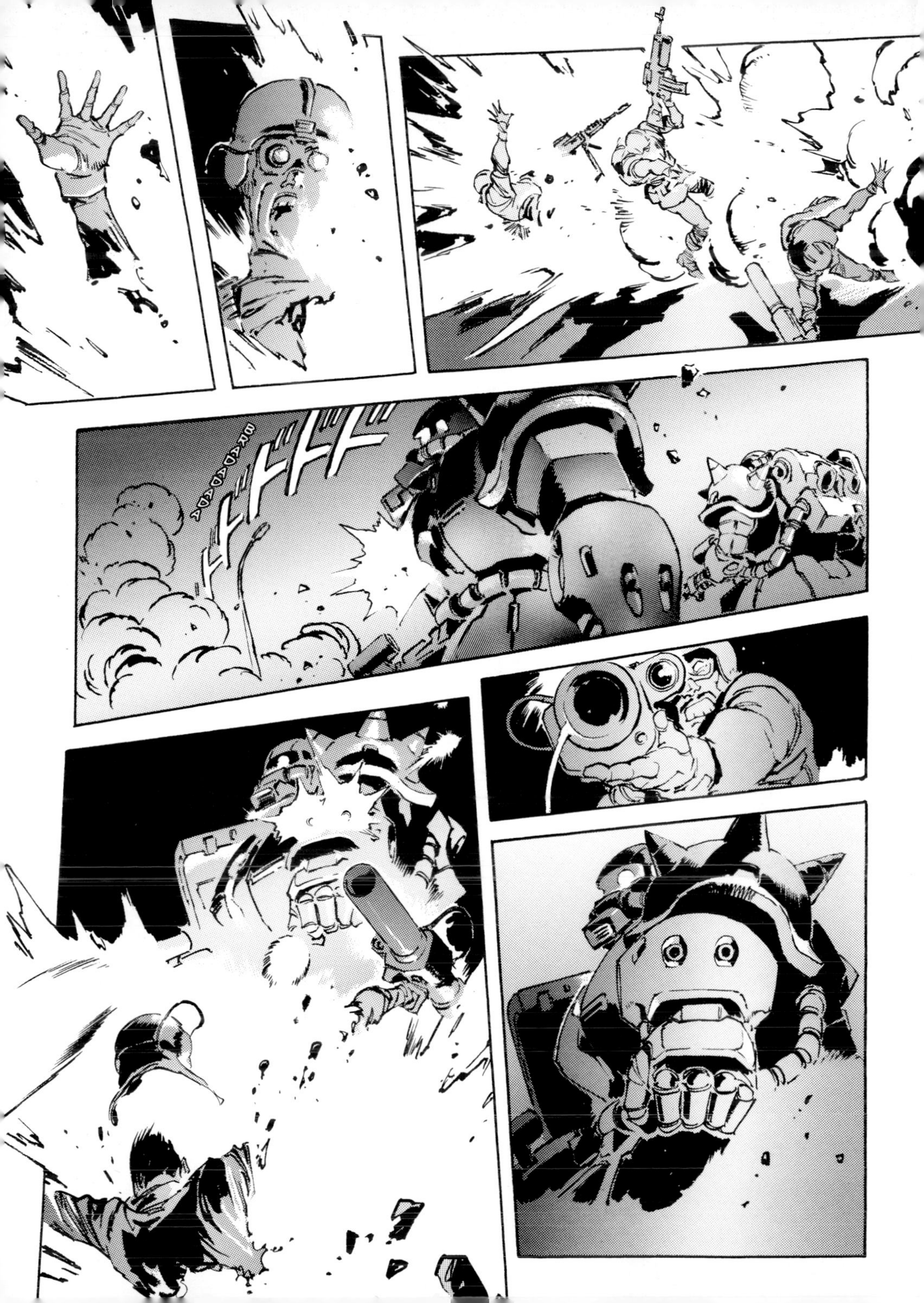
ドドドドドッ
BRADADADA

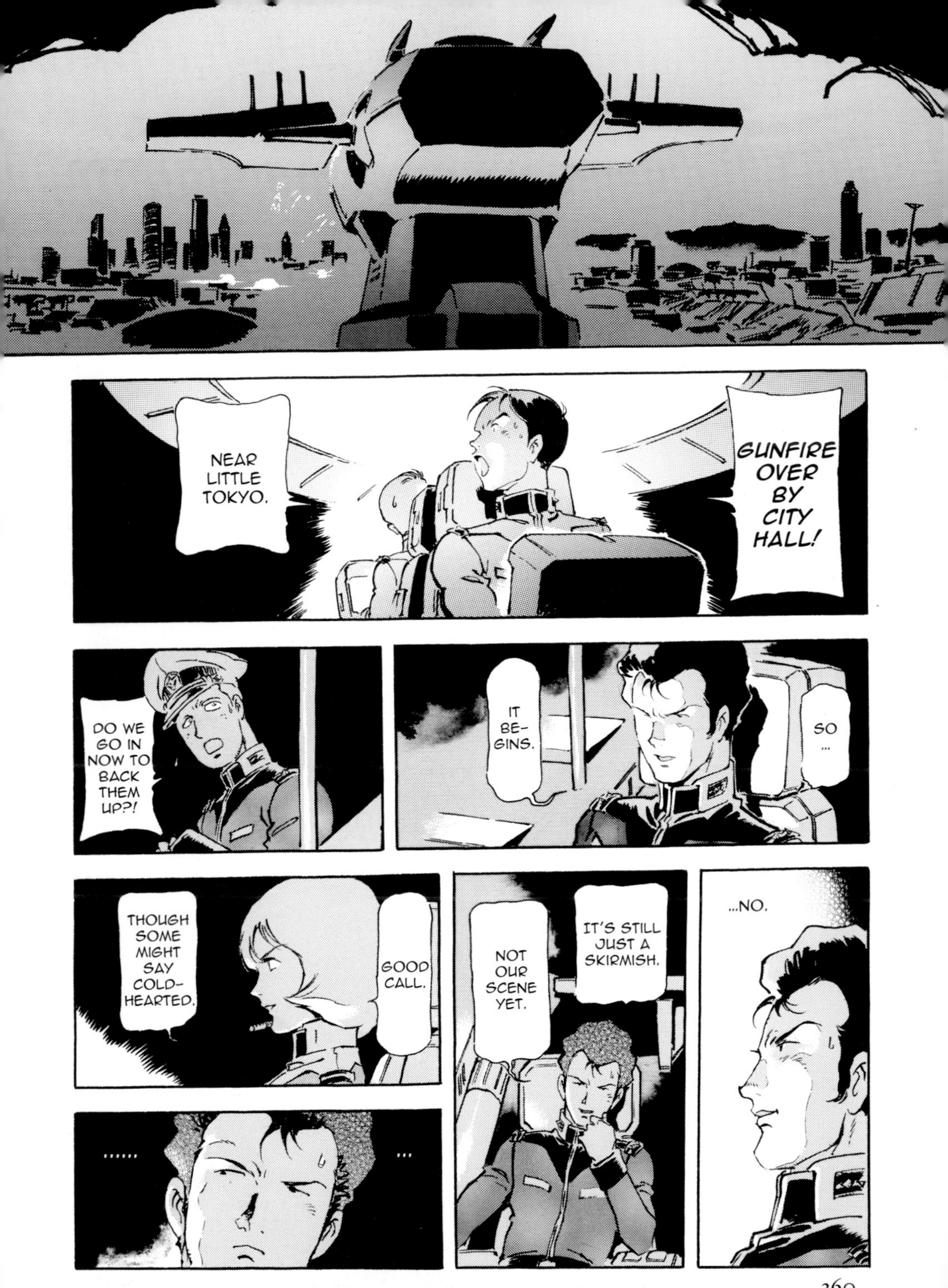
GUNFIRE OVER BY CITY HALL!
NEAR LITTLE TOKYO.
SO ...
IT BE-GINS.
DO WE GO IN NOW TO BACK THEM UP?!
...NO.
IT'S STILL JUST A SKIRMISH.
NOT OUR SCENE YET.
GOOD CALL.
THOUGH SOME MIGHT SAY COLD-HEARTED.
...
......

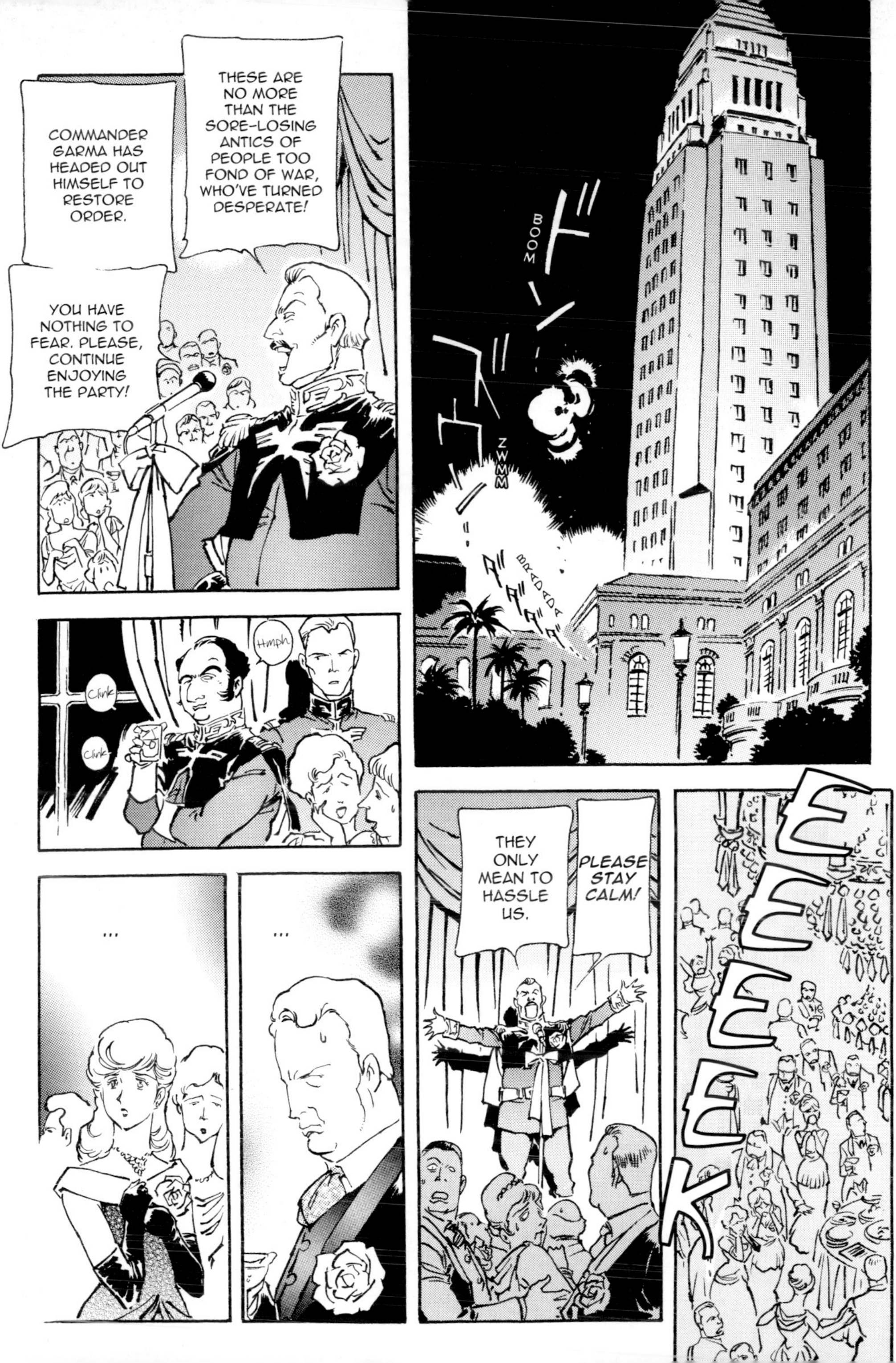
BOOM
ZWMM
BRADADA
THESE ARE NO MORE THAN THE SORE-LOSING ANTICS OF PEOPLE TOO FOND OF WAR, WHO'VE TURNED DESPERATE!
COMMANDER GARMA HAS HEADED OUT HIMSELF TO RESTORE ORDER.
YOU HAVE NOTHING TO FEAR. PLEASE, CONTINUE ENJOYING THE PARTY!
Hmph
Clink
Clink
EEEEEK
PLEASE STAY CALM!
THEY ONLY MEAN TO HASSLE US.
...
...

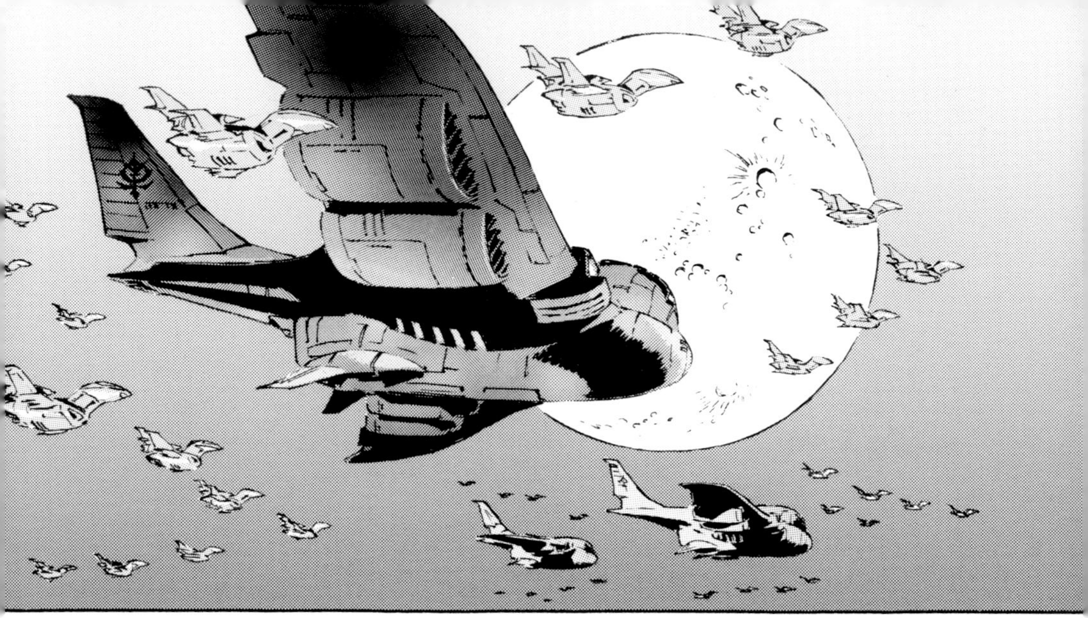

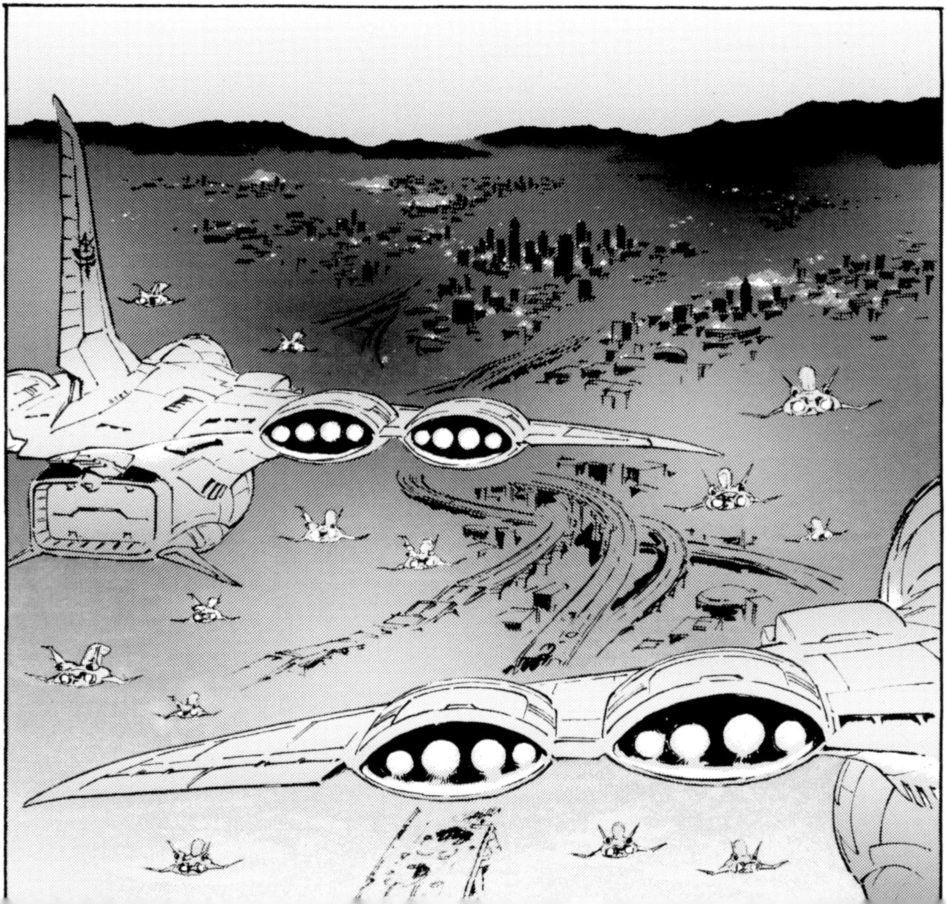

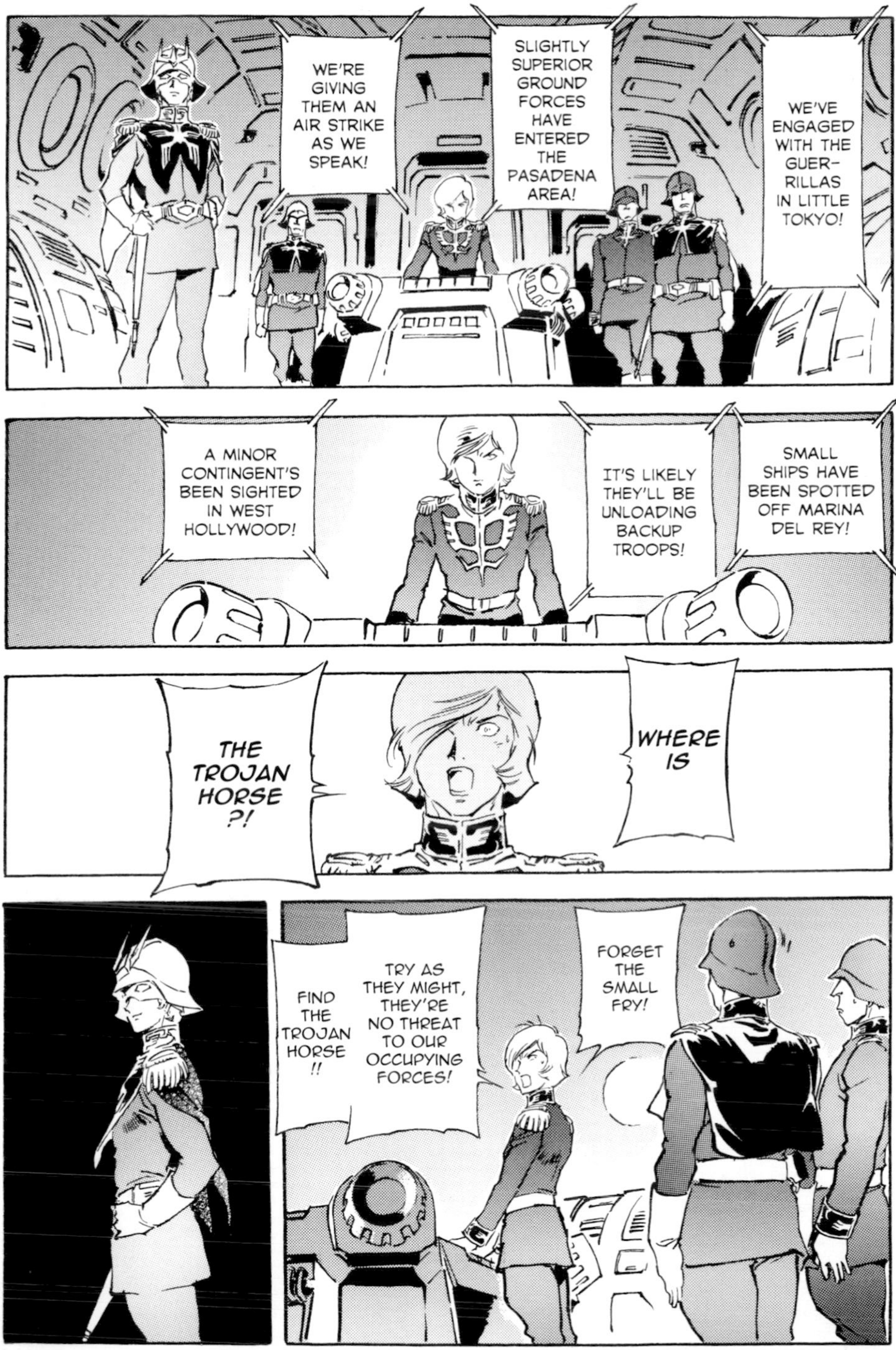
WE'VE ENGAGED WITH THE GUER-RILLAS IN LITTLE TOKYO!
SLIGHTLY SUPERIOR GROUND FORCES HAVE ENTERED THE PASADENA AREA!
WE'RE GIVING THEM AN AIR STRIKE AS WE SPEAK!
SMALL SHIPS HAVE BEEN SPOTTED OFF MARINA DEL REY!
IT'S LIKELY THEY'LL BE UNLOADING BACKUP TROOPS!
A MINOR CONTINGENT'S BEEN SIGHTED IN WEST HOLLYWOOD!
WHERE IS
THE TROJAN HORSE ?!
FORGET THE SMALL FRY!
TRY AS THEY MIGHT, THEY'RE NO THREAT TO OUR OCCUPYING FORCES!
FIND THE TROJAN HORSE !!

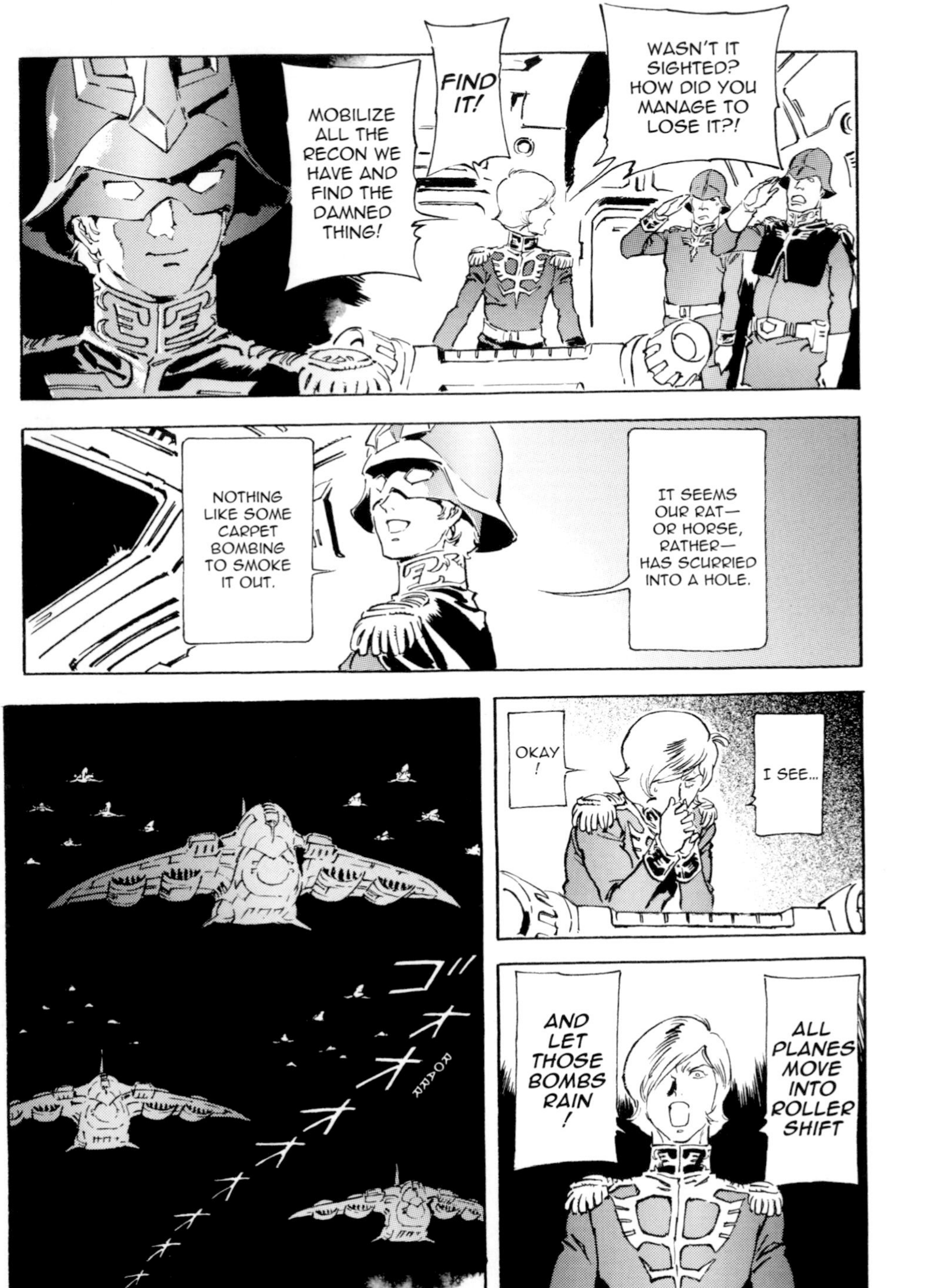
WASN'T IT SIGHTED? HOW DID YOU MANAGE TO LOSE IT?!
FIND IT!
MOBILIZE ALL THE RECON WE HAVE AND FIND THE DAMNED THING!
IT SEEMS OUR RAT— OR HORSE, RATHER— HAS SCURRIED INTO A HOLE.
NOTHING LIKE SOME CARPET BOMBING TO SMOKE IT OUT.
I SEE...
OKAY!
ALL PLANES MOVE INTO ROLLER SHIFT
AND LET THOSE BOMBS RAIN!
ROARR

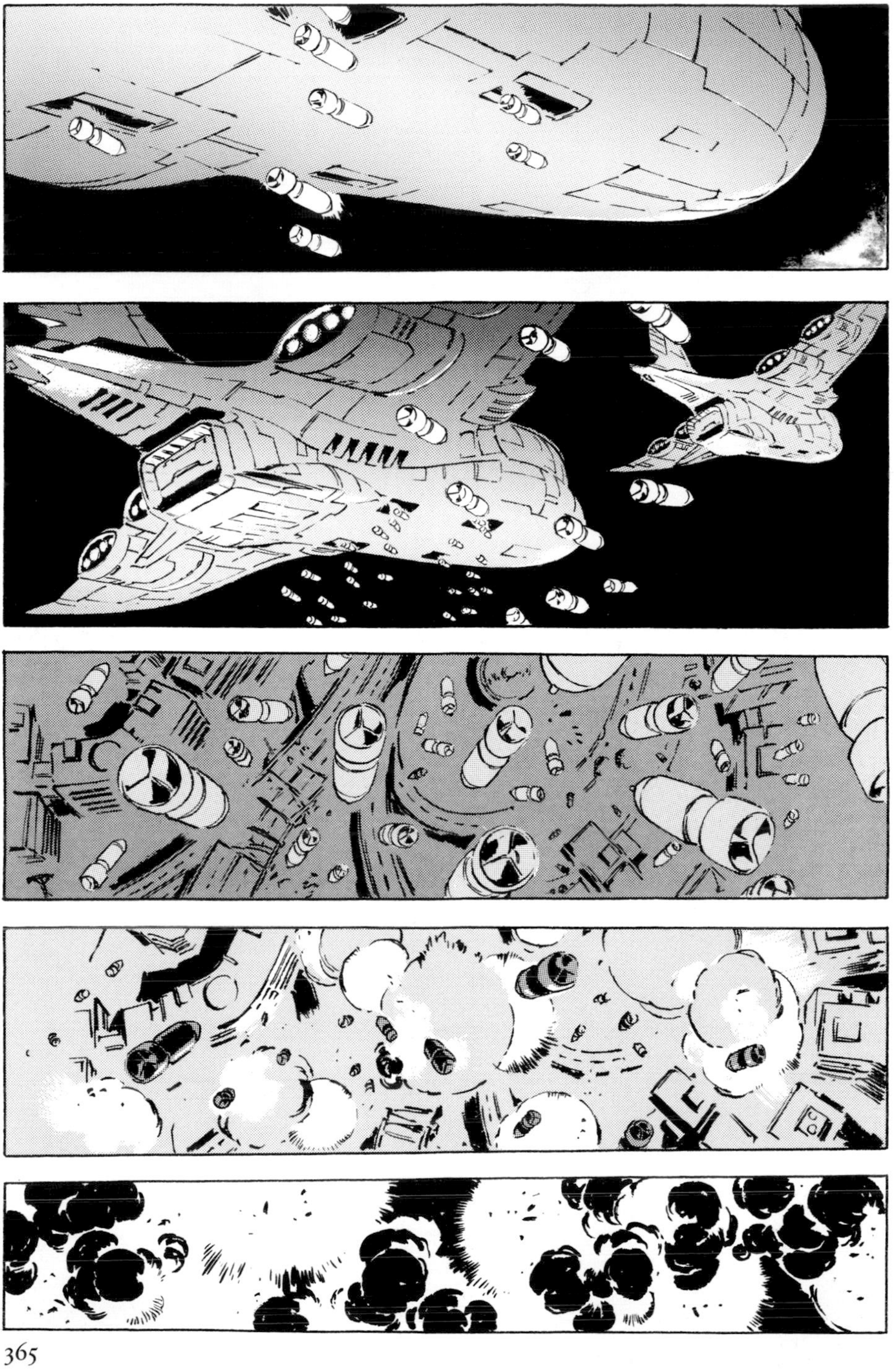

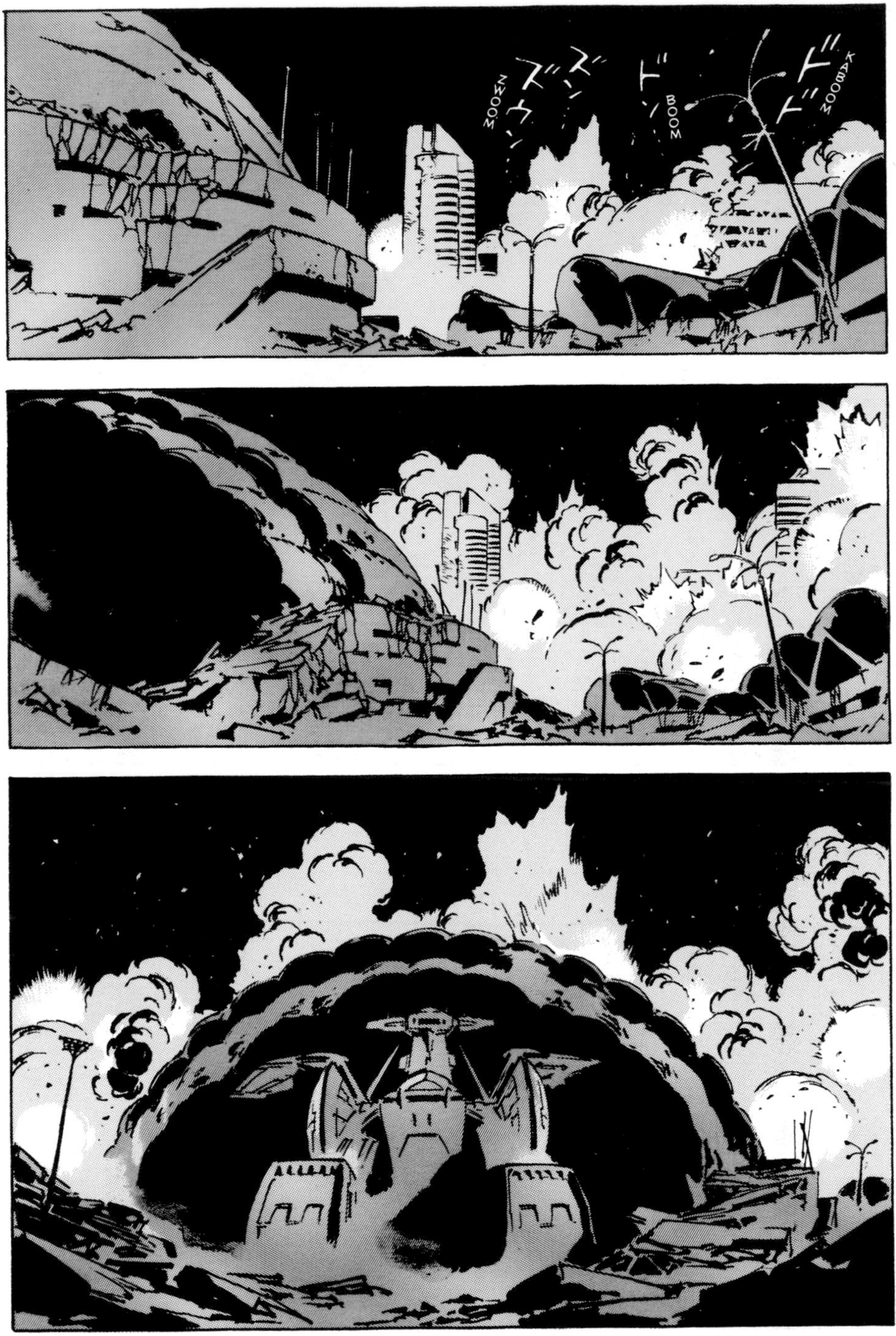
ドド
KABOOM
ドン
BOOM
ズン
ズウン
ZWOOM

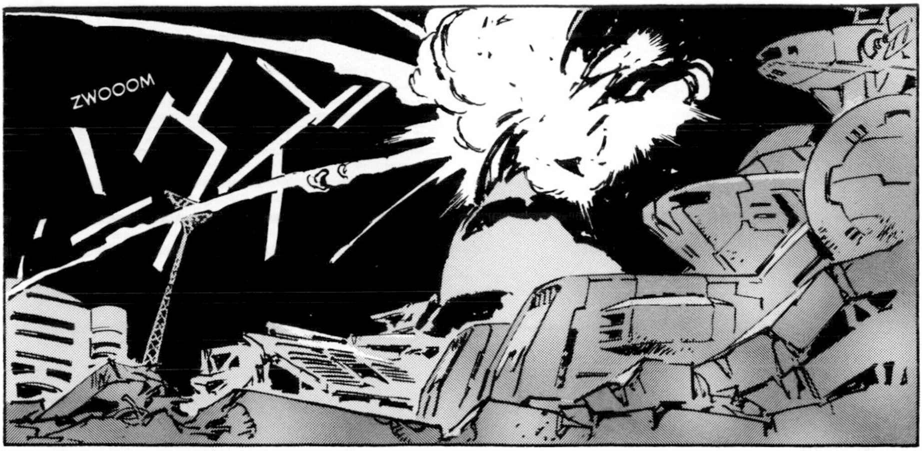
ZWOOOM

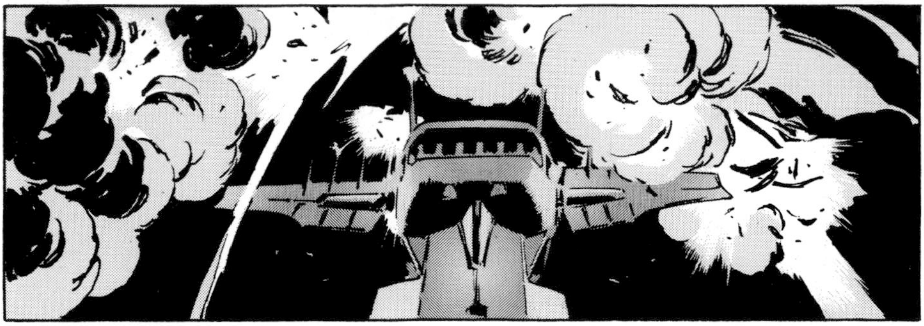

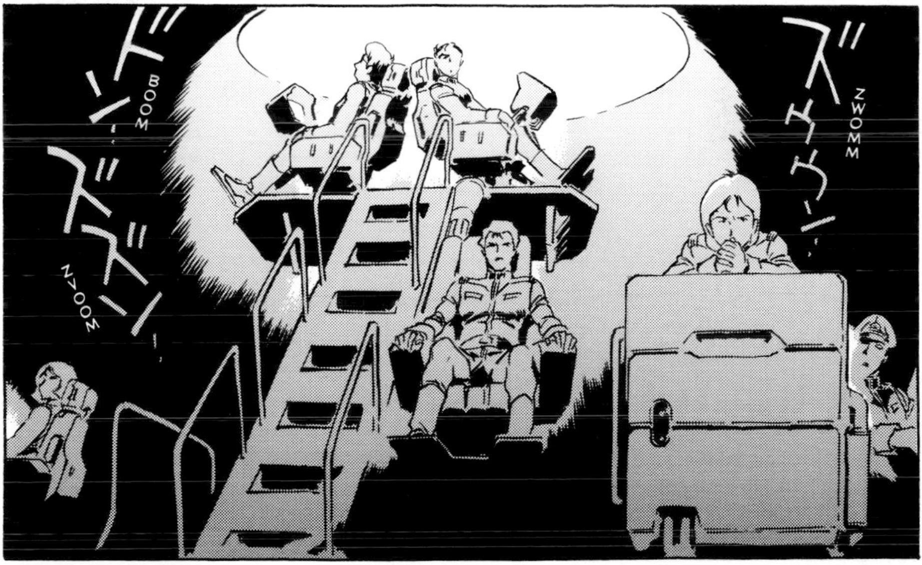
ZWOMM
BOOM
ZVOOM

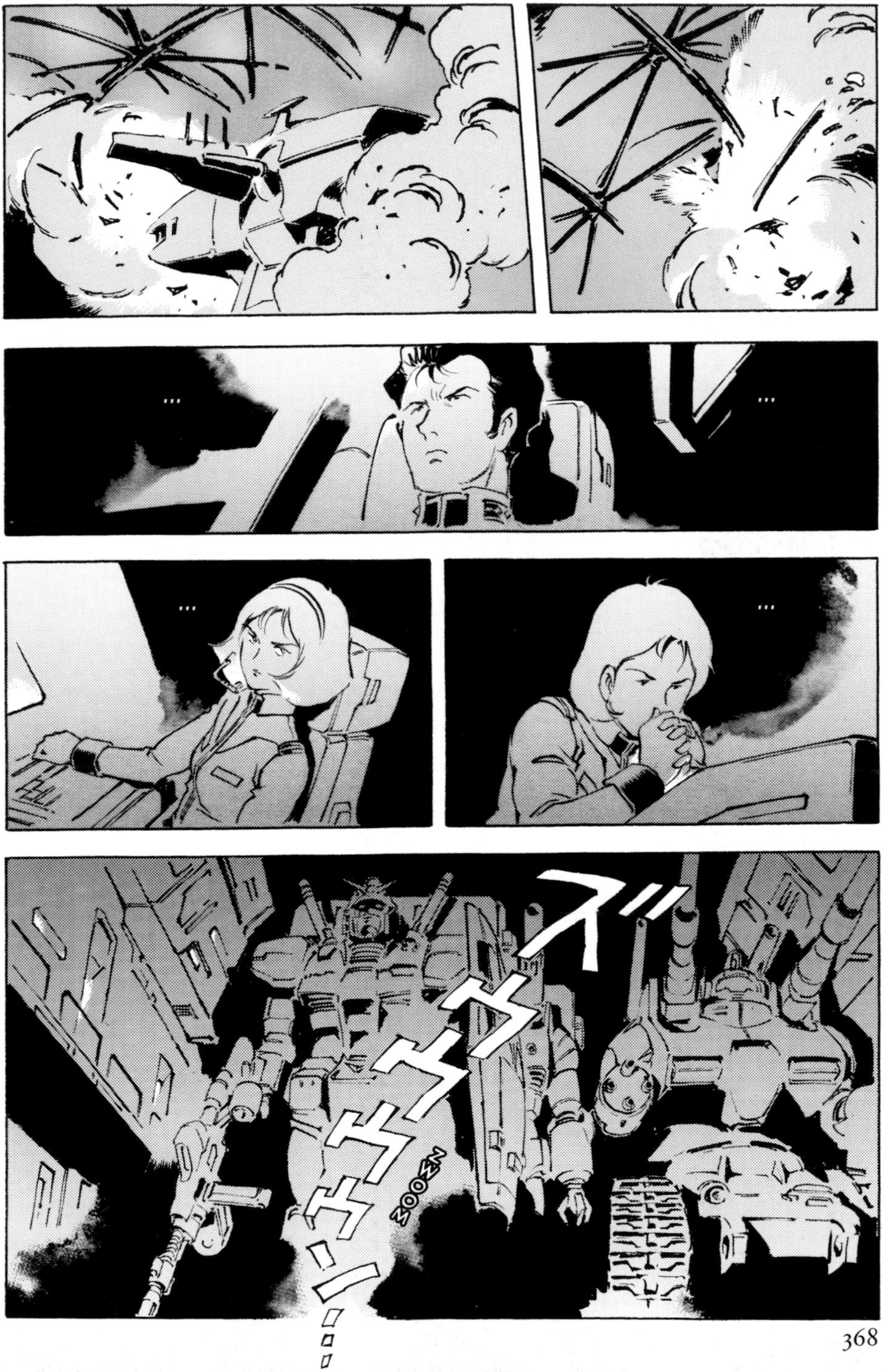
...
...
...
...

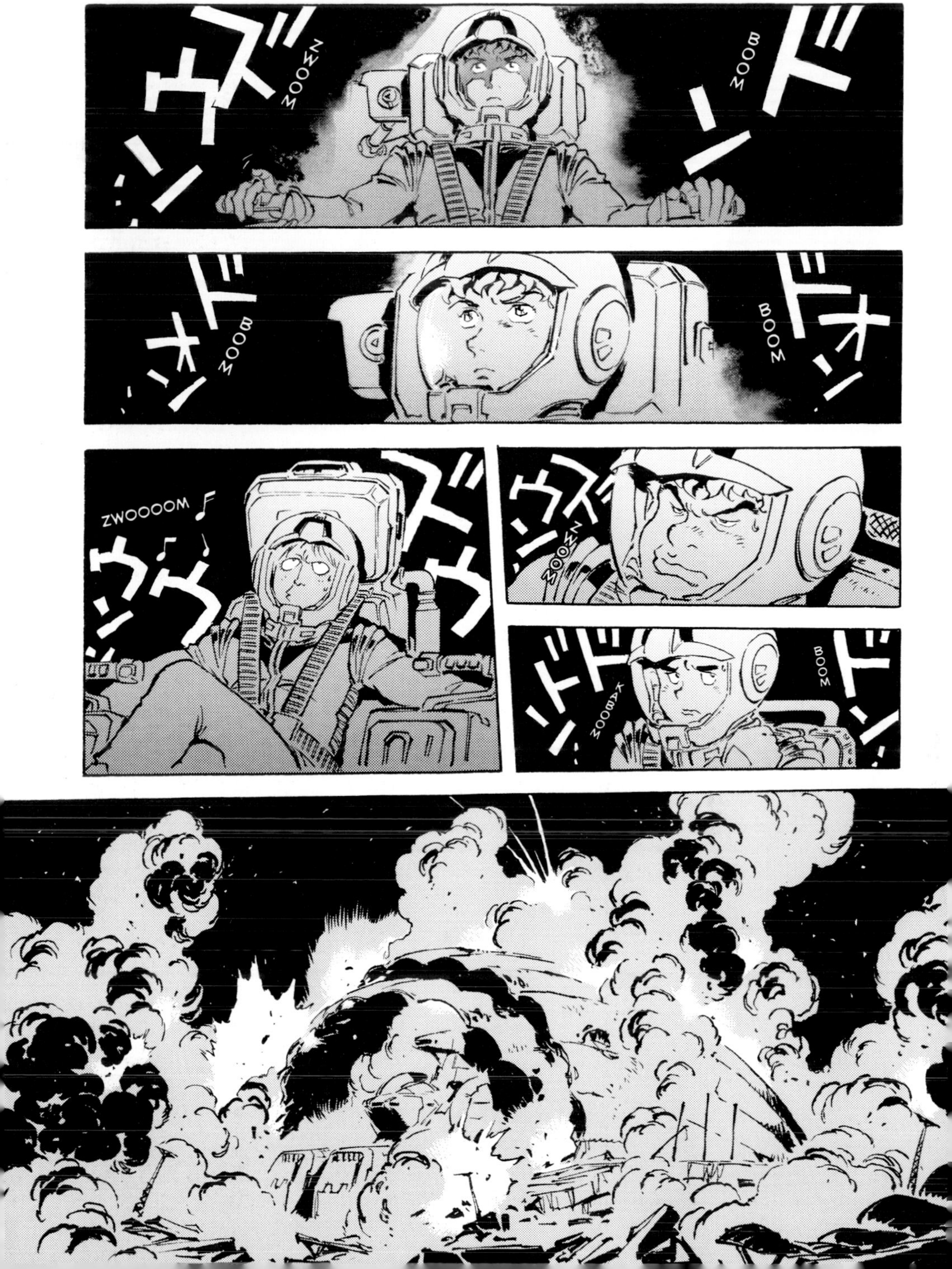

ドン
BOOM
ZWOOM
ズウン
ドオン
BOOM
BOOM
ドオン
ズウン
ZWOOM
ドン
BOOM
KABOOM
ドドン
ズウ
ZWOOOOM
ウウン

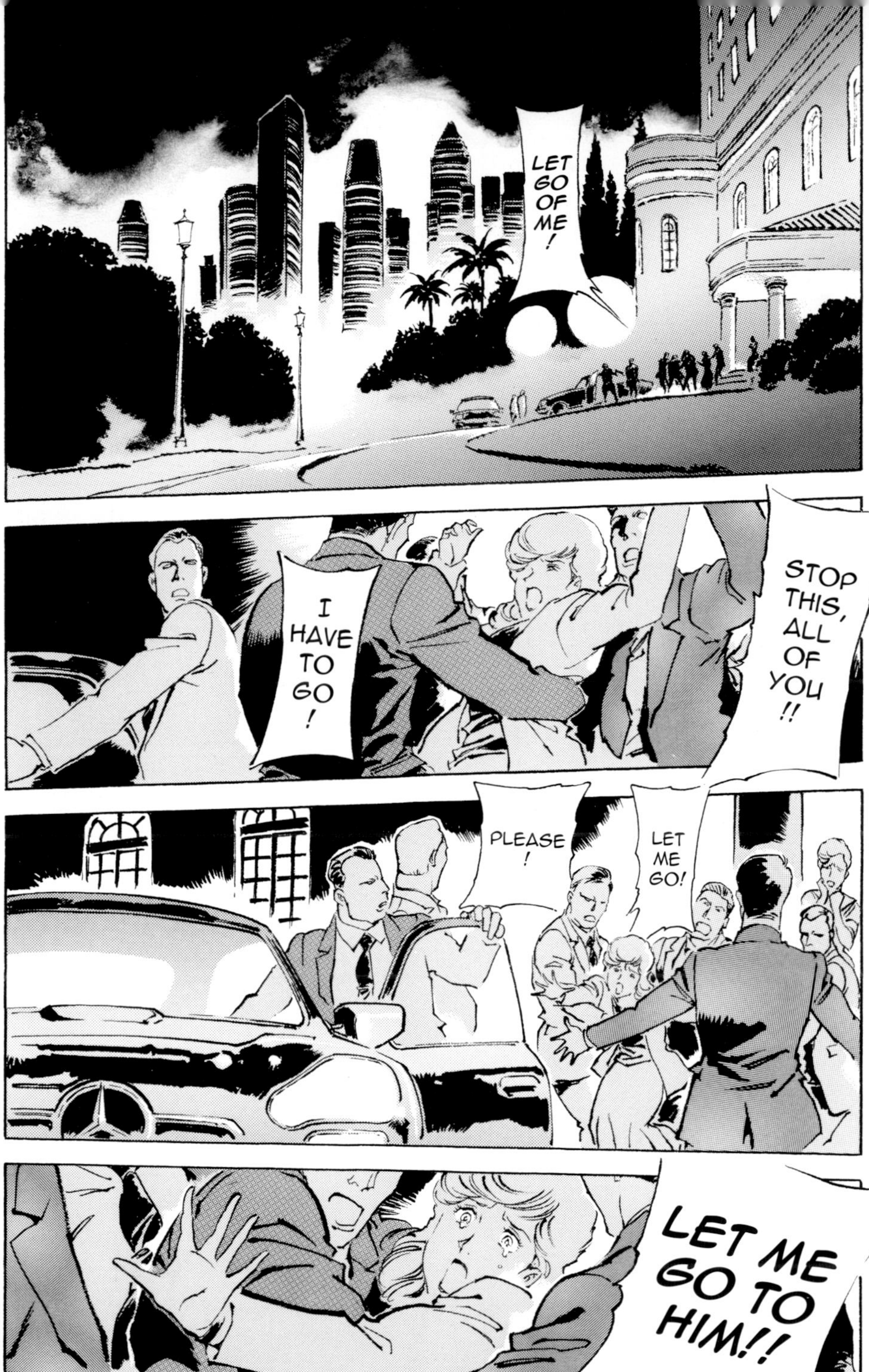
LET GO OF ME!
STOP THIS, ALL OF YOU!!
I HAVE TO GO!
LET ME GO!
PLEASE!
LET ME GO TO HIM!!

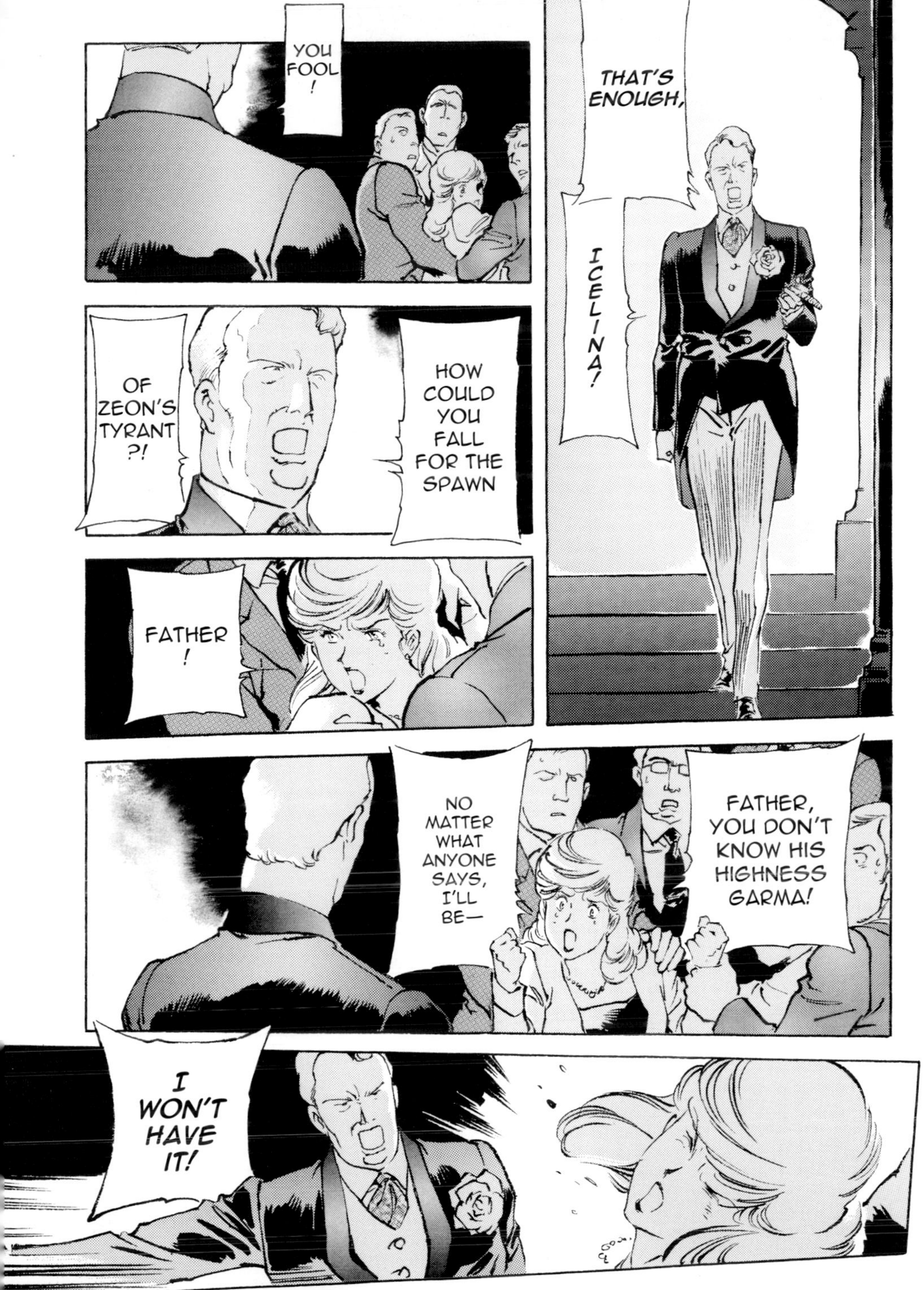
THAT'S ENOUGH,
ICELINA!
YOU FOOL!
HOW COULD YOU FALL FOR THE SPAWN
OF ZEON'S TYRANT?!
FATHER!
FATHER, YOU DON'T KNOW HIS HIGHNESS GARMA!
NO MATTER WHAT ANYONE SAYS, I'LL BE—
I WON'T HAVE IT!

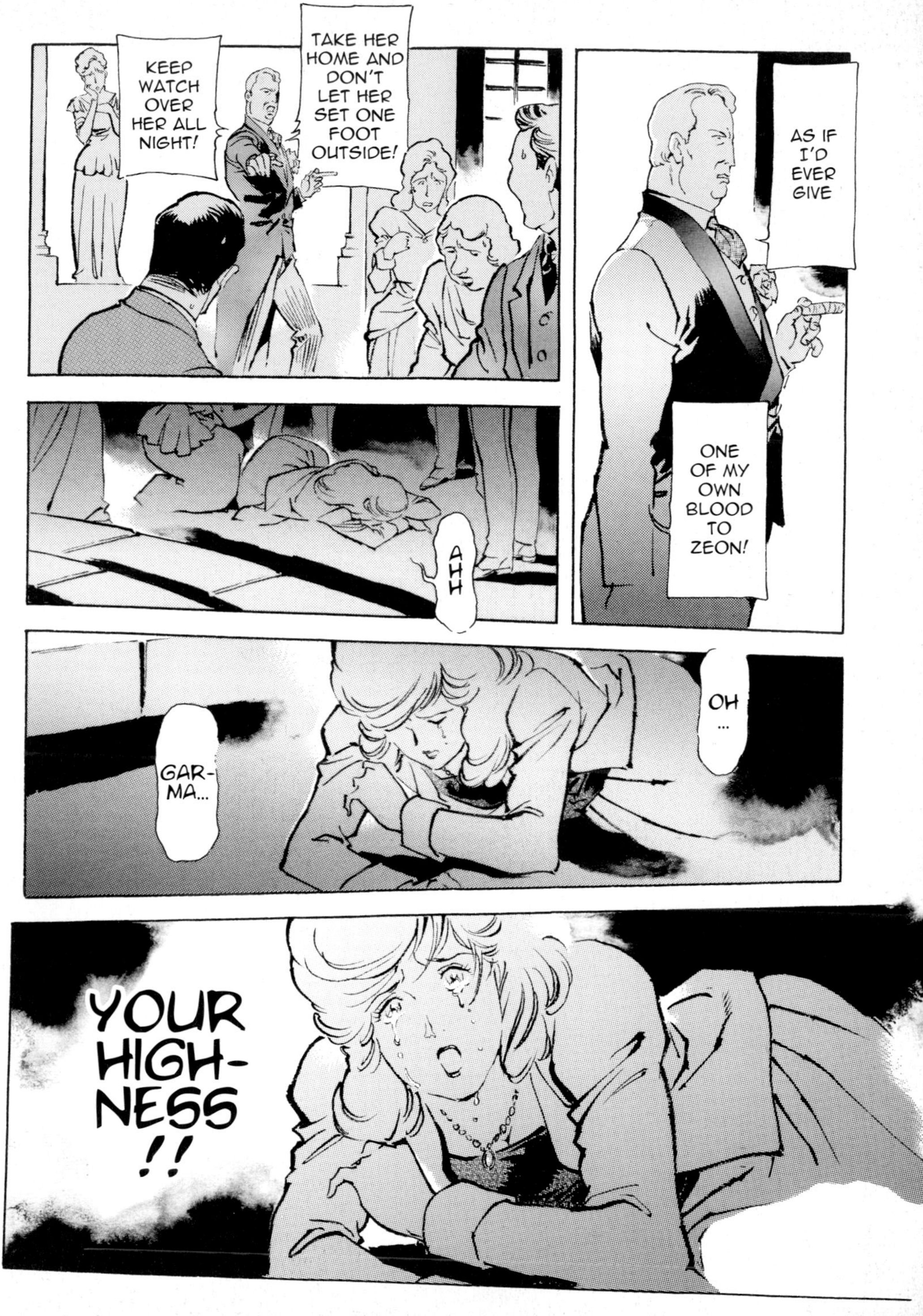
AS IF I'D EVER GIVE
ONE OF MY OWN BLOOD TO ZEON!
TAKE HER HOME AND DON'T LET HER SET ONE FOOT OUTSIDE!
KEEP WATCH OVER HER ALL NIGHT!
AHH
OH...
GAR-MA...
YOUR HIGH-NESS!!

SECTION
VIII

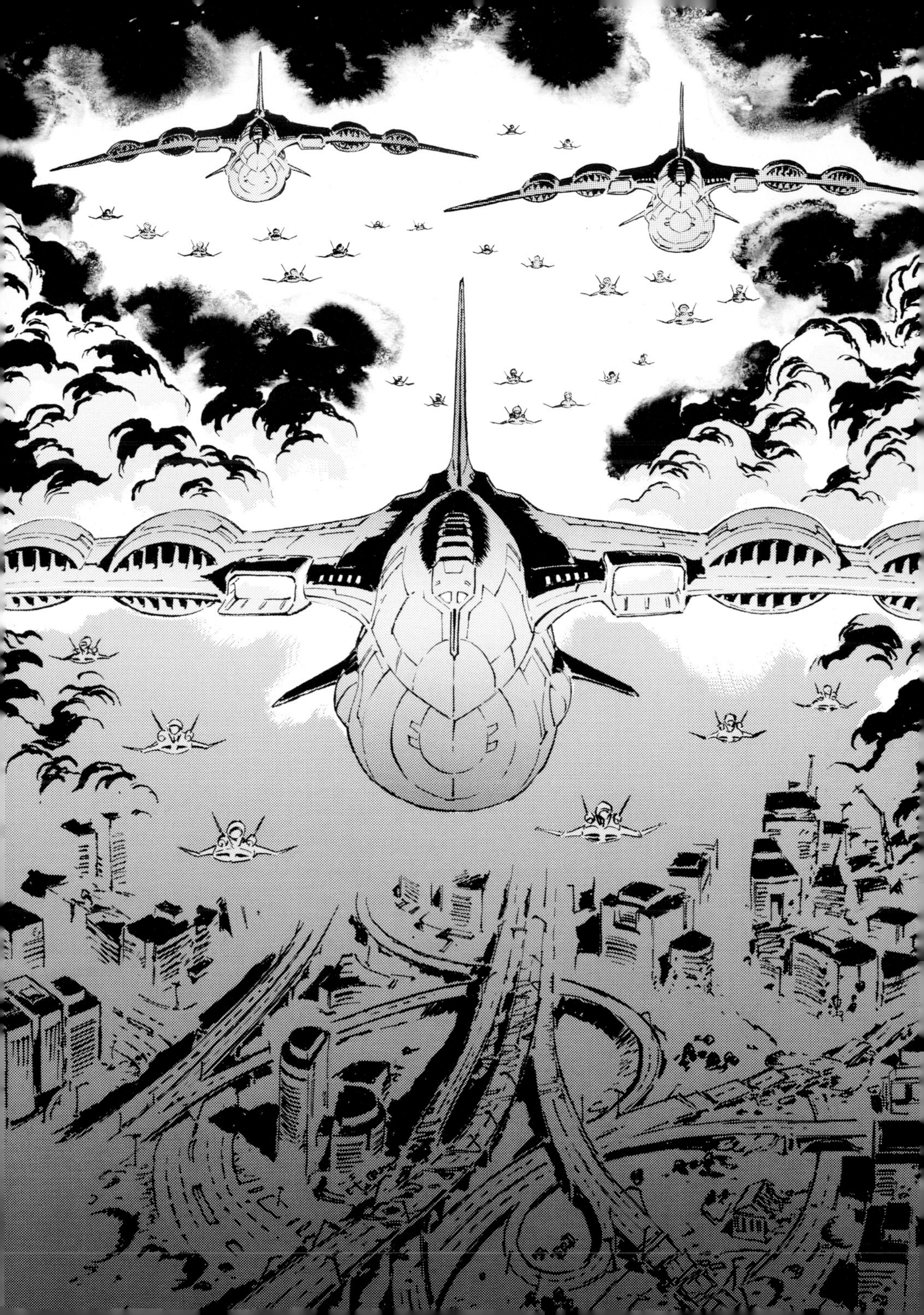

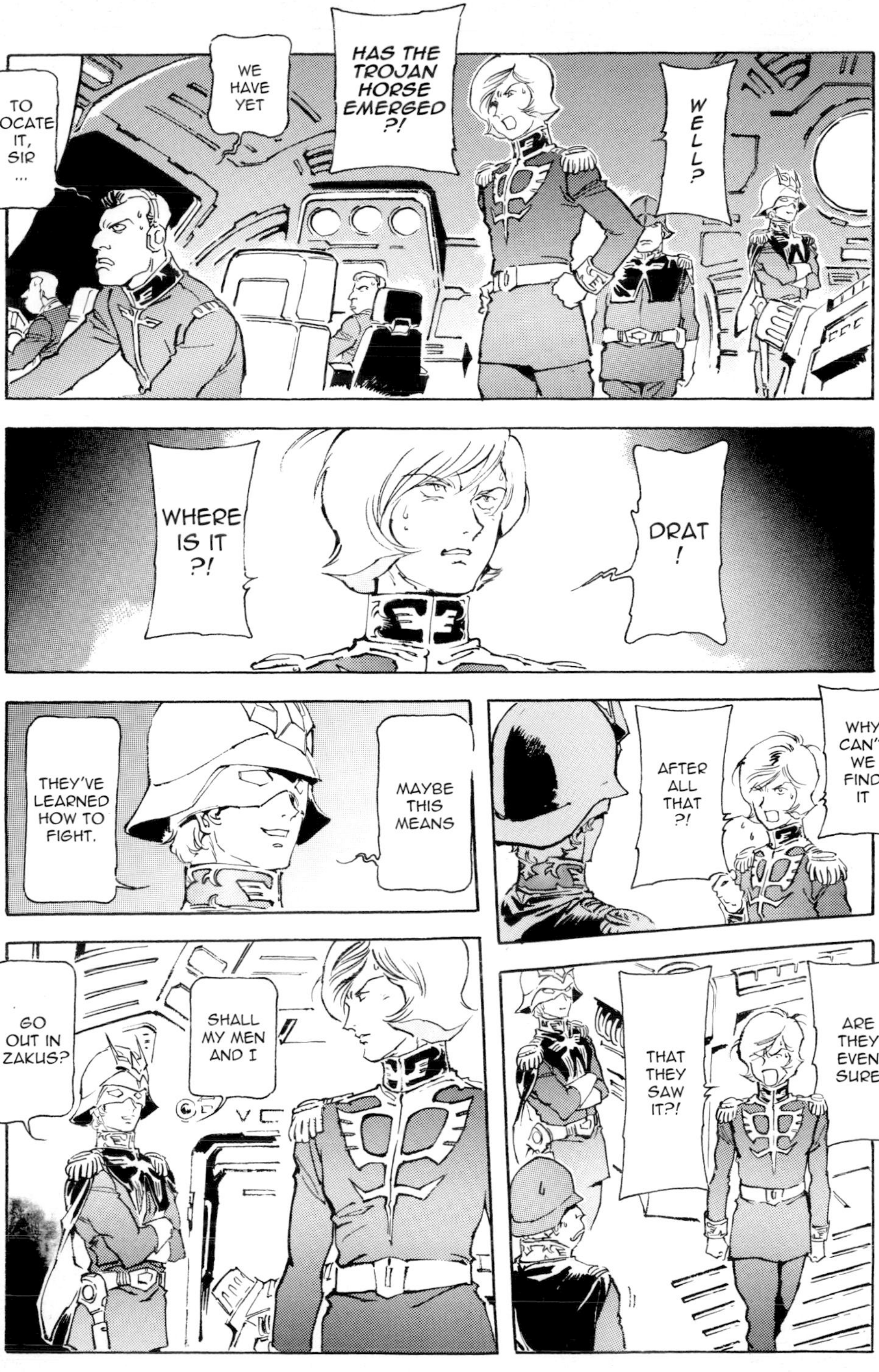
WELL?
HAS THE TROJAN HORSE EMERGED?!
WE HAVE YET
TO LOCATE IT, SIR ...
DRAT!
WHERE IS IT?!
WHY CAN'T WE FIND IT
AFTER ALL THAT?!
MAYBE THIS MEANS
THEY'VE LEARNED HOW TO FIGHT.
ARE THEY EVEN SURE
THAT THEY SAW IT?!
SHALL MY MEN AND I
GO OUT IN ZAKUS?

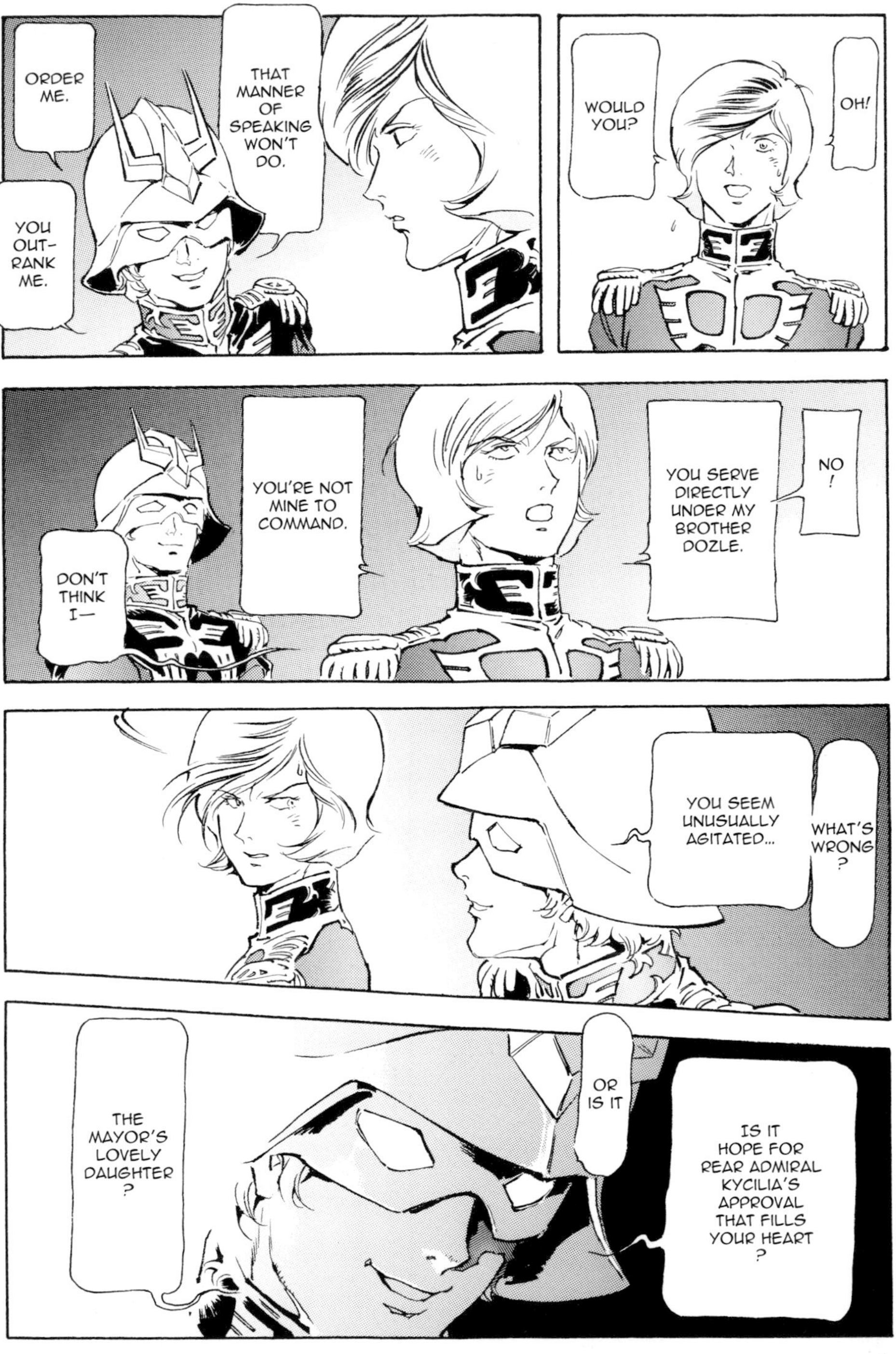
OH!
WOULD YOU?
THAT MANNER OF SPEAKING WON'T DO.
ORDER ME.
YOU OUT-RANK ME.
NO!
YOU SERVE DIRECTLY UNDER MY BROTHER DOZLE.
YOU'RE NOT MINE TO COMMAND.
DON'T THINK I—
WHAT'S WRONG?
YOU SEEM UNUSUALLY AGITATED...
IS IT HOPE FOR REAR ADMIRAL KYCILIA'S APPROVAL THAT FILLS YOUR HEART?
OR IS IT
THE MAYOR'S LOVELY DAUGHTER?

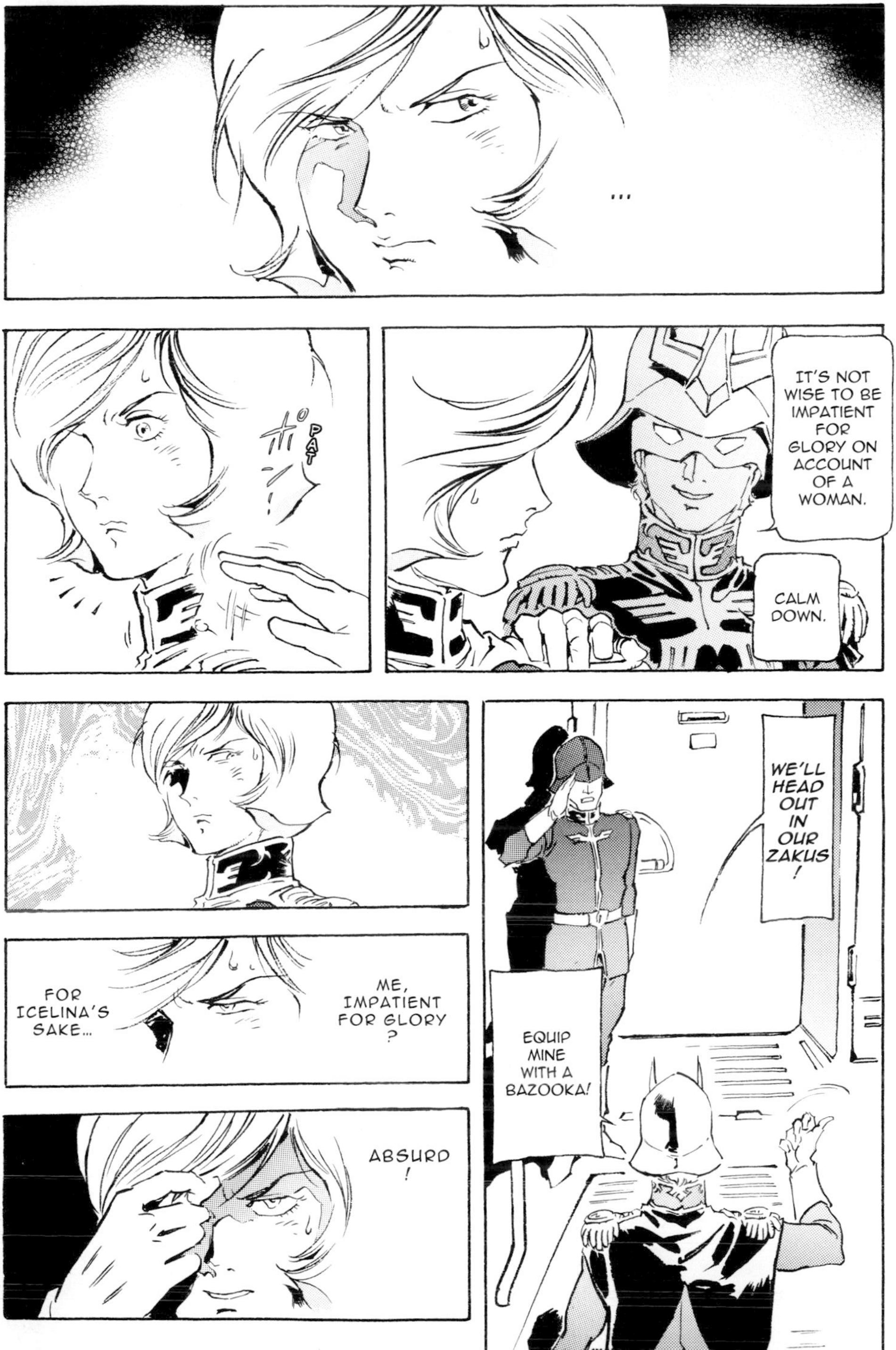
...
IT'S NOT WISE TO BE IMPATIENT FOR GLORY ON ACCOUNT OF A WOMAN.
CALM DOWN.
PAT
WE'LL HEAD OUT IN OUR ZAKUS!
EQUIP MINE WITH A BAZOOKA!
ME, IMPATIENT FOR GLORY?
FOR ICELINA'S SAKE...
ABSURD!

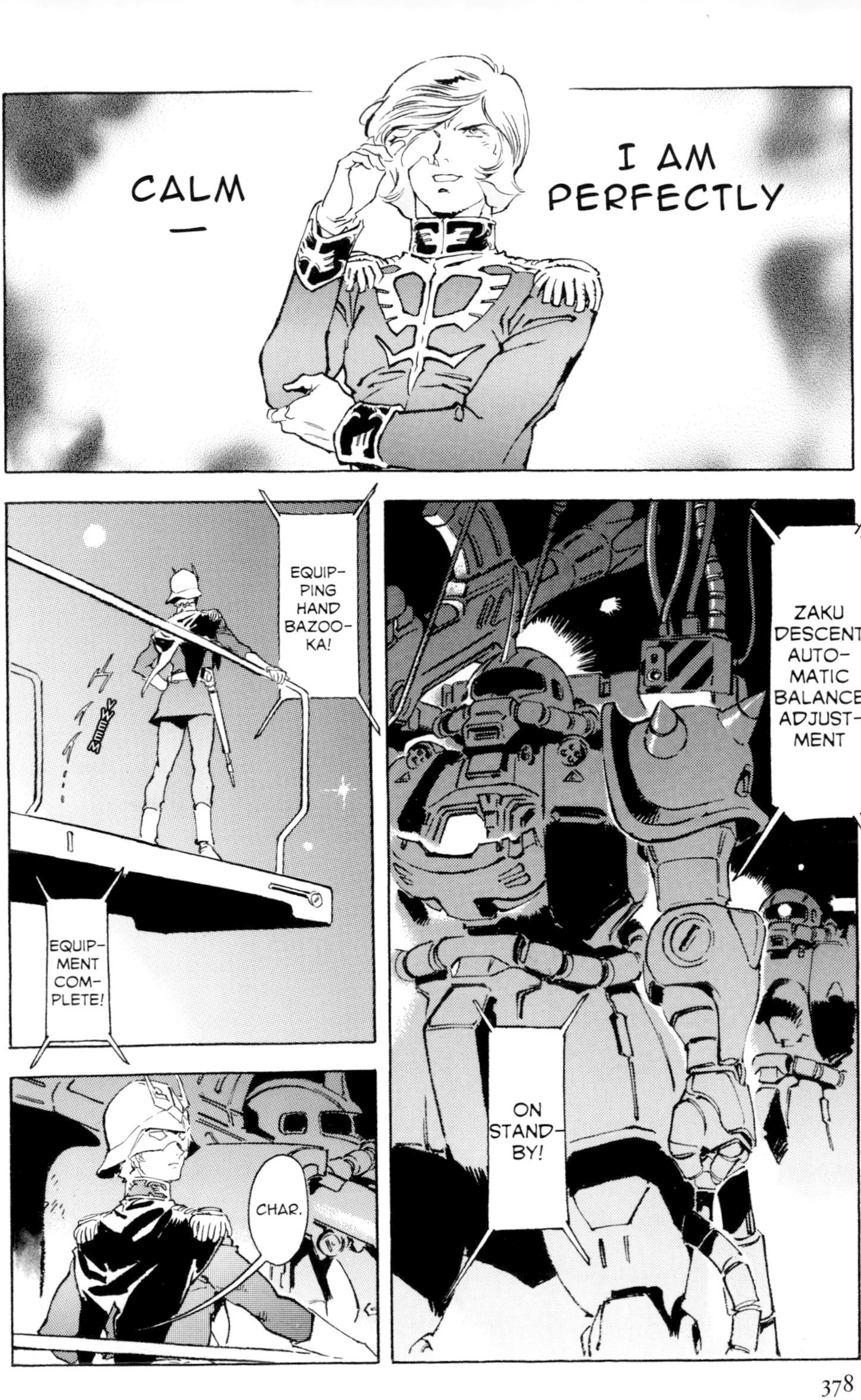
I AM PERFECTLY
CALM —
ZAKU DESCENT AUTOMATIC BALANCE ADJUSTMENT
ON STANDBY!
EQUIPPING HAND BAZOOKA!
EQUIPMENT COMPLETE!
CHAR.

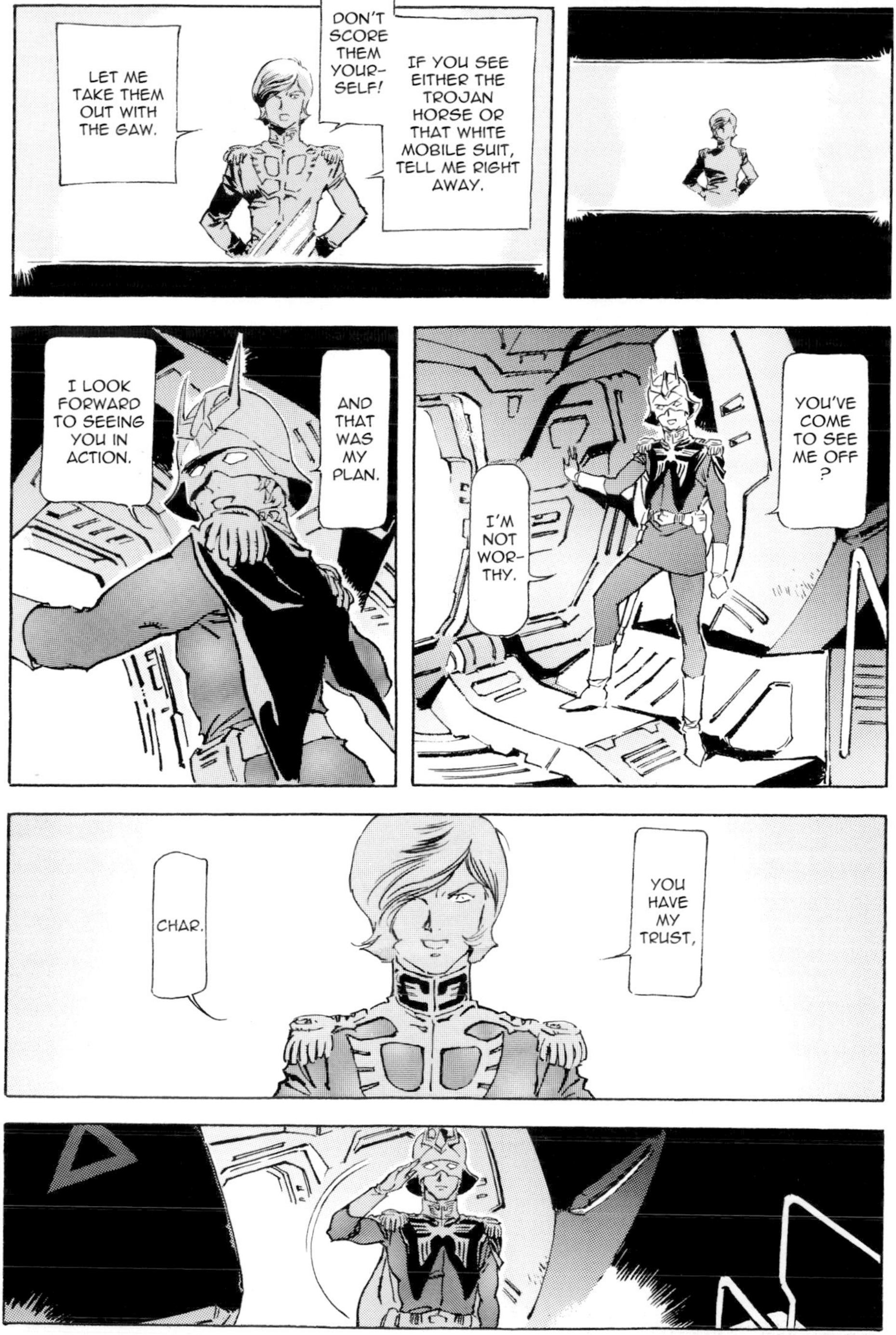
IF YOU SEE EITHER THE TROJAN HORSE OR THAT WHITE MOBILE SUIT, TELL ME RIGHT AWAY.
DON'T SCORE THEM YOUR-SELF!
LET ME TAKE THEM OUT WITH THE GAW.
YOU'VE COME TO SEE ME OFF?
I'M NOT WOR-THY.
AND THAT WAS MY PLAN.
I LOOK FORWARD TO SEEING YOU IN ACTION.
YOU HAVE MY TRUST,
CHAR.

WILL BE YOURS !

THE GLORY OF VIC- TORY

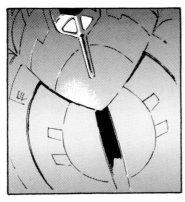

OPEN THE FORE DIVING HATCH!

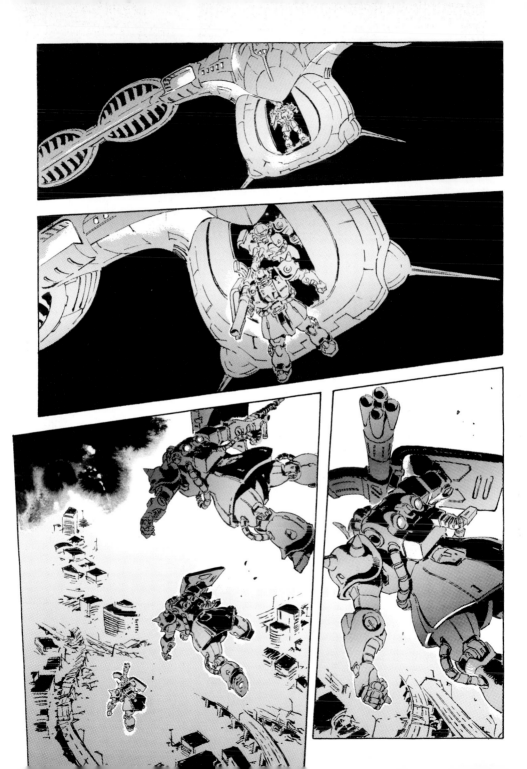

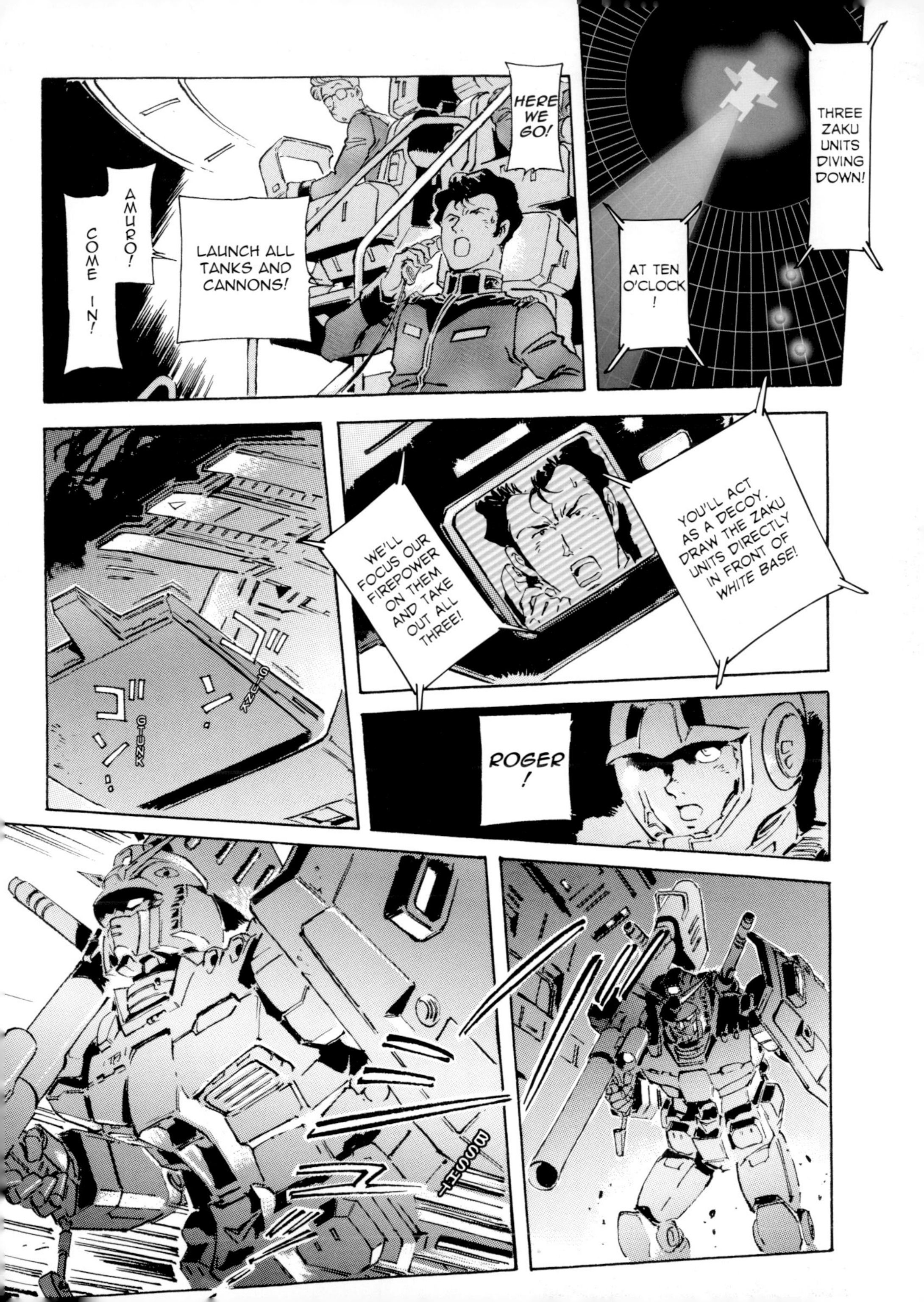
THREE ZAKU UNITS DIVING DOWN!
AT TEN O'CLOCK!
HERE WE GO!
LAUNCH ALL TANKS AND CANNONS!
AMURO! COME IN!
YOU'LL ACT AS A DECOY. DRAW THE ZAKU UNITS DIRECTLY IN FRONT OF WHITE BASE!
WE'LL FOCUS OUR FIREPOWER ON THEM AND TAKE OUT ALL THREE!
ROGER!
GTUNK
GTUNK

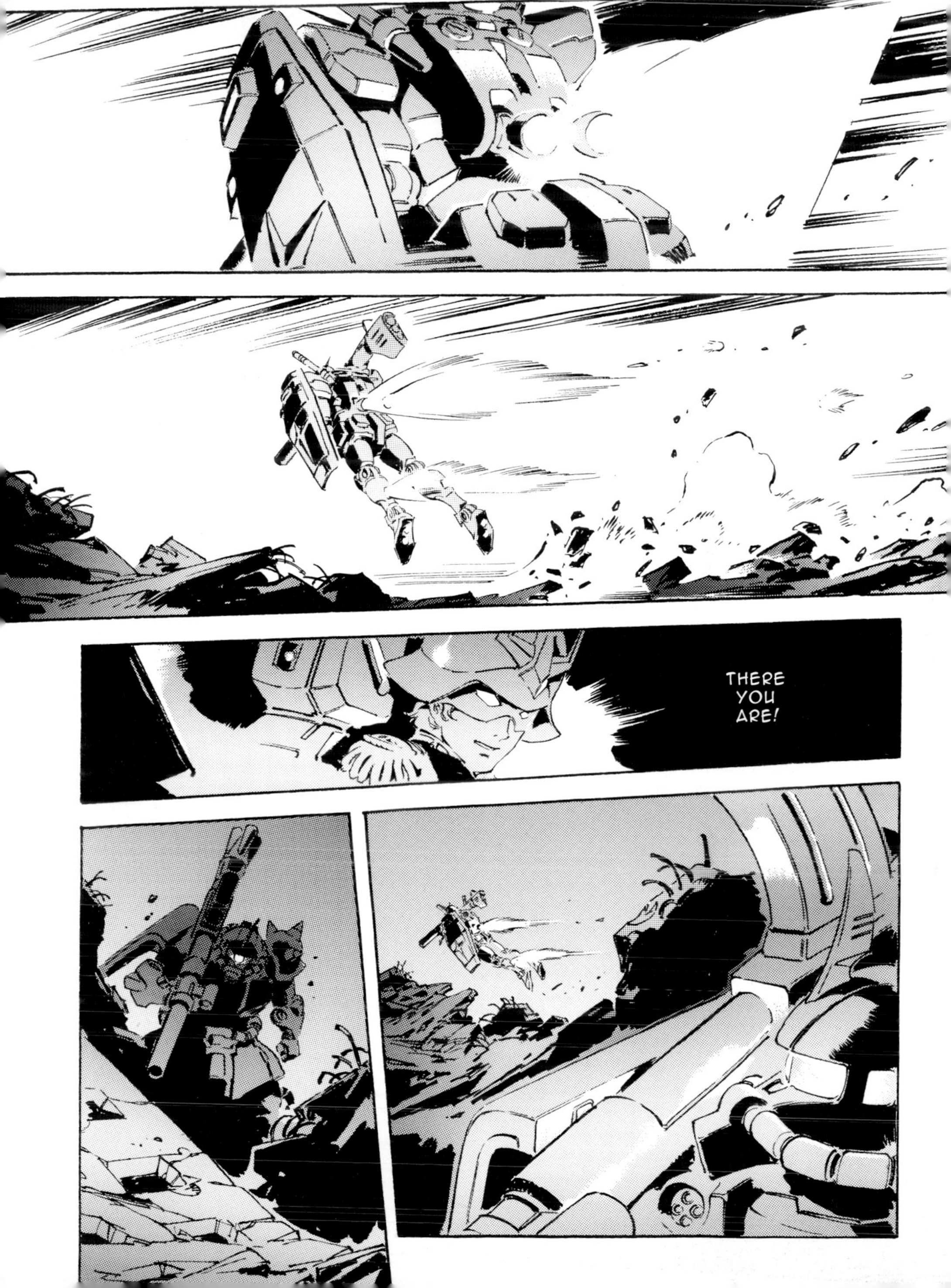
THERE YOU ARE!

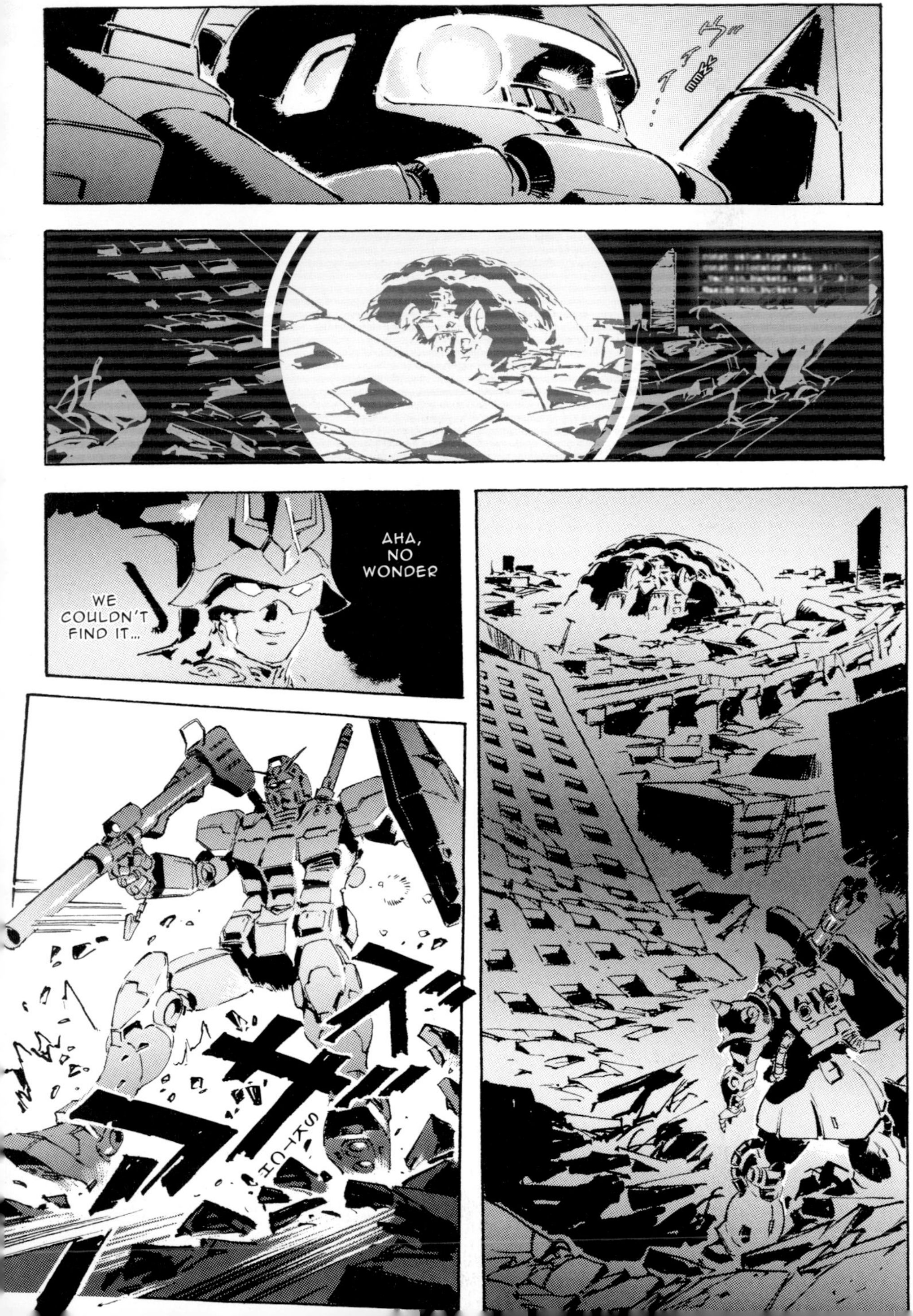
AHA, NO WONDER
WE COULDN'T FIND IT...
SKI-CH

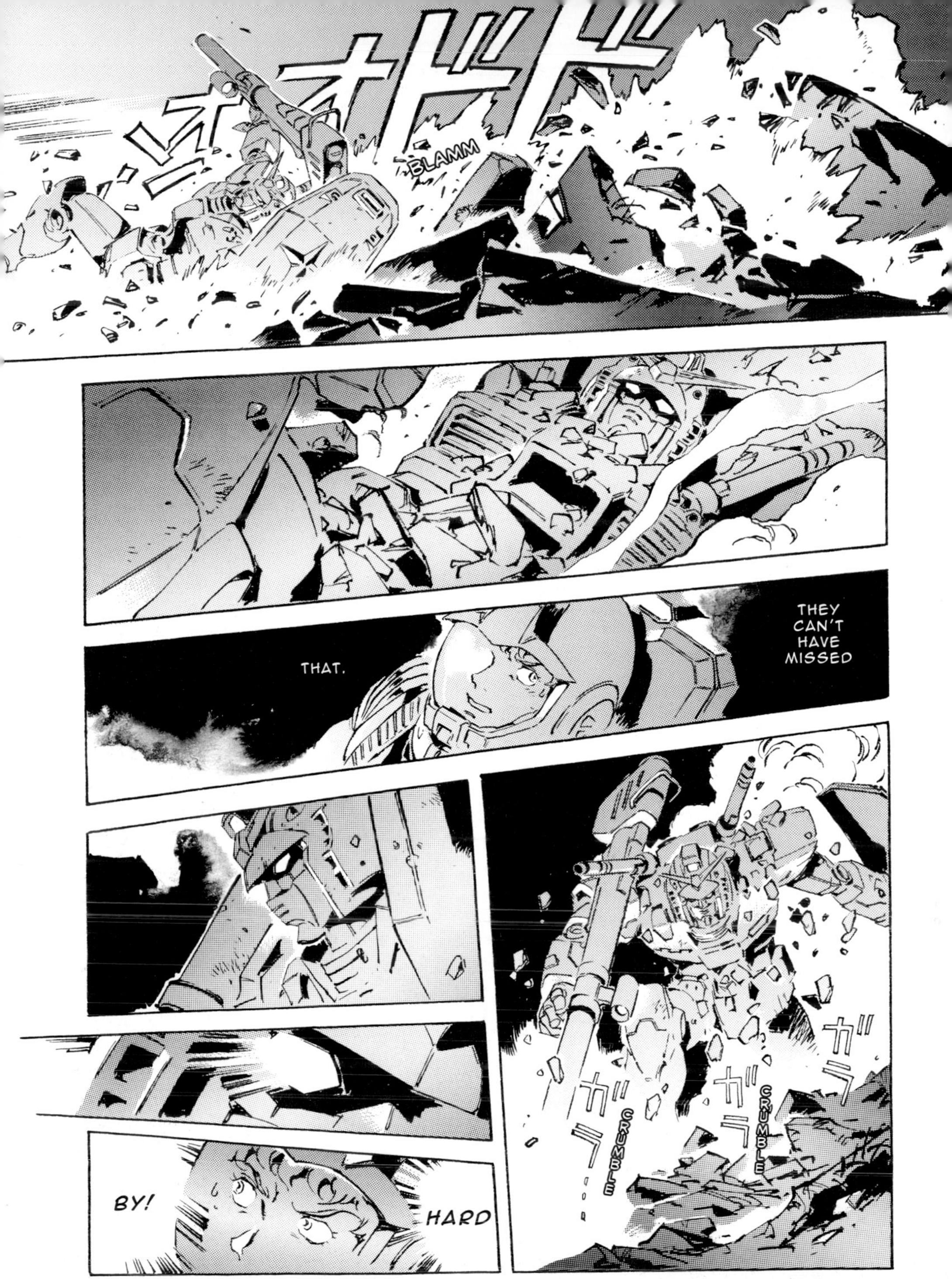
BLAMM
THEY CAN'T HAVE MISSED
THAT.
ガラ
ガラ
ガラ
CRUMBLE
CRUMBLE
HARD
BY!

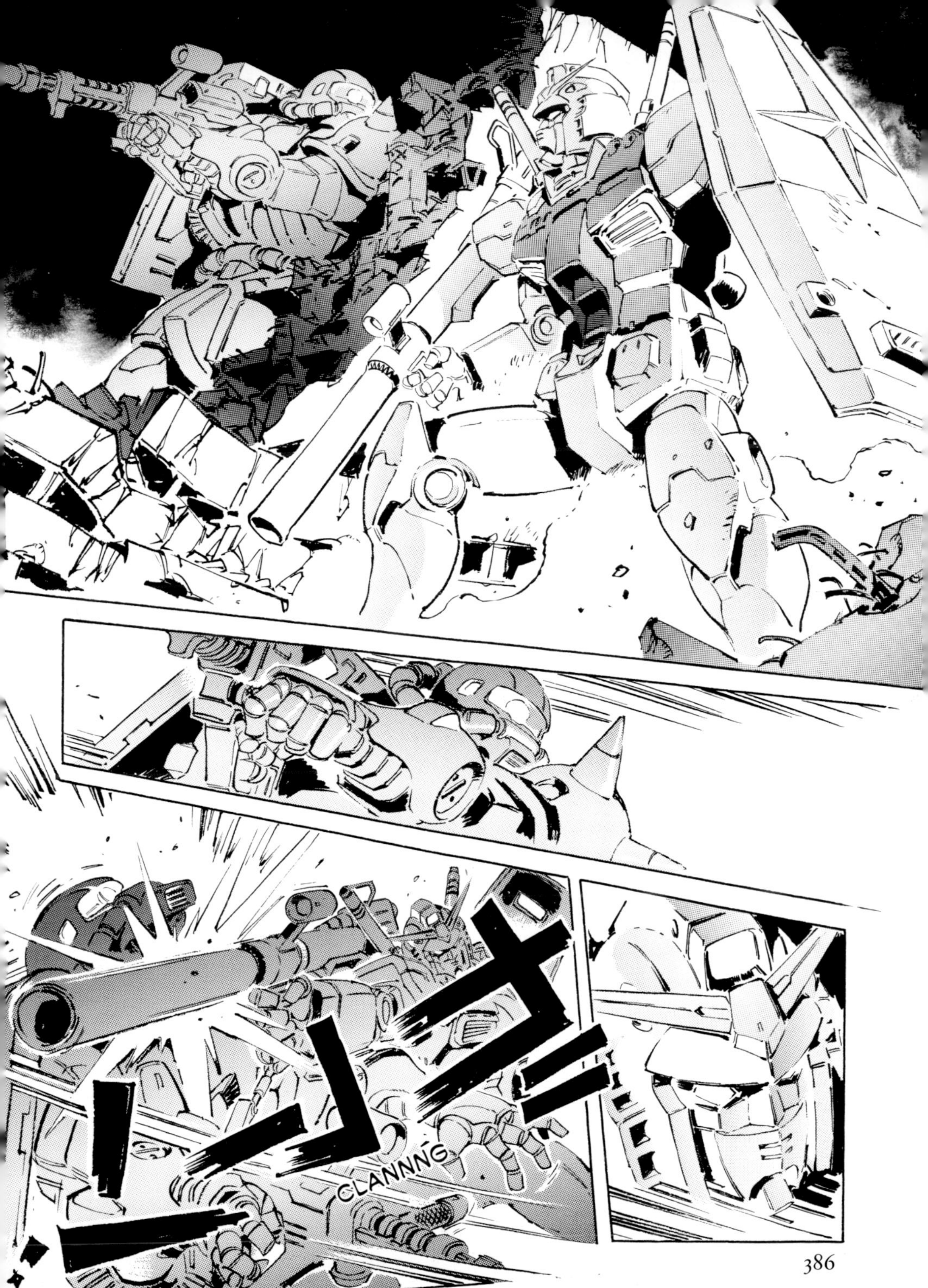
CLANNNG

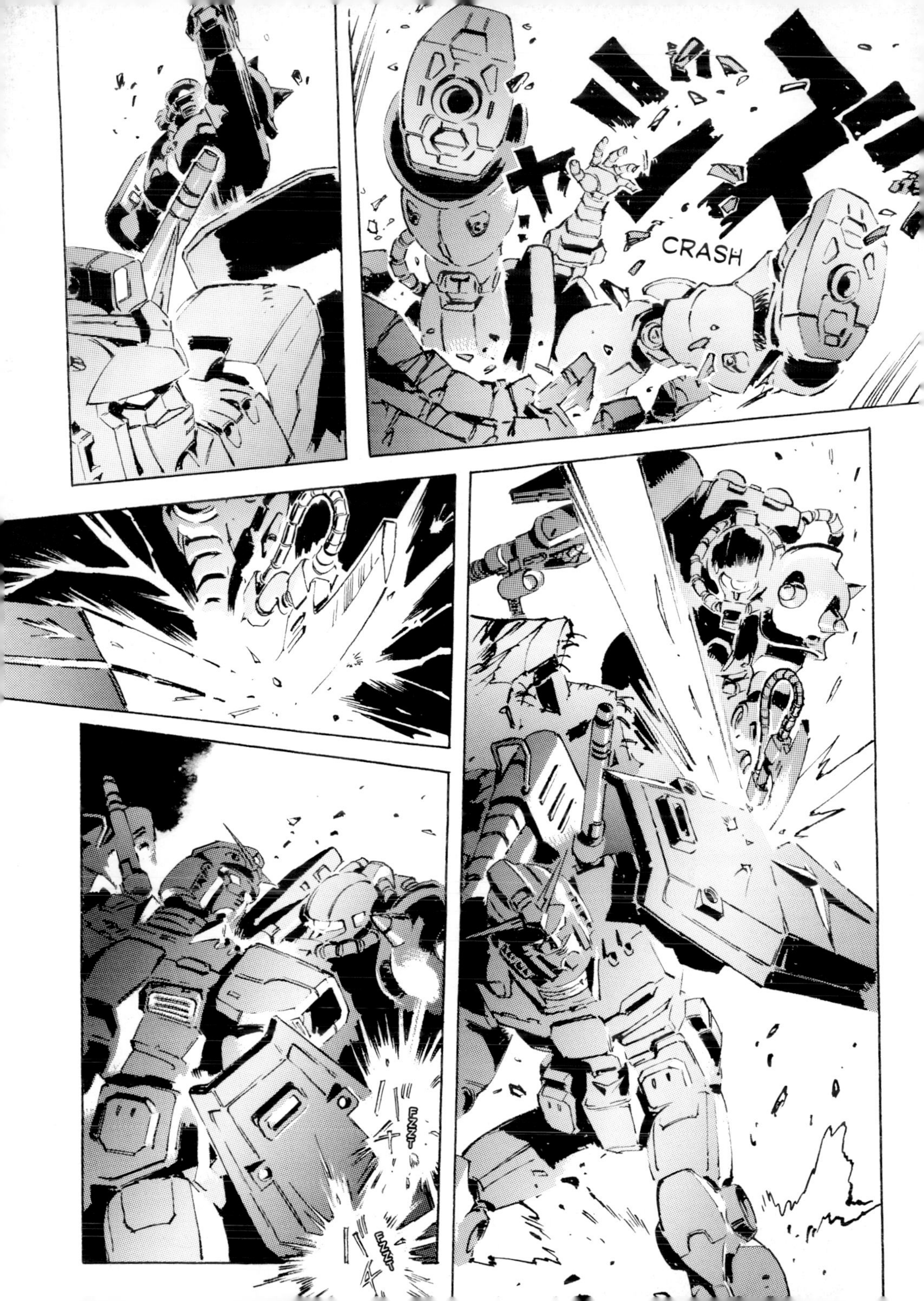
CRASH
FZZT
FZZT

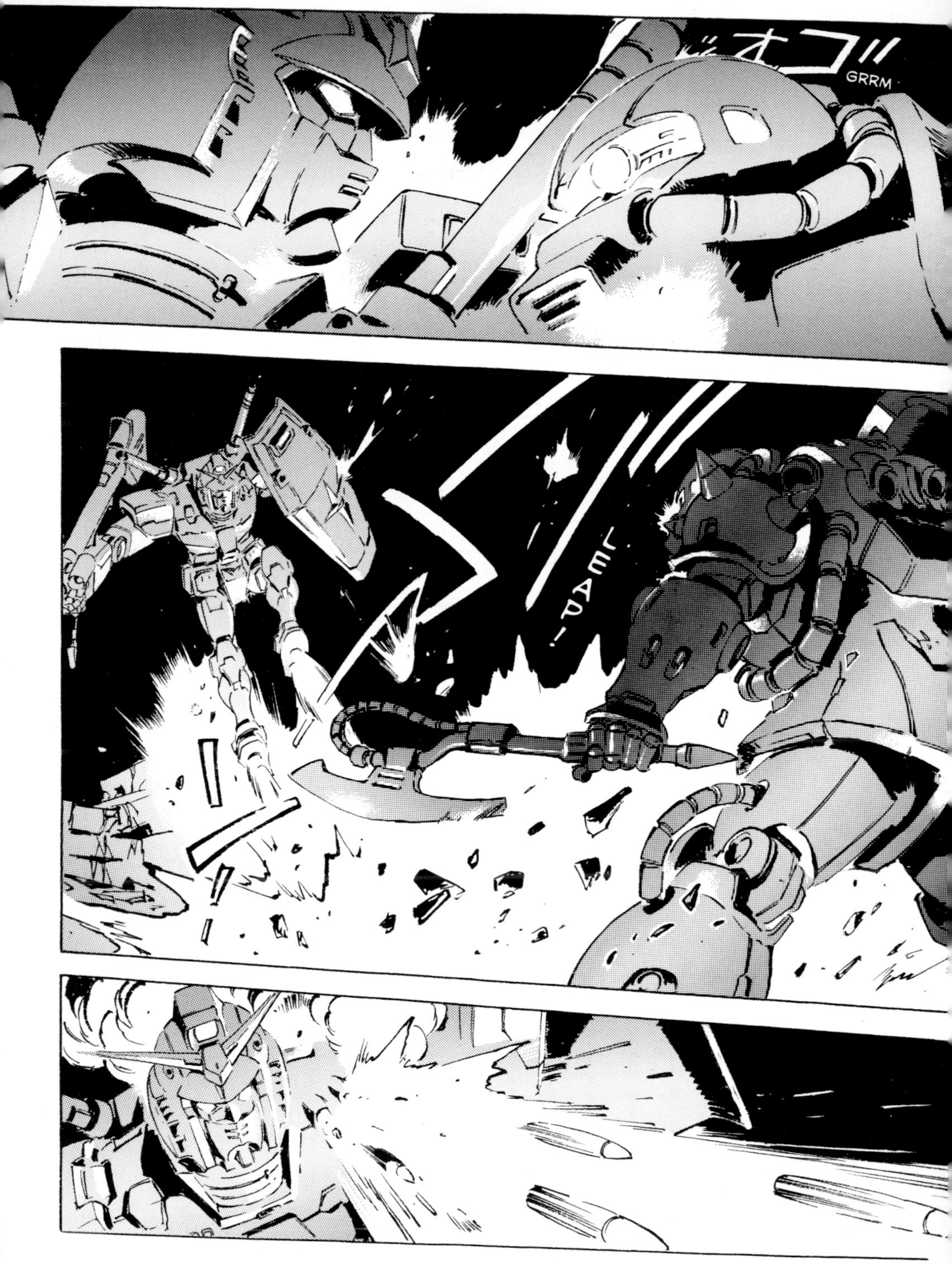
GRRM
LEAP!

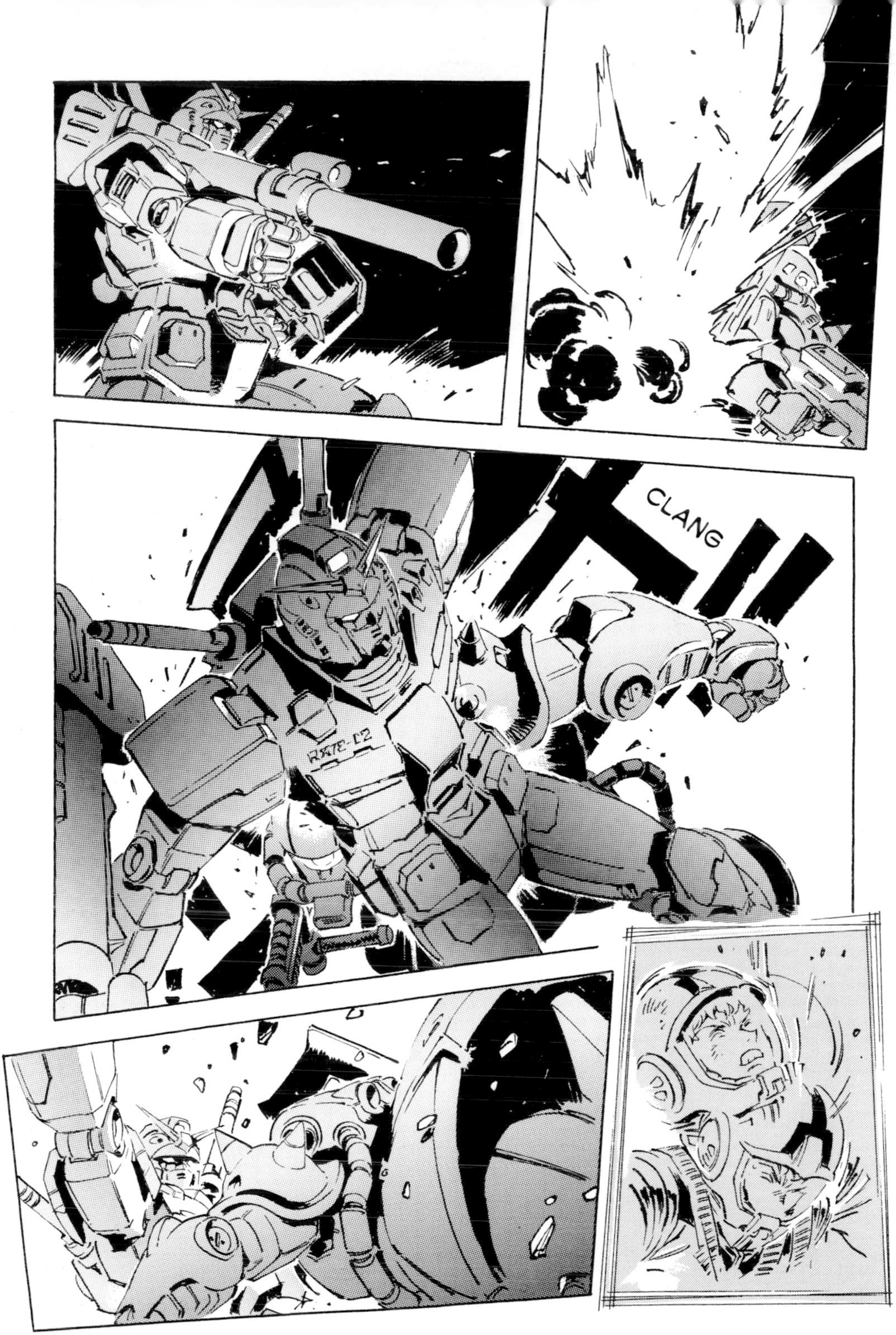
CLANG

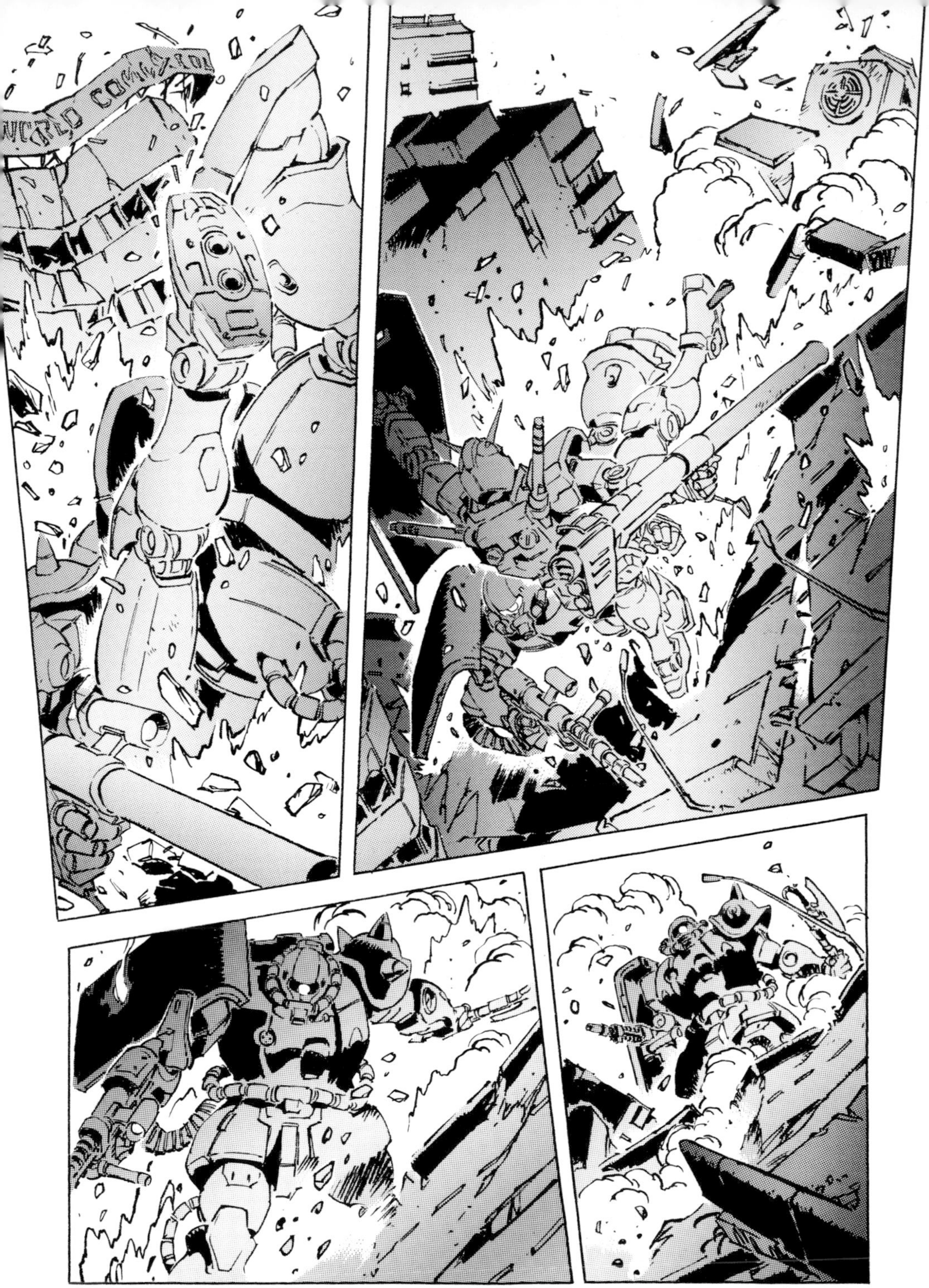

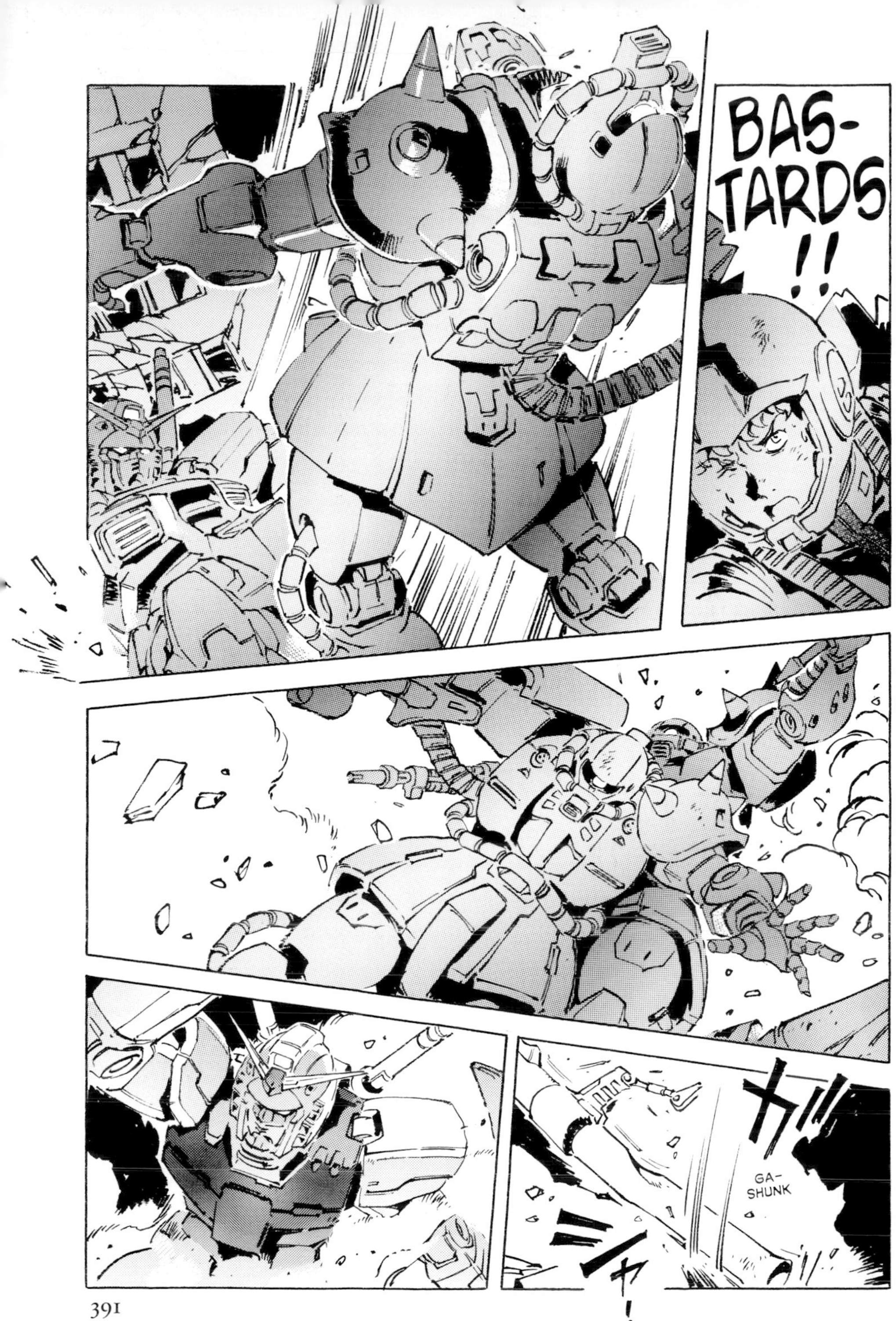
BAS-
TARDS
!!
ガ!!
GA-
SHUNK

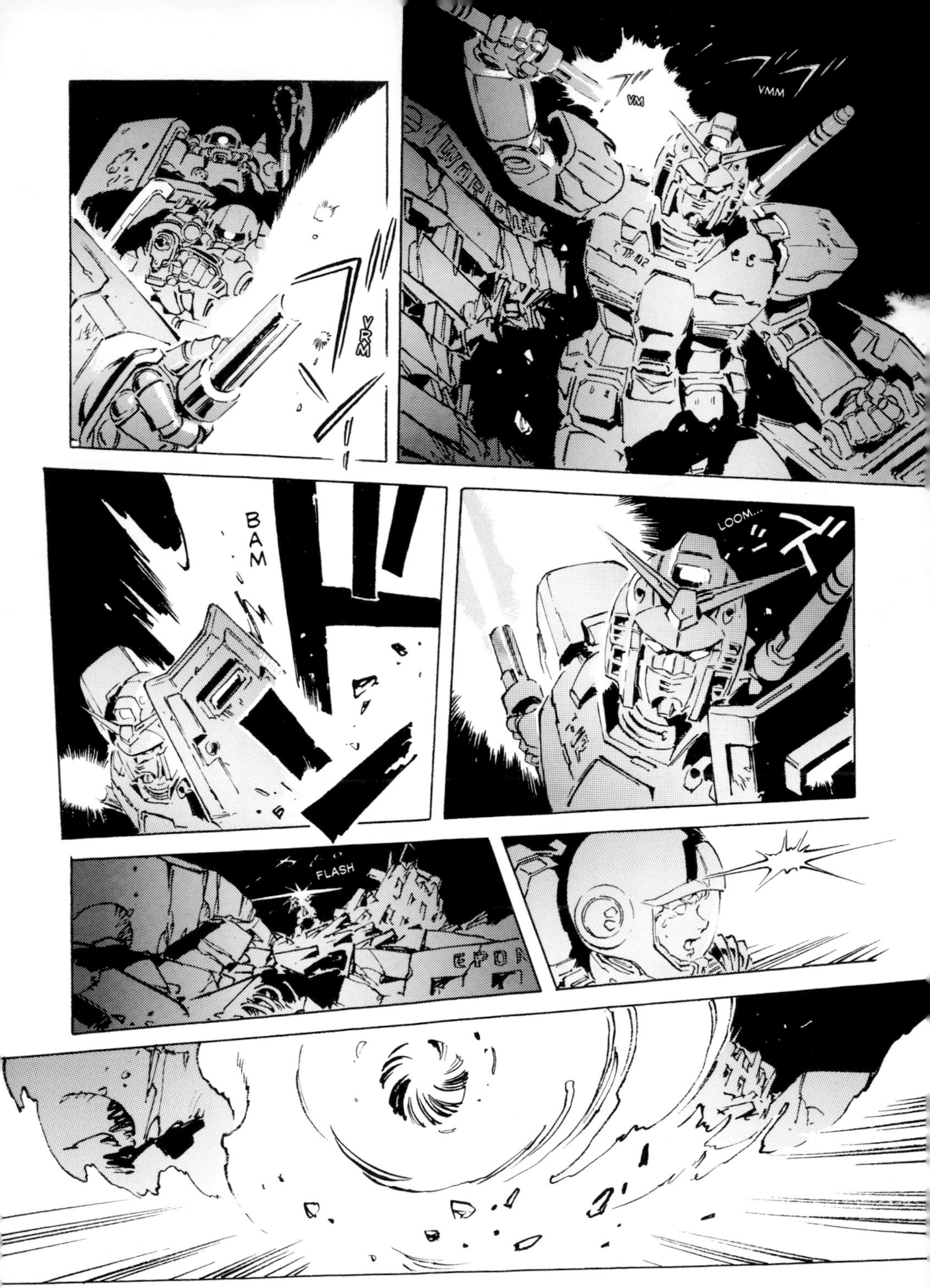
VMM
VM
VRM
LOOM...
BAM
FLASH

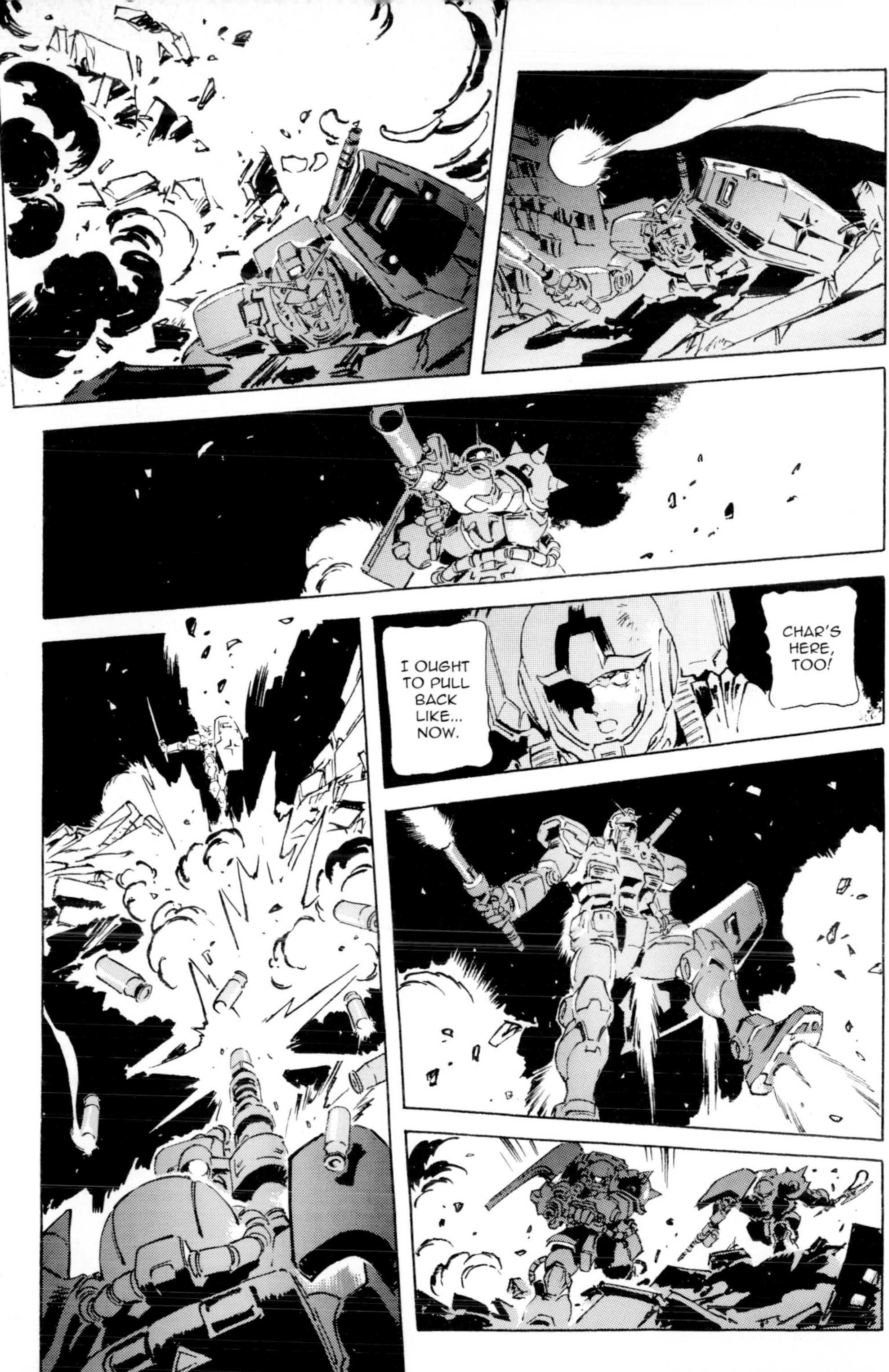
CHAR'S HERE, TOO!
I OUGHT TO PULL BACK LIKE... NOW.

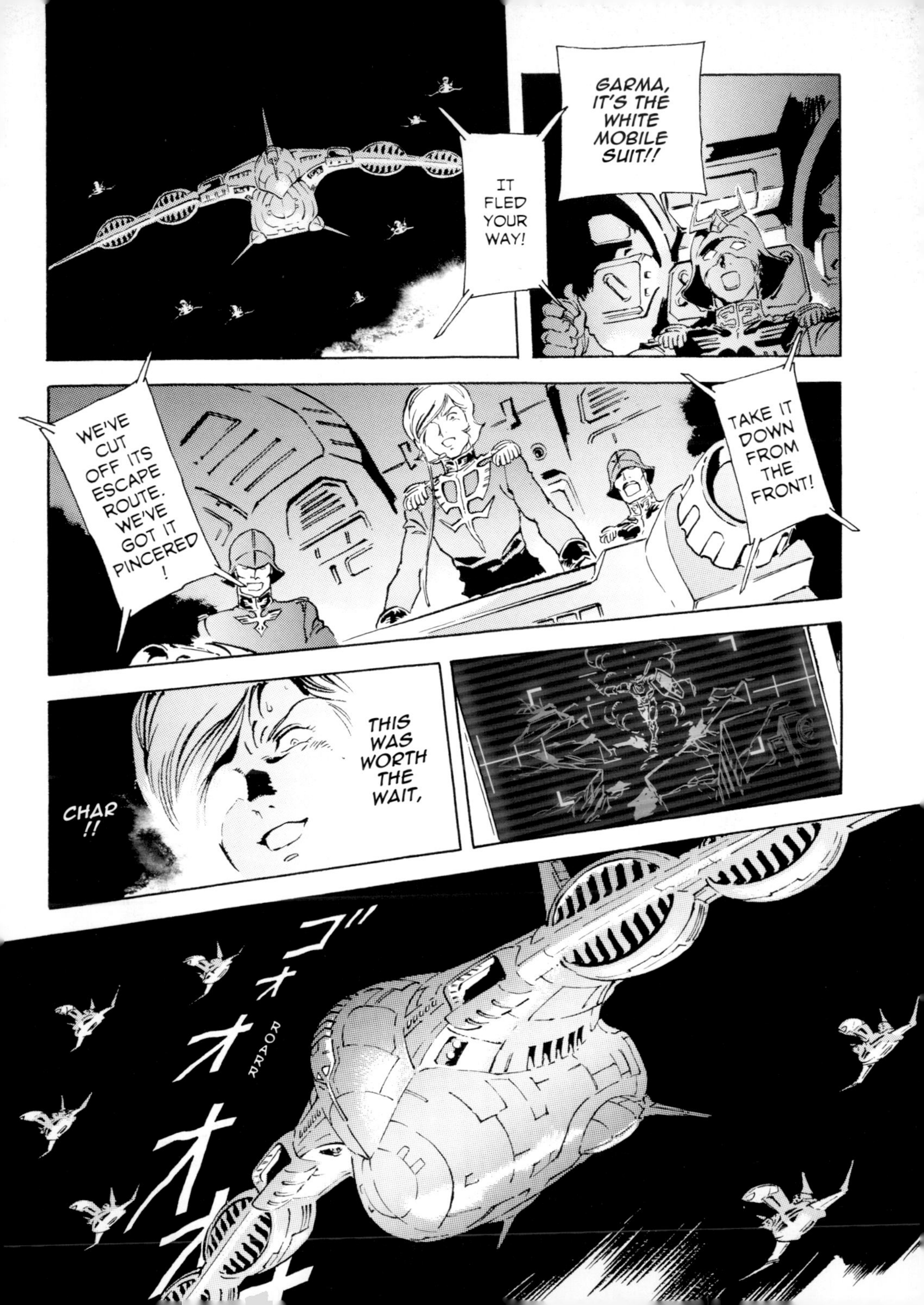
GARMA, IT'S THE WHITE MOBILE SUIT!!
IT FLED YOUR WAY!
TAKE IT DOWN FROM THE FRONT!
WE'VE CUT OFF ITS ESCAPE ROUTE. WE'VE GOT IT PINCERED!
THIS WAS WORTH THE WAIT,
CHAR!!
ゴオオオ
ROARR

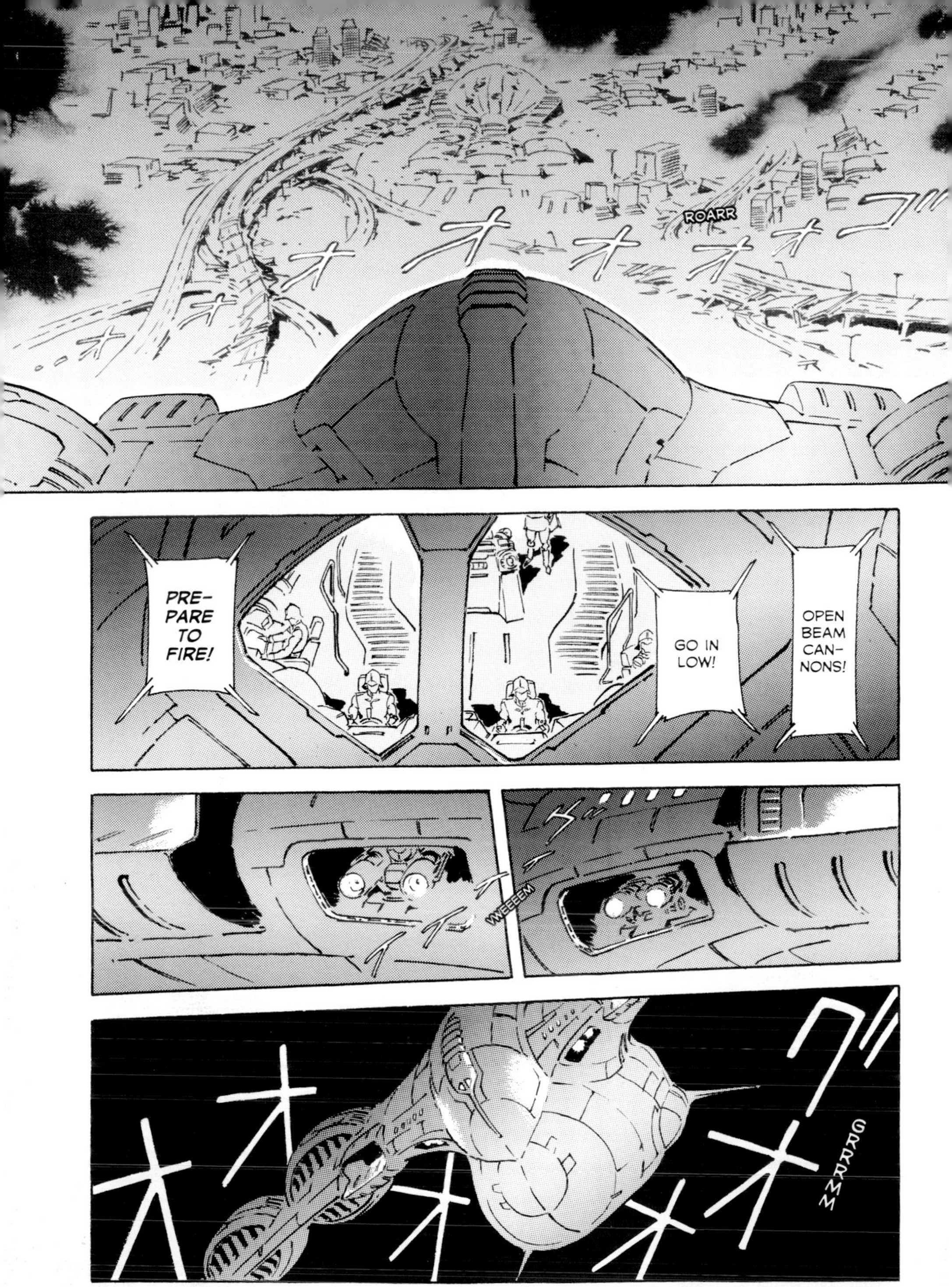
ROARR
OPEN BEAM CAN-NONS!
GO IN LOW!
PRE-PARE TO FIRE!
WEEEEM
GRRRMM

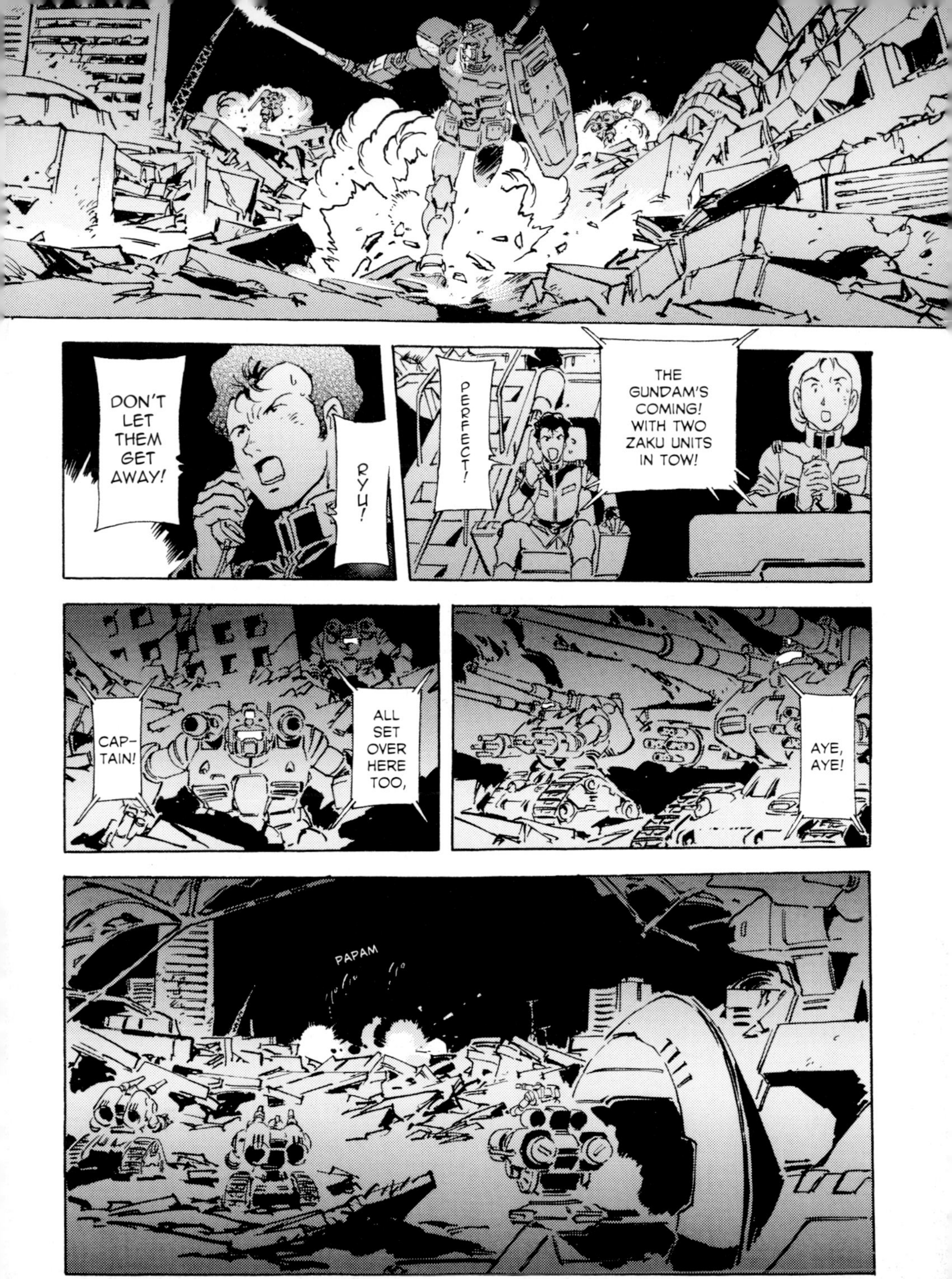
THE GUNDAM'S COMING! WITH TWO ZAKU UNITS IN TOW!
PERFECT!
RYU!
DON'T LET THEM GET AWAY!
AYE, AYE!
ALL SET OVER HERE TOO,
CAP-TAIN!
PAPAM

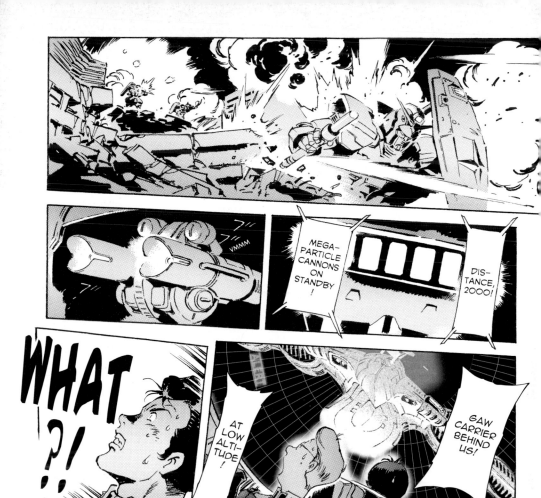

DISTANCE, 2000!
MEGA-PARTICLE CANNONS ON STANDBY!
VMMM
GAW CARRIER BEHIND US!
AT LOW ALTITUDE!
WHAT?!
GRRRMM

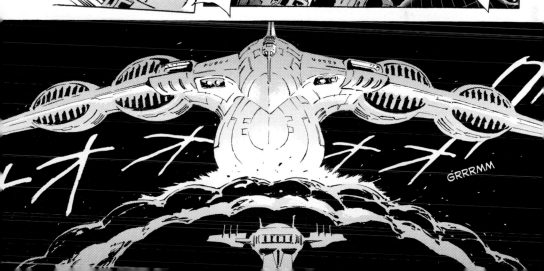

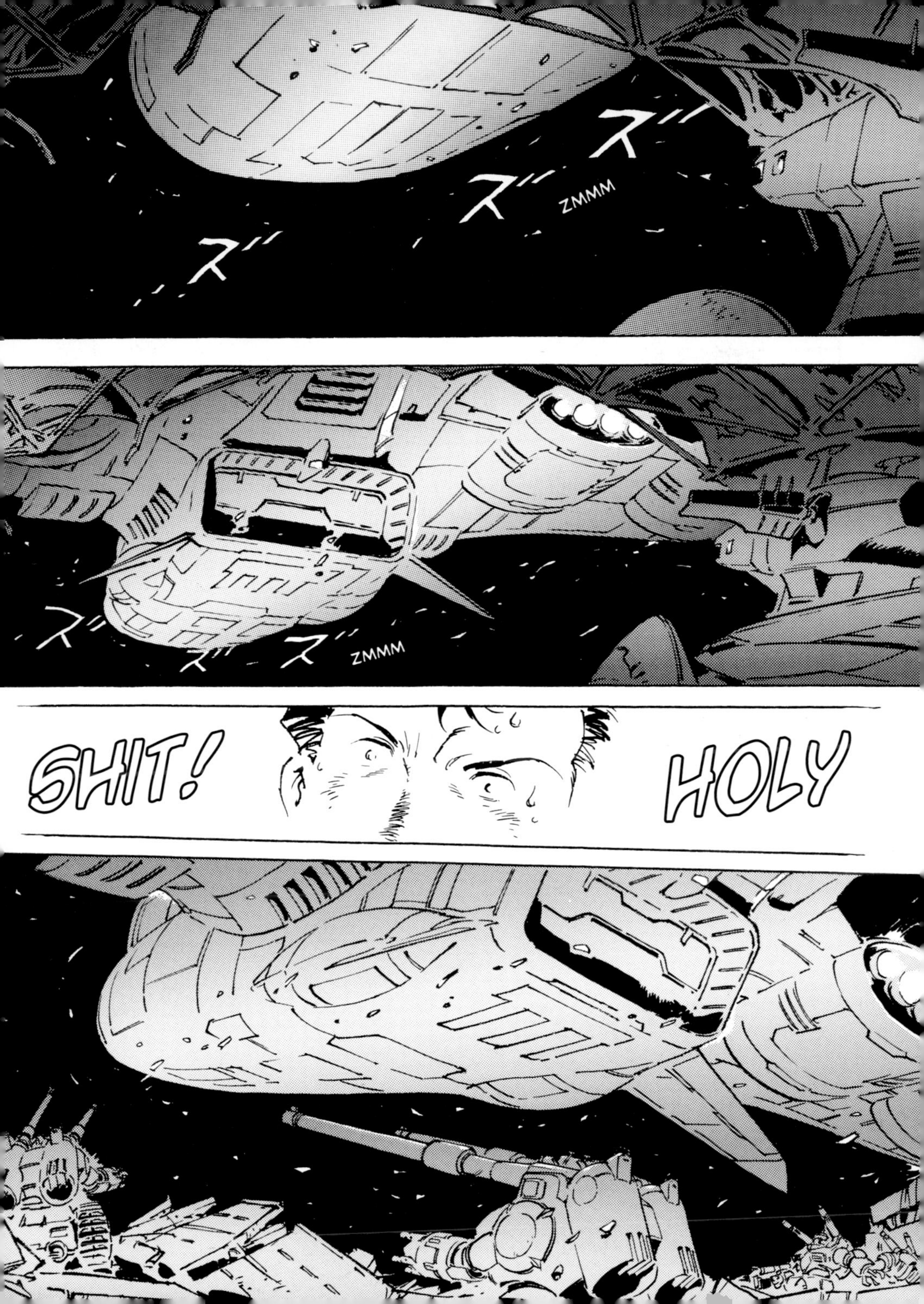
ズズズ
ZMMM
ズズズ
ZMMM
HOLY
SHIT!

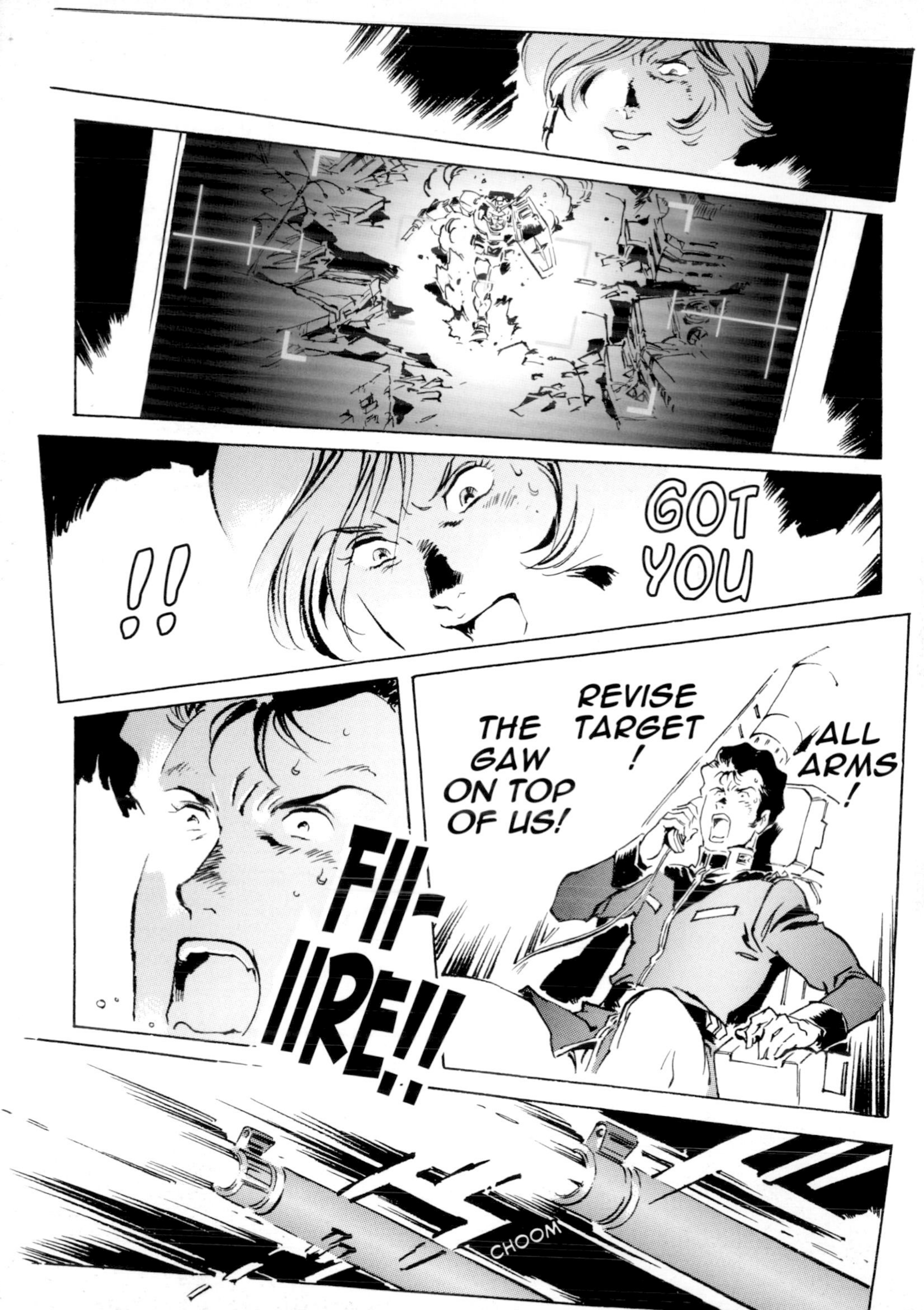
GOT YOU
!!
REVISE TARGET!
THE GAW ON TOP OF US!
ALL ARMS!
FII-IIRE!!
CHOOM

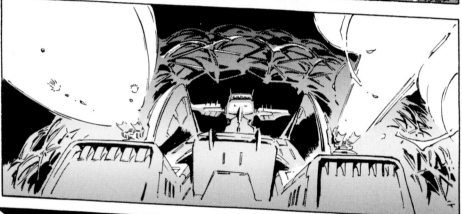

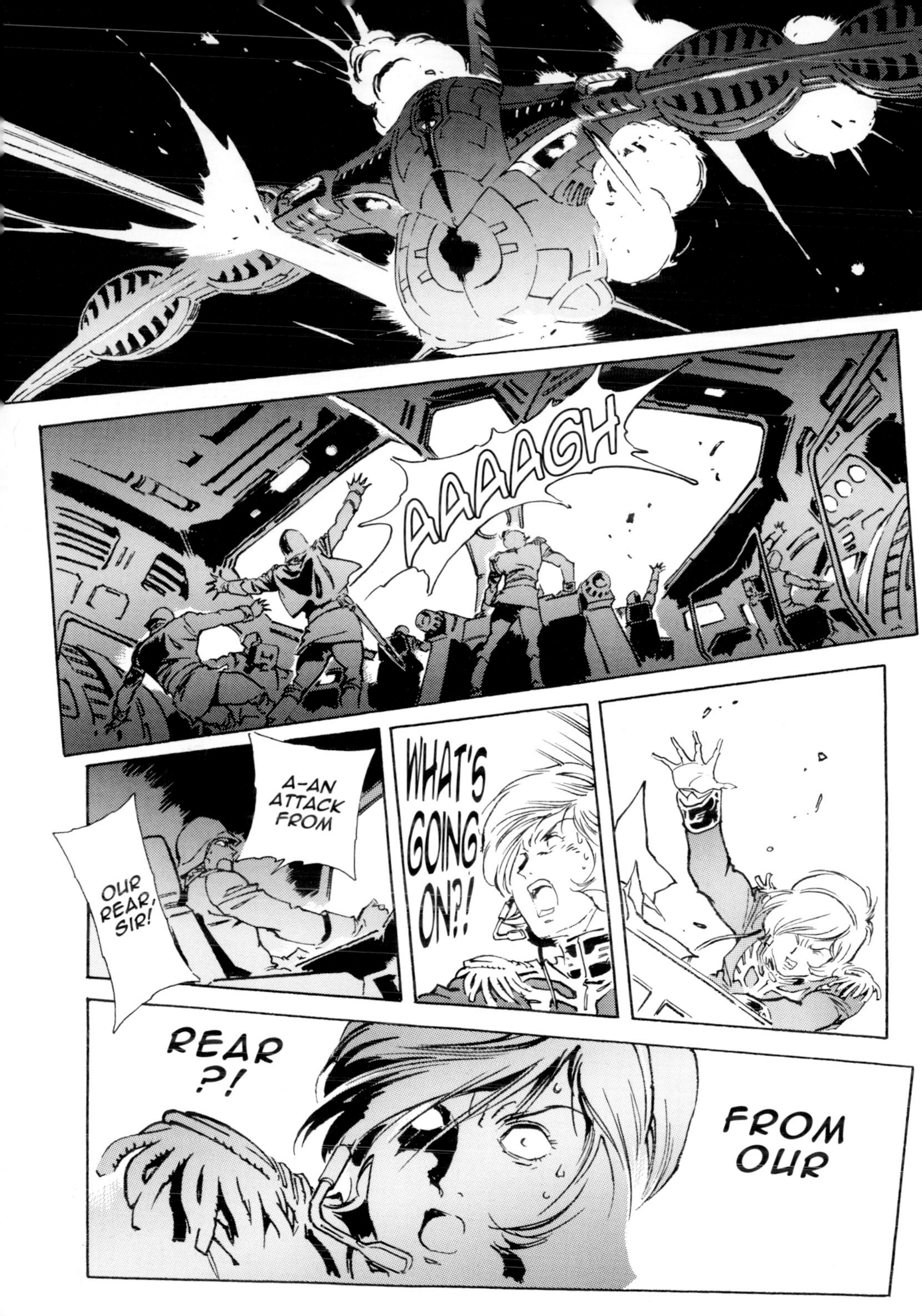
AAAAGH
WHAT'S GOING ON?!
A-AN ATTACK FROM
OUR REAR, SIR!
FROM OUR
REAR ?!

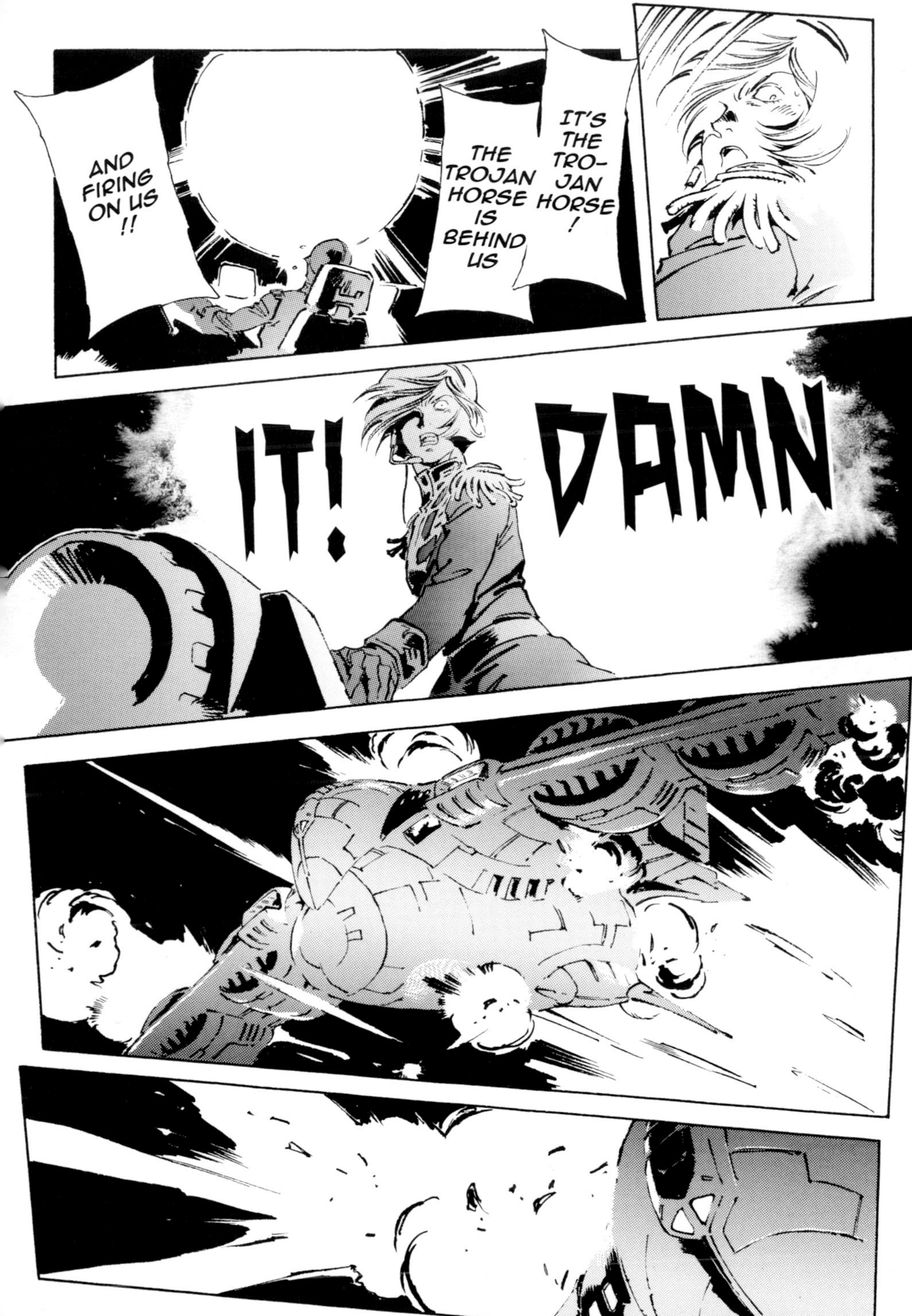
IT'S THE TRO-JAN HORSE!
THE TROJAN HORSE IS BEHIND US
AND FIRING ON US!!
DAMN
IT!

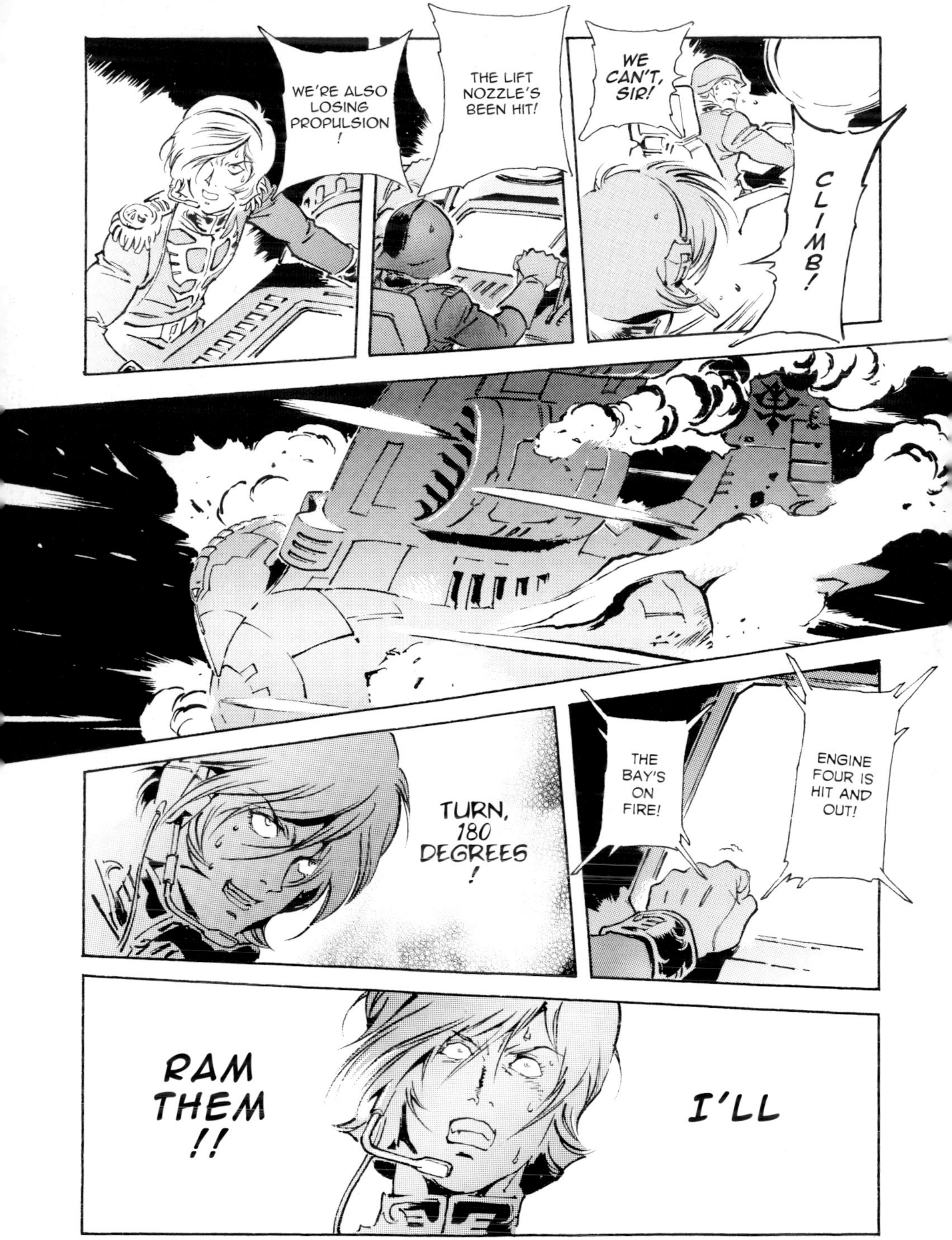
CLIMB!
WE CAN'T, SIR!
THE LIFT NOZZLE'S BEEN HIT!
WE'RE ALSO LOSING PROPULSION!
ENGINE FOUR IS HIT AND OUT!
THE BAY'S ON FIRE!
TURN, 180 DEGREES!
I'LL
RAM THEM!!

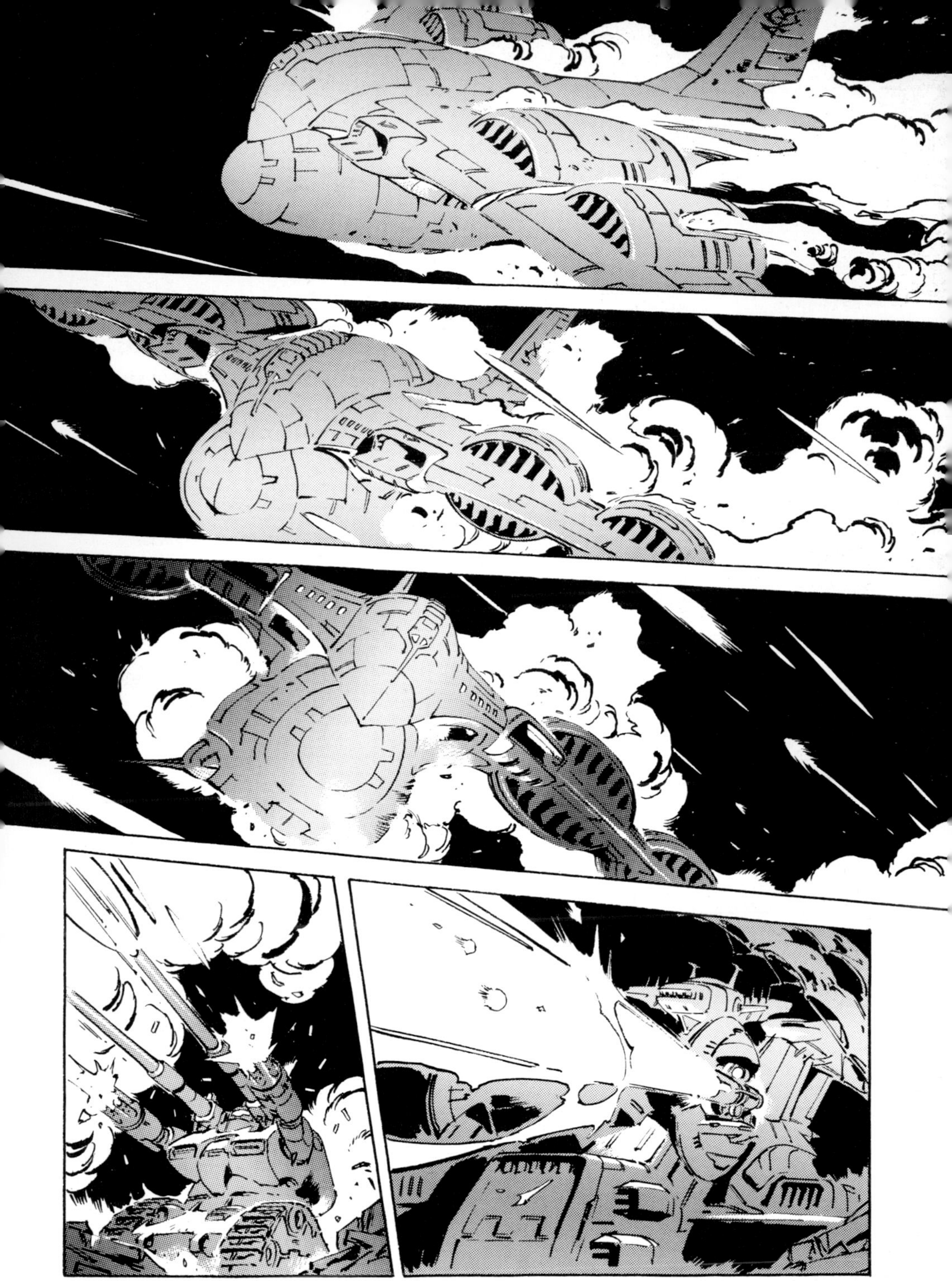

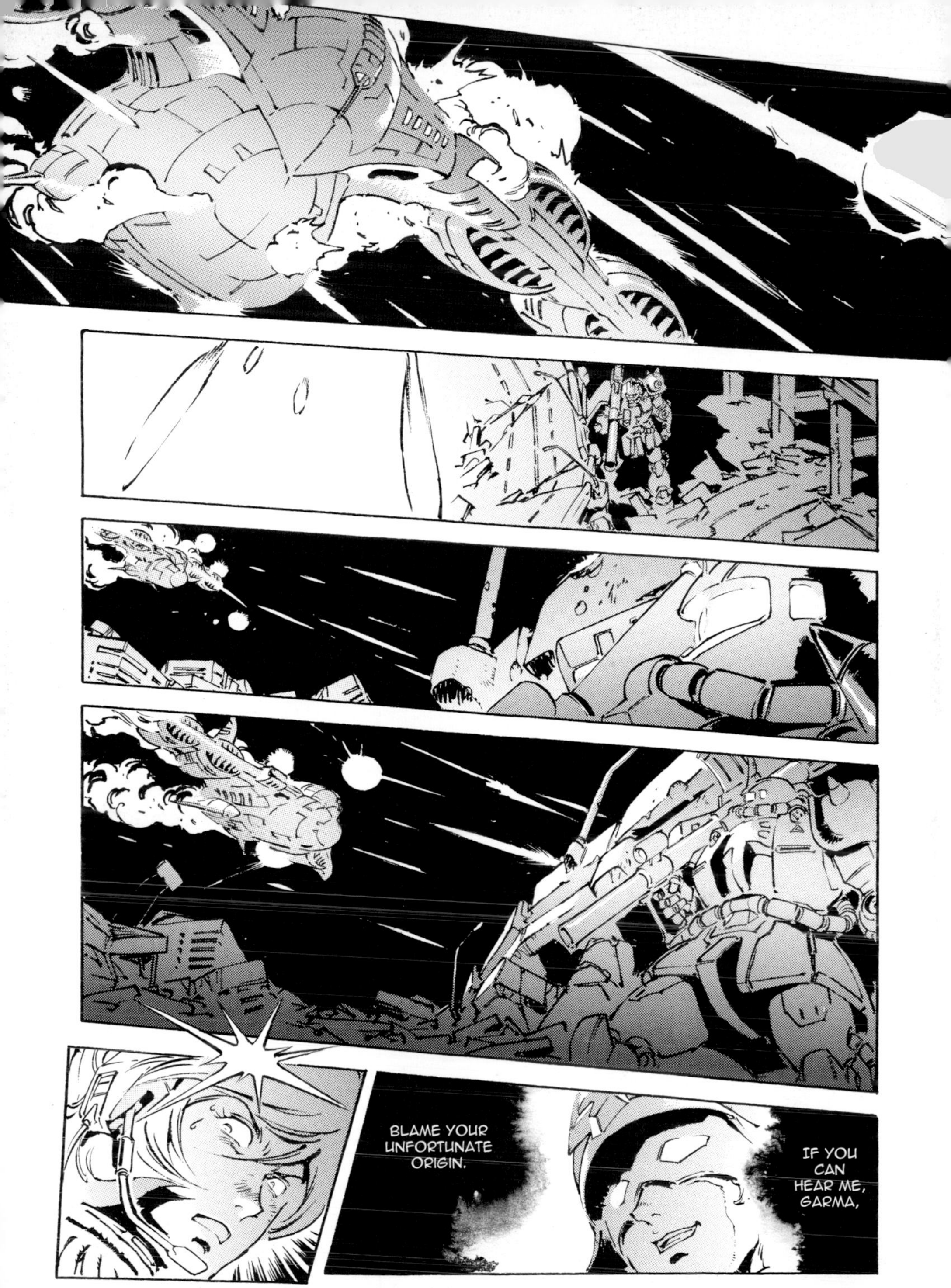
IF YOU CAN HEAR ME, GARMA,
BLAME YOUR UNFORTUNATE ORIGIN.

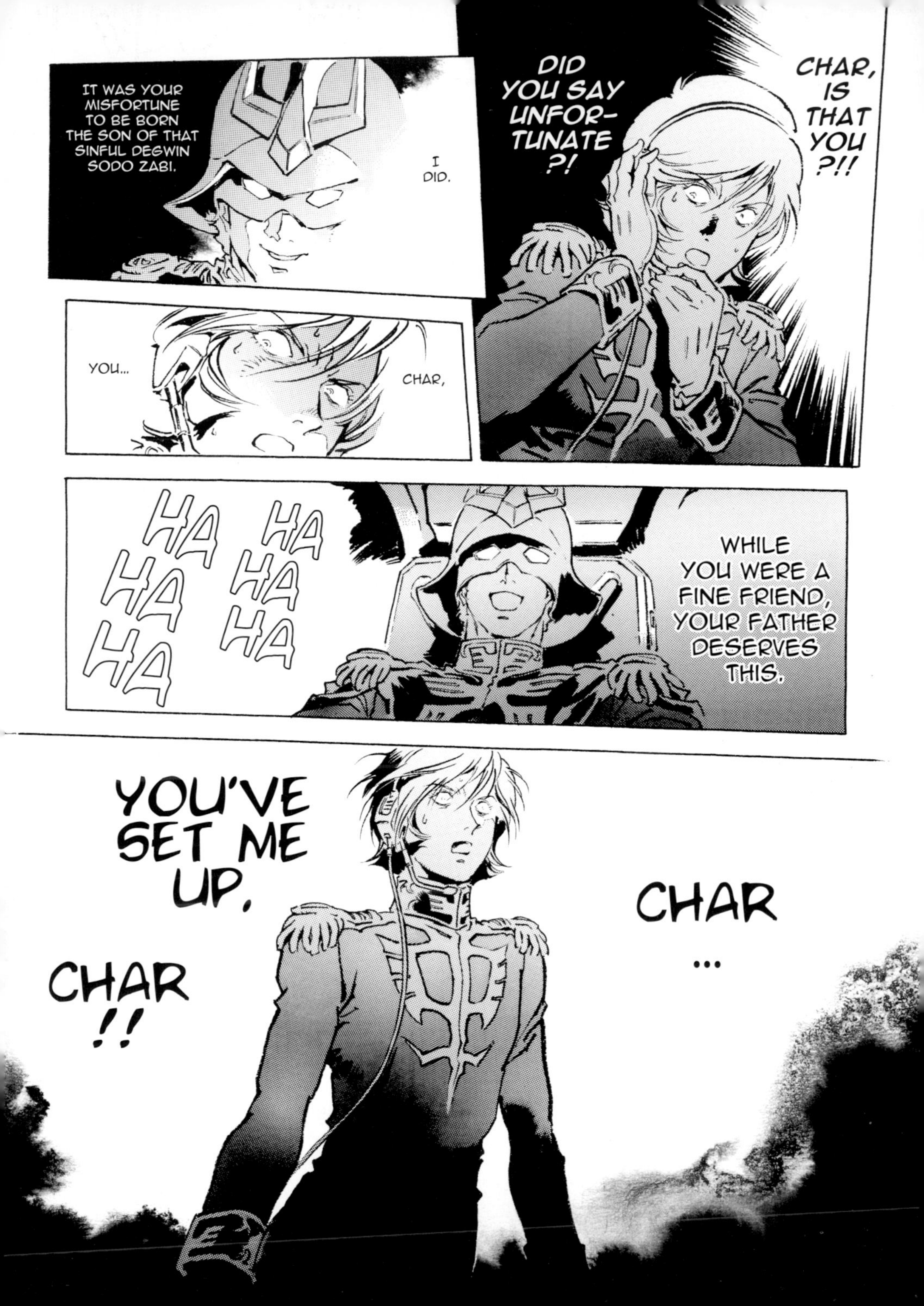
CHAR, IS THAT YOU?!!
DID YOU SAY UNFOR-TUNATE?!
I DID.
IT WAS YOUR MISFORTUNE TO BE BORN THE SON OF THAT SINFUL DEGWIN SODO ZABI.
CHAR,
YOU...
WHILE YOU WERE A FINE FRIEND, YOUR FATHER DESERVES THIS.
HA HA HA HA HA HA HA
CHAR...
YOU'VE SET ME UP.
CHAR!!

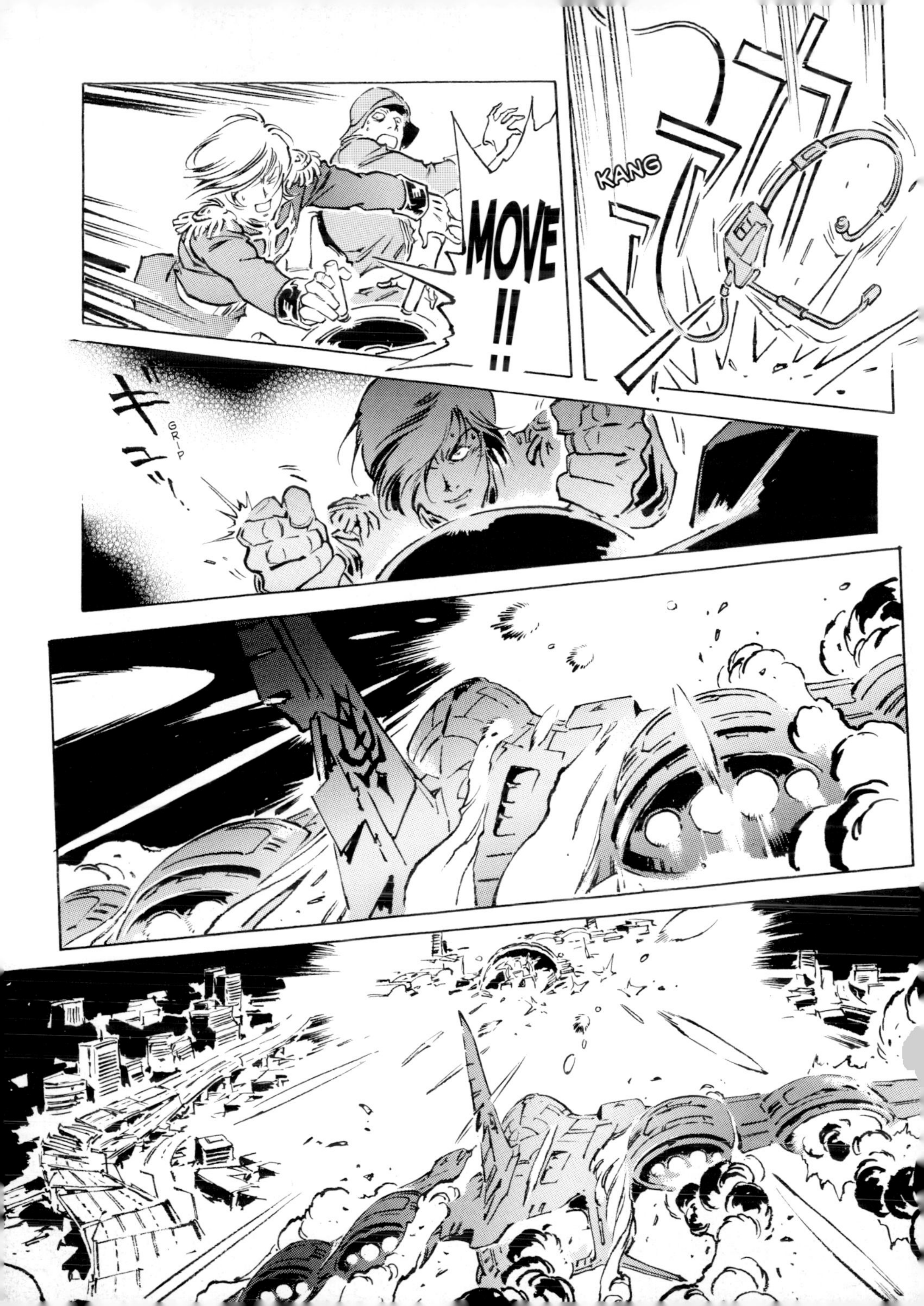
KANG
MOVE!!
GRIP

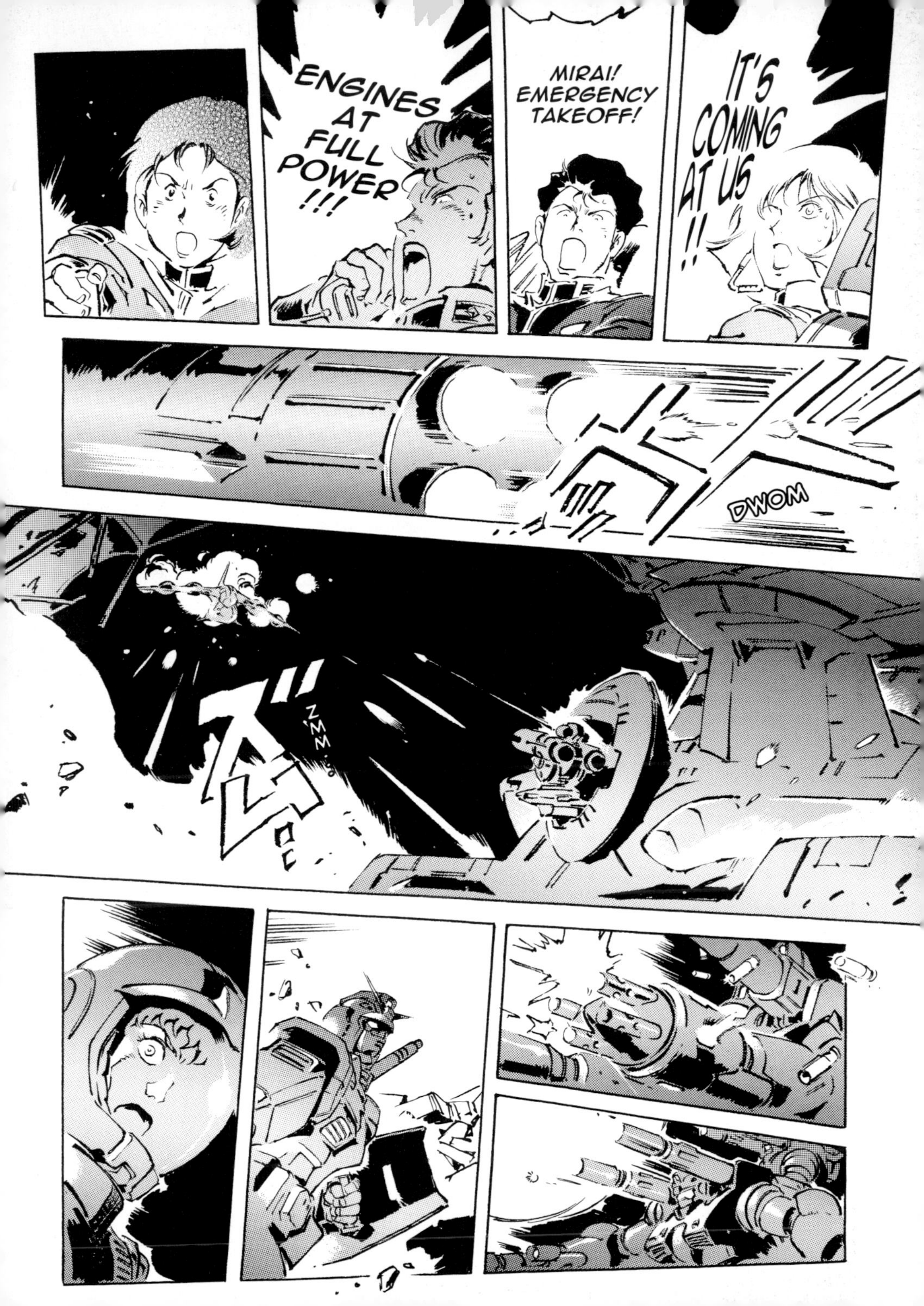
IT'S COMING AT US !!
MIRAI! EMERGENCY TAKEOFF!
ENGINES AT FULL POWER !!!
DWOM

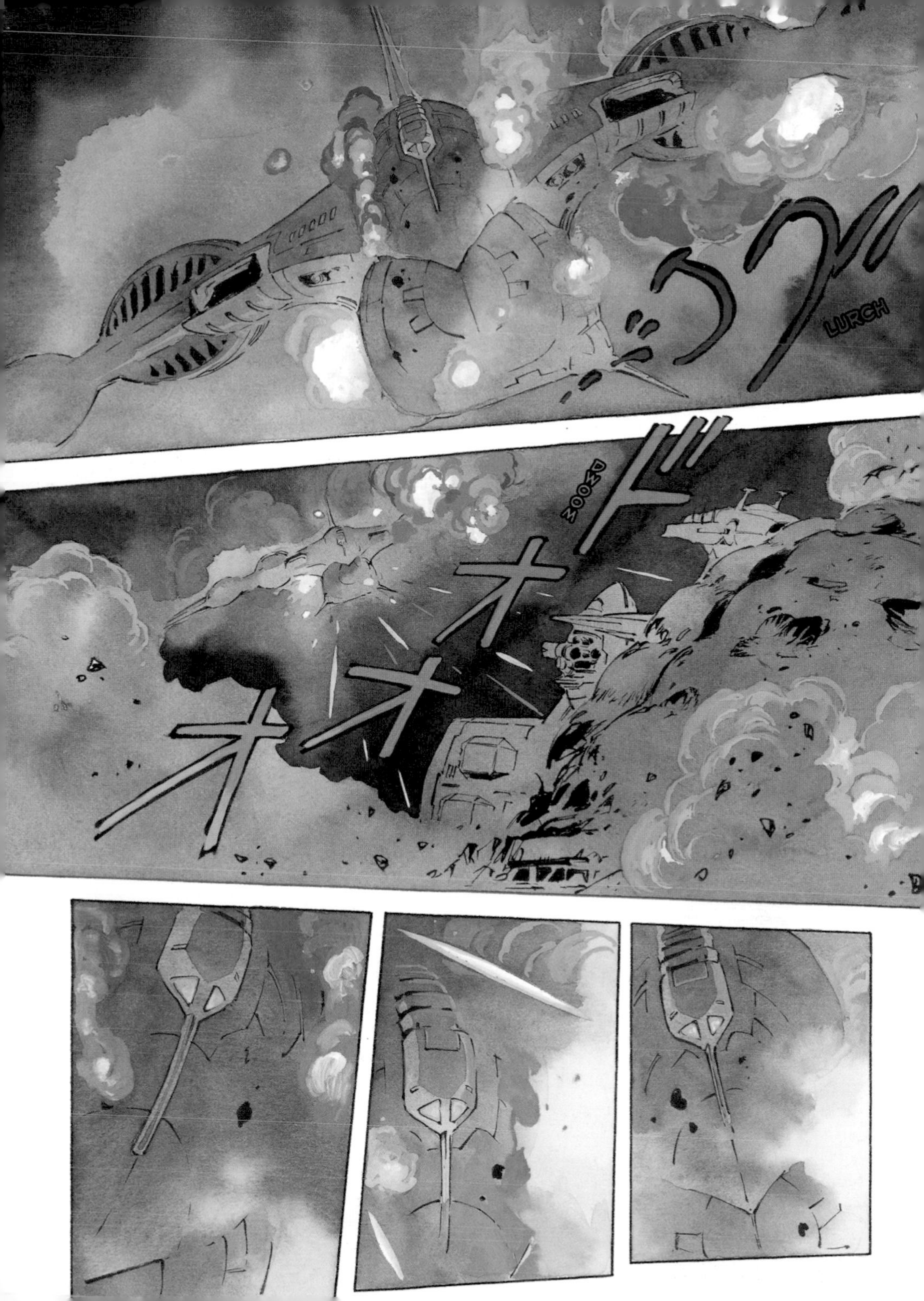
LURCH
ドオオオ
DWOOM

NRAAH!

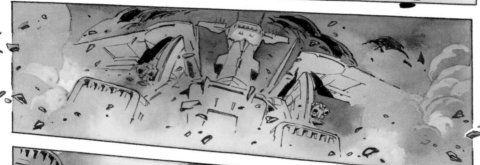

ALL HANDS PREPARE FOR IMPACT!!

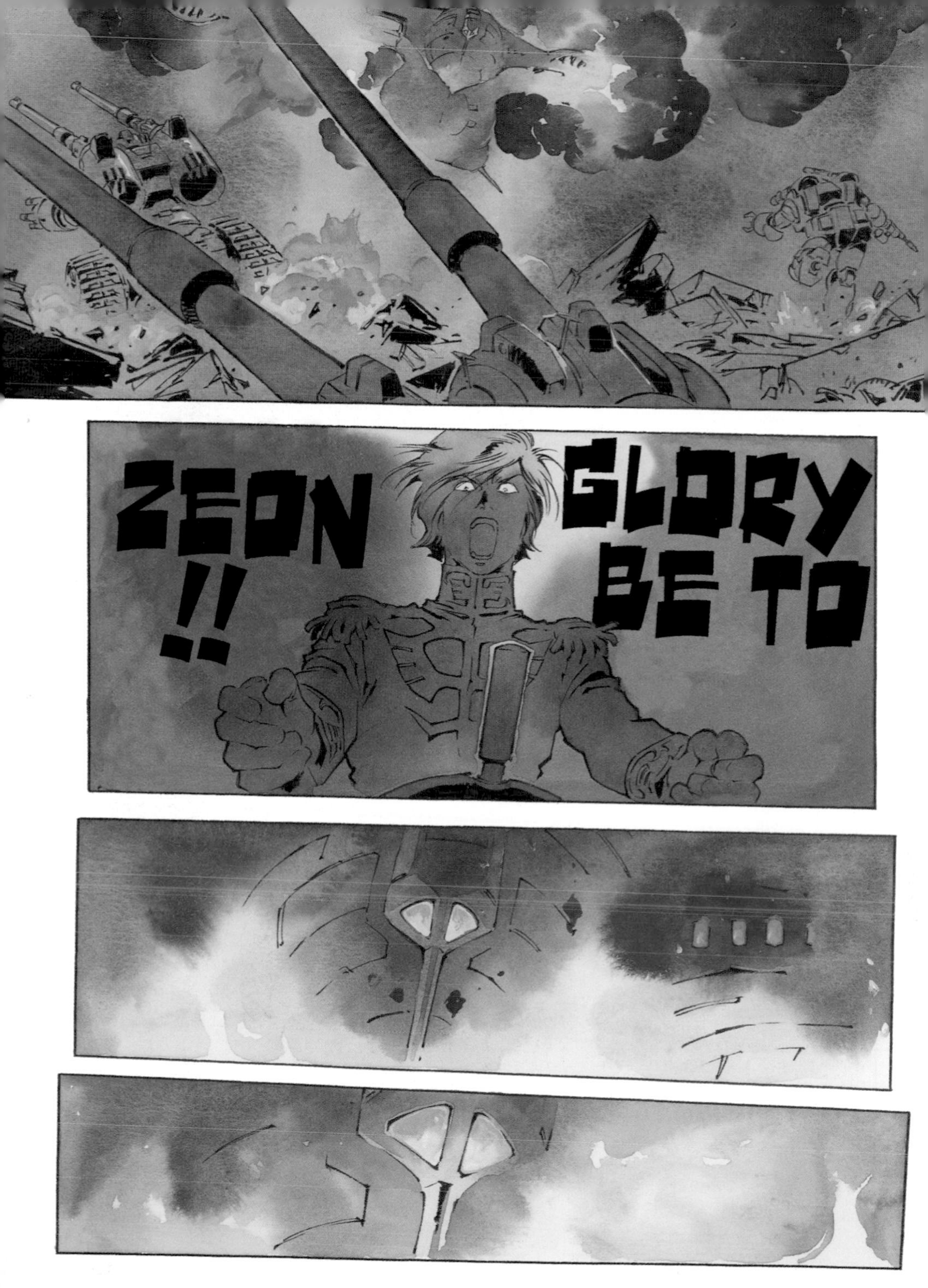
GLORY BE TO
ZEON !!

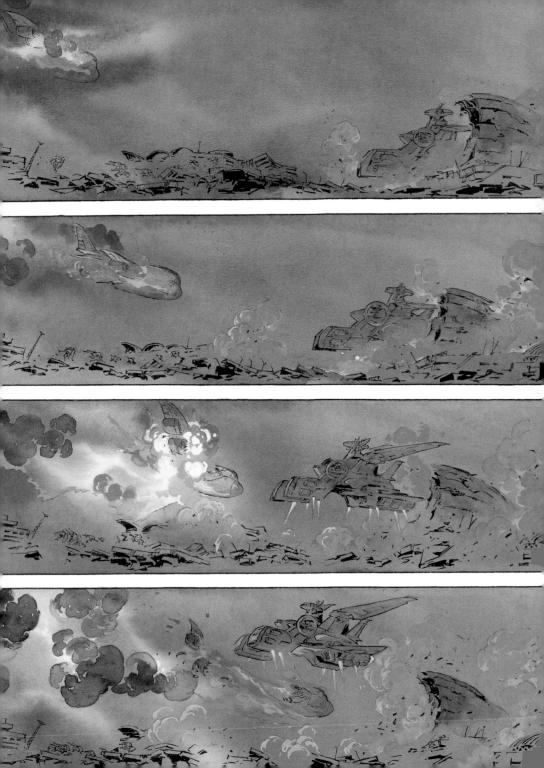

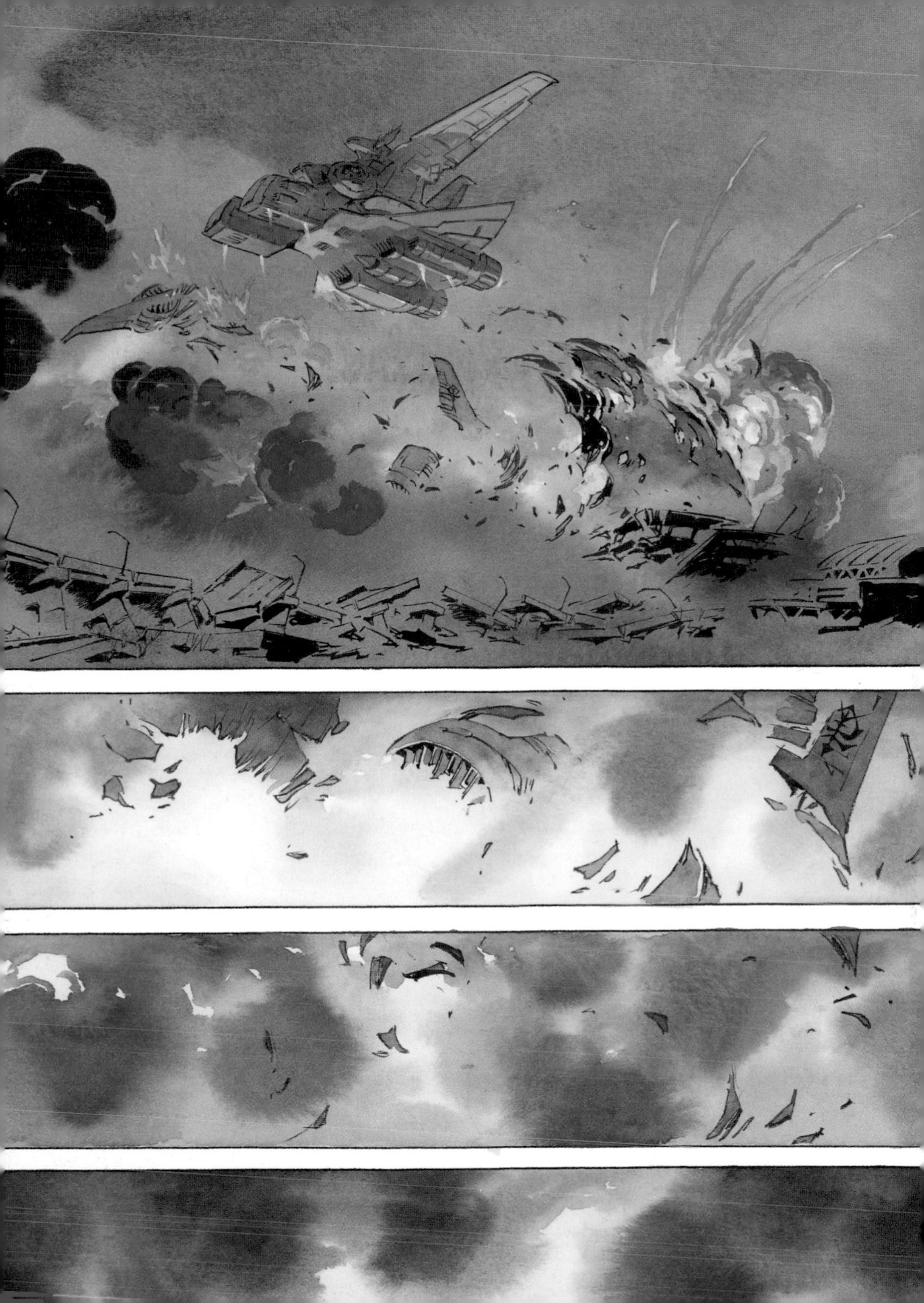

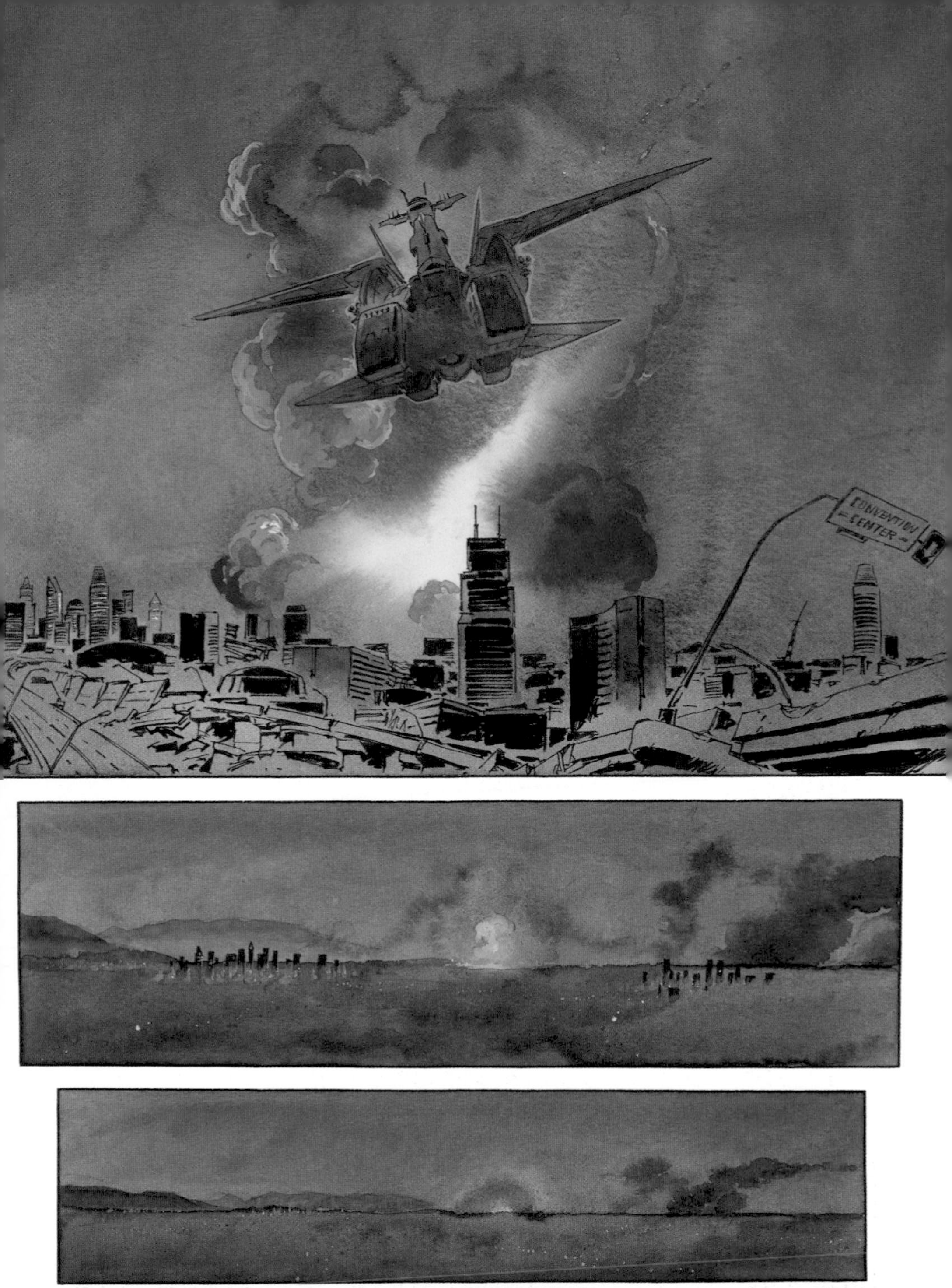
CONVENTION CENTER

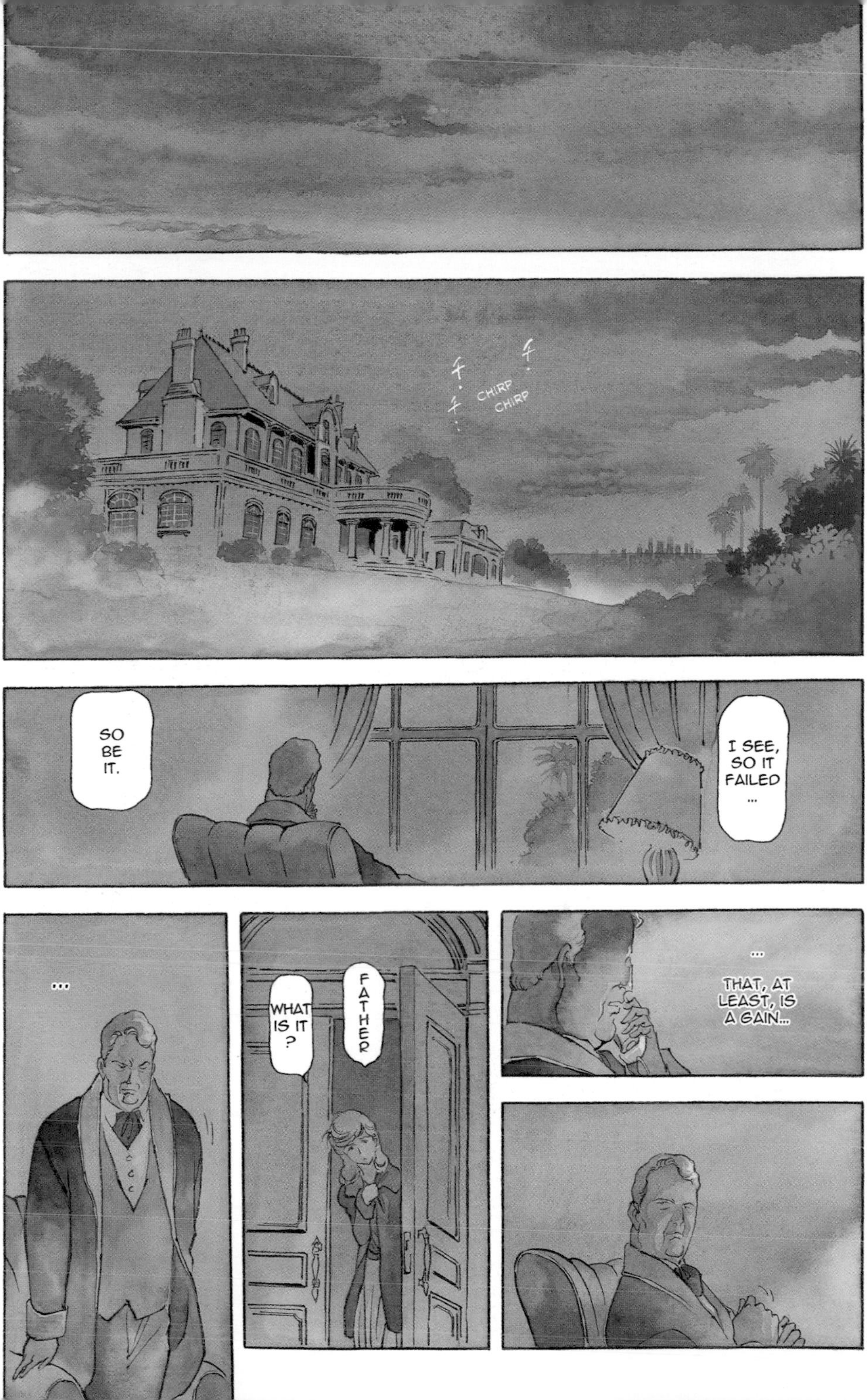
チ・チ・・
チ・
CHIRP CHIRP
I SEE, SO IT FAILED ...
SO BE IT.
... THAT, AT LEAST, IS A GAIN...
FATHER
WHAT IS IT?
...

GARMA ZABI

IS DEAD.

ºoº

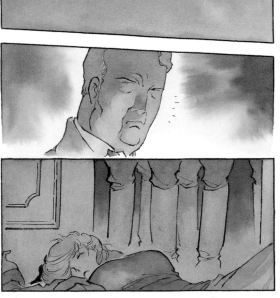

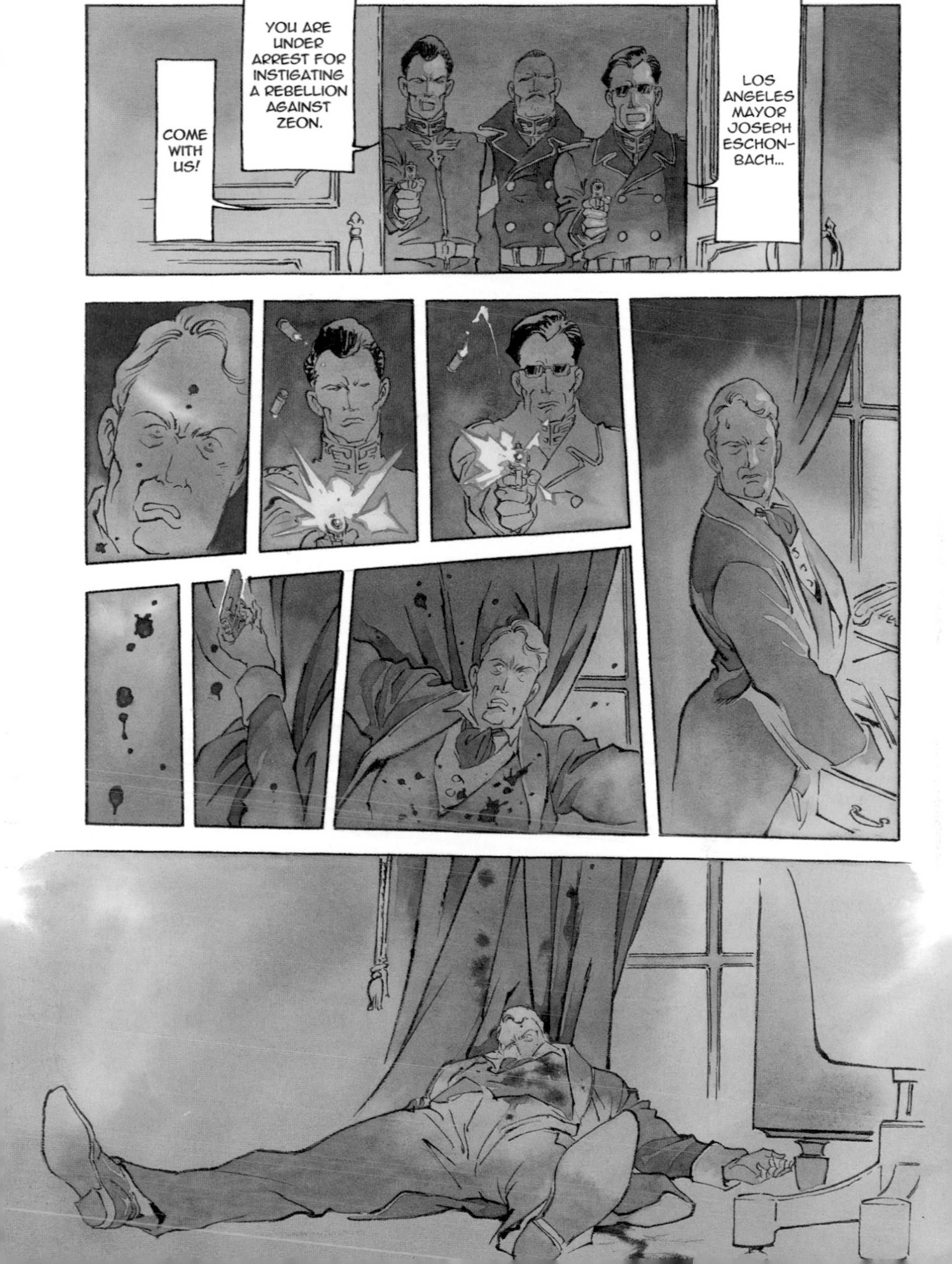
LOS ANGELES MAYOR JOSEPH ESCHON-BACH...
YOU ARE UNDER ARREST FOR INSTIGATING A REBELLION AGAINST ZEON.
COME WITH US!

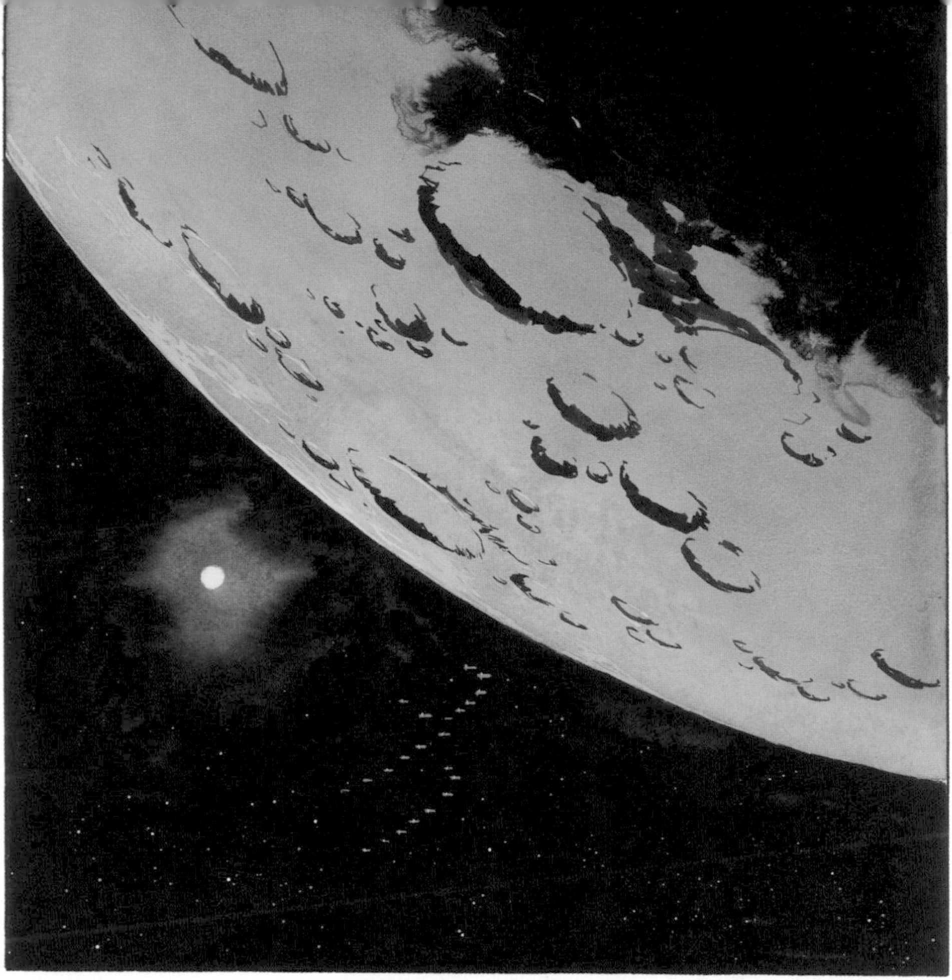
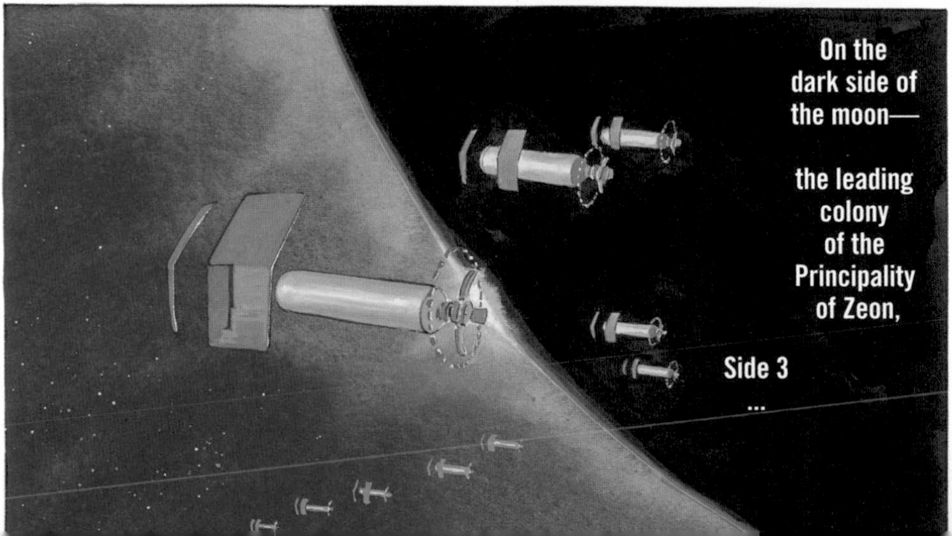
On the dark side of the moon—
the leading colony of the Principality of Zeon,
Side 3
...

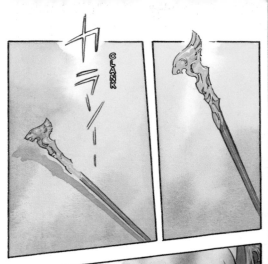

カ ラ ン

CLANK

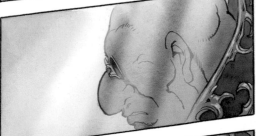

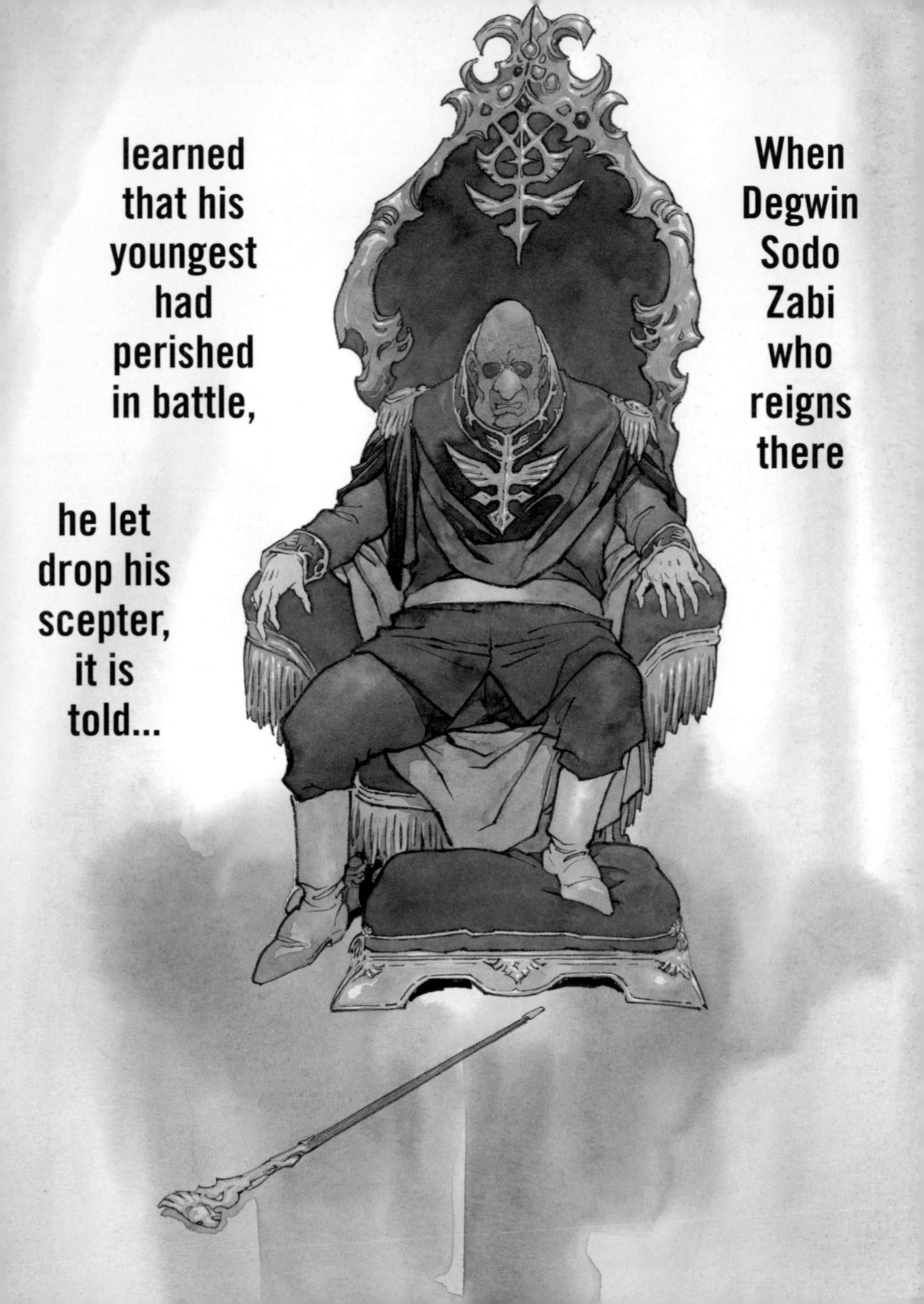
When Degwin Sodo Zabi who reigns there
learned that his youngest had perished in battle,
he let drop his scepter, it is told...

to be continued...

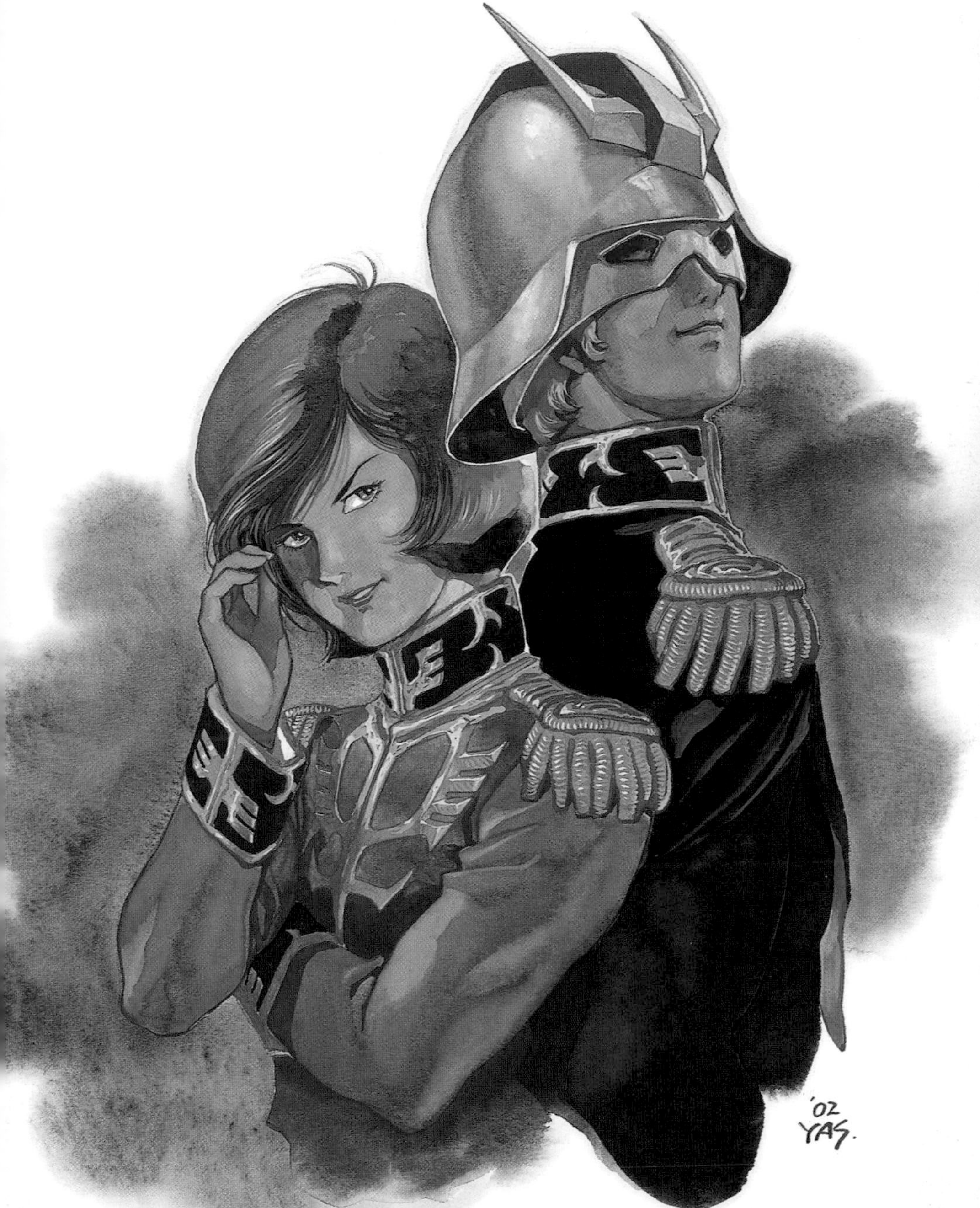
'02
YAS.

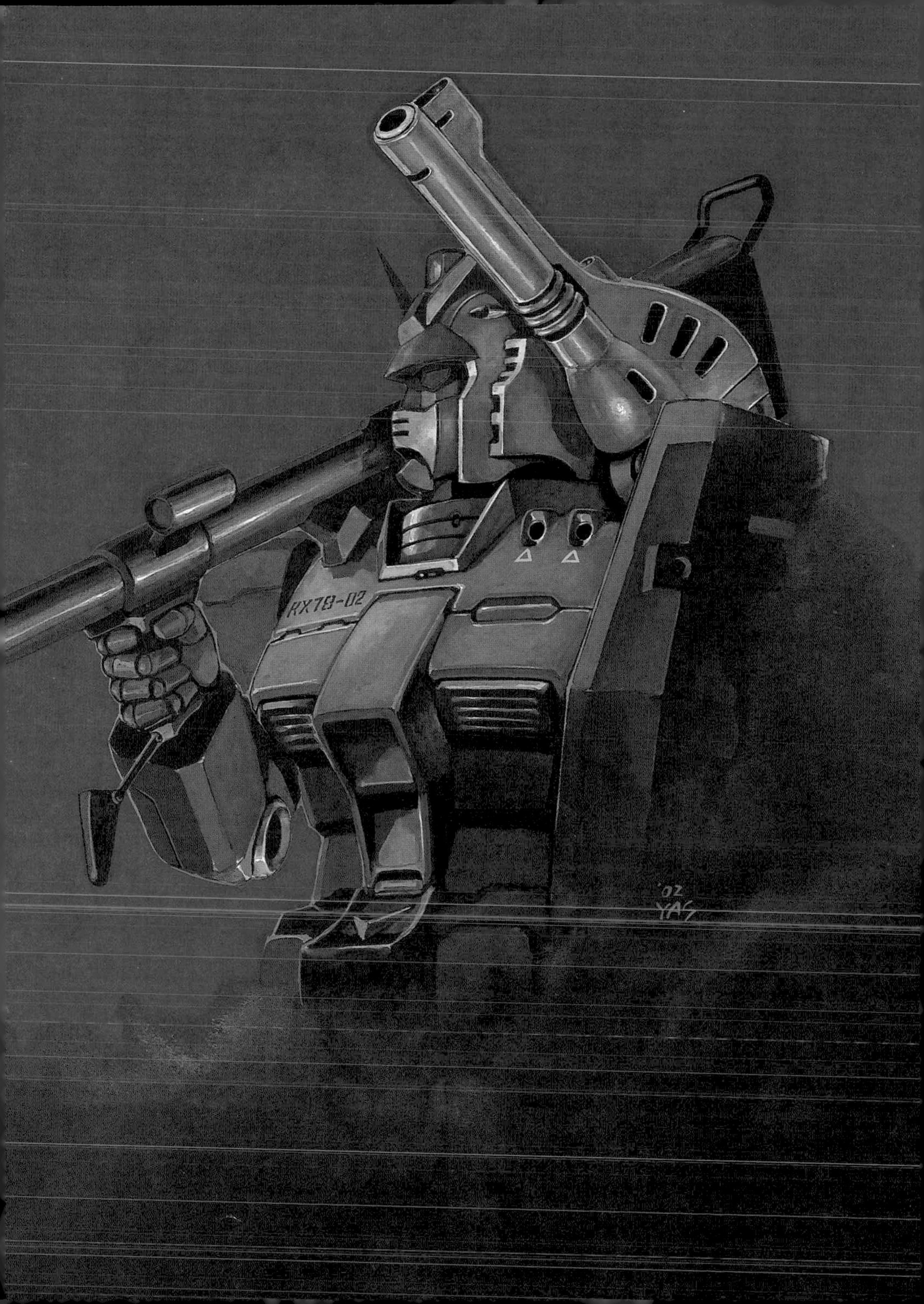
RX78-02
'02
YAS

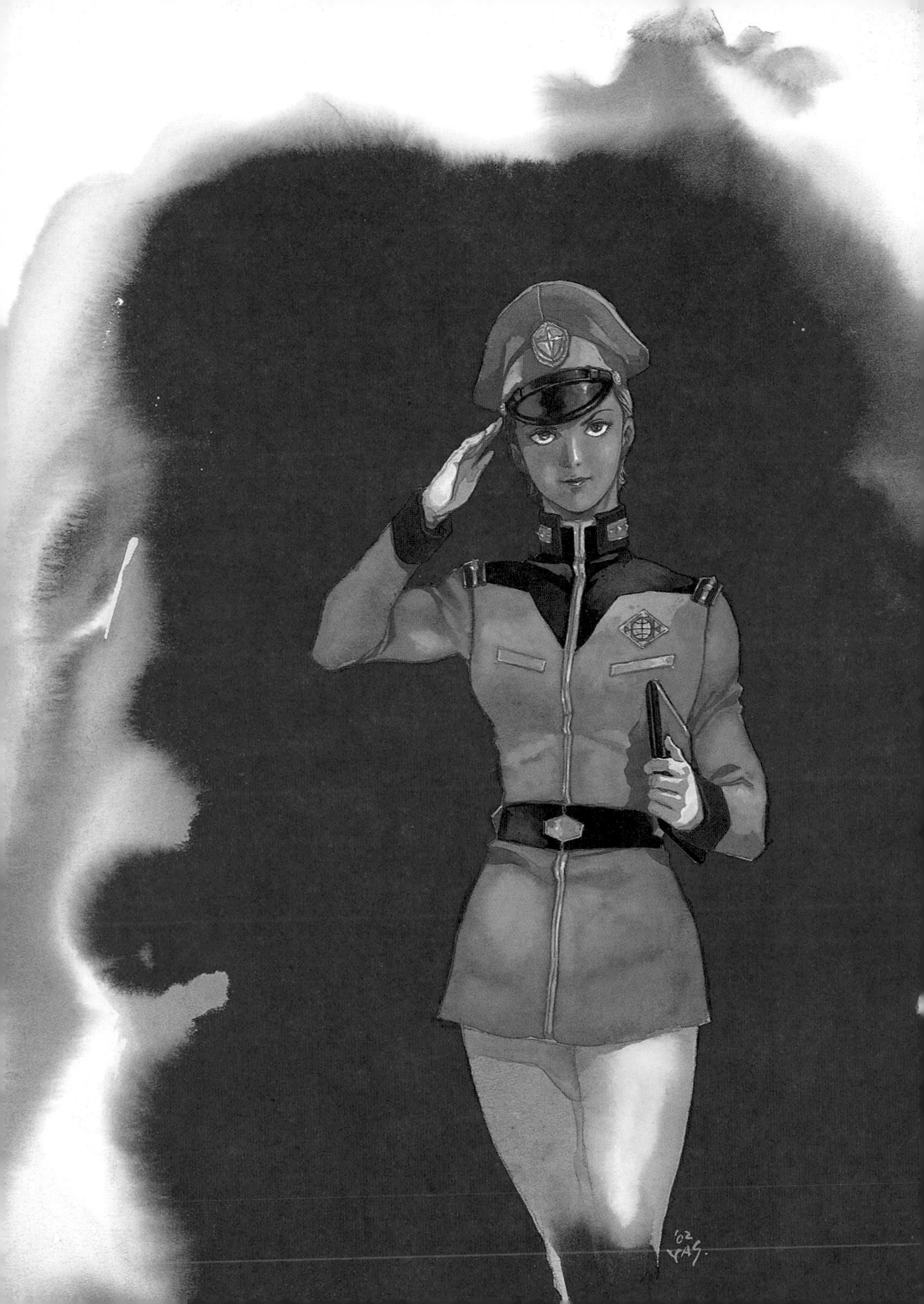
'02
YAS.

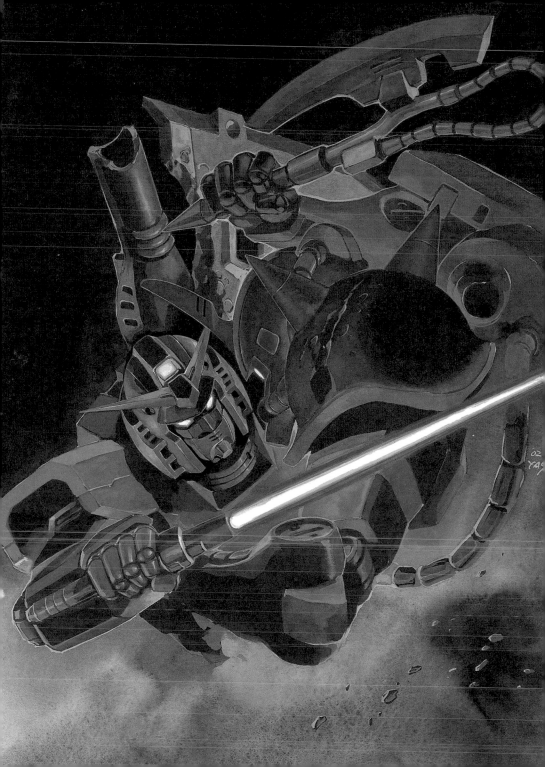

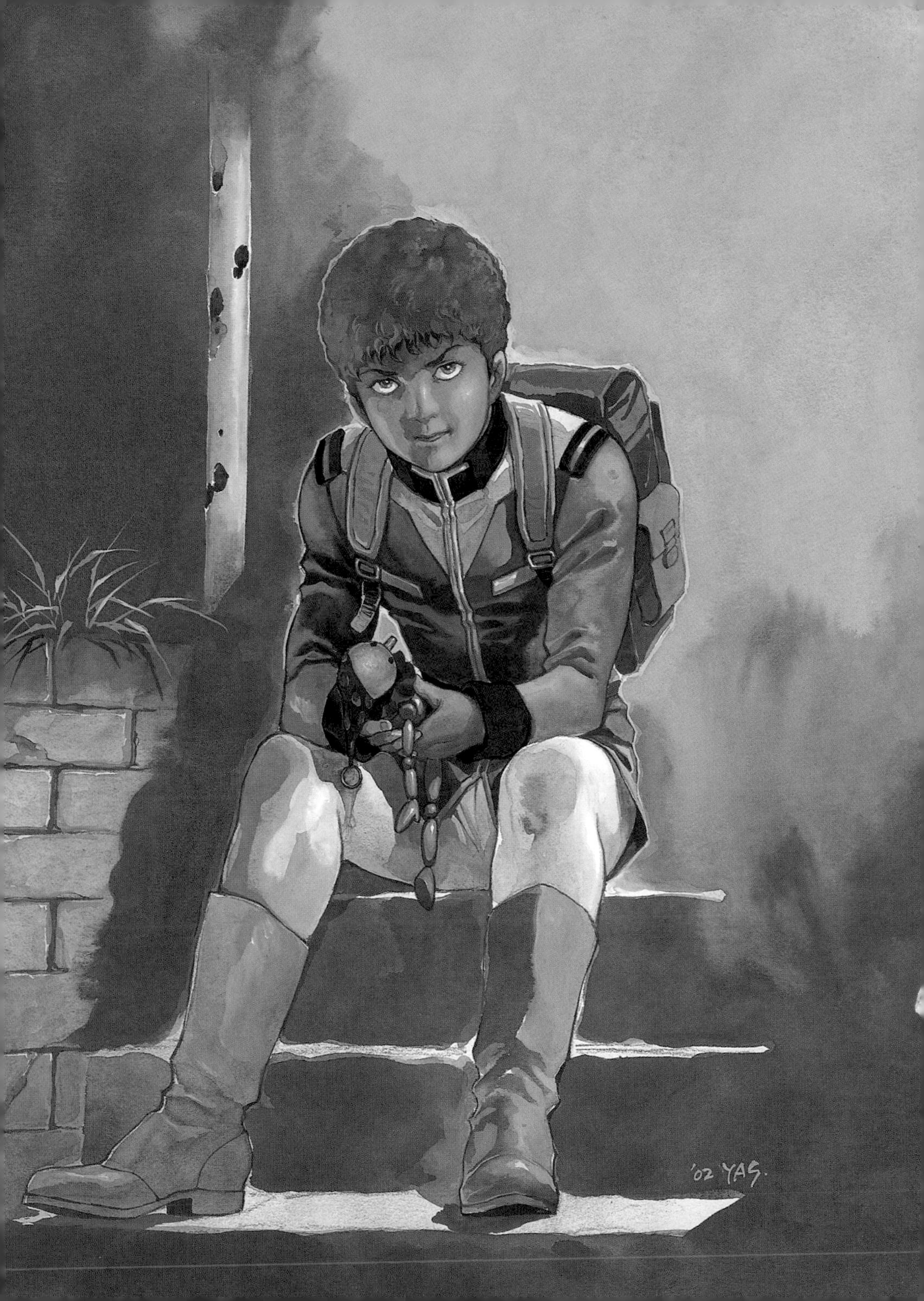
'02 YAS.

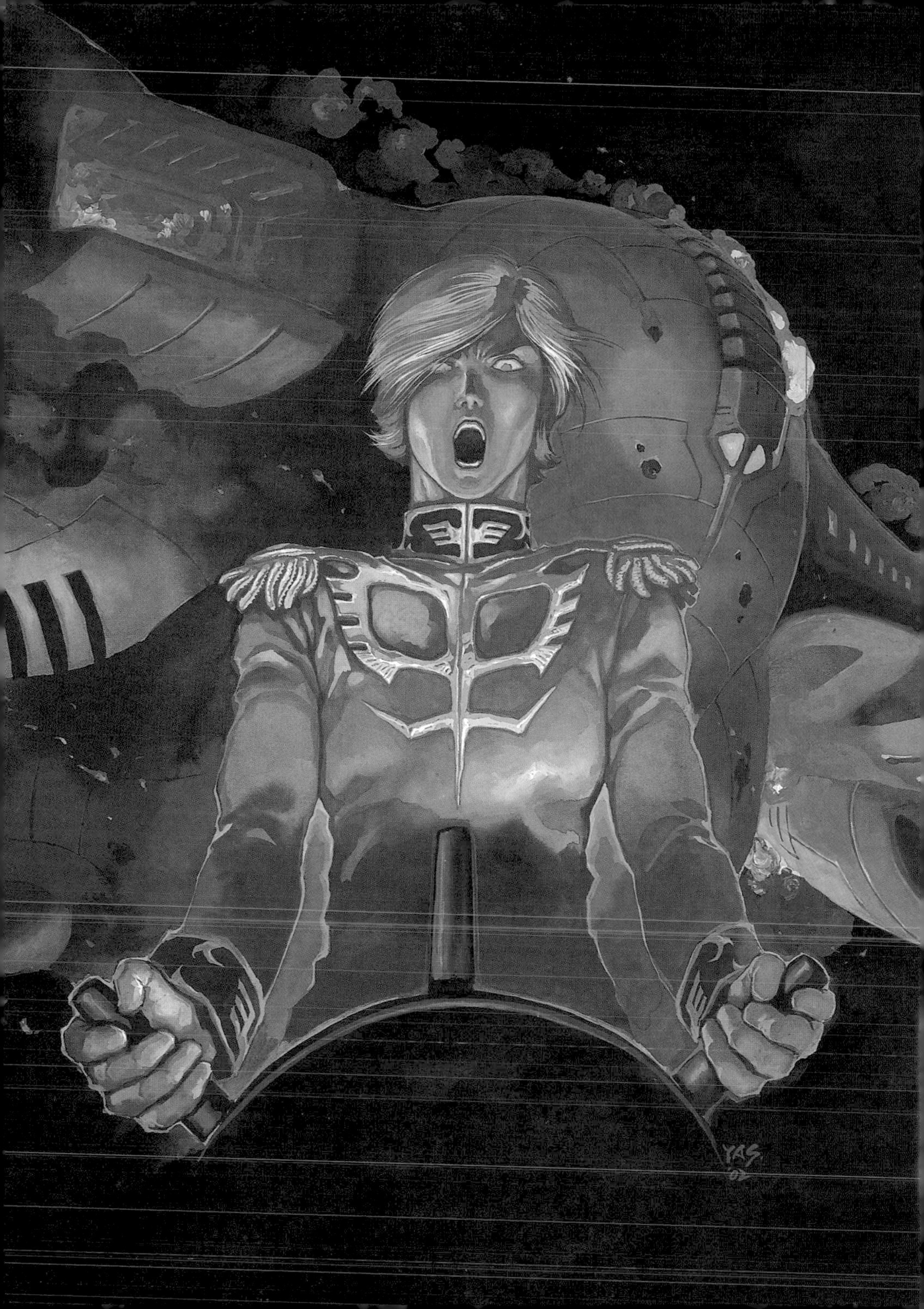
YAS.
'02

Hamon in it. I was startled, thinking, what's up with this anime? She's not an evil overlady? These mechas don't even do a rocket punch or combine or anything? *This is a really original giant robot anime,* I thought (laughs). And then when it got popular with the second broadcast, all the boys were going on about Gunpla models.

Nekoi: I like the original series the best, too.

Igarashi: I was really excited for *Zeta Gundam.* I watched it on the edge of my seat—the first episode, anyway.

Nekoi: But I just couldn't keep up with it. I was like, wait, Amuro isn't the main character? (laughs)

Mokona: Yeah, like, who's this brat? (laughs) And then Char cries, right? And he keeps trying and failing to assassinate people. Where's the dashing Char? But then, when I watched the original series again, Char seemed more cute than cool. Amuro and Bright and Kai—those guys were cooler.

Nekoi: That's a very mature opinion (laughs).

Mokona: But Char in *Origin* is cool again. He's ruthless. *Ooh, I'd fall hard for this guy,* I thought (laughs). *Origin* puts a different spin on the characters. Garma is really adorable. In the anime he was a pathetic spoiled kid, but *Origin* Garma is a lovable character, one you end up feeling pretty bad for (laughs).

Nekoi: And Ramba Ral is even more awesome. He just hogs all the good parts. Char is actually a lost cause, pretty much.

Igarashi: You can really see how broken he gets when he's grown up.

Nekoi: I can totally see why Sayla thinks he's too far gone (laughs).

Mokona: And it's like Amuro's far out alone and the best ever.

Nekoi: I guess that's what makes Char so cute, the contrast against his strengths.

Igarashi: I did like Garma, but he dies pretty early in the story, so I had to pin all my hopes on Char (laughs)… And he went in a weirder and weirder direction, until finally we got *Char's Counterattack* (laughs). But we're drawn to weird people, aren't we.

Nekoi: I was really identifying with Amuro when I watched. Kai, too, he got some depth in that storyline with Miharu.

Igarashi: Yeah, Kai is delicious (laughs).

Mokona: But when we go on about who we like, nobody ever mentions Hayato (laughs). Why not?

Nekoi: Hayato is a good kid—he's just *too* good. And I like mecha, so I was really into the idea of the realistic

mecha in *Gundam,* that people can get into and operate. I mean, before that, giant robots in anime were like, 57 meters tall.

Igarashi: Also, *Gundam* had somebody awesome in every scene. (laughs)

Nekoi: All the characters have backgrounds, their own dramas. Not everyone is stunningly handsome, but they all have their charms.

Mokona: Actually, the middle-aged men ranked higher on the coolness scale.

Igarashi: When you read *Origin* it makes you want to watch the anime again.

Mokona: There are things that you don't quite get in the anime that come through "properly" in *Origin.* Like the scene where Ryu kamikazes with his Core Fighter. Amuro's dealing with the bomb and gets attacked from behind by Lady Hamon, but nobody comes to help, not Kai or anyone. So Ryu has to do something. I always thought that was weird—what was everybody else doing? But the manga shows Kai and the others hard at work getting *White Base* ready for takeoff, so that made a lot more sense.

Nekoi: It's hard to get those kind of details into an anime. Mr. Yasuhiko must've been hounded by things like that.

At this point, Ohkawa returns.

Ohkawa: I hope your chat's been worthy of gracing the end of a collector's edition volume. We should each have a little message for Mr. Yasuhiko.

Igarashi: I'm starting to feel like I'm Amuro's mom. (laughs) I keep worrying for him like a mother would but am really excited. I'll be following *Origin* to the very end, so please keep up your amazing work!

Nekoi: I can't wait to see what'll happen next. I hope you keep drawing a ton of manga, so I have enough to enjoy to the end of my days!

Mokona: I absolutely love it. I'm saving space on my bookshelf for it! And I really want to see the new anime, too. Of course, the manga already has so much life in it, but I'd also like to see your art brought to life on the screen, Mr. Yasuhiko.

CLAMP

A creative team consisting of four women, Satsuki Igarashi, Nanase Ohkawa, Tsubaki Nekoi, and Mokona. In addition to manga, they are active in various fields including illustrations, graphic inserts, cover design, and scenario and essay writing.

A Special Contribution from CLAMP

It was my dream to draw with a touch like that.

Mokona: Hmm, what can I say about Mr. Yasuhiko? I mean, he's like a god to me. I respect him so much.

Igarashi: Sure, but when you met him at that wedding, you went into full-on fangirl mode (laughs).

Nekoi: Once you recognized him, you forced someone to change seats with you and basically clung to him the whole time (laughs).

Mokona: *A god stands before my very eyes! I'll never have another chance!* I thought.

Nekoi: I mean, I wanted to talk to him, too, but…

Igarashi: There was no way to get a word in edgewise past you.

Mokona: Ha ha ha ha!

Igarashi: His wife was gorgeous, too.

Nekoi: Someone wrote in an illustration collection that she's a beauty, and it was really true.

Mokona: Yup.

—*The editor suddenly sets the* Yoshikazu Yasuhiko Illustration Collection *and storyboard drafts for* Mobile Suit Gundam: THE ORIGIN *on the table!*

Everyone: OOOH! (They all reach for the drafts.)

Igarashi: A-Are these the storyboards? Wow… They're practically finished drawings. You could ink these and be good to go.

Mokona: If my storyboards came out like these, everyone would be thrilled (laughs).

Nekoi: They're just pencils, but the images are all right there. You can even actually read the dialogue (laughs).

Ohkawa: Now there's an example for you to follow, Mokona (laughs).

With that, Ohkawa returns to her meeting.

Nekoi: But if you put out storyboards on this level, it'd be hard for editors to suggest changes.

Igarashi & Mokona: Yeah.

Igarashi: These are in pencil, but he draws the actual drafts with a brush, right?

Mokona: At the storyboard stage, though, he's already established the touch he'll use in the finals.

Nekoi: Yeah. He draws with an awareness of how thick the lines will be when they're inked. And I bet he probably uses a brush so that he can get the perfect touch down in one stroke. With a pen, you have to use pressure and grip to vary the strength of the lines, but a brush lets your strokes flow more naturally.

Mokona: Right around the time when I first started drawing, I came across Mr. Yasuhiko's art, and it had such a huge influence on me. Seriously, it was my dream to draw with a touch like that. But it's really hard to draw with a brush… I worked at it, but I just couldn't pull it off…

Igarashi: Now that you mention it, your drawings back in high school had sort of a brush-like feel to them.

Mokona: Balance is the hard part, with a brush.

Igarashi: Right. Laying thick and thin strokes like this with the same brush—that really is hard.

Mokona: In the end, the best I could do was to imitate the way his characters stand (laughs).

Nekoi: That S-curve, right? (laughs)

Now they all reach for the illustration collection…

Igarashi: Ooh, *Dirty Pair* and *Crusher Joe*… I went to see those. Come to think of it, *Zambot 3* was Mr. Yasuhiko's work, too, wasn't it. Though I totally didn't realize it at the time.

Mokona: Mr. Yasuhiko's color illustrations overall have a kind of dark tone to them, but he really tends to use bright reds effectively, don't you think?

Igarashi: That's true, a lot of his art does make the red stand out.

Mokona: More like vermilion than just red. *(Looking at the illustration collection)* Whoa, he even worked on *Space Battleship Yamato*!

Igarashi: I remember being surprised to see Mr. Yasuhiko's name in some encyclopedia for *Yamato*. Oh, hey, I have a poster of this illustration. You could only get one if you bought advance tickets for the *Gundam* movies.

Mokona: And they would change the design every month. You had the worst time deciding when to buy the tickets to get the poster (laughs).

Nekoi: And being just a kid, you couldn't buy all of them… It was pretty frustrating, huh (laughs).

Mokona: If it were now, we'd totally just go every month and get all the posters (laughs).

Igarashi: You know the scene in *Crusher Joe* where the characters go to see *Dirty Pair*? Just around that time, the *Dirty Pair* anime was on TV. I was wondering why they didn't have Mr. Yasuhiko working on the TV series. So I remember being thrilled to see his *Dirty Pair* art in that movie.

Nekoi: Looking at this stuff now, though, we understand the circumstances behind it.

Igarashi: I feel bad for complaining about it at the time.

Nekoi: We haven't been talking about *Gundam* at all, here! Mokona, didn't you say you're proud of having watched the very first broadcast of the original series?

Mokona: I just happened to see an episode with Lady

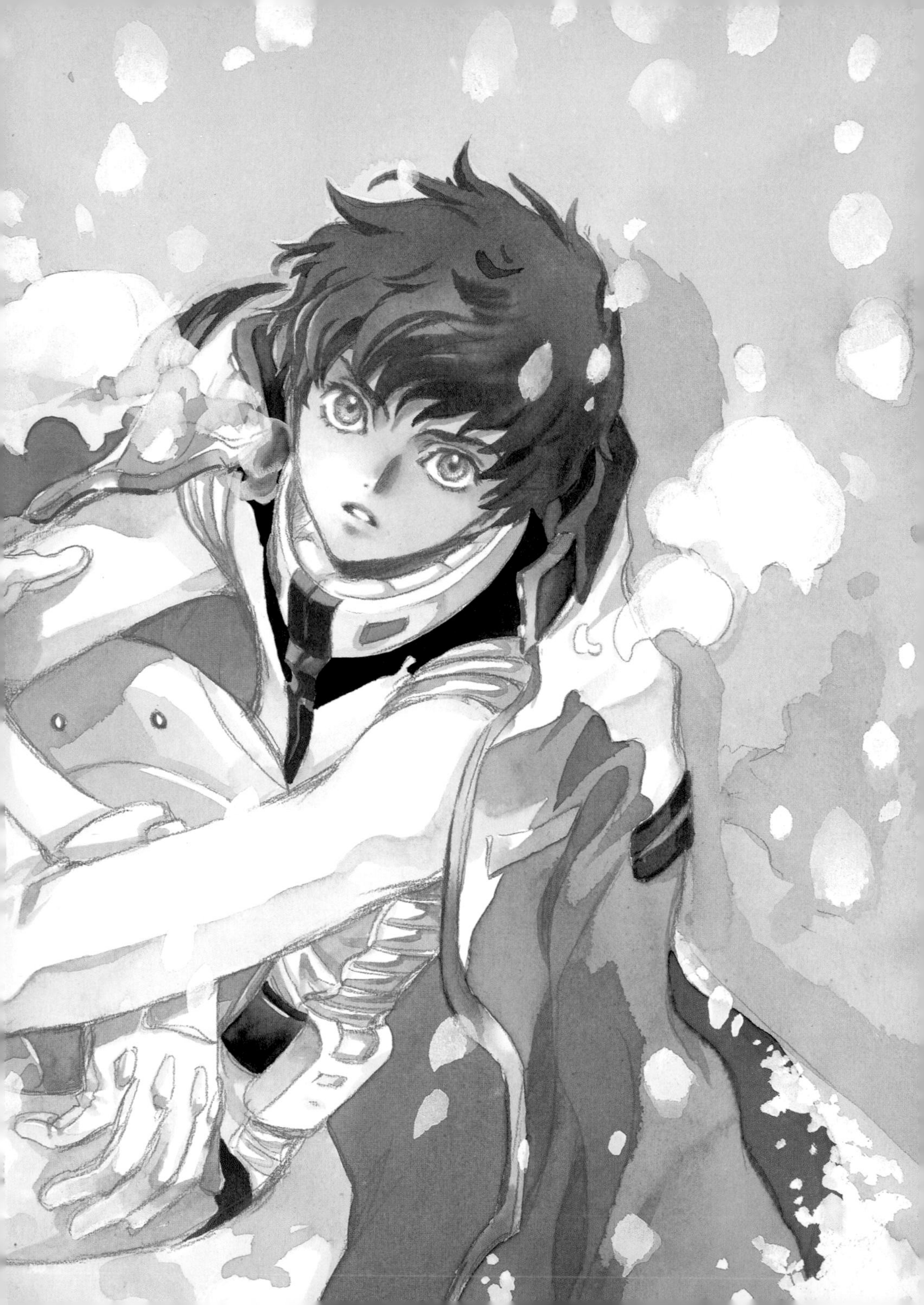

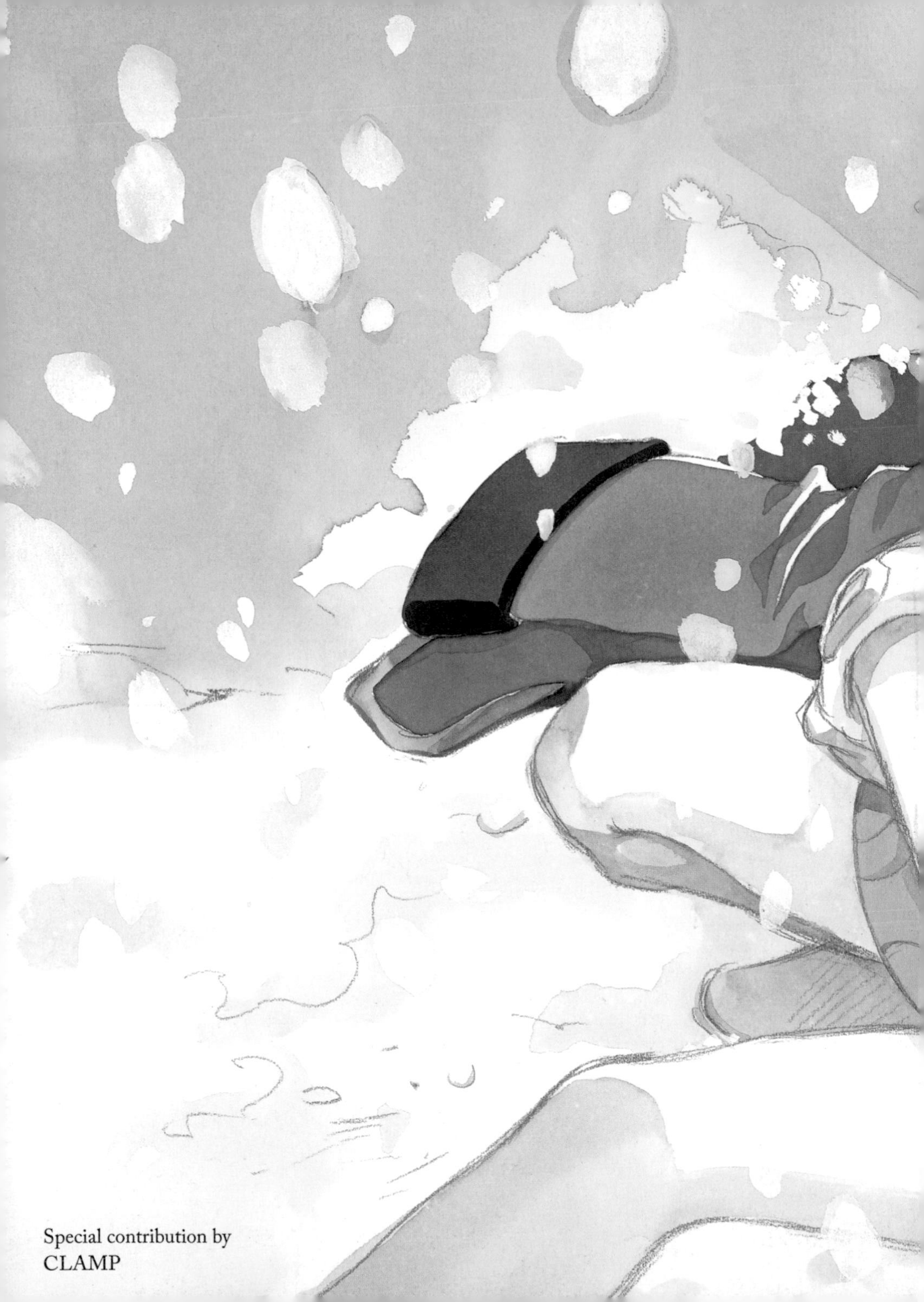

Special contribution by
CLAMP

AIZOUBAN MOBILE SUIT GUNDAM THE ORIGIN vol. 2

Translation: Melissa Tanaka

Production: Grace Lu
Hiroko Mizuno
Anthony Quintessenza

© Yoshikazu YASUHIKO 2006

© SOTSU • SUNRISE

First published in Japan in 2006 by Kadokawa Shoten, Co., Ltd., Tokyo

English translation rights arranged with Kadokawa Shoten, Co., Ltd.
through Tuttle-Mori Agency, Inc., Tokyo

Translation copyright © 2013 Vertical, Inc.

Published by Vertical, Inc., New York

Originally published in Japanese as *Kidou Senshi Gundam THE ORIGIN*
volumes 3 and 4 in 2002, 2003 and re-issued in hardcover as *Aizouban Kidou Senshi Gundam
THE ORIGIN II -Garuma-* in 2006, by Kadokawa Shoten, Co., Ltd.

Kidou Senshi Gundam THE ORIGIN first serialized in *Gundam Ace,*
Kadokawa Shoten, Co., Ltd., 2001-2011

ISBN: 978-1-935654-88-9

Manufactured in the United States of America

First Edition

Vertical, Inc.
451 Park Avenue South
7th Floor
New York, NY 10016
www.vertical-inc.com